E/1989/45
ST/ESA/211



Department of International Economic and Social Affairs

# WORLD ECONOMIC SURVEY 1989

## CURRENT TRENDS AND POLICIES IN THE WORLD ECONOMY

**UNITED NATIONS**
**New York, 1989**

NOTE

Symbols of United Nations documents are composed of capital letters combined with figures.

E/1989/45
ST/ESA/211

UNITED NATIONS PUBLICATION

Sales No. E.89.II.C.1

04500
ISBN 92-1-109116-0

## PREFACE

Global economic growth in 1988 confounded expectations. Not only was the expansion of world output larger than expected, but international trade and investments grew vigorously. However, this expansion failed to spread to many developing countries, particularly those in Africa and Latin America, which continued to stagnate or to grow very slowly. The *World Economic Survey 1989* reviews these trends and analyses their implications for the different regions of the world, including those that barely benefited from these positive developments.

The question remains whether the more favourable features of 1988, as well as the structural changes that have taken place in this decade, will provide the basis for more lasting achievements and, in particular, whether all economies, developing and developed, will eventually achieve sustained non-inflationary growth. Although domestic efforts will remain essential to this end, policies of international economic co-operation should make a critical contribution, as argued in chapter I.

Chapter II discusses production trends in the various regions of the world and the outlook for the world economy in the short term. Special attention is devoted to describing the diversity of the economic situation in developing countries, the longevity of the expansion in Western industrial countries, unemployment in those countries—including that of women—and the reform process in socialist countries. Recent trends in international trade and commercial policies, including the emergence of new blocs, are discussed in chapter III. Chapter IV studies the main developments in international finance and reviews financial flows among developed countries and related policy interventions. Special emphasis is given to assessing efforts to solve the debt crisis, the social and political costs of which are still mounting.

The continuing fluctuations in world energy prices, the changing structure of the oil industry and the link between fuel consumption and environmental change are discusssed in chapter V. Chapter VI studies the efforts being made during a period of rapid economic and political reform to achieve closer integration among socialist countries within the context of the Council for Mutual Economic Assistance. Chapter VII analyses the reasons for the persistently high interest rates in international markets and the divergence in those rates among major industrial countries.

The Economic and Social Council, in its decision 1988/160, requested the Secretary-General to continue to monitor the net transfer of resources from developing to developed countries and to devote a separate chapter of the *World Economic Survey 1989* to an analysis of this issue. Accordingly, in chapter VIII, recent trends in net financial flows from developing countries and their effects on domestic economies and, in particular, on investments and structural adjustment efforts are assessed.

Three special issues are discussed in the final portion of the *Survey.* The first has been included in accordance with Economic and Social Council resolution 1988/49, in which the Council called upon the Secretary-General to devote a separate section in the *World Economic Survey* to the economic aspects of the situation of women and their contribution to economic development, taking into account, *inter alia,* their participation in the evolution of labour markets. The second responds to Economic and Social Council resolution 1988/75, in which the Council requested the Secretary-General to prepare a survey of the mechanisms and means currently available within the United Nations system for the early indentification, analysis and monitoring of world economic developments and to include it in the *World Economic Survey 1989.* The third is a brief review of demographic indicators, with tables containing information for individual countries up to 1990.

As in previous years, the *World Economic Survey 1989* has benefited greatly from the surveys of the regional commissions and the analyses and studies of the United Nations Conference on Trade and Development, the International Monetary Fund, the World Bank, the General Agreement on Tariffs and Trade and other international institutions. It is our hope that the 1989 *Survey* will be of use to the public, to academic institutions and to the world community at large and, in particular, that it will assist the Economic and Social Council in its work of analysing current developments with a view to promoting a common understanding on how to improve economic and social conditions for all people throughout the world.

Rafeeuddin Ahmed
Under-Secretary-General for
International Economic and Social Affairs

## CONTENTS

**CONTENTS** *(continued)*

**CONTENTS** *(continued)*

TABLES *(continued)*

## CONTENTS *(continued)*

TABLES *(continued)*



FIGURES

## CONTENTS *(continued)*

### FIGURES *(continued)*

## EXPLANATORY NOTES

Symbols of United Nations documents are composed of capital letters combined with figures.

The following symbols have been used in the tables throughout the report:

Two dots (..) indicate that data are not available or are not separately reported.

A dash (—) indicates that the amount is nil or negligible.

A hyphen (-) indicates that the item is not applicable.

A minus sign (-) indicates a deficit or decrease, except as indicated.

A full stop (.) is used to indicate decimals.

A slash (/) between years indicates a crop year or financial year, for example, 1987/88.

Use of a hyphen (-) between years, for example, 1986-1988, signifies the full period involved, including the beginning and end years.

Reference to "tons" indicates metric tons and to "dollars" ($) United States dollars, unless otherwise stated.

Annual rates of growth or change, unless otherwise stated, refer to annual compound rates. In most cases, the growth rate forecasts for 1989 and 1990 are rounded to the nearest half of a percentage point.

Details and percentages in tables do not necessarily add to totals, because of rounding.

The following abbreviations have been used:

| | |
|---|---|
| ASEAN | Association of South-East Asian Nations |
| boe | Barrel of oil equivalent |
| CACM | Central American Common Market |
| c.i.f. | Cost, insurance, freight |
| CMEA | Council for Mutual Economic Assistance |
| COMIBOL | Corporación Minera de Bolivia |
| CPI | Consumer price index |
| ECE | Economic Commission for Europe |
| ECU | European currency unit |
| EEC | European Economic Community |
| EFTA | European Free Trade Association |
| ESAF | Enhanced Structural Adjustment Facility |
| ESCAP | Economic and Social Commission for Asia and the Pacific |
| FAO | Food and Agriculture Organization of the United Nations |
| f.o.b. | Free on board |
| f.t.c. | Foreign trade corporation |
| GATT | General Agreement on Tariffs and Trade |
| GCMB | Ghana Cocoa Marketing Board |
| GDP | Gross domestic product |
| GEMS | Global Environmental Monitoring System |
| GNP | Gross national product |
| GSTP | Global System of Trade Preferences |
| Habitat | United Nations Centre for Human Settlements (Habitat) |
| IAEA | International Atomic Energy Agency |
| IBRD | International Bank for Reconstruction and Development |
| IDA | International Development Association |
| IDF | International debt facility |
| ILO | International Labour Organization |
| IMF | International Monetary Fund |
| INSTRAW | International Research and Training Institute for the Advancement of Women |
| kWh | Kilowatt hour |
| LAFTA | Latin American Free Trade Association |
| LIBOR | London interbank offered rate |
| LNG | Liquefied natural gas |

| | |
|---|---|
| mbd | Million barrels per day |
| mboed | Million barrels of oil equivalent per day |
| MFA | Multifibre Arrangement |
| MW | Megawatt |
| OECD | Organisation for Economic Co-operation and Development |
| OPEC | Organization of the Petroleum Exporting Countries |
| PAMSCAD | Programme of Actions to Mitigate the Social Costs of Adjustment of the Government of Ghana |
| ppm | Parts per million |
| PPP | Purchasing power parity |
| SAF | Structural Adjustment Facility |
| SDR | Special drawing rights |
| UIP | Uncovered interest parity |
| UNCTAD | United Nations Conference on Trade and Development |
| UNEP | United Nations Environment Programme |
| UNICEF | United Nations Children's Fund |
| UNIDO | United Nations Industrial Development Organization |
| WHO | World Health Organization |
| WIDER | World Institute for Development Economics Research of the United Nations University |
| WIPO | World Intellectual Property Organization |
| WMO | World Meteorological Organization |

The designations employed and the presentation of the material in this publication do not imply the expression of any opinion whatsover on the part of the United Nations Secretariat concerning the legal status of any country, territory, city or area or of its authorities, or concerning the delimitation of its frontiers or boundaries.

The term "country" as used in the text of this report also refers, as appropriate, to territories or areas.

For analytical purposes, the following country classification has been used:

*Centrally planned economies:* Eastern Europe, Union of Soviet Socialist Republics.

*Developed market economies:* North America, southern and western Europe (excluding Cyprus, Malta and Yugoslavia), Australia, Japan, New Zealand, South Africa.

*Developing countries:* Latin America and the Caribbean, Africa (other than South Africa), Asia (excluding Japan), Cyprus, Malta, Yugoslavia; for some analyses, China has been shown separately.

For particular analyses, developing countries have been subdivided into the following groups:

*Capital-surplus countries:* Brunei Darussalam, Iran (Islamic Republic of), Iraq, Kuwait, Libyan Arab Jamahiriya, Qatar, Saudi Arabia, United Arab Emirates

Deficit countries (or capital-importing countries), subdivided into the following two subgroups:

*Other net energy exporters (or deficit energy exporters):* Algeria, Angola, Bahrain, Bolivia, Cameroon, Congo, Ecuador, Egypt, Gabon, Indonesia, Malaysia, Mexico, Nigeria, Oman, Peru, Syrian Arab Republic, Trinidad and Tobago, Tunisia, Venezuela.

*Net energy importers:* All other developing countries.

The designations of country groups in the text and the tables are intended solely for statistical or analytical convenience and do not necessarily express a judgement about the stage reached by a particular country or area in the development process.

# Chapter 1

## THE STATE OF THE WORLD ECONOMY

### Short-term prospects

In 1988, the output of the world economy grew by about 4.3 per cent, considerably more than in 1987 (3.3 per cent), and world trade increased by 8.3 per cent, which was faster than it had since the early 1970s. Total world population probably increased at 1.7 per cent, so that output per head increased by 2.6 per cent. For most of the 1980s, the gross world product has grown more slowly than in the 1960s and 1970s. There was a spurt in 1984 but only in 1988 did it regain the rhythm of the 1970s.

In 1989, this rapid expansion is likely to give way to more moderate increases in world output and trade. The measures taken to contain inflationary pressures in the industrialized countries in late 1988 and early 1989, and more cautious attitudes on the part of investors and consumers in the big industrial countries are slowing the growth of aggregate demand. Growth in the world economy is thus expected to slacken from more than 4 to 3.5 per cent in 1989 and to stay at about that level in 1990.

As has been the case throughout the 1980s, the fastest growing economies in 1988 were in Asia, where a great many countries, including China and India, showed per capita growth rates considerably higher than those in the old industrialized countries. In much of Africa and Latin America, on the other hand, per capita income was declining instead of growing. Many of the poorest countries were getting poorer or standing still, so the gap between them and the richest countries was widening. Average per capita income in the industrial countries is about 50 times that of the least developed countries, and the annual increase alone in the richer countries is about as large as the whole annual per capita income in the poorest countries, which is of the order of $300.

The most probable short-term scenario for 1989 and 1990 is one of a modest slow-down in output and a gradual deceleration of inflation in major industrial countries beginning in 1990 (see chapter II). The risk is that a sudden change in expectations in international financial markets may put an even heavier burden on monetary policy to counteract destabilizing price or exchange rate movements, which might make for an abrupt contraction.

Such a scenario, with an adverse change in world trade and a rise in interest rates, would make adjustment efforts much more difficult. Many heavily indebted countries increased their exports swiftly as international demand for manufactures and industrial raw materials expanded in 1988. Nonetheless, debt service ratios rose since interest rates went up in international financial markets. The net financial transfer from developing countries increased and it is likely to rise further in the course of 1989 as average interest rates exceed 1988 levels.

### The changing structure of the world economy

The challenges faced by policy makers at the present time are very different from those of a decade ago. The economies of the world have become more tightly linked through the globalization of financial markets, and the role and even the character of the main players in the world economy have changed.

Among the large economies, the United States has retained its predominance, but its persistent external deficit has led to a shift in policy preoccupations. Japan has become a major supplier of international finance, and in the second half of the 1980s has moved from a heavily export-led growth pattern to one of rapidly growing domestic expenditure. The European Communities have become the scene of great structural change in preparation for the steps toward closer integration by 1992. The Soviet Union, as well as other Eastern European countries, have initiated a process of reforms to decentralize economic decisions and deepen commercial, financial, and technological interchange with other industrial countries. China, which started a process of reforms in the rural economy in the late 1970s, has doubled per capita incomes and tripled exports and imports in the 1980s, and has turned to reforming its industrial structures. In these socialist countries, economic reform has also had far-reaching political consequences. A few smaller Asian countries have been able to increase exports of manufactures so rapidly that they have built trade surpluses large enough to have an impact on the world economy. India and Pakistan still have vast poverty problems but their economic growth in the 1980s has been fast. Much of Latin America and Africa, on the other hand, presents a picture of severe economic stress.

All in all, the world economy has changed dramatically in the course of the 1980s, and approaches to international economic policy issues must evolve accordingly.

### World-wide adjustment in the 1980s

Overcoming stagflation was the main objective of economic policies in the major industrial economies at the start of the decade. Much attention was given to the reduction of structural rigidities, and there were widespread efforts to resist rising fiscal pressure and limit the role of fiscal policy in demand management. The shift towards greater reliance on monetary policy led to an increase in real interest rates. This took place at a time of rapid technological progress, swift changes in patterns of comparative advantage, and an accelerated relocation of industrial production world-wide. As a consequence, the fortunes of many countries in the world, whether developed or developing, changed quite suddenly.

The capacity to adapt and adjust to new conditions varied greatly. In old industrialized countries, the range of industries is wide and the economic capacity to adjust the structure of production is very great, but closing down old industries and adjusting real income levels has social costs for many and often runs into political resistance to adjustment. In the many developing countries whose export revenues depend on a few primary commodities, the economic capacity to adjust is more restricted, and changes in terms of trade are usually greater, so that adjustment may involve very large cuts in real income, the responsibility for which is easily projected on the Government or on international institutions. The countries that adjusted most quickly were those which were flexible enough to gear their economies to new opportunities in world markets: their capacity to adjust and their development success sprang from the same sources.

Fluctuations in oil prices were an important source of shocks in the 1980s. The escalation of energy prices in 1980-1981 produced reactions in key policies of most countries. Later, the collapse of oil prices in 1986 caused havoc in many oil exporting countries where revenues were halved and per capita incomes fell by one third. The structure of oil markets has changed, as new suppliers have entered the market, but substantial reserves exist in only a few countries, and prices in energy markets remain unstable.

In the second half of the 1980s, new relations among the superpowers measurably improved the international political climate. The partial dismantling of nuclear forces and a gradual reduction in conventional forces has been accompanied by the end or mitigation of local conflicts which were extremely costly both in terms of loss of life and material destruction. These advances in political co-operation have not yet been greatly reflected in enhanced economic co-operation, but they already have important economic implications. They provide policy makers and investors with new prospects and new opportunities. The opportunity to reduce defence expenditures and redirect resources to human development has been long awaited, and by 1989 it seemed to have arrived.

### Internationalization of markets

The new and largely market based exchange rate and interest rate régimes are changing the character and scope of financial policies. Governments as well as private agents have more room for manoeuvre as the pool of credit and the diversity of financial instruments has widened. On the other hand, risks have increased as actual costs of international capital fluctuate greatly with changes in exchange rates and with developments in international money centres. For those developing countries that participated in the new international financial environment and contracted substantial debts, the experience proved costly when creditors withdrew after the Mexican debt crisis of 1982.

The shift from demand management towards supply-side policies has led countries all over the world to undertake extensive deregulation and rely more heavily on the market. Industrial countries liberalized capital markets and tried to slow down the increase in public spending. Similar policies were followed in many developing countries, many of which also privatized public sector activities, particularly parastatals engaged in trade and industry. In socialist countries, decentralization and devolution of decision-making power to enterprises has come to be seen as ways to improve productivity.

Increasingly the role of the Government in the economic field is perceived as one of enabling enterprise to thrive. Enlarging the economic freedom of individuals is seen as a way of promoting entrepreneurship. There is a growing recognition of the contribution of women in economic and social life, and institutions and policies are being changed in order to facilitate their greater participation.

Participation by countries in the multilateral system also increased during the 1980s, as new members entered the General Agreement on Tariffs and Trade (GATT), the International Monetary Fund (IMF), and the World Bank. Several creditor countries joined regional development banks. Gradually, the multilateral system is becoming truly universal. The large socialist economies which presently are not participating in GATT or in the Bretton Woods institutions have indicated their desire to do so in the future.

On the other hand many countries feel excluded from the Group of Five co-ordination process and some of them perceive it to be contrary to their interest. There is also considerable concern that the realization of a unified internal market in the European Economic Community and the creation of other trading blocs might lead to inward-looking and protectionist postures. But if the past is any guide, the increase in trade intensity observed in all countries, the formation of such blocs need not result in increased protectionism (see chapters III and VI).

### Unsettled issues

While there has been great progress in many areas, serious problems remain. The instability in the key parameters of the world economy—interest rates, exchange rates, energy prices—still persists. There are as yet few indications that the world economy will be more predictable or less unstable in the coming decade, raising concerns among several countries over prospects for increased international economic security. The external debt and the widespread unemployment in countries of all income levels have not yet found a solution. Nor has the risk of a new energy shock been removed: there are no indications of a *rapprochement* between consumers and producers. In the late 1970s, consumers were trying to engage producers in a dialogue on price stabilization. Today, some of the large producers have suggested that such a dialogue might be helpful, but they have found no echo among consumers. The concerns about global warming and the need to hold back the consumption of fossil fuels might give a new impetus to the search for a dialogue of this kind (see chapter V).

## Global patterns of trade and finance

The pattern of trade balances that emerged among the three largest economies of the world in the early 1980s has not been fundamentally modified. In 1989, the trade deficit of the United States will be about the same as in 1986 and well above that of 1983-1985, and the same will be true of the trade surpluses of the Federal Republic of Germany and Japan.

These trade deficits and surpluses have their counterparts in financial flows. The causal relationship between the trade side and the financial side is not self-evident, and there are different ways of interpreting the prevailing situation.

For many years, the United States trade deficits and the accompanying increases in United States borrowing and indebtedness have been termed "unsustainable", but they have lasted and remain very large by historical standards. Two different concerns have prompted this description. One arises from the dynamics of continued borrowing and the rising interest burden on the foreign debt which, as in all indebted countries, makes the debt service burden rise very fast when the interest rate is higher than the rate of growth of exports. The other concern arises from the financing of the deficit, and the worries that the United States might have to raise interest rates to attract funds and that eventually the confidence of foreign investors might erode, with the consequence of a great upheaval in the international economy.

However, the capacity of international capital markets has been greatly enlarged in recent years, and the rise in real interest rates was in large part a result of the reliance on monetary rather than fiscal policy to contain inflation. There are even those who argue that the inflow of foreign capital is the cause of the trade deficit rather than the other way around. It does not seem likely that the financial markets will in the near term impose an end to United States borrowing. But "unsustainability" can also mean that policy makers come to the conclusion that a trend must be arrested because it is contrary to the public interest.

In this sense there would seem to be both national and international reasons to seek to reverse the trends of the 1980s. In a global view it is an anomaly that the richest country in the world is absorbing a large part of the savings of other countries instead of contributing to the flow of capital to the rest of the world, as it used to do. In the medium to long term, an adjustment is likely to come about. However, given the magnitude of the deficit—35 per cent of exports in late 1988 and early 1989—and the size of the United States in the world economy, it is in no country's interest that this adjustment is so sharp as to be disruptive.

A redirection of surplus savings in the world economy towards the vast needs for infrastructure investments in developing countries is a very great challenge for the years ahead. It calls for reforms in those countries themselves as well as a greater capacity to channel funds to them.

## The debt crisis and the transfer problem

So far, virtually none of the countries with serious debt-servicing problems in 1982-1983 have managed to restore a workable balance of payments position, let alone their creditworthiness. They have not regained their capacity to increase investment on the basis of their own resources (see chapter VIII). After years of efforts to improve their trade balance at a heavy social and economic cost, adjustment fatigue is setting in. Even countries that have produced large trade surpluses seem more vulnerable today than at the onset of the debt crisis.

For many countries, the crisis has its roots in the 1970s. For others, it was a consequence of the energy shocks in the early 1980s. But a chief reason for the simultaneous eruption of the crisis in so many developing countries in the early 1980s was the unexpected deterioration in terms of trade and the high real interest rates.

Initially the debt problem was seen by many as a liquidity problem. It was expected that a reasonable dose of adjustment and a gradual return to normal commodity prices and interest rates would solve the problem for most countries. But primary commodity prices remained depressed and real interest rates remained high. In the second half of 1985, the initiative taken by the then Secretary of the Treasury of the United States cast the solution in terms of renewed growth, counting on increased resources from commercial banks and multilateral institutions. However, it was soon apparent that additional private finance was not forthcoming. The multilateral institutions responded to the call but were not in a position to supply much additional finance. By 1988, IMF, the World Bank and the Inter-American Development Bank (IDB) were absorbing net financial resources from countries with debt-servicing difficulties. The maturity of their loan cycle coincided with the difficulties of most of those countries.

New initiatives were taken in June 1988, at the Toronto Summit of the Group of Seven, which addressed the debt problems of low-income countries, most of which are in sub-Saharan Africa, and agreed on more lenient rescheduling of their debts in the Paris Club. In the autumn of 1988, the Governments of Japan and France put forward new initiatives to deal with the debts of the middle-income countries in Latin America and elsewhwere, and in early 1989 the United States made important proposals in the same direction. The common feature of these initiatives was the new role attached to debt reduction as one part of the approach to the debt problems. But large questions remain about the mechanisms to implement debt reduction, the appropriate magnitude of it, and the time frame (see chapter IV). There will have to be a great deal of learning by doing, but delay in tackling the problem would be costly.

The economic and social costs of drawn-out stagnation have in several cases led to political upheavals and loss of human lives. The rate of investment in the countries with debt-servicing difficulties remains well below that in 1980. The transfer problem resulting from the debt crisis of the 1980s will be a burdensome legacy for the 1990s.

## The positive signals

For many countries the 1980s have been years of frustration or even tragedy, but for others they have been years of great success. The reasons for these differences are complex, but they have spurred much rethinking and revision of policies and approaches to development throughout the world. Two observations may be in place:

First, the successful growth experiences in countries of great diversity obviously deserves great attention. Most of them have put heavy emphasis on the development of their human resources. The role of people themselves in making development come about stands out more sharply today, and along with it a development agenda that puts human needs and resources at the top, with all that this implies in terms of nutrition, education, health, shelter and technology. Participation—of men and women—in economic and political life is coming to be seen as an essential dimension of development, and the large numbers of the desperately poor are beginning to be regarded as a resource to be developed rather than as a burden.

Second, the intensification of world communication has contributed to the extraordinary growth of the network of private citizens and nongovernmental organizations in countries throughout the world who are actively engaged in international development on all fronts. Their contributions to new and experimental approaches on a human scale, their insistent support of human rights, and their vigilance in matters of global environmental hazards have created a vibrant international development constituency in which the peoples of the world speak directly both to one another and to their Governments and to the intergovernmental organizations.

## The economic and social policy agenda

The domestic and international policies that seem called for at the present time in order to revive growth and development where it is faltering and to consolidate the gains that have been made in other areas add up to an agenda which has changed greatly in the course of the 1980s. New issues have come to the fore and, as emphasized earlier, both theory and practice have changed in such important fields as macroeconomic policy-making and development.

The distinction between domestic and international policies has become increasingly blurred. Domestic policies in the key currency countries affect conditions in the whole world economy. Domestic policies in developing countries are of deep concern to their creditors. Conflicts between domestic and external objectives have been sharpened. In countries with open access to international credit markets monetary policies called for to control inflation may affect exchange rates in an unwanted direction. In countries with debt-servicing difficulties, rapid external adjustment tends to be at the expense of investment and domestic price stability.

On the other hand, there is, as the debt crisis has demonstrated, an essential complementarity between domestic economic management and international support. One of the reasons for the lack of progress in reaching lasting solutions to the problems of countries with serious debt-servicing difficulties is the vicious spiral of worsening economic conditions, mounting political tension and short-term emergency policies in the debtor countries, and loss of confidence on the part of creditors or donors of all kinds. The repeated rounds of rescheduling call for a very great negotiating effort to put together short-term packages without much hope that they will not have to be repeated very soon. In themselves, they impose a heavy cost on both debtors and creditors.

The problems raised by the debt crisis are not primarily technical. They arise from the need of simultaneously improving domestic policies and rebuilding the mutual confidence on which credit and aid relationships rest. Governments have great responsibilities for taking a long view of the consequences of the prolongation of the stultifying deadlock that still prevails, and in this sense the generalized debt crisis is essentially a political problem.

The acceptance in 1988 of the admissibility of reductions of debt or debt service widens the menu of debt renegotiations, but perhaps not as much as one might believe. A special institutional facility for debt conversion might be called for. However, discussions about new arrangements or facilities for debt rearrangement, however interesting, have no significance unless there is a genuine intention to tackle the debt crisis—in which case they might well turn out to be unnecessary. The debt crisis can be overcome, but only by the efforts and co-operation of all parties involved, and not by mutual reproaches.

One of the functions originally attributed to the system of international financial co-operation was to provide buffers in order to cushion the impact of external shocks on its members. These shocks have increased in magnitude, but the capacity of IMF and other agencies to cushion them has decreased in relation to the growth of the world economy. The destabilization of the world economy from the shocks in the early 1980s raises the question whether the original objective is to be abandoned. If it is to be retained, the resources of IMF should be enlarged and the distinction between automatic compensatory support and that which is subject to conditionality should be upheld.

In international trade negotiations, the ongoing talks have tackled new and important issues which will remain on the table well beyond the Uruguay Round. The liberalization of agricultural trade and the formulation of régimes for trade in services and for intellectual property will be on the international agenda for many years to come. With the emergence of stronger trading blocs, it remains essential that the rules of the game be respected and that access to markets, particularly of exports from developing countries, is not hampered. Overall efforts towards liberalization should continue. The decision recently taken to set up a policy review mechanism in GATT is a welcome step and should be strictly adhered to.

The least developed countries, not necessarily restricted to those so formally designated but in the sense of the weakest in the world community, have in the course of the 1980s come to stand out as posing the most difficult problems of international development. Their situation has for the most part not improved but worsened further. Many of them are already alarmingly dependent on external aid, but nonetheless need more to make up for their losses of commodity export earnings and to support the necessary reorientation of their development strategies. Donor countries who are contributing signally less than others to the international development effort should reconsider their capacity of increased support to their bilateral aid programmes as well as to the multilateral ones.

In the course of the adjustments in recent years, government spending on education and health have been cut back, often sharply, with troubling consequences not only for present living conditions but for future development prospects. As a reaction, there is a new consensus on the need to see people as the principal resource and potential of a country and not as a burden. The translation of this understanding into programmes and policies is only beginning, and it puts social issues high on the agenda for development co-operation.

The ambitious reform programmes in countries moving away from central planning to more flexible forms of economic organization raises the question of transitional arrangements to facilitate international trade and investment between them and other countries. The eventual objective ought to be the universalization of the international agencies for monetary, financial and commercial co-operation, but it is clear that this cannot be achieved in the near term. Here too is a new and challenging addition to the international agenda.

The special session of the General Assembly which has been convoked in the spring of 1990 provides the members of the United Nations with an opportunity to take stock of the many new features of the world economic and social situation and to seek agreement on the principles that should guide their co-operation in the years to come. This would lay the foundations for the elaboration and adoption later in 1990 of an International Development Strategy which would meet the demand for a realistic and genuine agreement on the commitments and responsibilities for a joint attack on the vast problems of poverty, development and ecological threats that beset the planet. In the meantime, the revitalization of growth in those economies that have been stagnant or have regressed in the 1980s remains the most urgent challenge.

# Chapter II

## GLOBAL ECONOMIC TRENDS AND PROSPECTS

### Recent developments

Global economic growth in 1988 confounded expectations. Whereas a slow-down was widely anticipated at the beginning of the year, growth of output accelerated from 3.3 per cent in 1987 to 4.3 per cent in 1988 (see table II.1). This high rate of global growth reflected the strong performance of the world's largest economies, which outweighed the lower rates of growth in many of the smaller countries.

Led by the largest members of the group, the developed market economies expanded output by more than 4 per cent in 1988, the highest rate of growth since the post-recession expansion in 1984. The Soviet Union grew faster than the previous year, while the other centrally planned economies of Europe roughly maintained their rate of growth.

The growth rates of developing countries have taken on an increasingly regional pattern. In South-East Asia, high growth continues unabated: even if they decline in the next few years, rates of growth in this region are expected to remain above those of other developing regions for the foreseeable future. The rapidity and longevity of growth in these countries is unprecedented in modern development experience.

The world's two most populous countries also attained high rates of growth in 1988. Output in both China and India grew by over 8 per cent, implying a tangible increase in average living standards for some 40 per cent of the world's population, which comprise the overwhelming majority of the world's poorest. China has achieved rapid growth continuously since 1982, but was intended to slow down in 1988. India's rapid acceleration in 1988 was to some extent a process of catching up following the drought-induced slowdown in 1987, but previous experience suggested that the adverse effects of the drought would be more prolonged. Instead, there is now evidence in India, as in China for some time, of overheating, manifested in higher inflation and a deteriorating external position. The rest of Asia grew at a more moderate rate in 1988 but, with a few exceptions, improved on performance in 1987.

The experience of most of Asia contrasts with the continuing difficulties in Africa and Latin America. In the latter region, there was a small increase in per capita output in 1987, but this was reversed in 1988. In Africa, there was an increase in the growth of output in 1988, but per capita output continued to decline.

The stagnation in these two regions is particularly disturbing in view of the fact that the international economic environment was more favourable in 1988. In addition to vigorous growth in the rest of the world, there was a strong expansion of world trade and few new and hostile external

Table II.1. Growth of population and output by region, 1981-1990

| | Population 1985 (Millions) | Population growth rate 1985-1990 (Annual percentage) | Gross domestic product 1985 (Billions of 1980 dollars) | Rate of change of gross domestic product (Annual percentage) | | | | | |
|---|---|---|---|---|---|---|---|---|---|
| | | | | 1981-1985 | 1986 | 1987 | 1988[a] | 1989[b] | 1990[b] |
| World | 4 837 | 1.6 | .. | 2.7 | 3.3 | 3.3 | 4.3 | 3.5 | 3.4 |
| Developed market economies | 789 | 0.6 | 7 640 | 2.2 | 2.7 | 3.0 | 4.1 | 2.8 | 2.6 |
| North America | 264 | 0.9 | 2 866 | 2.4 | 2.9 | 3.0 | 3.9 | 2.2 | 2.5 |
| Western Europe | 353 | 0.2 | 3 467 | 1.5 | 2.6 | 2.6 | 3.6 | 2.8 | 2.4 |
| Developed Asia | 121 | 0.5 | 1 060 | 3.6 | 2.5 | 4.0 | 5.4 | 4.2 | 3.2 |
| Centrally planned economies of Europe[c] | 394 | 0.8 | .. | 3.3 | 4.3 | 2.6 | 4.0 | 3.7 | 3.5 |
| Developing countries | 2 595 | 2.3 | 2 217 | 1.5 | 2.9 | 2.7 | 3.3 | 3.5 | 4.5 |
| Western hemisphere | 405 | 2.2 | 822 | 1.0 | 3.6 | 2.5 | 0.7 | 0.5 | 3.5 |
| West Asia | 108 | 3.2 | 343 | −0.9 | 0.1 | −1.3 | 1.4 | 2.5 | 3.5 |
| South and East Asia | 1 486 | 1.9 | 606 | 4.8 | 5.5 | 5.5 | 9.4 | 6.5 | 6.0 |
| Africa | 523 | 3.1 | 305 | −0.9 | −2.1 | 0.9 | 2.4 | 2.5 | 3.0 |
| Mediterranean | 74 | 1.6 | 141 | 2.9 | 5.6 | 3.7 | 3.6 | 3.0 | 4.5 |
| China[c] | 1 060 | 1.2 | .. | 9.4 | 7.4 | 9.3 | 11.4 | 10.0 | 9.0 |

*Source:* Department of International Economic and Social Affairs of the United Nations Secretariat. Data on population and population growth rates are those published by the Department in *World Demographic Estimates and Projections, 1950-2025* (United Nations publication, Sales No. E.86.XIII.3).

a Preliminary estimates.

b Forecast, based on Project LINK and Secretariat estimates. For the groups of developing countries, estimates are rounded to the nearest half percentage point.

c Net material product; data for 1981-1988 are government estimates.

Figure II.1. Rate of growth of per capita GDP of developing countries by region, 1971-1980 and 1981-1988

(Percentage)

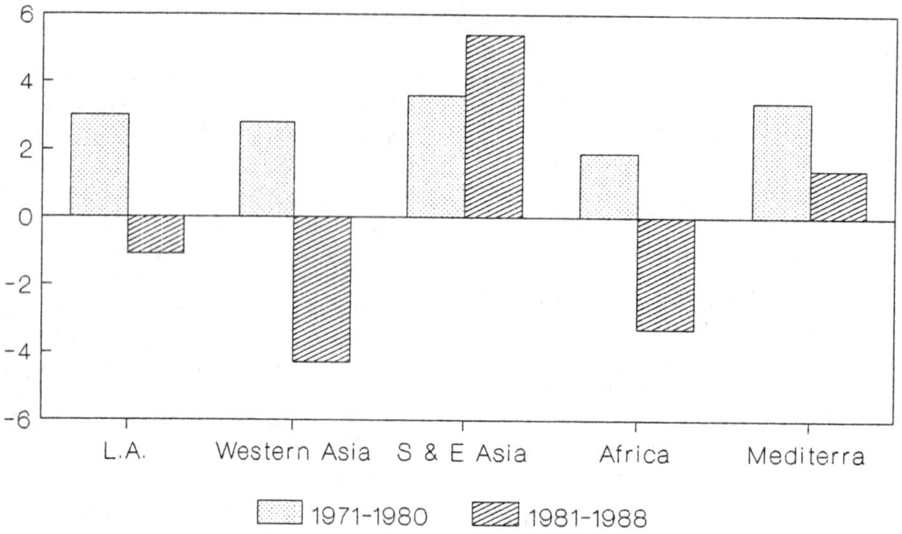


*Source:* Department of International Economic and Social Affairs of the United Nations Secretariat.

economic developments. However, the growth of world trade had different effects on the various groups of developing countries. The newly industrializing countries, particularly those in Asia but also some in Latin America, were able to increase exports, in some cases considerably. Less diversified economies had less success: in several African countries, export revenues fell in 1988. In Latin America, several countries achieved large increases in both the volume and value of exports but were unable to translate these gains into enhanced growth.

During the 1970s, all regions enjoyed rates of growth in per capita output broadly similar to that of South and East Asia in the 1980s (see figure II.1). In the 1980s, Asia has not only increased its rate of growth of output, but has also had a lower rate of growth of population than the other two regions, with the result that the divergence in rates of growth of output per capita is even greater than that of total output. This phenomenon has been characteristic of most of the present decade and is becoming increasingly entrenched.

Many are inclined to interpret this situation in simplistic terms. Some will say that the success of many developing countries demonstrates that the key to development lies in the right kind of domestic policies. Others will point to the enormous and adverse external shocks imposed on many countries and argue that the international economic environment is at fault.

The controversy about the relative roles of domestic policies of developing countries and of developed countries in maintaining a stable and favourable environment for growth and development has put its stamp on deliberations in the United Nations for decades. Any attempt to analyse and understand the process of international development must conclude that domestic development effort and a favourable international economic environment are both essential, and that there is also a natural interaction between them. On the one hand, Governments in control of their development process have easier access to external support. On the other hand, Governments of countries that have received particularly harsh external shocks may not be in a position to retain or reassume control of their development.

At the same time, external shocks, particularly the upheavals to which the world economy has been subjected during the 1970s and 1980s, act as an incentive to adjust domestic policies to the new environment. Economic adjustment, restructuring and reform have been applied to an ever wider range of activities in an increasing number of countries, developed and developing, over the past decade. The nature and extent of the economic changes under way vary widely among countries: different countries have adopted different types of measures at different times with different horizons. Nevertheless, the broad objectives have been similar, namely, to raise economic efficiency, *inter alia,* by improving the functioning of markets and access to them. Some of these improvements in efficiency are now being reflected in enhanced economic growth; others have yet to pay such dividends; and still others are giving rise to doubts about their efficacy. The challenge to national Governments and the international community in the 1990s will be to identify and consolidate beneficial changes while sidestepping dogma and discontinuing those of doubtful merit.

## Developed market economies: unexpected strength in 1988

The economic upswing in the developed market economies entered a record-breaking seventh year in 1988, belying forecasts that the collapse in equity prices in October 1987 presaged a slow-down in real economic growth in the following year. All the developed market economies experienced more rapid growth than was expected. In 20 of these 22 economies, the rate of growth was as high as or higher than in 1987, the exceptions being Ireland and the Netherlands. The seven largest economies grew faster on average than the smaller members of the group (see table A.1): all the former increased output by 3.5 per cent or more, whereas only three of the 15 members of the latter group did so.

This growth has to be seen against the background of the less encouraging outlook that prevailed at the end of 1987. Prospects were considered likely to be adversely affected by a number of factors with different time horizons. From a long-term perspective, there was an emerging view that the higher rates of economic growth that had prevailed during the 1960s and early 1970s might have been an aberration and that the "natural" long-term rate of growth of the world economy might be the lower rate experienced in the first half of the 1980s.

A more immediate concern was that the large imbalances among and within the developed market economies might have negative consequences for economic growth. Such an outcome was feared for a number of reasons. First, it was thought that a failure to correct the United States' current account deficit might result in, or require, an increase in interest rates in the United States, to the detriment of growth in that economy and also in the rest of the world. On the other hand, there was fear that any direct attempt to correct the United States' trade deficit, for example by reducing imports, would also slow world trade and the world economy generally. Finally, it was feared that reduction in the United States' fiscal deficit would reduce overall growth in that country and have similarly adverse effects on the world economy as a whole.

Superimposed on these structural concerns, the short-term outlook in early 1988 was darkened by the sharp world-wide decline in prices on equity markets that had taken place in October 1987. It was widely believed that this would have a negative effect on the real sectors of the economies concerned, in part because the paper loss of wealth by equity-holders would bring about a decline in consumption but also because a loss of confidence by the business sector would reduce investment.

These various fears regarding the developed market economies proved to be unfounded: some of the anticipated events did not materialize and those that did failed to have the negative effects that were feared. Long-term and medium-term factors are among those that have sustained the continuing expansion (see box II.1). From a short-term perspective, the rise in interest rates since mid-1988 has not been a consequence of the United States' continuing trade deficit, but rather the result of rapid growth. There have been some measures to control United States imports but world trade nevertheless grew at its fastest rate of the decade in 1988 (see chap. III). There was some reduction in the United States budget deficit, but the economy was still able to increase its rate of growth compared to 1987. Even the global collapse in equity prices had few discernible negative macro-economic effects.

The unexpectedly high growth attained by the developed market economies in 1988, despite these anticipated difficulties, can be ascribed in part to government economic policy, both short-term and medium-term and as applied by countries both individually and collectively. From a short-term perspective, the international economic policy co-ordination that has been taking place among the major industrial countries since 1985 has contributed to the avoidance of the possible adverse developments identified earlier. In particular, the collective response in late 1987 and early 1988 to the disturbances in both equity and foreign exchange markets helped to counter their potential negative consequences.

Most components of demand contributed to the acceleration of growth in 1988, but investment and exports played a disproportionately large role in comparison with recent years (see figure II.2). As a consequence of the former, there was a vigorous expansion of industrial output in several countries. The rapid growth of exports was not only a source of growth, but also a result of it, since growth stimulates international purchases.

Most of the developed market economies benefited from the decline in oil prices in 1988. They were affected only marginally by the increase in non-fuel commodity prices and by changes in exchange rates and thus improved their terms of trade for the third consecutive year (see table A.5). Even those European countries that were adversely affected by a decrease in international oil prices increased output more than on previous such occasions: the United Kingdom was second only to Japan in overall growth, while Norway, although remaining well below average, reversed the decline in GDP in 1987. For the developed market economies as a group, their low rates of population growth, coupled with the favourable movement in their terms of trade, meant that per capita incomes increased by about 3.5 per cent in 1988.

The United States continued to be among the fastest growing of the developed market economies, with output expanding by 3.9 per cent compared to 3.4 per cent in 1987. Business investment has been an important source of the recent growth, prompted by the pressure on capacity created by the steady increases in demand over the past several years. On the other hand, the latter part of 1988 brought a drought which is estimated to have reduced GDP for the year by as much as one percentage point and to have been responsible for some of the acceleration in inflation in the latter part of 1988 and early 1989. This development prompted policy makers to raise interest rates by two percentage points, albeit in stages.

Box II.1. Reasons for the prolonged expansion

Even from an *ex post* perspective, short-term factors seem insufficient to explain the unexpectedly robust growth displayed by the developed market economies since late 1987, particularly since it follows a historically long period of peace time expansion. This suggests that longer-term factors have also been at play. These include exogenous factors, structural changes within and between economies and national and international policy measures.

A major exogenous influence on growth during the 1980s has been technological progress. The lead time between innovation and mass market penetration has been drastically cut, as exemplified in the first half of the 1980s by videocassette recorders and in the latter half by facsimile machines. These new products buoy consumption and thereby serve as a stimulus to investment. At the same time, new technologies act as a direct encouragement to investment by making production technologies obsolete. Firms ignore such technological advances at their peril since improved communications and the globalization of markets have given more vigour and a new dimension to competition in most industries.

Structural changes in the developed market economies have been another factor dampening fluctuations in growth during the 1980s. In the past, inventory investment was very volatile and produced cyclical movements. The inventory cycle now seems less important than previously. This is partially because new technologies (computerized inventory control systems, more efficient communications and faster transportation) have enabled manufacturing companies to reduce stocks of raw materials and intermediate inputs (as in the "just-in-time" approach). In addition, raw materials and semi-processed goods account for a smaller proportion of value-added in output, further reducing the importance of inventories of intermediate goods.

There has also been a trend towards lower inventories of finished products. The rapidity of change in both technology and consumer tastes means that products quickly become obsolete, which discourages the holding of inventories. Moreover, as with inputs, modern inventory systems allow both manufacturers and distributors to maintain lower stocks without the danger of running out of merchandise. Finally, the high interest rates of the 1980s (see chap. VII) have raised the cost of inventories. The relative importance of inventories in the developed market economies has also fallen because of the increase in the importance of the service sector. This sector is less inventory-intensive than manufacturing because its final outputs are not susceptible to storage, but have to be produced as the demand arises.

The corollary of the relative decline in the importance of inventories has been an increase in other, more stable elements of aggregate demand. Government consumption, as opposed to public investment, rather than introducing or compounding fluctuations in an economy, is frequently used as a counter-cyclical device. The weight of this element of national expenditure has also increased over time in many countries,[a] adding a further element of stability to aggregate demand. Private consumption expenditure also tends to be more stable than investment demand in most countries and has risen as a share of GDP in the developed market economies as a group.[b] Moreover, there has been an increase in the stability of private consumption because transfer payments, which fluctuate less than earned income, have become a larger proportion of total income, itself the major determinant of private consumption.[c]

An important source of the sustained growth in the developed market economies over the past several years has been the increase in consumer demand, also brought about in part by some structural changes. One is a trend towards lower personal savings rate in some of the developed market economies, especially the United States (see figure VII.3). Of the many explanations advanced for this secular decline,[d] the apparent increase in consumer confidence is both a cause and an effect of the longevity of the current expansion. Higher levels of income and larger personal stocks of accumulated assets (increasingly in the form of real estate and often arising from inheritances) mean that economic setbacks are unlikely to impose the personal hardship that they did in the past. The "safety nets" in place in the developed market economies reinforce this personal economic security. Confidence in the expansion has been reinforced by the disavowal of many Governments of any new restrictive fiscal measures, suggesting to consumers that existing levels of income are unlikely to be reduced.

The trend towards higher personal consumption ratios has also been facilitated by government policy towards domestic consumer credit markets and financial innovation. The relaxation of restrictions on borrowing and the introduction of numerous new consumer credit instruments in several developed market economies have resulted in the rapid growth of consumer credit, particularly in the form of credit card debt and housing-related borrowing. Sustained confidence in the economic outlook has been one of the factors encouraging consumers to take advantage of the new opportunities to incur larger amounts of debt. This stimulus to consumption may be fading in some countries as households reach the limit of their debt-carrying capacity and Governments also become concerned about the possible repercussions of high levels of consumer indebtedness.[e] On the other hand, countries with lower levels of personal indebtedness and higher household savings rates (notably the Federal Republic of Germany and Japan) might continue to receive a stimulus to consumption from this source.

Prior to late 1985, domestic expenditure in the United States was an important engine of growth in the world economy. The subsequent shifts in global demand and in interna-

a The share of government consumption expenditure in the GDP of the developed market economies as a group increased from an average of 16.7 per cent in 1974-1979 to 17.3 per cent in 1980-1986.

b The increase was from 60.3 to 61.7 per cent of GDP between 1974-1979 and 1980-1986.

c Social security transfers increased from 12.4 to 13.6 per cent of the GDP of the developed market economies between 1974-1979 and 1980-1986.

d See, for example, L. Summers and C. Carroll, "Why is US national savings so low?", *Brookings Papers on Economic Activity,* 1987.

tional trade, brought about by the realignment of the exchange rates of the major currencies, have been additional factors sustaining short-term growth and also providing a basis for medium-term growth by stimulating business investment. The avoidance of a recession between 1985 and 1989 has been possible largely because the United States economy has not slowed to the extent anticipated, while other economies, most notably Japan, have reacted to the change in relative international prices more positively and rapidly than was expected. Japan has assumed the earlier role of the United States, with domestic demand growing by 4 per cent, 5.1 per cent and an estimated 7.5 per cent in 1986, 1987 and 1988, respectively. As with the United States in the earlier period, part of this increase in domestic demand has been channelled into imports, which grew by 9 per cent in 1986, a further 9 per cent in 1987 and 18 per cent in 1988. This, in turn, has induced growth in partner countries.

Another consequence of the realignment of exchange rates has been the rapid increase in Japanese foreign direct investment (see chap. III). This investment has been prompted by two considerations: first, the efforts of Japanese companies to replace and augment exports by producing within former export markets, and, secondly, the fact that foreign assets became cheaper in terms of yen. Fears of protectionist measures (such as voluntary export restraints and local content requirements) and their escalation have reinforced the first of these considerations. Although an increasing proportion is being allocated to developing countries in Asia, the majority of Japanese direct investment is in other developed market economies. In particular, the prospect of a united European market in 1992 has promoted foreign investment in that region, not only by Japan but also by countries from within Europe and by North America.

Micro-economic policy measures have also sustained growth through structural, so-called "supply-side", reforms. Foremost among these have been the tax reforms that have been undertaken in several of the developed market economies since the early 1980s. These have had the effect of increasing the share of profits in GNP in several countries and have acted as an incentive to the business sector, in particular to investment. The trend towards deregulation has also provided increased opportunities (and increased risks) for investment. In many countries, deregulation of the financial sector, including the reduction in restrictions on international financial transfers, has facilitated capital investment by making financial resources more readily available. This has been the case with both small companies requiring limited amounts of seed capital and large companies requiring huge sums to finance industrial restructuring.

The deregulation, liberalization and innovation in international capital markets has also facilitated the switching of growth poles from the United States to Japan. The result of these developments in financial markets has been that, as long as confidence is maintained, the private sector has been willing to finance current account imbalances of a magnitude that would be beyond the reach of public authorities. Despite the dollar's position as a reserve currency, it seems unlikely that the United States would have been able to finance its large and prolonged current account deficit if international capital markets did not exist in their present form. The same applies, by and large, to the deficits of other countries (such as Australia and the United Kingdom at the end of 1988). With less responsive private capital markets, each of these Governments would have been required to adopt restrictive policy measures in order to restore external imbalance. Experience indicates that corrective measures such as these may not only reduce demand directly but also prompt a loss of private sector confidence and reinforce any economic slow-down. The existence of both policy and institutional mechanisms which have allowed the avoidance of such action by Governments on any significant scale over the past several years has been an important factor explaining the continued expansion.

The lower rate of inflation that has been a primary policy objective in the developed market economies since the early 1980s has also contributed to the sustained growth of the period, as it did in the expansion from 1961 to 1969. The average annual rate of change of consumer prices has been 5.5 per cent between 1982 and 1988 (see table A.3) compared to 8.5 per cent during the 1970s, when growth was more erratic.

Lower inflation is conducive to growth in part because it reduces the costs of the resource misallocation that results from inflation-induced inaccuracies in relative prices. Low inflation also facilitates growth because it is usually associated with lower and more stable interest rates. Although real interest rates remain high (see chap. VII), nominal interest rates have declined fairly steadily during the 1980s, with the rate of inflation. Although investment would be still higher with lower real rates of interest, interest-sensitive components of demand, notably business investment and private housing, have been stronger and more stable than was the case in the 1970s.

Tight monetary policy, especially in the early years of the decade, takes a large part of the responsibility for the low inflation of the developed market economies in the middle and later 1980s. Policy measures have not only reduced inflation but have had an important psychological effect because economic agents have become convinced of the determination of Governments to hold inflation in check. This enhanced credibility and confidence in economic policy has reduced inflationary expectations, thereby sustaining low inflation.

Although monetary policy has played a major role in reducing inflation, it has been reinforced by a number of other factors. In Western Europe low rates of capacity utilization and high unemployment have reduced the scope for price and wage increases. Deregulation and globalization have increased competition and have acted as a further anti-inflationary force. Finally, the decline in international commodity prices until 1987, particularly the intermittent collapses in oil prices, have reduced the costs of raw materials and energy and helped hold inflation in the developed market economies in check.

[e] It remains to be seen, for example, whether the consumer debt burden will exacerbate any future slow-down in economic activity as decreases in income force heavily-indebted households to reduce consumption by a disproportionately large amount.

Figure II.2. Contributions to changes in real GNP/GDP of the developed market economies, 1985-1988

(Percentage)

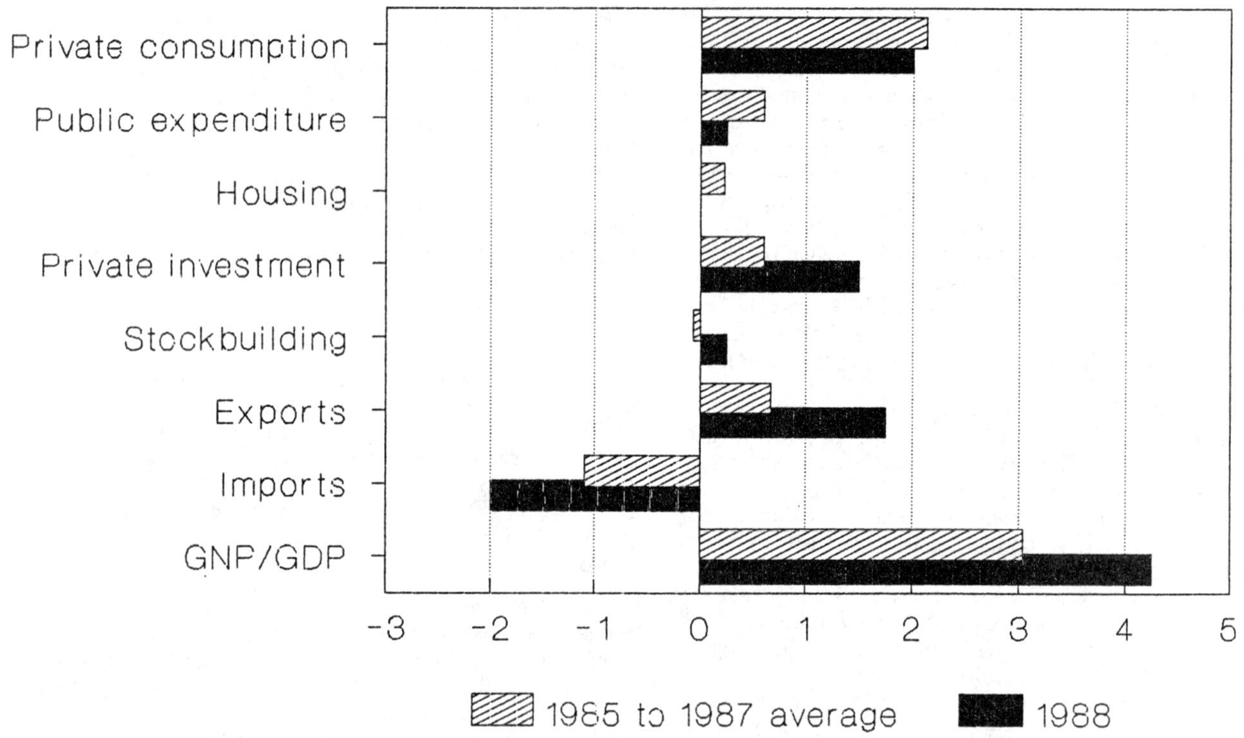


*Source:* Organisation for Economic Co-operation and Development, *Economic Outlook,* various issues.

Japan continues to be the most vigorous of the developed market economies, with output increasing by about 5.7 per cent in 1988. Both the magnitude and the changing composition of this growth were surprising. It was widely expected that Japan would be unable to increase domestic demand sufficiently to offset the decline in export volume that was anticipated as a result of the appreciation of its currency. However, stimulated by fiscal relaxation and the terms-of-trade benefits of currency appreciation on income, domestic demand in Japan has increased faster than in any other developed market economy over the past two years and has more than offset the net decline in foreign demand. An unprecedentedly high proportion of the increase in domestic demand has been directed towards purchasing imported industrial inputs, such as components and machine tools, as well as finished manufactured consumer goods. An increasing proportion of these imports originates in the newly industrializing countries in South-East Asia. This has been an important source of growth in those economies which, in turn, have relied heavily on Japan for the investment goods required to enhance their manufacturing capacity.

It was hoped that the Federal Republic of Germany, as the other major surplus country, would also switch demand from the export to the domestic sector, but domestic demand in the Federal Republic of Germany grew more slowly than in Japan, while its exports have remained vigorous. The investment boom in Europe provides part of the explanation for the sustained increase in the volume of exports by the Federal Republic of Germany. The Federal Republic of Germany is an important source of capital goods in Europe and its exports benefit from surges in investment such as that in 1988. It seems likely that the stimulus provided to investment in the region by the prospect of a unified market in 1992 will continue and this component of the exports of the Federal Republic of Germany will remain vigorous. As a result, its surplus is likely to be increasingly with its partners in Western Europe and correspondingly less with the United States.

Canada and the United Kingdom continued to grow faster than the average, but both began to show signs of overheating. In both countries, excess demand caused inflation to increase in the latter part of 1988 and early 1989 and also resulted in a sizeable current account deficit in 1988. Both Governments have adopted restrictive monetary measures, particularly in the United Kingdom where short-term interest rates rose more than four percentage points during 1988.

France and Italy both grew faster than in 1987 but more slowly than the other large economies, and neither encoun-

Figure II.3. International interest rates, 1980-1988

(Percentage)

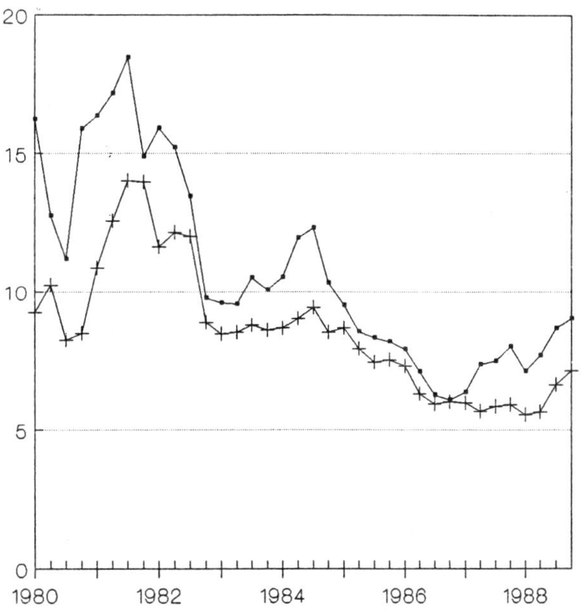


—•— London interbank offered rate (LIBOR) on six-month dollar deposits.

—+— Rate on special drawing rights. This is a weighted average of short-term interest rates in France, the Federal Republic of Germany, Japan, the United Kingdom and the United States.

*Source:* IMF, *International Financial Statistics*, various issues;

Figure II.4. Real effective exchange rates of the Federal Republic of Germany, Japan and the United States, 1982-1988

(1985=100)

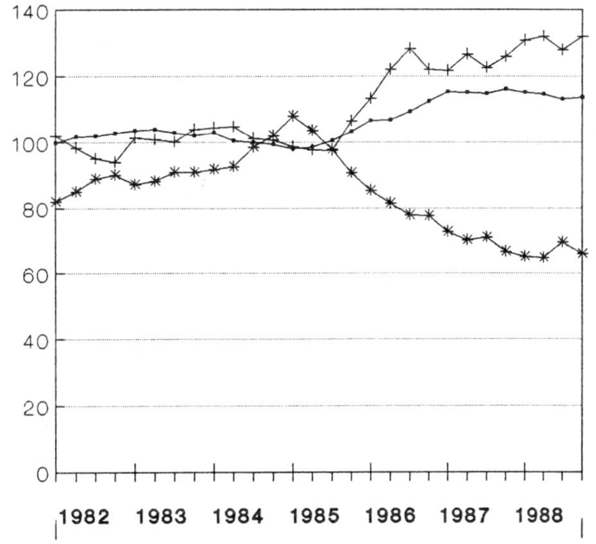


—•— Federal Republic of Germany —+— Japan —✳— United States

*Source:* IMF, *International Financial Statistics*, various issues.

tered the pressures manifested in Canada and the United Kingdom. The smaller industrial economies displayed more mixed results than the seven largest, but the majority did better than in 1987. Greece staged a sizeable turnaround following virtual stagnation in 1986 and 1987, while Denmark and New Zealand showed less dramatic signs of emerging from their recent recessions. The faster-growing economies in this group included Australia, Portugal and Spain. The former benefited from higher prices for its raw materials, but this was insufficient to offset the increased demand for imports and Australia became another of the developed market economies with a large current account deficit in 1988. In Portugal and Spain, growth has been fostered by their joining the European Economic Community (EEC) and the prospects of a unified market in much of Western Europe in 1992. There has been a surge of foreign investment in these countries as firms respond to their lower wage costs and establish facilities intended to service the new market.

Growth caused employment in the developed market economies to rise in 1988—by over 2 per cent in the United States, almost 2 per cent in Japan but less than 1 per cent in Europe. Within this last group of countries, Spain's growth caused employment to increase by over 2 per cent, whereas total employment in France fell, despite the accelerated pace of economic activity.

The growth of employment exceeded the growth of the labour force in most countries in 1988, causing unemployment rates to continue their previous decline (see table A.2). The general decrease in unemployment did little to change the prevailing differences among regions. Unemployment in the large economies in Europe continues to be high by historical standards, while in Japan it remains low. In both Canada and the United States, unemployment has decreased steadily for the past several years, reaching its lowest level of the decade in the United States in early 1989. Only in the United Kingdom since the end of 1986 has a similar trend been apparent in Europe.

**External imbalances: justifiable complacency?**

There was only modest adjustment of the imbalances among the developed market economies in 1988. The trade and current account surpluses of the Federal Republic of Germany and Japan combined remained largely unchanged in absolute amount. There was a 20 per cent improvement in the United States trade deficit, but it was partially offset by a deterioration in its balance on invisibles (see tables III.3 and A.8). However, the growth of both output and trade meant that these surpluses and deficits diminished in relative terms.

The trade and current accounts of some of the other developed market economies have deteriorated rapidly as a result of the recent build-up of domestic demand. Australia, Canada, Portugal and the United Kingdom are encountering unprecedented deficits in their trade balances (see table III.3). Belgium, the Netherlands and Switzerland had current account surpluses that exceeded 2 per cent of their GDP in 1988, but were relatively small in absolute amount.

The evolution of the external imbalances in 1988 was determined by the nature and pattern of global growth and by certain policy actions. Early in 1988, both the magnitude and composition of economic activity in the United States appeared to be consistent with a growth-oriented narrowing of the imbalances, with the main sources of expansion being higher capital investment and, most importantly, increased exports. The latter was initially thought to be the long-awaited response to the depreciation of the dollar that had commenced more than two years earlier and it stirred the hope of a steady narrowing of the trade deficit. However, the strength of United States exports faded as the year progressed, while imports remained robust. Nevertheless, by the end of 1988, the imbalance issue appeared to be of lesser concern to Governments, which instead turned their attention to the reappearance of inflationary pressures.

Inflation in the developed market economies as a group for the whole of 1988 was only slightly higher than in 1987 (see table A.3), but was increasing in a number of countries towards the end of the year and in early 1989. In several countries, this prompted Governments to raise interest rates and by the end of 1988 average short-term interest rates in the leading industrial economies were, on average, some two percentage points higher than a year previously (see figure II.3).

Governments have resorted almost exclusively to monetary policy to control inflation. Most of them have discarded fiscal policy as an instrument of economic management. In part, this is because monetary policy is believed to be faster-acting and more selective. In addition, the prevailing political objective among the Governments of the developed market economies has been to reduce taxes whenever possible. This general trend in fiscal policy has contributed to the continued expansion in these countries, but it has also muted the role of fiscal policy in the event of an excessively rapid build-up of economic activity. In the case of the United States, the magnitude of the fiscal deficit has contributed to the current account deficit and has had an impact on global interest rates (see chap. VII).

Heavier reliance on monetary policy as an instrument of demand management has been facilitated by the liberalization of capital markets. In the less versatile domestic and international capital markets that existed prior to the 1980s, excess domestic demand would have been reflected in an increase in inflation within the country concerned and downward pressure on its exchange rate. Such developments would, in turn, probably have elicited a restrictive monetary and fiscal response from the authorities, dampening domestic demand and relieving the pressure on the exchange rate. In the 1980s, reliance on monetary policy to restrain demand manifests itself in higher domestic interest rates which, combined with the increased availability and mobility of international finance, attract capital inflows. These inflows can finance current account deficits which formerly would have been implausible, or at least unsustainable at the prevailing exchange rate. Excess demand is thus channelled into imports, rather than inflation. However, the differential in international interest rates may produce an appreciation of the exchange rate, rather than the depreciation that would be desirable to encourage the economy move towards current account balance over the longer term. Indeed, in addition to using interest rates for domestic policy purposes, Governments are simultaneously using them as part of their efforts to influence exchange rates. On occasion, these domestic and international policy objectives may not be consistent.

In 1988, this conflict applied in the case of the United States. The successive increases in short-term interest rates in the United States in late 1988 and early 1989, while tending to dampen inflation, complicated the correction of the country's external imbalance in two ways. First, the United States' recent transition to net foreign debtor status means that higher interest rates have a deleterious effect on net investment income: in 1988, the country recorded a net deficit on such flows for the first time in recent economic history (see chap. IV and table A.8). Secondly, higher interest rates in the United States prompted an appreciation of the dollar *vis-à-vis* the deutsche mark and the yen during 1988 and early 1989 (see figure II.4.).

Although fairly small, this appreciation was contrary to the declared objectives of the Group of Seven and there was official intervention to halt the rise on a number of occasions. The strong demand for the dollar, however, tended to allay the fears that the United States deficit posed a threat to stability in financial markets.

### Developments in labour markets in the 1980s

Unemployment has been a pervasive and continuing problem in many developed market economies since the early 1980s, but it is not shared equally among countries or among the different segments of the population. Unemployment has now reached its lowest level of the decade in the United States and has held comparatively steady at a low level in Japan, but in most of Western Europe it continues to be higher than at the beginning of the decade. Nevertheless, there seems to be less preoccupation with the problem than a few years ago. One reason for this may be that the continued economic expansion has resulted in some decline in unemployment and steady increases in employment in most developed market economies since 1984. Unemployment on average reached a peak of 8.6 per cent in developed market economies in 1983; in 1988 it stood at 6.8 per cent.

In a broad view of an economy, those who work generate incomes which produce a demand for goods and services and for people to produce them. There is no immediately obvious reason why there should have to be more unemployment than that sometimes described as "frictional". Such unemployment is that accounted for by the waiting time and the search process involved as job seekers canvas available job offers and employers interview them. This process is inherent to the working of the labour market and is one reason why the first approaches to employment policy have always involved attempts to assist employers and job applicants in getting the right person in the right place.

Unemployment on a large scale poses different problems. It is still not seen the same way by all those who study it and the policies proposed to deal with it have always been controversial. However, in the 1960s there emerged a consensus with two basic components. Regional and local employment problems would have to be dealt with by special measures. Overall unemployment problems, on the other hand, were considered to arise from fluctuations in business investment, which Governments were expected to counter by adjusting fiscal and monetary policies in order to maintain a level of demand that would ensure full employment. These ideas were based on assumptions of an economy which, while far from closed, could still resolve its domestic problems first.

One of the important changes in labour markets in industrial countries in the 1980s is that this approach has been generally abandoned, as markets have opened up. Government spending to stimulate domestic employment was found to produce balance-of-payments crises and the issues of national employment came to be seen in terms of competitive real wages and technological growth.

The employment policy dilemmas facing industrial countries were examined in the *World Economic Survey 1987.*[1] The factors that influenced the demand and supply for labour were also discussed, including the explanation that unemployment breeds unemployment (or "hysteresis").[2] The following provides further information on some aspects of the 1987 analysis.

### Changes in the labour force

If the labour force suddenly grows much faster than the rest of the economy, it is not unreasonable to expect that the problems of absorbing it will produce higher unemployment. Between 1960 and 1975, the population aged 15 to 24 rose by some 29 million in the developed market economies, while the increase from 1975 to 1990 will be only 6 million. With a slower growth of population in this age group, youth unemployment in most developed market economies is decreasing (see table II.2).

Young people generally have much higher unemployment rates than older workers, in both good times and bad, so that changes in the proportion of younger job seekers affect overall unemployment rates. For the United States, it has been estimated that the increasing share of younger people in the labour force raised the overall unemployment rate by 0.3 percentage points in the 1970s, while the decreasing proportion of younger workers has reduced it by 0.4 or 0.5 percent-

1 United Nations publication, Sales No. E.87.II.C.1, chap. VII.

2 For a more recent discussion of hysteresis, focusing on the Federal Republic of Germany and the United Kingdom, see *IMF Survey,* vol. 17, No. 16 (15 August 1988).

Table II.2. Youth[a] unemployment in selected developed market economies, 1982-1988

(Percentage of youth labour force)

| | 1982 | 1983 | 1984 | 1985 | 1986 | 1987 | 1988 |
|---|---|---|---|---|---|---|---|
| North America | | | | | | | |
| Canada | 18.8 | 19.9 | 17.9 | 16.5 | 15.2 | 13.7 | 11.5 |
| United States | 17.0 | 16.4 | 13.3 | 13.0 | 12.7 | 11.7 | 10.5 |
| Europe | | | | | | | |
| Finland | 31.9 | 32.4 | 31.8 | 29.8 | 29.4 | 28.0 | 28.0 |
| France[b] | 19.0 | 19.7 | 24.4 | 25.6 | 23.4 | 23.0 | 24.0 |
| Germany, Federal Republic of[c] | 9.5 | 10.7 | 9.9 | 9.5 | 8.4 | 7.9 | 7.3 |
| Italy | 28.0 | 30.5 | 32.9 | 33.9 | 34.5 | 35.5 | 37.8 |
| Norway | 48.1 | 44.9 | 40.0 | 41.8 | 45.2 | 46.7 | 54.0 |
| Spain[d] | 36.7 | 38.7 | 44.4 | 44.7 | 43.1 | 38.9 | 37.0 |
| Sweden | 7.6 | 8.0 | 6.0 | 5.8 | 5.6 | 4.2 | 4.0 |
| United Kingdom[e] | 23.1 | 23.4 | 22.1 | 21.8 | 20.8 | 17.4 | 14.8 |
| Developed Asia | | | | | | | |
| Australia[f] | 12.9 | 17.9 | 16.1 | 14.3 | 14.5 | 14.6 | 13.0 |
| Japan | 4.4 | 4.5 | 4.9 | 4.8 | 5.2 | 5.2 | 5.0 |

*Source:* OECD, *Employment Outlook 1988* (Paris, September 1988).

a Generally aged 15 to 24.

b Data refer to March of each year. Conscripts are included in the youth labour force.

c Data refer to the registered unemployed at the end of September of each year.

d Data refer to the last quarter of each year.

e Data refer to July of each year and are based on registrations in 1982 and claimants from 1983 on. The data for 1983 and later include non-claimant school-leavers registered at Career Offices.

f Data refer to August of each year.

age points in the 1980s.[3] Moreover, youth participation rates in many developed market economies are expected to decline between 1987 and 2000, partly reflecting a trend towards increased education.[4]

The counterpart of the fall in fertility rates in developed market economies since the mid-1960s is the aging of the populations of these countries and of the work-force (see Special Issues, sect. III below). The population of working age (15-65 years) will be shrinking in some European countries and Japan by the end of the century. They will also have an older work-force. By 2020, about 43 per cent of the working population in the seven largest industrialized countries will be aged 45 or over, compared with 30 per cent in 1988. In contrast with youth, participation rates for the 55-64 age group are expected to rise in some countries as a result of insufficient retirement income, better health and cultural changes.[5]

Another trend on the supply side of the labour market has been the inflow of women into the labour market. The male participation rate dropped between 1973 and 1987 in all developed market economies for which data are available; it is expected to fall further by the year 2000, but the female participation rate has risen and is expected to continue to do so (see box II.2).

### Some effects of employment policies and structural change

Employment- and income-creating programmes have suffered from the curtailment of government spending. At the same time, unemployment compensation from fiscal budgets has increased and remains high in many countries. Unemployment compensation, including various other income maintenance payments to the unemployed, is the largest single category of labour market expenditure in developed market economies. Its relative magnitude partly reflects the national unemployment rate. In 1987, for example, Belgium, Denmark, Ireland, the Netherlands and Spain spent between 2.5 and 3.5 per cent of their respective GDPs on unemployment benefits; all, except Denmark, had especially high unemployment and all, except Spain, also stand out as leading spenders—after Sweden—on measures to help the jobless get work. Such measures include employment services and

3 Lynn E. Browne, "The labour force, unemployment rates, and wage pressures", *New England Economic Review,* Federal Reserve Bank of Boston, January/February 1989.

4 A participation rate is defined as the share of the labour force of a specific age in the total population of that age.

5 OECD, *Employment Outlook 1988* (Paris, September 1988), p. 40.

Table II.3. Unemployment rates in the developed market economies, by sex, 1983, 1985 and 1987

(Percentage)

| | Females | | | Males | | |
|---|---|---|---|---|---|---|
| | 1983 | 1985 | 1987 | 1983 | 1985 | 1987 |
| Australia | 9.9 | 8.0 | 8.3 | 9.9 | 7.8 | 7.5 |
| Belgium | 17.9 | 17.7 | 17.4 | 8.1 | 7.3 | 7.0 |
| Canada | 11.6 | 10.7 | 9.4 | 12.1 | 10.3 | 8.5 |
| Denmark | 10.1 | 9.2 | 8.0 | .. | 6.1 | 5.3 |
| Finland | 5.2 | 4.6 | 4.4 | 5.8 | 5.5 | 5.9 |
| France | 11.1 | 12.9 | 13.7 | 6.6 | 8.6 | 8.6 |
| Germany, Federal Republic of | 9.3 | 9.5 | 9.3 | 6.7 | 6.6 | 6.3 |
| Greece | 11.7 | 11.7 | 11.5 | 5.8 | 5.6 | 5.1 |
| Ireland | 15.0 | 19.7 | 22.1 | 14.2 | 17.1 | 18.1 |
| Japan | 2.7 | 2.7 | 2.8 | 2.7 | 2.7 | 2.8 |
| Luxembourg | 4.7 | 4.4 | 2.3 | 2.7 | 2.2 | 3.1 |
| Netherlands | 14.0 | 12.3 | 12.2 | 11.1 | 9.2 | 7.7 |
| New Zealand | .. | .. | 4.3 | .. | .. | 3.9 |
| Norway | 3.9 | 3.2 | 2.7 | 3.3 | 2.2 | 1.8 |
| Portugal | 12.7 | 12.1 | 9.0 | 5.2 | 6.8 | 4.9 |
| Spain | 21.3 | 25.8 | 27.9 | 16.5 | 19.8 | 15.6 |
| Sweden | 3.7 | 2.9 | 1.9 | 3.5 | 2.8 | 1.9 |
| United Kingdom | 9.8 | 10.9 | 9.6 | 11.9 | 11.8 | 10.8 |
| United States | 9.2 | 7.4 | 6.2 | 9.9 | 7.0 | 6.2 |

*Source:* OECD, *Employment Outlook 1988* (Paris, September 1988).

administration, labour market training of adults, special youth measures, direct job-creation and employment subsidies, as well as special measures for the disabled.

It is noteworthy that European countries with generous unemployment insurance systems (such as Belgium, France, the Federal Republic of Germany, the Netherlands and the United Kingdom) have suffered larger and more persistent increases in unemployment during the 1980s than the United States. There is also evidence of a positive relation between the level of such benefits and the length of time recipients remain unemployed. According to one estimate, an increase in the potential duration of benefit from six months to one year will increase the average period of unemployment by four to five weeks; an increase from six months to two years is predicted to generate a 13- to 16-week increase in the duration of unemployment.[6]

It is also interesting to note that, in the 1980s, employment has grown most in the industrial countries where productivity and real wages grew the least. Real wages and productivity have grown slowly in Canada, Norway, Sweden and the United States during the 1970s and 1980s, while employment has grown markedly. By contrast, wages and productivity grew rapidly in Belgium, Spain and the United Kingdom, but there was little expansion in employment.

The changing structure of the developed market economies may have implications for the overall level of employment since expanding industries may be less labour-intensive than those that are shrinking. There is evidence to suggest that increases in output may be generating less employment than previously. In particular, the increasing use of computer-driven automation will have an impact on the demand for labour. Although the evidence supports a wide range of views concerning the employment effects of new technology, levels of employment are likely to decline in the long term, either in terms of the numbers fully employed or through part-time employment or shorter working hours.[7]

Another aspect of structural change in the industrialized economies is that the demand for labour in expanding industries does not coincide with the qualifications of those released by contracting industries. At the same time, a shift in the structure of economic activity may open up employment opportunities for individuals who were not employed previously. The growth of the service sector, for example, partially explains the increasing role of women in the labour force.

Although the employment of women has been rising rapidly, female unemployment has consistently been higher

6 Lawrence F. Katz and Bruce D. Meyer, "The impact of the potential duration of unemployment benefits on the duration of unemployment", National Bureau of Economic Research, Working Paper No. 2741 (October 1988).

7 Raphael Kaplinksy, *Micro-electronics and employment revisited: A Review* (Geneva, ILO, 1987).

Table II.4. Part-time employment in the developed market economies, 1979, 1983 and 1987

(Percentage)

| | Part-time employment as a proportion of: | | | | | |
|---|---|---|---|---|---|---|
| | Total employment | | | Female employment | | |
| | 1979 | 1983 | 1987 | 1979 | 1983 | 1987 |
| Australia | 15.5 | 17.2 | 20.0 | 34.5 | 35.9 | 39.2 |
| Belgium | 6.0 | 8.1 | 9.4[a] | 16.5 | 19.7 | 22.6[a] |
| Canada | 12.5 | 15.4 | 15.2 | 23.3 | 26.2 | 25.3 |
| Denmark | 22.7 | 23.7 | 23.7[a] | 46.3 | 44.7 | 41.9[a] |
| Finland | 6.7 | 8.3 | 8.1[a] | 10.6 | 12.5 | 11.5[a] |
| France | 8.2 | 9.7 | 11.8[a] | 17.0 | 20.1 | 23.2[a] |
| Germany, Federal Republic of | 11.2 | 12.6 | 12.9[a] | 27.6 | 30.0 | 29.8[a] |
| Greece | .. | 6.5 | 5.8[a] | .. | 12.1 | 10.4[a] |
| Ireland | 5.1 | 6.7 | 6.2[a] | 13.1 | 15.7 | 14.2[a] |
| Italy | 5.3 | 4.6 | 5.0[a] | 10.6 | 9.4 | 9.5[a] |
| Japan | 15.4 | 16.2 | 16.6 | 27.8 | 29.8 | 30.5 |
| Luxembourg | 5.8 | 6.7 | 6.6[a] | 17.1 | 18.8 | 15.4[a] |
| Netherlands | 11.1 | 22.0 | 25.3[b] | 31.7 | 50.5 | 55.2[b] |
| Norway | 22.2 | 24.5 | 23.1[a] | 43.5 | 46.5 | 43.0[a] |
| Portugal | .. | .. | 4.1[a] | .. | .. | 6.6[a] |
| Sweden | 23.6 | 24.8 | 25.2 | 46.0 | 45.9 | 45.1 |
| United Kingdom | 16.4 | 19.1 | 21.6[a] | 39.0 | 42.4 | 45.0[a] |
| United States | 16.4 | 18.4 | 17.3 | 26.7 | 28.1 | 26.1 |

*Source:* OECD, *Employment Outlook 1988* (Paris, September 1988).

a 1986.

b 1985.

than male unemployment in all the developed market economies except Finland (see table II.3). One reason for this is that women are less geographically mobile than men and hence more likely to be affected by spatial mismatches.

Another trend is the proliferation of part-time employment. Part-time work is largely a female phenomenon (see box II.2). Over the period 1979-1986, it increased as a share of total employment in every developed market economy except Italy (where it remained low) and Norway (where it held roughly steady at a high level) (see table II.4). The increases have been most notable in the Netherlands and the United Kingdom. The proportion of workers in part-time employ tends to be high for older workers and teenagers, both male and female, especially in Canada, Denmark, Norway and the United States. For older people, working part-time may be a means of overcoming the detrimental effects of full retirement on a person's social contacts, self-esteem and income. For younger workers, part-time employment may be a way of getting a foothold into the labour market and of combining work with education.

Measures directed at youth are an important element of labour market policies in Denmark, France, Ireland, Italy, Spain and the United Kingdom, where special schemes have been launched in response to the combination of high youth unemployment and perceived deficiencies in the educational systems. Direct job-creation and employment subsidies account for 0.7 per cent of GDP in Belgium and substantial expenditures also in Finland, Ireland, Spain, Sweden and the United Kingdom. The Netherlands and Sweden, meanwhile, devote more than 0.7 per cent of GDP to special labour market measures for the disabled.

## Centrally planned economies: focusing on reform

### Growth of output in 1988

The expansion of total output in the centrally planned economies of Eastern Europe and the USSR reached 4.0 per cent in 1988 after 2.6 per cent in 1987 (see table II.1). The upturn was due mostly to the near doubling of growth in the Soviet economy.[8] In Eastern Europe, the change was only from 3.3 per cent in 1987 to 3.5 per cent in 1988 (see table

8 These data are based on official statistics. However, the growth of total output in table II.5 does not appear consistent with the growth rates in the two major sectors of industry and agriculture. Questions have also arisen regarding the methodology for the estimation of the price deflator used to calculate the growth of Soviet output in real terms (see, for example, *Economic Survey of Europe 1988-1989* (United Nations publication, Sales No. E.89.II.E.1), pp. 120-122.

## Box II.2. Women in the labour force

In all industrial countries, more and more women, including those who are married, have entered the labour force. In the United States, for instance, the participation rate for women aged 25 to 54 who have never been married was slightly over 80 per cent in 1987 and the rate for married women was 68 per cent. It is obviously difficult for mothers with young children to take jobs outside the house, but they are increasingly finding ways of doing it even though few countries have comprehensive child-care strategies to assist working mothers. In the United States, more than 55 per cent of all mothers with children under three years of age were in the labour market in 1987. Nevertheless, women are more likely than men either to be unemployed or to drop out of the labour force owing to difficulties finding work.

Many women take part-time work. Women's share of part-time work in 1986-1987 ranged from 61 per cent in Greece to 93 per cent in Belgium (see table 1). However, many jobs, particularly in management, are often closed to part-time workers and promotion prospects are limited. In many countries, part-time work is legally regarded as temporary and employees may have limited entitlement to unemployment, sickness and other social security benefits. If unemployment rises, the drop in part-time employment opportunities tends to be greater than the drop in full-time employment offerings and part-time workers become the first to be made redundant during a recession.

During the 1960s and early 1970s, many Governments passed legislation making it unlawful to pay women less than men for the same job, but women's earnings are far from parity with men's (see table 2).

Job opportunities for women are concentrated in particular industries and in a rather narrow band of occupations and women are found in relatively low-level positions within each occupation. Women are highly represented in clerical jobs and in the service sector, while men are strongly represented within transport and within the manufacturing sector. Women have penetrated virtually every occupation in recent years, but this has not so far produced much convergence in the overall distribution of male and female employment across occupations and industries.

It should be noted, however, that women own and run an increasing number of firms. It is reported that in the United States women now own 25 per cent of the business firms, while 30 per cent of all entrepreneurs in Finland are women, 25 per cent in Sweden, 20 per cent in France and 21 per cent in the Federal Republic of Germany. Canadian women own nearly one enterprise in three and about half the new jobs created come from these businesses.[a]

Table 1. Female share of part-time employment, 1979, 1983 and 1987

(Percentage)

| | 1979 | 1983 | 1987 |
|---|---|---|---|
| Australia | 78.8 | 77.8 | 78.2 |
| Belgium | 89.3 | 84.0 | 93.3[a] |
| Canada | 72.1 | 71.3 | 71.9 |
| Denmark | 86.9 | 84.7 | 80.1[a] |
| Finland | 74.7 | 72.1 | 68.4[a] |
| France | 82.0 | 84.6 | 82.2[a] |
| Germany, Federal Republic of | 91.6 | 91.9 | 90.3[a] |
| Greece | .. | 61.7 | 61.0[a] |
| Ireland | 71.2 | 72.0 | 72.6[a] |
| Italy | 61.4 | 64.8 | 64.2[a] |
| Japan | 69.7 | 72.7 | 73.3 |
| Luxembourg | 87.5 | 90.0 | 79.3[a] |
| Netherlands | 82.5 | 76.2 | 75.3[b] |
| Norway | 76.8 | 77.3 | 81.5[a] |
| Portugal | .. | .. | 64.0[a] |
| Sweden | 87.5 | 86.6 | 85.9 |
| United Kingdom | 92.8 | 89.6 | 88.7[a] |
| United States | 67.1 | 66.8 | 67.6 |

*Source:* OECD, *Employment Outlook 1988* (Paris, September 1988).
a 1986.
b 1985.

Table 2. Ratio of female to male earnings in selected developed market economies, 1960 and 1980

(Percentage)

| Country | 1960 | 1980 |
|---|---|---|
| Australia | 59 | 75 |
| Canada | 59 | 64 |
| France | 64 | 71 |
| Germany, Federal Republic of | 65 | 72 |
| Italy | 73 | 83 |
| Japan | 46 | 54 |
| Sweden | 72 | 90 |
| United Kingdom | 61 | 79 |
| United States | 66 | 66 |

*Source:* Adapted from Morley Gunderson, "Male-female wage differentials and policy responses", *Journal of Economic Literature,* vol. 27, No. 1 (March 1989), p. 47.

a As reported in *Employment Gazette,* United Kingdom Department of Employment, vol. 97, No. 1 (January 1989), p. 60.

Table II.5. European centrally planned economies: growth of output, 1982-1989

(Annual percentage change)

| | 1982 | 1983 | 1984 | 1985 | 1986 | 1987 | 1988[a] | 1989[b] |
|---|---|---|---|---|---|---|---|---|
| Total output | | | | | | | | |
| Eastern Europe | 0.1 | 3.9 | 5.3 | 3.7 | 4.6 | 3.3 | 3.5 | 4.5 |
| USSR | 3.9 | 4.2 | 2.9 | 3.5 | 4.1 | 2.3 | 4.4 | 6.0 |
| Industrial output | | | | | | | | |
| Eastern Europe | 1.2 | 4.4 | 4.8 | 4.1 | 4.6 | 3.5 | 3.7 | 3.9 |
| USSR | 2.9 | 4.2 | 4.1 | 3.9 | 4.9 | 3.9 | 3.9 | 4.0 |
| Agricultural output | | | | | | | | |
| Eastern Europe | 1.6 | 0.9 | 7.0 | -1.1 | 5.3 | -0.9 | 0.9 | 3.0 |
| USSR | 5.5 | 6.2 | -0.1 | 0.1 | 5.3 | -0.6 | 0.7 | 7.7 |
| Investment | | | | | | | | |
| Eastern Europe | 1.2 | 4.7 | 2.0 | 3.2 | 7.1 | 5.4 | 4.3 | .. |
| USSR | 3.5 | 5.6 | 1.9 | 3.0 | 8.4 | 5.6 | 4.8 | 4.2 |

*Source:* Department of International Economic and Social Affairs of the United Nations Secretariat, based on national and international sources.

a Data are based on official statistics (see footnote 8).

b Planned.

II.5). The strengthening of growth in the Soviet Union was largely attributable to the improvement in labour productivity which grew by 5.1 per cent in 1988 compared with 2.4 per cent in 1987 and an annual average of 3.2 per cent for the period 1981-1986. The revival was not, however, evenly distributed across sectors: industrial output attained the same rate of growth as in 1987, but the improvement in agricultural production was only 0.7 per cent.

Growth in Eastern Europe in 1988 varied from a high of 6.2 per cent in Bulgaria to 0.5 per cent in Hungary (see table A.4). The objective of quantitative growth appears to have been given lower priority in most of these countries and the focus of policy deliberations is now on institutional and structural reforms aimed at improving the quality of economic development. *Perestroyka* in the Soviet Union has become a powerful catalyst for reformist aspirations in the majority of East European countries, but the formulation of reforms has proved to be difficult and implementation remains uneven.

The plans for these economies in 1988 assumed that industrial output and agricultural production would increase by between 0.5 and 2.5 per cent. The weather interfered with these targets and agricultural production grew by only 0.7 per cent in the Soviet Union and fell by 3.8 per cent in the German Democratic Republic. Agricultural growth for the region as a whole was about 0.8 per cent in 1988. Growth of overall industrial production in the Eastern European economies in 1988 was less than planned, but better than in 1987, mostly because of increases in Bulgaria, the German Democratic Republic and Poland. The overall industrial picture was marred by the limited availability of energy, the sluggishness of construction and slow progress in the conservation of energy and material inputs. The energy situation, however, was less tight than in previous years.

For the region as a whole, the growth of investment in 1988 was less than in the previous year. There was a more modest approach to investment planning in 1988. The average planned rate of growth ranged from a 2.4 per cent decline in Czechoslovakia to about 4 per cent growth in Bulgaria and Poland. The Soviet Union aimed at investment growth of 5.7 per cent but reached only 4.8 per cent.

In the foreign trade sector, the rate of growth in the volume of exports increased after a downturn in 1987 and imports increased in volume after two years of decline.[9] Bulgaria, Czechoslovakia and Hungary transformed their trade deficits of prior years into surpluses. The six Eastern European economies had a surplus of about $1.5 billion in trade with the developed market economies and a surplus of $4.4 billion with the Soviet Union. The adjustment of the external sector, as reflected in the increasing trade surpluses, meant lower availability of resources for domestic purposes. On the other hand, a liberal import policy in the Soviet Union turned the foreign trade balance from a small surplus in 1987 to a deficit of $2.7 billion in 1988, but increased the supply of much needed technology.

After the increase in foreign debt in 1987, the Eastern European economies were cautious in their international hard currency borrowing in 1988. The indebtedness of the region decreased, owing to the strong foreign trade performance. Romania paid back all its external debt by March 1989, after a very aggressive export policy. Hungary and Poland also slowed the growth of their indebtedness.

9 For a detailed analysis of recent trends in the trade of the centrally planned economies, see *Economic Survey of Europe 1988-1989*, (United Nations publication, Sales No. E.89.II.E.1), pp. 158-165.

Substantial domestic imbalances remain in several of the centrally planned economies. Accentuated pressures in 1988 resulted in shortages, queues and the extension or introduction of rationing in some countries. In Hungary and Poland, there were substantial price increases. A major concern in all these economies was the restoration of balance in consumer markets, in particular for food.

## Continued economic reform

Soviet reforms served to deepen and broaden the scope of acceptable economic policy changes in other centrally planned economies in 1988. The common denominator of these economic reforms has been the emphasis on market discipline, although the degree to which full-fledged market-type mechanisms have been pursued has varied from country to country.[10] Bulgaria, Hungary and Poland have adopted an ambitious approach, coupled with substantial political change. Czechoslovakia has also strengthened its stance towards reform, but the German Democratic Republic and Romania have directed their efforts towards improving existing economic mechanisms.

### Enterprise reform

Attempts to decentralize planning and to strengthen the autonomy of industrial enterprises, through such principles as self-financing, have been at the core of many Soviet reforms. In 1988, 19,000 industrial associations and enterprises, employing about 55 per cent of the industrial workforce and producing about 60 per cent of industrial output, were operating on the basis of full economic accountability and self-financing.[11]

The reform provides for an enterprise's right to determine its areas of activity and to adapt its production and delivery plans in accordance with contractual obligations and agreements. It also places enterprises on an equal legal footing in their relations with government agencies. Enterprise management has been given wider latitude in deciding on labour remuneration and in financing the expansion of social services from enterprise funds. There has also been greater democratization of the internal decision-making process.

So far, the measures adopted by the Soviet Government have had a smaller impact than expected in terms of growth of output.[12] Moreover, there have been widely criticized deviations from the reform policy. One issue has been the abuse of planning prerogatives and state orders by the branch ministries. The reform regulations state that annual plans will be independently drawn up and ratified by enterprises on the basis of their five-year plans and delivery contracts. According to this reform, the State has to offer a profitable contract when it deems it necessary to develop lines of production.[13] Nevertheless, attempts by enterprises to depart from output targets assigned by the ministries have been overruled. Even cases where enterprise management contested state orders in a court of law were stifled by ministries employing the administrative and economic coercion still at their disposal.[14]

In addition, infringements by ministries on the self-financing status of enterprises remains a common practice. The self-financing of enterprises implies that the expenses they incur have to be covered by their own resources and that income from the sale of surplus fixed capital and other property belongs to the enterprise in the same way as profits. This concept is incompatible with restrictions on the enterprise's rights, since these can worsen its financial position through no fault of its own.

By the end of 1988, it appeared that, while the old mechanisms were no longer in effect, there was still no new, internally consistent, economic arrangement in its place. This situation stems from the contradiction between the enterprises' rights of increased autonomy and the fact that central administrative and planning bodies have retained responsibility for supplying key products to the economy.

Another shortcoming is that reform has not been accompanied by more widespread and active competition and is being carried out within a protected market in which enterprises take full advantage of their monopoly position, despite the emphasis in the Law on State Enterprise on their operating competitively. Such circumstances, permit the inflation of producer prices, since enterprises often choose to comply with the new requirements on self-financing by introducing "new" products, with higher price mark-ups, rather than by improving the quantity of their output.[15]

These problems have been taken into account in drawing up the Soviet plan for 1989, when all sectors are expected to switch to full economic accountability and self-financing. Compulsory output quotas have been reduced to less than 60 per cent of output in most large sectors and as low as 25 per cent in the machine-building complex.[16]

In response to the stifling of enterprise autonomy, the long-term leasing of enterprises by employees from state agencies is being promoted as one of the most promising and

10 For analysis of economic reforms in the centrally planned economies, see *World Economic Survey 1988* (United Nations publication, Sales No. E.88.II.C.1), pp. 93-120.

11 *Izvestiya,* 9 December 1988, p. 2.

12 *Izvestiya,* 3 September 1988, p. 1.

13 P. Bunich, "Samofinansirovanie: sushchnost', problemy, tendentsii", *Material'no-teknicheskoe snabzhenie,* No. 4 (April 1988), pp. 20-25.

14 Reports to this effect are numerous; for the most vivid, see A. Druzenko, "Dvadtsat' protsentov . . . nezavisimosti", *Izvestiya,* 15 March 1988, p. 2; V. Krivosheev "Gibel' idej", *Izvestiya,* 17 June 1988, p. 2; and "Dve nedeli na khozraschete", *Ekonomicheskaya gazeta,* No. 3 (January 1989), p. 5.

15 For a discussion of these problems, see, for example, *Sotsialisticheskaya industriya,* 11 May 1988, p. 3; 3 and 4 August 1988, p. 2; and 5 January 1989, p. 1.

16 D. Valovoy, "Piramida", *Pravda,* 19 September 1988, p. 2.

effective avenues of reform. Under this arrangement, employees lease enterprises for 10 to 20 years for an annual fee to be determined through negotiation. Management has the final authority for the distribution of enterprise earnings (after fixed deductions and taxes). Leasing has been in existence only since the latter half of 1988, but is reported to have increased productivity and efficiency and is being contemplated by many industrial managers. The State is giving priority to the leasing of unprofitable and inefficient enterprises.[17]

The Government is also putting pressure on inefficient producers. In September 1988, in an effort to reduce the state deficit, the Soviet Government called for a plan of action to liquidate loss-making enterprises. This is the first official recognition of the inevitability of some form of bankruptcy, which is a necessity if genuine self-financing is to work.

Wholesale trade is expected gradually to replace the system of rationing of investment goods. In 1988, enterprises were allowed to exchange surplus goods and those produced above planned output through wholesale distribution centres. To strengthen contracts, sanctions for non-delivery were increased. The result was that the volume of wholesale trade increased fourfold over the previous year.

Another element of the Soviet reforms is the expansion of co-operatives, with the total number of co-operatives growing from 3,700 in July 1987 to 48,500 in October 1988. While total employment in co-operative and individual enterprises is still no more than 1 per cent of the total labour force,[18] it is estimated that they have the potential to employ several million more workers and expand their share of retail turnover to more than 20 per cent in the next few years.

The legal and fiscal regulations of this sector were made more liberal in 1988, allowing the diversification of co-operatives into additional sectors of the economy. As a result, when some co-operatives experienced difficulties obtaining credit, they established co-operative banks. Such banks, which first appeared in August 1988, are free from most credit regulation, having been given the right to set credit terms mostly as they see fit.[19]

Reform in Poland has similarly focused on the three principles of enterprise autonomy, self-management and self-financing. The previous subordination of the enterprise is to be replaced by an equal partnership within a framework of mutually binding regulations. Workers' councils, elected by the work-force, are to obtain decision-making power in their economic unit, while the enterprise director will retain control of operations. By enforcing self-financing, profit is to be the cornerstone of the financial system.

The process of reform in Poland has been erratic because of the contradiction between the goals of economic growth and market equilibrium. Thus far, reform has remained mostly legislation and has had little influence on the behaviour of economic entities. The main reason for this is that the market has not been efficient in allocating and distributing resources. State intervention has become more and more common. This has amounted to the reintroduction of the traditional planning system through individual control measures and direct regulations. A number of non-price instruments continue to be employed to ensure sufficient resources for priority purposes. Investment continues to be subject to central controls and to be influenced by policies aimed at self-sufficiency in key products and by established trading patterns within the CMEA area. Administrative control of prices and discretionary individualization of taxes have remained largely intact, while the subsidization and rationing of industrial supplies have not been greatly curbed.

Poland faces a number of constraints to economic liberalization. One is the fact that it has to run a substantial trade surplus with the convertible currency area to finance its debt-servicing obligations. On the domestic front, because of price distortions, shortages and the limited usefulness of financial indicators, administrative intervention has continued to play an important role in economic management. Moreover, it has always been intended that certain enterprises and sectors (including the energy sector) should be excluded, wholly or partly, from the reform. Finally, the commitment to other social policy objectives (such as the desire to limit price increases and to maintain full employment) has tended to slow the pace at which central controls have been dismantled. The continued emphasis on the central plan suggests that Polish economic reform needs greater attention if it is to succeed.

Reform in Hungary has included a reduction in central control, the reduced subsidization of enterprises and an increase in their autonomy. Appropriate guarantees are provided by the Law on Economic Associations adopted in October 1988.[20] This is intended to encourage the creation of enterprises through the private and state issuance of stocks, to allow limited liability enterprises to be capitalized through the sale of shares and to increase the number of limited liability companies in general. Private firms are allowed to employ up to 500 workers, compared with the previous range of 13 to 25, depending on the nature of the business.[21] The new laws improve the legal status of non-socialized enterprises and limit the business risks involved in the investment of private capital.[22]

In Czechoslovakia, subsidies are being eliminated gradually and producers are being introduced to the influence of

17 T. Rysina, "Arenda", *Ekonomicheskaya gazeta,* No. 48 (November 1988), p. 5.

18 *Ekonomicheskaya gazeta,* No. 52 (December 1988), p. 4.

19 *Izvestiya,* 26 August 1988, p. 1.

20 The full text of the Law was published in *Heti Világgazdaság* (Budapest), 21 December 1988, pp. 3-20.

21 *Heti Világgazdaság* (Budapest), 10 September 1988.

22 Private stock enterprises can be formed with a minimum capital of 10 million forints, half of it in cash, and can have any combination of domestic (either private or state) and foreign participation. The minimum capital required for limited liability enterprises would be 1 million forints.

world market prices. Greater efficiency is also being introduced in the labour market. On 1 January 1989, an amendment to the Labour Code was promulgated, which foresees greater flexibility in changing jobs and in implementing labour rationalization policies at the micro-economic level.

In Bulgaria, a comprehensive and detailed programme for developing a market-oriented economic system was introduced in January 1989.[23] The first component of this package transforms state-owned enterprises into joint stock companies. A second component will replace administrative controls with indirect policy instruments, such as taxation, price policies and credit and foreign exchange regulations. Market-oriented price-setting has been established, fiscal policies have been streamlined with the introduction of uniform profit and value-added taxes, and the exchange rate is expected to be adjusted and to become more flexible. A third major component of reform will be the overhaul of property relationships, with the introduction of diversified forms of ownership, including private. It has been reported that Bulgaria expects to have its own stock exchange in two to three years.

### Agricultural reform

Compared to developments in other sectors, Soviet agricultural reform has been limited. Independence still eludes Soviet farm managers and infringements on farms' legally established rights are widespread, making it difficult to implement the changes envisaged.

Hopes for increasing efficiency in the agricultural sector remain weak, due in part to inconsistencies in the policies introduced in 1986 and 1987 to overcome the sector's difficulties.[24] These measures sought to reduce the number of centrally determined norms and to give more leeway to regional authorities and production units in planning, investment and financial control. Dissatisfaction with the outcome of these reforms prompted the discussions on possible new directions in farm policy. It was recognized that the failure of the existing measures stemmed from a command system that gave farmers little autonomy and few incentives and that often issued instructions that suited planners, but not producers. It was also recognized that piecemeal measures could hardly change the situation.

The corrective actions taken in March 1989 allowed individual farmers and farmers' associations to take long-term leases on land and fixed assets and gave more backing to small co-operatives and family and private plots. Inefficient farms are to be put up for competitive tender, under rules that are to be fixed by a new law on land use. Generally, large-scale farms are expected to become more loosely organized, providing oversight and services instead of direct control. Central and regional agro-industrial bureaux have been abolished, with joint management bodies set up in their place by local farms if they deem it necessary. There is to be an overhaul of the price and credit system and eventually an end to the régime of food subsidies that has become an ever-growing burden on the state budget.[25]

As a part of Polish agricultural reform, the Government has dismantled the state monopoly on agricultural procurement and is allowing co-operatives and private firms to compete with state enterprises for the purchase of farm products for further processing.

In the Czechoslovakian agricultural sector, a new mode of management is being introduced in 1989 and the independence of enterprises and agricultural co-operatives is being enhanced.

Agricultural complexes in Bulgaria have received greater autonomy by becoming self-financing entities and land can now be leased for 50 years to private farmers. A move to auction off land for personal use is also in the offing. In order to stop the migration of labour from rural to urban areas, further industrialization of agricultural complexes is envisaged.

### Price reform

The issue of price reform is among the most controversial debates surrounding the restructuring of the Soviet economy. Attitudes have undergone a dramatic turnaround and radical calls for immediate action died out as the magnitude of the problem and its political sensitivity became more apparent.

A number of changes in the Soviet price system have been made recently. However, one remaining deficiency is that industrial producer prices are still set primarily from the cost side and do not generally reflect demand. However, as part of the foreign trade reform, domestic prices of import goods are to be more closely related to foreign prices. Similarly, the revision of agricultural procurement prices has established a more reasonable relationship between prices and costs. Moreover, the latter remain distorted because of agricultural subsidies and the prices themselves become meaningless if farms are expected, if ordered, to deliver products at a loss. State retail prices are frequently below market-clearing levels. Decision makers intend to correct these inconsistencies by altering the levels and structures of industrial wholesale prices and agricultural procurement prices. In turn, state retail prices may be modified in conjunction with changes in industrial wholesale and agricultural prices.

Reform policy now emphasizes the need for price decontrols to increase the efficiency of the Soviet economy. At the same time, it is recognized that, unless decontrols are accompanied by policies to absorb excess purchasing power and to overcome supply shortages, there is a risk of inflation. This problem is moving into the forefront of the policy agenda as public awareness of inflationary pressure becomes more acute. The situation is aggravated by pent-up demand for consumer products, large cash holdings, increases in wages in excess of productivity gains and the

23 *Rabotnichesko delo* (Sofia), 11 January 1989 (Supplement) and *Népszabadság* (Budapest), 17 January 1989, p. 3.
24 V. Tikhonov, "Time for land reform", *Moscow News Weekly,* No. 32 (1988), p. 10.
25 *Pravda,* 16 March 1989.

emergence of a budget deficit of at least 5 per cent of net material product.[26]

In the light of these pressures, the Government is adopting a guarded approach to price decontrol, stretching the reform over a longer period than initially intended—probably five to eight years. Some unspecified form of wholesale price change has been set as a goal by 1993. Until then, measures to expand productive capacity to meet growing consumer purchasing power are to be implemented. On the supply side, recent disarmament measures are expected to allow some military production facilities to be converted to the production of consumer goods, relieving some pent-up demand. Other avenues being tested include opening the sale of state-owned housing to individuals already in occupancy and allowing employees to buy shares in state-owned industries.

In Poland, the reluctance of the Government to allow prices to rise to market-clearing levels has affected the conduct of external economic policies, such as limiting the linkage between domestic and world prices and requiring the retention of controls over exports and imports. The major constraint to implementing reforms has been the reluctance to allow economic activity to be restrained by financial concerns. Direct and indirect subsidies continue, as do budget deficits. Credit policy also continues to play an active role in allocating resources within the economy, with interest rates remaining negative in real terms and with priority activities having preferential access to bank credit.

In early 1988, the Polish Government adopted a wide range of institutional, legal and policy changes, together with a modified price reform involving a slower rationalization of the price structure. Emphasis has been put on stimulating entrepreneurship and activating the market mechanism. The reforms aim at reducing reliance on price controls and administrative intervention, at adjusting prices to market-clearing levels while ensuring that inflation is contained, at giving enterprises flexibility and incentives to respond to price signals, and at strengthening financial discipline by making the threat of bankruptcy real. They also envisage greater competition by dismantling some existing conglomerates, by making it easier to establish new enterprises (including participation by foreign investors) and by liberalizing the import régime. The last is to be combined with more active use of the exchange rate as part of a strategy to raise the relative price of tradables.

### Financial sector reform

The emergence of co-operative banks (see above) is part of the current Soviet reorganization of the credit and banking system. During 1988, 41 new commercial banks were created, 24 of them co-operative.[27] The creation of commercial banks was actively encouraged when it became clear that the reorganization of banking at the beginning of 1988 had done little to improve the decentralization and flexibility of the banking sector.[28]

The sale by enterprises of stock-like instruments to employees appeared around mid-1988.[29] This measure aims at using "plant shares" both as an investment vehicle and as a means of mobilizing the cash holdings of the population, thus helping to restore market balance.

In the Polish banking system, nine regional state-owned commercial banks were established in 1988 and greater flexibility in obtaining credit was introduced. In addition, permission was granted to set up a number of independent regional credit and banking organizations to be funded by enterprises, co-operatives and private capital. Finally, legislation adopted in December 1988[30] provides for the free movement of financial resources between economic agents, both to create a capital market with trade in bonds and shares and to introduce competition into the new banking system.

In the Czech banking sector, the State Bank has been acting as the central bank since 1 January 1989, but some central bank functions have been delegated to other commercial banks. Henceforth, the State, ministries, banks and enterprises can establish financial institutions; the Government is also considering the establishment of joint ventures with foreign participation in the banking sector.[31]

### External sector

The changes in the external sector in the Soviet Union in 1988 were aimed at decentralizing the traditional trade monopoly, giving authority to some enterprises to import and export on their own account and to maintain foreign currency bank accounts, and permitting joint ventures with foreign equity within the country.

The plan endorsed by the Politburo in October 1988 called for a radical expansion of foreign trade up to the year 2000, as well as a gradual move to full convertibility of the rouble. These new reforms were elaborated in a decree adopted at the beginning of December. As of 1 April 1989, this decree permits any enterprise or state or co-operative organization to engage in export and import activities, as well as allowing the establishment, on a joint stock basis, of trading firms and consortia for that purpose. These organizations are to exist as self-financing entities. New tariff and non-tariff regulations are to be worked out and a new law on foreign trade is to be prepared. The decree provides for deductions from

26 *Pravda*, 28 October 1988, p. 4 and *Literaturnaya gazeta*, 25 January 1989, p. 11.

27 V. Zakharov, "Novye banki. Zachem oni?", *Ekonomicheskaya gazeta*, No. 2 (January 1989), p. 9.

28 A critical assessment of the current state of banking reform is offered in I. Sheludko, "Bank: chto meshaet stat' partnerom", *Ekonomicheskaya gazeta*, No. 50 (December 1988), p. 10 and S. Bogdonkevich and V. Zayash "A nuzhny li spetsbanki?", *Ekonomicheskaya gazeta*, No. 51 (December 1988), p. 19.

29 It was officially approved on 15 October 1988. See "O vypuske predpriyatiyami i organizatsiyami tsennykh bumag", *Ekonomicheskaya gazeta*, No. 45 (November 1988), p. 23.

30 *Trybuna ludu*, 8 December 1988, p. 8.

31 *Figyelő* (Budapest), 3 November 1988, p. 18.

enterprises' foreign currency earnings to the state budget after 1991, for a new uniform exchange rate and for foreign currency auctions for enterprises under the supervision of the State Bank. It also outlines a new system of trade credits and insurance and envisages the development of free zones in order to attract foreign capital. Finally, an effort is being made to phase out some 3,000 different currency coefficients and move closer to a realistic exchange rate, first by adjusting the rouble downwards by 50 per cent on 1 January 1990 and then by establishing a new exchange rate one year later.

Foreign companies have been allowed to gain majority control of joint enterprises for the first time; labour laws affecting them have been relaxed to allow for more flexible hiring and dismissal. The joint venture law provides for the repatriation of profits and property and the Ministry of Finance has been given the right to waive taxation of repatriated profits for a set period. Joint ventures operate outside the state plan and receive a two-year tax holiday, investment tax rebates and other tax concessions. About 200 such ventures had been set up as of early 1989.

In Bulgaria, the legal procedures for joint ventures with foreign participation have been amended and the regulation of domestic and foreign enterprises has been made more similar. Majority ownership in a limited liability company with foreign capital requires state approval and 50 per cent of the employees have to be of Bulgarian nationality. State approval is mandatory if more than 20 per cent of the stock in a national company is to be acquired by a foreign firm. In Hungary, reform of foreign trade is to involve the gradual expansion of import possibilities, as well as an exchange rate policy that more accurately reflects the national currency's purchasing power.

## Developing countries: the growing dichotomy

The reports of the regional commissions have in recent years emphasized the great diversity among the major regions and the reports for 1988 suggest no change in earlier trends (see figure II.5). In Latin America, Africa and West Asia, per capita output declined in 1988. On the other hand, in South Asia and East Asia, most countries have grown rapidly in the 1980s and they grew even faster in 1988 than in 1987.

The number of developing countries with growth rates over 5 per cent increased in 1988 (see table II.6). Nevertheless, several developing countries declined or showed no growth. This is particularly worrisome since it occurred at a time when output in the industrial countries and international trade were buoyant.

For the first time in the 1980s, the rate of growth of the gross domestic product of the developing countries (excluding China) exceeded 3 per cent, rising to about 3.3 per cent in 1988 from 2.6 per cent in 1987. Despite the uncertainty about the future, it appears that the average rate of growth of output of the developing countries in the second half of the decade will be an improvement on the first half, when total output was almost stagnant while population continued to increase. Nevertheless, for a large number of developing countries, even the second half of the decade will see a continued fall or stagnation in per capita output.

During the 1970s, per capita output in all developing regions grew faster than in the developed market economies, and the gap was narrowing. In the 1980s, the situation has been more complex. An important group of Asian countries, large and small, has been growing faster, in both overall terms and per capita terms, than the developed market economies. Other developing countries have been growing more slowly.

One outcome of these trends is that the distribution of income among developing countries, weighted by population, has become more even, as some of the large low-income countries have been growing fast. Another one, however, is that, for a large number of developing countries, the economic gap between them and the developed countries is widening rapidly.

Some developing countries, mostly in Asia, have maintained a strong development momentum in the 1980s, even in the early years when the international environment was distinctly unfavourable, and they have benefited from the stimulus of the revival in world markets and world trade. Others, mostly in Africa and Latin America, have been caught in a slow-growth trap and their international linkages have been negative rather than positive.

Nevertheless, for most developing countries, the international economic environment since 1987 has been more favourable than in the earlier years of the 1980s. Fluctuations in the prices of both fuel and non-fuel commodities continued in 1988, but there was not a continuation of the deterioration in non-fuel commodity prices that has characterized much of the 1980s (see table II.7). On average, non-fuel commodity prices increased in 1988 in both nominal and real terms (see chap. III). This benefited many oil-importing developing countries, particularly those producing metals and, to a lesser extent, those producing agricultural raw materials. On the other hand, average prices of tropical beverages, a major export for several countries, did not increase as much; cocoa prices declined.

In the case of oil, international prices at the beginning of 1988 were about $16 per barrel; at the end of the year, they were in the same range and gradually eased higher in the early months of 1989. In mid-1988, however, they had fallen close to $10 per barrel (see chap. V), with the result that the average price during 1988 was some 20 per cent lower than in 1987. Despite the deterioration in their terms of trade (see table A.5), economic growth in the energy-exporting countries as a group improved by almost two percentage points in 1988 (table II.8). This contrasts with the effects of the previous, albeit larger, decline in oil prices in 1986 when there was a reversal of economic growth in the energy-exporting countries as a group.

Figure II.5 Rates of growth of output of developiong countries by region, 1981-1988

(Annual percentage rate)

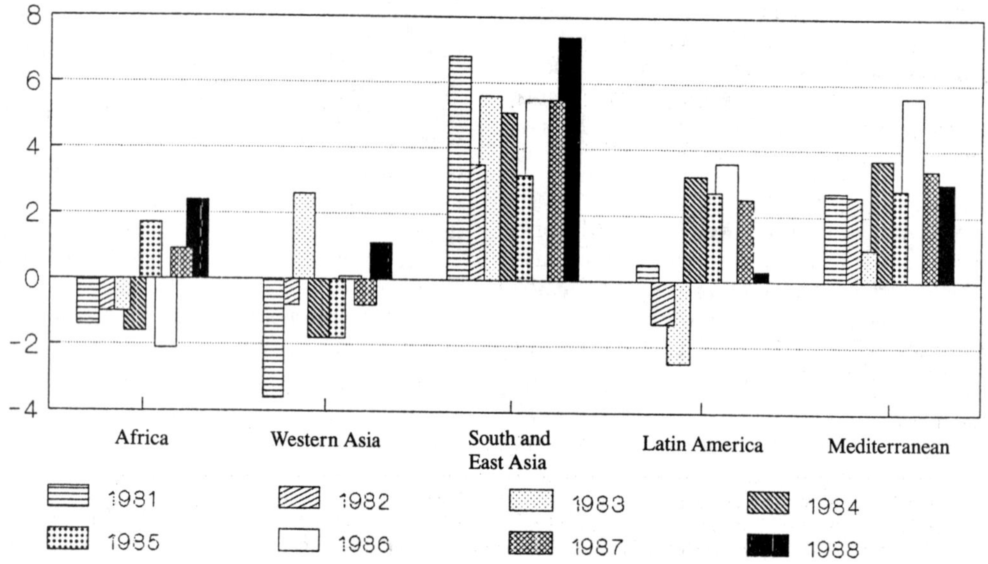


*Source:* Department of International Economic and Social Affairs of the Untied Nations Secretariat

For many developing countries, the overriding concern in 1988 continued to be the impediment to development presented by external indebtedness (see chap. IV). Although there were signs of potential progress, there were few tangible results in reducing the debt burden; in some countries, it worsened in 1988. An inadequate and, in many cases, negative net transfer of external resources remained a constraint on imports and investment in debtor countries. Adjustment efforts continued, but successes under such conditions have often been matched, or even followed, by failures.

**Latin America: a further set-back**

Output in Latin America and the Caribbean grew by only 0.7 per cent in 1988. This compares with a population growth rate of 2.2 per cent. Medium-term prospects offer negligible respite (see below), which highlights the long-

Table II.6. Developing countries:[a] frequency distribution of rates of growth of output, 1982-1988

(Number of countries)

| | 1982 | 1983 | 1984 | 1985 | 1986 | 1987 | 1988[b] | Population of countries in 1988 column: Number (millions) | Population of countries in 1988 column: Percentage of total |
|---|---|---|---|---|---|---|---|---|---|
| Zero or below | 40 | 33 | 27 | 25 | 19 | 18 | 13 | 328 | 12.4 |
| 0.1-2.5 per cent | 18 | 17 | 19 | 21 | 19 | 22 | 26 | 436 | 16.5 |
| 2.6-5.0 per cent | 11 | 20 | 21 | 25 | 33 | 31 | 29 | 625 | 24.7 |
| 5.1-7.5 per cent | 9 | 8 | 10 | 8 | 7 | 8 | 11 | 303 | 11.5 |
| 7.6 per cent and over | 5 | 5 | 6 | 4 | 5 | 4 | 4 | 918 | 34.8 |
| Total | 83 | 83 | 83 | 83 | 83 | 83 | 83 | 2 638 | 100.0 |

*Source:* Department of International Economic and Social Affairs of the United Nations Secretariat. The data on population and population growth rates are those published by the Department in *World Demographic Estimates and Projections, 1950-2025* (United Nations publication, Sales No. E.86.XIII.3).

[a] Based on data for 83 countries that account for 97 per cent of the population of developing countries, excluding China.

[b] Based on preliminary data.

Table II.7. Indicators of the international economic environment, 1980-1988

| | 1980 | 1981 | 1982 | 1983 | 1984 | 1985 | 1986 | 1987 | 1988 |
|---|---|---|---|---|---|---|---|---|---|
| | | | | (Annual percentage change) | | | | | |
| *World trade* | | | | | | | | | |
| Volume of world exports | 0.8 | 0.1 | -2.1 | 1.6 | 7.8 | 2.9 | 3.8 | 5.7 | 8.3[a] |
| *World prices* | | | | | | | | | |
| Oil | 65.8 | 11.5 | -4.3 | -10.3 | -4.3 | -3.5 | -45.6 | 16.4 | -20.4 |
| Non-fuel primary commodities | 13.4 | -15.4 | -16.1 | 6.4 | 1.2 | -10.7 | 5.3 | -3.8 | 18.4 |
| Manufactured exports | 11.1 | -6.0 | -2.1 | -4.3 | -3.2 | -1.1 | 15.7 | 11.7 | 6.1 |
| Effective exchange rate of dollar[b] | 0.1 | 12.7 | 11.7 | 5.8 | 7.9 | 4.1 | -19.1 | -11.8 | -5.8 |
| Interest rate[c] (percentage) | 14.0 | 16.7 | 13.6 | 9.9 | 11.3 | 8.6 | 6.8 | 7.3 | 8.1 |
| | | | | (Billions of dollars) | | | | | |
| *World financial flows* | | | | | | | | | |
| Net transfer of resources to developing countries[d] | 41.7 | 42.6 | 11.3 | -0.7 | -9.6 | -25.5 | -20.7 | -25.6 | -32.5 |
| Capital flows into the United States | -28.0 | -27.9 | -27.4 | 34.0 | 80.3 | 97.2 | 123.2 | 135.5 | 118.8 |

*Source:* Department of International Economic and Social Affairs of the United Nations Secretariat, based on IMF, *International Financial Statistics,* various issues; United Nations, *Monthly Bulletin of Statistics,* various issues; UNCTAD, *Commodity Price Bulletin,* various issues; and United States Department of Commerce, *Survey of Current Business,* various issues.

a Preliminary estimates.

b Based on the IMF Multilateral Exchange Rate Model.

c London inter-bank offered rate on six-month dollar deposits.

d For details, see table IV.2.

term nature of the development crisis that has engulfed Latin America throughout the present decade.

One characteristic of the region in the 1980s has been the small number of economies in which high growth has been sustained over a period of more than three years. Brazil achieved an average rate of growth of more than 5 per cent from 1984 to 1986 and Chile has expanded output by more than 5 per cent in each of the past three years, but it is the first country in the region to have done so this decade.[32] Colombia has been able to maintain a steadier, but lower, rate of growth throughout the 1980s and is the only country in the region that has not had negative growth in at least one year during the decade. The consequence of this erratic and low growth is that per capita income for the region as a whole remains below the level of 1980.

The two largest economies account for a large part of the poor economic performance of the region in 1988. There was practically no growth in Brazil, and Mexico grew by only 0.5 per cent, after a series of low or negative growth rates. Stagnation and decline were not confined to the large economies: national and international political difficulties were at the heart of a severe decline in output in Panama and of smaller decreases in Haiti and Nicaragua. Trinidad and Tobago registered its sixth consecutive year of negative growth. Peru suffered the consequences of the unsustainably rapid growth it enjoyed in 1986 and 1987, and strikes caused decreases of 25 and 20 per cent in the output of copper and zinc respectively, the country's two leading exports. Ecuador, on the other hand, staged a partial recovery from the set-back created by its oil pipeline disaster in 1987. Paraguay and some of the Central American countries have shown promise over the past two years.

The decline in oil prices led to lower export earnings and a deterioration in the terms of trade of the region's subgroup of energy-exporting countries in 1988. On the other hand, the situation of the energy-importing countries and major exporters of metals improved. In addition, the rapid growth of world trade and the need for debt-servicing made for larger export volumes; Argentina and Brazil, for example, increased their export volumes by about 20 and 10 per cent, respectively. The result of these price and volume changes was large increases in the export revenue of Argentina, Brazil, Chile and some other countries. Most of these countries achieved large trade surpluses in 1988, but these were absorbed by the service on their external debt. In the case of Argentina, for example, export revenue increased by about 40 per cent in 1988, but imports were reduced.

These trade surpluses reflect the external debt-related net transfer of resources which inhibits the resumption of economic growth in the majority of Latin American economies.

32 However, gross domestic product in Chile fell by some 14 per cent in 1982-1983.

Table II.8 Developing countries: rates of growth of gross domestic product by analytical country groupings, 1981-1990

(Annual percentage change)

| | 1981 | 1982 | 1983 | 1984 | 1985 | 1986 | 1987 | 1988[a] | 1989[b] | 1990[b] |
|---|---|---|---|---|---|---|---|---|---|---|
| Market economies | 1.1 | 0.2 | 0.8 | 2.2 | 2.0 | 2.9 | 2.6 | 3.3 | 3.5 | 4.5 |
| Large market economies | 3.0 | 1.2 | -0.8 | 3.6 | 4.9 | 3.1 | 2.3 | 3.1 | 3.5 | 4.5 |
| Bangladesh[c] | 6.8 | 0.8 | 3.6 | 4.2 | 4.1 | 4.5 | 3.0 | 1.5 | .. | .. |
| Brazil[c] | -2.0 | 1.4 | -2.7 | 4.8 | 8.2 | 8.0 | 2.9 | 0.0 | .. | .. |
| India[c] | 5.9 | 2.9 | 5.4 | 4.9 | 4.5 | 4.8 | 2.2 | 9.0 | .. | .. |
| Indonesia[d] | 7.9 | 2.2 | 4.5 | 4.2 | 1.9 | 3.0 | 3.6 | 4.0 | .. | .. |
| Mexico[d] | 8.3 | 0.0 | -5.2 | 3.5 | 2.7 | -3.5 | 1.4 | 0.5 | .. | .. |
| Nigeria[d] | -5.9 | -1.9 | -6.4 | -5.5 | 2.4 | -5.0 | -2.0 | 3.0 | .. | .. |
| Pakistan[c] | 7.7 | 4.3 | 6.5 | 5.3 | 8.2 | 7.0 | 6.2 | 5.4 | .. | .. |
| Other market economies | -0.2 | -0.4 | 1.9 | 1.3 | 0.2 | 2.8 | 2.9 | 3.4 | 3.5 | 4.5 |
| Net energy-exporting countries | -2.2 | -0.4 | 0.8 | -1.1 | -1.3 | -0.6 | -0.2 | 1.6 | 2.5 | 3.5 |
| Net energy-importing countries | 1.5 | -0.4 | 2.7 | 3.2 | 1.3 | 5.4 | 5.0 | 4.6 | 4.5 | 5.0 |
| China[e] | 4.9 | 8.3 | 9.8 | 12.0 | 12.3 | 7.4 | 9.3 | 11.4 | 10.0 | 9.0 |
| Memorandum items | | | | | | | | | | |
| Fifteen heavily indebted countries | 0.1 | -0.9 | -2.5 | 2.1 | 2.5 | 3.1 | 2.0 | 1.2 | 1.5 | 3.5 |
| Sub-Saharan African countries[f] | 2.1 | -1.1 | 1.1 | 0.8 | 3.0 | 2.3 | 1.5 | 2.2 | 3.0 | 3.0 |

*Source:* Department of International Economic and Social Affairs of the United Nations Secretariat, based on project LINK.

a Preliminary estimates.

b Forecast, rounded to the nearest half percentage point.

c Net energy-importing country.

d Net energy-exporting country.

e Net material product.

f Excluding Nigeria.

For the first time in the decade, the stock of outstanding debt decreased marginally in a few countries, but the increase in international interest rates more than offset the impact of that on debt-service obligations (see chap. IV). The ratio of debt service to exports for the region increased in 1988. This ratio has averaged more than 40 per cent throughout the 1980s and, in the absence of new external finance, it has constrained imports heavily. For the energy-importing countries, the volume of imports declined in 1988, although the opposite was the case for the energy-exporting group, mostly because of the large increase in the case of Mexico. From a longer-term perspective, the volume of imports of the region as a whole continues to be less than in 1981.

Another characteristic of the region in the 1980s has been the decline in the share of output allocated to gross investment. Following a modest recovery in the region's investment ratio in 1987, it declined again in 1988 to below 17 per cent, compared to some 22 per cent at the beginning of the decade. The main reason for this is that a net transfer of resources necessarily involves a curtailment of domestic expenditure and investment is easier to reduce than consumption (see chap. VIII). Investment is also adversely affected by the reduced availability of imports, since the region relies on imports for a large proportion of its capital goods.

A disturbing feature of the economic situation in Latin America in 1988 was the deterioration in the internal macroeconomic balance in many countries. One manifestation of this was the increase in consumer prices in the region which was more than double that in 1987 (see table II.9). In a number of countries, the rate of inflation approached the four-digit level, in some cases despite stabilization policies and, in others, perhaps as a result of them. Among the larger economies, only Chile and Mexico succeeded in reducing the rate of inflation.

The fundamental reason for these inflationary surges was that, as so often in the past, Governments in need of resources and unable to raise them by fiscal means resorted to increasing the money supply. Such an approach enables Governments to meet obligations for which there is not the necessary consensus, but the resulting inflation is a form of taxation which reduces the real income of the population. Numerous experiments have been made in Latin America in recent years which have successfully halted inflation for a short period, but only a few countries have set firm limits to the money supply and adhered to them. In 1988, many of the surges in inflation occurred after the breakdown of a "social pact" involving freezes on wages and prices.

Efforts to overcome the region's debt problem through structural adjustment have gone on for several years, but the lack of tangible results has led to "adjustment fatigue" in many countries. The success of economic policy has become

Table II.9. Developing countries:[a] annual rates of inflation, 1982-1988[b]

(Percentage)

| | 1982 | 1983 | 1984 | 1985 | 1986 | 1987 | 1988[c] |
|---|---|---|---|---|---|---|---|
| All countries | 39.9 | 65.5 | 93.6 | 126.7 | 53.2 | 68.0 | 150.1 |
| (Median) | (11.1) | (11.5) | (11.8) | (10.5) | (8.7) | (9.5) | (8.8) |
| Net energy exporters | 22.6 | 33.7 | 31.1 | 101.1 | 42.0 | 39.4 | 42.1 |
| Net energy importers | 52.3 | 88.3 | 138.6 | 145.2 | 61.2 | 88.7 | 219.0 |
| Western hemisphere | 78.8 | 136.3 | 198.4 | 290.0 | 97.6 | 144.6 | 314.6 |
| (Median) | (11.8) | (16.7) | (20.4) | (25.7) | (19.5) | (21.8) | (24.5) |
| West Asia | 17.1 | 18.9 | 33.1 | 24.3 | 46.6 | 4.7 | 4.3 |
| South and East Asia | 8.0 | 8.9 | 10.0 | 5.8 | 5.3 | 6.5 | 8.0 |
| Africa | 11.7 | 23.2 | 23.4 | 11.1 | 12.5 | 14.2 | 36.1 |
| Frequency distribution | | | | | | | |
| 5 per cent or lower | 6 | 14 | 18 | 21 | 26 | 24 | 21 |
| 5.01-10 per cent | 23 | 20 | 14 | 13 | 13 | 15 | 18 |
| 10.01-20 per cent | 25 | 21 | 16 | 16 | 11 | 12 | 10 |
| 20.01-50 per cent | 13 | 11 | 14 | 14 | 12 | 14 | 12 |
| 50.01-100 per cent | 4 | 2 | 7 | 4 | 9 | 4 | 5 |
| Over 100 per cent | 3 | 6 | 7 | 6 | 3 | 5 | 7 |

*Source:* Department of International Economic and Social Affairs of the United Nations Secretariat, based on IMF, *International Financial Statistics.*

a Based on a sample of 74 countries (73 in 1988).

b Annual rate of change in consumer prices.

c Preliminary estimates.

more dependent on the domestic political climate. Governments in the region have less economic and political room for manouevre and success is becoming increasingly elusive.

The burden of the net transfer has required most countries to be more outward-looking. However, less success has been achieved in reducing fiscal deficits and state participation in the economy. In some countries, the fiscal deficit increased as a proportion of gross national product in 1988. Part of the reason for this has been the increased cost of servicing the country's internal and external debt. The increase in domestic interest rates, introduced as a stabilization-cum-adjustment measure in many countries, has raised the cost of servicing public sector domestic debt, exacerbating existing budget deficits. These have often been financed by issuing new debt, compounding the problem. In addition, much of the region's external debt is public or publicly guaranteed. As a result, increases in international interest rates since mid-1987 have contributed to the growth of fiscal deficits in the region.

### Africa: emerging opportunities amid persistent constraints

In Africa, the rate of growth of output of 2.4 per cent in 1988 was the highest achieved in the 1980s (see table II.1). Nevertheless, as output grew by half a percentage point less than population, per capita output declined again.

Growth in the region as a whole was bolstered both directly and indirectly by the improvement in Nigeria, which reversed its declines of the previous two years and grew by about 3 per cent, despite the decline in oil prices. Egypt, which receives much external assistance, slowed in 1988, but nevertheless increased output by over 4 per cent. A number of other economies in the region grew at rates that were high by comparison with recent history: Ghana, Morocco and Zimbabwe grew by 5 per cent or more. On the other hand, a number of countries, such as Cameroon, Liberia and the Sudan, had negative rates of growth.[33]

Africa's economies remain highly vulnerable to circumstances that are largely beyond their control. Few of them have the size, resilience or momentum to absorb a set-back to a key sector. As a result, differences in annual growth rates usually reflect short-term factors. In 1988, for example, favourable weather played a large part in the improvement in the agricultural sector of several countries. Other countries, such as Mauritania and Senegal, were adversely affected by locusts.

Regional wars and unrest seriously disrupt the region and famine remains a scourge on the continent. More than

33 For a more detailed analysis of the differentiated performance of African economies, see Economic Commission for Africa, *Economic Report on Africa 1989.*

200,000 people died of starvation in the Sudan in 1988, primarily because of hostilities rather than an absolute shortage of food. Civil strife also had a negative effect on the agricultural sector in Angola, Mozambique and Uganda.

The poor performance of the agricultural sector has been the principal development problem for many African economies. Climatic and environmental factors make agricultural development in some African countries difficult, but the sector has great potential, which remains unrealized in large part because of inadequacies in policy formulation and resource allocation. The dependence of most African countries on developments in their export markets remains undiminished. In contrast to every other region except West Asia, Africa's export earnings declined in 1988 and provide one reason for the region's continued low overall rate of growth. Oil accounts for about 70 per cent of the region's export revenue and the decline in oil prices in 1988 reduced export earnings.

The benefits to African countries of the increase in non-fuel commodity prices in 1988 were limited. Tropical beverages, on which Africa is heavily dependent, did not increase as much as other commodity prices: coffee strengthened, but cocoa declined to its lowest level in many years. The major metal-producers in the region were unable to increase supply in response to the rapid escalation in international prices, largely because of the deterioration in plant and equipment during years of declining prices and profits. Output of copper in Zambia has declined steadily from a monthly average of 58,000 tons in 1982 to 36,000 tons in the first half of 1988. In Zaire, the decline has been from 42,000 tons monthly during the period 1982-1986 to 28,000 tons in the first six months of 1988, although the world price of copper increased from its low of $0.62 per pound in 1986 to about $1.18 in 1988.

The dominance of primary-producing sectors is a major weakness of most African economies. The manufacturing sector is small, overly dependent on imported raw materials and intermediate inputs and its market is almost entirely domestic. Moreover, falling export earnings and rising debt service have reduced imports of industrial inputs, resulting in chronic underutilization of productive capacity.[34] Industrial output in the region is estimated to have increased by only 3 per cent in 1988, despite the stimulus provided by the agricultural sector in many countries and the heavy domestic demand for manufactured goods.

For sub-Saharan Africa, debt-service as a proportion of exports of goods and services essentially remained at its 1987 level in 1988, but for Africa as a whole there was a noticeable increase. As in Latin America, Africa's debt-service obligations and stagnant export earnings restrict the imports that are necessary for the revival of investment and the utilization of existing agricultural and manufacturing capacities.

Although the majority of African countries face debt problems, the situation varies among countries. Nigeria's economic prospects, for example, have improved as a result of the agreement reached in the third quarter of 1988 regarding the rescheduling of its debt. Ghana has benefited from the increased flow of external resources that has been forthcoming over the past few years (see chap. VIII).

Severe external resource constraints are a major reason for the broad process of economic adjustment and reform now sweeping Africa. As of the end of 1988, some 30 African countries were undertaking adjustment programmes supported by the World Bank and IMF. There are also a number of national programmes unsupported by external assistance.

In agriculture, many of the measures adopted involve increased price incentives and reduced subsidies on food and agricultural inputs. Some countries have given a greater role to the private sector and to co-operatives in the distribution of inputs and the marketing of agricultural output. Allocations to agriculture in development programmes have been increased in a number of countries.

There is scattered evidence that such measures are producing results, although the good weather of 1988 makes it difficult to distinguish the effects of reforms on output in that year. Over a somewhat longer period, there has been a doubling of output of ground-nuts in the Gambia following a large increase in producer prices. Farmers in Nigeria have increased their production of cocoa after a fivefold increase in the price they receive. In Guinea, since the removal of price controls in 1986 and a large increase in the prices of imported rice, the area under rice cultivation has increased substantially. In Ghana, increasing the share of the world price received by the producer (from 30 per cent in 1982 to 50 per cent at present) has led, after years of decline, to an increase in the production of cocoa from 158,000 tons in 1983-1984 to an estimated 305,000 tons in 1988-1989. Better producer prices have also produced a positive supply response from cocoa producers in Ethiopia, Malawi, Togo and Uganda. However, these increased outputs have contributed to the decline in world prices for cocoa, reducing the foreign exchange benefits to the producing countries.

Adjustments of exchange rates have been important in improving the functioning of the price mechanism in the region. Many African countries entered the 1980s with overvalued currencies and came to realize that their balance-of-payments problems were magnified by distortions in the prices of tradable and non-tradable goods and in the profitability of productive versus rent-seeking activities. As a result, there have been sizeable nominal devaluations in recent years, resulting in real foreign exchange depreciation for the continent as a whole.

The weakness in international markets for African exports and the low price elasticity of demand for its essential im-

34 A number of countries have reported capacity utilization rates of well below 50 per cent in recent years (see UNIDO, *Industry and Development: Global Report 1988/89* (United Nations publication, Sales No. 88.III.6), p. 71.)

ports have tempered the response to these devaluations. The deterioration in the region's terms of trade, particularly taking the oil price into account, has had a negative impact on the purchasing power of exports. As a consequence and as in Latin America, the volume of the region's imports is now less than at the beginning of the decade.

In addition, efforts to align domestic and world prices and to expose African economies to world markets may not have the beneficial results intended if world prices and markets are themselves distorted. It is universally recognized that this is so in the case of agriculture, which is the single most important sector for African recovery and development and one in which the trade-off between subsistence (food) and cash (export) crops is crucial. There is a danger that exposure to artificially low world food prices may encourage African farmers to place excessive emphasis on cash crops, aggravating the excess supply in those markets and impeding Africa's attainment of food security.

While the distortions in Africa's relative prices may have been reduced, factors such as these go some way to explaining why devaluation has so far proved insufficient to deal with the external and domestic forces that are contributing to the continued vulnerability of many African economies. Most notably, devaluation has failed to remove the external constraint faced by most African countries.

A general evaluation of African reform measures is difficult. In many cases, programmes of reform have not been pursued long enough to form a judgement; in other cases, changed circumstances or a lack of resources have already led to their abandonment. Most importantly, however, the susceptibility of economic development in Africa to exogenous factors—notably, the dependence of agriculture on weather conditions and the vulnerability of export earnings to the vagaries of international commodity markets—makes it difficult to distinguish the causes of improved economic performance. As discussed in chapter VIII, Ghana, for example, has been pursuing a vigorous programme of economic reform for several years, but nevertheless suffered a serious decline in the production of cocoa—its major export—in 1987-1988. Despite improvements in the pricing and marketing of cocoa, weather—in the form of a drought—took the upper hand.

A second complicating factor is that flows of external concessional resources (and the limited non-concessional flows) are increasingly being directed towards countries undertaking reform. The study of Ghana shows that the net transfer of external resources averaged over 4 per cent of GDP over the period 1983-1988. The reforms alone would have been insufficient to sustain the improved growth that Ghana has achieved over this period (see chap. VIII), but it is unclear how much of the growth is attributable directly to the reforms, how much to the resource inflows that they attracted and how much to other factors.

Finally, the reforms aim at structural change and can only be evaluated over the longer term when such changes have taken effect. In the meantime, the key question is whether African countries will be able to persevere in the reforms because tangible benefits are still small and may take some time to become meaningful.

**West Asia: the resuscitation of economic growth**

Discussions of economic growth in West Asia are usually dominated by developments in the international oil market, but in 1988 even oil's gyrations were outweighed in terms of long-term economic consequences by the cessation of hostilities between the Islamic Republic of Iran and Iraq. The prolonged war had wreaked untold human and economic damage; reconstruction should reverse the economic decline of these two countries and provide a stimulus to the region. In the Islamic Republic of Iran, for example, output decreased in each of the years 1984 to 1987, but stabilized in 1988 and is expected to increase in 1989. On the other hand, a deteriorating political situation in Lebanon is bringing further devastation to that economy and neighbouring countries continue to suffer the economic consequences of their own political deadlock.

In 1988, the energy-exporting countries in the region achieved a positive rate of growth of output for the first time in five years. Their preceding slump was initially the result of the negative effects of the decline in oil prices on other components of output, notably construction, and subsequently a reflection of these countries' efforts to reduce oil production in order to bolster its price. The recovery of total output in 1988 was partially a result of increases in oil production in the early part of the year (which, in turn, gave rise to the decline in price). Other sectors also contributed to these countries' recovery, reflecting the increased diversification of the region. In some cases, returns on foreign investment have also reduced the energy-exporting countries' dependence on their primary export; Kuwait, for example, now receives more income from its overseas investments than from its oil revenues.

Not all the energy-exporting countries have a strong external position. Some of them continue to face balance-of-payments constraints because of their heavy dependence on imports for almost all categories of goods and many services. As with some of the countries exporting other primary commodities, these poor balance-of-payments situations may not be improved by increasing the volume of exports if such an expansion depresses world prices. Similarly, diversification is difficult because balance-of-payments constraints limit the availability of the capital goods that are required for investment to create new industries and activities. These factors explain why Saudi Arabia, despite being a major oil-producer, now faces balance-of-payments difficulties that are restricting its growth.

The balance-of-payments constraints faced by some of the other countries in the region, notably Iraq and Jordan, are debt-related. In the former case, the lack of capital, both domestic and foreign, is one reason why the rebuilding of the country has been slow to start.

Some of the countries of the region have been undertaking various forms of economic adjustment and reform in recent years. In the energy-exporting countries, this was prompted by the collapse in oil prices in the mid-1980s and primarily took the form of a curtailment of public sector investment. In some cases, the policy changes have been more wide-ranging and have included a more liberal policy towards foreign investment (for example, in the United Arab Emirates) and privatization (in Iraq). In 1988, the Syrian Arab Republic launched a comprehensive programme of economic reform.

The recent increase in regional political stability not only contributed to the improved growth in the region in 1988, but also was supplemented by other developments that should produce greater results in future. The agreement reached in the Organization of Petroleum Exporting Countries (OPEC) in November 1988 regarding output quotas (see chap. V) should give more stability to economic growth in the region. The changed political environment and the activities of the Gulf Co-operation Council and the Arab Economic Co-operation Council provide further opportunities to expand regional co-operation and thereby sustain economic growth.

**South and East Asia: continued vigorous growth**

Most developing economies of South and East Asia continued to grow rapidly in 1988, in some cases faster than before. Excluding China, GDP for the region as a whole increased by almost 8 per cent, compared with 5.5 per cent in 1987 and an average of 5.0 per cent during the period 1981-1987. The acceleration of growth was due partly to recovery by India from a poor, drought-affected performance in 1987. In addition, more countries enjoyed high growth than in previous years: 10 of the 14 major economies in the region grew at a rate of 5 per cent or higher in 1988 (compared to seven in 1987), with the most rapidly growing countries slowing somewhat and the others accelerating. The exceptions to the general improvements included Bangladesh, which achieved little increase in output, in large measure because of especially severe flooding.

The dominance of the large countries and the rapid growth of some other economies of the region often causes the smaller least developed, island and land-locked Asian countries to be overlooked in a general assessment. These economies are more akin to their peers in other regions, particularly Africa, than their neighbours within the region. They have exhibited erratic growth during the 1980s. They are less diversified, heavily reliant on agriculture and susceptible to external developments, both natural disasters and economic forces. In 1988, floods, droughts, cyclones and tidal waves afflicted some of these countries to an unusual degree; they saw little or no improvement in their terms of trade and, as their external concessional assistance also tended to stagnate or decline, their ability to acquire essential imports, including food in some cases, deteriorated.

One factor contributing to the high rate of growth in several Asian countries was the increase in agricultural production in 1988, largely as a result of better weather. This was particularly true of India, where agricultural output increased by 10 per cent after a 6 per cent drought-induced decline in the preceding year. Neighbouring Bangladesh, however, suffered the consequences of unusually severe flooding. Elsewhere in the region, substantial increases in agricultural production were recorded in Indonesia, Nepal, the Philippines, Sri Lanka and Thailand and came on top of a long-term rising trend. The improvement in the prices of the region's agricultural commodity exports in 1987 and 1988, again in broad contrast with Africa, contributed to the expansion in output.

The increase in industrial production was more pronounced than in agriculture. Rates of growth of industry in India, Malaysia, the Republic of Korea, Singapore and Thailand varied from 9 to 17 per cent. Although the agricultural sector provided some stimulus in 1988, there are signs that industrial expansion in the region may have become less dependent on agricultural growth, even in countries where the latter sector remains large. In India, for example, industrial output continued to increase rapidly despite the fall in agricultural production in 1987. More generally, and in contrast with the situation in Africa, the increased dynamism of their industrial sectors has reduced the susceptibility of the South and East Asian countries to fluctuations in agricultural output, even though they too continue to be subject to the vagaries of the climate.

A sharp increase in exports, achieved in part through diversification in their direction and composition, contributed to the growth of output in many of the South and East Asian economies in 1988. Manufactured exports increased by over 20 per cent in value terms in 1988 and now account for about 70 per cent of the region's total exports. The region has benefited from the fact that neighbouring Japan has not only been the most rapidly growing of the developed market economies, but has become increasingly import-oriented. This has produced some redirection of Asia's trade from Europe and North America towards Japan. However, trade among the developing countries of the region is also expanding rapidly: spurred by increasing domestic demand within the economies of the region, imports have increased almost as fast as exports.

The high rate of investment in many countries of the region gathered strength in 1988. It was accompanied by a substantial flow of foreign investment, especially in some of the East Asian economies. A large part of this foreign investment originated in Japan, as companies from that country established facilities abroad in order to remain competitive in export markets in the face of the appreciation of the yen. However, some of the more advanced countries in South-East Asia are also responding to similar incentives and are becoming important sources of foreign investment in other countries of the region.

Most of the countries of South and East Asia have a moderate burden of external debt; the Republic of Korea has even been able to repay some of its debt. This low debt burden is both a result of these countries' earlier development strategies and a factor behind their growth in the 1980s. The rapid growth of exports enabled these countries to avoid excessive debt-service ratios, allowing imports to increase and to support the growth of output. However, the debt-service ratio has been high in a few countries in the region where export growth has been less vigorous, particularly Burma (about 60 per cent) and the Philippines (over 20 per cent); in other countries, such as Bangladesh, India and Pakistan, it is about 18 per cent and becoming potentially critical, as reflected in the pressure on the balance of payments of India and Pakistan in 1988.

The centrally planned economies in Asia are undertaking economic reforms comparable to those in Eastern Europe. The reshaping of the economic mechanism in Viet Nam is based on a market-oriented development model, giving greater autonomy to production units and liberalizing the foreign trade sector. A detailed package of reform measures for 1988-1990 was adopted at the end of 1987 and included measures to liberalize the distribution of goods, to encourage the development of small-scale private enterprises and to dismantle the system of state subsidies. Reform of agriculture and related sectors is being emphasized. A strong commitment has also been made to promote the direct access of producers to foreign markets and to encourage foreign ventures in Viet Nam.

Notwithstanding these measures, economic circumstances, including acute food shortages during the first half of the year, were not conducive to the implementation of reform in 1988. The country's fiscal and current account deficits greatly complicate market-oriented liberalization, while high inflation inhibits price reform. While some measures aimed at removing the State from direct economic management were implemented in 1988, more far-reaching institutional changes had to be delayed. Nevertheless liberalization produced some tangible results, especially in the production of consumer goods. There was also an increase in the volume of resources flowing into agriculture which, together with stronger incentives for farmers, resulted in an improvement in food supplies in the second half of the year.

In the Democratic People's Republic of Korea, attention has focused on streamlining the administrative structures for economic management and planning and fine-tuning the system of incentives in order to raise output.

In Mongolia, the main direction of the economic reform adopted in 1987 also involved increasing the autonomy and self-financing of enterprises.[35] The reform strategy entails some decentralization in economic decision-making and envisages greater flexibility in price-setting procedures. Though the pace of reform is still seen as rather slow, the Government is cutting subsidies to inefficient enterprises, promoting collective contracts and the leasing of land in agriculture and strengthening incentives for the development of co-operative and individual labour activity.[36]

### Performance and policy in China

China's macro-economic policy objective for 1988 was to moderate growth in order to mitigate material shortages and inflation while continuing to use price reforms to reduce distortions in demand and relative prices.[37] Following growth of 9.4 per cent in GNP and 16.5 per cent in industrial output in 1987, the targets for 1988 were 7.5 per cent and 8 per cent respectively. Notwithstanding these objectives, the effects of the macro-economic measures adopted in 1988 continued to be stimulative and output increased by over 11 per cent (see table II.10). Total fixed investment increased by almost 19 per cent. However, there was drought in several regions of the country and grain output declined by 2.2 per cent. Output of cotton and oil crops also declined, while sugar production fell behind target.

In conformity with the Government's priorities, light industry grew at a faster rate than heavy industry, with rural industrial enterprises growing fastest of all. The growth in the output of final goods far exceeded that in the subsectors of energy, transportation and other intermediate goods and materials, exacerbating shortages in these areas. The chronic energy shortage intensified during the year, disrupting industrial production.

Table II.10. China: selected economic indicators, 1986-1989

| | 1986 | 1987 | 1988[a] | 1989[b] |
|---|---|---|---|---|
| | (Annual percentage change) | | | |
| GNP | 7.8 | 9.4 | 11.2 | 7.5 |
| Net material product | 7.4 | 9.3 | 11.4 | .. |
| Industrial output | 9.2 | 14.6 | 17.7 | 8.0 |
| Agricultural output | 4.0 | 4.7 | 3.2 | 4.0 |
| Gross fixed investment | 4.5 | 16.5 | 18.5 | -22.0 |
| Value of retail sales | 15.0 | 17.6 | 27.8 | .. |
| Retail price index | 6.0 | 7.3 | 18.5 | 13.5-15.5 |
| | (Billions of dollars at year-end) | | | |
| Foreign exchange reserves | 10.5 | 15.2 | 17.5 | .. |
| Foreign debt outstanding | 21.2 | 29.4 | 35.0[c] | .. |
| | (Yuan per dollar) | | | |
| Official exchange rate (annual average) | 2.94 | 3.45 | 3.72 | .. |

*Source:* State Statistical Bureau; *Economic Daily,* 1 March 1989, p. 2; IMF, *International Financial Statistics;* and estimates by the Department of International Economic and Social Affairs of the United Nations Secretariat.

a Preliminary.

b Planned.

c Estimate.

35 *Novosti Mongolii,* No. 61 (28 July 1987), p. 2. For a more detailed analysis, see "Sovershenstvovanie upravleniya v MNR", in *Novoe v upravlenii ekonomikoj. Po materialam s'ezdov kommunisticheskikh i rabochikh partij,* R. Belousov and O. Nekrasova, eds. (Moscow, Ekonomika, 1988), pp. 176-198.

36 "5 plenum tsentral'nogo komiteta MNRP" (Ulan-Bator, Gosizdatel'stvo MNR, 1988), pp. 103-118.

37 *Renmin Ribao* (Beijing), 17 April 1988, p. 3 and China Daily (Beijing-New York), 28 April 1988, p. 3.

## Box II.3. China: balancing reform and rapid growth

China's efforts at slowing economic growth and inflation through more centralized means are to involve much slower economic reform and some recentralization.[a] However, the long-term goal of economic reform is being retained, as is the continuation of an open foreign economic policy.

Initially, the centre-piece of economic reform in 1988 was to be the decontrol of prices. However, accelerating inflation has caused policy makers to adopt several measures aimed at directly controlling prices and reducing the growth in aggregate demand and in money supply. Price reform has now been postponed indefinitely and a target national inflation rate of 15 per cent or lower has been set for 1989. Monitoring of prices has been strengthened to ensure adherence to state-controlled prices and price ceilings for decontrolled goods. Fixed investment, primarily outside the central budget, is to be selectively reduced by about 20 per cent from its level in 1988, with continued emphasis being put on agriculture, infrastructure, intermediate goods, light industries producing goods in short supply and export-oriented industries.

Emphasis has thus shifted from price reform towards continued enterprise and employment reform, reform of the monetary system, and reform of the foreign trade system. Enterprise reform was launched on a full scale early in 1988 when the Industrial Enterprise Bill was passed; this was followed by the Enterprise Bankruptcy (Trial) Law in November. The objective was to raise the efficiency of enterprises, particularly those in the state sector, by increasing their autonomy and improving incentives for performance, while also enforcing financial accountability. To date, the results have been disappointing and there are discussions and experimentation with privatization through shareholding.

The urgency of slowing down economic growth and inflation has also resulted in varying degrees of recentralization in other areas. For example, the contract system was supposed to give autonomy to factory managers and provide them with incentives to improve efficiency. Under this system, the State retains ownership, but managers and the State agree on the profits to be remitted to the State in return for the authority of managers to operate the enterprise and to retain the rest of the profits. Rapid inflation has undermined the fulfilment of these contracts, but the main problem is the failure to stop government and party intervention in the operation of enterprises. Moreover, under this system, the Government has no recourse when the enterprise fails to fulfil the contract or becomes insolvent.[b]

Under the new Enterprise Bankruptcy Law, bankruptcy status makes enterprises eligible for tax reduction and exemption, low-interest loans and reprieve from debt repayment. However, in this area also, the inability to discontinue government and party intervention in decision-making makes it difficult to pinpoint responsibility for bankruptcy. The problem of accountability remains unresolved.

The continued search for measures to improve the efficiency of enterprises resulted in an alternative reform of ownership being implemented on an experimental basis in 1988. The basis of this reform is the conversion from state to private ownership through shares sold to workers, the public and local governments.[c] This is expected to reduce govern-

a *China Daily* (Beijing-New York), 21 March 1989, p. 1 and *The New York Times*, 21 March 1989, pp. A1 and A14.

b *Economic Reporter* (Hong Kong), 1 January 1989, pp. 78-79 and *The Asian Wall Street Journal Weekly*, 13 February 1989, p. 18.

c FBIS, *Daily Report - China*, 13 February 1989, p. 47 and *The Asian Wall Street Journal Weekly*, 13 February 1989, p. 18.

---

The major adjustment and decontrol announced in May 1988 focused on prices of non-staple foods in urban areas, namely, pork, eggs, vegetables and sugar, with experimentation in the decontrol of cigarette and liquor prices and of grain prices in selected areas.[38] Nevertheless, excess demand for foodstuffs, as well as for some consumer goods and most intermediate materials and goods, persisted and manifested itself in shortages where prices were controlled and in price increases where prices were decentralized. Consumption increased in anticipation of further price increases and resulted in the drawing down of savings in urban areas in response to price decontrols. At the same time, higher prices and shortages of inputs resulted in further underutilization of the manufacturing capacity that had been created by several years of high capital investment.[39]

By the end of the year, the economy was exhibiting rapid price and wage increases and a high rate of industrial growth, accompanied by lagging production of infrastructure and intermediate goods, a decline in grain output and a mounting trade deficit. Nominal wages kept ahead of the price increases, mainly as a result of higher subsidies financed by a larger central budget deficit. Increases in some non-staple food prices owing to price decontrol also raised rural incomes. Extrabudgetary fixed investment, financed by increased bank credit, continued to grow rapidly.

The difficulty of simultaneously achieving decentralization of the economic system, rapid growth and stable prices became increasingly evident in 1988 and resulted in some moderation of the original objectives in each of these dimensions of policy (see box II.3). Central fiscal and monetary policies have so far failed to reduce the rate of investment. The State controls only about 20 per cent of capital construc-

38 *China Daily* (Beijing-New York), 7 May 1988, p. 1.

39 *China Daily* (Beijing-New York), 23 July 1988, p. 2.

ment intervention and to create accountability to shareholders. However, the creation of a market for such shares remains a problem, given the rudimentary capital market and the lack of a sizeable pool of private investors.

The problem of the estimated 15 million to 20 million redundant workers in state enterprises also remains unresolved.[d] The implementation of contract employment of up to five years was intended to replace the lifetime employment system in state enterprises, but only about 8 per cent of those concerned are under the new system. Furthermore, social and political pressure at the enterprise level often prevents a reduction of the work-force. As a result, other experimentation in streamlining the work-force has begun. Surplus workers are removed from their jobs and redeployed within the enterprise (with or without retraining) or placed in other enterprises with assistance from the local government. Those who are not placed are entitled to unemployment insurance paid from a locally established fund based on contributions from the local government and enterprises.

The plan for 1989 is to select several cities as test cases for extending this reform,[e] but the political and social pressures that may be generated by increased unemployment represent a potential obstacle. The problem of unemployment is likely to be aggravated by the current objective of slowing down the economy. The development of a comprehensive and viable unemployment insurance system has been inhibited by problems in obtaining adequate contributions, even where the systems are based on payments by local enterprises. This has put pressure on local governments and the State to redeploy workers in other enterprises or to become directly involved in setting up insurance plans.

The priority placed on stabilizing the economy has also resulted in a slow-down in reform of the external sector, although official support for continued opening up of the economy has been reiterated. Certain aspects of the foreign trade system are becoming more decentralized, but others have not changed or have become more centralized. Local foreign trade corporations (FTCs) and selected local enterprises have replaced the central FTCs in directly carrying out foreign trade. These new units have greater autonomy in trading functions and in the retention and usage of foreign exchange. The management of foreign exchange has also become more localized. However, the rapid growth of the economy caused strict controls on imports of consumer goods to be retained in 1988 and export controls were extended, particularly to raw materials and metals in short supply. The number of local FTCs is being limited, as is the authority of local governments to approve the formation of FTCs.[f]

The opening of the economy to foreign investment has also slowed as moderating domestic growth and stabilizing prices have taken priority. The "special economic zones" are not going to be expanded in 1989.[g] Some joint venture contracts will be postponed as credit restrictions have affected the ability of Chinese partners to put up their share of the capital. While there have been official reassurances regarding the availability of capital for joint ventures, it appears that only projects approved by the Government will be given priority, with others being postponed for at least two years.[h]

d *China Daily* (Beijing-New York), 25 October 1988, p. 1.
e *Beijing Review* (Beijing), 19-25 December 1988, pp. 23-25.
f *China Daily* (Beijing-New York), 10 March 1989, p. 1.
g FBIS, *Daily Report - China*, 9 December 1988, p. 36.
h *The Wall Street Journal* (New York), 7 December 1988, p. A11.

tion through its budget, while negative to slightly positive real interest rates create incentives for investment. Greater use is being made of credit created by the banking system to finance investment and other operating expenditures of production units and so the major instrument being used to slow investment is the reduction in the growth of bank credit. This has produced results, but has also led to some disruption of industrial production, a lack of funds to pay for state procurement of agricultural commodities and a decline in funds for wage and bonus payments. As a result, there has been resistance to continued financial austerity.

With the devolution of economic decision-making, the central government budget, which previously was used to control investment and consumption directly, is becoming a progressively smaller proportion of aggregate demand. The retained profits of enterprises and farmers, local government revenues and the earnings of workers have become more important sources of demand. Chinese economists themselves are sceptical about the effectiveness of the wage freeze and the possibility of reducing the growth of the money supply.[40] The problem with the former is that centrally controlled wages now constitute a smaller proportion of total non-agricultural wage income, particularly with the increasing tendency to hold second jobs. Controlling the growth of the money supply is also difficult because of the liquidity outside the banking system and the fact that the Central Bank lacks autonomy and can be subject to political pressure to loosen the money supply.

The overall result is that the institutions and price and incentive systems crucial to the macro-economic management of a decentralized economy are still lacking. The lack of

40 *South China Morning Post* (Hong Kong), 15 February 1989, pp. 1 and 10.

complete autonomy and inadequate financial accountability of enterprises and of the banking system lead to persistently high demand for investment and for credit to finance it, regardless of efficiency. Similarly, enterprises are prone to increase workers' wages and benefits beyond productivity growth. The objectives of these different micro-economic units are likely to be at variance with the State's goals of moderating economic growth and stabilizing prices as long as the indirect policy instruments to bring about the necessary reconciliation remain ineffective.

### The global food situation

Food production not only plays a key role in determining human well-being, but is an important component of economic activity. In 1988, the increase in food production in Africa was an important major reason for the acceleration in the region's growth. Even in the large diversified economy of the United States, food production is significant: the set-back to cereal production in 1988 reduced economic growth and contributed to inflation. Economies relying on the importation of food are more prone to effects resulting from changes in food availability and prices on world markets. Because of the global shortfall in production in 1988, the volume of food aid will likely be reduced in 1989 and commercial prices will increase, imposing an estimated additional burden of $2.5 billion to $5 billion on the foreign exchange resources of the developing countries.

Current developments are of special concern since, for the first time in more than 40 years, world food production fell significantly for the second consecutive year in 1988. Also for the second consecutive year, global consumption of cereals outstripped production and global stocks of cereals fell by more than a quarter (from about 400 million tons to under 300 million tons). The fall was not only the largest ever recorded, but reduced the world stock of cereals to below the 17-18 per cent of consumption that FAO considers necessary for global food security. Stocks are now at the lowest level in relation to consumption since the world food crisis of 1974-1975. Although production will recover from this set-back, it is likely to be some time before stocks return to desirable levels.

The deterioration in the world food situation in 1988 was almost exclusively related to adverse weather conditions, although hostilities disrupted production in a few countries. However, there are also long-term trends that give cause for concern. These concerns had dissipated in the earlier 1980s (particularly compared to the 1960s), partly because food production in the most populous regions of the world had been increasing more rapidly than population. This was the result of a variety of factors, including the 'green revolution' and improved policies towards agriculture, among others. In India, wheat production more than tripled in the 20 years ending in 1985. In China, economic reforms contributed in large measure to an increase of almost 50 per cent in grain production between 1976 and 1984. More generally, production of cereals in the developing countries as a group is estimated to have increased at an annual rate of 3.8 per cent over the period 1970-1985.

This favourable long-term trend not only suffered short-term set-backs in 1987 and 1988 but is also showing signs of slowing. India and China suffered droughts in 1987 and 1988 respectively, but in both cases the growth of food production had already stalled. India's food production increased by almost 20 per cent in the 1983/84 season, but there was no growth during the next four years. Output in 1987/88 was only 137 million tons, because of the drought, but is believed to have recovered strongly in 1988/89 to an estimated 170 million tons. China's output of staple food crops also peaked in 1984 (at over 407 million tons). In 1988, output was 394 million tons, having been reduced by the drought.

In both countries, notwithstanding the recovery in India in 1988, the long-term rate of growth of food output seems to have slowed. Overall, the annual rate of growth of cereals production in the developing countries is expected to average only 2.6 per cent to the year 2000. The main reasons for the decline are an increasing shortage of agricultural land in some countries, ecological deterioration (such as erosion and the over-pumping of ground water for irrigation) and diminishing returns to the "green revolution".

These unfavourable developments call for national and international policy attention. There remains great scope for technological progress in agriculture (most particularly in the area of biotechnology) and for the wider application of existing technologies. However, reaping the benefit of these technical possibilities requires an appropriate economic environment at both the national and international levels, most particularly in ensuring that prices give appropriate signals to the millions of food producers around the world.

Notwithstanding such more favourable developments, there will continue to be food-deficit countries, among which the low-income countries are likely to face serious difficulties. The net food import requirements of all food-deficit developing countries are forecast to increase by some 70 per cent by the end of the century to about 95 million tons. Within this group, the situation is likely to be most problematic in sub-Saharan Africa, but other countries may also face diffficulties.

Africa has not increased food output commensurately with population over the past two decades. This is now a major constraint on the region's overall development, particularly since its rate of growth of population has increased during this period (in contrast with Asia's decline). Climatic factors have also produced short-term variations in Africa's agricultural output, although data suggest that these short-term fluctuations have been less than in some other regions during the 1970s and 1980s. In addition to climatic and environmental factors, the technologies developed during the

1960s and 1970s were not always appropriate for African crops and this contributed to the lower long-term rate of growth of food production in the continent. However, inadequacies in policy formulation and resource allocation were also important in some cases.

As illustrated in the first half of the 1980s, this slow growth of food production places Africa in a vulnerable position, particularly in the light of the apparent slow-down in the growth of global food output. This situation calls for a reaffirmation of the priority now being attached to the agricultural sector in most African countries. It also suggests that attention should be given to improving the links between food-deficit developing countries and food surplus developing countries, some of which are in Africa.

The short-term food outlook is difficult to forecast because of the overwhelming role of the weather. In the United States, the spring and summer drought in 1988 has been followed by a winter drought in 1989 in some food-producing areas and the winter crop, which accounts for about three quarters of total United States wheat production, is likely to be reduced by up to 10 per cent. Drought has also reduced the prospective harvest in Latin America, particularly in Argentina where wheat output may fall by 20 per cent in 1989. In addition, the experience of the 1980s suggests that possibility of a weather-related set-back to food production in either Africa, China or India has to be constantly borne in mind. In view of the depleted state of world food stocks, simultaneous declines in food output in two or more of these areas could be disastrous, pointing to the present precarious state of world food security.

## Short-term outlook for the world economy

### Policy assumptions in the forecasts

In making the forecasts for the growth of world output in 1989 and 1990, it has been assumed that the United States fiscal deficit will increase slightly in the 1989 fiscal year and then fall by somewhat more than $25 billion in fiscal year 1990. The tight monetary policy that has been introduced in the United States in late 1988 and early 1989 is expected to be maintained throughout 1989 (to the extent of an increase in interest rates of more than two percentage points compared with their average level in 1988) and then to ease somewhat in 1990. Higher interest rates in the United States are expected to lead to moderately higher rates in other developed market economies as a result of co-ordinated efforts to moderate, but not eliminate, differences in national interest rates and thereby encourage depreciation of the dollar. In the Federal Republic of Germany, it is assumed that a reduction in income tax equivalent to about 1 per cent of GNP will be implemented in 1990 as scheduled. In Japan, the Government's continued policy of stimulating domestic demand is expected to be reflected in a reduction in corporate tax rates in 1989. In most of the remaining developed market economies, neutral fiscal policies are assumed.

Developing countries experiencing debt-servicing difficulties are assumed to exercise budgetary and monetary restraint and to undertake other measures necessary in order to contain import demand and, in several cases, to reduce inflation. A few newly industrializing economies are expected to allow their exchange rates to appreciate further to facilitate a reduction in their current account surpluses. In the centrally planned economies of Eastern Europe and in China, the implementation of additional economic reform measures is expected.

The average price of oil exported by OPEC countries has been assumed to be 10 per cent higher in 1989 than in 1988 and to increase in nominal terms by 4 to 5 per cent in 1990 in line with world inflation. Non-oil commodity prices are expected to be stable in 1989 and 1990, but with considerable volatility for individual commodities. The prices of copper, tin and nickel are expected to exhibit large declines which, except in the case of nickel, will largely offset the increases in 1988. Grain prices, which increased in 1988 because of drought in the United States, are also expected to fall in both 1989 and 1990. Coffee and cocoa prices, on the other hand, are expected to increase, with the price of coffee continuing to advance and that of cocoa recovering from its fall in 1988. The price of sugar is expected to continue to increase in 1989, but to decline in 1990.

### Growth of output in 1989 and 1990

On the basis of these assumptions, growth of output in the developed market economies is projected to slow to about 2.8 per cent in 1989 and about 2.6 per cent in 1990 (see table II.1). The slow-down is expected to be more pronounced in Japan and in the United States than in Europe. Aggregate growth of GDP in Western Europe is projected to fall by only about a half a percentage point because the prospect of a unified internal market in 1992 will sustain the optimistic investment climate and result in stronger growth in private investment than in the United States.

Owing to slowing world demand, the rate of growth of world trade is expected to fall to slightly less than 6 per cent in 1989 and to about 4 per cent in 1990. Exports of manufactures are expected to increase at a faster pace than the average for total world trade, while the growth in exports of raw materials is expected to slow markedly.

In Canada and the United States, the higher interest rates are expected to have a negative impact on consumer demand, housing and private investment. In the United States, more slowly growing world demand is expected to cause export growth to be less buoyant than in 1988. In Japan, the main source of growth is expected to continue to be domestic demand, with both private consumption and private investment benefiting from tax reductions. Nevertheless, these two components of demand will both slow in 1989 and 1990.

With capacity utilization rates at high levels in most developed market economies, inflation, as measured by consumer prices, is expected to increase to an average of about 4

Table II.11. Developed market economies: short-term outlook for inflation and unemployment rates, 1988-1990

| | 1988[a] | 1989 | 1990 |
|---|---|---|---|
| Consumer price index (annual percentage) | | | |
| All developed market economies | 2.8 | 4.1 | 3.4 |
| Western Europe | 1.8 | 3.2 | 2.9 |
| Developed Asia | 1.0 | 2.9 | 2.2 |
| North America | 4.2 | 5.8 | 4.7 |
| Unemployment rate (percentage) | | | |
| All developed market economies | 7.0 | 7.0 | 7.1 |
| Western Europe | 11.0 | 10.8 | 10.7 |
| Developed Asia | 3.3 | 3.2 | 3.3 |
| North America | 5.6 | 5.7 | 5.9 |

*Source:* Department of International Economic and Social Affairs of the United Nations Secretariat, based on projections of Project LINK and other national and international sources.

a Preliminary estimates.

per cent in 1989 before subsiding in 1990 as a result of the slower growth. Recent and expected increases in inflation have already led to moderately restrictive monetary policies. As indicated above, these policies will contribute to the slow-down in growth. Indeed, if monetary policy in the United States becomes excessively restrictive and is followed by other major countries, the slow-down could be severe (see box II.4).

In some of the major developed market economies, slowing domestic demand is expected to be partially offset by an improvement in net exports, especially in the United Kingdom and the United States. The reductions in trade deficits, however, will come largely at the expense of other developed market economies, so that the contribution of the external sector to growth in the group as a whole is expected to be small.

The forecast is for unemployment rates to continue at their current levels in 1989 and 1990 (see table II.11). For EEC as a whole, the unemployment rate is expected to remain above 10 per cent, with significant differences among countries, partly owing to different trends in labour force participation and in demographic factors (see earlier section of this chapter). Unemployment rates in Japan and in North America will continue to be considerably lower than in Europe.

The large capital flows among the developed market economies—the counterpart of their current account imbalances—will continue to dominate international capital markets. The trade imbalances are expected to remain large but to decline considerably. In the United States, slower growth will have a negative impact on import demand, while there will continue to be some growth in exports, albeit slower than in 1988. These factors are expected to reduce the United States current account deficit by about $16 billion over the period 1989-1990. The corollary of this is expected to be a large reduction in the surplus of Japan, with much smaller decreases in the surpluses of the Federal Republic of Germany, the Republic of Korea and Taiwan Province of China. The expected widening in the differential in interest rates in favour of dollar-denominated instruments should be sufficient, even after the discount for further depreciation of the dollar, to attract a net inflow of external capital large enough to finance the expected United States current account deficits in 1989 and 1990.

Net capital flows to developing countries are expected to exhibit some slight improvement. Increased lending by multilateral financial institutions and official bilateral sources is anticipated, with no further reduction in the net assets of private banks *vis-à-vis* developing countries. However, the indebted countries' need to rebuild foreign exchange reserves and to continue to pay interest on external debt is expected to prevent large increases in their domestic demand. If the new phase of debt renegotiations now under way results in a reduction in debt service of the heavily indebted developing countries (see box II.5), the negative net transfer of resources from developing to developed countries may be reduced. However, these improved prospects for net capital flows are expected to be more than offset by the effects of increases in international interest rates and by the slow-down of world demand for developing countries' exports. Countries heavily dependent on primary commodities or those heavily burdened with debt are unlikely to be able to increase their rate of growth, with the result that the recent divergences in rates of growth among developing countries are expected to persist.

Growth in Africa is expected to be only marginally higher in 1989 than in 1988. Per capita income will again fall. Growth is expected to accelerate to about 3 per cent in 1990 as agricultural production responds further to the adjustments in relative prices and other economic reforms being implemented. A larger increase in growth will require a broadening and deepening of the recent instances of success in economic reform, normal agricultural growing conditions and donors' fulfilment of pledges to augment the currently planned net flows of official development assistance to sub-Saharan Africa.

Growth in Latin America is expected to continue to be impeded by the manifold problems stemming from its external debt and by the need to reduce the high rates of inflation prevailing in several countries. These adversities will be compounded by a deceleration in the rate of growth of ex-

## Box II.4. The effect of more restrictive monetary policies

The baseline forecast includes an assumption of higher interest rates which partially explains the anticipated slowdown in private consumption, housing and private business investment in the developed market economies. However, there is concern that anticipated inflation may be considered too high and that a further tightening of monetary policy will result. This scenario examines the implications of such developments by assuming that interest rates in the United States rise by 200 basis points above the baseline forecast in 1989 and remain 100 basis points higher in 1990; other developed market economies are assumed to conform with this rise in interest rates. Fiscal policies are assumed to remain unchanged.

Simulations indicate that the results of this adjustment in policy would be a cumulative decrease in world output over the three-year period of 0.6 per cent (see the table). Most of the decrease would occur in the first year; the growth rate of global GDP would be reduced by 0.4 per cent and the slowdown forecast in the baseline would be accentuated. The effect on the developed market economies would be more severe than in the developing countries, lowering growth rates by 0.5 per cent in 1989 and a further 0.6 per cent in 1990. This makes it highly likely that 1990 would include a period of recession. The impact on inflation would, however, be slight, reducing it by only one tenth of a percentage point. Unemployment would be half a percentage point higher in 1990, before moderating slightly in 1991. Equally importantly, the current account balance of the United States would deteriorate, increasing the possibility of further deflationary measures to remedy the problem.

For the developing countries, this more restrictive monetary policy would reduce the growth rate of GDP by one tenth of a percentage point in 1989 and by two tenths of a percentage point in 1990. The rate of growth of world trade would fall by 0.5 per cent in the first year and by a cumulative 1 per cent over the three-year period.

### Impact of more restrictive monetary policies in the industrial countries on the world economy, 1989-1991

(Differences from baseline)[a]

| | 1989 | 1990 | 1991 |
|---|---|---|---|
| | *Percentage deviation from baseline level* | | |
| Real GDP | | | |
| World | -0.4 | -0.7 | -0.6 |
| Developed market economies | -0.5 | -1.1 | -0.8 |
| EEC | -0.6 | -1.3 | -1.0 |
| Japan | -0.5 | -1.0 | -1.1 |
| United States | -0.6 | -1.1 | -0.8 |
| Developing countries | -0.1 | -0.2 | -0.2 |
| World trade volume | -0.5 | -1.2 | -1.0 |
| | *Percentage point difference from baseline* | | |
| Inflation rate | | | |
| Developed market economies | 0.0 | 0.0 | -0.1 |
| EEC | 0.1 | 0.0 | -0.2 |
| United States | 0.0 | -0.1 | -0.4 |
| Unemployment rate | | | |
| Developed market economies | 0.2 | 0.5 | 0.4 |
| EEC | 0.0 | 0.2 | 0.2 |
| United States | 0.3 | 0.8 | 0.6 |
| | *Billions of dollars difference from baseline* | | |
| United States current account balance | -14.6 | -20.3 | -9.0 |

*Source:* Project LINK.

a Figures for output and trade represent a percentage change relative to the baseline level. The figures for 1989 may also be interpreted as additions to the baseline growth rates. For subsequent years, the additional growth may be calculated by taking the difference between one year's figure and that of the previous year. For example, in 1989 the level of real world GDP in this scenario is 0.4 per cent below the baseline level. The reduction in the growth rate in 1990 relative to the baseline is 0.3 of a percentage point, which is the difference between -0.7 and -0.4.

Box II.5. The impact of debt relief on developing countries

It has become widely recognized that it is necessary to reduce the debt-servicing burdens of many developing countries if their growth is to accelerate. The initiative presented by United States Secretary of the Treasury in March 1989 and discussed in the Interim Committee of the Board of Governors of the International Monetary Fund in April appears to ensure that debt reduction will be included among the options of commercial banks when renegotiating their debt-servicing obligations with developing countries. However, it is likely that any debt relief to developing countries will result only from country-by-country negotiations spread over several months or years. If the process could be speeded up, the impact on aggregate growth in developing countries and on the world economy could be both larger and more immediate.

To investigate this possibility, this scenario assumes that (a) interest rates on the outstanding debt of the 15 countries classified as heavily indebted are 3 percentage points lower in each of the years 1989-1991; (b) the stock of outstanding debt is reduced by 3 per cent per year over the same three-year period; (c) gains realized from this relief by the indebted countries are spent on importing manufactured goods; and (d) this package would have no discernable impact on conditions in capital markets in developed countries.

The effect of assumptions (a) and (b) would be to reduce interest payments by 33 per cent in the first year, increasing to 41 per cent in the third year. This accelerated programme of debt reduction would raise the aggregate GNP of the developing countries by about 1 percentage point over a two-year period and that of the developed market economies by less than half as much. The growth of world trade would increase by 1 percentage point in the first year and by 0.3 per cent in the second year. Inflation would increase by one tenth of a percentage point and the unemployment rate in the developed market economies would fall by two tenths of a percentage point.

Impact of debt relief for developing countries on the world economy, 1989-1991

(Differences from baseline)[a]

| | 1989 | 1990 | 1991 |
|---|---|---|---|
| | *Percentage deviation from baseline level* | | |
| Real GDP | | | |
| World | 0.3 | 0.4 | 0.5 |
| Developed market economies | 0.3 | 0.4 | 0.5 |
| Developing countries | 0.6 | 1.0 | 1.1 |
| World trade volume | 1.0 | 1.3 | 1.4 |
| | *Percentage point difference from baseline* | | |
| Developed market economies | | | |
| Inflation rate | 0.0 | 0.1 | 0.1 |
| Unemployment rate | −0.1 | −0.2 | −0.2 |

*Source:* Project LINK.

a See footnote to table in box II.4.

port earnings as a result of the slow-down in the growth of world demand. Moreover, the anticipated increase in international interest rates will aggravate debt-servicing problems and further reduce growth in import capacity. For the region as a whole, expectations are for almost no growth in output in 1989 for the second year in a row because of likely stagnation or negative growth rates expected for the larger and medium-sized economies of Brazil, Mexico, Peru and Venezuela. A rebound in these countries and a continuation of slow to moderate growth in other countries is expected to increase growth to 3.4 per cent in 1990 for the region as a whole.

The slow-down in world growth will also reduce growth and export earnings in South and East Asia, but export performance is still expected to outpace that of other regions and it is forecast that growth of GDP will be 6 per cent or higher in both 1989 and 1990. In West Asia, having adjusted government expenditures downward in response to declining oil revenues, countries are poised to continue the growth which resumed in 1988 and to expand GDP by about 2.5 to 3.5 per cent per year in 1989 and 1990. The trend towards expansion has been buttressed by the cease-fire in the Iran-Iraq conflict.

Official plan figures point to an acceleration of economic growth in Eastern Europe in 1989 to 4.5 per cent for the smaller member countries of CMEA and about 6 per cent for the Soviet Union, with individual countries differing quite substantially. Apart from the targeted rate of economic growth, details of policy objectives for 1989 are scanty. It is certain, however, that external adjustment, structural change and economic reform will remain the most important issues on the agenda. The expected economic slow-down in the world economy, continuing internal imbalances in Eastern Europe, further terms-of-trade changes with the Soviet Union in favour of Eastern Europe and the possible positive effects of the economic reforms suggest growth in the net material product in the region of 3.7 per cent in 1989 and 3.5 per cent in 1990 for the seven countries as a group.

In China, targets for 1989 (see table II.10) reflect the urgency of slowing growth and stabilizing prices. Prospects for attaining these two objectives depend on many factors. Excess demand is likely to persist and does not bode well for reducing inflation. Moreover, a grain shortage is forecast for at least the first half of 1989 as a result of the natural disasters in 1988. This will lead to higher market prices for food, while persistent shortages of energy, raw materials and manufactured inputs are likely to lead to higher prices in extra-plan markets. Wages, bonuses and subsidies will be frozen until at least the end of 1989 to reduce consumer demand. Money supply is targeted to grow at a much slower rate than in 1988, the aim being to reduce the inflation rate to 13.5-15.5 per cent in 1989. These measures are expected to reduce the overall rate of growth to less than 10 per cent in 1989 and less than 9 per cent in 1990, somewhat in excess of the Government's target.

# Chapter III

## INTERNATIONAL TRADE

### Overview

International trade in 1988 was characterized by a sharp increase in the volume of world exports, a substantial improvement in non-fuel commodity prices, large shifts in trade flows and major developments in trade policy.

The most important feature of international trade during the year was its surprisingly high rate of growth. As the estimated growth in 1987 has been revised upward, and a fairly high rate of growth is expected in 1989, the rate of growth of world trade in the last three years of the decade seems far to exceed the average growth in the earlier years. Although it is too early to suggest that this is a lasting break with the earlier trend, the recent upsurge of trade represents a positive development for the world economy. It is still unclear whether fundamental changes underlie the recent growth, but an attempt to trace its sources will nevertheless be made in the following pages.

The volume of world exports surged by 8.3 per cent in 1988, after a 5.7 per cent increase in 1987, which was itself an improvement over 1986. The rate of growth in 1988 exceeded the 7.8 per cent growth in 1984, the highest rate achieved so far in the 1980s. Growth is expected to decelerate to about 6.0 per cent in 1989. Nevertheless, the average rate of growth of world trade over the period 1987-1989 would be about 6.5 per cent, compared with 2.2 per cent for the period 1981-1986.

The improvement in the growth of world trade in 1988 was accompanied by an unexpected 4.3 per cent growth in world output, which was also the best since 1984. The growth of trade was thus much faster than the growth of production. Trade grew twice as fast as output, whereas it grew at about the same rate as output during the period 1981-1986. Part of the explanation was the large shifts in export and import demand resulting from the realignment of major currencies. Another significant factor was the continued fast growth of the newly industrializing countries which have a large income elasticity of trade.

The value of world exports increased by about $330 billion or by 13 per cent, raising it to over $2,800 billion (see tables III.1 and A.5). The share of the developed market economies, which had been increasing till 1986, levelled off at about 70 per cent. Despite weak oil prices, the share of the developing countries, which had been declining since 1981, stopped falling and remained at about 20 per cent because of a surge in prices of non-fuel exports and a large increase in exports of manufactures. China's exports grew rapidly which raised its share of world exports from 1 per cent to 2 per cent over the 1980s. The share of the centrally planned economies of Europe remained virtually constant over the period.

The large realignments in exchange rates that have taken place since late 1985 have produced significant shifts in the flows of trade between the major developed market economies. Yet the trade imbalances among these economies remain very large and improvements that have been taking place during 1987 and 1988 seem to have stalled. More important, concern with external balance often tends to be seen as a matter of trade policy in deficit countries. This has resulted in national actions that emphasize bilateralism, regionalism and reciprocity, and contributed to the erosion of the multilateral system.

A major feature of international trade in 1988 has been a significant increase in the prices of non-fuel primary commodities. After having declined sharply and remaining at record low levels for much of the 1980s, nominal prices started to increase towards the end of 1987 and by the end of 1988 were close to their average 1979-1981 level. The increase was also substantial in real terms. For many developing countries, this improvement represented an increased capacity to import, which had been stagnating for many years. By early 1989 most prices appeared to be levelling off. Oil prices, on the other hand, declined over most of 1988 and were beginning to recover at the end of the year.

While trade expanded fast, many developments in the multilateral trading system continued to cause concern. A number of actions taken by national Governments led to trade tension. Bilateralism appeared to strengthen. Non-tariff barriers to trade continued to proliferate and there were few instances of rollback of existing barriers. The Uruguay Round of trade negotiations, while achieving substantial progress in some areas, ended the year with a set-back in others at the Montreal mid-term review. Significant progress in the negotiations was, however, made in April 1989.

### Sources of growth of world trade

The remarkable growth of world trade over the past two years has puzzled forecasters. Rising incomes would probably account for a large part of the growth of trade but the rest remains difficult to explain. Revolutionary changes in technology are taking place. They have greatly reduced distance between countries by cheapening transport and communication, quickened the response to changes or new information, introduced new products and led to an integration of world financial markets. These forces may be contributing to the growth of world trade, especially of new products and services. It is, nevertheless, doubtful that the sudden, and possibly short-term, upsurge of trade can be adequately explained by these forces, which are longer-term in nature. While a fully satisfactory explanation is not yet available, some of the sources of growth may be traced to changes in world output, commodity composition and trade flows between countries.

A major source of the buoyancy of world trade was the acceleration of world income. The rate of growth of output

Table III.1. World trade, 1980-1988

| | 1980 | 1981 | 1982 | 1983 | 1984 | 1985 | 1986 | 1987 | 1988 |
|---|---|---|---|---|---|---|---|---|---|
| Value of world exports (billions of dollars) | 1 998 | 1 972 | 1 830 | 1 808 | 1 902 | 1 925 | 2 126 | 2 485 | 2 816 |
| Developed market economies | 1 252 (0.63) | 1 228 (0.62) | 1 151 (0.63) | 1 148 (0.63) | 1 221 (0.64) | 1 266 (0.66) | 1 478 (0.70) | 1 732 (0.70) | 1 975 (0.70) |
| Developing countries | 587 (0.29) | 584 (0.30) | 512 (0.28) | 479 (0.26) | 502 (0.26) | 484 (0.25) | 453 (0.21) | 539 (0.22) | 606 (0.22) |
| Centrally planned economies | 159 (0.08) | 160 (0.08) | 168 (0.09) | 181 (0.10) | 180 (0.09) | 176 (0.09) | 196 (0.09) | 214 (0.09) | 235 (0.08) |
| Volume of world exports (annual percentage change) | -0.8 | 0.1 | -2.1 | 1.6 | 7.8 | 2.9 | 3.8 | 5.7 | 8.3 |

*Source:* Department of International Economic and Social Affairs of the United Nations Secretariat.

Notes: Figures between parentheses are shares of country groups in world exports. Developing countries include China.

a Preliminary estimate.

in the developed market economies increased from 2.7 per cent in 1986 to 3.0 per cent in 1987 and 4.1 per cent in 1988. Growth also improved in the developing countries, rising to 4.8 per cent in 1988 from an average of about 4 per cent during 1986-1987. Even with the relatively low response of world trade to growth of output during the 1980s, this meant a large absolute increase in the volume of trade. Furthermore, the rate of growth of trade in manufactures during the 1980s has been proportionately much higher than the rate of growth of world income.[1] With manufactures now accounting for 70 per cent of world merchandise trade, the improvement in world income could thus be seen as accounting for a more than proportionate increase in the volume of world trade. However, while the growth of world trade was undoubtedly stimulated by rising incomes, it in turn contributed to the growth of output. The experience of the past two years demonstrates the interdependence between a high level of world economic activity and a high level of world trade.

Manufactures led the growth of world trade. World output of manufactures also grew faster than in recent years: in the developed market economies by about 3.6 per cent in 1988, compared with an average of 2.5 per cent during 1986-1987; and in the developing countries by over 8 per cent in 1987 and probably by as much in 1988. Exports of the developed market economies increased by about 8.5 per cent,[2] while exports of the developing countries, led by the newly industrializing countries, probably grew much faster. Preliminary estimates suggest that the growth of world exports of manufactures grew by about 10 per cent, the highest rate since 1984,[3] accounting for the bulk of the growth of world trade during the year.

In contrast to the trend of the early and mid-1980s, however, exports of primary commodities, spurred by an increase in world demand, also increased significantly in 1988. Agricultural exports increased by about 4 per cent and exports of minerals, dominated by oil, by about 7 per cent.[4]

Large changes in the composition of trade flows were caused by the realignments of major currencies, which altered the international competitiveness of the countries, the partial success of macro-economic co-ordination among the major economies, and the emergence of a growth pole in South and East Asia.

Of particular significance was the process of correction of trade imbalances among the major developed economies. Exports of the United States increased very fast over the past two years as the dollar depreciated. After an increase of about 13 per cent in 1987, the volume of exports rose by over 20 per cent in 1988, providing a major impetus to the growth of world trade during the year. The growth of United States exports accounted for almost a quarter of the 8 per cent

1 The elasticity of world trade in manufactures with respect to world output was about 1.8 during the period 1980-1987. The elasticity for 1988 was 1.9, close to the average of the 1980s.
2 United Nations, *Monthly Bulletin of Statistics,* vol. XLIII, No. 3 (March 1989).
3 GATT, Press Release, 21 February 1989.
4 *Ibid.*

Box III.1. Growth and changing pattern of Japan's trade

Partly as a result of the rising value of the yen and the compelling need to reduce its large surplus, Japan's structure of demand and production and the direction of its trade and investment have been undergoing significant changes in recent years. In 1987 and 1988 the economy grew strongly and at a higher rate than any other major industrial economy. The expansion was in part based on the $40 billion fiscal package put into effect in 1987, a relatively liberal credit policy and lower import prices resulting from the appreciating yen. Domestic demand increased much faster than total demand, diverting production from exports to home consumption and investment, and increasing imports.

Japan's imports, which account for about 6 per cent of world imports, increased little during the first half of the 1980s but have been growing fast since 1986. The value of imports increased from $126 billion in 1986 to $187 billion in 1988, or by 48 per cent. Imports of manufactures increased faster, from $53 billion to $92 billion or by 74 per cent. The share of manufactures in total imports increased from 31 per cent in 1986 to 48 per cent in 1988. The import penetration of the Japanese economy, though still relatively small, has been increasing fast and has spread to a variety of goods, including consumer goods as the following table suggests. The increasing importance of manufactures in the country's imports, which have earlier been dominated by raw materials and fuel, and the increased diversity of these imports, appear to be significant developments in international trade.

These changes have been accompanied by noticeable shifts in the direction of trade. Changing currency values led to a relative increase in trade with the European Economic Community (EEC) and the developing countries although the United States remained by far the largest trading partner. The EEC share of Japan's exports increased from about 11 per cent in 1985 to 18 per cent in 1988, while its share in the country's imports increased from 7 per cent to 13 per cent. Non-oil imports from the developing countries increased fast, raising their share from 26 per cent of Japan's total imports in 1985 to about 32 per cent in 1988. Trade with East and South Asia has been increasing particularly fast.

The strengthening of economic ties with developing, particularly Asian, countries is also reflected in a large expansion of Japan's foreign direct investment in these countries. Investment in the Asian developing countries doubled in 1987, raising the total Japanese foreign direct investment in manufacturing in 1987 to about $10 billion. A significant part of Japanese imports of manufactures from these countries arose from intra-industry trade between Japanese firms and their affiliates in Asia.

Degree of import penetration in Japan in selected industrial items

*(Percentage)*

| | 1980 | 1986 | 1987 |
|---|---|---|---|
| Iron and steel: | | | |
| Hot-rolled sheets and coils | 2.1 | 23.9 | 31.0 |
| Cold-rolled sheets and coils | 0.0 | 3.1 | 6.8 |
| Machinery: lathes | 20.5 | 30.4 | 40.2 |
| Calculators | 12.9 | 44.7 | 49.0 |
| Portable radios | 38.8 | 39.9 | 55.7 |
| Bicycles | 0.0 | 2.6 | 7.7 |
| Cameras (55 mm.) | 7.7 | 19.4 | 46.6 |
| Automobiles | 1.6 | 2.2 | 3.0 |
| Plastic toys | 29.8 | 31.8 | 37.7 |
| Outerwear | 20.8 | 34.8 | 46.3 |
| Underwear | 12.2 | 25.4 | 36.2 |

*Source:* Ministry of International Trade and Industry (MITI), *News from MITI,* NR-354 (88-02), May 1988.

Note: Degree of import penetration is defined as (import)/(production - export + import).

growth of world exports in 1988. Imports also rose strongly, though at a slower pace than exports, as domestic demand continued to expand.

Imports of Japan increased by about 16 per cent, following a 9 per cent increase in both 1986 and 1987. This represented a sharp acceleration of the growth of imports, which had been virtually static during the first half of the 1980s. This growth of imports over the past three years has been a major factor behind the recent growth of world trade. Japanese imports in 1988 contributed almost 1 percentage point to the 8 per cent growth of world imports. Significantly, the country's imports of manufactures have grown at a faster rate than its total imports (see box III.1) and are becoming more diversified, providing a growing market for the world trade in manufactures.

A recent phenomenon of potentially far-reaching significance for the world economy is that the high rate of growth of the economies of South and East Asia and a large expansion of both their imports and exports are beginning to exert a major influence on world trade. These economies, including China, have been growing at twice the rate of growth of world income during the 1980s. Their exports already account for well over 10 per cent of world exports and increased by about 25 per cent in nominal terms in 1988. Their imports grew even faster, by about 30 per cent,[5] which is beginning to turn these economies into major markets for the developed economies as well as other developing countries. These high rates of growth added about 2 percentage points to the 8 per cent growth of world trade in 1988.

## The trading system

In spite of—and sometimes owing to—the strong growth of world trade over the past two years, the multilateral trading system was subject to considerable strain. Various national actions appeared to strengthen the trend towards bilateralism in trade relationships and led to a proliferation of the already numerous quantitative restrictions to trade. International efforts to strengthen the system continued.

Barriers to trade continued to spread. The number of "voluntary" export restraints and other export restraint measures recorded by the General Agreement on Tariffs and Trade (GATT) shot up from 135 in September 1987 to about 290 in September 1988.[6] These numbers, moreover, exclude export restrictions under the Multifibre Arrangements (MFA). Some of these measures appear minor and in a few cases restraint measures may only have averted a total import ban. Nevertheless, the proliferation of these measures is evidence of a shift towards bilateralism and managed trade. Eighty-seven of these agreements were obtained by the European Economic Community, 62 by the United States and 47 by other developed market economies and were aimed at restraining exports from both developing and developed countries. The largest proportion of the restraints were accounted for by textiles and clothing, followed by agriculture and steel. Increasing use is also being made of countervailing duties and anti-dumping measures. Developing countries continued to use a wide range of non-tariff barriers as well as tariffs that are often very high and are imposed for balance-of-payments and other reasons, especially raising government revenue.

Non-tariff trade barriers now affect a larger proportion of world trade than before. The proportion of non-fuel trade subject to various forms of such barriers increased from about 19 per cent in 1981 to 23 per cent in 1987.[7]

The proliferation of such measures has been accompanied by new trade frictions, while many old disputes continued. Trade tension between EEC and the United States increased over the Community's ban on hormone-treated beef. The amount of import from the United States that was affected was only $150 million and the restriction was not considered by the Community as a trade measure. But it resulted in United States retaliation under which punitive import duties were imposed on $100 million worth of Community food exports. EEC counterretaliated by restricting $360 million worth of United States farm exports.

In another trade conflict, the United States claimed that Japan had not sufficiently opened its market to foreign semiconductors. It therefore refused to lift trade restrictions it had earlier imposed on certain Japanese exports to the United States. The protection of Japanese agriculture, despite some recent liberalization, also remained a source of friction between Japan and its major trading partners. The United States, seeking voluntary export restraint, has expressed its intention to impose countervailing duties and quotas on imports of beef, veal and mutton from Australia and New Zealand. A number of countries have complained against restrictions by EEC on imports of apples. The threat of anti-dumping measures forced the Republic of Korea to stop temporarily exporting colour televisions and video cassette recorders to EEC and to accept voluntary restraints on knitwear exports to Japan. EEC enforced one of the largest anti-dumping measures ever taken, imposing duties of up to 44 per cent on Japanese exports of dot-matrix computer printers. In May 1989, the United States announced that it would retaliate against Japan for having failed to open its telecommunications market to United States competition.

However, a number of trade liberalization measures have also been taken. Under the rollback commitments made at Punta del Este, the European Economic Community became the first trading group to offer to eliminate quantitative restrictions and import quotas on 121 industrial processed goods, excluding Japanese and Eastern European exports. Japan has agreed to take a number of steps to liberalize its imports of beef, citrus and seven categories of processed

5 Figures relate to January-September 1988 and exclude Taiwan Province of China.

6 GATT, *Review of Developments in the Trading System,* April-September 1988 (L/6435). Information on most of the developments reported here was obtained from this document and earlier documents in the series.

7 UNCTAD, "Protectionism and structural adjustment" (TD/B/1160 and Add.1), 1988.

food. The Republic of Korea has reduced tariffs, eliminated the licensing system for some imports and relaxed foreign exchange regulations. A ban on imports of beef was replaced with quotas. A number of other developing countries, including Brazil, Colombia, India, Mexico and Pakistan, as well as Australia, New Zealand and Poland, have unilaterally reduced tariffs on imports.

A major development during the year was the enactment of the United States Omnibus Trade and Competitiveness Act of 1988. The legislation, which sets rules of trade for the largest trading nation, will have a large impact on the trading system. The United States administration and Congress have viewed it as an instrument of liberalization of trade. Others, however, have seen its emphasis on reciprocity and provisions for retaliation as a threat to the system of international rules.

The United States administration announced, in early May 1989, a list of countries which it considers to have erected unfair barriers against United States exports. Under the provisions of the law, countries were to be selected from the list for United States sanctions if they failed to remove the barriers within a specified period. Prominent on the list were EEC, Brazil, India and Japan. The announcement of the list has given rise to concerns about increased frictions in international trade.

Among the positive developments, greater use is being made of the GATT machinery for settlement of trade disputes, although bilateral agreements far outnumber such settlements. In 1988, 14 dispute settlement panels were set up, compared with 7 in 1987 and an annual average of 2.4 in the pre-Uruguay Round years.[8]

The final legislative approval of the Canada-United States free-trade agreement was another major development in the trading system. Under the agreement, tariff barriers between the two countries will be dismantled and non-tariff barriers lowered. The agreement also provides for liberalization of a range of trade in services. Trade between the two countries will increase substantially as a result of these measures.

In April 1988, 48 developing countries, meeting at the ministerial level in Belgrade, adopted an agreement setting up the Global System of Trade Preferences (GSTP) to increase trade among themselves through mutual concession on tariffs and other trade measures. In the first round of negotiations, concessions on a large number of products were exchanged.

### The Uruguay Round of trade negotiations: Montreal and after

The launching, at a GATT ministerial meeting at Punta del Este in September 1986, of a new round of multilateral trade negotiations was an urgently needed step to strengthen the trading system. The need arose from the rapid spread of protectionism in the 1980s which accompanied a slowing down of growth of world trade and the changing structure of trade which had been giving rise to major new issues. The urgency was reflected in the decision to complete the negotiations in four years. The round of trade talks initiated surpasses its predecessors in its scope and complexity. An accumulation of unresolved systemic problems and short-term conflict between national interest and freer international trade added to the magnitude of the task. The progress in the first two years of negotiations should be viewed against this background.

Fifteen negotiating groups, 14 on goods and one on services, were formed soon after Punta del Este to negotiate a freer world trade and a strengthened GATT system. A mid-term review of the progress of their work was undertaken at Montreal in December 1988. The results showed considerable progress in some areas and were disappointing in others. In most cases, the achievement so far has been in broad agreements on procedures and framework of negotiations. The major results of the Montreal review are summarized here.[9]

Although tariffs are now far less important as trade impediments than non-tariff barriers, in many cases they remain high. The reduction or elimination of high tariffs and tariff escalation is a major objective of the negotiations. Detailed procedures and methods needed for the negotiations have not yet been agreed on and are to be finalized by July 1989.

On non-tariff measures, a crucial area of concern for the Uruguay Round, there was agreement on guidelines for the conduct of the negotiations. These guidelines emphasize transparency in negotiations, recognize the complexity of the problem and hence the need for trying various negotiating approaches, and call for the use of tariffs in place of non-tariff measures wherever possible. A framework of negotiations is to be established by mid-1989.

Considerable progress has been made in negotiations on tropical products of export interest to developing countries. The work has proceeded beyond procedural into substantive matters. Offers of tariff and non-tariff concessions on a range of tropical products have been made by a number of countries and EEC and an agreement was within reach at Montreal.

On natural resource-based products, there was consensus on pursuing the objective of the fullest liberalization of trade. Examination of the issues involved, including coverage of products, is to continue. Some developing countries wish to limit the coverage to non-ferrous metals and forestry and fishery products, while some developed countries prefer an open-ended approach and would like to include mineral fuels. The developed countries also emphasize the question of access to supply of these products.

---

8 GATT, *Focus,* Newsletter 58, November/December 1988.

9 The assessment is based in part on GATT document "Multilateral trade negotiations, the Uruguay Round", *Trade Negotiations Committee Meeting at Minsterial Level,* Montreal, December 1988 (MTN.TNC/7(MIN)); and UNCTAD, *Review of Developments in the Uruguay Round,* part II (UNCTAD/MTN/INT/CB.7/Rev.1/Add.1), January 1989.

Trade-related investment measures remain a difficult area of negotiations but there was agreement to identify further trade-restrictive or distortive effects of measures that are or may be covered by existing GATT articles and to continue examination of the other issues involved. The issues of contention include the question of regulation of transnational corporations, their export performance and local content requirements which many host countries insist on, and the extent to which trade-related investment falls within GATT jurisdiction.

The dispute settlement mechanism of GATT has often been considered as a weakness of the system. The group on negotiations in the area has come to substantial agreement on ways to improve the organization's dispute settlement rules and procedures.

Significant progress has been made on the related but broader issues of improving the functioning of the GATT system. A package of decisions have been taken on surveillance of trade policies of member countries. This includes the setting up of a trade policy review mechanism under which trade policies of member countries and their impact on the functioning of the trading system will come under scrutiny. These reviews will be undertaken every two years for the first four major trading entities, counting EEC as one, and at longer intervals for other countries. The decisions also include greater ministerial involvement in GATT affairs and co-operation between GATT and international monetary and financial institutions.

The aim of negotiations in the entirely new and complex area of trade in services has been to come to an agreement on a framework of principles and rules of this trade. The work of the negotiating group on services over the first two years was devoted to the examination of a number of issues: statistical and definitional questions; coverage of the multilateral framework for trade in services; broad concepts on which principles and rules for trade in services might be based; existing international disciplines and arrangements concerning trade in services; and existing practices contributing to or limiting the expansion of trade in services, to which the conditions of transparency and progressive liberalization might be applied. Given the complexity of the subject and its contentious nature, considerable progress has been made in negotiations in the area. A broad agreement has been reached on the set of guidelines to carry the work forward.

The results of the work of the negotiating groups must be considered positive even where they did not extend beyond an agreement to continue to negotiate or build a framework for negotiation. But negotiations broke down in four critical areas: agriculture, textiles and clothing, safeguards, and trade-related aspects of intellectual property.

There was general agreement that trade in agriculture should be freed from the high degree of protection that distorts it at present, but there was a wide divergence of views on how to achieve this. The United States urged a total elimination of agricultural subsidies within a specific time-frame. This was considered unrealistic by EEC, which advocated short-term measures. The "Cairn" group of countries (Argentina, Australia, Brazil, Canada, Chile, Colombia, Fiji, Hungary, Indonesia, Malaysia, New Zealand, the Philippines, Thailand and Uruguay) submitted their own set of proposals to liberalize trade in agriculture in stages. Some developing countries were apprehensive about the impact of liberalization on their agriculture and on the cost of import of food. The conflicting positions, particularly those of EEC and the United States, proved irreconcilable at Montreal and the negotiations broke down.

Much of the trade in textiles and clothing is regulated through MFA and lies outside the GATT framework. The basic question before the negotiators was the phasing out of MFA and bringing trade in textiles into the framework of the normal rules of GATT. The divergence of the position of the developed and the developing countries was too great to be resolved at Montreal.

In the negotiation on the trade-related aspects of intellectual property rights, the major area of dispute concerned the competence of the GATT forum to discuss these issues. Most developing countries, though willing to discuss the trade-distorting aspects of the subject, maintained that such issues are more properly discussed in such forums as the World Intellectual Property Organization (WIPO).

The question of the safeguard provisions of GATT, under which a country may temporarily protect domestic industry from the damaging consequences of a sudden surge in imports, has long been a contentious issue and was carried forward as a major unresolved issue at the Tokyo Round. Little progress has so far been made under the Uruguay Round on the important questions, such as non-discrimination, selectivity, treatment of grey-area measures and commitment to a specified time-frame for removal of such measures, on which past negotiations foundered.

The failure to reach agreement on these four areas rebounded on agreements in other areas. It led to a hardening of positions at Montreal and all results of the review were put "on hold" till the Trade Negotiations Committee, the main committee for the conduct of the negotiations, had met in April 1989. The Director-General of GATT was to hold high-level informal consultations on the four sectors where negotiations had broken down.

The Trade Negotiations Committee met in the first week of April and succeeded in reaching agreement on the four sectors, which enabled the negotiations on all fronts to proceed.[10] On agriculture, there was agreement that the long-term objective of negotiations was to establish a fair and market-oriented agricultural trading system through progressive reductions in agricultural support and protection over an agreed period of time. The special circumstances of developing countries, including the necessity for provision of government assistance for agricultural development, and the needs of many of these countries for import of food, were to be an integral part of the negotiations. Among the most significant of the agreements on agriculture was the decision to freeze agricultural subsidies and present trade barriers at current levels. A final agreement was also

10 GATT, *News of the Uruguay Round of Multilateral Trade Negotiations* (NUR 027, 24 April 1989).

reached on strengthening the dispute settlement procedure of GATT, including the speeding up of the work of the dispute settlement panel. Negotiations on textiles and clothing, trade-related aspects of intellectual property, and safeguards were to continue.

Following up on the agreement on surveillance of trade policies of member countries, the GATT secretariat set up a trade policies review division in May 1989.

## The emergence of free-trade areas and the trading system

The European Economic Community, already by far the largest trading bloc, is moving towards the goal of a single market by 1992. The recent free-trade agreement between Canada and the United States makes the two countries a large trading bloc, while the Eastern European countries have special arrangements of their own. As table III.2 shows, trading blocs with various degrees of free-trading arrangements already account for a large proportion of world trade. The unification of European markets and the Canada-United States free-trade agreement have thus given rise to concern about the proliferation of free-trade areas and their implications for the multilateral trading system.

Table III.2. Major trading blocs in world trade

| | Value of intra-bloc trade (Billions of dollars, 1987) | Share of world trade (Percentage) | Share of intra-bloc trade in the bloc's total trade (Percentage) |
|---|---|---|---|
| EEC | 1 111 | 22.3 | 58.4 |
| Canada-United States | 127 | 2.6 | 17.0 |
| EFTA | 46 | 0.9 | 14.1 |
| European centrally planned economies | 275 | 5.5 | 53.0 |
| Total | 1 559 | 31.3 | |

*Source:* Department of International Economic and Social Affairs of the United Nations Secretariat, based on GATT, *International Trade 87/88*, Geneva, 1988.

*Note:* Trade is defined as exports plus imports.

Trade between Canada and the United States is the largest bilateral trade flow in the world. In 1987, United States merchandise exports to and imports from Canada amounted to $57 billion and $70 billion respectively. Together, they amounted to 2.6 per cent of world imports and exports. The importance of the trade is much higher for Canada than for the United States. In 1987 Canada received a quarter of United States exports, while the United States accounted for three quarters of Canada's exports. United States exports to Canada amounted to only 1.3 per cent of United States GNP, while Canada's exports to the United States were equal to 20 per cent of its GNP. The two economies are already significantly integrated through trade and investment. The agreement will greatly enhance the process through elimination of tariffs, reduction of non-tariff barriers and liberalization of trade in services.

The single market in EEC is to be achieved by doing away with all remaining barriers to trade between member countries by 1992. The removal of non-tariff barriers is the main instrument of unification of the markets. This involves the elimination of border controls and technical and fiscal barriers to trade and removal of controls on flow of capital between countries. Restrictions on trade in goods between member countries have already been greatly reduced. The impact of the unification will thus be felt more on trade in services. While the actual liberalization by 1992 may fall short of the objective, a large step towards it will have been taken.

A number of other, far smaller, preferential trading arrangements already exist. The European Free Trade Association (EFTA) is the other major free-trade arrangement among the developed market economies. Among the developing countries, preferential trading arrangements include the Association of South-East Asian Nations (ASEAN), the Latin American Free Trade Association (LAFTA), the Central American Common Market (CACM), the Andean Pact and the East African Community.

In recent months a number of moves have been made to strengthen some of the existing arrangements and form new preferential trading areas.[11] ASEAN announced moves to boost intra-regional trade. Australia and New Zealand signed an agreement which accelerates the implementation of their Closer Economic Relations Agreement and the possibility has been mentioned of extending this co-operation to include ASEAN countries. In Latin America, Argentina and Brazil are moving towards establishment of a common market, which will later be extended to include Colombia and Uruguay. In the Middle East, Egypt, Iraq, Jordan and Yemen agreed to form a new economic bloc, the Arab Co-operation Council, while the Maghreb countries are discussing a regional grouping.

A voluminous literature exists on the consequences of such free-trade arrangements for the constituent economies, but less attention has been given to their impact on the external world. Yet a proliferation of regional trading arrangements, though perceived as beneficial to member countries, may not be so for the growth of international trade, the most efficient allocation of the world's resources, and the multilateral trading system.

Formation of a free-trade area raises two related but distinct issues: its impact on the growth of world trade and on the working of the multilateral trading system.

A free-trade area may create trade, that is, increase trade between partners made possible by specialization among them. It may also divert trade, i.e., substitute trade among partners for trade with third countries, as imports from an

11 Some of this information is based on GATT, *Developments in the Trading System* (C/W/548 and L/6435).

inside producer become cheaper than those from an outside producer that was a former supplier. It may have both these effects. Whether total world trade increases as a result depends on the relative importance of the two. Even when world trade increases as a result of trade creation being greater than trade diversion, though, world allocation of resources will be less efficient than in the absence of the union, if the outside country is the more efficient producer.

This is a static analysis. But formation of a trading group will normally increase real income of member countries through increased specialization. This will increase their demand for imports, and trade with the rest of the world will also increase, provided tariffs or other trade barriers against outsiders are not excessive.

The arguments above are mostly illustrative. Empirical evidence on the trade-creating and trade-diverting effects of free-trade areas and customs unions are not very clear. Changes in trade are also due to other factors than the formation of the trade area, including changes in trade policies and in the world economy, and free-trade areas differ greatly in the nature of their free-trade arrangements or in the structure of the economies of the member countries. The formation of EEC did divert trade in its early phases, but trade creation outweighed diversion, and total trade increased. The enlarged EEC internal and external trade increased equally fast during the 1970s.[12] The latest enlargement of the Community to include Greece, Portugal and Spain, may have had the effect of diverting some trade, especially in agriculture, from a number of developing countries.

The completion of the single market in EEC will lead to a net gain in economic welfare and higher growth of GDP of the member countries through better exploitation of economies of scale, improvement in efficiency, fuller utilization of comparative advantage among members and an increased flow of innovations.[13] Preliminary studies suggest that intra-EEC imports will increase while extra-EEC imports are likely to decline, implying a net diversion of trade.[14] The number of products in which extra-EEC imports may decline is likely to be large. The major items may include high-technology products among machinery and equipment, and imports of some services, such as banking and insurance, may also decline.

Much of what will eventually happen to the external trade of EEC will depend on the trade policies to be followed by the Community. While apprehension has often been expressed about the possible evolution of the unified market into a "fortress Europe", this outcome is not inevitable. Indeed, the standard of openness of the unified market might be set by member countries that are the most open to trade with third countries. On the other hand, the formation of a free-trade area has rarely been a precursor to liberalization of trade with the rest of the world. It has been argued in this context that the trade régime of EEC over the past two decades has moved in a "non-liberal" direction.[15] It instituted the Common Agricultural Policy, which is one of the major instruments of protectionism in the developed countries, and its use of non-tariff barriers, bilateralism and discrimination in trade relations has, along with those of its trading partners, increased.

This leads to the second major issue: the impact of the free-trade areas on the working of the multilateral trading system. Opinions are divided on this subject. Regional integration can be welcomed as a way of reducing the collective cost of protection and exploiting numerous economies of scale, and when the region is recognized as taking the place of its members in a non-discriminatory system. The venerable language of the most-favoured-nations principle must then be understood to refer either to nations or to the new entities taking their place. If the members pursue their commercial policies in a truly concerted manner, and if the rights and obligations were transferred to the new entities, principles of multilateralism would not be threatened.

But as regional integration stops short of political union, this is not the case. In addition to pursuing some of their interests through free-trade areas or customs unions, Governments continue to press other interests on their own, and the ambiguity weakens the system of rules and restraints on commercial policy.

Free-trade areas are permitted under GATT rules. Yet, as a major study on the trading system pointed out, the exceptions and ambiguities that have been permitted in the examination of the conformity of the free-trade arrangements to the GATT rules have set a "dangerous precedent for further special deals, fragmentation of the trading system, and damage to the trade interests of nonparticipants".[16]

### Trade flows and trade balances among country groups

The growth of world trade in 1988 was widely shared. The rates of growth, nevertheless, varied considerably among countries and produced, together with the considerable divergence in price movements, significant changes in their

12 This, of course, does not prove that total trade would not have grown even faster in the absence of the enlargement.

13 Commission of the European Communities, *European Economy: The Economies of 1992*, No. 35 (March 1989).

14 *Ibid.*, annex A. Calculations based on data for a selected number of EEC countries, including the four largest, suggest a 2.2 to 2.6 per cent decline in extra-EEC imports and a 3.7 to 4.5 per cent increase in intra-EEC imports as a direct result of removal of the internal trade barriers. The direct and indirect effects show a decline of 5.7 to 7.7 per cent in extra-EEC imports. The study points out that these figures are broad orders of magnitude.

15 David Henderson, *1992: The External Dimension*, Group of Thirty, Occasional Papers 25, New York, 1989.

16 GATT, *Trade Policies for a Better Future: Proposals for Action*, report of an independent group of experts (GATT publications, Sales No. GATT.1985-1), p. 41.

balance of trade.[17] The changes in the value of the major currencies were relatively modest for the year as a whole though there have been disturbingly large short-term fluctuations. But the large changes in the preceding years, along with macro-economic policy shifts, produced large changes in the relative growth of imports and exports of the major industrial countries, as already noted. The increase in non-fuel commodity prices during the year contributed to a large increase in the value of exports of the non-oil-exporting developing countries. Falling prices of oil had the opposite effect on exports of the energy-exporting countries. The persistent debt crisis was a powerful reason for many developing countries to push exports and restrain imports.

### Developed market economies

The volume of exports of the developed market economies increased by about 8 per cent in 1988, only slightly less than the growth of imports. The balance of trade for the countries taken as a whole remained practically unchanged, but large imbalances persisted in the trade relations of the major economies and remained a source of trade tension.

The volume of United States exports increased at an extraordinary rate of over 20 per cent in 1988, which was a large acceleration over the 13 per cent growth in 1987. The volume of imports also increased, though much more slowly than exports, as a result of strong domestic demand. These changes led to the first reduction of the United States trade deficit in the 1980s, from $160 billion in 1987 to $126 billion in 1988. However, current projections indicate a widening of the gap in 1989. The persistence of the large United States trade gap has become a major cause of protectionist sentiment and the pressure to use trade policy as an instrument to narrow the gap has been mounting.

The main counterparts of the United States deficit are the large surpluses of Japan and, to a lesser extent, the Federal Republic of Germany. Japan's imports increased in real terms by about 16 per cent in 1988, after a 9 per cent increase in 1987, while its exports grew by about 4 per cent. Despite the large differential in the rates of growth of imports and exports, the trade surplus of the country shrank by only $2 billion, from $97 billion in 1987 to $95 billion in 1988. The volume of exports and imports of the Federal Republic of Germany, on the other hand, increased at about the same rate and the country's trade surplus widened somewhat, from $70 billion to $74 billion. Although much of the Federal Republic of Germany's trade surplus was with other European countries, Japan's large trade surplus mainly reflected the imbalance of the country's trade with the United States.

Among other developed market economies, strong growth of domestic demand led to a sharp deterioration of the trade gap of the United Kingdom. The country's exports failed to grow, while its imports increased sharply, resulting in an increase of the trade deficit from $17 billion in 1987 to $37 billion in 1988. The trade deficits of France and Italy also increased (see table III.3).

Table III.3. Developed market economies: trade balance,[a] 1980-1988

(Billions of dollars)

| | 1980 | 1986 | 1987 | 1988 |
|---|---|---|---|---|
| All countries | -70.0 | -3.3 | -22.8 | -18.9 |
| Excluding the United States | -44.5 | 141.2 | 137.4 | 107.6 |
| Major industrial countries | -33.5 | 0.9 | -10.9 | 1.2 |
| Canada | 8.0 | 7.6 | 8.8 | 6.2 |
| France | -13.4 | -2.4 | -9.3 | -10.3 |
| Germany, Federal Republic of | 8.9 | 55.7 | 70.0 | 73.8 |
| Italy | -16.9 | 4.5 | 0.1 | -0.2 |
| Japan | 2.1 | 92.8 | 96.5 | 94.8 |
| United Kingdom | 3.3 | -12.8 | -16.7 | -36.7 |
| United States | -25.5 | -144.5 | -160.3 | -126.5 |
| Other countries | -36.5 | -4.3 | -12.0 | -20.0 |

*Source:* Table A.7.

a On an f.o.b. basis.

### Developing countries

The volume of exports of the developing countries increased by about 10 per cent in 1988, about the same rate as in 1987. Much of this increase was due to a large increase in the exports of manufactures, but exports of primary commodities, especially fuel, also increased. The changes in the volume and prices of exports varied widely among countries and regions. Exports of Africa increased only marginally while there was a large increase in exports from Latin America, much of it from the heavily indebted countries, especially Argentina, Brazil, Mexico and Venezuela. The volume of exports of West Asia increased significantly, but this was more than offset by the decline in oil prices. As in recent years, the largest increase in exports came from South and East Asia. The volume of exports from the region increased by about 14 per cent after a 17 per cent increase in 1987.

Imports also increased rapidly. For the developing countries as a whole, the volume of imports increased by about 10 per cent in 1988, about the same rate as exports, after a 5 per cent increase in 1987. Imports of South and East Asia increased even faster than their exports, and this largely determined the high rate of growth of imports of the developing countries as a whole. Nevertheless, the growth of imports has been fairly widespread. Imports of the African countries increased, only marginally, for the first time since 1981. Imports of Latin America increased, owing to a very large increase in the imports of Mexico, which was the result of policies to liberalize imports to keep inflation under control and meet food shortages caused by drought. Imports

17 Regional and country trade data were obtained mainly from the regional commissions of the United Nations, including the Economic Commission for Africa, *Economic Report on Africa 1989,* the Economic Commission for Europe, *Economic Survey of Europe in 1988-1989,* the Economic Commission for Latin America and the Caribbean, *Preliminary Overview of the Latin American Economy 1988,* and the Economic and Social Commission for Asia and the Pacific, *Economic and Social Survey of Asia and the Pacific 1988.*

of some of the large countries, for example, Argentina and Brazil, declined. Imports of the energy-exporting developing countries increased slightly in 1988 after many years of decline.

The terms of trade of the developing countries as a whole deteriorated by about 3.5 per cent in 1988. This was entirely due to the large decline in oil prices, which led to a fall of about 17 per cent in the terms of trade of the energy exporters. For the energy-importing countries, the terms of trade improved by about 4.5 per cent, the first such improvement since 1984.

Increased imports and a deterioration of their terms of trade reduced the trade surplus of the developing countries as a group. Most of the deterioration was in the energy-exporting group whose trade surplus fell from $48 billion in 1987 to $32 billion in 1988. Exports and imports of the energy-importing countries were evenly balanced in 1988, for the first time in the 1980s, largely as a result of a sharp increase in the trade surplus of the Latin American economies, mainly Argentina, Brazil and Chile.

The rate of growth of China's external trade during the 1980s has been very high, with the volume of its exports increasing by about 12 per cent annually. Following a 27 per cent increase in 1987, exports in real terms increased by about 20 per cent in 1988, led by a large increase in manufactured exports. A rapidly growing economy also led to a 25 per cent increase in import volume during the year, resulting in a marked deterioration in the country's balance of trade (see table III.4).

Table III.4. Developing countries: trade balances,[a] 1980-1988

(Billions of dollars)

| | 1980 | 1986 | 1987 | 1988 |
|---|---|---|---|---|
| Developing countries | 112.4 | -2.7 | 32.6 | 26.5 |
| Energy-exporting countries | 173.2 | 18.8 | 48.1 | 32.0 |
| Surplus | 140.8 | 8.5 | 25.2 | 19.0 |
| Deficit | 32.4 | 10.3 | 22.9 | 13.0 |
| Energy importers | -58.0 | -12.5 | -13.9 | 0.0 |
| China | -2.8 | -9.1 | -1.7 | -5.5 |

*Source:* Table A.12.

*Note:* Developing countries exclude Taiwan Province of China.

a On an f.o.b. basis.

## Centrally planned economies

The growth of foreign trade of the centrally planned economies of Europe improved slightly in 1988 after an exceptionally slow growth in 1987. The external trade (average of imports and exports) of these economies grew by less than 1 per cent in volume in 1987 and by about 4.5 per cent in 1988, which was a little over half the rate of growth of world trade.

Most of the centrally planned economies proposed or undertook changes in their foreign trade mechanism, in step with their general policy of economic liberalization. In general, these measures can be characterized as efforts to decentralize foreign trade. They include a set of organizational changes which aims at transferring the right to conduct foreign trade to the enterprises. While in some countries these changes are still at their inception, in others steps have already been taken towards decentralization. The effects of these measures on the growth of trade will be apparent only in the longer run.

The volume of exports from the seven European centrally planned economies rose by some 5 per cent in 1988 following a 2 per cent increase in 1987. The increase was more widely spread among these economies than before. In 1987 much of the increase in exports came from the Soviet Union, while exports from the other economies stagnated. The growth of exports in 1988 was much more balanced, exports of the Soviet Union growing at 5 per cent and those of the rest of Eastern Europe growing at about 4.2 per cent. Much of the growth of Soviet exports derived from exports to the developed market economies which increased at about 12 per cent in volume, continuing the high rate of expansion of the past few years. Exports of the other centrally planned economies to the developed market economies also increased faster than their total exports. The volume of exports of the Soviet Union and other centrally planned economies to the developing countries also increased fast during the year.

Soviet imports increased by about 5 per cent in real terms in 1988, after two years of import contraction. Most of the increase stemmed from the developed market economies but imports from the developing countries increased as well. Imports of the centrally planned economies as a whole increased by some 4 per cent, after a decline of 0.4 per cent in 1987.

Intra-CMEA trade accounts for more than half of the total trade of the centrally planned economies and increase in this trade remains a major collective objective of these countries. Nevertheless, the critical need for hard currencies, partly to service external debts, has led to an emphasis on exports to the market economies and restraint on non-essential imports from them. Increased imports in 1988 and a deterioration of terms of trade led to a worsening of the trade balance of the centrally planned economies with the developed market economies. Their terms of trade worsened by about 3 per cent, largely because of the decline in oil prices and hence a fall in unit prices of Soviet exports. The balance of trade of the centrally planned economies with the developed market economies turned from a small surplus in 1987 to a small deficit in 1988 (see table III.5). These economies usually have a large trade surplus with the developing countries. The surplus declined somewhat in 1988.

The intra-CMEA trade balance underwent a significant change in 1988. The usual trade surplus of the Soviet Union with the rest of the Eastern European centrally planned economies turned into a deficit. This was largely the result of the movement of the terms of trade of the Soviet Union *vis-à-vis* the other six. (For policies affecting intra-CMEA trade, see chapter VI.)

## Commodity prices: short-term improvement and uncertain future prospects

For a large number of developing countries, the prices of their primary exports rose significantly in 1988, the first such increase since the mild upturn of 1983-1984 which was followed by an almost continuous decline. The overall index of dollar prices of non-fuel primary commodities exported by these countries started to increase from the third quarter of 1987, rose sharply in the last quarter of the year and continued on a milder upward trend in the first half of 1988. In the second half of the year, prices appeared to have stabilized, with a weakening in the third quarter and a pick-up in the next (see figure III.1 and table A.6). By December 1988, the index was only 5 per cent below its 1979-1981 average. For the year as a whole, it was about 18 per cent higher than in 1987.

Table III.5. European centrally planned economies: trade balance, 1980-1988

(Billions of dollars)

| | 1980 | 1986 | 1987 | 1988 |
|---|---|---|---|---|
| European centrally planned economies | | | | |
| World | 2.2 | 8.9 | 15.6 | 11.2 |
| Centrally planned economies | 2.3 | 4.0 | 4.2 | 4.7 |
| Developed market economies | -3.6 | -3.5 | 1.6 | -1.2 |
| Developing countries | 3.5 | 8.3 | 9.9 | 7.6 |
| Eastern Europe | | | | |
| World | -5.8 | 0.7 | 3.9 | 7.8 |
| Centrally planned economies | -1.8 | -1.4 | 0.9 | 5.5 |
| Developed market economies | -3.8 | 0.4 | 1.1 | 1.5 |
| Developing countries | -0.2 | 1.7 | 2.0 | 0.7 |
| USSR | | | | |
| World | 8.0 | 8.2 | 11.7 | 3.4 |
| Centrally planned economies | 4.1 | 5.4 | 3.3 | -0.8 |
| Developed market economies | 0.2 | -3.9 | 0.5 | -2.7 |
| Developing countries | 3.7 | 6.6 | 7.9 | 6.9 |

*Source:* Department of International Economic and Social Affairs of the United Nations Secretariat, based on national and international data.

Technological changes and the changing structure of the industrial economies had a depressing effect on the world demand for primary commodities during the 1980s. Together with a general oversupply of commodities, it led to a sharp fall in commodity prices during the period. An important contributory factor was, however, the slow-down of the world economy itself. The significant improvement in world growth during 1987-1988 was an important factor behind the recent increase in commodity prices. Reduced supply, in some cases resulting from elimination of excess capacity, also contributed to the rise in prices.

Evidence also suggests that demand in developing countries, and the high rate of growth of some of the more industrialized among them, have helped to sustain the demand for primary commodities over recent years. Most developing countries remain intensive users of raw materials, and while many developing countries have stagnated or declined during the 1980s, a number of them have grown fast. These economies have partly offset the stagnation in the demand for commodities in industrial countries. The increased importance of the demand for commodities in developing countries is evident from the changing destination of their exports (see table III.6). The change is pronounced in raw materials and fuels which are directly related to the level of industrial activity.

Table III.6. Changing destination of exports of primary commodities from developing countries

(Percentage share of intra-developing country exports in total developing country exports)

| | 1973 | 1980 | 1986 |
|---|---|---|---|
| Food | 17.9 | 23.5 | 19.9 |
| Raw materials | 22.7 | 26.1 | 27.7 |
| Ores and minerals | 6.7 | 11.5 | 18.2 |
| Non-ferrous metals | 11.0 | 15.7 | 22.7 |
| Fuel | 18.6 | 22.2 | 27.9 |
| Total primary products | 18.0 | 22.1 | 24.9 |
| Excluding food and fuel | 16.0 | 19.3 | 23.6 |

*Source:* Department of International Economic and Social Affairs of the United Nations Secretariat, based on data in GATT, *International Trade 86-87.*

The increase in the prices of non-fuel commodities in 1988 was widespread. Of the 40 commodity prices in the UNCTAD price index, 37 increased, many of them sharply. This contrasted with price behaviour in the preceding two years when changes in the prices of a limited number of commodities dominated the change in the overall price index.[18] Nevertheless, the changes in prices varied considerably among commodities (see figure III.1).

Prices of food and beverages, which account for over 50 per cent of the value of exports of primary products from the developing countries, increased by about 12 per cent over their average 1987 level (see table A.6). Wheat and rice prices rose sharply from the low levels of the mid-1980s. Weather-related supply factors, especially drought in the United States and some Asian countries, and low stocks contributed to the increase. Sugar prices also recovered from the very low levels of the mid-1980s. On the other hand, there were only marginal increases in prices of tropical beverages, which account for over half of the value of exports in the group. Coffee prices rose following agreement on export quotas under the International Coffee Agreement in October 1987. Cocoa prices reached record low levels in 1988. As the largest producers continued to increase production in the

18 *World Economic Survey 1988* (United Nations publication, Sales No. E.88.II.C.1), p. 39.

Figure III.1. Non-fuel commodity price indices, 1980-1988

(1979-1981 = 100)

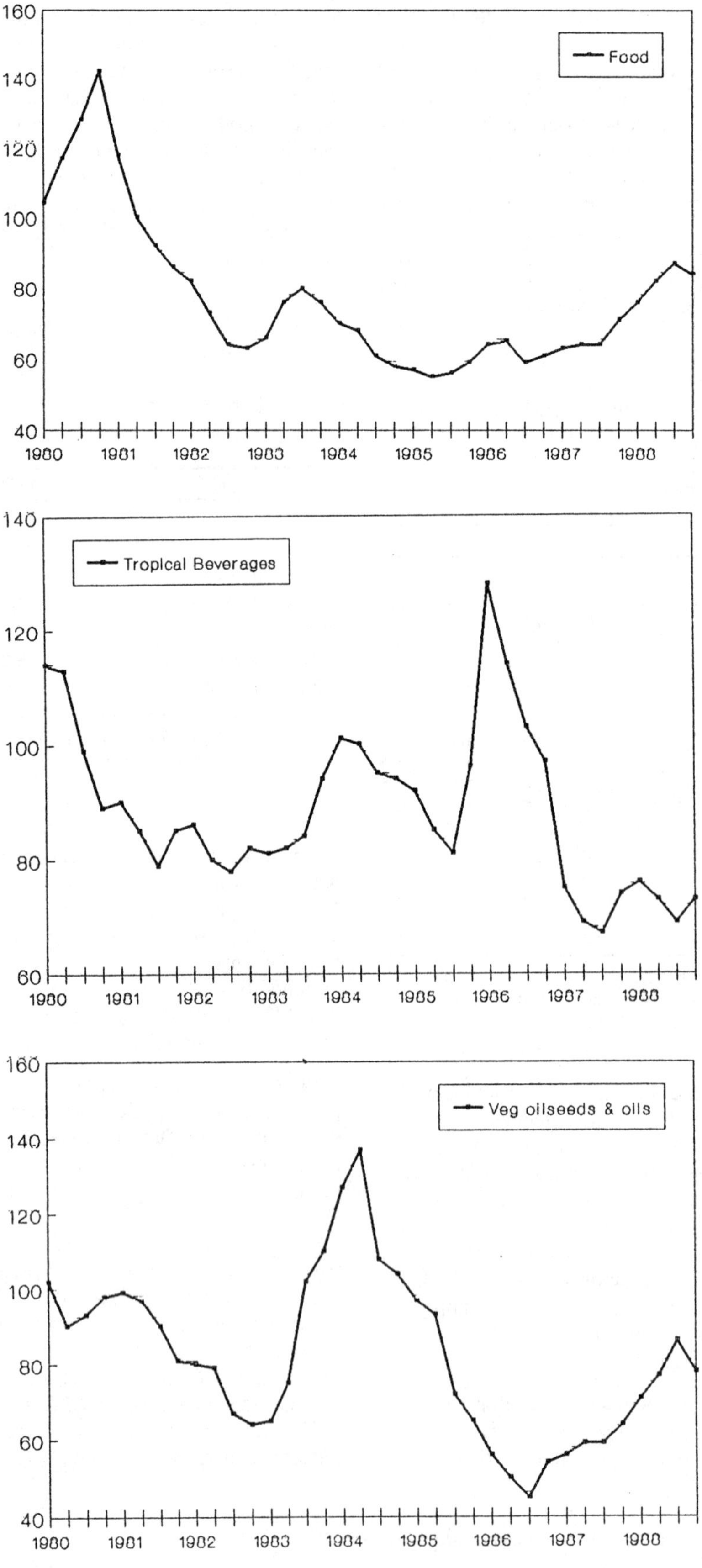

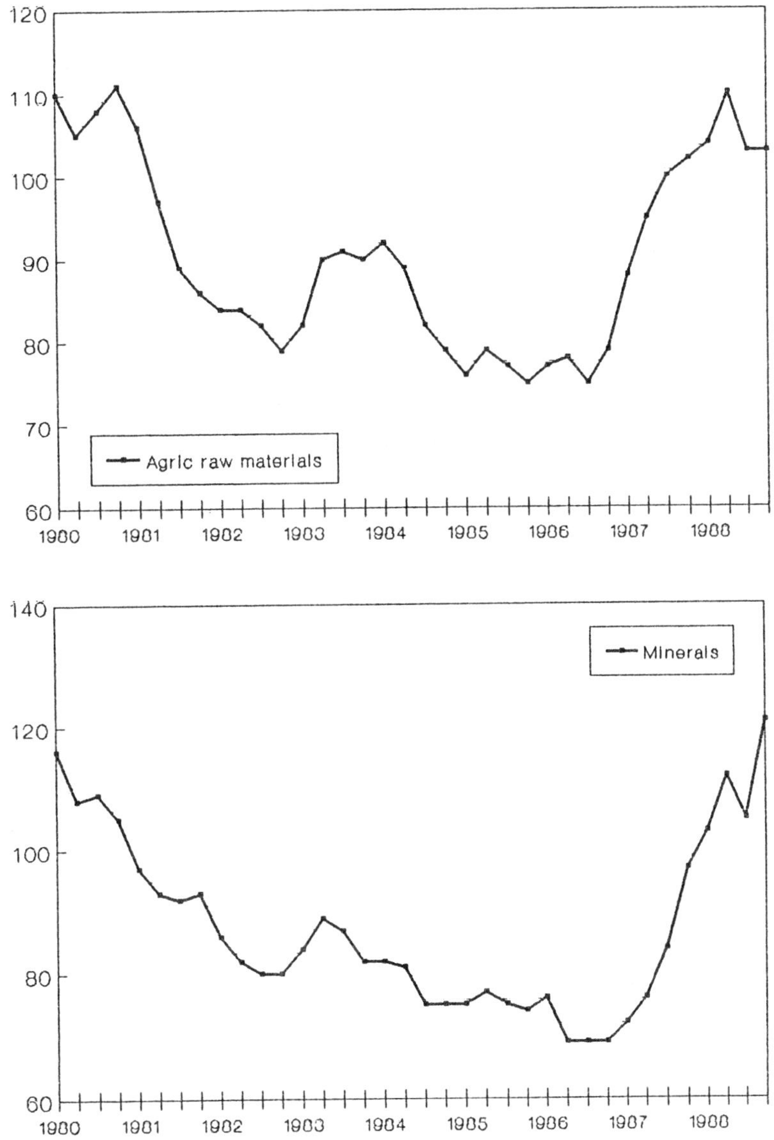


*Source:* UNCTAD, *Monthly Commodity Price Bulletin.*

face of stagnant demand, prices fell below the floor set under the International Cocoa Agreement, despite a large buffer stock purchase by the International Cocoa Organization. Tea prices remained weak since 1984 as supply increased, but rose modestly in 1988 in dollar terms.

Agricultural raw materials account for about 20 per cent of non-fuel primary exports of the developing countries. Prices, which had increased significantly in 1987, rose by about 8 per cent in 1988. Prices of oil and oilseeds, a much smaller group, increased sharply, by 30 per cent on the average.

The sharpest increase in prices occurred in minerals and metals which account for a fifth of the exports of primary products of developing countries. These prices increased by an average of 34 per cent over their 1987 levels. Increased demand from world manufacturing activity, as well as a decline in capacity over the years of low prices, contributed to this. Prices of all major metals rose. Copper, the most important in the group, was about 45 per cent higher in 1988 than the average for 1987. There were also large increases in aluminium and nickel. Among the major metals, prices of tin showed only a modest increase.

Non-fuel commodity prices increased not only in dollar terms but in real terms as well, that is, in terms of manufactured imports that a unit of primary commodity would buy. Prices of manufactured exports of developed market economies increased by about 7 per cent in 1988. The real prices of non-fuel commodities thus increased by about 11 per cent in 1988, the first such increase since 1984. Despite this improvement, it remained 30 per cent below its 1979-1981 average (see figure III.2 and table A.6).

Figure III.2. Nominal and real prices of non-fuel commodity exports, 1980-1988

(1979-1981 = 100)

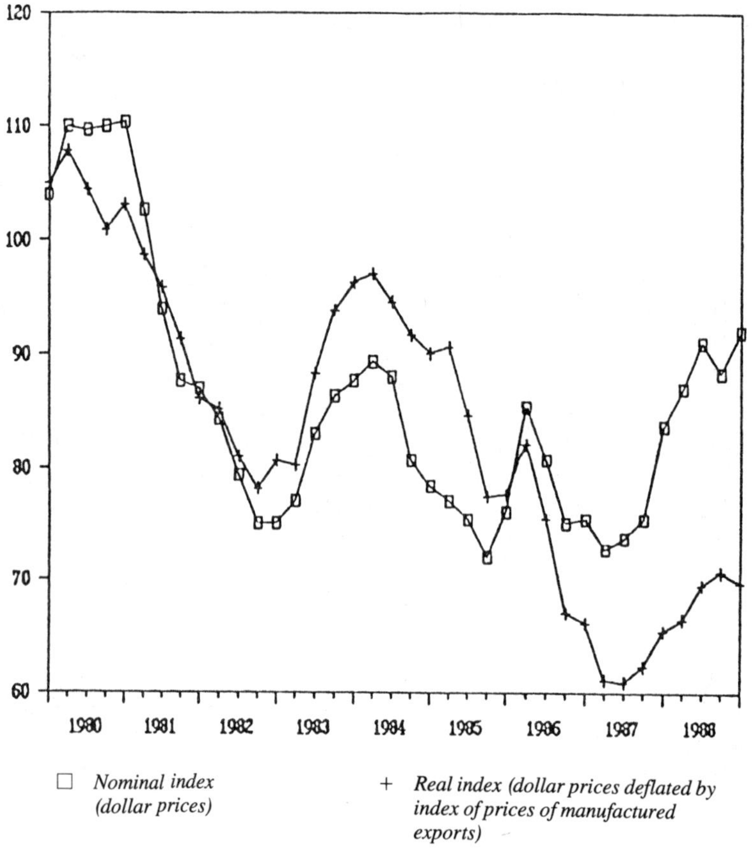


*Source:* UNCTAD, *Monthly Commodity Price Bulletin* and United Nations, *Monthly Bulletin of Statistics*.

A great deal of uncertainty surrounds the course of prices of primary commodities in the near future. Prices appeared to have already peaked by the end of 1988. A slower projected growth of world output in 1989, and an improvement in the supply of a number of commodities in response to high prices, suggest that commodity prices may be somewhat lower in 1989 than in 1988 and fall again in 1990.

While prices of non-fuel primary commodities increased by about 18 per cent in 1988, there was a fall of almost the same magnitude in the price of oil, which accounts for over 30 per cent of the total exports of developing countries. After a partial recovery in 1987, oil prices declined in dollar terms by an average of about 20 per cent in 1988. In real terms, the decline was even sharper. Towards the end of 1988, prices were starting to rise and, following a return to production restraint by the OPEC countries and an announcement of cut-back of production in other exporting countries, they rose in the first quarter of 1989 (see chap. V).

# Chapter IV

## INTERNATIONAL FINANCE AND DEBT

Two related issues of international finance are currently key global policy concerns. The first is foreign indebtedness. The developing countries that are in protracted debt crisis have necessarily been a major focus of world attention, and certain centrally planned economies also have had major debt crises. The country with the largest absolute amount of foreign debt, however, is the United States. Although, of course, it is not a country with debt-servicing difficulties, concern has been raised about the sustainability of the growth of its net foreign debtor position.

The availability of financing is the second area of broad concern to policy makers. In the developing countries, the major focus is on obtaining adequate external financing to support economic adjustment and development. In the centrally planned economies it is experimenting with ways that countries with non-market economic structures might better draw on private international financing. In the developed market economies, attention focuses on the changing capital flows and their impact on exchange rates and on the official financial movements made in response to changing private international flows.

The present chapter surveys these issues, which it sees in the context of an integrated world financial system. The developed market economies collectively seek to manage their exchange rates and stabilize them. The centrally planned economies seek to develop more intensive financial linkages with the rest of the world and the developing countries—or more precisely, the countries heavily constrained by debt crisis—seek to remove financial obstacles to their own adjustment and return to a more normal place in the global system. In support of the latter, specific policy recommendations are put forward in this chapter in order to speed the resolution of the international debt crisis and promote the development of the developing countries.

### A multipolar world financial system

The international economy, as set in motion once again after the end of the Second World War, was unusually dependent on a single country and a single currency. The United States produced roughly half the world's output and its currency became the single major vehicle for international trade and finance. Indeed, the international monetary system that was established when the International Monetary Fund was created, took the United States dollar as the explicit anchor of the system. Europe and Japan were rebuilding their economies, the third world was only beginning to define itself through decolonization and non-alignment, and China was emerging from a great civil war.

The world today has become a multipolar one. The United States accounts for about one quarter of world output, and the dollar—while still the most widely used currency in international transactions—increasingly shares the role of international money with other currencies, notably the deutsche mark and the yen. In recent years, the trend toward multipolarity in currency and other financial matters seems to have accelerated.

In particular, whereas 80 per cent of international bonds—bonds placed simultaneously in more than one national market—were denominated in dollars as recently as 1984, by 1987 only 41 per cent of international bonds were dollar-denominated, and 43 per cent were so denominated in 1988. The rest were in deutsche mark (13 per cent), pounds sterling (12 per cent), yen (9 per cent), Canadian dollars (7 per cent), ECUs, the currency unit of the European Community (6 per cent), and several other currencies.[1] The fall in the dollar's share of international bank lending has also been marked: from 72 per cent of cross-border loans outstanding of banks in developed market economies at the end of 1984, the dollar's share fell to 52 per cent at the end of 1988. As in the case of bonds, however, the shares of other currencies remained far behind that of the dollar, the largest being that of the deutsche mark (8.5 per cent).[2]

The receding role of the dollar can be traced to several factors. One is the growth and development of other developed economies relative to that of the United States. Besides this measure of catching up, which increased the attractiveness of other currencies, the instability of exchange rates themselves has been a force pushing people to diversify the currency composition of their assets and their debts. Moreover, as the current account deficit of the United States balance of payments swelled in the 1980s (see table IV.1), it became increasingly necessary for the United States to mobilize foreign financing. A positive real interest differential in favour of the United States increasingly was needed so that some of the savings in high-saving countries would be attracted into the relatively low-saving United States economy.[3] Dollar denominated financial instruments became a relatively expensive vehicle for borrowing, and this led borrowers to search for non-dollar instruments. Finally, countries that had traditionally been major users of dollars, in particular developing countries, reduced their operations in the dollar-based market. In the case of Middle Eastern oil

1 Data from Organisation for Economic Co-operation and Development, *Financial Market Trends,* No. 42 (February 1989), p. 109.

2 It might be charged that these figures are a distortion in that they convert bank loans in non-dollar currencies using current exchange rates. Indeed, at end-1988 exchange rates, the bank loan share never really changed (56 per cent of foreign currency and domestic currency cross-border loans of banks in industrial countries at the end of 1984 versus 52 per cent at end-1988). But the fact of the matter is that exchange rates did change and the value of the bank portfolio of loans (and thus the dollar share of that value) should be measured in actual terms (estimates calculated from data from Bank for International Settlements, *International Banking and Financial Market Developments,* various issues).

3 See chapter VII for an elaboration of this issue.

Table IV.1. World balance of payments on current account,[a] by country group, 1980-1989

(Billions of dollars)

| | 1980 | 1981 | 1982 | 1983 | 1984 | 1985 | 1986 | 1987 | 1988[b] | 1989[c] |
|---|---|---|---|---|---|---|---|---|---|---|
| Developed market economies | -35.7 | -4.8 | -6.2 | -1.9 | -39.1 | -24.8 | 15.8 | -7.9 | -23.4 | -37.5 |
| Large industrial countries | -11.3 | 20.8 | 14.3 | 2.2 | -40.0 | -24.9 | 14.0 | -5.6 | -15.0 | -22.5 |
| of which | | | | | | | | | | |
| Germany, Federal Republic of | -7.1 | 2.4 | 11.1 | 10.6 | 16.1 | 22.5 | 46.5 | 55.0 | 60.0 | 59.0 |
| Japan | -9.5 | 6.2 | 8.1 | 22.2 | 36.4 | 50.5 | 87.3 | 89.7 | 82.5 | 75.5 |
| United States | 7.4 | 12.0 | -2.6 | -39.9 | -98.4 | -103.8 | -127.0 | -143.9 | -125.2 | -122.5 |
| Other industrial countries | -24.4 | -25.6 | -20.5 | -4.1 | 0.8 | 0.1 | 1.8 | -2.3 | -8.4 | -15.0 |
| Developing countries | 32.3 | -38.0 | -75.8 | -56.5 | -28.5 | -28.9 | -47.5 | -6.1 | -25.5 | -28.5 |
| Capital-surplus countries | 104.3 | 61.4 | 17.9 | -5.2 | -0.3 | 7.2 | -9.8 | 4.8 | -1.5 | 4.0 |
| Capital-importing countries | -72.0 | -99.4 | -93.7 | -51.3 | -28.2 | -36.1 | -37.7 | -10.9 | -24.0 | -32.5 |
| Energy exporters | -0.4 | -29.4 | -34.9 | -10.6 | -1.0 | -1.8 | -20.3 | -3.6 | -16.5 | -12.5 |
| Energy importers | -69.2 | -72.0 | -64.6 | -45.2 | -29.6 | -22.8 | -10.2 | -7.6 | -4.5 | -16.0 |
| Recent surplus economies[d] | -8.9 | -7.1 | -2.9 | 1.5 | 6.7 | 10.4 | 23.1 | 30.5 | 26.0 | 17.0 |
| Other | -60.3 | -64.8 | -61.7 | -46.7 | -36.3 | -33.2 | -33.3 | -38.1 | -30.5 | -33.0 |
| China | -2.4 | 2.0 | 5.9 | 4.4 | 2.4 | -11.5 | -7.2 | 0.3 | -3.0 | -4.0 |
| Centrally planned economies of Europe[e] | -4.3 | -7.4 | 3.7 | 7.7 | 9.9 | 1.7 | -0.2 | 7.3 | 4.5 | 1.5 |
| Eastern Europe | -6.6 | -5.1 | 0.7 | 2.2 | 3.7 | 1.3 | -0.9 | 1.2 | 1.1 | 1.0 |
| Soviet Union | 2.8 | -1.7 | 3.5 | 5.9 | 6.6 | 0.6 | 0.9 | 6.6 | 3.8 | 1.0 |
| World residual[f] | 7.8 | 50.2 | 78.3 | 50.7 | 57.7 | 51.9 | 31.9 | 6.7 | 44.4 | 64.5 |
| of which | | | | | | | | | | |
| Trade residual (imports, f.o.b.) | -43.2 | -32.8 | -18.0 | -23.5 | -31.7 | -4.6 | -5.0 | -40.5 | -21.0 | -16.0 |
| Services and private transfers | 51.0 | 83.0 | 96.3 | 74.2 | 89.4 | 56.5 | 36.9 | 47.2 | 65.4 | 80.5 |

*Source:* Department of International Economic and Social Affairs of the United Nations Secretariat, based on data from the International Monetary Fund, and other official national, international and private sources (see tables A.7 to A.12).

a Balance on goods, services and private transfers.

b Preliminary estimate; developing countries rounded to nearest half-billion dollars.

c Forecast, rounded to nearest half-billion dollars; based in part on Project LINK (see chapter II for assumptions underlying forecast).

d Hong Kong, Republic of Korea, Singapore and Taiwan Province of China.

e Balance with market economies; total including estimated investment income deficits of Council for Mutual Economic Assistance (CMEA) banks.

f Unreported trade, services and private transfers, or errors and timing asymmetries in reported data.

Table IV.2. Funds raised on international credit markets, 1981-1988

(Billions of dollars)

| | 1981 | 1982 | 1983 | 1984 | 1985 | 1986 | 1987 | 1988 |
|---|---|---|---|---|---|---|---|---|
| Grouped by borrower | | | | | | | | |
| Developed market economies | 137.2 | 123.2 | 113.3 | 182.5 | 231.3 | 285.2 | 263.0 | 329.2 |
| European planned economies | 1.6 | 0.7 | 1.1 | 3.4 | 5.3 | 3.9 | 3.7 | 4.2 |
| Developing countries | 55.1 | 46.7 | 35.8 | 33.1 | 29.3 | 22.2 | 28.8 | 26.3 |
| Multilateral institutions | 6.7 | 8.5 | 7.7 | 9.8 | 13.2 | 10.1 | 11.9 | 10.7 |
| World total | 200.6 | 179.1 | 157.8 | 228.8 | 279.1 | 321.4 | 307.4 | 370.5 |
| Grouped by instrument | | | | | | | | |
| Bonds, of which | 52.8 | 75.5 | 77.1 | 111.5 | 169.1 | 228.1 | 180.8 | 227.4 |
| International bonds | 31.3 | 50.3 | 50.1 | 81.4 | 136.5 | 187.7 | 140.5 | 177.2 |
| Foreign and special placements | 21.5 | 25.2 | 27.0 | 30.1 | 32.5 | 40.4 | 40.3 | 50.2 |
| Loans | 147.7 | 103.6 | 80.7 | 117.3 | 110.1 | 93.3 | 126.7 | 143.1 |
| Bank loans | 94.6 | 98.2 | 67.2 | 62.0 | 61.1 | 63.2 | 95.4 | 127.6 |
| Other facilities | 53.1 | 5.4 | 13.5 | 55.3 | 48.9 | 30.0 | 31.2 | 15.5 |
| World total | 200.6 | 179.1 | 157.8 | 228.8 | 279.1 | 321.4 | 307.4 | 370.5 |

*Source:* Data from Organisation for Economic Co-operation and Development, *Financial Statistics Monthly.*

exporters, their investable surplus fell as oil prices receded in the 1980s and there was a political as well as economic premium on asset diversification. In the case of much of Latin America and elsewhere, the debt crisis cut off most access to new credit.

At the global level, international finance continues to grow quite strongly, with a 20 per cent increase in 1988 alone, as table IV.2 illustrates. Although the amount of cross-border lending arrangements has risen or fallen in the various years of the 1980s, it has in the end roughly doubled since the decade began. Lending has been increasingly concentrated, however, on the industrialized countries, as many developing countries lost access to the market through debt crisis, while a few others became net suppliers of funds to the market by developing substantial surpluses in their balance of payments.[4]

The vehicles by which international credit is accorded have also diversified markedly during the 1980s. Whereas there was almost three times as much bank lending as bond financing in the beginning of the decade, there is now about 60 per cent more bond financing than bank lending (see table IV.2). This in part reflects the growing securitization of financial markets,[5] but it also reflects the greater dominance of developed country borrowers which generally have the high credit ratings needed for access to bond markets.

The stock markets of several countries have also become more important vehicles of international finance. In the United States, in particular, foreign equity purchases became a significant source of foreign financial resources for two years, 1986 and 1987 (see table A.8). After the stock market crash of October 1987, however, that source of financing disappeared.

Nevertheless, more than a year later the United States and some major foreign stock markets have begun to recover and significant foreign flows might resume across borders.[6] There was, after all, little evidence that international transactions in stocks had much to do with the 1987 crash—rather, it was more an international transmission of panic—and certain reforms in specific markets that would help to stabilize market behaviour have been identified in several studies after the crash (see box IV.1).

Finally, not only have credit and equity markets diversified as they grew in the 1980s, but direct investment activity has as well. Indeed, although the United States owned almost half the world's stock of foreign direct investment in 1960 and even 40 per cent in 1980, its share had fallen to 35 per cent by 1985. The share of the United Kingdom has also fallen, from 18 per cent in 1960 to 15 per cent in 1985. The share that has grown most and accounts for most of the shift is that of Japan (from 7 per cent to 12 per cent).[7]

The United States has also become an increasingly important host for direct investment from other countries. Whereas the United States was the location of 12 per cent of world foreign direct investment in 1975, it accounted for almost 30 per cent by 1985. These investments rose from 2 per cent of United States gross domestic product (GDP) to 5 per cent. Japan, the most dynamic source of foreign direct investment, remains insignificant as a host, accounting for 1 per cent of the total (0.5 per cent of its GDP).

Together, these investment flows have comprised the major sources of financing to cover the balance-of-payments deficits on current account and to provide the outlets for the current account surpluses. Table IV.1, showing the international pattern of current account balances, can equally be viewed as a table of net flows of funds. Thus, the United States may be seen as the single largest net absorber of funds and the Federal Republic of Germany and Japan as the largest identifiable net sources.[8] The developing countries continue to absorb a diminished flow of funds compared to the early years of the 1980s, and the centrally planned economies—both fewer in number and smaller in degree of integration into the international market economy than other groups—run generally small current-account balances with the market economies.

---

4 Four developing countries have earned large current-account surpluses in recent years, as indicated in table IV.1. They have arisen, first, on the strength of their merchandise trade balance, but there is also a contribution from services that are in part the earnings on overseas construction and other labour activities, but also from reduced interest on foreign debt that is being repaid and increased interest earned on foreign assets (see table A.12).

5 See, "The changing institutional character of international financial markets in the 1980s", *Supplement to World Economic Survey 1985-1986* (United Nations publication, Sales No. E.86.II.C.2), pp. 28-51.

6 The United States index of stock market prices rose 15 per cent (December 1987 to December 1988), while that of the Federal Republic of Germany rose 24 per cent and Japan's rose 21 per cent, based on local currency indices of Organisation for Economic Co-operation and Development, *Financial Statistics Monthly.* In several developing country markets, dollar price indices almost doubled (Brazil, Mexico, Republic of Korea and Taiwan Province of China), while in others, dollar prices rose 20 per cent or more (Argentina, Chile, India, Malaysia/Singapore, the Philippines and Thailand), according to the International Finance Corporation of the World Bank, *Emerging Stock Markets Factbook.*

7 Data in this and the subsequent paragraph are from United Nations Centre on Transnational Corporations, *Transnational Corporations in World Development: Trends and Prospects* (United Nations publication, Sales No. E.88.II.A.7), pp. 24-25.

8 The sum of the current accounts of all the world's countries does not come to zero in table IV.1 as it would if all data were correctly and fully reported. The table shows, in particular, that $44 billion of current account surplus—and thus of financial flows—were unaccounted for in 1988 and a larger residual is forecast for 1989 (equivalently, the reported current account deficits may have been overstated so the "missing" financing may have been smaller than the data indicate). Although there is much room for error in data for recent years given their preliminary nature, even data from many years before show comparable residuals. It is possible to decompose the residual into trade and services components which indicate that the errors are mainly in the services accounts, and probably in the financial services components (for a comprehensive analysis of this problem, see International Monetary Fund, *Final Report of the Working Party on the Statistical Discrepancy in World Current Account Balances* (September 1987)).

## Box IV.1. The world's major stock markets, viewed from the perspective of 1989

The stock market crash of 19 October 1987 is now receding into the distance, and it should be possible to gain a better perspective on exactly what happened in the world's equity markets at that time. There is still no consensus, however, as to whether the crash of 1987 was or was not a "correction" of overpriced securities, whether rapidly appreciating stock prices in the 1980s did or did not represent a "speculative bubble", whether the markets are or are not currently overvalued, or whether market overvaluation is or is not a world-wide phenomenon in which speculative excesses are transmitted across borders. What does seem clear, however, is that the sustained buoyancy of the world's major stock markets during the one and one half years since the crash seems to indicate that the market is again behaving in more traditional ways.

The performance of a stock market essentially reflects the demand and supply of the hundreds of individual stocks that are traded in that market. The price of a stock is generally believed to reflect fundamental economic factors that affect the value of that stock. If participants in the market for securities are assumed to be rational—meaning they use all available information that might affect the value of a stock—the price of a stock today should equal the future cash flow of dividends it is expected to provide, each year's flow discounted by an appropriate interest rate. On average, prices of equities over the past 25 years seem to have reflected these fundamentals.[a] A notable exception, however, is seen in the months preceding October 1987. At that time, industrial share prices in the equity markets of the Group of Seven countries rose to levels that no longer seemed to reflect economic "fundamentals". This can be seen for Japan, the United Kingdom and the United States in the figures given below in this box, where the hypothetical curves represent an estimate of what stock prices would be if they were to reflect certain fundamental economic factors. The hypothetical curves, which are based on 25 years of behaviour, generally seem to trace a path around which actual prices have fluctuated. Although the hypothetical departure from behaviour in Japan has been relatively large in recent years, it became especially marked in 1987, suggesting that Japan shared in the same phenomenon as elsewhere. While the reasons for the 1987 divergence in all three countries are still widely debated, a recently proposed theory advancing the concept of "rational speculative bubbles" offers a tenable explanation.

### Rational speculative bubbles

Theoreticians have shown that even when expectations are "rational", prices of securities will be influenced by expectations of future prices.[b] These expectations can become self-fulfilling, and can significantly influence current stock prices. It may thus be "rational" for stock prices to make continuously-increasing deviations from the prices that fundamentals would dictate. In such a case, investors would be aware that the market was making an incorrect valuation, but the expected returns (including the possibility of a crash) would be high enough to keep them in the market. Although the "bubble path" is unsustainable and will eventually lead to a crash, rational and efficient market actors none the less find it in their interest to follow the path. Thus, a "bubble" is created whereby the actual stock prices are considerably higher than economic "fundamentals" would suggest. It is possible that the prices of stocks in the months leading up to October 1987 were, in fact, buoyed by something resembling a rational speculative bubble, and on October 1987 that bubble burst (although the market retreated less in Japan and has since recovered).

### Globalization

Globalization of world equity markets has become an important concern of policy makers, especially after the events of 1987. One major question is whether or not the globalization of equity markets had a significant effect upon the crash. Globalization of these markets has clearly been on the rise in the 1980s, as market mechanisms and electronics-based developments have created a trading environment in which portfolio managers and arbitragers can move quickly between different countries' stock exchanges. Financial market deregulation in several countries has opened up trading to multinational securities firms. Volatility in exchange rates has created the need to hedge portfolios across markets as well as incentives to speculate. Exchange rate variations have greatly affected exchange rate adjusted returns from cross-market investing. And macro-economic imbalances—

a The ensuing analysis is based on T. Thurston and B. Herman, "Recent issues and evidence on the behaviour of world equity markets", Department of International Economic and Social Affairs of the United Nations Secretariat Working Paper No. 12 (forthcoming in 1989). The analysis is carried out for the stock markets of each country in the Group of Seven; space limitations preclude presenting all those results here.

b See Olivier J. Blanchard, "Speculative bubbles, crashes and rational expectations," *Economic Letters*, vol. 3 (1979), pp. 387-389. For a statistical application of the theory to the 1987 crash, see Gikas A. Hardouvelis, "Evidence on stock market bubbles: Japan, the United States, and Great Britain", Federal Reserve Bank of New York, *Quarterly Review* (Summer 1988), pp. 4-16.

Prices of industrial shares, 1980-1988
(Index, 1980=100)

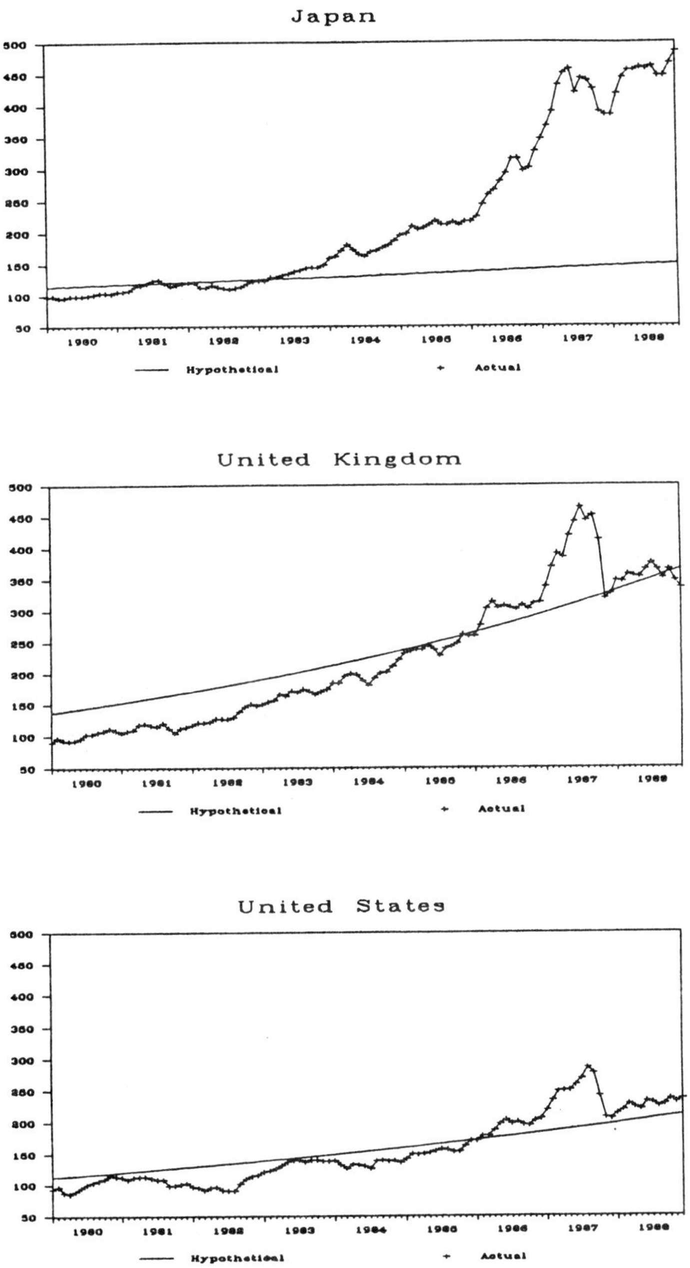


*Source:* T. Thurston and B. Herman, "Recent issues and evidence on the behaviour of world equity markets", Department of International Economic and Social Affairs of the United Nations Secretariat, Working Paper No. 12 (forthcoming in 1989).

especially between the United States with its large current account deficits, and Japan with its large surpluses—helped to induce an unprecedented volume of cross-border equity ownership.

There is no clear answer yet as to whether globalization has been distorting equity flows between markets in different countries. As noted above, average stock prices have been periodically mispriced relative to fundamentals. It seems that this mispricing may move in sympathy across markets. However, in the period since globalization of equity markets came into being (sometime during the 1980s) there is no evidence of a greater degree of sympathy of movement than was the case in earlier periods.

### Panic psychology

Even if globalization has not clearly led to heightened price-sensitivity among equity markets in different countries, the October 1987 crash has posed an instance of near-simultaneous panic selling in many markets. The repatriation of funds undeniably contributed to declines in most markets. This must, however, be kept in perspective. Even at the peak of cross-border activity in 1987, the share of such activity was never large relative to domestic participation. A recent study by the Federal Reserve Bank of New York could find few instances of cross-border activity's having spread the crash among markets on 19 October.[c] Rather, the principal cross-border impacts appear to have resulted from investors having observed sharp price declines in each others' markets, which led to a panic psychology.

### Policy implications

Under the experience thus far, it is difficult to show that global techniques or trading practices *per se* have either substantially tightened international linkages or contributed substantially to the late-1987 decline. This suggests that the need to control cross-border activity or internationally coordinate regulation of such activity may not be as soundly based as many had presumed. On the other hand, studies seem to support stricter regulation and improvements in market mechanisms at the domestic level.[d]

c See Robert Aderhold, Christine Cumming and Alison Harwood, "International linkages among equities markets and the October 1987 market break", Federal Reserve Bank of New York, *Quarterly Review* (Summer 1988), pp. 34-46.

d For example, see *Report of the Presidential Task Force on Market Mechanisms* (The Brady Commission Report), (Washington, D.C. United States Government Printing Office, 8 January 1988); *The October 1987 Market Break,* Securities and Exchange Commission Staff Report (Washington, D.C., United States Government Printing Office, February 1988); and United States General Accounting Office, *Preliminary Observations on the Market Crash of October 1987* (26 January, 3 and 5 February 1988).

For 1989, the international pattern of recent years is expected to continue. The United States, Japanese and German current accounts are expected to move slightly in the direction of greater equilibrium,[9] although changes of such small small magnitude cannot be forecast with any degree of certainty. Exporters of petroleum are expected to see a strengthening of their current account balances, although the Soviet Union is forecast to use the opportunity to strongly step up imports from convertible currency markets in support of its economic reform programme described in chapter II above. The developing countries that have been so successful in building trade and payments surpluses in recent years are forecast to show a strong reduction of their surpluses, a direction that they have indeed been encouraged to take by other countries. Other developing countries are expected to follow a pattern similar to their recent one. The capital-importing developing countries as a whole would thus once again find themselves transferring net financial resources to the rest of the world.

### The net transfer of financial resources from developing countries, and the debt problem

In each year since 1983, the capital-importing developing countries have transferred financial resources overall to the rest of the world. In 1988, far from a correction of the flow, the net outward transfer grew to more than $30 billion, measured as the total financial flows in and out of these countries minus the net payment of interest, dividends and other capital-servicing. Measured in an alternate way—in terms of the shortfall of expenditures below income produced in their economies—the net outward transfer was even greater, exceeding $40 billion (see table IV.3).[10]

As in recent years past, the outward transfer can be largely attributed to transactions relating to credit flows. In contrast, for the first time this decade, the net transfer related to direct foreign investment became significantly positive in 1988, owing to a strengthening of net direct investment. Official flows also provided a significant inward transfer, although the net transfer related to foreign official credits *per se* was more strongly negative in 1988 ($7 billion) than in 1987 ($5.5 billion).

The net transfer out of the developing countries is closely related to the slow-down in lending to these countries and thus to the slower growth in their gross foreign debt. In 1988, the debt grew by less than 3 per cent, the smallest annual increase in the 1980s. And, the ratio of debt to GNP finally seems to have stopped rising (see table IV.4).

As in previous years, the net outward transfer was an economic burden for most developing countries experiencing it, as is detailed in chapter VIII. But it was a sign of economic strength in a few countries. Among the latter, the Republic of Korea applied a portion of its current account surplus of approximately $14 billion to retiring some $2 billion of its outstanding bank debt.[11]

For the many other developing countries that have been struggling under a tight external capital constraint, there were no signs in 1988 that international credit flows would soon improve, neither official nor private.

#### Multilateral finance and the need for a refinancing mechanism

Multilateral development financing continued to grow slowly in 1988, but even then only in nominal terms. Overall commitment levels in dollars rose 5 per cent, but this was less than the international rise in prices (see table A.14). Measured in real terms, multilateral development commitments fell in 1988, leaving them 18 per cent below their peak in 1985 (see figure IV.1). The fall has been concentrated on the non-concessional component of multilateral lending, as concessional multilateral flows have, in essence, kept pace with inflation.

For countries whose per capita income place them outside the criteria for concessional lending, the decline in the real value of non-concessional commitments denies them potentially important assistance for development and adjustment. And as the obligation to pay debt-servicing on already outstanding debt is not subject to rescheduling, the net flow and the net transfer tend to diminish. Indeed, in 1987 the aggregate net transfer had already turned negative for the main non-concessional lending programme of the World Bank, conventionally denoted as lending by the International Bank for Reconstruction and Development (IBRD). As IBRD-lending itself accounts for almost half of all multilateral development flows (see figure IV.2), this is an extremely significant development. It is also not likely to be reversed soon. The 1988 agreement to expand the capital stock of the World Bank by $75 billion is considered sufficient to allow IBRD

9 As a share of GDP the correction would be somewhat greater than in absolute dollar terms: from 2.7 per cent of GDP in 1988 to 2.2 per cent in 1989 for Japan, and from 2.8 per cent of GNP in the United States in 1988 to 2.5 per cent in 1989. The degree of correction in the case of the Federal Republic of Germany would be from 4.8 per cent of GNP to 4.6 per cent (based on forecasts of Project LINK).

10 The difference between the two flows is the net use or accumulation of official reserve assets. In 1988, in particular, about $9 billion were added to reserves, which required a reduction in expenditures beyond what was required for transactions relating to all the different types of foreign capital flows (for a formal derivative of these relationships, see *World Economic Survey 1986* (United Nations publication, Sales No. E.86.II.C.1), pp. 163-164).

The continued need for reserve accumulation is highlighted by the fact that despite the addition to reserves that took place, end-1988 reserves (valued in dollars at current exchange rates) fell to about 2.5 months' coverage of import expenditures from almost three months in 1987, as may be seen in table A.13 (expenditures include interest payments on foreign debt and other services, as well as merchandise imports). This notwithstanding, the proportion of countries with less than two months' coverage of import expenditures—a rule-of-thumb minimum security level—fell to one half in 1988 from about 55 per cent of capital-importing countries in each of the preceding two years.

11 Based on data from the Bank for International Settlements.

Table IV.3. Net transfer of financial resources of the capital-importing developing countries,[a] 1980-1988

(Billions of dollars; sample of 98 countries)

| | 1980 | 1981 | 1982 | 1983 | 1984 | 1985 | 1986 | 1987 | 1988[b] |
|---|---|---|---|---|---|---|---|---|---|
| Transfer through direct investment | | | | | | | | | |
| Net investment flow | 6.5 | 11.3 | 8.1 | 7.0 | 6.6 | 7.4 | 6.1 | 8.3 | 12.5 |
| Net dividends and other income | -11.0 | -10.5 | -10.1 | -9.8 | -9.0 | -8.3 | -7.4 | -7.9 | -8.5 |
| Net transfer | -4.5 | 0.8 | -2.0 | -2.8 | -2.4 | -1.0 | -1.3 | 0.4 | 4.0 |
| Transfer through private credit | | | | | | | | | |
| Net credit flow | 36.5 | 37.8 | 23.9 | 12.4 | 9.0 | -1.6 | 1.5 | -3.0 | -14.0 |
| Net interest paid | -19.3 | -30.4 | -42.6 | -39.0 | -42.0 | -39.3 | -33.6 | -31.7 | -32.0 |
| Net transfer | 17.2 | 7.5 | -18.7 | -26.5 | -33.0 | -40.9 | -32.1 | -34.7 | -46.0 |
| Transfer through official flows | | | | | | | | | |
| Official transfers (grants) | 13.2 | 13.6 | 11.1 | 11.4 | 12.4 | 15.0 | 14.5 | 14.2 | 15.0 |
| Net official credit | 21.9 | 27.8 | 29.6 | 27.4 | 25.0 | 14.9 | 14.3 | 12.0 | 14.0 |
| Interest paid | -6.2 | -7.1 | -8.8 | -10.2 | -11.7 | -13.6 | -16.1 | -17.5 | -21.0 |
| Net transfer | 29.0 | 34.3 | 32.0 | 28.6 | 25.8 | 16.3 | 12.7 | 8.7 | 8.0 |
| Overall net transfer | 41.7 | 42.6 | 11.3 | -0.7 | -9.6 | -25.5 | -20.7 | -25.6 | -32.5 |
| Memorandum item | | | | | | | | | |
| Use of official reserves[c] | -16.2 | 3.4 | 22.6 | -2.3 | -18.7 | -5.2 | 5.4 | -8.0 | -9.0 |
| Net transfer on expenditure basis | 25.5 | 46.0 | 33.9 | -3.1 | -28.4 | -30.8 | -15.3 | -33.6 | -41.5 |

*Source:* Department of International Economic and Social Affairs of the United Nations Secretariat, based on data from the International Monetary Fund (IMF), the World Bank and United Nations Secretariat estimates.

a Definitions: Direct investment is net of re-invested earnings (cash flow approach); official credits include use of IMF Credit and interest includes Fund charges; net private credit flow includes arrears on interest as well as principal, and outflows of capital by residents.

b Partly estimated; rounded to the nearest half-billion dollars.

c Additions to reserves are shown as negative numbers.

to expand its lending by about 10 per cent a year in nominal dollar terms, reaching an annual lending level of more than $20 billion by the early 1990s.[12] But debt-servicing payments to IBRD have already grown at twice that rate since 1970, and they grew 24 per cent a year on average from 1980 to 1987.

If the net transfer of resources of IBRD is negative, the net capital flow (i.e., excluding interest payments) remains positive. This is not the case for lending by IMF, where the net capital flow has been a net repayment to the Fund since 1986 (see figure IV.3). The Fund has been a net recipient of capital from each of the main developing country regions since 1987 (see figure IV.4).

In contrast to the World Bank and other development agencies, IMF is primarily an agency for providing relatively short-run support for balance-of-payments adjustment programmes that are typically expected to be completed in one to three years, with credits to be repaid within five (or up to ten years for extended arrangements). The loans of the early 1980s are thus being repaid, although few cases could be cited in which the adjustment process has now been successfully completed.

In this context, the decision of several countries to suspend debt-servicing payments to the Fund, the World Bank and other institutions is an important signal. As at 1 April 1989, 11 countries were over six months in arrears to the Fund, 8 to the World Bank and 3 to the Inter-American Development Bank. The international community has insisted on the privileged status of debts owed to the multilateral institutions and has no method for rescheduling them. For some heavily-indebted countries, there seemed little alternative to arrears, as they did not have significant reserves and virtually no private or bilateral official credit to draw upon. In some cases the major creditor in the past had been precisely these multilateral institutions.

The countries that have built up substantial arrears to the multilateral institutions have all been countries in crisis. Analysts can attribute the difficulties in each one to domestic economic, social and political strains, but the fact that there are so many is a signal that there is some failing at the international level as well. Other countries that have not yet incurred arrears could be forced into doing so if their circumstances deteriorated. It would be better to anticipate that problem and assist those not able to extricate themselves at this time.

The IMF has implicitly recognized the difficulties of some of its member countries that borrowed significant sums from it on regular, commercial terms in the early 1980s when their situation actually warranted longer-term and highly concessional lending. The Fund did not then have an active concessional window, but the Structural Adjustment Facility (SAF) and later the Enhanced Structural Adjustment Facility

12 World Bank, *Annual Report 1988*, p. 33.

Table IV.4. Foreign debt of the capital-importing developing countries,[a] 1980-1988

| | 1980 | 1981 | 1982 | 1983 | 1984 | 1985 | 1986 | 1987 | 1988[b] |
|---|---|---|---|---|---|---|---|---|---|
| | | | | | *Billions of dollars* | | | | |
| Medium-term and long-term debt | 430.8 | 499.2 | 563.0 | 654.2 | 696.1 | 770.4 | 871.3 | 969.7 | 991 |
| Official concessional | 107.3 | 114.1 | 122.7 | 131.0 | 133.4 | 152.9 | 177.8 | 211.9 | 217 |
| Official non-concessional[c] | 69.6 | 87.2 | 103.3 | 128.0 | 140.1 | 171.9 | 210.6 | 250.0 | 256 |
| Private | 253.9 | 297.8 | 337.0 | 395.2 | 422.6 | 445.5 | 482.9 | 507.9 | 518 |
| Short-term debt | 121.4 | 143.3 | 159.0 | 129.0 | 122.5 | 120.2 | 107.4 | 119.4 | 126 |
| Total debt | 552.2 | 642.4 | 722.0 | 783.2 | 818.5 | 890.6 | 978.7 | 1 089.2 | 1 117 |
| | | | | | *Percentage* | | | | |
| Total as a ratio to GNP[d] | 28.3 | 31.1 | 35.9 | 41.1 | 42.1 | 45.2 | 48.3 | 49.5 | 47.4 |
| Total as a ratio to exports[e] | 127.1 | 139.5 | 166.0 | 183.0 | 177.1 | 198.1 | 227.3 | 214.5 | 189.7 |
| Memorandum item | | | | | | | | | |
| Debt of a larger grouping of capital-importing countries (billions of dollars)[f] | 656 | 755 | 831 | 894 | 933 | 1 051 | 1 152 | 1 281 | 1 320 |

*Source:* Department of International Economic and Social Affairs of the United Nations Secretariat, based on data from the World Bank, the International Monetary Fund and the Organisation for Economic Co-operation and Development.

a Sample includes China, but not Hong Kong, nor Taiwan Province of China.
b Estimate.
c Including use of IMF credit.
d Sample of 106 countries.
e Sample of 112 countries; exports of goods and services.
f World Bank grouping of the developing countries other than high-income oil-exporting countries (principal difference with above total is inclusion of certain countries of Western and Eastern Europe classified as "developing" by the World Bank).

(ESAF) sought to remedy that. For some countries, an important component of SAF and ESAF programmes was that they informally refinanced outstanding non-concessional IMF credits on concessional terms. In the World Bank, a comparable use can be made of IDA loans.

To the degree that adequate funds are available under these lending programmes, an important contribution can be made to providing official finance to ease the foreign capital constraint, epitomized by the outward net transfer of resources. But a group of countries cannot draw on these resources because their economic situation has not yet deteriorated enough to make them eligible for special assistance for low income countries. To assist countries that seek to regularize their international financial situation and are ready to embark upon a major adjustment and development effort, as well as to protect the future financial strength of the multilateral institutions, it would be appropriate to mobilize the requisite resources for refinancing obligations to the multilateral lenders on appropriate terms.

When countries fall into crisis conditions, private foreign creditors withdraw from extending new loans, which is natural as they fear for the safety of their earnings and have no wider responsibility. The same cannot be said for official institutions. But it is up to the major shareholders of those institutions to supply the institutions with means adequate to the task.

## Commercial credit and the debt overhang

The financial markets seem to evaluate lending to most developing countries as a relatively risky undertaking and developing country borrowers that have access to this market are themselves wary about the amount of new debt they take on. One result is that gross borrowing arrangements by capital-importing countries on international capital markets remain at the depressed level of recent years, especially if the involuntary lending by banks arranged as part of debt-rescheduling negotiations is excluded (see figure IV.5).

In addition, the secondary market in developing country loans that has grown to a significant level of activity in recent years continues to downgrade the debt of heavily indebted countries. Figure IV.6 illustrates trends in secondary market prices commonly experienced by developing countries. The debt of a few countries has been rated highly, although with some recent slippage, as Algeria shows; the debt of other countries has fallen sharply as is the case for countries as different as Brazil and Côte d'Ivoire; and the debt of yet other countries has long been heavily discounted, as exemplified by the Dominican Republic. In no case has the debt of a country that had been heavily discounted in recent years risen appreciably in the market.

The commercial banks that had earlier been attracted into lending to developing countries have instead reduced their exposure in recent years in large part through the secondary market. In the case of the United States banks, for example, total exposure has fallen from $138 billion at its peak at the end of 1983 to $89 billion at the end of December 1988. Banks that have had a relatively smaller stake in this lending have reduced their exposure the most, leaving the exposure of United States banks concentrated heavily on that of nine money-centre banks whose holdings are, in turn, concentrated on a small number of the heavily-indebted countries (see figure IV.7). And the major theme of how to treat the debt of the countries that are over-indebted to the banking

Figure IV.1. Multilateral development commitments in real terms, 1970-1988

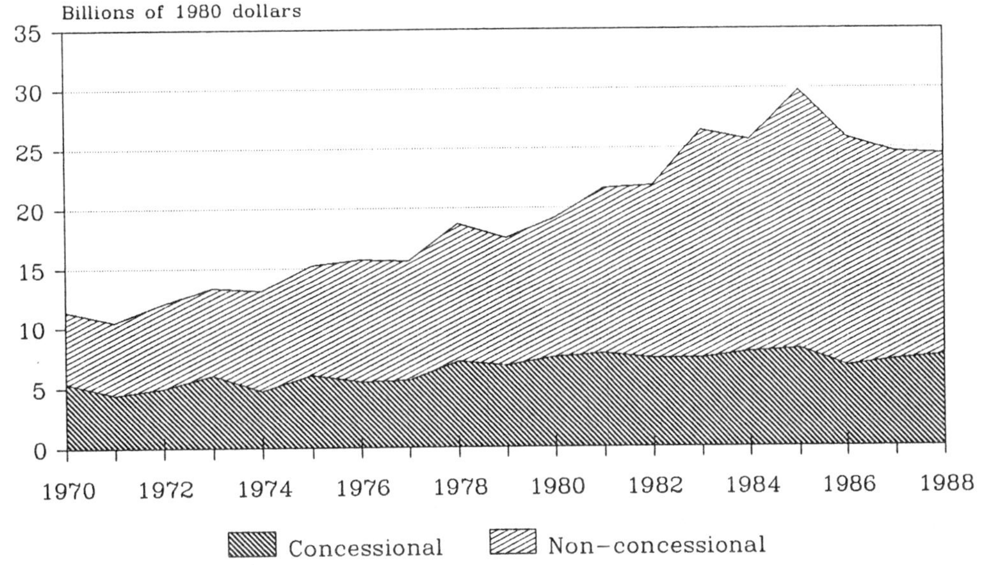


*Source:* Department of International Economic and Social Affairs of the United Nations Secretariat.

Figure IV.2. Multilateral resource commitments, 1988 (Total = $30.0 billion)

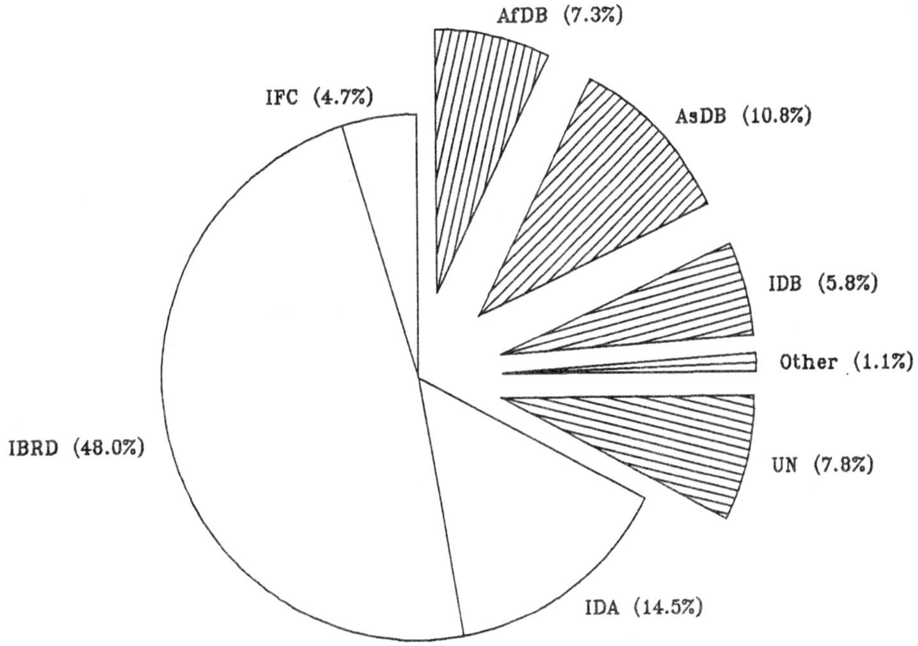


*Source:* Table A.14.

Figure IV.3. Developing country drawings and repayments from the International Monetary Fund,[a] 1980-1988

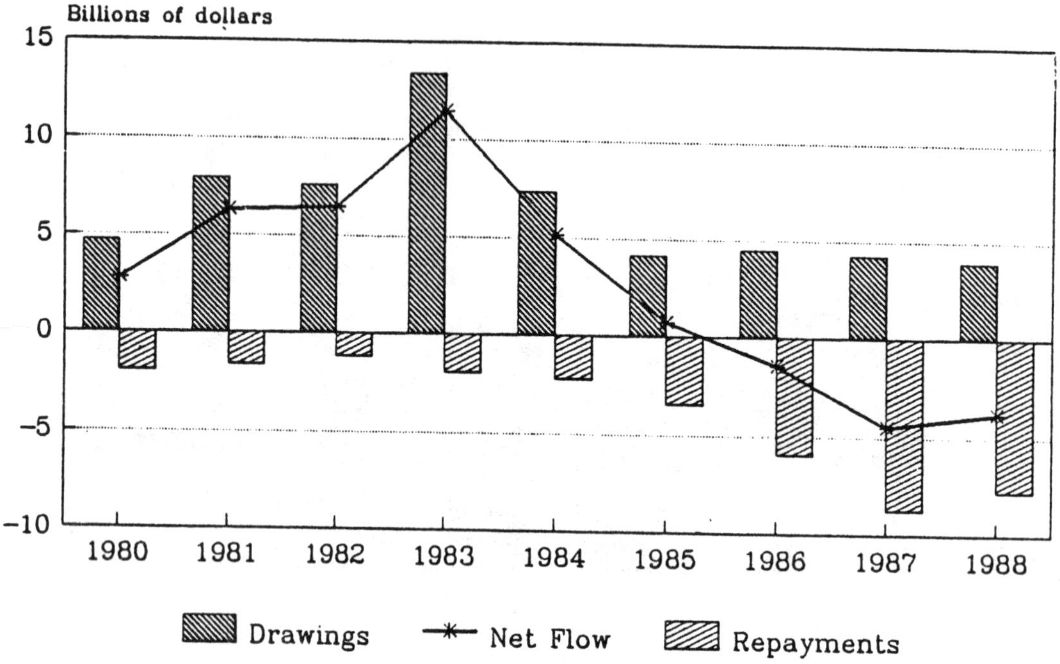


*Source:* Data from International Monetary Fund, *International Financial Statistics.*

[a] Use of Fund credit and reserve tranche.

Figure IV.4. International Monetary Fund net lending to the developing countries, by region,[a] 1981-1988

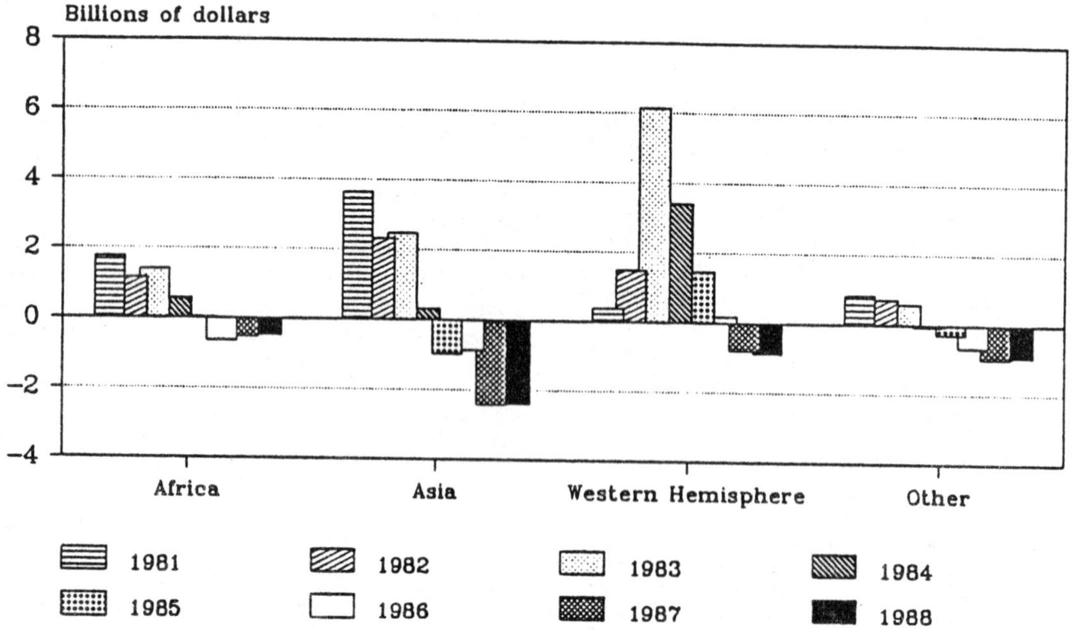


*Source:* Data from International Monetary Fund, *International Financial Statistics.*

[a] Use of Fund credit and IMF Trust Fund.

Figure IV.5. Gross borrowing arrangements on international capital markets by capital-importing developing countries, 1981-1988

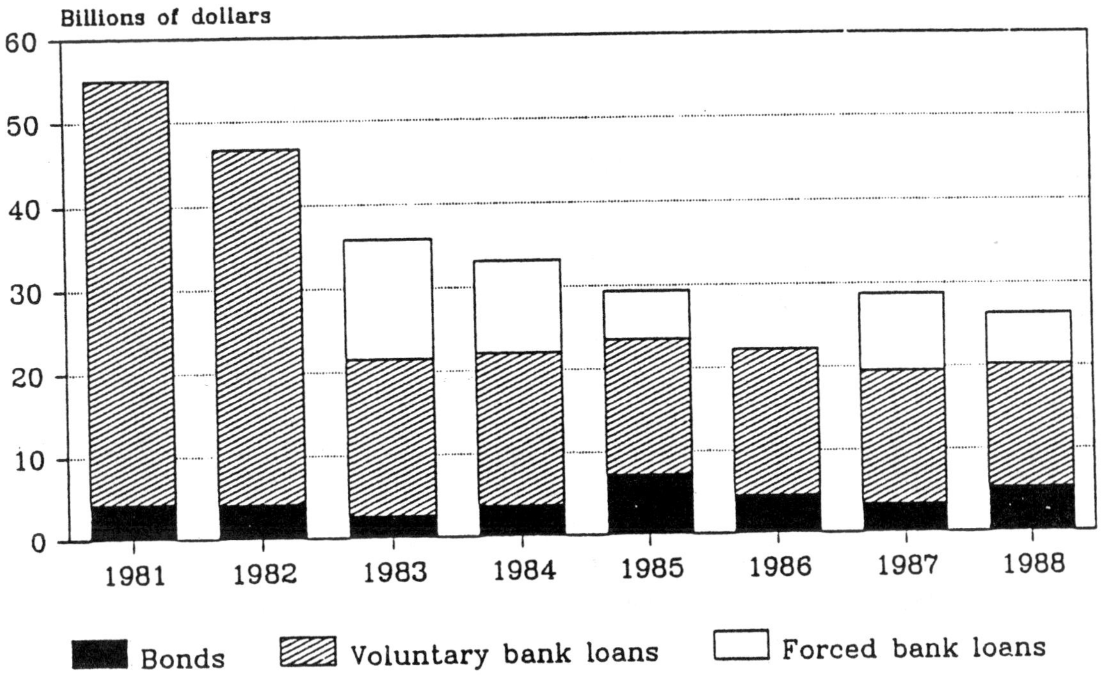


*Source:* Data from The Organisation for Economic Co-operation and Development and the World Bank.

sector has now become how to reduce the debt, not how to entice, cajole or force the banks to extend new loans.

The international community has been actively grappling with the external debt problem of developing countries since debt-servicing difficulties became a widespread phenomenon in the early 1980s. It has been a major focus of attention in technical, financial and political forums.[13] International policy has gone from short-term crisis management to efforts to mobilize new financial flows along with debt-rescheduling on increasingly better terms for debtors, to an expanding menu of financing and debt relief options, and finally to broad recognition of the need for significant debt reduction in a wide variety of situations faced by heavily-indebted developing countries. In the last year the area of agreement on the need for a permanent reduction of debt-service—reducing the present value of the debt—has broadened appreciably.

**Debt owed to bilateral official creditors.** A major step was taken on 21 June 1988 at the Toronto Summit of seven major industrial countries (the Group of Seven) when the Heads of State or Government reached consensus on new terms for rescheduling the debt owed to official creditors by the poorest developing countries which were also undertaking internationally approved adjustment programmes. The new step was to create a "framework of comparability" in which Government creditors could choose among concessional interest rates, usually on shorter maturities, longer repayment periods at commercial rates of interest, partial write-offs of debt-service obligations being rescheduled, or a combination of these.[14] The understanding was that concessions of different kinds should involve comparable burdens.

By the autumn of 1988, the Paris Club of official creditors agreed to how the various new options would work, namely:

13 Monitoring and analysing emerging developments in the external debt situation of the developing countries has been a major concern of many official international organisations and the secretariats that service them. Indeed, the analysis presented here may be considered an extension of that in earlier *World Economic Surveys* and the series of reports on the external debt crisis and development prepared for the General Assembly, the most recent of which was "Toward a durable solution of the debt problem" (A/43/647 30 September 1988). Annual reports to other global bodies that monitor the developing country debt situation include International Monetary Fund, *World Economic Outlook,* United Nations Conference on Trade and Development, *Trade and Development Report;* and World Bank, *World Debt Tables,* 1988-1989 edition, vol. I, Analysis and Summary Tables.

14 Economic declaration issued by the seven major industrial countries at the end of their three-day summit, 21 June 1988, para. 30 (see, *IMF Survey,* 27 June 1988, pp. 219-223).

Figure IV.6. Secondary market prices of foreign bank debt of selected developing countries, 1987-1989

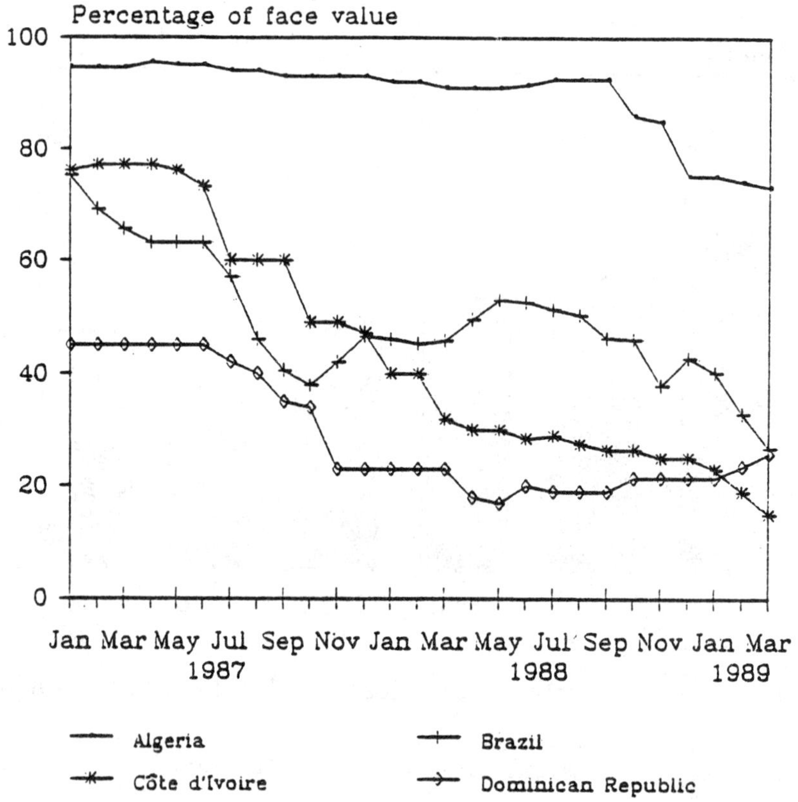


*Source:* Data from Salomon Brothers, New York.

(a) *Partial write-off.* One third of debt service originally due during the period being renegotiated would be forgiven and the remainder would be rescheduled under fairly standard terms for low-income countries (14-year maturity with 8-year grace period at market interest rates);

(b) *Extended maturities.* The full amount of debt service being renegotiated would be rescheduled, at market interest rates, but with a 25-year maturity and 14-year grace period;

(c) *Concessional interest rate.* The full amount would be rescheduled as in (b) above, but at the shorter term of option (a) and at an interest rate that is 3.5 percentage points below market rates or one half of market rates, whichever gives the smallest reduction.

Options (a) and (c) are considered to have comparable degrees of concessionality, and although option (b) involves no concession in terms of discounted present value if the longer-term claims are paid in full, it clearly is more risky for the creditor.

From the debtor's perspective, however, the short-term cash flow benefits of the new package were not large. The World Bank has estimated that for the countries participating in its Special Programme for Africa, debt-service payments during the period 1988-1990 would fall by less than 5 per cent compared with recent rescheduling standards.[15] This notwithstanding, the options approach had been applied in several cases by early 1989 (namely, Central African Republic, Madagascar, Mali, Niger, United Republic of Tanzania and Uganda). It is clearly a step forward, but it only begins to address the needs for debt relief of low-income countries.

Additional debt relief measures for low-income countries that would go further in improving the net financial resource transfer to these countries in the short run have been proposed and still warrant consideration by the creditor countries. This applies in particular, to the recommendations of the Advisory Group on Financial Flows for Africa, convoked by the Secretary-General of the United Nations in 1987. These recommendations entailed a three-part policy approach to Paris Club debt:

15 See, World Bank, *World Debt Tables ...*, box I-2.

Figure IV.7. Exposure of United States banks to developing country debt, 1982-1988

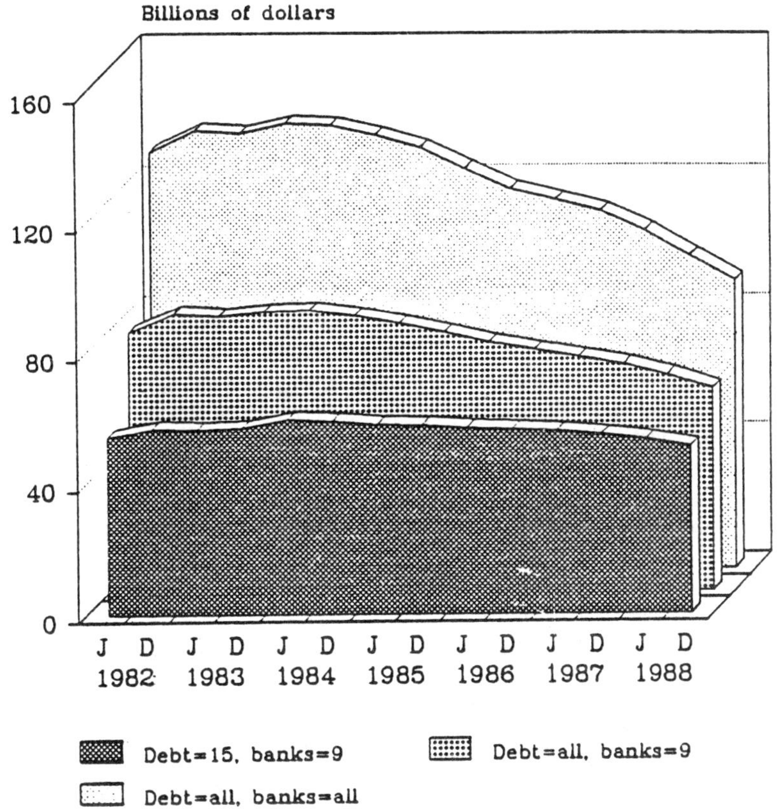


*Source:* Data from the United States Federal Financial Institutions Examination Council.

(a) For countries that are not expected to become creditworthy in the foreseeable future in the eyes of commercial creditors and in which there is an agreed medium-term framework for adjustment, all servicing of bilateral official debt scheduled for the next three years should be rescheduled at the highly concessional rate of interest charged on loans from the World Bank's IDA and at the favourable maturity and grace periods already being accorded by the Paris Club (up to a 20-year repayment period with up to a 10-year grace period);

(b) For countries with better prospects of regaining creditworthiness, conventional annual rescheduling should be made available, but at a below-market interest rate that brings their debt-servicing burden into reasonable conformity with debt-servicing capacity;

(c) Countries with stronger prospects would continue under terms of rescheduling already available and export credit agencies should renew cover for new lending as soon as debt relief and adjustment are under way.[16]

**Debt owed to commercial banks.** The other milestone in broadening the consensus on debt relief in 1988 came when first Japan, and then France, made new proposals for commercial bank debt relief for middle-income countries undergoing adjustment programmes. The proposals included actions that would reduce the present value of their debt to the banks. The Japanese proposal, presented formally at the Joint Annual Meetings of IMF and the World Bank in September and reiterated in the United Nations General Assembly,[17] included the idea that some of the outstanding bank debt might be converted into securities and the rest rescheduled, with certainty of repayment enhanced for creditors by each debtor country establishing a special reserve account at the IMF to serve as collateral. The presumed advantage for the debtor country, especially as it was expected to put its own resources into the IMF account, was that the securities or rescheduled debt would carry lower interest obligations

16 See, *Financing Africa's Recovery: Report and Recommendations of the Advisory Group on Financial Flows for Africa*, (published by the Department of Public Information of the United Nations Secretariat, 1988), paras. 141-142.
17 See summary records of the Second Committee of the General Assembly (A/C.2/43/SR.16, paras. 60-66).

than those obtainable under conventional rescheduling practices.

The proposal of the President of France[18] is complementary to that of Japan in that he proposed establishing a fund in IMF to guarantee interest payments on bonds converted from commercial bank loans owed by the eligible heavily-indebted countries. The resources for that fund would come from the developed countries' share of a proposed issue of IMF special drawing rights. This proposal raised the possibility both of lower interest obligations and of new resources to underwrite interest guarantees.

In March 1989, the United States made a proposal that also allowed the possibility of international financial suport for negotiated reduction of commercial bank debt. The United States suggestion was acted upon by the Interim Committee of the IMF and the joint World Bank/IMF Development Committee at their spring meetings, wherein the Committees agreed, *inter alia,* that part of the resources committed under Fund-supported arrangements or policy-based financing at the Bank could be set aside for use in facilitating debt reduction operations; and the Fund and Bank were also asked to consider as a matter of urgency the issues and action involved in the major proposals that had been put forward.[19] Several heavily-indebted developing countries have begun consultations with a view to drawing on the opportunity provided by the new initiative and leading—as is already the case for Mexico—to a new round of negotiations with their commercial bank creditors.

Given the attention paid to this new international initiative on debt—which has been coined the "Brady Plan", after the United States Secretary of the Treasury who had proposed it[20]—it is thus important to examine it in some detail. Like its predecessors, the new initiative envisions debt reduciton taking place on a case-by-case basis in voluntary agreements negotiated between the debtor country and its creditor banks. Secretary Brady's plan proposes to support this process through four key innovations.

First, the plan suggests that the private banks waive, for a period of three years, the negative pledge and sharing clauses, which have been a pervasive presence in the international banks' loan agreements with developing countries. These clauses provide for equal treatment among the creditor banks: the borrower promises not to pledge assets to any of the banks on a preferential basis or to pay debt-servicing preferentially. The clauses have tended to slow debt reduction because a prior waiver of them by a majority of banks has been needed to initiate buy-backs and securitization of debt.[21] An across-the-board waiver would be expected not only to accelerate the negotiation of debt reduction, but also to enhance the terms for the debtors, since in principle there would be a more competitive environment on account of the developing country's ability to negotiate individually with its different creditors.

Second, the Brady Plan also calls for the creditor Governments to explore ways to reduce regulatory, accounting and tax impediments to the banks' participation in debt reduction schemes.

Third, the plan would permit, for the first time in the management of the international debt problem, an explicit commitment of public resources to support a debt reduction process. World Bank resources would come out of the its recent $75 billion capital increase; the Fund would use existing resources, although the plan also promised to study an increase in that institution's quotas. Countries in balance-of-payments surplus also would be asked to contribute to the plan's financing. Indeed, Japan had earlier proposed extending additional finance in the form of untied loans of the Export-Import Bank of Japan in support of Fund arrangements and Japan announced that these would be available under the strengthened debt strategy.

The fourth key innovation of the Brady Plan involves a delinking of the disbursements of IMF programmes from the management of the private banks' balance sheets. In effect, the Fund and a developing country would be able to move ahead with their adjustment programme even if there were no prior commitments from private banks to contribute to its financing through rescheduling, debt reduction or new money packages. This would reverse a policy in place since 1982 in which IMF programmes have generally been contingent on a country's attaining a prior agreement with its banks to close the financing gap through a combination of debt relief and new money.[22]

The Brady Plan's proposals represent an important advance in the conception of how to manage the commercial bank debt problems of the highly-indebted countries. The positive aspects of the proposal can perhaps be best appreciated by examining the scope and limitations of the Brady Plan's predecessor, the Baker Plan, and more specifically, the second stage of that Plan, the so-called market menu approach.

---

18 See preliminary verbatim records of the General Assembly (A/43/PV.10, 30 September 1988), pp. 6-20.

19 See communiqué of the Interim Committee of the Board of Governors of the International Monetary Fund, 4 April 1989, para. 3; and communiqué of the Joint Ministerial Committee of the Boards of Governors of the Bank and the Fund on the Transfer of Real Resources to Developing Countries, 4 April 1989, para. 10 (as published in *IMF Survey,* 17 April 1989, pp. 118-121).

20 "Remarks by the Secretary of the Treasury Nicholas F. Brady to the Brookings Institution and the Bretton Woods Committee Conference on Third World Debt", *Treasury News* (United States Department of the Treasury, 10 March 1989).

21 A waiver of the negative pledge usually requires the consent of between 50 and 66 per cent of a country's creditor banks, while the sharing provisions generally call for consent of between 95 and 100 per cent of the banks (see Michel Bouchet and Jonathan Hay, "The Rise of the Market-Based Menu Approach and Its Limitations" (Washington, D.C., World Bank, 1989).

22 For analysis of the traditional relationship between the banks and the IMF during the management of the crisis, see United Nations Economic Commission for Latin America and the Caribbean, "Politicas de ajuste y renegociación de la deuda externa en américa latina," *Cuadernos de la CEPAL,* No. 48 (United Nations publication, Sales No. S.84.II.G.18), published in English as *External Debt in Latin America,* (Boulder, Colorado, Lynne Rienner Publishers, 1985), pp. 47-86.

### Debt restructuring experience under the market menu approach

The market menu approach emerged in 1987 on account of the shortcomings of the Baker Plan's original formula for restoring growth in the highly-indebted developing countries, which involved intensification of economic reforms in the debtor countries, coupled with a redoubled effort to mobilize concerted loans for them from commercial banks and official lenders.[23] As it became evident taht the commercial banks were unwilling to support the Baker Plan's lending commitments, the official focus shifted to the menu approach as a way to overcome the developing countries' financing constraint.[24]

The menu concept essentially supplemented concerted lending packages by the banks with other financing options. On the one hand, the menu proposed the use of alternative instruments such as trade and project loans, bond placements and limited capitalization of interest payments. On the other, it introduced for the first time in the management of the debt problem the possibility of financing the debtor countries through debt reduction techniques such as debt-equity swaps, exit bonds and buy-backs. The items on the menu had to emerge voluntarily from the market on a case-by-case basis in negotiations between the debtor country and its creditor banks. Moreover, the creditor Governments were emphatic that their support of the menu could not involve costs for their taxpayers, i.e., public guarantees to enhance financing packages were explicitly excluded from the official management strategy.

While appearing in 1987, the menu did not gain concrete form until 1988 when an array of its market-based options emerged from the negotiations between debtors and creditors. Financing schemes tended to stress debt reduction techniques, in part because net lending by the banks had become ever more difficult to mobilize. Indeed, according to World Bank estimates, net bank financing to the highly-indebted countries, after adjustment for the net movement of arrears, was only $500 million in 1988, compared to an already low figure of $7 billion in 1987.[25] There were, however, certain notable efforts at debt reduction

**Mexico.** An innovative operation was tried in Mexico in early 1988 in which the Government proposed to trade up to $20 billion of restructured public debt for $10 billion of bonds having a single maturity of 20 years and an annual interest rate of 1.63 per cent over the London interbank offered rate (LIBOR), compared to 0.81 per cent over LIBOR for already restructured debt. To enhance the attractiveness of the new bond, Mexico indicated a willingness to guarantee its principal by using the country's foreign exchange reserves to make a parallel purchase of a specially-issued United States. Treasury zero-coupon bond with a face value and a maturity identical to that of the Mexican instrument.[26]

Gaining the necessary waivers from the banks to initiate the conversion operation was not as difficult as it might have been because protracted negotiations over the latest rescheduling agreement had already exempted public debt from the sharing clause, which had earlier required approval of 100 per cent of the banks. The remaining obstacle was the negative pledge clause which had to be waived to collateralize the new bonds. Since this waiver required approval of only 51 per cent of the banks, it was secured within two months. But major problems arose on other fronts.

First, Mexico's collateral was for principal only, which represented just 18 per cent of the discounted present value of the 20-year Mexican bond. In other words, the banks perceived that over 80 per cent of the income stream on the bond was unsecured Mexican risk. The Mexican authorities tried to overcome this problem by asserting that the new bond would be senior to existing loans, but most banks were apparently unconvinced by seniority created by *fiat*. Second, the attractiveness of the offer to United States banks also was reduced by a ruling of the United States Securities and Exchange Commission which stated that United States banks would have to write down all loans tendered for the exchange, even if they ultimately were not accepted by the Mexican Government. Third, the announcement of an offer to exchange up to $20 billion of debt for $10 billion of bonds implied a discount of 50 per cent on outstanding bank loans; yet many institutions in the United States had loan loss reserves sufficient to cover discounts of only 25-30 per cent, while the formal reserve cover of the Japanese banks for loan losses was even lower.[27] Fourth, for many European banks there was little or no advantage in recognizing the lower value of their assets in an exchange, as they had already received a tax reduction when setting up reserves against possible losses (in contrast, say, to the United States where the tax loss is taken only when the debt is written

---

23 The Baker Plan was announced in September 1985 and sought to mobilize $29 billion over three years for heavily-indebted developing countries. Of that, $20 billion were to come from commercial banks and $9 billion from official lenders. However, bank financing proved difficult to mobilize, in part because by 1986 commercial banks had substantially reduced their vulnerability to default and therefore had less incentive to lend in concerted fashion to problem borrowers. Indeed, World Bank data suggest that net lending by banks totalled only $6 billion over the period 1986-1988, in contrast to $15 billion for official lenders (see World Bank, Debt and International Finance Division, *Quarterly Review*, March 1989, p. 3).

24 For a more complete analysis of the evolution of the official debt management strategy and the emergence of the market menu approach, see United Nations Economic Commission for Latin America and the Caribbean, *The Evolution of the External Debt Problem in Latin America and the Caribbean*, Estudios e Informes de la CEPAL No. 72, United Nations Publication; Sales No. E.88.II.G.10); and Robert Devlin, *Debt and Crisis in Latin America: The Supply Side of the Story* (Princeton, Princeton University Press, forthcoming 1989), chaps. 5 and 6.

25 World Bank, Quarterly Review..., p. 3.

26 For more detail on the Mexican proposal, see Ruben Lamdany, "Voluntary Debt Reduction Operations: Bolivia, Mexico and Beyond...", (Washington, D.C., World Bank, June 1988).

27 See Economic Commission for Latin America and the Caribbean, "Economic survey of the United States", (LC/G.1477, 28 February 1989), table 32; and Bouchet and Hay, *op. cit.*, p. 19.

down). Fifth, the placement confronted "free-rider" problems, since some banks were tempted to withhold their participation in anticipation of having the value of their loans rise as the absolute amount of Mexican debt fell. Finally, it is well known that the market reacts cautiously to new instruments such as this one and therefore conversions of this type should normally be expected to start quite small.[28]

The reaction of the market to the Mexican offer fell far short of initial expectations. In the auction Mexico received 320 bids from about a quarter of the country's nearly 500 creditor banks for a total value of $6.7 billion. The Government accepted just 95 of those bids valued at $3.7 billion and traded them for $2.6 billion of the Mexican bonds. Thus, the average discount on the operation was 30 per cent and debt was reduced by $1.1 billion. The Government had to set aside about $490 million of foreign exchange reserves to collateralize the new bonds, and about another $100 million had to be drawn upon to collateralize the country's bonds already in circulation among bondholders in order to avoid discrimination.

The results of the Mexican exchange offer disappointed creditors and debtors alike. Nevertheless, because of the way the programme was financed, not even the most optimistic scenario of a $10 billion debt reduction would have produced dramatic relief for Mexico's harried balance of payments.[29] With an interest rate on rescheduled debt of LIBOR plus 0.81 per cent and with LIBOR then at 8 per cent, every dollar of debt reduction brought with it, at that time, 8.8 cents of cash flow relief in the form of lower interest payments. However, this interest savings was partially offset by the fact that Mexico enhanced the new bond with a higher spread over LIBOR than was found on the old debt and also had to use liquid, interest-earning foreign exchange reserves to purchase the collateral instrument that, while earning a competitive interest rate, would not generate any cash flow for 20 years and had to be held until maturity. Thus, at a 50 per cent discount, $10 billion of debt swap would have produced only $660 million annually in net interest savings, compared to an annual interest bill with the banks in excess of $7 billion. Moreover, in view of the need to set aside $1,985 million for collateral, the net cash flow on that operation would have been negative for Mexico for the first three years of the 20-year life of the bonds.[30] The benefits received from the actual programme were of course much more modest. The net interest saving was $35 million per year (calculated at 1988 interest rates) and the full cash flow pay-back would not be reached until the seventeenth year of the programme.

**Bolivia.** Another debt reduction operation was arranged in March 1988 by Bolivia. Because of economic and political problems, this nation unilaterally suspended its debt service in mid-1984 (see the case study in chapter VIII). After rescheduling its Paris Club debt in July 1986, Bolivia began to actively negotiate a buy-back of its bank debt, worth about $670 million (excluding interest on arrears), or 15 per cent of the country's total public foreign debt. The country's bank debt had been circulating in secondary markets at about 6 cents on the dollar, but with news of a potential buy-back, secondary market prices quickly rose to 11-12 cents.

A year after initial contacts, in July 1987, Bolivia won waivers of its restrictive clauses which had been contained in a 1981 rescheduling agreement. Among the conditions established for the buy-back were that the resources for the purchase had to come from third party donors; the contributions had to be placed in an IMF trust fund, and an identical price would have to be offered to all the country's bank creditors. The banks also won the option to accept, in lieu of cash, 25-year collateralized peso-denominated zero-coupon bonds, which were indexed to the United States dollar and eligible for conversion into local equity at a 50 per cent premium over their face value.[31]

The buy-back was formally announced in January 1988 with an offer price of 11 cents on the dollar. In March, Bolivia announced that 53 of its 131 creditor banks had made bids; nearly $270 million of debt was exchanged for cash and $64 million for notes for a total settlement of almost $37 million, involving a draw-down of $28 million from the IMF Trust Account (the rest supplied in Bolivian bonds). The outstanding bank debt thus was reduced by about half.

The buy-back clearly illustrated how assistance from the international donor community can assist in a reduction of outstanding bank debt. Indeed, the entire operation would not have been feasible without the resources provided by donor Governments and the IMF's good offices. Nevertheless, the operation was not an unqualified success and re-

---

28 See K. Telljohann, "Analytical Framework", *Prospects for Securitization of Less Developed Country Loans* (New York, June 1987), Salomon Brothers, p. 11.

29 On recent balance-of-payments and net-resource-transfer difficulties, see the Mexican case study in chapter VIII.

30 With LIBOR at 8 per cent and a spread of 0.81 per cent, the interest saving on a $20 billion reduction of bank debt would be $1,762 million per year. If the debt had been swapped at a 50 per cent discount, the Government would have to emit $10 billion in bonds paying an interest rate of 9.63 per cent, which meant an interest cost of $963 million per year (the bank debt would have had a shorter number of years to maturity, but it can be assumed it would have been rolled forward again by a subsequent debt renegotiation). This marks a direct gain of $799 million per year. But there were losses too. Mexico would have needed to purchase $1,885 million of United States Treasury bonds to have the $10 billion collateral in 20 years (at 8.7 per cent a year interest, the rate then prevailing). While the $1,885 million would still be a Mexican asset, it would no longer be liquid as are reserves and would thus be a cash loss of $1,885 million in the first year. In addition, however, Mexico put up at least another $100 million of reserves to accord comparable treatment to its existing bond holders, so its total purchase of United States Treasury bonds would have been $1,985 million. If these reserves had themselves been invested in United States Treasury bills paying, say, 7 per cent interest (a highly conservative investment assumption), then the interest income foregone — or the cash flow foregone — would be $139 million a year. The net interest gain per year would therefore have been $660 million. As the cash drain in the first year would have been $1,985 million, Mexico would not have recovered its cash flow loss until the end of the third year of the programme.

31 For a more detailed summary of the Bolivian operation, see Lamdany, *op. cit.*

vealed shortcomings of the market menu approach as then conceived.

In particular, it is striking that facing an unquestionable state of insolvency in Bolivia, an offer price that nearly doubled that prevailing in the secondary market before the announcement of a buy-back, and the availability of third parties to finance a full scale repurchase, only 40 per cent of the country's creditor banks volunteered to participate in the operation. The reasons for this sluggish response are varied. Some banks clearly preferred to ride free, thinking that with a reduced debt Bolivia might eventually be willing to settle the remaining outstanding obligations on terms more favourable to them. Other banks which were fully reserved against Bolivian portfolio risk expected little immediate tax or accounting benefits from formally recognizing a loss; indeed, by sitting tight a bank might achieve a windfall benefit if, say, the country's terms of trade unexpectedly rose sharply and renewed its ability to service the debt. Other banks, with inadequate reserves against their developing country exposure, wanted to avoid the losses implied by participation in a buy-back and thereby keep their loans at book value. Finally, some institutions undoubtedly preferred to avoid the precedent of debt forgiveness.

Another problem was the rise in the secondary market price itself. At 6 cents on the dollar the secondary market had been valuing the country's $670 million bank debt at $40 million. However, anticipating the buy-back the market price rose to roughly 11 cents, so that at the new price, the remaining unpurchased debt of $336 million had a market value of $37 million. Thus, slightly less than $37 million of cash and Bolivian notes bought only a $3 million reduction in the market value of outstanding obligations; in other words, Bolivia paid 11 cents on the dollar for a debt with a marginal value of less than one cent per dollar of debt.[32]

Buying back a debt under such circumstances is not necessarily the best use of resources for a country with a foreign exchange constraint. Nevertheless, what made the Bolivian operation attractive was that donor resources were earmarked for the purpose of a buy-back and the country already had a significant pipeline of commitments of foreign loans and grants which it was able to absorb only gradually. Another problem, however, is that even a partial buy-back as large as that in Bolivia did not dramatically alter private investors' perception of Bolivian risk; since after the buy-back the country was still unable to service its remaining bank debt. Banks continued to offer those outstanding obligations for trade in secondary markets at only 11 cents per dollar. Potential new investors would undoubtedly still fear a long embattled queue for available foreign exchange.

**Brazil.** Perhaps the fullest expression of the menu approach emerged in June 1988 when Brazil announced a new financial package with its creditor banks that would lead the country out of the moratorium which it had declared in February 1987. The agreement included the traditional rescheduling of principal on commercial terms and a new money commitment. However, what was notable about the agreement was the impressive array of menu items incorporated into the financing.

As part of a new money package of $5.2 billion, Brazil offered to issue, in lieu of new loans from the banks, up to $1 billion of bonds in bearer form which would carry the same terms as the loans. Moreover, $2.9 billion of the new money subscribed in the form of loans would become eligible over the period 1989-1991 for conversion into local equity at par, up to a limit of $50 million per month.

Brazil also offered the banks an "exit" option on restructured debt. In lieu of rescheduling, the creditors could exchange public sector medium-term debt for exit bonds valued at par with a 25-year maturity and a fixed, below-market interest rate of 6 per cent. The bonds were designed to offer those banks that wished to avoid future reschedulings and requests for a new money package a chance to exit from the process, but at the cost of accepting financial instruments with lower interest rates and longer maturities. To further enhance the instruments, Brazil allowed the banks to convert the exit bonds at par into cruzado-denominated Brazilian Treasury notes indexed, at the choice of the bank, to domestic inflation or to the dollar exchange rate.

The entire new money package, as well as the exit bonds, were also eligible to participate in Brazil's newly introduced debt-equity swap auctions, which began in February 1988. Other menu items in the agreement involved a retiming of interest payments from a quarterly to a semi-annual basis and relending provisions for restructured debt.[33]

The Brazilian agreement clearly was innovative and the best expression to date of the menu approach. But again as a vehicle for debt relief it was only a qualified success. The subscription to the new money package was unusually quick, about one month. Yet only 308 of Brazil's 500 creditor banks entered into the agreement. Moreover, the participating banks' chief motivation for taking up the loans was that it helped Brazil to liquidate more than $3 billion of arrears.

The subscription to the exit bond, while much more successful than a similar instrument promoted by Argentina in 1987,[34] only attracted 108 banks for a total value of $1 billion, or 20 per cent of the amount that Brazil had originally

32 That is, $334 million in reduction of the face value of the debt lowered the market value by only $3 million or $0.009 per $1 reduction of the face value. See Jeremy Bulow and Kenneth Rogoff, "The buy-back boondoggle," *Brookings Papers on Economic Activity* No.2 (1988), pp. 675-704.

33 For an analytical review of the retiming and relending provisions, see Ruben Lamdany, "The Market Based Menu Approach in Action: the 1988 Brazil Financing Package" (World Bank, December 1988).

34 In 1987 Argentina offered exit bonds with a 25-year maturity and a fixed 4 per cent rate of interest. Only two banks subscribed. See Lamdany, *op. cit*, p. 36.

offered to exchange. At that time, the conversion implied a savings of about $30 million per annum in interest payments, which would not have a significant impact on the then $8 billion annual interest burden on the debt with the banks.[35]

In addition, considering that the new money eligible for conversion into equity at face value corresponded closely to the amount of interest payments in arrears, and that the market then valued Brazilian obligations at 50 cents on the dollar, a swap at par was an extremely generous arrangement for the creditor banks. Moreover, the conversions—which are an addition to the official debt-equity programme—also undoubtedly would make management of the country's severe inflationary problem more difficult.

**Chile.** In April 1988 Chile had begun negotiations with its creditors to amend loan contracts so as to introduce more flexibility into the country's debt management. Six months later, in September, the requested amendments were approved by the banks to allow: (a) direct buy-backs of the debt at a discount for an amount not to exceed $500 million to be funded exclusively from the country's foreign exchange reserves; (b) debt exchange offers for up to $2 billion; (c) pre-payments in pesos in cases where receipts are re-lent to new investment projects; and (d) the awarding of preferential guarantees on new debt up to an amount of $500 million. The pre-payment provision was used during 1988 to extend $35 million in financing to a local mining project, and in November Chile deployed $168 million of its reserves to purchase $299 million of debt, capturing a discount of 44 per cent.[36]

The Chilean initiative certainly did introduce needed flexibility into the loan agreements. Yet the banks put severe limits on the volume of resources that could be managed in this new way. Moreover, like any buy-back operation, there is the question of efficient allocation of resources. At that time the repurchase brought about $16 million per annum in net interest savings; however, since the country was required to make an outlay of $168 million in reserves, the cumulative net cash flow on the operation would remain negative for the next 10 years.[37]

**Other activities.** In contrast to these negotiated debt reduction schemes, the most dynamic source of debt reduction in developing countries in 1988 involved formal debt-equity swap programmes as well as informal swaps, which are operations that do not directly involve a debtor country's monetary authorities. The World Bank estimated total swaps to have been about $14 billion in 1988, compared to $7 billion in 1987 and $1.5 billion in 1986. Most of the swaps occurred in four countries: Argentina, Brazil, Chile and Mexico. Brazil carried out by far the biggest volume of swaps; estimates place them at $8 billion, of which about $3.6 billion were in the country's formal programme. Mexico also had a large number of informal swaps, estimated at $3 billion in 1988. Meanwhile, Chile converted about $2 billion of external debt into peso-denominated assets under its formal chapter 18 and 19 programmes. Argentina registered $1 billion in formal swaps, plus an undisclosed amount of informal transactions. In addition, Nigeria began operating debt-equity auctions in late 1988 and the Philippines has begun informal transactions.[38]

While the volume of debt-equity swaps has risen markedly in recent years, so have the polemics surrounding them.[39] One of the major concerns raised by the debtor countries has been related to their weak fiscal situation and the inflationary effects of converting foreign debt into currency and notes. These and other problems with swaps caused Mexico to halt its formal programme in 1987, while both Brazil and Argentina temporarily suspended their operations in early 1989. On the other hand, Chile, with a relative sound fiscal situation, continued to aggressively promote its swap programme, but maintained a ceiling on total operations to be held per year for anti-inflationary reasons.

**Conclusion.** This review of some of the major financial operations in heavily-indebted countries highlights some of the shortcomings of the menu approach. Most important, the time-path of effective cash flow relief granted by market-based voluntary debt reduction techniques tended to be the inverse of what was needed by problem debtors. They have a very high need for an improvement in their current net transfer of financial resources. Most of the techniques focused on reducing principal, the payment of which had already been pushed off into the future by restructurings or moratoria, and which at the margin had an extremely low expected value. The effective balance-of-payments relief therefore was limited to lower interest payments; however, these fell by only a tenth or less of every dollar of debt reduction.

Second, the voluntary responses of the banks to the debt reduction schemes were very poor. This was due to a complex constellation of factors: free riding, sharp differences in the ability of the banks to absorb losses, disincentives arising from bank regulatory and tax codes, fears of precedent, and difficulties in creating preferential status for new debt instruments.

Third, the ability of the debtor-country Governments to undertake direct buy-backs, or to enhance exchange offers was limited by the scarcity of their own foreign exchange reserves, legitimate questions about the best use of those

35 Evaluated at LIBOR in mid-1988 (8 per cent) and a spread of 0.81 per cent on restructured debt.

36 Ricardo Ffrench-Davis, "Recompra de la deuda de Chile," CIEPLAN (Corporación de investigaciones económicas para américa latina) (Santiago, Chile), September 1988.

37 Here, November's LIBOR of 9 per cent plus a spread of 0.81 per cent for restructured debt and interest earnings of 8 per cent on the foreign exchange reserves are applied.

38 World Bank, *Quarterly Review...*, pp. 8-9.

39 For an evaluation of some of the potential negative effects of swaps, see David Roberts and Eli Remolona, "Debt swaps: a technique in developing country finance", in Richard Debs *et al.*, *Finance for Developing Countries* (New York, Group of Thirty, 1987), pp. 15-40.

resources, and in the particular case of debt-equity swaps, the implications of those conversions for expansion of the domestic money supply and inflation. The only case in which new foreign resources were made available to a swap scheme was that of Bolivia which, if made general, would require more substantial direct budgetary outlays by the Governments of creditor countries than seems politically feasible at this time.

Fourth, negotiations with the banks for voluntary debt reduction were usually protracted, owing in part to the need to gain waivers on restrictive clauses in loan contracts. This, coupled with the uncertain response of the banks to exchange offers even when they were approved, created great uncertainties regarding the volume and timing of financing via voluntary debt reduction techniques.

When financial instruments that act more directly on interest payments were deployed by the debtors, such as exit bonds, interest savings tended to be marginal. This was because of the factors cited above, and the fact that the uncertain return of exit bonds had to compete with the certain return of an exit via a cash sale in secondary markets (which does not have any direct benefit for the debtor). When countries tried to enhance the response to their exchange offers through collaterization, the net balance between the use of foreign exchange and the savings of foreign exchange was initially unfavourable for the debtor and not rectified for many years.

Fifth, new loans were increasingly difficult to raise from the banks after they added to their loan-loss reserves and became more interested in reduction of exposure.

Sixth, the menu's options, whether in the form of new resources or debt reduction, tended to be applied very unevenly across the debtor countries, with its limited benefits being concentrated in only a handful of countries.

### The Brady Plan: new stage of the international debt strategy

The Brady Plan is clearly a welcome response to the plight of the overly indebted countries; however, it is still mostly an outline that will gain concrete form only in the months ahead as specific financing schemes emerge from case-by-case negotiations. It has raised expectations that the Governments of creditor countries will give much needed assistance to the market through institutional and financial support of the debt reduction process. Government action on a waiver of restrictive clauses, modification of regulatory and tax impediments to debt reduction, and the allocation of public resources to enhance financing packages could all, in principle, improve the volume of conversion schemes and their terms for the debtors. However, the success of the initiative will depend on three key factors: (a) an allocation of enough new public resources to induce a quick elimination of the debt overhang; (b) strong public co-ordination of the banks to ensure that an adequate number of them participate and that benefits are spread equitably among countries willing to undertake structural reform; and (c) effective growth-oriented adjustment programmes in the debtor countries.

Unfortunately, expectations about debt reduction have already been raised that might exceed what the plan will be able to finance. Informal discussions of the plan in official circles suggest that IMF and World Bank funding of debt reduction on the order of $12 billion per institution over the next 3 years is under consideration. Another $4.5 billion in parallel lending has been committed by the Government of Japan. Of this total of $29 billion, about $15 billion would be additional resources, with the remaining $14 billion involving money that would be reallocated from policy-based lending of the Fund and Bank that is already programmed.

Although a total of 39 countries have been discussed as potential users of the plan, if one just considers the 15 countries that are commonly grouped together as a sample of heavily-indebted countries,[40] it is clear that the $29 billion already committed to the Brady Plan could support no more than a very partial reduction of the debt overhang. For example, if used in a straight buy-back of those countries' debt at the April 1989 weighted average of secondary market prices of 36 cents per dollar, the above-mentioned public funding could reduce commercial debt by some $80 billion. Even this magnitude of debt reduction—which is highly optimistic because it assumes that secondary market prices would not rise once the concrete plan was announced—would bring a fall in government interest payments to private creditors of 36 per cent, because most of the $221 billion debt owed to these institutions in 1989 would be left untouched.

Moreover, the $29 billion is to be provided as loans at non-concessional interest rates, and so the cash flow relief will be less than the reduction in interest payments to the banks. There are two cases. Loans that are a reallocation of funds that would anyway have gone to the debtor country entail an initial cash-flow loss from the inability to use the loan to raise imports.[41] Loans that are additional funds to which these countries would not otherwise have had access add to the debt-servicing burden, reducing the benefit of making lower interest payments to the private creditors. If the $29 billion for the Brady Plan were all new official loans, the net reduction of government foreign interest payments would be

40 The 15 countries are Argentina, Bolivia, Chile, Colombia, Côte d'Ivoire, Ecuador, Mexico, Morocco, Nigeria, Peru, the Philippines, Uruguay, Venezuela and Yugoslavia (the 1989 forecast of debt and interest payments of this group of countries used in the ensuing exercise is drawn from International Monetary Fund, *World Economic Outlook*, April 1989).

41 At a price of 36 cents per dollar of debt, a $100 Fund or Bank loan can repurchase $278 of debt. At a 10 per cent interest rate, the reduced debt eliminates $28 per annum of interest payments to the banks. Interest and amortization on the new loan does not adversely affect cash flow since the country would have been lent the funds anyway. But the $100 is now not available for general support of the balance of payments owing to the rechannelling of the cash to the buy-back. The cumulative nominal cash balance on the transaction would be negative until year four.

### Box IV.2. Why establish an international facility for debt reduction?

Many proposals for a comprehensive solution to the debt problem envisage an institutional innovation in the form of an international debt facility (IDF).[a] While the the details of the proposals differ, in all of them a significant part of the outstanding debt obligations to private creditors would be eliminated and the new IDF would guarantee much of the remaining debt-servicing. Also, a common assumption is that the debt owed to banks that did not participate in the restructuring would be subordinated to the debt covered by the IDF; in other words, non-participating banks would come after participating banks in the queue for debt-servicing payments.

One frequently discussed approach involves the purchase of commercial bank debt by the IDF at secondary market prices. The IDF would then renegotiate the debt-servicing obligations with the debtor, either voiding a portion of the loan contracts, or retaining their original face value as the nominal value, but reducing the interest rate on the loans. In either case, the intention is that the debtor country would receive the benefit from the market discount on the debt and would be able to redirect some of its own resources from debt-servicing to financing an internationally agreed adjustment programme.[b]

The finance for the facility's purchases of the bank debt could be mobilized by issuing bonds, which would be guaranteed by the Governments that owned and established the facility (in effect, the Governments of creditor countries). The creditor banks are assumed in most proposals to buy a substantial portion of the bonds. The banks would thereby be given the opportunity to dispose of an outstanding loan that is subject to significant default risk, in exchange for an asset of a lower contractual value that is subject to a substantially reduced risk of default and is itself tradable on a secondary market, as are bonds of the World Bank and other international financial institutions.

The basic benefit to a participating country in an IDF programme or any debt-reduction scheme is a long-run improvement in the cash flow of debt-servicing. The value today of a future cash flow stream—the present value of the cash flow—would be expected to fall under an IDF programme. But the present value is subjectively assessed and depends on the probability that the contracted payments will actually be made. Some Governments have been accumulating arrears on debt-servicing. In these cases, the benefit to the debtor country of participation in an IDF programme would not necessarily be a reduction in the present value of its debt, but a reduced risk of creditor countermeasures against unilateral moratoria and possibly increased access to other lending. By the same token, creditors' perceptions of the present value of a country's outstanding debt might rise as a result of the country's participation in an IDF programme.

Even if from the debtor's perspective the present value of debt-servicing is reduced by an IDF programme, in some cases the present value of the net financial transfer of the country *vis-à-vis* all private creditors together might not improve substantially. In some debt-restructuring negotiations, particularly involving the largest debtor countries, banks have agreed to provide "new money" and to maintain short-term credit lines and other credit facilities. They have been increasingly reluctant to put up such funds, but have seen it as necessary in some cases to help protect the value of their past loans. One attraction of a debt-reduction package to the banks is that it relieves them of the obligation to extend new money and provides a means to disengage from the debt problems of the debtor country.[c] In any case, the object of the debt-reduction exercise should be to substantially improve the overall net transfer of resources of the debtor country in the near term.

#### Pros and cons of a facility

A first argument for establishing a facility to carry out debt reduction is that neither the market menu approach nor the recent enhancement of it in the Brady Plan seems able to provide more than marginal measures of debt-servicing re-

---

a The concept of a debt reconstruction facility was first broached in the *World Economic Survey* in 1987 (United Nations publication, Sales No. E.87.II.C.1), p. 10, based in part on the report of a study group convoked by the World Institute for Development Economics Research (WIDER) of the United Nations University (see S. Okita, L. Jayawardena and A. Sengupta, *Mobilizing International Surpluses for World Development: A Wider Plan for a Japanese Initiative,* WIDER Study Group Series, No. 2 (Helsinki, May 1987)). For a concise summary of several proposals and their publication sources, see United Nations Conference on Trade and Development, *Trade and Development Report 1988* (United Nations publication, Sales No. E.88.II.D.8), pp. 125-131.

b A related approach would assign a reduced role to the international debt facility (IDF), and a reduced need to raise its own cash. Here, the debt burden of the debtor countries would be reduced by lowering interest charges on outstanding obligations or partially writing off the debt, which would be agreed through direct negotiations between the debtor country and its bank creditors. The debt would continue to be owed to the commercial banks. The IDF would guarantee those reduced debt-service payments to the private creditors for a fee and it could even operate a concessional window through which it would subsidize interest payments made by lower income countries (the latter would require a special set of cash donations, as the facility itself is envisaged as self-financing). This proposal would in essence provide only the insurance aspect of the main proposal.

c A widely felt sentiment in the market today seems to be that sovereign-risk lending to Governments for general balance-of-payments financing will not return soon for the countries that have had debt-servicing crises; but with hindsight it is clear that this was an inappropriate form of financing for such needs anyway. Trade and project financing in which collateral for a loan could be established is seen to be more likely, at least initially, for shorter maturities. This notwithstanding, experience suggests that the return to the market even of countries that have undertaken considerable adjustment efforts will be painfully slow.

duction. The establishment of an international facility may be the only way to galvanize the world financial system into action that cannot be taken in individual negotiations when creditors are fearful of establishing precedents and are unable to meet the economic needs of the specific countries whose cases are being negotiated. The IDF would replace the complicated *ad-hoc* process of co-ordinating concerted debt relief by many private and official creditors with the force of a single institution.

A second argument in favour of a facility is that it could introduce greater consistency into the international treatment of debt problems. Membership in the facility could be open to creditor and debtor countries on appropriate terms, as in the cases of the International Development Association and the Multilateral Investment Guarantee Agency of the World Bank. All debtor country members would have access to the same debt relief arrangements (or special subsidies might be provided for low-income countries), which would be a major improvement over the current situation in which smaller countries are not in general able to extract the same concessions from creditors as the largest debtors.

Third, to the degree that the benefits of participation in the facility are attractive, the probability of debtor countries adopting *ad-hoc* and unilateral policies on servicing their debt would be reduced. The intent would be to replace contractual obligations that exceeded the repayment capacities of debtor countries with obligations that carried a reduced default risk. Thus, an IDF should add a measure of predictability to relations between debtors and creditors and make for a more orderly management of the international debt situation.

Several arguments have also been raised against establishing an IDF. One is that it could require large financial outlays by official creditors and thus by the public in creditor countries. If true, this would greatly compromise the political feasibility of the proposal, especially if it were seen as bailing out the commercial banks. But possible official outlays under an IDF must be set against expenditure prospects under a continuation of the current approach, the basic tenet of which has been to "bail in" the banks by putting up official funds to show the strength of official commitments to the adjustment strategies of the debtors.

In fact, the banks have not been bailed in, except with considerable and persistent official pressure at high levels, and much of the banking community wants to exit, albeit with minimal financial losses. Furthermore, continuing the current strategy without better success in raising the net transfer of resources enough to finance the investments and inspire the confidence needed for effective adjustment means that official as well as private credits outstanding will increasingly be at risk of default. Arrears to multilateral agencies have already reached unprecedented amounts.

The resources needed for a facility would only be large if it were indeed used to bail out the banks by overpaying them for their holdings of developing country loans and continuing to saddle the countries with excessive debt-service obligations. The bonds issued by an IDF would trade on a secondary market only if potential purchasers believed the debtors were likely to be able and willing to meet their debt-service payments. Internationally-agreed adjustment efforts would undoubtedly be a condition for using the facility and some of the adverse consequences of unanticipated international shocks could be ameliorated by access to the enhanced IMF Compensatory Financing Facility and other arrangements. Thus, the formal guarantee of IDF bonds should be of marginal importance in establishing their liquidity.

The size of total capital subscriptions to an IDF would depend on how much of the bank debt of how many countries would be eligible for IDF programmes. Rough orders of magnitude can be indicated. The total value of public or publicly-guaranteed medium-term debt owed to commercial banks by the 73 countries identified by the IMF as having had recent debt-servicing problems is approximately $245 billion.[d] Recent trends in secondary market prices for developing country debt suggest that bank loans might be purchased by an IDF at half or less of their face value. If for the sake of argument all of the outstanding debt were to be converted by an IDF at half the face value, the facility would have to issue $123 billion in bonds. Following the very conservative World Bank practice of requiring 100 per cent capital backing of loans and guarantees, the capital of the IDF would have to be $123 billion. The paid-in portion of the capital—the only direct budgetary cost—would be far less. Again looking to World Bank practice, the paid-in portion of its total capital subscriptions is about 8 per cent (although the paid-in portion of the recent capital increase was only 3 per cent). Thus, the budgetary impact of establishing an IDF might be on the order of $10 billion.

The contingent claims on donor countries, as guarantors, would be much higher; but if IDF programmes were properly designed, the probability of drawings on those resources would be very low. The amount of official resources needed to establish an IDF should be small when equitably shared among the major countries of the international financial community. It would also be small relative to the prospective financing of the Brady Plan, which comes out of forgone multilateral lending or new loans directly from Governments.

Another criticism of IDF proposals is that only few banks would participate. It is argued that it would be in the interest

*Continued...*

d International Monetary Fund, *World Economic Outlook* (Washington, D.C., April 1989), Statistical appendix.

*...Box IV.2 continued*

of each bank to strongly encourage the participation of other banks in IDF programmes while remaining on the sidelines itself. The incentive to do so is the probable increase in the secondary market valuation of the bank debt that remains after the bulk of debt is reduced through an IDF programme. The non-participant in a successful programme is thus a free-rider that benefits without incurring any costs.

Governments would be able to pressure their banks to participate in IDF schemes, but there are limits to the powers of Governments to coerce the banks to give up claims to full servicing of their loans to borrowers that are not formally bankrupt. There is obviously a strong case for debt-reduction arrangements that are voluntarily entered into by most creditor banks and do not set off protracted legal struggles. In addition to the tax and regulatory measures already proposed in the Brady Plan, an informal understanding that the debtor country would subordinate the servicing of loans of non-participating banks to the servicing of IDF obligations would help to discourage free riders.

Another argument is that the expected establishment of an IDF might reduce the incentive for creditors and debtors to arrive at appropriate debt-restructuring agreements on their own. But no such agreements have been worked out yet in the existing forums, so there is little reason to believe that any lasting solutions would be postponed.

about 13.5 per cent for the 15-country sample,[42] and of course less if the $29 billion were spread among 39 countries.

In any event, the resources currently being discussed for the Brady Plan suggest a debt reduction that will be piecemeal and which will fall far short of achieving the broad cut in interest burdens that the heavily-indebted countries need to return to a growth rate of output and investment that could get them out of the present impasse. Certainly, these countries would continue to transfer substantial resources to the rest of the world.

The debt-reduction process that can be expected to evolve out of an underfinanced international debt-reduction plan would, therefore, have limited benefits for the debtor countries. The partial buy-back or securitization of the debt overhang over a three-year period would bolster the secondary market price of old debt, but the discounts are likely to remain substantial. Those discounts, which reflect continued uncertainty about the normal servicing of financial claims, would generate adverse incentives for the repatriation of capital flight, new lending, and new private sector investment. Moreover, subsequent piecemeal debt reduction would cost even more on account of the higher market price for the remaining debt. In that case, the debtor country might be better advised to channel scarce foreign exchange—including World Bank and IMF money—into domestic programmes supporting reforms, investment and economic growth.

The financing of a piecemeal debt-reduction process may not be in the interest of the World Bank and IMF either. Extending loans at a quasi-commercial interest rate to finance a marginal debt buy-back with little or no quick return for the debtor country might weaken these institutions' loan portfolio. Their loans from existing or even additional resources, would have a better prospect of repayment if they were channelled directly into reforms, investment and growth.

Indeed, on the terms currently under discussion, the major beneficiaries of the new plan might be the banking community, since those banks wishing to voluntarily withdraw from the debt problem would be able to do so with the added enhancement of new public collateral, while those that did not wish to participate would get a free ride in the form of a higher market value of their outstanding claims in the developing countries. Assessment of the plan from the bank creditors' point of view must begin with the fact that they are holding claims on highly troubled economies whose Governments have not been able to service the claims normally for almost a decade and are not expected to be able to begin regular servicing any time soon under the existing menu of debt renegotiation options. That these loans are still on the books of the banks at face value is a tribute to the successive international strategies for managing the debt and the unending sequence of debt renegotiations they have set in motion.

There is one element of the Brady Plan, however, that could cause a major change in the distribution of benefits. When the plan proposed that the IMF consider severing the link of IMF stand-by programmes to agreement with the banks on a debt-restructuring package, it opened up the possibility of an improvement in the cash flow in the short run through growth of arrears on the interest and principal of bank loans. Accumulation of arrears would not have to be openly endorsed by the IMF; but even that would be feasible if they could be interpreted as an appropriate exchange restriction under Article VIII(2)(b) of the Articles of the International Monetary Fund.[43] It also would put pressure on the banks to be more forthcoming with proposals to lower the outward transfer of resources from the debtor countries. Indeed, that seems to have been the intent of this part of the proposal.

42 This assumes a 10 per cent interest rate on the commercial bank loans and 8 per cent on the new World Bank loans. The overall cash flow would become even less advantageous as amortization on the World Bank loans began after the grace period ended. For example, a new $100 World Bank loan could repurchase up to $278 of bank debt and generate annual interest savings of $28. Yet, with an 8 per cent interest rate and a 20-year amortization period and five years of grace on the loan, cash flow relief would be $20 for the first five years ($28 interest relief minus $8 interest paid to the World Bank) and then fall to $14 in the sixth year as amortization of the loan kicks in.

43 See Whitney Debevoise, "Exchange controls and external indebtedness: a modest proposal for a deferral mechanism employing Bretton Woods concepts", *Houston Journal of International Law,* vol. 7, No. 1 (Autumn 1984), pp. 157-168.

In sum, the Brady Plan is clearly an encouraging initiative that was long overdue. To be fully successful, however, it would require greater official financial commitments than have thus far been made. Also, to ensure an adequate response from the commercial banks, strong official action might be required to broaden and deepen their participation in debt reduction. Waivers of restrictive clauses, coupled with guarantees on new debt instruments, could reward co-operating banks with assets of preferred status. Changes in regulatory and tax codes could provide additional incentives to prod recalcitrant lenders. Commercial banks also might be more willing to co-operate if their Governments applied similar debt reduction techniques to the Paris Club obligations of these countries. This would also promote greater symmetry for the smaller debtor countries, most of which are relatively more dependent on Government-to-Government loans than on commercial bank debt.

Finally, if the international debt strategy were to seriously set its sights on all these objectives, they probably could be achieved more efficiently in the context of a multilateral debt-reduction facility, perhaps organized as an affiliate of the World Bank. An independent facility which did not have to contend with institutional precedents and the difficult interpretation of existing statutes in the international organisations, could be more agile in the task of debt reduction and also more easily accountable for its successes and failures. The creation of a separate facility would also conveniently avoid contamination of the World Bank and IMF loan portfolios (see box IV.2).

## Debt, borrowing and foreign investment in the centrally planned economies of Europe

A sea change in the economic strategies of the centrally planned economies of Europe has been building over more than a decade, with the pace of reform accelerating significantly in recent years.[44] As part of this change, these econo-economies are becoming more involved in the international economy and their relations with the international financial system of the market economies is becoming more intensive and transparent. In all, the experiences of these countries have been quite diverse. Certain Eastern European countries face major foreign debt difficulties, the general appearances of which are quite similar to those of developing countries. Other countries have been very cautious in their use of financial resources from market economies, but all are anxious to make more productive use of such resources. Important developments have occurred over the past year in two financial areas, namely, the debt policies of heavily-indebted countries, and the policies on direct foreign investment across the region. These steps point the planned economies of Europe towards gradual integration into the international financial system.

### The foreign debt situation

At the end of 1988, the total indebtedness of the seven Eastern European countries to market economy creditors stood at $122 billion.[45] More than half the debt was owed by two countries, Poland, with $38 billion, and the Soviet Union, $37 billion (see figure IV.8). Three other countries—Bulgaria, Czechoslovakia and Romania—had relatively small amounts of debt, although that of Bulgaria has been growing significantly in recent years, doubling from $3 billion in 1985 to $7 billion in 1988.

Romania, on the other hand, having been burdened by excessive debt-servicing requirements in recent years, has been implementing a unique policy of debt reduction through repayment of outstanding loans and eschewing new ones. Its gross foreign debt has been reduced from about $10 billion in 1981 to less than $3 billion by the end of 1988. In 1988 alone, Romania applied $2 billion of its $4 billion trade surplus to repaying loans, including to private banks ($700 million) Governments of developed market economies ($350 million, under a Paris Club agreement), IMF ($200 million), and the World Bank ($200 million), among other creditors. The goal of the Government was to totally repay its foreign debt by 1990, and it announced that it had met that goal as at the end of March 1989.[46]

While Romania's policy represents the sharpest reaction to high foreign debt levels, other countries of the region have become increasingly cautious in their policy toward foreign debt. The borrowing from foreign commercial banks, net of repayments, by the six Eastern European countries was $2 billion in 1987 and about $2.5 billion in 1988, which is an increase of less than 5 per cent of their bank debt in each year. Net borrowing by the Soviet Union, however, was $5.5 billion last year (and virtually nil the year before), an increase of over 16 per cent of its bank debt outstanding at the beginning of the year.[47]

The Soviet Union has increased its use of foreign credit since prospects for its terms of trade are not considered propitious and desired changes in the structure of exports are slow in coming. To support the expansion of imports essential for carrying out its programme of industrial modernization, and in order to relieve shortages in consumer markets, a substantial increase in external borrowing is being undertaken. This is reflected in the increased commercial bank borrowing and in agreements concluded in the autumn of 1988 to open lines of credit from Western European and

44 For detailed discussion of the overall development of economic reforms in centrally planned economies, see United Nations, *World Economic Survey 1988* (United Nations publication, Sales No. E.88.II.C.1), pp. 93-120; for latest developments, see chapter II of the current *Survey.*

45 The ensuing discussion is restricted to the debt of the European planned economies that is denominated in convertible currencies and in particular excludes transferable rouble debt.

46 See *Scînteia* (Bucharest), 18 April 1989, p. 1.

47 Data are changes in liabilities to foreign banks at constant exchange rates, as reported by the Bank for International Settlements in its quarterly reports on international banking developments.

Figure IV.8. Indebtedness in convertible currencies of European planned economies, 1988

Gross debt
(Billions of dollars; end-year)

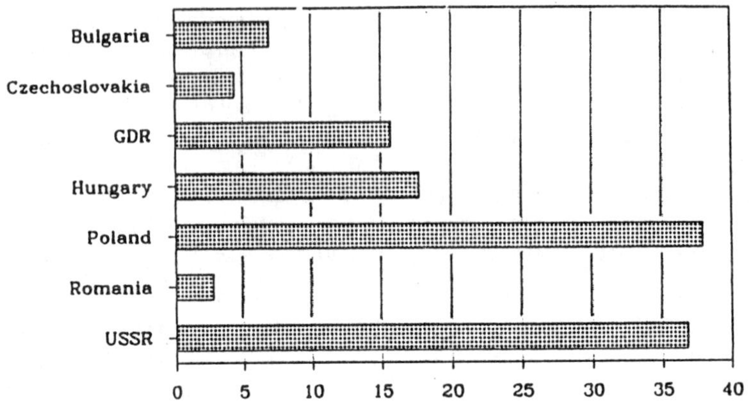


Net debt
(Billions of dollars; end-year)

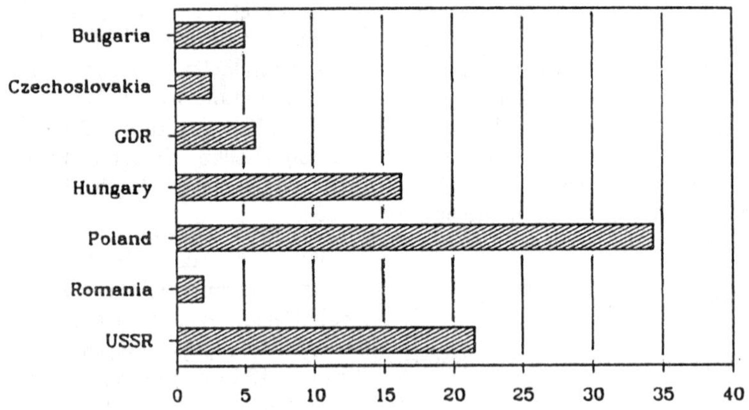


Net debt to export ratio
(Percentage of convertible currency merchandise exports)

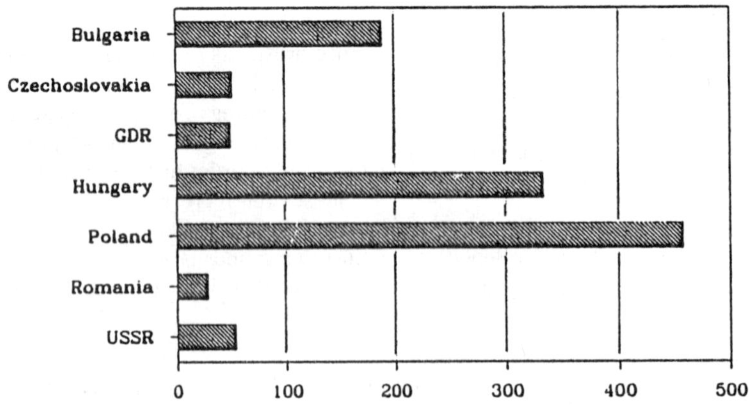


*Source:* Department of International Economic and Social Affairs of the United Nations Secretariat, based on official national and international data.

Japanese lenders of about $9 billion, earmarked mostly for re-equipment of consumer-oriented production. At the same time, new ways of mobilizing private international funds are being studied, encouraged by the successful floating of a bond issue denominated in Swiss francs of SwF 100 million in early 1988 and the fact that the possibility of issuing Euro-notes, bonds and other marketable securities seems to have won acceptance. Nevertheless, Soviet decision-makers are expected to make cautious use of these credit commitments in order to ensure that reforms of economic structures are advanced enough to make effective use of foreign resources.

That the Soviet Union does have room for manoeuvre in international financial markets is made clear by the indicators of foreign indebtedness. In particular, the large foreign currency holdings of the Soviet Union, not to mention its monetary gold stock, make its net foreign debt position *vis-à-vis* the rest of the world substantially less than its gross position. This may be seen in the middle panel of figure IV.8 which shows a conservative estimate of the net debt position of each of the European planned economies in which the only assets set against the gross foreign debt are deposits in international commercial banks.[48]

Another indicator of the state of indebtedness is the ratio of the net debt position to exports to convertible currency markets. By this measure, as may be seen in figure IV.8, the foreign indebtedness of the Soviet Union is modest, while the debt situation of Hungary and Poland is by far the most precarious.[49]

Poland's debt crisis stems from the early 1980s. Its first rescheduling of debt owed to bilateral official creditors was arranged in April 1981 and its first rescheduling of commercial bank debt one year later. Poland has had 10 debt rescheduling agreements in all, and further ones are anticipated. The last Paris Club agreement was in December 1987, but as at the end of 1988, none of the implementing bilateral agreements with official creditors had been signed and arrears continued to mount. In 1989, negotiations are expected to regularize the debt situation.

Like many developing countries that have lost access to international credit, Poland has been making a net transfer of financial resources to the market economies; in 1987 it amounted to $2 billion or about 3 per cent of gross national product (GNP) and in 1988 it was of a similar order of magnitude.[50] In 1989, Poland is scheduled to repay $1.7 billion of amortization on its medium-term debt and make interest payments of $3.5 billion. Without new capital inflows, this would be a heavy drain of financial resources and the Government is thus seeking a new rescheduling of the debt.

A package of debt restructuring and new loans has been under discussion in the international creditor community, and recent political developments in Poland have made the prospects more favourable. Besides a Paris Club rescheduling, proposals have been made for an IMF stand-by arrangement and World Bank financing, as well as increased bilateral commitments, all in support of economic adjustment and decentralization.

In the case of Hungary, a major new adjustment programme with IMF support is under way to help the country reduce its vulnerability to debt crises and give market processes a more central role in the economy. The Government of Hungary has set for itself the target of no further increases in debt after 1990, although new loans would be undertaken to help retire outstanding debt and to make the economy self-financing in the 1990s; but for the short run, additional loans must be incurred to help cover the growing interest payments.[51] Although it has been possible in the recent past to cushion the impact of a negative transfer of financial resources to the market economies by drawing down foreign exchange reserves, this is a self-limiting option. The net transfer to the market economies in 1987 was 6 per cent of Hungary's GNP which was tempered by a reduction of about $1.5 billion of official reserves. In 1988, the loss of reserves was $300 million, but the net transfer itself dropped to roughly 3 per cent of GNP.

One major plank in Hungary's adjustment programme is a substantial change in ownership structure of Hungarian industry. The intention is to turn existing enterprises into joint stock companies, with ownership either by Hungarian or foreign investors. Hungarian authorities are also interested in developing ideas that have been used in other heavily-indebted countries, in particular, to develop a debt-for-equity swap scheme.[52] Hungary, like Poland, has recently introduced legal changes affecting foreign ownership of local firms and foreign direct investment.

All in all, the European planned economies that have accumulated a heavy foreign debt burden have been facing a dilemma comparable to that of indebted developing countries, namely, the need to adjust under a sharp foreign resource constraint. The adjustment imperative has affected all the centrally planned economies to a greater or lesser degree. In the late 1970s, these economies had a fairly wide range of policy choice; but with the critical events of 1981-

48 A more complete accounting of the gross assets of the planned economies of Europe in convertible currencies—or even official reserves—defined on a comparable basis for all countries is not available. Thus, the data in figure IV.8 should be understood as rough indicators; in particular, the net debt of the Soviet Union is undoubtedly less than the $22 billion shown.

49 The indicator is perhaps somewhat misleading in that some exports to other CPEs might be arranged in convertible currency and only merchandise exports are included; but in any case, the ratios for Hungary and Poland are of a comparable order of magnitude to that, for example, for the sample of 15 heavily-indebted developing countries, which was 383 per cent in 1988.

50 The net transfer in the first three quarters of 1988 was $1.6 billion (based on data in IMF, *Balance of Payments Statistics;* GNP data for 1987 are as published in World Bank, *World Debt Tables,* 1988-1989 edition).

51 Speech delivered by Rezsö Nyers, State Minister and Member of the Politbureau of the Hungarian Socialist Workers Party on 27 January 1989 (*Magyar Hírlap* (Budapest), 28 January 1989, p. 5).

52 See, for example, the interview with the Secretary of the Central Committee of the Hungarian Socialist Workers Party and now Prime Minister, Miklós Németh, in *Magyar Hírlap* (Budapest), 28 May 1988, p. 3.

1982, it became difficult to finance their external deficits. As a result, several Eastern European economies had to introduce restrictive adjustment policies, generally on an emergency basis, like many of the capital-importing developing countries.[53] There have been two phases of adjustment: one between 1982 and 1985, and the second starting around 1985 and still continuing.

In the first phase, external pressures for adjustment were most pronounced in Hungary, Poland and Romania. The latter two were forced into debt-rescheduling, but shifts in policies were induced across the group. Throughout most of the adjustment phase, export volume expanded steadily while the import volume contracted or grew only very slowly. Within the CMEA, the six European countries experienced a steady terms-of-trade decline of a moderate 2 to 4 per cent a year, but there was little change in their terms of trade with market economies. Terms-of-trade losses *vis-à-vis* CMEA partners reduced the capacity to import from member countries, but this was in part compensated for by substantial increases in export volume, especially to the Soviet Union. The brunt of the adjustment burden was undoubtedly borne by investments.[54]

Until early 1985 there was a deceleration of growth. Consumers were generally protected, while there was an absolute decline in the level of net accumulation (net investments in fixed assets and changes in inventories). The magnitude of the decline was strongly correlated with the external imbalance.

In the second phase of economic adjustment, a recovery of investment was made possible by restructuring the trade sector and cutting back the external debt burden through successive trade surpluses that financed much of the interest servicing requirements and allowed a slower growth in overall borrowing. Between 1984 and 1988, the region borrowed $19 billion from foreign banks, net of repayments. But total indebtedness to foreign banks rose by $50 billion, owing to the fall of the dollar against other creditor country currencies.

In summary, adjustment policies arrested the modernization and expansion of an already outdated industrial base. As a result, the technological gap between East and West widened, particularly in the area of more sophisticated technologies. To cope with the situation, Eastern European countries turned increasingly toward outward-oriented policies, but their stringent foreign exchange constraints limit their ability to undertake import liberalization on a large scale, and shortages of capital limit industrial investment in export industries.

**The evolving role of direct foreign investment**

In all those countries, there is increasing interest in drawing on direct foreign investment for national economic development. Earlier views on the role of foreign ownership and control have been substantially revised and joint ventures with foreign equity participation are now seen as desirable and promising, especially to promote exports and curb hard currency imports. Joint ventures are also viewed as an important source of access to new technology and know-how—including marketing and management techniques—which can help to modernize selected economic sectors and improve domestic supply.

In the late 1960s and early 1970s, the European planned economies used industrial co-operation agreements with the developed market economies to encourage technology import and increase hard currency exports. By the mid-1970s, industrial co-operation agreements were being hampered by protectionist measures and balance-of-payments constraints. Product buy-back and counter-purchase arrangements became common, as debt-servicing obligations of some of the centrally planned economies created shortages of the convertible currency required to buy needed imports. The authorities of the centrally planned economies then looked for direct capital import and transfers of high-level technology that would not jeopardize their hard-currency balance-of-payments.

The development of direct investment depends on institutional arrangements, financing facilities, the local availability of complementary technology, management and organisation, ability to transfer earnings abroad and the contractual framework. Institutional arrangements have evolved, but restrictions on the transfer of technology and the lack of transparency in legal regulations concerning ownership and profit transfer have acted as limiting factors. After several years of experience and experiment, managerial, marketing, servicing and legal changes have taken place, which are now raising confidence both among Western investors and the Eastern host countries.

New laws on foreign investment régimes have been enacted in recent years across Eastern Europe (see box IV.3). The new laws have changed the conditions for operation of joint ventures.[55] National differences still remain, however, They revolve around the problem of reconciling foreign capital participation with socialist principles and the practice of State ownership and planning.

As a result of the measures taken in the Soviet Union and other European planned economies, joint ventures in the re-

---

53 The successive measures adopted were discussed in detail in *World Economic Survey 1985* (United Nations publication, Sales No. E.85.II.C.1), pp. 89-101.

54 The interrelationship between adjustment, investment and structural change in the centrally planned economies has been discussed in detail in *World Economic Survey 1986* (United Nations publication, Sales No. E.86.II.C.1), pp. 121-134.

55 Two recent reviews of these conditions are: Economic Commission for Europe, *East-West Joint Ventures* (United Nations publication, Sales No. E.88.II.E.18); and United Nations Centre on Transnational Corporations, *Joint Ventures as a Form of International Economic Co-operation* (United Nations publication, Sales No. E.88.II.A.12).

**Box IV.3. Joint venture legislation in the USSR and Eastern Europe**

The recent history of joint venture legislation in the European planned economies has reflected the evolution of policy in those countries. The case of the USSR provides one important example. On 19 August 1986, the Presidium of the Council of Ministers of the USSR passed a decree which authorized the reorganisation of Soviet organisations involved in foreign economic relations and the restructuring of foreign trade practices and procedures. One of the most significant changes was the new possibility of entering into joint ventures. The initial regulations of January 1987 limited the foreign share in joint-venture capital to a maximum of 49 per cent, and required both the chairman of the board and director general to be Soviet citizens. Personnel management and employee benefits were to be regulated by Soviet law. To establish a joint venture, potential partners had to go through a centralized procedure where the final approval was to be made by the Council of Ministers. These and many other features of the legislation proved an impediment to foreign companies' preparedness to enter into joint ventures with a Soviet partner.

In September 1987 the joint-venture regulations were amended. Approval procedures were simplified by granting ministries and agencies the right to independently take decisions on setting up joint ventures. A more favourable tax scheme was also provided.

On 2 December 1988 another significant step was taken. A new Decree lifted limitations on foreign equity participation, paving the way for joint ventures with majority foreign ownership. Foreign nationals may also be appointed to top positions in joint venture boards. Recruitment and dismissal of personnel and the amount and forms of payment to employees are to be determined by the joint venture itself. Additional tax incentives for joint ventures were provided. The right to enter into joint venture agreements with foreign partners was given to State enterprises and organisations and also to production co-operatives.

In addition, the Eastern European countries have revised legislation in order to stimulate greater direct investment inflows. Thus, as of 1 January 1986, Hungary liberalized its 1982 joint venture law. As a result, a preferential tax rate of 20 per cent instead of the general 40 per cent rate applies to joint ventures in electronics, production of spare parts in transportation, agricultural machinery, pharmaceuticals and other sectors. These entities are also free of tax liabilities for five years; thereafter, they pay the 20 per cent rate mentioned above. If 50 per cent of profits in a year are reinvested, 50 per cent of that year's tax is cancelled. If 100 per cent of profits are reinvested, 75 per cent of the tax is reimbursed. If the foreign partner imports productive assets, there is a five-year customs deferral, as opposed to the previous three years. Further incentives are offered for investment in export processing zones. Also, to ease administrative constraints, starting 1 January 1989, joint ventures with less than 50 per cent foreign capital no longer need permits; court registration is enough.

In the Polish law of 23 April 1986 on companies with foreign capital participation, joint ventures were exempted from income tax during the first two years. Tax exemption is granted on that part of the profit that is reinvested. There is also an import duty exemption for three years on contributions to the joint venture's capital stock. Poland's latest law on economic activity with the participation of foreign parties entered into force on 1 January 1989.

The Bulgarian Decree No. 535 on economic co-operation between Bulgarian juridical persons and foreign juridical and physical persons, has also been modified. From 1988, tariff-free zones can and will be established. Bulgaria has also issued an extended and revised decree on economic activity, dealing with foreign capital participation as well.

In 1988, the Government of Czechoslovakia published the full text of its act on enterprises with foreign property participation, entering into force on 1 January 1989.

---

gion more than doubled their number in 1987 (from 75 to 166). They are estimated to have reached 500 by the end of 1988, with a total amount of foreign capital invested of more than $1.2 billion. In the USSR alone, their number increased from 23 in January 1988 to 199 in January 1989, with an amount of foreign investment of about $900 million.

However, as the rapid growth of joint venturing began at a very low starting point, the aggregate financial impact of direct investment has thus far not been substantial, and it will undoubtedly remain relatively modest for some years to come.

Many potential foreign partners remain ambivalent about direct investment in the European planned economies, pointing, in particular, to ambiguities remaining in the legal and administrative superstructure of joint ventures. Among the number of rigidities facing joint ventures in the centrally planned economies, five stand out. These are organisational issues, accounting problems, ambiguities of laws and regulations, financing questions and exchange rate problems.

As far as organisational issues are concerned, most Eastern European countries still strive for majority ownership in negotiations to establish joint ventures, which immediately compels the Western partner to use its managerial, technological and marketing leverage to offset unwanted effects. More often than not, the Eastern European Government considers itself the effective owner of the joint venture, although it is by definition an independent legal entity.

Transparency of joint venture laws in general is in need of improvement. Determination of the value of assets supplied by the partners is often ambiguous. Regulations on amortization are also difficult to assess. Not all countries even have a concise compendium of all the relevant laws and regulations, together with all subsequent amendments and interpretations.

Financing of joint ventures is another complicated issue. It is widely recognized that new methods of financing are needed to allow the financial independence of the joint venture. The exchange rate used to transfer profit abroad plays an important role in any calculations. A plethora of exchange rates makes it impossible to establish clear rules for external transactions.

## The dollar exchange rate, current account imbalances and the world financial system

The role of the United States dollar in the world financial system may be declining, as noted in the introduction to this chapter, but it is still the anchor of the system, the currency most widely accepted in international transactions in trade and finance, the most frequently used unit of account, and the most common currency in which to hold international financial assets. At the same time, the United States has become the world's most indebted nation and its debt continues to grow through large deficits in its balance of payments on current account. Despite this, private foreign demand for dollar assets was so strong in much of 1988 and in early 1989 that it brought up the exchange rate of the dollar without the need for large-scale official support, as had been the case in 1987.

### Debt and the net transfer of financial resources to the United States

Measured by The net international investment position, which indicates the net foreign financial claims on a country, the United States reached a net debtor position of approximately $500 billion at the end of 1988 (see table IV.5).[56] Gross foreign claims were, of course, much higher, reaching almost $1,800 billion, but those are set against United States foreign assets of $1,300 billion.

The figure for the United States that is most comparable to the gross debt statistics of developing countries presented in table IV.4 above would be gross foreign claims on the United States, excluding direct investment and foreign holdings of equity shares. By that measure, the foreign debt was roughly $1,300 billion at the end of last year, or the same order of magnitude as the total debt of all the capital-importing developing countries combined.

But if the United States foreign debt seems large in absolute amount, it has not deterred foreign investment in dollar assets. In 1988, investors purchased $172 billion of United States assets (and an indeterminate amount of dollar assets trading outside the country). Almost $80 billion of that were foreign bank lending to United States clients and almost $50 billion were United States debt securities sold abroad (see table A.8).

Foreign holders of dollar assets thus do not seem particularly concerned about the size of the United States foreign debt. Indeed, the data have well-known inadequacies which may overstate the size of the debt.[57] But other data series that attempt to adjust for various measurement problems also show a declining trend in the United States position even if it remains positive. Also, almost all the debt is denominated in dollars (the major exception being some corporate bonds denominated in foreign currency), so there is little danger that the United States economy would not be able to meet its contractual obligations to foreigners, as has been the case in the heavily-indebted developing countries. Furthermore, when set against the size of the United States economy, the foreign claims are still seen to be quite modest. The gross debt comes to roughly one quarter of United States GNP, or about half the ratio of the capital-importing developing countries.

This notwithstanding, the United States debt ratios have been growing rapidly. Four years ago, the ratio of gross debt to GNP was less than one fifth, and it was only 13 per cent as recently as 1981. That was the year in which the overall net international investment position of the United States had peaked at $141 billion or 5 per cent of GNP. By 1986, the position had swung to a net debtor position of over 6 per cent of GNP, taking only two more years to reach the level of 10 per cent. Thus, if the United States foreign debt situation is not yet severe, the direction and pace of change does not seem propitious.

Nor, it seems, is the United States current account deficit—the financing of which is the source of the growth of the net debt position—sustainable at its present order of magnitude. If the current account deficit net of investment income were to continue at roughly its 1988 level, and if interest rates and the growth of nominal GNP were at the plausible average annual rate of 7 per cent, then in the long run the current account deficit would stabilize at 3.25 per cent of nominal GNP, and the net international debtor position of the United States would reach $3,500 billion by the year 2000, close to 32 per cent of GNP, and approach $8,700 billion in 2010, or about 40 per cent of GNP.[58]

---

56 The estimate for 1988 in table IV.5 is based on data available as at March 1989. In June, the United States Commerce Department generally announces its data on the net investment position as at the previous year-end. It is then published in the June issue of the *Survey of Current Business,* which should be consulted for more up-to-date data than was possible to include in table IV.5.

57 Some of these factors were reviewed in *World Economic Survey 1988* (United Nations publication, Sales No. E.88.II.C.1), pp. 67-69.

58 This exercise is reported in Federal Reserve Bank of New York, *Seventy-Fourth Annual Report,* for the year ended 31 December 1988 (April 1989), p. 32. The exercise posits a more severe deterioration in the United States situation than is implied by the baseline forecast discussed in chapter II of this issue, wherein the United States current account deficit falls almost to 2 per cent of GNP by 1990, although it does not improve at all thereafter in the forecast.

Table IV.5. Net international investment position of the United States, 1980-1988

(Billions of dollars)

| | 1980 | 1981 | 1982 | 1983 | 1984 | 1985 | 1986 | 1987 | 1988[a] |
|---|---|---|---|---|---|---|---|---|---|
| I. United States foreign assets | 607 | 720 | 825 | 874 | 896 | 950 | 1 071 | 1 168 | 1 267 |
| Official assets | 91 | 99 | 109 | 113 | 120 | 131 | 138 | 134 | 133 |
| Official reserves | 27 | 30 | 34 | 34 | 35 | 43 | 49 | 46 | 48 |
| Other Government assets | 64 | 69 | 75 | 79 | 85 | 88 | 90 | 88 | 85 |
| Private assets | 517 | 621 | 716 | 761 | 776 | 819 | 933 | 1 034 | 1 135 |
| Direct investment | 215 | 228 | 208 | 207 | 211 | 230 | 260 | 309 | 329 |
| Securities | 63 | 63 | 75 | 84 | 89 | 113 | 133 | 147 | 159 |
| Banking and other | 239 | 329 | 433 | 470 | 476 | 476 | 541 | 578 | 646 |
| II. Foreign assets in the United States | 501 | 579 | 688 | 784 | 893 | 1 061 | 1 341 | 1 536 | 1 769 |
| Foreign official assets | 176 | 180 | 189 | 194 | 199 | 203 | 242 | 283 | 322 |
| Private assets | 325 | 398 | 499 | 590 | 693 | 858 | 1 091 | 1 253 | 1 448 |
| Direct investment | 83 | 109 | 125 | 137 | 165 | 185 | 220 | 262 | 304 |
| Securities | 90 | 94 | 119 | 148 | 185 | 290 | 400 | 423 | 493 |
| Banking and other | 151 | 196 | 256 | 305 | 343 | 384 | 478 | 568 | 651 |
| III. Net international investment position (I-II) | 106 | 141 | 137 | 89 | 4 | -111 | -269 | -368 | -502 |
| Memorandum item | | | | | | | | | |
| Indicators as a percentage of GNP | | | | | | | | | |
| Net position | 3.9 | 4.6 | 4.3 | 2.6 | 0.1 | -2.8 | -6.4 | -8.2 | -10.3 |
| Gross foreign debt[b] | 12.9 | 13.3 | 15.4 | 16.2 | 16.8 | 18.8 | 22.5 | 24.4 | 26.0 |

*Source:* United States Department of Commerce, *Survey of Current Business,* June 1988 for data to 1987; and for 1988, United Nations Secretariat estimates based on balance-of-payments data as at March 1989 and roughly approximated valuation adjustments.

a Preliminary estimates.

b Foreign assets in the United States, excluding direct investment and corporate stocks.

It is hard to assess whether even such a seemingly high debt burden would be difficult for the United States economy to absorb. Australia, Canada and Denmark, for example, have had ratios of their net international investment position to GNP of over 40 per cent in the 1980s. These countries have not, however, enjoyed the latitude that the United States has had in setting its macro-economic policies, nor does the world look to the stability of the currencies of those countries as the anchor of the international monetary system.

However, even if the threat to the world monetary system from the United States becoming ever more deeply-indebted lies only in the future, there is an additional reason to focus attention on the current deficits in the United States balance of payments and the growth of foreign debt that they entail. The reason is that the United States, in a very substantial departure from the long-run experience since the second World War, has become a major user of the world's savings, instead of contributing some of its own savings for investment in other countries. As may be seen in figure IV.9, there has been a net transfer of financial resources to the United States in recent years of over 3 per cent of United States GNP, although the net transfer in 1988 itself had fallen back to 2.6 per cent of GNP. This means that total spending in the United States has recently been about 3 per cent higher than total income generated by that country.

The rest of the world has transferred resources to the United States on a net basis—and thus helped finance an excess of spending over production—since the late 1970s, but the size and character of the transfer changed after the United States international payments deficit began to escalate in 1983. The net transfer now reflects continuation of some of the factors operating in the earlier period plus some additional ones. Thus, the net transfer arising from United States direct investment abroad has fluctuated, but on average has continued apace as the income from the outstanding stock of these investments exceeds the net additions to the stock through new foreign investment. The net transfer from foreign direct investment in the United States, in contrast, has made a rapidly increasing contribution to the total transfer, as United States earnings paid abroad are not very large—since the stock of investment is relatively small—and the inflow of investment has grown appreciably, reaching $42 billion in 1987 and 1988 (see again, table A.8).

The most significant change in the components of the net transfer to the United States, however, has been in the credit flows. The United States private sector has traditionally been a net supplier of financial resources to the rest of the world, and continued as such even as interest rates rose in the late 1970s and early 1980s, swelling United States net foreign interest income. But beginning in 1983, private lending abroad ground to a virtual halt,[59] while foreign lending to

59 Bank lending abroad net of amortization was $111 billion in 1982 and $1 billion in 1985 (see table A.8).

Figure IV.9. Net transfer of financial resources to the United States, 1960-1988

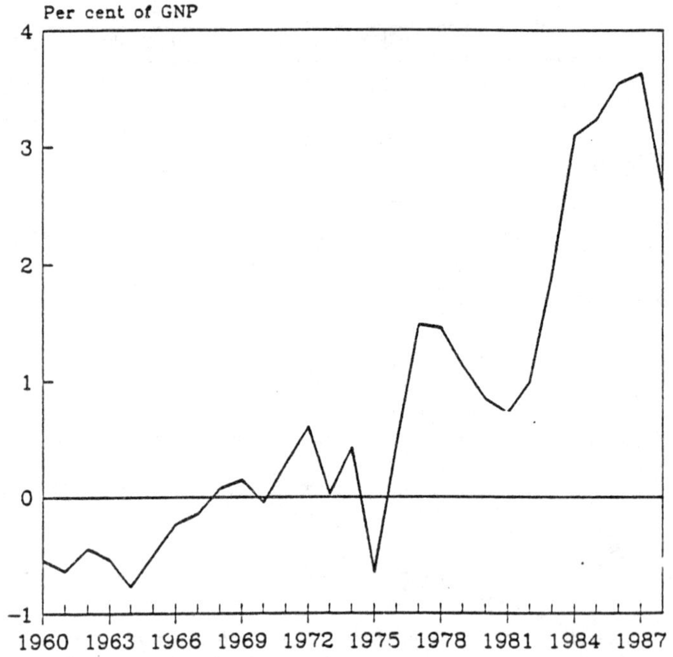


*Source:* Department of International Economic and Social Affairs of the United Nations Secretariat, based on United States data.

Figure IV.10. Net foreign payments of interest by the United States, 1960-1988

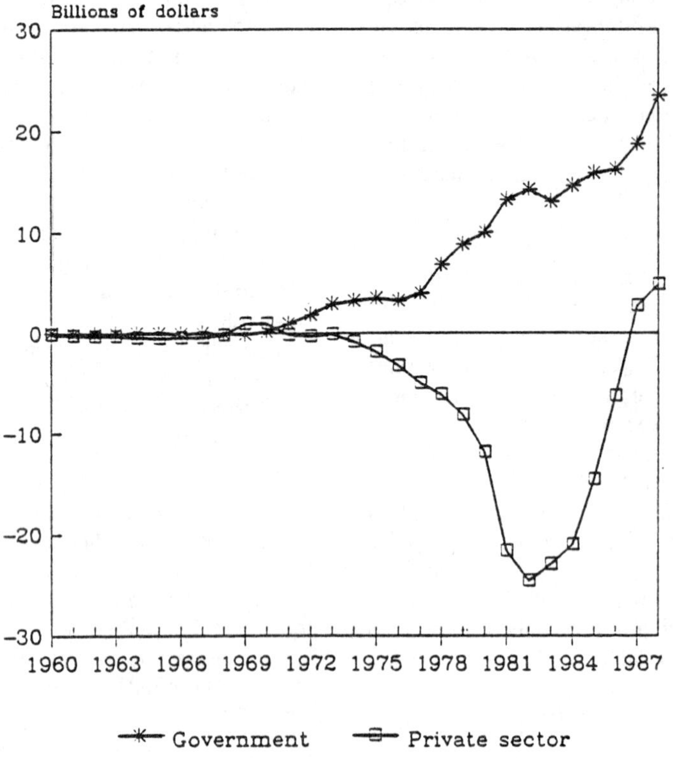


*Source:* Data from the United States Department of Commerce, *Survey of Current Business.*

Table IV.6. Net resource transfers to the United States, by regions, 1980-1988[a]

(Billions of dollars)

| | 1980 | 1981 | 1982 | 1983 | 1984 | 1985 | 1986 | 1987 | 1988[b] |
|---|---|---|---|---|---|---|---|---|---|
| Canada | -0.3 | 0.8 | 8.3 | 9.4 | 12.7 | 13.4 | 10.6 | 9.8 | 7.7 |
| Japan | 9.8 | 14.9 | 15.9 | 23.2 | 36.2 | 42.8 | 54.5 | 56.2 | 50.5 |
| Western Europe | -16.6 | -9.0 | -2.9 | 5.8 | 23.3 | 32.5 | 36.3 | 35.5 | 22.4 |
| of which | | | | | | | | | |
| Germany, Federal Republic of | 1.8 | 2.4 | 4.8 | 7.8 | 12.8 | 15.4 | 18.9 | 20.2 | .. |
| Latin America and Caribbean | -0.9 | -4.4 | 6.3 | 20.0 | 22.8 | 18.7 | 15.2 | 16.9 | 11.8 |
| of which | | | | | | | | | |
| Mexico | -2.4 | -5.1 | 4.5 | 10.4 | 8.3 | 7.9 | 7.9 | 8.8 | .. |
| Major oil exporters of Africa and Asia[c] | 36.1 | 26.6 | 7.6 | 2.7 | 6.2 | 4.0 | 2.5 | 7.6 | 4.7 |
| Other developing countries | -2.5 | 0.7 | 2.2 | 11.0 | 21.3 | 22.4 | 32.7 | 41.4 | 36.4 |
| European planned economies | -2.5 | -2.8 | -2.7 | -1.5 | -2.0 | -1.1 | 0.2 | 0.0 | -1.3 |
| Other countries[d] | -0.1 | -4.7 | -3.4 | -5.9 | -3.7 | -2.9 | -1.9 | -3.2 | -4.5 |
| Total | 23.0 | 22.1 | 31.3 | 64.7 | 116.9 | 129.8 | 150.1 | 164.3 | 127.8 |

*Source:* Department of International Economic and Social Affairs of the United Nations Secretariat, based on data from United States Department of Commerce, *Survey of Current Business.*

a Expenditure definition of the net transfer of financial resources, i.e., balance of payments on goods, private transfers and services other than investment income, with sign reversed.

b Preliminary; full country breakdown unavailable at this time.

c Comprises member countries of the Organization of Petroleum Exporting Countries, excluding Ecuador and Venezuela.

d Including net transactions with international organisations and unallocated amounts.

the United States began to increase, first in foreign purchase of securities (including Treasury bonds and bills, but also shares of stock in corporations and corporate and other bonds), and then in banking flows. However, foreigners were net sellers of United States equity shares last year, while United States purchases of foreign stocks grew by two thirds. The 1988 current account deficit was thus financed much more than in 1987 by international credit flows (and a decline in direct investment abroad).

The preponderance of the net international credit flows in the balance of payments turned the United States into a net payer of interest several years ago, the remaining positive overall balance of net investment income being mainly the result of the net earnings from overseas direct investment. But as figure IV.10 indicates, the private sector is no longer the large beneficiary of net foreign interest earnings that it was in the first half of the 1980s. In other words, the United States private sector, like the Government, has been borrowing heavily abroad and now is paying more interest abroad than it is receiving. As the net indebtedness of the economy grows, this situation will intensify.

Not all net transfers into the United States are of a voluntary nature. As table IV.6 shows, while the United States has been receiving net transfers in the second half of the 1980s on the order of $50 billion a year from Japan and $20 billion from the Federal Republic of Germany, it has also been receiving $12 billion or more from Latin America and the Caribbean.[60] The large transfer from the grouping labelled "other developing" appears to have been primarily the placement of balance-of-payments surpluses by the fast growing exporters of manufactures in Asia, especially the Republic of Korea and Taiwan Province of China. That is understandable, but the net transfer to the United States from the heavily-indebted countries in economic crisis must be a major cause for concern.

### International financial flows and international confidence

The ability of the United States to continue to absorb financial resources from the major creditor countries is not automatic, especially if it is to be done at roughly stable exchange rates. It hinges on the ability to maintain foreign confidence in the safety and real earnings of the direct and financial investments made in the country. This has both long-run and short-run aspects.

Confidence about the long run has many dimensions, including one involving attitudes toward foreign involvement in an economy. It is a feature of international integration that residents of one country own assets in another country. A more or less balanced build-up of cross-border claims may tie countries more tightly together. A preponderance of claims in one direction can promote nationalist tensions. The

60 As the data in table IV.6 are in terms of the expenditure definition of the net transfer, they reflect the net results of the resource transfers themselves and are not affected by whether the financial transfers were routed through off-shore centres or direct bilateral transactions.

United States has itself been at the centre of such tensions, especially in the post-war years when United States transnational firms seemed dominant in Europe and much of the rest of the world. The situation has been evolving, however, and the world now seems to be in a phase in which the balance is swinging back to a multiplicity of cross-border claims and that is a positive development to be encouraged. Nevertheless, if the net international investment position of the United States continues indefinitely to deteriorate at a rapid rate, at some point the build-up of international claims may become too one-sided again, this time with the United States potentially subject to the self-perception of national weakness, which can raise tensions, resentments and distrust of foreign holders of the domestic assets.

The process of building up foreign claims on the United States may, however, be self-limiting if the confidence of creditors slackens. Perhaps a major reason for the strong capital flow into the United States during the 1980s is the confidence investors have that the reputation of the United States as the economic core of the developed market econo-

**Box IV.4. Constructing a unified European financial market by 1992**

Over the past several years, financial integration of the European Community (EC) into a single, unified market has made substantial headway. By the end of 1988, of the 27 directives proposed by the Commission aimed at financial integration, 10 had already been approved, 12 were under discussion, and five were being prepared. And, although many obstacles stand in the way of the single financial market, irrevocable steps in that direction have been taken.

There are two aspects of the financial integration process under way in Europe and both aspire to the same goals: lower prices and increased efficiency through heightened levels of competition. The first aspect, the liberalization of the movement of financial services, strives to eliminate all barriers to cross-border competition among European financial service firms (insurance, banking, brokerage firms etc.). The second aspect of European financial integration, the liberalization of capital movements, is aimed at removing all controls on financial flows. In particular, this would affect transactions involving stocks, bonds and other investment funds, including short-term as well as long-term instruments.

**Building financial competition**

Efforts at achieving the free flow of financial services within the EC countries are focused on three distinct areas of the financial services industry: banking, securities, and insurance. A common approach, called the "single-license principle," has been adopted in each of these areas. This principle is based on the idea that any financial institution licensed in one member country will be allowed to operate freely in any other member country. These operations, with several notable exceptions, would be licensed, regulated, and supervised by the country of origin, or the "home" country.

The home country principle, while eliminating the otherwise cumbersome paperwork surrounding cross-border licensing, voluntarily reduces the authority of sovereign States over foreign firms operating within their borders. Controversial issues, such as differing levels of investor protection and widely divergent rules governing minimum capital requirements of financial institutions, must be addressed. Thus, a key aspect of the movement towards financial integration is how the regulations of different EC countries will be harmonized. Even with such harmonization and acceptance of home country supervision, however, the host country will continue to have the final say in the regulation of foreign firms within its borders by evoking its right to protect the "public good". A lengthy process of litigation, most likely extending beyond 1992, may be required before the uses and limitations of the "public good" argument are established.

The three main branches of the financial services industry—banking, securities and insurance—are at different stages of the integration process. The European banking industry, for one, is undergoing extensive transformation in preparation for 1992. It is widely held that for banks, the competitive key to 1992 will be controlling channels of distribution. With this in mind, cross-border mergers and various types of cross-border service contracts have become commonplace. Many large national banks have made moves to acquire, in foreign countries, smaller banks with already established reputations and distribution centres. In addition, the financial sectors of many EC countries are experiencing mergers between domestic banks, producing very large and potentially dominant, banking companies. These occurrences are undoubtedly altering the face of European banking. However, as much of banking is consumer-oriented, regional banks with cultural and social links to a community are likely to retain an important niche in the European banking industry even after 1992.

Many directives freeing cross-border investment services in securities have already been approved, and numerous others are being drafted. A possible impediment to full securities integration, however, could appear if the member countries are unable to establish compatible standards restricting insider trading activities. Insider trading is a formidable element of EC investment markets. The problem is twofold: each country has its own idea of acceptable trading practices, and the penalties for infractions have traditionally been lenient. So far, the EC's attempts to prohibit insider trading have been mostly unsuccessful. But with so much at stake, member countries may be expected to look at the situation more intensively.

mies is still sound, that it remains the world's largest trading nation, that its economy is so large that it is still not very dependent on trade, that it remains the centre of technological development and that the management of its economy and currency will remain sound and its borders kept unreservedly open to international trade and capital flows. However, economic and political forces and time have already begun to attack these views.

The industrialized market economies have already been developing into a multipolar system in which, eventually, no one pole may be seen as clearly dominant in any of the aforementioned areas. The European Economic Community has already grown into a coherent regional economy and is poised to add new dimensions of integration, leading to a single market for financial transactions—and perhaps eventually adopting a single currency—as well as a single market for trade in goods (see box IV.4).

The comparatively strong growth and dynamism of the Japanese economy has continued in the 1980s and the pace

Integration in the insurance industry, while progressing at a steady pace in certain areas, has been plagued by a number of issues. Traditionally the most regulated of the financial services industries, it has encountered stiff resistance to the cross-border insurance of individuals. The most significant areas not yet open to foreign involvement—and not likely to be in the near future—are life and automobile insurance. Intra-European competition has been greater in the commercial insurance fields, where it is assumed that a firm will be able to make more informed decisions about a foreign insurance firm's reliability than will an individual consumer.

**Allowing free capital flows**

The second aspect of European financial integration, the removal of obstacles to cross-border capital movements, has been necessitated and reinforced by the global trend towards financial deregulation.[a] Although there have already been significant advances in this direction by the EC with respect to long-term capital market instruments, the biggest test will come next year. An EC directive adopted in June 1988 has set 1 July 1990 as the date when all remaining controls on capital flows and commercial transactions must be removed by member countries[b] (with the exception of Greece, Ireland, Portugal and Spain, which were given extensions on the deadline to better prepare their economies for the potentially disruptive effects of completely mobile capital).

One of the most important concerns that accompanies the EC's bold move towards liberalizing capital movements is the fear that when the remaining controls are abolished, huge imbalances in capital flows will disrupt the financial markets. The treatment of capital and investment differs widely among EC countries. There will be a strong incentive to move financial assets from countries with strict restrictions and withholding taxes towards countries with more favourable capital and investment policies. For example, Luxembourg does not impose withholding taxes on non-resident income from capital, nor does it report the income to foreign tax authorities. Thus, when the barriers are removed, it is possible that Luxembourg will attract a great deal of capital from individuals in other countries within the EC. This possibility raises two concerns: (a) if huge imbalances in capital flows develop, countries negatively affected will be tempted to re-impose capital controls, which could severely damage the system's credibility; and (b) without an agreement on the sharing of tax information on investments of foreign citizens, investors would be able to conceal their wealth from their home governments, and tax evasion could become a serious drain on government revenues.

To assure a smooth transition to free capital movements, one of two changes seem to be required, neither of them politically easy. One is that the EC could adopt Community-wide tax code harmonization on foreign investments. The difficulty of this task, however, is suggested by the recent failure to mandate an EC-wide withholding tax of 15 per cent on foreign investments. The other is that the bank secrecy laws currently in place in several member countries could be reformed. However, both moves will continue to encounter strong opposition from countries with financial communities that would suffer from their implementation.

**The gains anticipated**

The potential gains from successful European financial integration are indeed significant. A recent study performed for the European Commission measured the price differentials among typical banking, brokerage, and insurance services across the EC[c] The study estimates that new pan-European competitive pressures would lower the cost of financial services across the board by approximately 10 per cent, with those countries that have fostered uncompetitive financial services markets seeing the greatest price reductions. For example, it was estimated that the cost of financial services in Spain could fall by as much as 21 per cent due to increased competition.

Similarly, the liberalization of capital flows is expected to stimulate substantial economic benefits by increasing the availability of capital to relatively high productivity sectors. This, in turn, should bolster both output and income across the EC.

a See, "The changing institutional character of international financial markets in the 1980s," in *Supplement to World Economic Survey 1985-1986* (United Nations publication, Sales No. E.86.II.C.2.), pp. 28-50.

b European Community Directive 88/361/EEC.

c See, Commission of the European Communities, *European Economy,* No. 35 (March 1988), p. 219.

Figure IV.11. Long-term foreign investment of Japan, 1980-1988

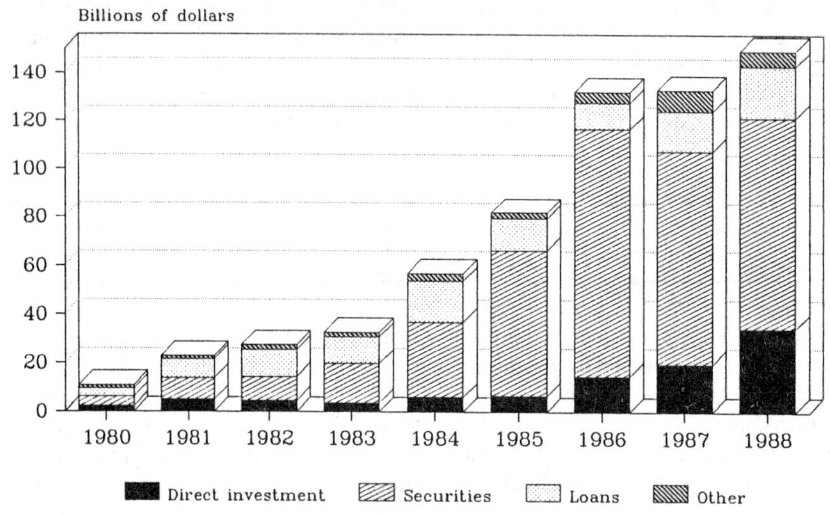


*Source:* Data from the Bank of Japan.

Figure IV.12. Long-term foreign investment of the Federal Republic of Germany, 1980-1988

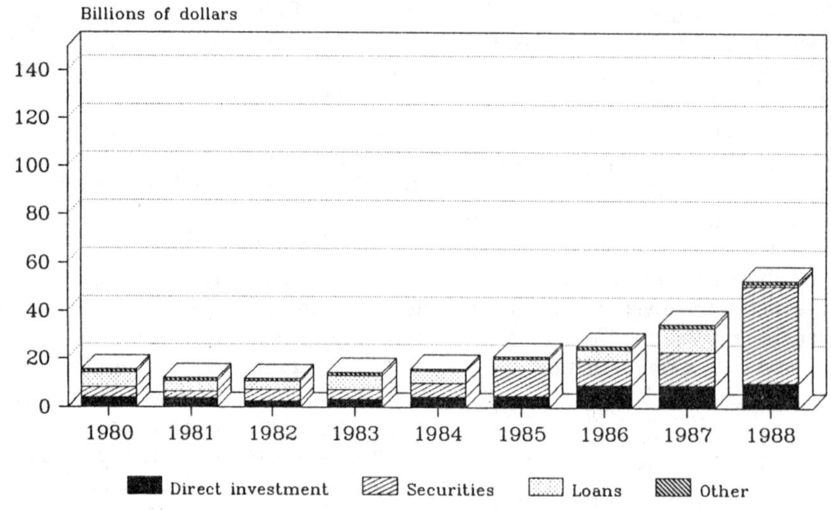


*Source:* Data from the Deutsche Bundesbank.

of long-term Japanese investment has grown to globally important dimensions. In 1988, it reached almost $150 billion and has been above $130 billion since 1986. The long-term foreign investment of the Federal Republic of Germany, to cite another large capital-exporting country in contrast, was $53 billion last year and half that in 1986 (see figures IV.11 and IV.12).[61]

The implication is that the best means to ensure the continued confidence of foreign creditors in the long-run performance of the United States economy is to diminish more rapidly the need for the continued large-scale net capital inflow from them, i.e., to demonstrate appropriate progress in the macro-economic and structural adjustment of the United States economy, which entails more rapid correction of the

61 The current account surpluses of Japan and the Federal Republic of Germany do not differ by as much as the long-term outflows from each country; the ability of Japan to maintain such large outflows stems, instead, from the larger foreign flows into Japan than into the Federal Republic of Germany, including especially in 1988 foreign purchases of Japanese long-term securities and short-term banking inflows (see tables A.9 and A.10).

Table IV.7 Exchange-rate adjusted changes in non-United States official holdings of foreign exchange reserves, 1987-1988[a]

(Billions of dollars)

| | 1987 quarters | | | | 1988 quarters | | | |
|---|---|---|---|---|---|---|---|---|
| | I | II | III | IV | I | II | III | IV |
| Member countries of the Group of Seven, of which | 28.9 | 12.8 | 2.6 | 35.3 | -0.4 | -5.0 | -2.2 | 9.4 |
| Canada | 3.0 | 1.3 | 0.9 | 0.5 | 2.9 | 2.8 | -1.1 | 0.7 |
| France | 0.4 | 0.2 | -0.9 | 1.3 | -1.1 | -1.0 | -1.1 | -2.3 |
| Germany, Federal Republic of | 6.5 | 1.8 | 1.2 | 11.2 | -4.1 | -5.8 | -5.1 | 0.4 |
| Italy | 4.0 | -1.9 | -1.1 | 6.4 | -0.2 | -2.0 | 1.6 | 4.2 |
| Japan | 12.6 | 8.2 | 2.2 | 6.6 | 2.3 | 1.8 | 2.4 | 4.6 |
| United Kingdom | 2.5 | 5.8 | 0.4 | 9.4 | -0.2 | -0.8 | 1.1 | 1.8 |
| Other countries (excluding United States) | 14.6 | 21.1 | 17.1 | 21.2 | 1.7 | 0.3 | -3.9 | 12.2 |
| World (excluding United States) | 43.5 | 33.9 | 19.8 | 56.5 | 1.3 | -4.7 | -6.1 | 21.6 |

*Source:* Data supplied by the International Monetary Fund..

a Measured as changes in stocks of reserves at constant exchange rates.

trade and budgetary imabalances, as discussed elsewhere in this *Survey,* and a reinvigoration of investment to promote more rapid productivity increases, especially in the sectors producing tradable goods and services.

However, even if confidence is strong in the long-run direction of the United States economy, there is also a short-run dimension of confidence that can short-circuit the willingness of international creditors to transfer resources. Indeed, lack of that confidence was manifest in 1987 but it returned in 1988.

In 1987, as discussed in the *World Economic Survey 1988,*[62] net private financial inflows to the United States fell far short of what was needed to finance the United States current account deficit. If the foreign exchange markets had been left to their own devices, the dollar would have tumbled. However, the seven major industrialized countries (the Group of Seven) had committed themselves to stabilize key foreign exchange rates in the February 1987 Louvre Accord and thus they intervened heavily in the market by buying dollars and adjusting interest rate differentials in favour of the dollar. The total amount of official intervention is not readily determined and in any case, official purchases of dollars even without the express intent of stabilizing the dollar have the same effect as explicit intervention. What can be said is that in 1987, world reserves outside the United States rose by more than $150 billion, of which $80 billion were accounted for by member Governments of the Group of Seven (see table IV.7). With the dollar share of reserves at 55 to 60 per cent in the Group of Seven, excluding the United States, this implies over $44 billion in support by the Group of Seven, and world official support, in effect, on the order of $85 billion or more. The United States Government also intervened in 1987, drawing down its reserves by a net amount of $9 billion for the year.[63]

The experience in 1988 was entirely different. The confidence that had weakened appreciably in 1987, especially in the fourth quarter, was rebuilt in the first quarter of 1988. Thus, as table IV.7 shows, the build-up of reserves outside the United States almost came to a halt, with a net amount of only $2 billion accounted for by the Group of Seven. United States reserves rose by almost $4 billion and private capital flows to the United States on a balance-of-payments basis continued at the same levels as 1987, while the current account deficit shrank by almost $20 billion.

The confidence that was rebuilt in 1988 pertains specifically to the short-run stability of the dollar relative to the other major currencies. After the global stock market crash in October 1987, this confidence about the short-run was shattered by fears of economic recession, especially in the United States where shares of stock form a larger per cent of personal wealth than in other developed countries. Also, to shore up the sagging stock market, the United States monetary authorities had added considerably to monetary liquidity. Both factors pointed to declining interest rates in the United States relative to its major financial partners, which would reduce the attractiveness of holding dollar assets to individuals who make their financial calculations in yen, deutsche marks, pounds sterling and so on. Foreign exchange traders had to fear that if others decided to reduce their dollar holdings, the dollar would start to fall and those still holding dollars would suffer substantial losses. The Louvre Accord had promised that the major countries would step in to stabilize exchange rates, but the private sector could only wonder how strong the commitment was, how

62 See, *World Economic Survey 1988,* chap. IV, pp. 67-76.

63 Based on balance-of-payments data (see table A.8).

much would be expended by official authorities or for how long, especially if doing so was seen to conflict with other policy commitments. Furthermore, as progress in reducing the United States trade deficit had been halting, the wisdom or ability to maintain exchange rates at levels that might not yet be the equilibrium could be questioned.

As it turned out, however, there was no recession in the United States, Europe or Japan. The United States trade deficit began to show more signs of adjusting and with aggregate demand still strong in the United States, it was possible to rebuild interest rate differentials in favour of the United States.[64] Moreover, not only had the Group of Seven collectively and individually made repeated reassurances of the commitment to the Louvre Accord, but the large-scale intervention in late 1988 and the early weeks of 1989 had demonstrated their resolve.

The result was that for much of 1988, foreign demand for dollar assets was strong and even pushed the dollar exchange rate higher despite intervention to slow the rise through dollar sales. Exchange rate confidence, however, can also be undermined by fear that the pace of adjustment of the economic fundamentals would slow down, and that also seemed to occur in the last quarter of 1988 when the United States election resulted in a President from one political party and the Congress more firmly in control by the opposition. The outlook for speedy budgetary correction was clouded and international financial flows and thus the dollar again weakened.[65] Nevertheless, with new official intervention by the Group of Seven to support the dollar and with inflationary pressures making it attractive to the monetary authorities to raise interest rates anyway, the markets were again calmed. An optimistic mood on the dollar thus returned in early 1989, but its continuation remains dependent on actually achieving significant progress in United States budgetary correction, still the major missing piece of the macro-economic policy package viewed as essential for increased world economic stability.

64 On the role of interest differentials and other factors in the determination of exchange rates in recent years, see chapter II.

65 Other short-term factors, such as a slowing of United States economic growth, also seemed to help pull the dollar down (for a detailed narrative of changes in the confidence of market participants and the role of policy changes and official intervention, see the quarterly reports to the United States Congress by the Federal Reserve System, "Treasury and Federal Reserve foreign exchange operations", as published in the *Federal Reserve Bulletin* and Federal Reserve Bank of New York, *Quarterly Review*).

# Chapter V

## THE INTERNATIONAL ENERGY SITUATION

Energy developments during the past two decades have involved fundamental changes in patterns of energy production and consumption, with different but significant effects on national economies (see table V.1). Volatility in energy prices and apprehensions about security of supplies have led to extensive misallocation of resources in the development of high-cost energy sources.

Considerable progress was achieved in energy conservation and efficiency as a result of the energy crises of the 1970s. This has been especially welcome in view of the scientific evidence that fossil fuels are major culprits in the so-called greenhouse effect as well as in acid rain.

Technological developments contributing to energy conservation and efficiency have been notable in the developed market economies, which are the main energy consumers. Provided conditions are right in the future, further progress may be expected in this field.

The emergence of the current global energy situation has been characterized by sharp conflicts of interest between energy importing and exporting countries. Attempts to promote dialogue and co-operation have been fitful. In view of the economic and environmental costs at stake and the structure of the world energy economy, international co-operation is imperative. Future energy developments should be marked by rationality and equity rather than by national rivalries leading to environmental degradation and global economic penalties. After an analysis of the international oil market, this chapter focuses on natural gas, coal and electricity and on the environmental consequences of energy use in the world energy economy.

### Developments in oil markets in 1988

#### Oil price plunge and recovery

Apprehensions about a repetition of the 1986 collapse in oil prices characterized practically the whole of 1988. During the first 10 months of 1987, prices stayed close to the target price of $18 per barrel set at the OPEC meeting in December 1986, but in the last two months of 1987 another decline began.

Expectations of a slow-down in the world economy after the stock market crash of October 1987, and the difficulties of OPEC members in reaching an agreement during their December meeting at Vienna, owing to the intensification of the Iran-Iraq conflict, made prices drop to $14-$15 per barrel (f.o.b. Middle East) by the end of the first quarter of 1988. By October 1988, prices had fallen to $10-$11 per barrel. For the year as a whole the average price is estimated at $14 a barrel (see figure V.1). Oil export revenues of OPEC member countries contracted accordingly. However, increases in export volume by a few countries compensated them for the per barrel loss in revenue.

Table V.1. Composition of commercial primary energy consumption

(Million tons of oil equivalent)

| | | Coal | | Oil | | Gas | | Electricity | | Total | |
|---|---|---|---|---|---|---|---|---|---|---|---|
| | | Consumption | Percentage share | Consumption | Percentage share | Consumption | Percentage share | Consumption | Percentage share | Consumption | Percentage share |
| Developed market economies | 1976 | 660.8 | 20.8 | 1 661.5 | 52.4 | 737.1 | 23.2 | 111.4 | 3.5 | 3 170.8 | 100 |
| | 1986 | 873.4 | 26.4 | 1 516.3 | 45.8 | 711.1 | 21.5 | 209.2 | 6.3 | 3 309.9 | 100 |
| Centrally planned economies | 1976 | 593.7 | 45.2 | 396.7 | 30.2 | 305.9 | 23.3 | 17.6 | 1.3 | 1 313.9 | 100 |
| | 1986 | 655.4 | 37.9 | 447.9 | 25.9 | 587.3 | 33.9 | 40.8 | 2.4 | 1 731.4 | 100 |
| Developing countries | 1976 | 394.9 | 42.5 | 419.7 | 45.2 | 85.1 | 9.2 | 29.9 | 3.2 | 929.4 | 100 |
| | 1986 | 629.4 | 42.4 | 626.8 | 42.2 | 166.4 | 11.2 | 61.3 | 4.1 | 1 484.0 | 100 |
| Member countries of OPEC | 1976 | 1.3 | 1.2 | 71.9 | 65.3 | 35.3 | 32.1 | 1.6 | 1.5 | 110.1 | 100 |
| | 1986 | 3.4 | 1.5 | 143.1 | 64.1 | 72.9 | 32.7 | 3.7 | 1.7 | 223.1 | 100 |
| Other oil-exporting countries | 1976 | 242.2 | 57.5 | 142.7 | 33.9 | 27.5 | 6.5 | 8.6 | 2.0 | 420.9 | 100 |
| | 1986 | 444.4 | 60.1 | 226.9 | 30.7 | 49.2 | 6.7 | 18.8 | 2.5 | 739.4 | 100 |
| Oil-importing countries | 1976 | 151.4 | 38.0 | 205.1 | 51.5 | 22.3 | 5.6 | 19.7 | 4.9 | 398.4 | 100 |
| | 1986 | 181.6 | 34.8 | 256.8 | 49.2 | 44.3 | 8.5 | 38.7 | 7.4 | 521.5 | 100 |
| Total world | 1976 | 1 649.3 | 30.5 | 2 477.8 | 45.8 | 1 128.1 | 20.8 | 158.9 | 2.9 | 5 414.1 | 100 |
| | 1986 | 2 158.2 | 33.1 | 2 591.0 | 39.7 | 1 464.8 | 22.4 | 311.3 | 4.8 | 6 525.3 | 100 |

*Source:* Department of International Economic and Social Affairs of the United Nations Secretariat, based on *Energy Statistics Yearbook*, various issues.

Figure V.1. Crude oil prices

(Dollars per barrel)

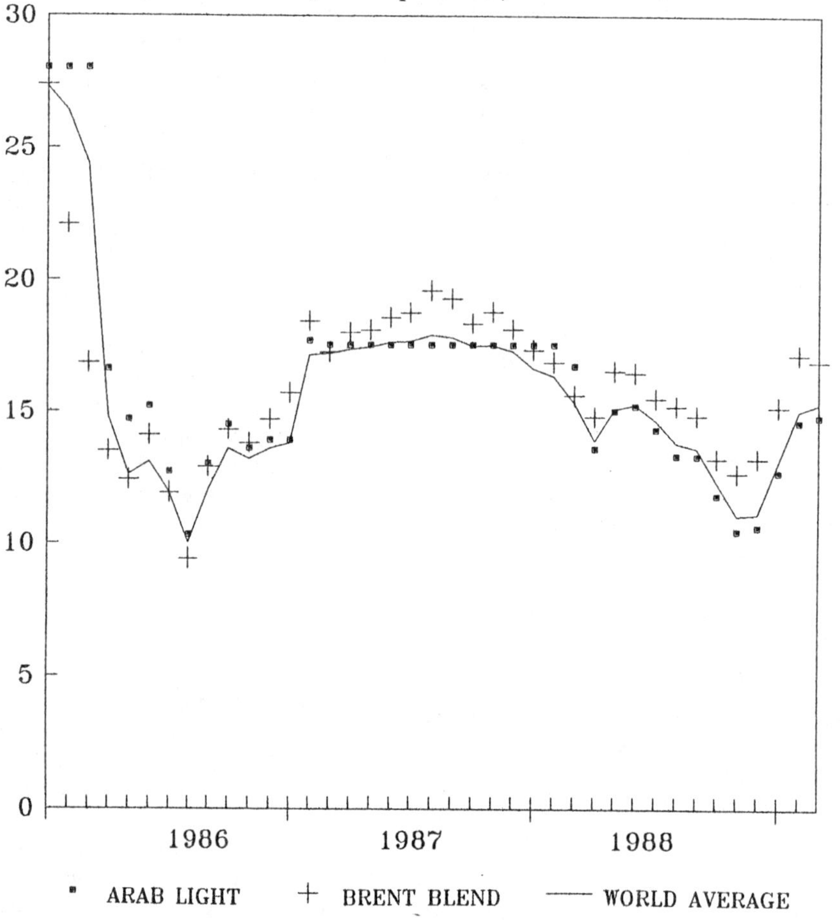


*Source:* Department of International Economic and Social Affairs of the United Nations Secretariat, based on United States Department of Energy, Energy Information Administration, *Weekly Petroleum Status Report,* 1986-1989 issues.

During the second half of the 1980s, lower oil prices have had a dramatic impact on the foreign exchange revenues of the member countries of OPEC. Population growth has also been considerable. As shown in table A.17, oil revenues between 1980 and 1987 dropped from $287 billion to $96 billion. Per capita oil revenues dropped from $816 to $221.

Oil revenues for OPEC as a whole are estimated at $77 billion in 1988, as compared to $96 billion in 1987. Export prices declined by an average of $3 a barrel, and production increased by 11 per cent. While the target price of $18 a barrel was not abandoned by OPEC, trading in oil throughout 1988 was based on a variety of formulae related to market conditions, often including comparisons with prices of key grades such as Brent and Dubai on the spot market and netback values (i.e., value of refined products less refinery fee, freight and insurance).[1]

More recently, trading practices in crude oil reveal a return to long-term supply relationships between oil-exporting countries and refining companies in importing countries. Such contracts, representing as much as 10 million barrels a day in total, are flexible with regard to prices in order to meet rapidly changing market conditions. The net effect is less trading through intermediaries and lower volumes on the spot market.[2]

With the return to production restraint by the OPEC member countries at the beginning of 1989 and announced cutbacks in exports by 5 per cent from the main non-OPEC oil-exporting developing countries, as well as Norway and the Union of Soviet Socialist Republics, oil prices climbed to a level above $16 a barrel, f.o.b. Middle East, by the end of the first quarter, with prospects of reaching the target price of $18 a barrel during 1989.

1 "Updated price scorecard for key world crudes", *Petroleum Intelligence Weekly,* Special Supplement Issue, 23 January 1989.
2 "Crude oil contracts: who's who in 1989", *Petroleum Intelligence Weekly,* Special Supplement Issue, 13 February 1989.

## Growth in oil consumption surpasses expectations

In view of the instability in the world financial markets, prospects for economic growth looked subdued at the beginning of 1988 and oil consumption was only expected to grow by 1 per cent. However, unexpected rapid growth in the developed market economies, as well as persistently lower oil prices throughout the year, led to a 2.6 per cent increase in oil consumption. As a result, consumption reached an average of 36.8 million barrels a day, an increase of 1.0 million barrels a day over 1987.

Reflecting regional differences among the developed market economies, oil demand was particularly strong in Japan. As a result oil consumption increased by 6.3 per cent in the Pacific region, 2.7 per cent in North America and 0.4 per cent in Western Europe.

Much of the increase in oil demand in the developed market economies in 1988 was due to gasoline and aviation fuel. Lower prices for heavy fuel oil, especially during the last quarter of 1988, led to a switch from natural gas in the United States of America and from coal in the United Kingdom for electricity generation. In Japan, temporarily reduced nuclear operation resulted in increases in the use of heavy fuel oil and crude oil for direct burning in electric power plants. In France, oil-fueled power stations were reopened when nuclear power generation was reduced by strike action, and in Spain, sharply reduced hydro-electric supplies were made up by electricity generated with heavy fuel oil.

In the developing countries, preliminary estimates indicate that oil consumption increased by 3 per cent or 0.4 million barrels a day and reached 13.4 million barrels a day in 1988.

In the centrally planned economies of Eastern Europe, no increase in oil consumption occurred in 1988 mainly because of conservation policies in the Union of Soviet Socialist Republics.

World oil consumption increased by an average of 2.3 per cent or 1.4 million barrels a day, reaching a total of 61.9 million barrels a day or 22.7 billion barrels in 1988. This was the highest level of world oil consumption since 1980.

In 1989, oil consumption in the developed market economies is expected to increase by 2.1 per cent or 0.8 million barrels a day, reaching 37.6 million barrels a day, on the assumption that economic growth will slow down from 4 per cent in 1988 to 3.25 per cent.

Oil demand trends in the United States of America are of particular significance: the United States consumed 17 million barrels a day in 1988 or about 28 per cent of the world total. Decreasing domestic oil production and increasing demand have raised oil imports by 50 per cent between 1985 and 1988 and they are expected to increase further in the future for the same reasons. Such increases of oil imports in the biggest oil market in the world are bound to have an impact on the world market.

In the developing countries, oil consumption may reach 13.9 million barrels a day in 1989, 4 per cent higher than the previous year.

In the centrally planned economies of Eastern Europe, oil conservation policies by the Union of Soviet Socialist Republics are expected to persist, with consumption remaining static.

World oil consumption in 1989 will therefore increase by about 2 per cent or 1.3 million barrels a day, reaching a total of 23.1 billion barrels (see table V.2).

Table V.2. World oil consumption, 1985-1989

(Million barrels a day)

| | 1985 | 1986 | 1987 | 1988 estimate | 1989 projected |
|---|---|---|---|---|---|
| Developed market economies | 34.2 | 35.2 | 35.8 | 36.8 | 37.6 |
| Centrally planned economies | 11.5 | 11.6 | 11.7 | 11.7 | 11.7 |
| Developing countries | 12.2 | 12.6 | 13.0 | 13.4 | 13.9 |
| Total | 57.9 | 59.4 | 60.5 | 61.9 | 63.2 |

*Source:* Department of International Economic and Social Affairs of the United Nations Secretariat.

While the fall in crude oil prices since 1986 has undoubtedly reversed oil consumption trends, its effect was restrained by a variety of policies in importing countries. The price of crude oil is only one of the factors in the price of petroleum products. Excise taxes usually constitute a large proportion of the final price of petroleum products paid by consumers. Thus, in order to restrain demand, all the developed market economies have increased taxes on gasoline (see table V.3).

## More pronounced production shift to developing countries

Persistent over-production by the OPEC member countries in the second half of 1987 was corrected during the first quarter of 1988 when production was reduced to about 17.6 million barrels a day. From April to December 1988, however, over-production again accelerated and, by the end of the year, total OPEC production had reached 22.8 million

Table V.3. End-use gasoline taxes and price indices in selected countries

| | Indices of gasoline prices (1985=100) | | | | Percentages of taxes in gasoline prices | | | |
|---|---|---|---|---|---|---|---|---|
| | 1985 | 1986 | 1987 | 1988[a] | 1985 | 1986 | 1987 | 1988 |
| Canada | 100 | 90 | 97 | 108 | 26.7 | 33.0 | 36.2 | 36.2 |
| France | 100 | 109 | 130 | 126 | 62.3 | 73.9 | 75.3 | 76.0 |
| Italy | 100 | 124 | 145 | 142 | 64.4 | 78.2 | 78.2 | 78.3 |
| Japan | 100 | 124 | 143 | 147 | 38.6 | 43.9 | 44.6 | 47.0 |
| Spain | 100 | 107 | 115 | 110 | 39.2 | 67.6 | 65.3 | 63.0 |
| United Kingdom | 100 | 99 | 112 | 116 | 54.3 | 63.9 | 64.1 | 67.0 |
| United States | 100 | 77 | 79 | 82 | 23.0 | 32.7 | 30.8 | 29.5 |
| Germany, Federal Republic of | 100 | 101 | 119 | 113 | 48.7 | 61.5 | 62.8 | 63.4 |

*Source:* International Energy Agency, *Energy Prices and Taxes* (Paris, OECD, 1989).

a Third quarter 1988.

barrels a day, about 5 million barrels a day above the agreed production levels.

OPEC production was influenced by the Iran-Iraq conflict until the cease-fire of August 1988, by higher than expected oil demand owing to vigorous economic growth in the developed market economies, by pressing needs for revenues leading to higher export volumes to make up for declining prices, and by competition for market shares, with most of the increase in output during 1988 occurring in Iraq, Kuwait, Saudi Arabia and the United Arab Emirates.

Oil production in the member countries of OPEC increased by 11 per cent to about 7.2 billion barrels (19.8 million barrels a day) in 1988 from 6.5 billion barrels in 1987 (17.8 million barrels a day) (see table A.18 and figure V.2).

Repeated consultations among OPEC member countries about restoring production restraint were unsuccessful until their Vienna meeting (21-28 November 1988). Agreement was then reached on a level of OPEC production for the first half of 1989 of 18.5 million barrels a day, distributed among all member countries as shown in table A.19.

This agreement included Iraq for the first time since 1986 and stipulated new allocations of production levels for each of the member countries. In addition, a monitoring committee (Algeria, Indonesia, Islamic Republic of Iran, Iraq, Kuwait, Nigeria, Saudi Arabia and Venezuela) was given the task of preparing a long-term strategy, including the allocation of permanent quotas, which were defined for the first time as follows:

"The quota of a member country is defined as crude oil production plus stock movements. Quota consists of (a) domestic consumption (which is the sum of local sales of crude oil and refined petroleum products inclusive of bunkers and aviation fuels sold to national flag carriers as well as refinery fuel and loss and own use by the oil industry); (b) net export sales of crude oil and refined products from national borders; (c) withdrawal of stocks of crude oil and refined products from inventories held outside of national borders."[3]

Another significant development in 1988 was the co-operation between OPEC member countries and other oil-exporting countries in the co-ordination of production, with a view to stabilizing prices.[4] The meeting of OPEC member countries (Algeria, Indonesia, Kuwait, Nigeria, Saudi Arabia and Venezuela) and other oil-exporting countries (Angola, China, Colombia, Egypt, Malaysia, Mexico and Oman) in Vienna on 26 and 27 April 1988 was hailed as the beginning of a new stage of co-operation among oil-producing countries; it was hoped that others would join. The non-OPEC countries undertook to continue their efforts to secure the participation of other countries.

The independent producers and the OPEC members stated that their objective was a stable market, beneficial to producers, consumers and the world economy at large. They expressed the hope that consuming countries would recognize the mutual benefit of such a policy.[5]

Apparently, the non-OPEC oil-exporting countries offered to cut their exports by 5 per cent, provided that OPEC member countries would commit themselves to a proportional response, but no agreement was reached.[6]

At the OPEC meeting in November 1988, at which unity was restored and new production levels agreed, member countries reiterated that the preservation of the oil price in the world market also required a serious and genuine effort

3 Resolution LXXXIV.286, adopted by the OPEC Conference at its 84th meeting (Vienna, 21-28 November 1988), annex I, as reported in *Middle East Economic Survey,* Supplement, vol. XXXII, No. 8 (28 November 1988).

4 Youssef M. Ibrahim, "New hopes for a global oil coalition", *The New York times,* 11 April 1988.

5 OPEC press release No. 3/88, 27 April 1988.

6 *Middle East Economic Survey,* 2 May 1988.

Figure V.2. OPEC crude oil production and f.o.b. crude oil prices

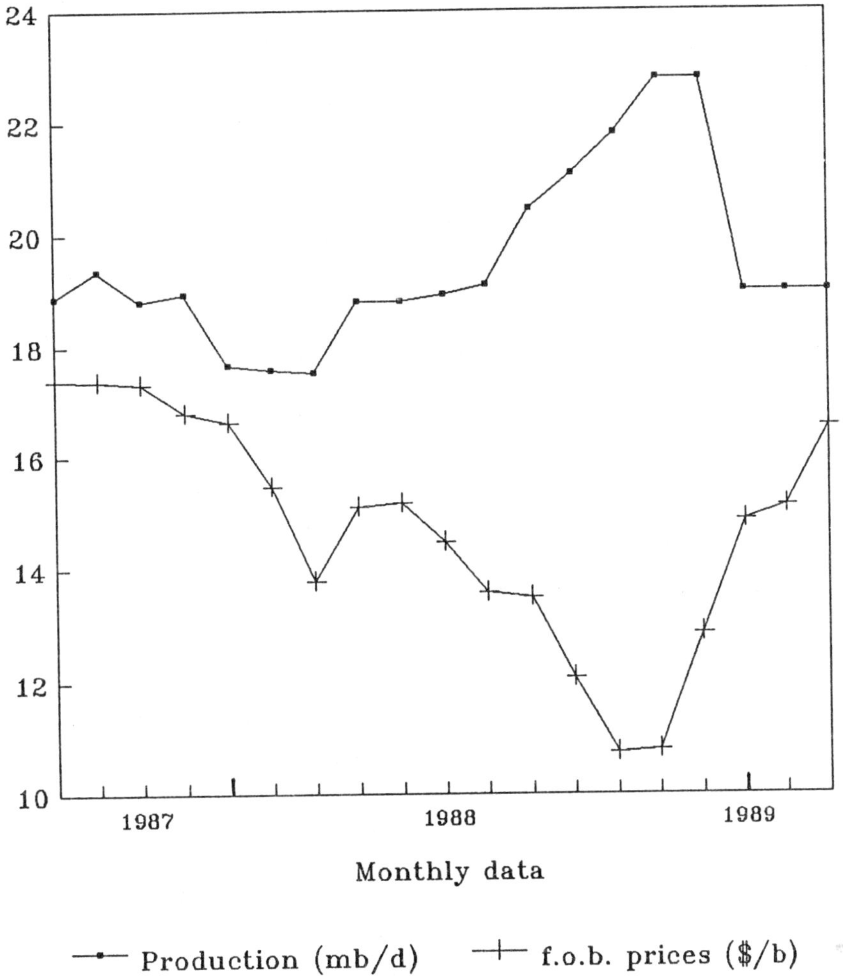


*Source:* Department of International Economic and Social Affairs of the United Nations Secretariat, based on United States Department of Energy, Energy Information Administration, *Weekly Petroleum Status Report,* 1987-1989 issues; and *Petroleum Economist,* March 1988 and March 1989.

on the part of the non-OPEC oil-producing countries. They stressed that the restoration of market stability was the joint responsibility of oil producers as well as consuming countries.[7]

Following this, a meeting of technical experts of OPEC member countries and non-OPEC oil producers took place in London on 26 January 1989.[8] The experts agreed on the need for further steps to strengthen the oil market. Technical experts from the non-OPEC oil producers agreed to recommend to their appropriate authorities necessary co-operative measures.

The technical meeting was followed by higher-level consultations in late February 1989 in London. In March 1989 most of the non-OPEC participants and observers at the meeting mentioned previously announced either a freeze or reductions of 5 per cent in their oil exports for the second quarter of 1989. Norway continued a 7.5 per cent production restraint. On 3 March 1989, Tass reported that "Soviet oil exports for freely convertible currency will be reduced approximately by 5 per cent in the first six months of 1989 as against the same period in 1988".[9]

In 1988 the growth of oil production in non-OPEC oil-exporting developing countries was uneven: the overall increase was 3.6 per cent (see table V.4). Output expanded in Angola, China, Congo, Malaysia, Oman, the Syrian Arab Republic and Yemen, but in Bahrain, Colombia, Egypt,

7 OPEC press release No. 13/88, 28 November 1988.

8 OPEC countries attending the meeting were: Algeria, Indonesia, Kuwait, Nigeria, Saudi Arabia and Venezuela. Non-OPEC countries were: Angola, China, Colombia, Egypt, Malaysia, Mexico and Oman. In addition, the Province of Alberta (Canada), the States of Alaska and Texas (USA), Norway, the USSR and Yemen attended as observers.

9 *The New York Times*, 4 March 1989, p. 45.

Table V.4. World crude oil production

(Millions of barrels)

| | 1980 | 1985 | 1986 | 1987 | 1988 |
|---|---|---|---|---|---|
| Developed market economies | 4 598.9 | 5 242.7 | 5 202.7 | 5 205.7 | 5 210.5 |
| Centrally planned economies | 4 525.3 | 4 466.2 | 4 606.4 | 4 711.6 | 4 708.1 |
| Developing countries | 12 622.4 | 9 710.0 | 10 630.0 | 10 454.6 | 11 043.7 |
| OPEC countries | 9 781.8 | 5 869.6 | 6 712.7 | 6 458.9 | 6 920.3 |
| Other oil-exporting countries | 2 439.0 | 3 135.4 | 3 202.7 | 3 298.4 | 3 417.2 |
| Oil-importing countries | 401.6 | 705.0 | 714.6 | 697.3 | 706.1 |
| Total world | 21 746.6 | 19 418.8 | 20 439.1 | 20 371.8 | 20 962.2 |

*Source:* Department of International Economic and Social Affairs of the United Nations Secretariat, based on *Energy Statistics Yearbook, 1982* and *1986* (United Nations publications, Sales Nos. 84.XVII.4 and 88.XVII.3); and *Oil and Gas Journal,* 28 December 1987 and 26 December 1988.

Mexico, Peru, Trinidad and Tobago, Tunisia and Zaire production declined.

Output expansion in 1989 and beyond is expected in some non-OPEC oil-exporting developing countries (Angola, Congo, the Syrian Arab Republic and Yemen) as the result of accelerated exploration and development of recent discoveries. Future output in Colombia, Egypt, Malaysia, Mexico, Oman and Yemen will be influenced by a combination of factors, including OPEC/non-OPEC co-operation. Efforts are being accelerated in other countries in order to arrest production declines.

In the oil-importing developing countries, oil production stagnated in 1988. Argentina registered a modest increase but Brazil's output declined because of an offshore platform fire. India and Pakistan also increased production and Democratic Yemen produced oil for the first time. In view of the drop in investments in oil exploration and development in the oil-importing developing countries, their production performance in the longer term is not promising.

Oil production in the Soviet Union appears to have reached a plateau at 4.6 billion barrels in 1988 (12.6 million barrels a day). Future production will depend on the application of new technologies in exploration, production and secondary recovery methods and techniques, possibly in joint ventures with specialized firms and international oil companies. Nevertheless, expectations are that the energy mix will shift more towards gas, coal and nuclear electricity during the 1990s. In other centrally planned economies of Eastern Europe, low production levels were maintained in Albania, Bulgaria, Czechoslovakia, the German Democratic Republic, Hungary and Poland, and output in Romania dropped to 204,000 barrels a day in 1987 from 214,000 in 1985.[10]

In the developed market economies as a whole, crude oil production in 1988 remained unchanged at about 5.2 billion barrels. There was a decline of 2.2 per cent in the United States of America, almost made up by an increase in Canada. In the North Sea, reductions in United Kingdom production as a result of offshore accidents were offset by greater output from new fields in the Norwegian sector.

In the United States of America crude oil output declined from 9.0 million barrels a day in 1985 to 8.2 million barrels a day in 1988. This drop is expected to continue; forecasts indicate production at 7.7 and 7.3 million barrels a day respectively for 1989 and 1990.[11] Trends in the production of domestic oil in the United States of America deserve close scrutiny in the coming years because of the impact of that country on the global oil market (see table A.20).

**Investments remain depressed**

The persistence of lower, though volatile, oil prices since 1986 has led to a drastic decline in petroleum investments (see table V.5). Investments dropped by about 50 per cent in the United States of America in 1986 and remained at a low level in 1987. Investments outside the United States of America were lower by 25 per cent in both 1986 and 1987 as compared to 1985.

These investment figures pertain to 28 large United States energy companies and two of the major oil companies of Western Europe, but they are representative of world-wide trends. The drop in financial investments was tempered by a sizeable decline in the costs of exploration and development as a result of lower prices for petroleum services such as geophysical surveys, drilling and production facilities. Nevertheless, a variety of physical statistics, such as the number of wells drilled, confirm the severity of the decline.[12] In the United States of America, completions of oil and gas exploration and development wells dropped by 59 per cent, from 83,889 in 1982 to 34,579 in 1988 (see table A.20). Between 1982 and 1986 the number of wells completed in the developed market economies outside North America dropped by

10 Department of International Economic and Social Affairs of the United Nations Secretariat, based on *Energy Statistics Yearbook,* various issues.

11 *Oil and Gas Journal,* 20 February 1989.

12 See report of the Secretary-General on energy exploration and development trends in developing countries (A/43/476), tables 8 and 9.

Table V.5. Investments in petroleum exploration and development, 1980-1987

(Millions of dollars)

| Year | United States | Rest of the world | Total |
|---|---|---|---|
| 1980 | 28 364 | 13 974 | 42 338 |
| 1981 | 35 315 | 15 336 | 50 651 |
| 1982 | 35 506 | 17 950 | 53 456 |
| 1983 | 29 576 | 14 515 | 44 091 |
| 1984 | 31 916 | 13 906 | 45 822 |
| 1985 | 29 935 | 15 212 | 45 147 |
| 1986 | 15 830 | 11 380 | 27 210 |
| 1987 | 14 264 | 11 834 | 26 098 |
| Total | 220 706 | 114 107 | 334 813 |
| of which | | | |
| Property acquisitions | 51 573 | 8 879 | 60 452 |
| Exploration | 68 814 | 44 109 | 112 923 |
| Development | 100 319 | 61 119 | 161 438 |

*Source:* Salomon Brothers, Inc., *Proved Petroleum Reserves of 30 Large Energy Companies, 1980-87,* 1988 edition (New York, October 1988).

Table V.6. Oil and gas finding costs

(Dollars per barrel of oil equivalent)

| Area | 1980 | 1985 | 1986 | 1987 | 1980-1987 Average |
|---|---|---|---|---|---|
| United States | 7.31 | 15.63 | 14.06 | 6.12 | 8.47 |
| Rest of the world | 5.95 | 5.50 | 6.09 | 3.15 | 5.33 |

*Source:* Salomon Brothers, Inc., *Proved Petroleum Reserves of 30 Large Energy Companies, 1980-87,* 1988 edition (New York, October 1988).

18 per cent, from 1,342 to 1,099 wells. In the developing countries, it fell by 33 per cent, from 7,748 to 5,199 wells, during the same period.[13]

Finding costs of new oil and gas reserves declined to $6.12 per barrel of oil equivalent (boe) in the United States of America in 1987, with foreign operations retaining a significant advantage with costs at $3.15 per barrel of oil equivalent (see table V.6). Although no comprehensive data are available, lower finding costs have attracted new investments from national and private sector oil companies of developed market economies in Western Europe (e.g., Finland, France, the Federal Republic of Germany and Spain), Asia (e.g., Japan), Oceania (e.g., Australia) and of developing countries (e.g., Brazil, Kuwait and the Republic of Korea).

For the 30 large energy companies, the depressed level of investments has led to an overall decline in their total new discoveries so that their petroleum replacement rate has dropped significantly (table V.7). For the United States of America, the conclusion of a prominent United States investment firm is that:

> "in view of the currently depressed oil and gas prices, and the poor investment returns from exploration, it seems all but certain that United States oil and gas production replacement rates will remain low, reserves will deplete rapidly and the production capacity of domestic oil producers will fall".[14]

**Changes in the structure of the petroleum industry**

As a consequence of the nationalization of oil reserves during the late 1960s and the 1970s by some OPEC members, major oil companies redirected their exploration and development investments to the developed market economies and non-OPEC developing countries. High oil prices made these investments attractive, and independent oil companies were active in both the North Sea and North America until prices declined in the early 1980s and collapsed in 1986. This produced bankruptcies, take-overs and consolidations in the industry, which have continued through 1988.

13 *World Petroleum Trends, 1987,* Petroconsultants (UK) Ltd.

14 Salomon Brothers, Inc., *Proved Petroleumk Reserves of 30 Large Energy companies, 1980-87,* 1988 edition (New York, October 1988), p. 12.

Table V.7. Petroleum replacement rate

(Percentage)

| Year | United States Oil | United States Natural gas | Rest of the world Oil | Rest of the world Natural gas | World-wide Oil equivalent |
|---|---|---|---|---|---|
| 1980 | 55 | 66 | 60 | 103 | 74 |
| 1983 | 68 | 67 | 67 | 77 | 71 |
| 1984 | 86 | 89 | 87 | 83 | 86 |
| 1985 | 57 | 65 | 60 | 70 | 64 |
| 1986 | 41 | 49 | 44 | 56 | 49 |
| 1987 | 45 | 42 | 44 | 64 | 52 |

*Source:* Salomon Brothers, Inc., *Proved Petroleum Reserves of 30 Large Energy Companies, 1980-87,* 1988 edition (New York, October 1988).

Structural change was not limited to the private sector. Public oil companies were equally affected. Their role was also affected by change in political perceptions which, in the case of the United Kingdom, led to the privatization of British Gas and the British National Oil Corporation.

A number of oil-exporting developing countries have embarked on programmes for downstream integration into refining and marketing operations in Western Europe and the United States. Kuwait has established such operations in Western Europe on its own and the Libyan Arab Jamahiriya, Nigeria, the United Arab Emirates and Venezuela have entered into joint ventures in industrialized countries. In 1988, the trend towards downstream integration into refining and marketing was confirmed by an agreement between Saudi Arabia and Texaco for a joint venture involving a 50 per cent interest in all the refining and marketing facilities of Texaco in 23 east coast and Gulf Coast States in the United States of America at a cost of nearly $2 billion.[15] Saudi Arabia indicated that similar joint ventures were being considered in other areas.[16] China entered into its first joint venture involving refining and marketing in the west coast of the United States of America.

Kuwait, which pioneered downstream integration, continued its investment policy by purchasing 21.6 per cent of the stock of British Petroleum, which was later scaled down to 9.9 per cent after the intervention of the Government of the United Kingdom. The United Arab Emirates purchased an 8 per cent interest in Total-CFP.

Investments in oil exploration and production in the developed market economies have been stepped up by the national oil companies of Western Europe and the private sector oil companies of Japan. In the case of Japan, financial assistance covering 70 to 80 per cent of total investment has been provided by Japan National Oil Company in support of the policy to augment the share of equity oil in Japanese imports. Foreign oil exploration and development ventures are also engaged in by private oil companies of the Republic of Korea and the national oil company of Brazil.

Meanwhile, traditional oil companies from the United States of America and Western Europe have redirected their investments towards prospects in oil-exporting developing countries. In some cases, they have expressed readiness to enter into new relationships with countries that had previously resorted to nationalization.

Different perceptions and expectations regarding the future of the world petroleum industry thus affect strategic planning by the oil companies and their respective Governments.

The older oil companies resort to mergers and consolidations and concentration on their main line of business by divesting a variety of non-petroleum operations they had acquired during the period of high prices and profits. In this manner, they position themselves to preserve their historical role and to seek new co-operative arrangements with petroleum-exporting developing countries.

As shown in table A.21, the relative strength of OPEC countries, in terms of ownership of proved oil reserves, has increased in recent years. This is likely to continue for some time because of the unique geological prospects of the Middle East and the drastic reductions in petroleum investments in higher-cost areas.

Changes in the structure of the petroleum industry may affect the price of oil on the world market, as well as of petroleum products in national markets. Some evidence already suggests that oil company consolidations in the United States had an effect, with gasoline prices remaining or even rising slightly in 1988, reflecting little of the reduction in crude oil costs which amounted to about 20 per cent.[17] Similarly, the Monopolies and Mergers Commission of the

15 "Texaco, Saudis formalize downstream venture", *Oil and Gas Journal,* 21 November 1988.

16 Hisham M. Nazer, Minister of Petroleum and Mineral Resources, Saudi Arabia, "The need for stability and predictability in the oil market", *Middle East Economic Survey,* 20 February 1989.

17 Ronald S. Schmidt, "Crude oil and the price of unleaded gasoline", *Federal Reserve Bank of San Francisco Weekly Letter,* 30 December 1988.

Table V.8 Integration of oil companies, 1987

| Rank | Company | Country | Liquids output (Thousand barrels a day) | Integration index[a] (Percentage) |
|---|---|---|---|---|
| 1 | Saudi Aramco | Saudi Arabia | 4 348 | 27 |
| 2 | Pemex | Mexico | 2 540 | 60 |
| 3 | NIOC | Iran (Islamic Republic of) | 2 333 | 26 |
| 4 | INOC | Iraq | 2 244 | 30 |
| 5 | Exxon | United States | 1 835 | 221 |
| 6 | Royal Dutch/Shell | Netherlands/United Kingdom | 1 803 | 233 |
| 7 | PDVSA | Venezuela | 1 653 | 76[b] |
| 8 | British Petroleum | United Kingdom | 1 425 | 157 |
| 9 | Chevron | United States | 1 338 | 201 |
| 10 | Sonatrach | Algeria | 1 072 | 43 |
| 11 | Texaco | United States | 1 065 | 201 |
| 12 | KPC | Kuwait | 971 | 84 |
| 13 | NNPC | Nigeria | 960 | 25 |
| 14 | Amoco | United States | 797 | 130 |
| 15 | Mobil | United States | 781 | 265 |

*Source:* "PIW ranks top 50 oil companies", *Petroleum Intelligence Weekly,* Special Supplement Issue, 12 December 1988.

a Refining capacity divided by liquids production.

b Domestic refineries only.

Table V.9. Oil companies' reserves, 1987

| Rank | Company | Country | Liquids proved reserves | |
|---|---|---|---|---|
| | | | Million barrels | Year's output[a] |
| 1 | Saudi Aramco | Saudi Arabia | 167 400 | 105 |
| 2 | INOC | Iraq | 100 000 | 122 |
| 3 | KPC | Kuwait | 94 525 | 267 |
| 4 | NIOC | Iran (Islamic Republic of) | 92 860 | 109 |
| 5 | Adnoc | United Arab Emirates | 58 089 | 236 |
| 6 | PDVSA | Venezuela | 58 084 | 96 |
| 7 | Pemex | Mexico | 47 176 | 51 |
| 8 | Lybia NOC | Libyan Arab Jamahiriya | 22 800 | 101 |
| 9 | NNPC | Nigeria | 15 980 | 46 |
| 10 | Pertamina | Indonesia | 9 000 | 32 |
| 11 | Sonatrach | Algeria | 8 500 | 22 |
| 12 | Royal Dutch/Shell | Netherlands/United Kingdom | 7 939 | 12 |
| 13 | Exxon | United States | 6 634 | 10 |
| 14 | British Petroleum | United Kingdom | 5 005 | 10 |
| 15 | QGPC | Qatar | 4 500 | 40 |

*Source:* "PIW ranks top 50 oil companies", *Petroleum Inteligence Weekly,* Special Supplement Issue, 12 December 1988.

a Liquids proved reserves divided by 1987 output.

United Kingdom has initiated an inquiry into gasoline pricing.[18]

The position of national oil companies in oil-exporting developing countries is demonstrated in table V.8. Eight of them are among the top 15 companies in terms of world oil production outside the centrally planned economies. Table V.9 demonstrates their overwhelming ownership of oil reserves, with only three private-sector oil companies coming anywhere near their position. Table V.8 also indicates the degree of integration of both national and private-sector oil companies. The evidence also indicates that the number of independent oil companies with exploration activities in the United Kingdom sector of the North Sea has been significantly reduced in recent years.[19]

In view of the continuing volatility in oil prices, the direction of changes in the structure of the world petroleum industry remains uncertain but it deserves further analysis and monitoring because of its possible effects on prices in both global and national markets, as well as on oil exploration and development, particularly in the developing countries.

## Wider use of natural gas

Table V.10. World reserves, production and consumption of natural gas

(Billion cubic meters)

| | Reserves | | Production | | Consumption | |
|---|---|---|---|---|---|---|
| | 1980 | 1988 | 1980 | 1987 | 1980 | 1987 |
| Developed market economies | 12 777 | 14 281 | 847.1 | 807.1 | 908.2 | 888.2 |
| Centrally planned economies | 25 753 | 43 271 | 491.5 | 818.4 | 463.5 | 743.3 |
| Developing countries | 33 631 | 53 903 | 176.0 | 349.9 | 142.4 | 234.8 |
| OPEC countries | 27 573 | 43 912 | 83.8 | 179.9 | 60.5 | 107.5 |
| Other oil-exporting countries | 4 334 | 6 963 | 66.4 | 106.8 | 55.2 | 67.3 |
| Oil-importing countries | 1 724 | 3 028 | 25.8 | 63.2 | 26.7 | 60.0 |
| Total world | 72 161 | 111 455 | 1 514.6 | 1 975.4 | 1 514.1 | 1 866.3 |

*Source:* Department of International Economic and Social Affairs of the United Nations Secretariat, based on *Energy Statistics Yearbook, 1982* and *1986* (United Nations publications, Sales Nos. 84.XVII.4 and 88.XVII.3); *Oil and Gas Journal,* 27 December 1979 and 26 December 1988.

Natural gas is produced either independently or in association with oil. Reserves are of a similar magnitude and probably underestimated because of limited surveys and exploration of gas-prone areas, particularly in the developing countries where there are limited markets for natural gas. The high costs of the necessary infrastructure have so far restrained the development of this versatile fuel.

Where conditions have been favourable, as in North America, Western Europe and the Soviet Union, massive natural gas networks have been established for household consumption, production of petrochemicals and other industrial purposes, and increasingly for electricity generation.

Advances in the manufacture of large-diameter pipes and the construction of continental and intercontinental pipelines have facilitated the transport of natural gas to distant markets. The past 25 years have also seen the rise of extensive trade in liquefied natural gas (LNG), which requires investments in processing plants at the source, specialized LNG carriers for transportation at sea and regassification facilities in the importing countries.

Proved reserves of natural gas have increased by 54 per cent since 1980, mostly in the Union of Soviet Socialist Republics and in the member countries of OPEC (see table V.10).

In terms of oil equivalent, the proved natural gas reserves in 1988 amounted to about 725 billion barrels, equivalent to 73 per cent of proved oil reserves. However, the geographic distribution of natural gas reserves is different from that of oil. The share of the developing countries is 48 per cent for gas as compared to 89 per cent for oil, mainly because of the vast reserves of gas in the Union of Soviet Socialist Republics.

In liquefied natural gas trade, Japan is the main market, with supplies coming mainly from Brunei Darussalam, Indonesia and Malaysia, and lesser volumes from the United Arab Emirates and the United States of America (Alaska).

Natural gas has acquired the status of an independent fuel as the link between gas and oil prices has weakened. By the middle of 1988, delivered gas prices in Western Europe were about $100 per ton or $13.50 per barrel of oil equiva-

18 "UK majors begin 'gas' price hikes", *Platt's Oilgram News,* vol. 67, No. 64 (4 April 1989).
19 "Number of independents active off UK slips", *Oil and Gas Journal,* 30 January 1989, p. 26.

lent. In Japan they were considerably higher—about $139 per ton or $19 per barrel of oil equivalent—because of the higher cost of liquefied natural gas.

In the past few years, increasing attention has been paid to natural gas because of its relatively benign effect on the environment. Considerable progress has been made in conserving associated gas through re-injection rather than flaring it to waste as previously done. Gas utilization has also increased in oil-exporting countries. In oil-importing developing countries, new pricing policies in recent years have attracted investments from transnational corporations and multilateral organizations.

## Revival of coal

Table V.11. World production and consumption of coal

(Million metric tons)

| | Hard coal production | | | Lignite production[a] | | | Coal and lignite consumption | | |
|---|---|---|---|---|---|---|---|---|---|
| | 1973 | 1981 | 1987 | 1973 | 1981 | 1987 | 1981 | 1985 | 1987 |
| Developed market economies | 977.2 | 1 230.4 | 1 357.7 | 195.8 | 299.2 | 359.4 | 1 486.6 | 1 632.6 | 1 647.0 |
| Centrally planned economies[b] | 687.3 | 719.9 | 785.1 | 595.5 | 697.6 | 830.5 | 1 423.8 | 1 496.9 | 1 560.0 |
| Developing countries | 537.2 | 782.0 | 1 119.7 | 6.0 | 35.0 | 52.2 | 881.4 | 1 266.3 | 1 337.9[c] |
| Total world | 2 201.7 | 2 732.3 | 3 262.5 | 797.3 | 1 031.8 | 1 242.1 | 3 791.8 | 4 395.8 | 4 544.9 |

*Source:* Department of International Economic and Social Affairs of the United Nations Secretariat, based on *Energy Statistics Yearbook,* various issues; and International Energy Agency, *Coal Information 1988* (Paris, 1988), pp. I.50 and I.52.

a Includes brown coal.

b Includes Democratic People's Republic of Korea and Mongolia.

c 1987 lignite consumption for China is not available.

Declining oil prices during the 1950s and 1960s displaced coal as the premier fuel in the world economy, a position it gained already in the second half of the nineteenth century and maintained through the mid-1960s. Cheap and abundant oil met increasing energy demand and made inroads into traditional coal-using markets. This led to the decline of the coal industry in the developed market economies despite the availability of vast reserves. Protective measures and subsidies could not restrain the competition from oil.

However, higher oil prices and fears of security of energy supplies led to a revival of coal in the 1970s. Steam coal for the generation of electricity became a substitute for heavy fuel oil. The consumption of such oil dropped by 45 per cent during the period 1980-1986.[20]

The International Energy Agency has assessed accessible coal reserves in terms of the amount of coal that could be produced using currently available technology and transport infrastructure.[21] These estimates of accessible coal reserves are shown in table A.22. Normal losses during mining and beneficiation reduce by half to two thirds the amount of recoverable coal from these reserves which also include protected and subsidized coal (e.g., the Federal Republic of Germany, Japan and the United Kingdom). With world coal and lignite production in 1987 estimated at 3,263 and 1,242 million metric tons, respectively, accessible coal and lignite reserves are adequate for 40 to 50 years.

Coal reserves are unevenly distributed. About 41 per cent is in the centrally planned economies of Eastern Europe, where the Union of Soviet Socialist Republics has 30 per cent. The developed market economies have 39 per cent and the developing countries 20 per cent, owing mainly to reserves in China and India. Smaller reserves have been identified in recent years, as in Colombia, Indonesia and Venezuela.

World coal production has increased by 50 per cent since the first energy crisis of 1973 (see table V.11). The United States of America retained its predominant position, with about 56 per cent of total production in the developed market economies.

Hard coal production doubled in the developing countries, mainly because of an increase of 108 per cent, to 870 million

20 *World Economic Survey 1988* (United Nations publications, Sales No. E.88.II.C.1), p. 86, table V.4.
21 International Energy Agency, *Coal Information 1988* (Paris), p. I.81.

tons by 1987 in China and an increase of 127 per cent, to 177 million tons in India. Since 1983, China has moved ahead as the biggest hard coal producer in the world.

Lignite production has also increased steadily since 1973, with about two thirds of world output in the centrally planned economies of Eastern Europe. Output in the developing countries was limited to less than 5 per cent of the world total, mostly attributed to China and India (see table V.11).

Much of the increase in coal consumption and trade has been due to steam coal for electricity generation. Prices of steam coal have remained competitive throughout the 1980s, except for 1986 when the price of heavy fuel oil fell below the equivalent price for steam coal.

World consumption of coal and lignite has increased by about 20 per cent since 1981. Much of this was due to the 55 per cent increase in China and to a 46 per cent increase in India.

In the developed market economies, in 1987, the United States accounted for 45.7 per cent of coal and lignite consumption, at 752 million tons, the Western European countries for 32.5 per cent, at 535 million tons, and Australia, Japan and South Africa for 19.6 per cent, at 85.1, 102.9 and 134.5 million tons, respectively.

In the centrally planned economies of Eastern Europe, the Union of Soviet Socialist Republics accounted for 44.7 per cent of coal and lignite consumption, at 697 million tons in 1987. The second biggest consumer was Poland, at 236 million tons, followed by Czechoslovakia, at 124 million tons.

## The preference for electricity

Since the energy crises of the 1970s, energy input per unit of economic output has been reduced through conservation and improvements in efficiency. Sometimes this has even resulted in lower consumption of particular energy products. However, consumption of electricity has continued to grow, and it has grown faster than other energy products, which reflects its great versatility in uses in practically all economic sectors. As shown in table V.1., the role of electricity has been increasing practically everywhere.

Additional capacities during the past 20 years have largely been based on steam coal, nuclear power and hydropower, while the use of heavy fuel oil has been drastically reduced, particularly in the developed market economies.

Recently, the availability of natural gas at lower prices, persistent environmental concerns and the reversal of expectations for nuclear power have shifted energy policies in several countries towards coal and natural gas.

In the developed market economies, electric power generation capacity increased from 1,202.7 thousand megawatts (Mw) in 1979 to 1,428.6 thousand Mw in 1986 (see table V.12). About half of the increase was nuclear and a quarter each hydropower and thermal. The share of thermal capac-

Table V.12. Changes in the composition of electric power capacities[a] in developed market economies, 1979 and 1986

(Thousand megawatts)

| Energy source | 1979 | 1986 | Net change |
|---|---|---|---|
| *Total* | *1 202.7* | *1 428.6* | *225.9* |
| Nuclear | 109.0 | 219.6 | 110.6 |
| Hydro | 263.7 | 322.7 | 59.0 |
| Other | 1.5 | 2.4 | 0.9 |
| Thermal | 828.5 | 883.8 | 55.3 |
| Single fuel | | | |
| Coal | 333.2 | 352.3 | 19.1 |
| Oil | 247.4 | 183.6 | -63.8 |
| Gas | 99.0 | 36.3 | -62.7 |
| Other solid | 0.6 | 3.6 | 3.0 |
| Multi-fired | | | |
| Solid/liquid | 40.2 | 85.8 | 45.6 |
| Solid/gas | 17.4 | 31.2 | 13.8 |
| Liquid/gas | 78.8 | 177.1 | 98.3 |
| Solid/liquid/gas | 11.8 | 13.9 | 2.1 |

*Source:* Department of International Economic and Social Affairs of the United Nations Secretariat, based on International Energy Agency, *Coal Information 1988* (Paris, 1988).

a Power plants with capacity less than 30 Mw are not included.

Table V.13. Production of electricity by type

(Million kilowatt hours)

| | | Thermal | Hydro | Nuclear | Geothermal | Total |
|---|---|---|---|---|---|---|
| Developed market economies | 1980 | 3 584 575 | 1 058 599 | 581 798 | 10 097 | 5 235 069 |
| | 1986 | 3 558 078 | 1 128 925 | 1 276 744 | 18 896 | 5 982 643 |
| Centrally planned economies | 1980 | 1 438 188 | 236 581 | 82 577 | 0 | 1 757 346 |
| | 1986 | 1 659 270 | 275 238 | 209 072 | 60 | 2 143 640 |
| Developing countries | 1980 | 774 899 | 459 830 | 16 830 | 3 357 | 1 254 916 |
| | 1986 | 1 131 893 | 622 937 | 70 507 | 10 644 | 1 835 981 |
| Member countries of OPEC | 1980 | 117 935 | 26 106 | 0 | 0 | 144 041 |
| | 1986 | 187 236 | 42 993 | 0 | 254 | 230 483 |
| Other oil-exporting countries | 1980 | 324 722 | 117 325 | 0 | 915 | 442 962 |
| | 1986 | 461 075 | 180 283 | 0 | 1 715 | 643 073 |
| Oil-importing countries | 1980 | 332 242 | 316 399 | 16 830 | 2 442 | 667 913 |
| | 1986 | 483 582 | 399 661 | 70 507 | 8 675 | 962 425 |
| Total world | 1980 | 5 797 662 | 1 755 010 | 681 205 | 13 454 | 8 247 331 |
| | 1986 | 6 349 241 | 2 027 100 | 1 556 323 | 29 600 | 9 962 264 |

*Source:* Department of International Economic and Social Affairs of the United Nations Secretariat, based on *Energy Statistics Yearbook*, various issues.

ity decreased from 69 per cent in 1979 to 62 per cent in 1986. However, its composition changed considerably: single fuel fired plants increased by 19.1 thousand Mw for coal, decreased by 63.8 thousand Mw for oil and 62.7 thousand Mw for gas, and multi-fuel fired plants increased by 159.8 thousand Mw. The developed market economies have increased their nuclear and hydropower capacities while also doubling their multi-fuel thermal plants, thus providing increasing flexibility during periods of energy price volatility.

Projections indicate that electric power capacities in these countries may increase to 1,818 thousand Mw in the year 2000. Coal- and gas-fired electric power capacities are expected to increase, but total thermal capacity will decrease because of a further decline in the use of heavy fuel oil. Nuclear power and hydropower will increase further.

In developing countries in 1986, about 62 per cent of electric power production was thermal, and 34 per cent hydropower (see table V.13). Indigenous reserves make coal-fired plants particularly significant in the plans of China and India, as well as a few other developing countries (e.g., Botswana, Turkey and Zimbabwe). Recently increasing coal imports are also being used for electricity generation in the rapidly growing economies of South-East Asia—Hong Kong, the Republic of Korea, Singapore and Taiwan Province of China—as well as in other developing countries.

Most developing countries, however, continue to depend on oil, often imported, and on indigenous gas and hydropower for their electric power generation. The development of hydroelectricity in the developing countries is essential. Out of an increase in world hydroelectricity of 846 billion kilowatt hours (kwhs) since 1970, 397 billion kwhs were added in the developing countries, 299 billion kwhs in the developed market economies and 138 billion kwhs in the centrally planned economies. In 1986, the developing world produced 31 per cent of the world's hydroelectricity. However, only a small part of the hydro-power potential of developing countries has been exploited because of lack of markets near the sites and a variety of other factors, including the lack of capital and regional co-operation.

Nuclear power has disappointed the early hopes that it "would provide electricity too cheap to meter". By 1988, out of a total of 426 nuclear power plants in operation in the world, only 25 were in developing countries: Argentina (2), Brazil (1), India (6), Pakistan (1), Republic of Korea (8), Taiwan Province of China (6) and Yugoslavia (1). In addition, 20 plants were under construction: in Argentina (1), Brazil (1), China (3), Cuba (2), India (8), the Islamic Republic of Iran (2), Mexico (2) and the Republic of Korea (1).[22]

Over the past 20 years, demand for electricity in the developing countries has grown at an average of 7 per cent per annum, thus doubling required capacities every 10 years. It is estimated that in about 30 developing countries, electricity shortages are causing serious disruptions of economic activity and that these problems will continue, primarily because of the scarcity of capital and foreign exchange.[23] However,

22 International Atomic Energy Agency, *Bulletin*, vol. 30, No. 4 (Vienna, 1988).

23 United States Agency for International Development, *Power Shortages in Developing Countries: Magnitude, Impacts, Solutions and the Role of the Private Sector* (Washington, D.C., March 1988).

there are considerable opportunities for saving electricity. Efficiency in the consuming sectors could be raised by as much as 30 per cent. By raising efficiency, developing countries could reduce the growth rate for electricity consumption to 5.5 per cent. This would bring down investment requirements over the next 20 years from $3.1 trillion to $2.1 trillion.[24]

In the centrally planned economies of Eastern Europe, electricity production is still based mostly on thermal primary energy sources, although there has been a rapid expansion of nuclear power. Since the accident at Chernobyl in 1986, energy plans have been reassessed. The future mix of electric power capacities in the Union of Soviet Socialist Republics and other countries in the region is uncertain, but it may well come to rely more on coal and natural gas.

## Increasing environmental concerns

Growing environmental concerns have added significantly to uncertainties in energy investments which, in recent years, have also been influenced by excessive volatility in energy prices and interest rates. Because of their magnitude and long-term nature, investments in electric power plants have been especially vulnerable to these uncertainties. Lack of additional capacities may cause electricity shortages in a number of countries in the 1990s.

Following the serious accidents at Three Mile Island (1979) and Chernobyl (1986) and recent revelations of the spread of radioactivity from military nuclear stations, opposition to nuclear power has grown world-wide. Higher than expected costs, considerable decommissioning costs and difficulties in the disposal of radioactive wastes have aggravated uncertainties. As a result, in a few countries, nuclear power plants have been shut, and in others, plans for future capacities have been scaled down or cancelled altogether. While overall nuclear power is expected to grow further, it is mainly due to the completion of plants under construction.

Since the contribution of fossil fuels is paramount to world energy consumption, their environmental consequences are analysed below with regard to two main issues of international dimensions, namely, climate warming and acid rain.

In view of the opposition to nuclear power, which was previously considered the most promising alternative energy source, adjustments of the world energy mix in order to address environmental concerns will be difficult unless technological breakthroughs can provide benign alternative energy sources and/or radically improve energy efficiency. Such developments can at best be expected in the long term and adjustments in the medium term will by necessity be limited to greater reliance on the less malignant energy sources.

For the same energy output, the combustion of natural gas produces about 57 per cent of the amount of carbon produced from coal, and the combustion of oil produces about 83 per cent. The substitution of natural gas for coal is therefore advisable, and available technologies and reserves favour such an adjustment, particularly in the electric power sector.

### Fossil fuels and climate change

Mounting evidence concerning the degradation of the earth's ecosystem has led the scientific community to warn that a variety of human activities are likely to induce climatic changes that may have a far-reaching impact. The cause of concern is the global greenhouse effect—the warming of the climate by the increasing concentrations of trace gases in the atmosphere.

The most abundant of these gases is carbon dioxide ($CO_2$). This pollutant is emitted into the atmosphere mainly as a result of the combustion of fossil fuels (coal, oil and natural gas). Burning of biomass and deforestation also contribute significantly to the accumulation of carbon dioxide in the atmosphere.

Measurements of atmospheric composition indicate that the present concentration of $CO_2$ is about 340 parts per million (ppm) (0.034 per cent) of the atmosphere's volume. It has increased by more than 15 per cent since pre-industrial times[25] and by nearly 8 per cent in the past 25 years.[26] Between 1860 and 1985 cumulative carbon releases from fossil fuel combustion alone amounted to about 165 billion tons,[25] more than half of which was generated since 1960.

Several other trace gases such as chlorofluorocarbons, nitrous oxide, chloroform, methane and ozone also contribute to the greenhouse effect. Although present in the atmosphere in minute concentrations, recent analyses indicate that their global effect could warm the earth's climate by as much as carbon dioxide.[27]

Scientists have been aware of the greenhouse effect since the nineteenth century. They noted that carbon dioxide absorbs infrared radiations emitted from the surface of the earth which would otherwise escape to space, and then emits some of these radiations downward. As a result, the equilibrium between radiations entering the atmosphere from the sun and leaving it from the earth is established at higher temperature.

By the late 1960s, when it was evident that the concentration of $CO_2$ in the atmosphere was rising at an alarming rate, scientists began to develop quantitative theories aimed at an

24 Report of the Secretary-General on trends and salient issues in energy resources (E/C.7/1989/10), paras. 55-69.
25 Vaclav Smil, *Carbon, Nitrogen, Sulfur: Human Interference in Grand Biospheric Cycles* (New York, Plenum Press, 1985).
26 Gregg Marland, "Carbon dioxide emission rates for conventional and synthetic fuels", *Energy,* vol. 8 (1983).
27 United Nations Environment Programme, *The Greenhouse Gases,* UNEP/GEMS Environment Library No. 1 (Nairobi, 1987).

understanding of the atmospheric ozone reaction and the climate warming mechanism. Available climate models indicate that a doubling of the atmospheric $CO_2$ concentration from pre-1900 levels of 300 ppm to 600 ppm, in conjunction with increasing concentrations of other trace gases, should produce an average temperature rise of the earth's climate between 1.5 and 4.5 degrees centigrade by the year 2030.[28] According to some models, the increase in temperature will vary according to location. In the northern hemisphere, the change should be about four to six degrees centigrade. In the southern hemisphere, the warming should be much less.

The resulting changes in climate may cause thermal expansion of the oceans and melt some of the Antarctic ice sheet, resulting in a rise in sea levels, which could flood coastal areas throughout the world. It may also have adverse effect on human health and agriculture.

### Contribution of fossil fuels to carbon dioxide emissions

A fundamental problem in assessing and analysing the impact of atmospheric $CO_2$ on climate change is the uncertainty over the anticipated pattern of global energy demand and the role of fossil fuels in future supply. Equally important is the correlation between the rate of growth in the consumption of fossil fuels and the rate of increase in the emissions of carbon dioxide.

At present, about seven billion tons (oil equivalent) of fossil fuels are consumed annually, providing more than 80 per cent of global energy demand. On average, about two thirds of the fuels are carbon. Therefore, about five billion tons of carbon are discharged into the atmosphere annually from fossil fuels.

The pattern of global $CO_2$ emissions from fossil fuels during the period 1950-1986 is shown in table V.14. From 1950 to 1973, a period of rapid growth in primary energy consumption, the average annual growth in $CO_2$ emissions was nearly 4.5 per cent. In the wake of the 1973-1974 oil crisis and the subsequent rise in energy prices, this growth rate averaged slightly more than 1 per cent during the period 1974-1985. However, following the oil price collapse of 1986, the growth of $CO_2$ emissions accelerated again owing to higher fossil fuel consumption.

The developed market economies of North America, Western Europe and Japan produce 49 per cent of global $CO_2$ emissions, the centrally planned economies of Eastern Europe 25 per cent and the developing countries 26 per cent.[29] In addition to 5.3 billion tons of carbon from the combustion of fossil fuels, released into the atmosphere annually, some two billion to three billion tons come from the burning of biomass, deforestation and other sources of carbon. Assuming that $CO_2$ contributes 50 per cent to the global greenhouse effect, in 1986, $CO_2$ emissions from fossil fuel use were responsible for about 32 to 36 per cent of the total greenhouse effect, of which 13.3 to 15 per cent were contributed by coal, 14 to 15 per cent by oil and 5 to 6 per cent by gas (see table V.15).

Table V.14. Global emissions of carbon dioxide from fossil fuels[a]

(Million tons of carbon per year)

| Year | Total $CO_2$ Emissions | Gas | Petroleum Liquids | Solids | Gas Flaring | Cement Production |
|---|---|---|---|---|---|---|
| 1950 | 1 639 | 97 | 423 | 1 078 | 23 | 18 |
| 1955 | 2 050 | 150 | 625 | 1 215 | 30 | 30 |
| 1960 | 2 586 | 235 | 850 | 1 419 | 39 | 43 |
| 1965 | 3 154 | 351 | 1 221 | 1 468 | 55 | 59 |
| 1970 | 4 090 | 515 | 1 838 | 1 571 | 88 | 78 |
| 1975 | 4 628 | 620 | 2 131 | 1 686 | 96 | 95 |
| 1980 | 5 249 | 721 | 2 409 | 1 921 | 78 | 120 |
| 1981 | 5 113 | 730 | 2 274 | 1 930 | 58 | 121 |
| 1982 | 5 075 | 724 | 2 188 | 1 986 | 56 | 121 |
| 1983 | 5 066 | 730 | 2 167 | 1 992 | 52 | 125 |
| 1984 | 5 238 | 783 | 2 200 | 2 080 | 47 | 128 |
| 1985 | 5 338 | 807 | 2 182 | 2 173 | 46 | 130 |
| 1986 | 5 555 | 827 | 2 297 | 2 250 | 45 | 136 |

*Source:* Oak Ridge National Laboratory, Environment Sciences Division, *Estimates of $CO_2$ Emissions from Fossil Fuel Burning and Cement Manufacturing Using the United Nations Energy Statistics and the United States Bureau of Mines Cement Manufacturing Data*, report prepared for the United States Department of Energy, September 1988.

a Includes gas flaring and cement manufacturing.

28 United Nations Environment Programme, *The Ozone Layer*, UNEP/GEMS Environment Library No. 2 (Nairobi, 1987).

29 Stewart Boyle, "Global warming—a paradigm shift for energy policy?", *Energy Policy*, February 1989.

Table V.15. Contribution of $CO_2$ to the greenhouse effect in 1986

| | $CO_2$ emissions | | Greenhouse effect |
|---|---|---|---|
| | Billions of tons of carbon per year | Percentage | Percentage |
| Gas | 0.83 | 9.8-11.1 | 4.9-5.6 |
| Oil | 2.30 | 27.1-30.7 | 13.6-15.4 |
| Coal | 2.25 | 26.5-30.0 | 13.3-15.0 |
| Fossil fuel | 5.38 | 63.4-71.8 | 31.8-36.0 |
| Cement production | 0.14 | 1.6-1.9 | 0.8-1.0 |
| Others[a] | 2.0-3.0 | 35.0-26.3 | 17.4-13.0 |
| Total $CO_2$ | 7.5-8.5 | 100 | 50 |

*Source:* Department of International Economic and Social Affairs of the United Nations Secretariat.

a Includes deforestation, land exploitation and burning of biomass.

Available estimates of the cumulative mass of carbon produced from all sources since the middle of the nineteenth century range between 220 billion and 380 billion tons, with 300 billion tons being the most likely value.[25] About 165 billion tons of this carbon have been produced by fossil fuels. However, it has been demonstrated in different $CO_2$ monitoring stations that the amount of carbon remaining airborne in the atmosphere is equivalent to about one half of the total carbon produced. The other half is absorbed by oceans, trees and plants.

### Scenarios for global carbon dioxide trends

Two scenarios depicting low and high fossil fuel consumption have been used for this analysis in order to assess future incremental carbon dioxide concentrations from fossil fuel combustion until the year 2050.

As shown in figure V.3, about 5.3 billion tons of fossil fuel-derived carbon were produced in 1986, of which 2.81 billion tons were retained in the atmosphere (assuming an airborne fraction of 53 per cent). By the year 2000, some 6.8 billion tons will be produced, of which 3.6 billion tons will remain airborne. The low consumption scenario shows that by the middle of the twenty-first century, the annual emission of $CO_2$ will be roughly three times as much as the 1986 level. During the projection period 1986-2050, cumulative carbon remaining airborne in the atmosphere is estimated at 314 billion tons and the cumulative atmospheric carbon dioxide concentration at 147 ppm. The resulting increase in the annual growth rate of carbon release averages 1.6 per cent per year and of $CO_2$ atmospheric concentration 2.2 parts per million per year.

The high consumption scenario estimates an upper bound of $CO_2$ emissions of about 23 billion tons of carbon per year in 2050, of which 12.2 billion tons remain in the atmosphere. The cumulative amount of carbon generated from 1986 to 2050 totals some 403 billion tons. The resulting increase in $CO_2$ emissions averages 2.3 per cent per year, which corresponds to an average growth rate in atmospheric $CO_2$ concentration of 2.9 parts per million per year. The cumulative $CO_2$ concentration during the projection period is estimated at 189 ppm. When added to the current concentration of 340 ppm, about 529 ppm of carbon dioxide should be in the atmosphere by the year 2050. However, non-fossil fuel sources of carbon would contribute further to the total amount of carbon dioxide concentration during this period.

Therefore, according to these two scenarios, the pre-1900 $CO_2$ concentration of 300 ppm may not come close to doubling before the middle of the next century and probably not before the end of the next century.

Many climate-change models have assumed high fossil fuel consumption growth rates of about 4 per cent per year and concluded that the doubling date of $CO_2$ concentration would occur around the year 2030. However, assuming annual growth rates of 2 to 3 per cent, the doubling of $CO_2$ concentration extends the period to around the year 2060, while rates of 1 to 2 per cent would delay it far beyond the middle of the next century.

## Acid Rain and Fossil Fuels

Research on the effects of acid rain has intensified during the past several years. Acid rain is responsible for acidifying lakes and streams with profound damage to aquatic life, diminishing productivity of forests and crops, accelerating deterioration of materials and structures and contributing to human health hazards.

Acid rain is the result of acid precipitation in the atmosphere through chemical transformation of sulphur dioxide ($SO_2$) and nitrogen oxides ($NO_x$). These air pollutants are emitted into the atmosphere by both natural and man-made sources. Natural sources include sea spray, bacterial decompositon of organic matter, lightning, volcanic eruptions and

Figure V.3. Projected global $CO_2$ emissions from fossil fuel consumption

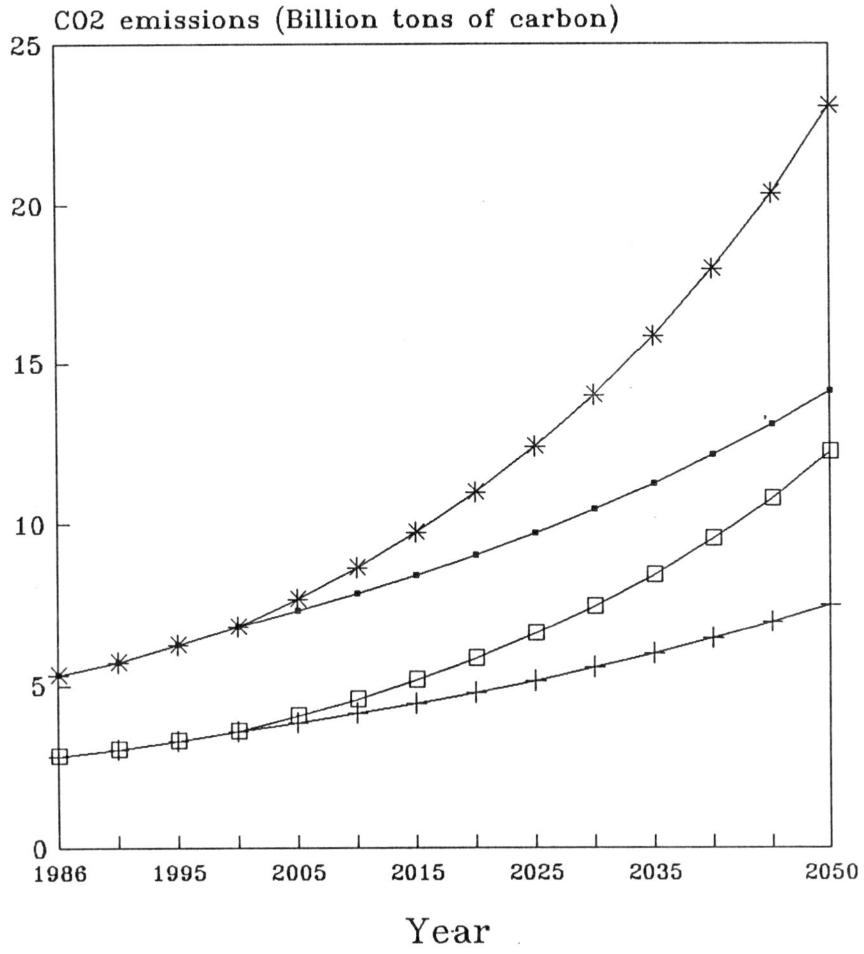


Scenario 1. Total carbon production
Scenario 1. Carbon retained in the atmosphere
Scenario 2. Total carbon production
Scenario 2. Carbon retained in the atmosphere

*Source:* Department of International Economic and Social Affairs of the United Nations Secretariat.

forest fires. Man-made sources include electric generating plants, smelting of ores, industrial installations, motor vehicles and residential and commercial establishments using fossil fuels.

When $SO_2$ and $NO_x$ are emitted in the air they become oxidized to form acid sulphate ($SO_4$) and acid nitrate ($NO_3$), respectively. These acids, sometimes travelling hundreds or even thousands of kilometres, return to the earth as precipitates in rain, snow and hail (wet deposition) and as dry microscopic particles (dry deposition).

**Sources of emissions**

Globally, natural emissions of the sulphur and nitrogen cycles are roughly equal or even larger than man-made emissions. However, studies conducted in North America and Europe indicate that man-made sources contribute more than 90 per cent of total emissions in these regions.[30,31]

Since the middle of the nineteenth century, increasing fossil fuel consumption has resulted in significant increases in nitrogen and sulphur emissions. Global man-made emissions of sulphur dioxide rose from about 7 million tons per year in 1860 to about 155 million tons per year in 1985.[32]

30 Frank Record and others, *Acid Rain Information Book* (New Jersey, Noyes Data Corporation, 1982).

31 J. N. Galloway and D. M. Whelpdale, "An atmospheric sulfur budget for North America", *Atmospheric Environment,* vol. 14 (1980).

32 *World Resources 1988-89,* a report by the World Resources Institute and the International Institute for Environment and Development, in collaboration with the United Nations Environment Programme (New York, Basic Books, Inc., 1988).

However, emissions of $SO_2$ during the period 1970-1985 were reduced substantially in several countries as strict pollution standards were imposed.

In most of the developed market economies, generation of electricity in power plants using fossil fuels is the largest single contributor to the emissions of sulphur dioxide, whereas the transportation sector is the largest source of nitrogen oxides. In 1986, the United States Environmental Protection Agency (EPA) estimated that about 57 per cent of all man-made emissions of $SO_2$ in the United States came from only 200 large coal-fired power plants.[32] In an earlier report, EPA estimated that about 20.8 million tons of sulphur dioxide were released over the United States in 1983, 14 million of which were accounted for by power plants.[33] Industrial processes and boilers emitted 4.1 million tons and smelters 1.1 million tons. The remainder was accounted for by other sources.

The amount of nitrogen released annually is almost as large as that of sulphur. On the average, about one third to one half of man-made emissions of $NO_x$ are attributable to mobile sources. In the United States, for example, the transport sector is responsible for 45 per cent of the estimated 20 million tons of nitrogen oxides emitted in 1985.[32] Similar patterns are observed in other countries. In Western Europe, about 50 per cent of the man-made $NO_x$ budget is caused by motor vehicles.

Although emissions of nitrogen oxides have been slightly reduced or stabilized over the period 1970-1985 in some of the developed market economies, the total amount of nitrogen released annually is still rising. The prime reason for this limited success is due to $NO_x$ emissions from motor vehicles, which are the major sources but numerous and difficult to control, as compared to the major sources of $SO_2$ emissions, which are large coal-fired electric plants which are easy to identify and regulate with less difficulty.

### Transportation and deposition of acids

The intensity of acid rain in many regions downwind of major pollution sources demonstrates the importance of long-range transport of air pollutants. Acid deposition in these regions far exceeds emissions from local sources. Sweden, Switzerland, Austria, eastern Canada and the Netherlands, for example, are responsible for less than 40 per cent of their domestic sulphur deposition.[34] In Norway, about 75 per cent of the sulphur deposition is carried downwind from other countries. Acid rain falling over the Atlantic as far out as Bermuda and the acidity of snow in the Arctic are other examples of long-range transport of acids.[35]

A small fraction of the dispersed sulphur dioxide is converted to acid sulphate and deposited within less than 100 kilometres of its sources. The remainder is transported long distances. This observation may be substantiated by the fact that most of the sulphur is emitted by fossil fuel power plants, which usually use tall smoke-stacks, dispersing air pollutants high in the sky and casting pollution problems to the wind. On the other hand, emissions of nitrogen oxides are thought to have more localized effects, since nearly half of the $NO_x$ is emitted at ground level by motor vehicles.

Attitudes towards acid rain are changing rapidly in the developed countries. Acid rain is currently receiving much attention not only within the environmental community but also at the highest governmental levels. Some progress has been made. Several international organizations, such as the United Nations Economic Commission for Europe (ECE), the European Economic Community (EEC) and the Organisation for Economic Co-operation and Development (OECD) have in the past few years adopted strategies to mitigate acid rain. The ECE sulphur-reduction protocol, agreed to at Helsinki in July 1985, entered into force in September 1987; it is the first international treaty specifying measurable reductions of air pollution.[36] The protocol binds the concerned countries to reduce their sulphur emissions by at least 30 per cent from 1980 levels as soon as possible and by 1993 at the latest. While the protocol has been ratified by most of the developed market economies, some of the largest sulphur emitters have not joined yet, including Poland, the United Kingdom and the United States. A similar protocol to limit nitrogen oxide emissions is being negotiated. This draft protocol calls for a freeze in $NO_x$ emissions at 1987 levels by 1994.[32]

A variety of approaches and technologies aimed at the reduction of atmospheric pollution are currently available. Selection of fuels low in sulphur and nitrogen content, combustion modification using limestone injection multi-stage burners (LIMB), fluidized bed combustion (FBC) and post combustion emission controls using scrubbers are all effective approaches, providing over 50 to 90 per cent $SO_2$ removal capacity in coal-fired electric power plants.

For mobile sources, pollution control measures and technologies are mainly aimed at reducing emissions of nitrogen oxides. One of the most effective of these technologies is the catalytic converter, a sophisticated control system used mostly in new automobiles burning unleaded gasoline. Improved car engines aimed at increasing fuel efficiency in themselves reduce pollutant emissions. Other approaches that are equally important in controlling pollutants from vehicles are not necessarily technological. Transport regulation, car pooling, limitation of private automobile use and use of gasoline low in sulphur and nitrogen content, all serve the purpose of reducing vehicle pollution.

Despite the availability of these control technologies, the acid rain problem has not been solved principally for two reasons. First, most of these technologies have been developed only recently and are not yet widely used. Secondly, the relative cost of emission control technologies is quite high. As of 1982, estimated emission control costs for large

33 Roger Thompson, "Acid rain: Canada's push for U.S. action", *Editorial Research Reports*, vol. 1 (1986).
34 Gregory Wetstone, "Acid rain: the international perspective", *Environmental Policy and Law*, vol. 11, No. 1/2 (October 1983).
35 Roy Gould, "Energy and acid rain", *Annual Review of Energy*, vol. 9 (1984).
36 "UN/ECE, 30% protocol in force", *Environmental Policy and Law*, vol. 17, No.5 (October 1987).

electric power plants in OECD Countries were about 10 to 20 per cent of the total cost of electricity generated by the plants.[37]

Perhaps a more serious problem is the fact that those who cause acid rain are unwilling to bear the costs since the victims are often far away in other areas or countries. Nevertheless, the ECE protocol and recent consultations between Canada and the United States indicate significant progress in international co-operation. They might be effective in accelerating preventive measures and in intensifying co-operation in other regions or countries as well.

## Outlook to the year 2000 and conclusions

Available forecasts of energy consumption and production to the year 2000 and beyond suggest a continuation of the patterns of the second half of the 1980s. Overall energy consumption is expected to increase by 2 to 3 per cent per annum on the assumption that economic growth rates will proceed in a similar range to the year 2000.

World energy consumption is expected to reach a level of 176 million barrels of oil equivalent per day (mboe/d) in the year 2000 as compared to 136 mboe/d in 1986, that is, to increase by about 30 per cent. Fossil fuels will continue to dominate the world energy picture although their share will diminish somewhat, declining from 85 to 78 per cent of world commercial energy consumption.

The growth rates of nuclear, hydro and geothermal electricity, as well as other renewable energy sources, will be considerably higher than that of fossil fuels. By the year 2000 their contribution to the world energy economy is expected to double to a level of 48 mboe/d.

This scenario assumes modest rates of economic growth, and also continued efforts and further progress in energy conservation and efficiency, especially in the developed market economies. It does not assume any drastic measures at either the national or the international level to constrain energy consumption in order to meet growing environmental concerns.

At the global level such a pattern of energy consumption by the year 2000 and beyond will not be constrained by availability of supplies. The magnitude of known energy reserves and the application of modern technologies in exploration and development and improving recovery factors will make for ample supplies. Nevertheless, at the national and regional levels, energy imbalances will be further accentuated, particularly with regard to oil.

A growing oil imbalance will be especially significant in the developed market economies, and production is even expected to decrease in the United States of America. Oil import requirements of these countries will increase to 34 million barrels per day in the year 2000 from 17 million barrels per day in 1986.

Because of high investment requirements in frontier areas and depletion of major fields in the Union of Soviet Socialist Republics there is also a possibility of an oil deficit in the centrally planned economies of Eastern Europe, where the current level of net exports of 2 million barrels per day will turn to an equivalent import requirement unless conservation and substitution measures in favour of natural gas and other energy sources are stepped up.

In view of the reliance on oil as the premier commercial energy source in most of the energy-deficient developing countries, the drastic reduction in investments by transnational oil corporations in exploration and development in these countries already experienced during the 1980s, the lack of alternative sources such as coal and the limited prospects of nuclear power and the difficulties of financing exploitation of their hydropower potential, their oil import requirements will also increase, especially if their economic growth revives.

A significant expansion of nuclear power, as well as a substantial increase of coal, mainly for electricity generation, hydropower and other energy sources, is postulated in this global energy scenario for the year 2000. This may not come about: environmental and safety concerns have already led to a slow-down of plans and, in a few countries, to the shutdown of nuclear power plants and the cancellation of new orders.

The increasing oil import requirements in the developed market economies and the energy-deficient developing countries can be met only from the reserves of the developing countries which are concentrated in the member countries of OPEC, particularly in the Middle East.

Developments in the international oil market during the first half of the 1980s, with lower demand for oil exports from the member countries of OPEC and drastic reductions in prices and oil revenues, have resulted in a drop of production capacities in those countries to less than 30 million barrels a day in 1988 from 39 million barrels a day in 1979.[38] The proved oil reserves in these countries could sustain much higher production capacities than even those of 1979, but this would require considerable investments. Whether or not such investments are made will be determined by the member countries themselves on the basis of their perceptions of future developments in the oil markets. Such developments will also be influenced by the plans and policies of the consuming countries, mainly the developed market economies.

While monitoring new developments, identifying patterns of change and assessing emerging trends from a global per-

---

37 Ian Torrens, "What goes up must come down: the acid rain problem", *OECD Observer,* No. 129 (July 1984).

38 Stanley Tucker, "The impact of lower oil prices", *Petroleum Economist* (March 1989).

spective remain critical, measures to face current and potential problems will in many instances require action at the multilateral level.

International co-operation and dialogue between oil exporters and importers will be necessary in order to avoid excessive volatility in energy prices and the consequent misallocation of energy investments. Suggestions for such a dialogue have been made by member countries of OPEC: the Minister of Petroleum and Mineral Resources of Saudi Arabia has stated that "co-operation and market management is sometimes essential if the anarchy of blind and powerful market forces is to be disciplined in the interests of both producers and consumers".[16]

Environmental concerns have added to suggestions for the initiation of such a dialogue. The Prime Minister of Norway declared last January:

> "To redirect world energy trends in the absence of direct market pressures is an unprecedented challenge ... Energy uses and climate are closely interrelated. Energy prices are at the core of the greenhouse problem as well. It is now high time that we all recognize the tight links between energy, economy and the environment ... Improved international dialogue in the energy field is vital. The World Commission on Environment and Development recommends that new mechanisms for promoting dialogue between producers and consumers be explored."[39]

---

39 Gro Harlem Brundtland, Prime Minister of Norway, "The vital issues of the 1990s", statement before the Davos Conference, 26 January 1989.

# Chapter VI

## ECONOMIC REFORM AND INTEGRATION OF CENTRALLY PLANNED ECONOMIES

In January 1989, the Council for Mutual Economic Assistance (CMEA) celebrated its fortieth anniversary at an unusual juncture in the history of its member countries. Previous national reform experience during most of the post-war period has had only a marginal impact on regional integration, on the organization and *modus operandi* of CMEA, and on the way in which CMEA policy intentions are translated into concerted action that enhances the economic performance of the component economies. In contrast, the reforms under way since about 1985 in the majority of CMEA member countries appear to exert significant pressure for change in regional integration policies and institutions and policy instruments.

Since the late 1970s, regional co-operation has suffered from economic malaise, due in part to the unanticipated external shocks and adjustment needs of a number of member countries, particularly in Eastern Europe. Long-term co-operation policies agreed upon in the second half of the 1970s were thus rendered obsolete. Furthermore, adjustment policies were formulated by each member country in isolation, with the common integration framework providing at best marginal support. The organization remained largely passive in the face of the emergencies of its members. Calls for regrouping CMEA to provide better support for growth were issued on a number of occasions. They were even placed at the top of the agenda of several high-level meetings, but no breakthrough was reached until late 1986.

CMEA policy makers have now decided to work resolutely for the creation of a unified common market of their own. This momentous decision was reached in late 1986 at the second, so-called working, CMEA economic summit of the 1980s (Moscow, 10 and 11 November 1986) and has since produced a number of changes that in time may lead to a sharp mutation in integration. This applies also to the less developed non-European CMEA member countries, which have traditionally remained on the periphery of integration policies but are now being co-opted into CMEA integration. Important decisions are expected to be endorsed at the next economic summit—the third of the decade—to be convened at Prague in mid-1989.

This chapter provides a perspective on the present phase of integration policies in the CMEA framework. It describes the evolution of CMEA as an organization and of the integration policies pursued during the past four decades; identifies the major determinants of the current transformation of CMEA; reviews the emergence of a general movement in favour of national economic reforms; provides details of the policy debate on CMEA reform until the economic summit in November 1986, summarizing the decisions reached there and at subsequent high-level meetings; touches on the implications for third countries; describes briefly the special features of the agreement between CMEA and the European Economic Community; and concludes by noting what is likely to be tabled for action under the heading "common market" at the summit in mid-1989 and beyond.

### Evolution of CMEA

The ties among the countries of Eastern Europe and the Soviet Union go back to the mid-1940s and the political, military and economic situation in the wake of the Second World War. The geopolitical situation then emerging was solidified by the Cold War, which contributed to moulding the region into a close alliance. However, CMEA trade in the post-war period was built on weak precedents. During the inter-war period, these economies found their external markets primarily in Western Europe; trade among them was minor, and with the Union of Soviet Socialist Republics almost negligible. The share of the USSR in Eastern Europe's trade in 1938, for example, was less than 2 per cent.

The decision to set up CMEA[1] in early 1949 is often seen as a retaliatory response to the Marshall Plan and the Western trade embargo, inspired by United States commercial and foreign policies that crystallized during the period 1947-1948, rather than as a momentous agreement with far-reaching implications. The second half of the 1940s was a very turbulent period in international relations, largely due to the basic incompatibility of the political and ideological objectives of global economic and political organization in East and West. Although by the late 1940s the prospect of a continental or Eastern European subregional economic co-operation plan had faded, this did not mean that the economic, organizational and other problems stemming in part from the tensions and the economic disarray in Europe that such plans were intended to tackle had been eliminated.

The evidence suggests that the Council's original objectives and agreed instruments of economic co-operation were far more ambitious, comprehensive, challenging and promising than now generally recalled. There is tentative evidence to the effect that the Council was meant to promote the creation of a strong economic bloc. But this was evidently only one subset of the motives behind the founding of a regional organization for the fostering of economic co-operation among the countries of Eastern Europe and the Soviet Union. Other objectives included countering the economic, political and strategic ramifications of the Marshall Plan; closing the involved debates about subregional federations, confederations or unions in post-war Eastern Europe; creating an economic arm of the Communist Information Bureau

1 This decision was taken by Bulgaria, Czechoslovakia, Hungary, Poland, Romania and the USSR at a conference held in Moscow from 5 to 8 January 1949. Albania joined in February 1949 and the German Democratic Republic in late 1950. The membership remained unchanged until 1961 when Albania became inactive. Mongolia was admitted in 1962.

(Cominform) in support of the ideological and political struggle against the West and dissension in Yugoslavia which had led to its expulsion from Cominform in mid-1948; and providing an effective institutional foundation for tight regional relations in the economic domain, in addition to already existing ideological and political links.

Far-reaching economic interdependence was to be fostered by a socialist industrialization strategy patterned after the inter-war experience of the USSR. It was clear, however, that development policies would depend on institutional links for trade and general economic co-operation within the region. Particularly relevant was the search for ways and means of plan co-ordination and trade and payments instruments tailored to the needs of economic interaction among planned economies, an issue that actively preoccupied the Council organs set up in 1949 until at least mid-1950. The objective was regional economic integration.[2] The process of dovetailing national economic policies would not, however, proceed through market interaction. Initially, key members of the Council aimed at a joint economic policy (including trade, investment and production co-ordination) to correct the growing obstacles to interregional trade and improve indigenous conditions for steady growth, but these efforts foundered.

Under the impact of the deteriorating political and military situation in the mid-1950s and the lingering struggles over effective political control in most of the CMEA countries, which by mid-1950 had firmly reverted to Communist Parties, the integration blueprint was abandoned and replaced by national development strategies. These were interlinked through bilateral co-operation with the USSR as anchor, and by national economic policies formulated under the direct supervision of the USSR. There was an interlink with the Soviet Union through the Council's organs as well. The co-operative efforts among the Eastern European members of CMEA were mainly driven by the perceived need to foster rapid industrialization in each country in isolation rather than by a search for a comprehensive regional development programme, which might have enabled member countries to overcome isolationism and the economic retardation in various regions.

It is paradoxical that the Council did not engage itself in practical economic measures for the development of the region as a whole. But this was apparently not due to shortcomings in the Council itself. In view of the small size of individual national markets and the inadequate domestic reserves of many fuels and industrial raw materials of Eastern European countries, regional co-operation imposed itself but was not pursued as a regional development programme. Rather than seeking multilateral co-operation within a preferential zone, member countries retrenched to a network of bilateral trade and payments agreements anchored to the Soviet economy. This had profound implications for domestic economic policies and narrowly restricted the Council's role. The Council was not revived until the second half of the 1950s, well after it had become clear that the cost of national autarky was too high, but by then it had become much more difficult to formulate a comprehensive, purposeful regional economic policy.

### Membership in the Council

CMEA comprises countries from Africa, Asia, Europe and Latin America. The full members are six Eastern European countries (Bulgaria, Czechoslovakia, the German Democratic Republic, Hungary, Poland and Romania), all of which, except the German Democratic Republic, are founder members; the Soviet Union, which is also a founder; Albania since 1949, though inactive since 1961; Cuba since 1972; Mongolia since 1962; and Viet Nam since 1978.

In addition to full membership, the Council has three types of association. They may be described as associate, co-operant and observer status, though the second designation is an informal one. Associate membership applies only to Yugoslavia. It is based on a special agreement with the Council by which the associate member pledges to participate fully in some of the Council's activities. This was found to be an acceptable way of bringing Yugoslavia, which had been an observer, into the CMEA fold without jeopardizing the country's position as a non-aligned, yet socialist country.

Co-operant status at present applies to Afghanistan, Angola, Democratic Yemen, Ethiopia, Finland, Iraq, Mexico, Mozambique and Nicaragua. It issues from an agreement between the co-operant and the Council, which may envisage chiefly the promotion of regular commerce, but is probably more significant in fostering technical assistance and in facilitating the reciprocal flow of pertinent economic information.

Observer status has been reserved for planned economies that are not CMEA members, developing countries and, on occasion, international economic organizations. Observers take part in meetings, usually of the Council Session; this status is generally granted for individual meetings.

This chapter focuses on the full members of the Council. In some cases, it will be helpful to distinguish between European and other CMEA members because for most of the post-war period the critical concern of socialist economic integration has involved only the European membership. This is not to deny the importance of CMEA for other participants. The presence of developing countries in CMEA permits the European planned economies to articulate an internationalist commitment and outlook. The economic benefits for the less developed countries derive from capital flows, trade price concessions and preferential access to markets. Though these benefits should not be overlooked, they are not a core concern of this chapter.

### Construction and evolution of the planning règime

When members tried to revive the Council in the second half of the 1950s, they found it difficult to formulate a truly

2 For details, see Sándor Ausch, *Theory and Practice of CMEA Co-operation* (Budapest, Akadémiai Kiadó, 1972), p. 44, and Nikolai V. Faddeev, *Sovet ekonomicheskoy vzaimopomoshchi - XXV let*, 3rd ed. (Moscow, Ekonomika, 1974), pp. 130-131.

regional economic policy. The reason was simple. By that time they had set up fully planned economies, in which domestic and external activities were sharply separated. Strict central planning of domestic economic activities was based largely on physical indicators with only minimal regard for static or dynamic comparative advantages. The typical development strategy had as its prime objective the elaboration of a substantially autarkic economic complex, in the hope of attaining a diversified industrialized economy that could function independently of foreign fluctuations and disturbances. Especially important was the state monopoly of foreign trade and payments, designed expressly to neutralize economic and other influences from abroad, whether positive or disruptive.

The disjunction of the domestic economy from external influences may have been inspired by the belief that an ambitious growth path could be trodden without taking into account all relevant internal and external market conditions. But for economies too small to be autarkic, severing domestic decision-making from world market criteria had serious consequences.

In the traditional planned economy, the level and composition of trade are intermeshed with the overall system of material balances. The question of whether to import or to produce domestically is usually resolved by considering the domestic availability of inputs and the need to pay for imports. Central planners have only a marginal interest in the potential benefits of export-led growth or in minimizing the real economic cost of import substitution. The technique of material balances is useful in ensuring that physical demand and supply in the economy even out, but it is not conducive to the exploitation of trade opportunities.

Trade is by definition a sector that eludes the control of one planning centre. Furthermore, it cannot be managed solely through quantitative instruments of assignment and control. To gain greater stability in domestic economic activity, the traditional planned economy tries to forecast and plan trade flows. But activities and fluctuations abroad are not easily predictable. Born out of necessity in the immediate post-war period, detailed bilateral trade and payments agreements among the planned economies—and, where possible, with market economies too—at stable, if artificial, prices suited the administrative planning system well. It also facilitated the implementation of the political aspirations regarding the promotion of regional cohesion.

Traditional planning thus insulates domestic processes from direct interaction with agents abroad. Actual trade events can have an impact on the domestic economy, but not through prices since domestic prices are set autonomously. The nominal gains and losses from trade are absorbed by fiscal means. But there are, of course, macro-economic repercussions.[3] A deviation from planned import costs and export revenues, if accommodated, affects the disposable budget, and ultimately consumer income, as well as the foreign exchange situation. Planners attempt to neutralize the impact of this perturbation by sterilizing trade results. Alternatively, they offset trade gains or losses through the variation of other budgetary expenditures and adjust the next plan accordingly. But this indirect influence does not play an overriding role in domestic economic decision-making.

A crucial implication of this model is that macro-economic decision makers are unaware of, or at least spottily informed about, the real economic cost of import-substitution policies. The micro-economic equivalent of this is that economic agents do not know the true scarcity costs in world markets. From a planner's point of view, this does not matter as long as autarky reigns supreme. But once a more active trade policy is given priority in the policy agenda, this trade model becomes a formidable obstacle.

As the development record of the past 40 years suggests, the Eastern European industrialization strategy has been suitable for radically restructuring relatively backward societies into moderately sophisticated economies, although at high cost. A tightly centralized organization may have been necessary for fast transformation of economic structures. The turbulence of the times, inexperienced management and a largely unskilled labour force may have favoured the adopted course of industrialization under strictly centralized control. However, once these conditions began to fade away as a result of social, economic and political change, the justification for maintaining the technical features of planning became less and less persuasive. Most of the planned economies arrived at this conclusion in the mid-1950s and were prepared to remedy their perceived deficiencies through broad-based economic reforms by the first half of the 1960s.

The blueprints for reform of the 1960s can be divided into three groups according to their impact on the organization of the economy, the use of indirect co-ordination instruments and the shifts in trade policies.[4] The first wave of economic reforms in the 1960s sought to endorse trade as a way of supporting domestic social and economic growth. Trade operations were to be better co-ordinated with domestic decision-making. The attention devoted to trade and foreign economic co-operation is underscored by the fact that, since the early 1970s, the gradual change in the organization of firms and in the methods of planning and control have continued in the foreign trade sector, in marked contrast to the reform measures affecting most other sectors of the economy which retrogressed and languished until the mid-1980s.

By the 1960s, the previous sharp separation of the trade sector from producers and users became increasingly more difficult to justify in view of the necessity in most countries, particularly in Eastern Europe, to expand exports of manufactured products. With the greater dependence on trade, the nearly complete disjunction between trade and production also became more and more wasteful. In consequence, there

3 For a useful elaboration, see Thomas A. Wolf, *Foreign Trade in the Centrally Planned Economy* (Chur, Switzerland, Harwood Academic Publishers, 1988), pp. 38-47.

4 For references to individual reforms and a summary of the reform experience of Eastern Europe, see *World Economic Survey 1988* (United Nations publication, Sales No. E.88.II.C.1), pp. 93-120.

Figure VI.1. Formal structure of CMEA

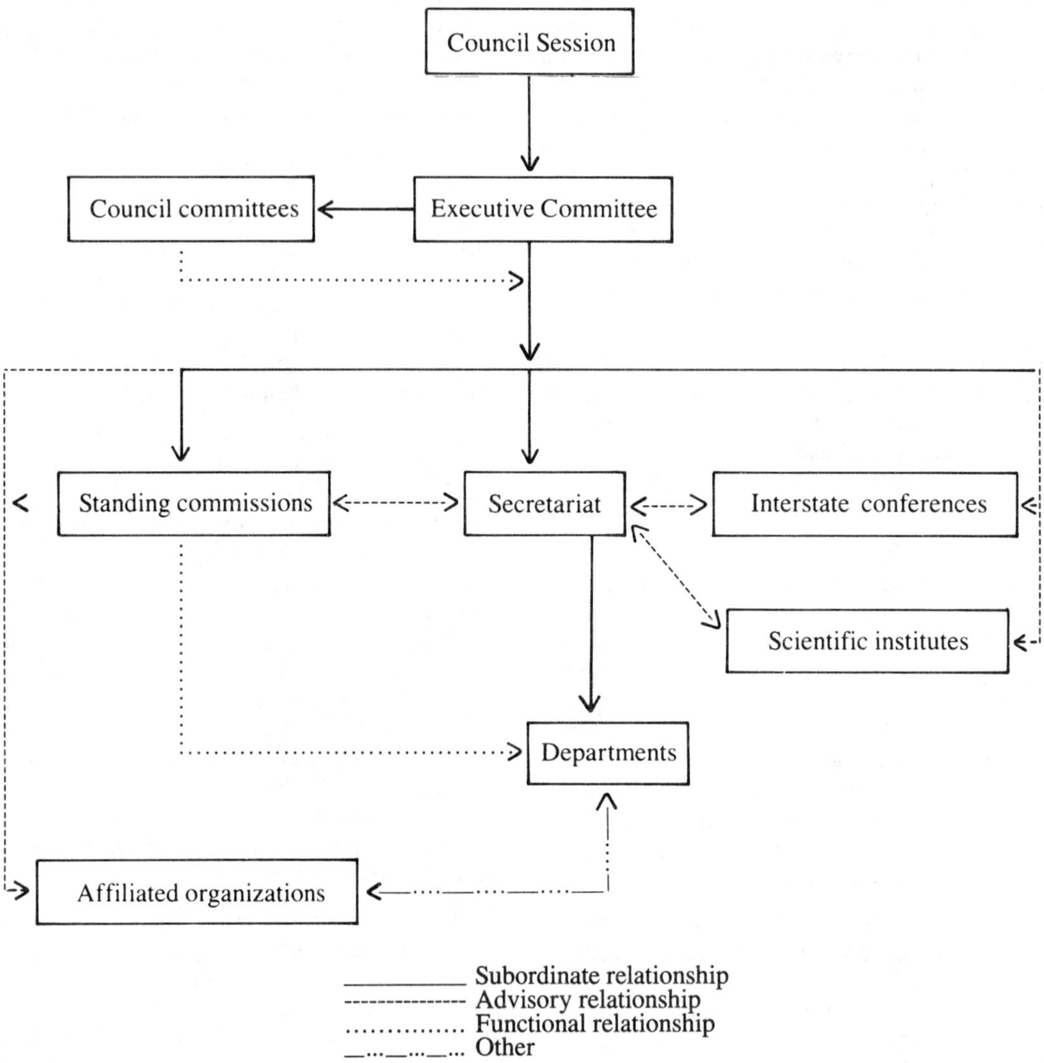


was a general trend toward the reinforcement of the organizational links between trade and production, and the strengthening of the role of trade prices both in domestic price reforms and, in some countries, in actual price formation.

The issues emanating from concerns about how to link trade and domestic decision making and foster regional economic integration have been high on the policy agenda since the late 1950's. The external adjustment efforts of the 1980s and the new willingness of policy makers to entertain far-reaching changes in organization and macro- and micro-economic policies have sharpened the attention to trade and regional co-operation. Hence the need to look at the ongoing reform attempts and the repercussions of organizational and policy reforms within the context of the Council.

### Organizational structure of the Council

CMEA obtained its official charter in 1959. Prior to that there may have been informal understandings to guide the work of the Bureau and its secretariat, which were put in place in 1949 but soon left to languish. The Council Session did not meet between November 1950 and March 1954; CMEA was essentially a weak intergovernmental consultative organ.

According to the charter, which has been revised and amended several times since it was first endorsed in 1959, the important CMEA organs are the Council Session, the Executive Committee and its subcommittees, the standing or permanent commissions and the Secretariat. In addition, the official tiers of the Council comprise formal and informal conferences, institutes and a large number of affiliated institutions that maintain tenuous links with the Council. In connection with the reform of CMEA institutions and policies currently under way, a sharp shift in the composition of and among these layers has occurred. In this section, the organizational structure of the Council until late 1987 will be clarified. The various layers are shown in figure VI.1. The innovations introduced during the period 1988-1989 are taken up in conjunction with the reform agenda discussed below.

The charter makes the Council Session the highest official organ of CMEA. National delegations in Session meetings are usually headed by prime ministers. Between these meetings, CMEA affairs are guided by the Executive Committee, which is composed of permanent representatives, generally deputy prime ministers. Day-to-day affairs are entrusted to the Secretariat. However, the pivotal problems of CMEA co-operation are in general discussed first in the framework of inter-party relations, and the important decisions are taken up in the CMEA economic summits, which are convened under the official title "Conference of First Secretaries of Communist and Workers' Parties and of the Heads of Government of the CMEA Member Countries". Preparations for summit meetings are guided by the Central Committee Secretaries of each country's Communist Party entrusted with economic affairs. The Secretaries meet as an informal CMEA body.

The range of topics for debate at summits is very wide, and decisions reached have been of seminal importance for the evolution of integration policies. This has been the case particularly in the past few years, which have shown that stagnation or crisis in the operation of intergovernmental organizations, such as CMEA, is not remedied through entrenched procedures and instruments. Extraordinary action is required to reconfirm at the highest political level a firm and unwavering commitment to the enhancement of co-operation.

Day-to-day affairs and the execution of established policies are entrusted to the formal CMEA organs, whose relationship is shown in figure VI.I. This organizational structure is still largely valid, although details have changed since early 1988, as discussed below.

Between Council Sessions, which are usually held once a year, CMEA affairs are guided by the Executive Committee and its subsidiary specialized committees. The Executive Committee is a non-permanent organ convoked at least once a quarter, usually in Moscow. It is composed of high-ranking officials—deputy chairmen of councils of ministers at the very least. Although originally designed to assume the paramount responsibilities of a supranational planning centre, the Executive Committee has largely remained a consultative organ concerned with the broad guidelines of national and regional macro-economic policies and their trade implications. Since 1971, it has been assisted by subsidiary committees, four of which had been established by the end of 1987: committees for planning (1971), scientific-technical co-operation (1971), material-technical supply (1974) and machine-building (1984). These are high-level bodies dealing with important target areas of the co-ordination of overall national plans.

The standing commissions are the true working organs of CMEA. The first were set up in 1956 to replace the *ad hoc* working parties and subdivisions of the Bureau and the Secretariat. Their number and field of authority have fluctuated. Starting with 12 commissions in 1956, their number rose to 23 in 1986-1987. The standing commissions that existed before the current reform movement are listed in table VI.1. Some are sectoral while others deal with general economic issues. Most of them have their headquarters in Moscow.

It is in the standing commissions that concrete proposals on common activities are worked out and detailed documents on the relevant sectors or general economic and organizational problems are distributed. National delegations to the standing commissions are headed by ministers or senior civil servants of the ministries concerned. This has implications for the topics that can be tabled, the deliberations and the eventual follow-up. The commissions meet at least twice a year, usually in Moscow.

The Secretariat in Moscow is the only permanent CMEA organ. The head of the Secretariat is assisted by a number of deputies in the upper echelon. These senior officials oversee a moderately large staff recruited from the various member countries. By late 1987, the CMEA civil service may have comprised about 2,000 persons. The Secretariat is officially responsible for organizing, contributing to and servicing the meetings of other CMEA bodies, particularly the Council Session. It also guides the implementation of recommendations and decisions. It may play a crucial role in charting the course of socialist economic integration by preparing the recommendations and decisions of the other organs and moulding them into a practical format.

Among other official organs, of importance for the gradual development of regional integration are the common enterprises and other international economic organizations, whose number had expanded from just a few in the late 1960s to over 100 by late 1987. They belong to a sprawling network of bilateral and multilateral agencies. The various kinds of organs involved are shown in figure VI.2. Most do not formally belong to the Council. But their contacts with the top levels are intimate and their routine operations are closely monitored by the relevant official Council organs. Some take the form of a common enterprise that produces commodities or essential financial services and are usually put on a self-financing basis (*khozraschet*). Others are entrusted with the co-ordination of production and research, and are normally financed by the central government budget of the participating members.

### Decision-making in the Council

This brief description of the organizational structure of CMEA suggests that, since the early 1970s, CMEA has possessed a diverse organizational infrastructure intended to deal with all the concrete problems involved in co-ordinating the economic development of its members. The main organizational problem is that many of the important Council organs were not constituted to prepare or to take economic decisions *per se*. In this respect, it is symptomatic that organizational and other reforms in member countries up until the second half of the 1980s have by and large failed to affect CMEA. The Council's central role as a clearing house for overseeing and promoting economic integration among members has on the whole remained unchanged since the early 1950s, despite the expansion of its formal structure and the more systematic and up-to-date codification of co-operation principles.

Table VI.1. Standing commissions of CMEA at the end of 1987

| | |
|---|---|
| Agriculture (Sofia, 1956) | Geology (Ulaanbaatar, 1963)[b] |
| Biotechnology (Moscow, 1986) | Light industry (Prague, 1958)[c] |
| Chemical industry | New materials and technology |
| (Berlin (East), 1956)[a] | (Moscow, 1986) |
| Civil aviation (Moscow, 1975) | Non-ferrous metallurgy (Budapest, 1956) |
| Coal industry (Warsaw, 1956) | Peaceful utilization of atomic energy (Moscow, 1960) |
| Construction (Berlin (East), 1958) | Post and telecommunications (Moscow, 1971) |
| Currency and finance (Moscow, 1962) | Public health (Moscow, 1975) |
| Electrical energy (Moscow, 1956) | Radio technology and electronics (Budapest, 1963) |
| Ferrous metallurgy (Moscow, 1956) | Standardization (Berlin (East), 1962) |
| Food industry (Sofia, 1963)[c] | Statistics (Moscow, 1962) |
| Foreign trade (Moscow, 1956) | Transportation (Warsaw, 1958) |
| Gas and oil (Bucharest, 1956) | |

*Note:* The headquarters or main meeting place of the commissions and the year in which they were established are shown in parentheses.

[a] Including the commission for timber and cellulose, which was independent from 1956 to 1958.

[b] Created in 1956, abolished in 1958, and re-created in 1963.

[c] Created in 1958 as the commission for food and light industries; in 1963, a separate commission for food processing was established.

Until late 1986, CMEA decisions typically failed to touch upon the key obstacles inherent in the internal organization of member countries. Similarly, changes contemplated or inaugurated in the participating economies proceeded without repercussions on CMEA organization and modes of behaviour. This was because the constitution of CMEA was weak. Until 1962, CMEA did not have a commonly agreed—and published—policy on how socialist economic co-operation should evolve. The only documents of intent were the vaguely phrased communiqué of January 1949 and the Council's charter ratified in 1960. Until the early 1960s, the goals of the Council were interpreted according to prevailing views on socialist internationalism, national development and mutually beneficial economic co-operation. The scope and content of socialist economic co-operation tended to be defined implicitly as the result of "historical experience".

The Council Sessions of the mid-1950s focused on attaining a higher level of specialization, especially in industries where CMEA members had been pursuing similar growth objectives. Agreements on intra-product and interproduct specialization were signed as early as 1956, but opinion on their implementation and effects is not very favourable. The failure to implement these agreed specialization measures, in part because of seminal transformations in Eastern Europe, provided a major incentive for reinforcing the Council's institutions, adopting a formal charter and issuing the first broad policy document to guide concrete action.

The charter stipulates the purpose of CMEA to be "the planned development of the national economy, the acceleration of economic and technical progress ... the raising of the level of industrialization in the industrially less developed countries, a steady increase in the productivity of labour and

Figure VI.2. CMEA organs

**Interstate economic organizations**

- Financial[a]
- Branch production[b]
- Transport and communication[b,c]
- Scientific-technological[b]

**International economic organizations**

- International economic associations[a,c]
- International economic partnerships[a,c]
- Joint enterprises[a]

**Interstate economic associations[b]**

- Co-ordination centres
- Co-operation commissions
  - Bilateral and multilateral for special questions
  - Commissions for co-operation with non-member countries

**International non-governmental associations[b]**

**International non-governmental organizations[b]**

*Source:* Based on Praskovya A. Tokareva, *Uchrejdenie mejgosudarstvennykh ekonomicheskikh organizatsii stran-chlenov SEV* (Moscow, Nauka, 1976), and Georgy M. Velyaminov, "Mejdunarodnye ekonomicheskie organizatsii sotsialisticheskikh stran" (*Byulletin inostrannoy kommercheskoy informatsii - prilojenie,* No. 1 (1977), pp. 3-37.

a Economic accounting units.

b Budget units.

c Possibly temporary budget units.

a constant improvement in the welfare of the peoples [of member countries]".[5] This general task is then specified to involve fostering a rational use of resources and acceleration of the development of the productive capacities of members. This is to be attained through plan co-ordination, the comprehensive examination of economic and scientific-technical problems, and the creation of common ventures in spheres of interest to members.

Since the early 1960s, the Council has been underpinned with policy documents that aim at facilitating the regional mobility of goods and production factors. Special attention should be devoted to two challenging documents—one on the goals and methods of the international socialist division of labour (ISDL) and the other on socialist economic integration (SEI). These documents are specific about the goals and purposes of CMEA, they set forth the principles and methods of economic collaboration endorsed by members and they provide some guidelines for concrete follow-up. But both documents are essentially statements of intentions to pursue research and negotiations for the purpose of fostering the objectives of ISDL and SEI.

The policy document on ISDL,[6] which was endorsed in 1962, emphasizes each member country's need to map out its development plans according to its own conditions and the effort to promote an optimal allocation of resources within a region-wide horizon. To attain a more efficient regional economy based on true comparative advantages, bilateral and multilateral plan co-ordination should be perfected. The important technical questions of how to assess comparative advantages in the region and to secure maxi-

5 The original version of the charter, with minor amendments introduced in 1962, is reproduced in *Mnogostoronnee ekonomicheskoe sotrudnichestvo sotsialisticheskikh gosudarstv - sbornik dokumentov,* edited by Praskovya A. Tokareva, Mikhail D. Kudryashov and Vasily I. Morozov, eds. (Moscow, Juridicheskaya literatura, 1967), pp. 45-54.

6 The full title is "Basic principles of the international socialist division of labour". The original Russian version is reproduced in *Mnogostoronnee ...*, pp. 23-29.

mum benefit for the region as a whole were not examined, but stated to be in need of clarification and to be settled through deliberations and negotiations. The document also alludes to the strengthening of mutual economic ties through "the creation in the future of the world communist economy ...according to one plan".[7] In accompanying and subsequent statements, this cryptic formulation was interpreted as a signal that ISDL would be the focus of a single socio-economic plan for the CMEA region as a whole, to be drawn up by a regional planning agency under the aegis of the Executive Committee.

Although the document paid lip-service to the national interests of member countries, the call for a common solution of shared problems, not only in trade but in general economic development, was at the forefront of the broad, and at times acrimonious, dispute shortly after the document was endorsed at the CMEA economic summit of June 1962. This debate questioned the very meaning, purpose and methods of socialist internationalism in the economic sphere. Strongly diverging views surfaced about the goals and means of uniform planning and the practical instruments of integration.

As a result of the first wave of economic reforms in the mid-1960s and the new ambitions for East-West economic co-operation, a number of CMEA members pressed the issue of more efficient specialization in the context of the global economy and insisted upon doing so according to more precisely defined economic criteria before entering into specific regional commitments. In the course of the debate about ISDL, however, an effort was made to tackle some of the fundamental problems of economic co-operation among planned economies, such as price formation, exchange rates, multilateralism and the mobility of labour and capital. Attempts were also made to come to grips with the practical obstacles to regional economic co-operation. Particularly noteworthy initiatives were the creation of the transferable rouble as the first international socialist currency and accounting unit as well as the establishment of the first CMEA bank—the International Bank for Economic Co-operation—to effect settlements of payment among CMEA members. This, together with the new economic and political realities of the late 1960s, led to a seminal change in the approach to CMEA integration.

This significant watershed in CMEA relations culminated in proposals on genuine economic integration. The new co-operation strategy was launched in 1969, on the occasion of the twentieth anniversary of CMEA, and crystallized in 1971 in the form of a comprehensive document on economic integration (hereinafter referred to as the Integration Programme).[8] CMEA members in 1971 agreed gradually to eliminate man-made obstacles to the free intra-regional flow of goods, services and, to some extent, production factors. Furthermore, they agreed to reduce impediments due to natural obstacles by purposeful co-ordination of all relevant aspects of economic policy. For this, due allowance needed to be made to reflect specific requirements of individual members, safeguarded by the so-called interestedness principle, first adopted in 1967, which means that each member is entitled to decide whether or not to participate in a particular project.

The Integration Programme stipulates two principal types of instruments of integration. The main one is the co-ordination of national economic plans when they are still in draft form and thus amenable to feedback and modifications in the proposed allocation of resources. Regular bilateral and multilateral consultations were to be held in order to specify preferred areas for co-ordination and joint planning. However, direct economic relations between the ultimate producer and user, as distinct from informal contacts, were not expected to play a key role.

The second type of instruments comprises those which harmonize economic decisions and activities indirectly. They include prices, exchange rates and interest rates. If they are to function properly, the required institutional infrastructure needs to be put in place. These instruments and institutions were expected to underpin integration in the drafting of plans and their implementation. Economic criteria as such, however, were not be allotted an exclusive or overriding role in selecting or formulating broad plans or common projects. Markets should not replace the conscious planning and centrally guided implementation of economic decisions. Socialist economic integration was to be sought in accordance with comparative advantage, but within the framework of common planning. The Integration Programme does not clarify the concrete means by which this would be achieved. Methods to synchronize national economic plans and delineate the scope for co-ordination are left vague, although they are recognized to be in need of further refinement. The Programme sets deadlines for study and resolution of these issues, particularly with a view to improving the financial and monetary aspects of integration. But all this was to be pursued without introducing new forms or institutions of regional co-operation for the duration of the Programme—a period of up to two decades. It was doubtful from the start whether this vague commitment would suffice to elicit the genuine economic integration on which some members had placed high hopes.

Although none of the basic components of a proper integration mechanism could be agreed upon in the Integration Programme, the ensuing search for operational modalities exhibited two features. First, the debate on the principles and methodology of plan co-ordination and joint planning, and on harmonizing monetary and financial co-ordination instruments was vigorous, although it failed to yield acceptable solutions to any of the fundamental issues. Second, in parallel with the examination of principles of socialist economic integration, practical co-operation issues were tackled within the traditional framework of plan co-ordination.

7 *Mnogostoronnee ...*, p. 24.

8 The full title is "Comprehensive programme for the further extension and improvement of co-operation and the development of socialist economic integration by the CMEA member countries". The original version is reproduced in *Mnogostoronnee ekonomicheskoe sotrudnichestvo sotsialisticheskikh gosudarstv - sbornik dokumentov,* 2nd ed., Praskovya A. Tokareva and others, eds. (Moscow, Juridicheskaya literatura, 1972), pp. 29-103.

This shift in emphasis was stimulated in the mid-1970s by world inflation, the global raw materials shortage and the recession in developed market economies, all of which curtailed the list of options available to market-minded planned economies.

During the latter part of the 1970s, integration discussions focused on improving plan co-ordination, especially for detailed projects about which specific specialization or co-operation agreements had been concluded. In this connection, two types of documents are of special consequence. In 1975, CMEA members endorsed the first Concerted Plan of Multilateral Integration Measures. Beginning in 1976, they embarked on the formulation of Long-Term Target Programmes of Economic Co-operation. Five Target Programmes had been endorsed by 1979, by which CMEA members committed themselves to a common development path in selected economic fields for a period of one to two decades.

These programmes were designed to come to grips with aspects of plan co-ordination that CMEA members had long found it difficult to accommodate within the framework for the dovetailing of annual and medium-term economic plans. They included (1) maintaining the balance in energy, fuels and raw materials; (2) region-wide specialization in existing engineering branches through modernization and structural change; (3) the balance in basic food supplies and self-sufficiency in each component economy and the region as a whole; (4) the supply and quality of a wide range of industrial consumer goods; and (5) a fully integrated transportation system.

This was essentially the state of affairs in regional economic integration in CMEA at the time the planned economies were putting the finishing touches to their medium-term development plans for the first half of the 1980s and beyond.

## Economic policies in the 1980s

The economic emergency measures embraced in the first half of the 1980s and reimposed in a different guise in 1986-1988, helped to whittle down external payments constraints by compressing domestic absorption, principally imports from convertible currency partners.[9] In the difficult situation that virtually all European planned economies faced in the medium-term and annual plans of the 1980s, austerity through import compression was achieved at the cost of uneven economic performance throughout the decade, particularly during its first half. Unfavourable domestic and external events put pressure on import demand, and Eastern European policy makers were compelled to compress imports to protect their external accounts. Set-backs in agriculture, transportation bottle-necks and inflexible supplies of fuels, energy and raw materials narrowed the room for policy manoeuvre. Adverse external developments included a sharp terms-of-trade slide for most Eastern European economies, sluggish Western demand for products from the planned economies, the global payments crisis, weak progress on integration and endogenous supply constraints within CMEA, chiefly with regard to raw materials and fuels from the Soviet Union.[10]

Emergency adjustment measures in most planned economies included slashing domestic absorption through steep investment cut-backs, holding back personal consumption, raising exports, and redirecting demand toward domestic substitutes. The volume of convertible currency exports was raised by some countries in 1983-1984, but this faltered in late 1984 and, in most countries, did not recover until 1988, owing largely to buoyant import demand in Western Europe (see chap. III). Although external imbalances were temporarily redressed and tensions in domestic supplier and service sectors eased, growth in Eastern Europe decelerated to the lowest pace of the post-war period and several countries sustained a decrease in per capita income levels in at least one year.

The difficulties encountered in the early 1980s stemmed in part from circumstances beyond the control of CMEA countries. But unforeseen external diversities were not the most central cause of the troubled planning cycle. Many of the growth obstacles emanated from deep-rooted structural problems. Some arose from below plan performance in key sectors, owing to structural and systemic features and others from shocks that narrowed the room for policy manoeuvre. Policy decisions in some CMEA members also had marked repercussions on the environment for economic policies in partner countries. These included the deliberate spurning of indirect co-ordination instruments and institutions in favour of a return to *dirigiste* policies, particularly the failure to rationalize economic structures in line with transformations in real domestic and external growth opportunities, and the culmination of successive delays in moving away from the engrained policies of favouring extensive growth.

The response to the global disturbances was not decisive. Key components of economic policies in most CMEA members were kept in place, in the hope that the worsening external environment would be a passing phenomenon. The delay in responding also stemmed from institutional characteristics, including the arrangements for CMEA trade and payments flows. Thus, the CMEA pricing mechanism eased the transmission of adverse global price developments by averaging fluctuations over a five-year period, which proved to be a two-edged sword since the resilience to external shocks justified, and in some countries encouraged, inertia in designing positive national and regional steps to overcome the slow-growth syndrome of the early 1980s.

The policies of the early 1980s failed to deliver on the socio-political commitment to steady increase in per capita

9 The adjustment efforts of the early 1980s are examined in detail in *World Economic Survey 1986* (United Nations publication, Sales No. E.86.II.C.1), pp. 121-134.

10 That is to say, the volume that the USSR was willing to transact at regular transferable rouble prices within the conventional settlements mechanism typical of CMEA.

incomes, which most planned economies have found difficult to sustain since the late 1970s. There is a need to develop a positive structural adjustment policy. This involves a combination of forward-looking development objectives and institutional as well as behavioural policy measures designed to regain higher growth without giving rise to chronic domestic or external payments imbalances in either transferable rouble or convertible currency relations. Such measures are currently being examined.

A number of policy makers in CMEA appear to advocate that, in the short to medium run, there is no feasible alternative to pursuing CMEA integration as a prime source of domestic growth, at least until these countries succeed in restoring domestic and external balances at a level and structure of economic activity that would allow them to enhance their competitiveness in world markets. On the other hand, economic reform to seek new ways and means of enhancing economic performance has received strong impetus from the *perestroyka* policies adopted in the Soviet Union.

### Towards a new wave of economic reforms

Under the impetus of the economic set-backs of the early 1980s, one CMEA member after another started to search for alternatives. The drift toward economic reform, which has gathered momentum in all CMEA members except Cuba, the German Democratic Republic and Romania, has received an important impetus from the discussion around *perestroyka* in the Soviet Union and the measures introduced there to bolster economic performance by decentralized decision-making and financial autonomy of firms. These measures have affected not only the domestic economy and Soviet society at large, but also the foreign economic activities of Soviet economic entities. Changes in the environment within which Soviet firms take part in foreign economic relations will affect the external behaviour and requirements of that economy profoundly, and other CMEA countries will also change. Four issues have an important bearing on CMEA reforms.

First, radical changes in socialist societies now call for greater emphasis on the quality of economic development rather than on the sheer rise in physical output of goods and services. This implies new priorities, including a lessening of Soviet dependence on export revenues from fuels and raw materials, strengthening the position in markets for manufactures and shifting import priorities with a view to exploiting existing comparative advantages, thereby opening export opportunities for other countries, including developing ones. It also implies a new attitude toward participation in global economic co-operation.

Second, Soviet *perestroyka* affects CMEA both directly and indirectly. Direct effects include the emulation of reform policies, not limited to the economic domain, in other CMEA members. Indirect effects flow from Soviet preferences regarding the reconstruction of CMEA as a regional economic organization as well as shifting priorities with respect to socialist economic integration. These trends have also been reinforced by the slowly emerging changes in the Soviet foreign trading systems and operations.[11] These are bound to elicit responses from Soviet partners who have to come to grips with the new environment of the Soviet economy, given that between 30 and 50 per cent of the trade of CMEA countries is transacted with the Soviet Union.

Third, Soviet perceptions of the key components of predictable and sustainable international economic relations have undergone marked modifications. Perhaps the most noticeable effect is the search for greater involvement in the global economy. One key concern has been how to place the Soviet economy on a faster growth path through the importation of technology and know-how without incurring a substantial external debt in a potentially still volatile East-West political climate. But there is also an apparent desire of the present Soviet Government to assume greater responsibility for world economic affairs, including ensuring stability and growth in the global economy.

Finally, whereas the East-West conflict since the Second World War has been driven predominantly by the rivalry between the Soviet Union and the United States, the Soviet Government is now building a global and pragmatic network of relations with all parts of the world and re-examining its relationship with developing countries.

Foreign trade reform in the Soviet Union has several dimensions. It aims first of all at devolving decision-making to individual firms and enabling them to make economically sound decisions. This requires better links between domestic prices, which themselves are in need of a comprehensive overhaul, and prices in world markets. Third, it is realized that the effective functioning of the foreign trade sector depends on proper exchange rates, a rational allocation of foreign exchange and steady progress towards currency convertibility for current account transactions. Finally, reforms envisage the opening up of domestic markets to foreign capital through joint ventures and the establishment of special economic or free trade zones.

The implementation of these reform intentions on external trade and joint ventures has been slow, as the external and the internal environments for this aspect of the reform are far from conducive to successful partial decentralization. This will remain true as long as wholesale trade with flexible domestic prices and dependable exchange rates is impeded—and thus withheld—from the arena within which firms formulate their external economic decisions. Moreover, inasmuch as about half of Soviet trade is committed in medium-term trade agreements with CMEA partners, two thirds of exports to developed market economies consists of fuels and raw materials, and trade with most developing countries has been severely constrained by the debt overhang, the opportunities for decentralized decision-making in

11 For a rounded view of Soviet reform ambitions, see *World Economic Survey 1988* (United Nations publication, Sales No. E.88.II.C.1), pp. 109-120, and the latest Soviet decree on foreign economic activity in *Pravda* (Moscow), 3 December 1988.

the short run have not been promising. But if domestic conditions change, as is already envisaged at this stage, the scope for foreign trade reform and genuine competition abroad may soon be greater.

In February 1986, at the time of the twenty-seventh Party Congress, it was made clear in the remarks of Mr. Gorbachev that the Soviet Union wished to end the CMEA's "armchair administration" and "endless committee deliberations". Such transformation would encompass not only CMEA as a regional organization, but also the priorities governing intra-CMEA economic relations, the instruments and institutions utilized to advance regional co-operation, and the longer-term strategic development goals coveted by the planned economies.

### Renewal of CMEA

Since the preparations for the June 1984 CMEA economic summit—the first since April 1969—the agitation for enacting profound changes in CMEA and regional integration can be grouped under three main target areas. First, there has been a broad debate about changing the institutional and organizational set-up of CMEA with a view to rationalizing the bureaucracy, streamlining procedures and making the deliberative organs more effective. Transforming CMEA into an effective regional organ that contributes to the enhancement of economic integration ranks highly on the policy agenda of the Soviet Union and several other key CMEA partners. Second, the ultimate purposes of CMEA integration and the means to pursue it have been slated as topics for re-examination. Finally, the institutional framework and the integration mechanism have become the focus of probing inquiries.

The key issues involved have been debated in the highest policy-making organs, including two recent CMEA economic summits (June 1984 and November 1986), most Council Sessions since 1983 and numerous meetings of the Central Committee Secretaries. Though consensus is only slowly emerging, some important decisions have been taken and, to a limited extent, already implemented. A critical layer of issues continues to form part and parcel of the ongoing policy agenda for debate.

Disclosures about intra-mural discussions have become noticeably more interesting since mid-1987 and the important "extraordinary" Council Session of 13 and 14 October 1987 in Moscow. This revealed *ex post* the seminal contribution of the November 1986 "working" summit, which had earlier appeared as a failed attempt at polarizing the movement towards CMEA reorganization and integration reform. It was clear at the time that the failure to move ahead quickly and decisively with the December 1985 guideline for policy action (hereinafter referred to as the Scientific-technological Programme[12] had led to new initiatives, but the formal debate on the future of CMEA remained confidential; few features were disclosed until mid-1987.

Before proceeding to the November 1986 summit and the October 1987 extraordinary Council Session,[13] a brief comment on the Scientific-technological Programme is in order. At its roots was the disappointing economic performance of the early 1980s and the lack of progress on CMEA economic integration. This had been the theme of the 1984 CMEA economic summit, at which it was resolved that CMEA members should work out a programme to invigorate technological progress. Some action was taken, including the identification of the so-called "head" or "lead" organizations (*golovnaya organizatsia*), which were placed in charge of 93 bundles of co-operation topics, embodying hundreds of projects and thousands of themes, coming under the provisions of the five areas identified in the Scientific-technological Programme for priority advancement through common efforts.

As regards the signing of the all-important bilateral implementation agreements concerning these measures, 1986 proved unfruitful. Equally disappointing was the overall economic performance, which lagged markedly behind the targets of the new five-year socio-economic plans. The difficulties were in inter-firm relations, common capital formation in the CMEA, the problems of dovetailing the Scientific-technological Programme with the already endorsed and harmonized five-year plans for 1986-1990 and the myriad problems of reconciling decentralized decision-making with central planning.

These inauspicious circumstances were behind the sudden convening of another economic summit only two and a half years after the seminal one of 1984 and just days after the long-delayed annual Session, the forty-second, of the Council. Reports on the deliberations at the time were exceedingly brief. The communiqué[14] of the working summit mentioned that the leaders of CMEA members had concerned themselves with the "cardinal problems of development and improvement of co-operation" in CMEA. They had considered "new, much more progressive forms of economic and scientific-technological co-operation in the interest of accelerating" socio-economic progress. This cursory information seemed to signal that the new summit had attempted to tackle the obstacles to effective integration, but that the results had been meagre. However, the ambiguity was removed when the forty-third extraordinary Council Session was finally convened in Moscow in October 1987, after several postponements. From that meeting it transpired that in

12 The full title is "Comprehensive programme to promote scientific and technological progress of the member countries of the Council for Mutual Economic Assistance up to the year 2000". It was published in all the main Communist Party papers of 19 December 1985.

13 It was identified as extraordinary because of the admittedly extraordinary agenda and the perhaps still tentative decisions made there even though the Session was a regularly scheduled one.

14 See *Izvestia* (Moscow), 13 November 1986, p. 1.

the course of the year, and perhaps even in 1986, vigorous discussions on the reorganization of CMEA and the policies and instruments of economic integration had been taking place. Their importance can best be gauged by referring to the key achievements reported in connection with the forty-third Session.

That seminal Council Session was both a revelation and a disappointment. It was disappointing because it failed to resolve a number of critical problems related to socialist economic integration that had been on the agenda for years. The debates were none the less quite informative. First of all, they confirmed that the November 1986 summit, perhaps with hindsight, had been very critical of CMEA policies. Furthermore, the Session issued a number of tentative recommendations that are bound to exert a major influence on the future of CMEA co-operation in five major areas.

### CMEA organization

The Session agreed to streamline the organizational structure of CMEA, abolishing organs that had not performed well over the years, consolidating overlapping units, cutting back staff and gearing the work of the organization less to day-to-day planning of resource allocation than to charting the medium-term and long-term strategic direction of structural change. The aim of separating the objectives and instruments of central planning for structural change from day-to-day economic decision-making at both the micro- and macro-economic levels in member countries evidently parallels the CMEA reform intention. Some reforms were introduced in early 1988.

As for official CMEA organs, some sources claim that 19 of the 36 official CMEA organs in place in October 1987 were abolished, amalgamated, transformed into committees of the Executive Committee or superseded by newly created ones, and that as of early 1988, 24 official organs remained.[15]

The 19 units were abolished or partly absorbed by existing institutions and six new ones were set up in early 1988. Three new committees of the Executive Committee were created and one (on material-technical supply) was abolished, so that the number of subcommittees of the Executive Committee was expanded to six in early 1988. The number of standing commissions was severely curtailed. Of the 23 existing at the end of 1987, only 12 were kept intact, two were merged and two new ones were added, so that the structure that existed before the end of 1987 was changed even more dramatically.[16] By early 1988, there were in all only 15 standing commissions. Finally, one of the conferences was transformed into a new standing commission (on legal affairs) and five others were abolished altogether, so that only one conference (water administration and shipping) remained. The three institutes were apparently not affected.

A sizeable portion, roughly 600 to 700 persons,[17] of the international civil service of CMEA was slated to be redeployed to the home civil services. How precisely this would be accomplished, and when, has remained unclear, however. Though staff cuts may have been enacted in early 1988, concrete evidence is lacking.[18] These changes were apparently to be one component of a much more sweeping, still ongoing, reform of the organization and personnel of CMEA.

### Role of the developing planned economies in integration

There was widespread, but not unanimous, agreement in Moscow to rechart assistance policies to the developing country members of CMEA (Cuba, Mongolia and Viet Nam). These non-European countries agreed with their European partners that past economic and technical development assistance efforts extended by the European CMEA members had not been as effective as they could have been. Disenchantment was evident for both recipient and donor. The donor countries promised to elaborate a comprehensive and consistent multilateral approach to assistance for the less developed partners. This was to be enshrined in a medium-term to long-term co-ordinated programme for economic assistance, in a coherent fashion, for the three non-European CMEA members. It would then become an integral component of the new CMEA integration strategy discussed below.

### A new integration strategy

In a similar vein, it was agreed virtually unanimously to work out a new integration strategy for the period 1991-2005. Because it would be based on a new concept of the international socialist division of labour, the new document would at least move beyond previous plans and programmes for CMEA co-operation. Efforts to set forth such a new integration programme have been on the table since the earliest calls for a top-level CMEA economic summit in the early 1980s. Nothing was proposed until late 1986, when it was deemed useful to take a fresh look at integration objectives, policies, instruments and basic institutional supports of regional economic co-operation. These appear to be jelling around the programme tentatively entitled "Collective con-

15 See, in particular, Igor Ikonnikov, "Sovershenstvovanie struktury SEV", *Ekonomicheskoe sotrudnichestvo stren-chlenov SEV* (Moscow), No. 2 (1988), pp. 20-21. These data, however, are difficult to reconcile with the statutory official CMEA organs reported as of late 1987. CMEA was then made up of 40 official organs (the Session, the Executive Committee and four committees, 23 standing commissions, the Secretariat, seven conferences and three institutes). If so, as of the first half of 1988, 28 rather than the reported 24 organs must have remained in place.

16 Ikonnikov (*loc. cit.*, p. 21) includes among these organs one commission for co-operation with developing countries, but this has never been reported among the CMEA standing commissions or other official organs.

17 The most up-to-date information from the forty-fourth Council Session at Prague in July 1988 indicates that the staffing table of the Secretariat was to be reduced by 31.7 per cent of the mandated contingent of late 1987. Details appear in *Hospodárské Noviny* (Prague), No. 23 (1988), p. 11.

18 See Yury S. Shiryaev, "SEV: sovremennaya strategia ekonomicheskogo i nauchno-tekhnicheskogo sotrudnichestva", *Izvestia akademii nauk - seria ekonomicheskaya* (Moscow), No. 1 (1988), pp. 7-8.

cept of the international socialist division of labour for the years 1991-2005" (hereinafter referred to as the Collective Concept).

The Collective Concept should ensure the "transition to a qualitatively new level of co-operation" in the years ahead.[19] In addition to reiterating old formulas for CMEA relations and strengthening the role of central planning in laying down structural guidelines for medium-term to long-term development, the new programme was intended to foster economic efficiency and buttress the role of economic analysis in the various forms of co-operation. It would aim at endorsing greater use of commodity and financial relations in CMEA affairs. Furthermore, it would endeavour to encompass more fully and actively all economic organizations in regional economic co-operation. All of these objectives were to be related to transparent criteria of economic efficiency.

### The integration mechanism

Directly related to the above programme are decisions that revolve around the integration mechanism to be elaborated by CMEA countries in support of the ongoing reform process in key member economies. Gaining concurrence on these matters at the forty-third Council Session was particularly difficult. Although there was broad agreement on the need to revise key elements of central planning as the traditional form of regional economic co-operation and to overhaul monetary and financial co-operation in a significant way, members were divided on critical economic issues. These included the introduction of a modified form of limited regional convertibility, multilateralism in trade and payments, determination of unified exchange rates, revision of the regional price-formation mechanism, linking of domestic prices with transferable rouble prices and the world market or at least East-West trade prices, and enhancing the role of capital movements within CMEA.

The Session also emphasized the need to reinvigorate the Scientific-technological Programme by improving the economics of and the organizational prerequisites for direct inter-firm relations. Micro-economic entities need to be given room to negotiate over prices and quantities, once central policy makers institute more general economic guidance rules and macro-economic policy instruments, and put in place institutional supports to facilitate genuine micro-economic decision-making. The measures envisaged, particularly by the USSR, include settlement of accounts for selected transactions, implying in fact some highly limited form of intra-group convertibility. The transactions qualifying for this type of settlement would be selected, presumably extending only to the most important forms of exchange within the boundary set for direct enterprise relations. Second, convertibility would be restricted to intra-regional transactions, such as forint against leva, but not leva against dollars. Finally, the envisaged variant of convertibility would be introduced gradually, starting in 1991, over a period of at least 10 years. No settlements of imbalances in convertible currencies would be envisioned in the near term. Agreement in principle on this point was reached by seven members, with the German Democratic Republic, Romania and Viet Nam abstaining.

In the meantime, some member countries have made more rapid progress with this part of the CMEA reform agenda than originally anticipated. In early 1988, Bulgaria, Czechoslovakia, Mongolia, Poland and the Soviet Union concluded bilateral agreements[20] for this type of convertibility—or rather the easing of selected types of intra-group settlement of accounts—to begin in late 1988 or early 1989. There is no evidence that the other members that concurred on moving towards limited convertibility will soon introduce similar measures. It is to be noted that the exchange rates used to clear these transactions at the national level differ, in some cases substantially, from any of the exchange rates already in place.[21]

### Future role of planning and plan co-ordination

Finally, the forty-third Council Session paid lip-service to the need for better co-ordination of economic plans and for support at the regional level for direct enterprise relations. The German Democratic Republic and Romania continued to emphasize the paramount role of plan co-ordination. The former stressed its critical role in fostering co-ordination in science and technology. The latter did so to ensure prompt deliveries of critical fuels and raw materials. There is a marked contrast between these policy stances and the muted role accorded to planning instruments for operational purposes by the commentators of the other CMEA member countries, which essentially focused on the kind of decentralization currently envisaged for their economies, with short-run planning essentially devolving upon the enterprise level, affecting the CMEA organization.

---

19 See *Izvestia* (Moscow), 15 October 1987, p. 6.

20 The Soviet Union has apparently concluded agreements with all the members mentioned. Bulgaria and Czechoslovakia have signed an agreement, and Czechoslovakia is to sign another one soon with Poland (see Jirí Vetrovsky and Vasil Hrinda, "Zúctováni primych vztahuv národních menách CSSR a SSSR - rubl a koruna", *Hospodárské Noviny* (Prague), No. 15 (1988), p. 3 and *Svět Hospodářství* (Prague), No. 88 (1988), p. 2). But there is no evidence of Bulgaria and Czechoslovakia having come to terms with Mongolia on the issue of limited convertibility. Both have recently indicated that agreement with Poland is imminent.

21 In the case of Czechoslovak-Soviet direct inter-firm relations, the partners have settled on a conversion rate of 10.4 koruny per rouble for 1989 and 1990, which implies a sharp depreciation of the koruna as the official commercial exchange rate is 8 koruny per transferable rouble. In relations between Bulgaria and Czechoslovakia, a conversion coefficient of 9.9 koruny per lev has been set for transactions between 1 September 1988 and 31 December 1990. This compares to the official exchange rate of about 6.5 koruny per lev. Finally, in relations between Bulgaria and the Soviet Union, a rate of 1.05 leva per rouble for 1989 and 1990 has been set which compares to 1.3 at the official exchange rate.

The discussions about the Council Session at Moscow made it clear that expectations regarding the follow-up (forty-fourth) Session, first planned for June 1988, were very high. There were to be drafts of key new programmes, including a new concept of long-term integration, and partners had committed themselves to elaborating on details of the new integration mechanism (including prices, direct wholesale trade, exchange rates, convertibility and regional settlements) and its institutions (including the two CMEA banks), and perhaps also on the further streamlining of the structure of the CMEA organization as such. The forty-fourth Session was held at Prague from 5 to 7 July 1988.

It is difficult to extract from the communiqués, reports and analyses what precisely the members agreed upon, as distinct from items on which there was disagreement or a call for further refinement of the proposals. None of the reported drafts examined at Prague have been released either in full or in summary form.[22]

### Socialist economic integration and the developing country members of CMEA

The least controversy arose over the further integration of the non-European members in CMEA. Three separate drafts of comprehensive economic co-operation with Cuba, Mongolia and Viet Nam were apparently endorsed. These drafts are now to be combined to form a document on the technical and economic assistance provided by CMEA to non-European members, which in turn will be an integral part of the Collective Concept.

Judging from the summaries of the speeches of the representatives of Cuba, Mongolia and Viet Nam, the draft programmes have progressed sufficiently to be ratified in the near future. The basic objective is to integrate these countries into mainstream CMEA affairs by involving them in concrete agreements on production co-operation and specialization, scientific and technological co-operation, and generally further commercializing their economic relations with the European members.[23] Some economic and technical assistance to the non-European countries will continue to be provided by the developed country members.

### Restructuring CMEA

In late 1987, members had endorsed broad-based reform of the CMEA organization. The follow-up Council Session at Prague welcomed the changes introduced in early 1988 and called for further restructuring of CMEA organs aiming at a complete change in the organization, as called for at the forty-third Session.[24] Under the new measures the standing commissions for ferrous metallurgy and for non-ferrous metallurgy were combined, as were the standing commissions for civil aviation and transportation;[25] the standing commissions for gas and oil, coal and geology were combined to form a new committee on energy attached to the Executive Committee.[26]

The proposed changes are apparently part and parcel of a sweeping reform, including reform of the specialized or affiliated CMEA organs. It was apparently decided to abolish a great number of specialized organizations, but details are lacking. Deputy Prime Minister Carlos Rafael Rodriguez, the chief delegate from Cuba,[27] referred to the "the reduction of the number of permanent bodies from 107 to 34", but it is unclear to which organs he was referring. If the numbers are correct, most of the organs abolished must be the so-called affiliated, quasi-autonomous international agencies. For the specialized organizations that will be retained, a new role will need to be carved out. There is little doubt that major changes will be carried out if the new system of management in CMEA members and CMEA itself is implemented.

The revamped structure of CMEA as it emerges from the specialized literature[28] consists of the Council Session, the Executive Committee with 7 specialized committees,[29] 11 standing commissions[30] and 2 institutes (for economic problems and standardization). Even the last remaining conference appears to have been abolished at the Prague Session, as does the Management Institute.

### The integration mechanism

The restructured integration mechanism is to form an integral component of the Collective Concept. It should support more intensive integration within the group, particularly among the European members. This requires that the economic tools of management be improved. Although macroeconomic co-ordination will continue to be implemented through national central planning bodies, firms are to play a much more significant role. A particularly critical task is reserved for the functions of the transferable rouble in enhancing direct inter-firm relations based on economic incen-

---

22 Perhaps the most dependable excerpt, though astonishingly bland and general, is "Kolektivní koncepce mezinárodní socialistické delby práce", published as an annex to Svêt Hospodářstvi (Prague), No. 110 (1988).

23 This is a significant shift of emphasis for, as recently as early 1987, CMEA observers had identified these countries as not being quite ready for full co-operation in the context of the Scientific-technological Programme. For details, see Galina A. Abolikhina, Oleg Bakovetsky and Boris I. Medvedev, "Sushchnost i novye formy sotsialisticheskoy integratsii", *Voprosy ekonomiki* (Moscow), No. 1 (1987), pp. 139-140.

24 Report of the speech of Lubomir Strougal, then Prime Minister of Czechoslovakia, in *Rudé Právo (Prague), 6 July 1988, p. 4.*

25 This measure had already been reported "realized" in early 1988 (Ikonnikov, *loc. cit.*, p. 21).

26 *Scînteia* (Bucharest), 8 July 1988, p. 5.

27 As reported in *Rudé Právo* (Prague), 6 July 1988, p. 2.

28 See "RVHP—nová struktura orgánu", *Svêt Hospodářstvi,* No. 106 (1988), p. 4.

29 Agrocomplex, electronization, engineering, foreign economic relations, fuels and raw materials, planning, and scientific-technological co-operation.

30 Chemical industry, currency and finance, electrical and nuclear energy, environment, legal affairs, light industry, metallurgy, post and telecommunications, standardization, statistics, and transportation.

tives and in improving the mechanism by which transferable rouble prices in intra-group trade are formed and negotiated. These and other elements are to be in place in time for the introduction of the next medium-term socio-economic plans in 1991.

As on previous occasions, the Session emphasized the need to reinvigorate the implementation of the Scientific-technological Programme by improving the organizational and economic conditions for direct interaction between firms from different countries. The room for genuine micro-economic negotiations is to extend to the determination of prices and quantities of both inputs and outputs so that enterprise profit will become a key guide to decision-making at the level of firms. The need to stimulate direct firm-to-firm relations was originally endorsed in 1985. The Moscow and Prague Sessions emphatically stressed the need to invest such relations with economic guidelines and institutional supports. In addition, improvements were envisaged in domestic and trade pricing, exchange rates, the credit mechanism of the International Investment Bank, trade and payments multilateralism through the International Bank for Economic Co-operation and other aspects pertaining to the indirect co-ordination of economic decisions.

Though concurrence on the Collective Concept was received from all CMEA members save Romania, no progress was reported on the settlement of accounts for selected goods exchanged through direct enterprise contracts or on the number of supporting countries. But the seven CMEA members that originally endorsed this idea, particularly Bulgaria, Czechoslovakia, Poland and the Soviet Union, report progress on negotiations on pricing and exchange rates in direct enterprise relations. Surprisingly, Hungary does not appear to have been in the vanguard of the movement; Cuba and Mongolia have not been enthusiastic about this new form of socialist integration.

The links of the reformed mechanism to the new integration programme should have been the focus of the forty-fourth Council Session. The Session highlighted the need to have in place economic instruments, institutions and macro-economic policies that can support and foster more intensive forms of economic development and integration.

Whether the transferable rouble as a regional unit of account in settling transactions and determining reciprocal pricing will survive all the suggested modifications in the regional economic machinery is by no means certain. Prime Minister Ryzhkov of the USSR spoke of the Soviet intention "gradually to expand the use of the Soviet rouble within the system of settling accounts within CMEA".[31] But this may have been an oblique reference to the special accounting in selected inter-firm relations examined above, rather than an announcement that rouble convertibility as such should become the backbone of regional multilateralism and transferability. At the June meeting of the Central Committee Secretaries at Budapest, in preparation of the Prague Session, the question of real convertibility was raised by the representatives of Czechoslovakia and Hungary, who argued for the introduction of partial settlement in convertible currency as an incentive for countries to bolster regional exports.[32] The issue was touched upon at Prague by the then Hungarian Prime Minister,[33] but genuine convertibility did not obtain wide support, except perhaps as a distant goal.

An unusual item on the agenda was the creation of socialist multinationals centred on key national firms of the members. This suggestion was apparently first endorsed at the June meeting at Budapest of the Central Committee Secretaries. Prime Minister Ryzhkov reportedly raised it at the Prague Session, saying that the Soviet Union was "prepared to study [it] thoroughly with [interested] partners".[34] One important Soviet commentator on the Session endorsed such transnational organizations as a way of overcoming "bureaucratic obstacles and the formalistic approach to [integration] tasks".[35]

Finally, the forty-fourth Council Session reiterated the need to improve the traditional forms of plan co-ordination and to provide support at the regional level for inter-firm relations. The co-ordination of plans was highlighted again in the statements of the German Democratic Republic and Romania, but it surfaced only marginally in other speeches. A critical role is meant to be played by production specialization, particularly in engineering, but not solely through planning at the intergovernmental level.

### The new integration programme

Perhaps the most important decision of the forty-third Session was the agreement to elaborate a new collective concept of the international socialist division of labour for the years 1991-2005 in time for consideration at the forty-fourth Session. A draft of the Collective Concept was tabled, in spite of the serious objections raised at the June meeting of the Central Committee Secretaries about the blandness of the proposals, the wordiness of the drafts and the lack of commitment to this kind of concept.

The document should contain a new mechanism for streamlining economic policy in the context of regional economic integration. As Prime Minister Ryzhkov affirmed, it should be:

> "a model of co-operation that, while preserving the forms that have proved valid, would be based on the criteria of efficiency, on the ever-increasing role of commodity-money relations and economic instruments and on engaging the countries' economic organizations in all areas of co-operation on a broad scale".[36]

31 *Pravda* (Moscow), 6 July 1988, p. 4.
32 See the reports in *Rudé Právo* (Prague), 3 June 1988, p. 3 and *Magyar Hírlap* (Budapest), 3 June 1988, p. 4.
33 See the summary of a speech by K. Grósz in *Magyar Hírlap* (Budapest), 6 July 1988, p. 4.
34 *Pravda* (Moscow), 6 July 1988, p. 4.
35 See Oleg T. Bogomolov in *Komsomolskaya pravda* (Moscow), 23 July 1988, p. 3.
36 *Pravda* (Moscow), 7 July 1988, p. 4.

## Towards a unified or common CMEA market

The idea of creating a unified market in Eastern Europe is by no means new. It loomed large over the debates at the Council's inception. The establishment of a uniform economic region with free movement of goods and services, including labour and capital, was one of the aims of the more visionary participants in the debates about the founding of CMEA during the period 1949-1950. If a regional planning centre had been entrusted with elaborating a plan for CMEA as a whole, such a plan would have been constructed around a single market concept.

At this stage, the following is new: first, the explicit endorsement of a unified common market as the central focus of CMEA policy was initiated at the forty-third Council Session by the Soviet Union; second, it was wholeheartedly endorsed at the forty-fourth Session by all CMEA members, save Romania, in some contrast to the weak support mustered less than eight months earlier. It might be important that it was adopted on the eve of the celebrations marking the fortieth anniversary of CMEA, in 1989.

A draft of the new integration programme was debated at Prague but it has not yet been published. The Secretary of CMEA made it clear that the programme focuses on accelerating technological progress; intensifying production; broadening production specialization, particularly in engineering sectors; and integrating more fully the non-European CMEA members.[37] His statement also singles out engineering and electronics for accelerated integration efforts and refers to the use of fuels and raw materials, the social repercussions of integration and the need for co-operation in environmental protection.[38] Prime Minister Ryzhkov noted that this common market aims at:

> "ensuring a high degree of uniformity of economic conditions, the relatively free movement of goods, services, manpower and finances among our countries' economic organizations, and the unified macro-economic regulation of economic processes—regulation based on a co-ordinated policy—are a matter for the remote future. But we must keep this prospect in mind even now. For us the unified market is not a fashionable slogan but an important guideline for the development of the integration process".[39]

The communiqué is worded cautiously. It states that the CMEA members, except Romania, reaffirmed an "earlier decision regarding the stepwise establishment of the conditions for the mutual free movement of goods, services and other production factors with the goal of creating eventually a unified market, after the preconditions thereof have been examined".[40] This examination is to take place between now and 1990, when the Executive Committee will prepare recommendations for further improving the mechanism of multilateral co-operation and effective economic integration.

## Renewal in CMEA and external impacts

The reforms contemplated or already under way in the majority of CMEA member countries and at the CMEA level itself raise a number of fundamental issues. One concerns the realism of the economic reforms, the probability that they will be implemented as envisaged and the determination with which the leaders of member countries will pursue the reform aspirations in spite of inevitable set-backs. This question will be taken up later. The second set of issues focuses on the implications of the reform debates for the integration of the planned economies singly or as a group into the global economic order, and the potential for their participation in the international financial, monetary and trading régimes.

The current leaders in Eastern Europe seem convinced that further growth in their countries depends on stepping up the participation of their economies in global economic interdependence. This goal is unrelated to the market type of reforms envisaged in some of these countries, although measurable progress with restructuring in the planned economies would obviously affect the pace and character of their integration into the world economy.

With regard to trade, the first policy priorities are more effective interaction within CMEA. If achieved, this might initially reduce the room for useful economic interaction with third countries, including both developed and developing market economies. But it can only be short term. CMEA countries are under severe constraints: either they diversify and enlarge their procurement of fuels and raw materials from non-CMEA partners or they must reduce their demand for imports of such products without reducing output growth. The latter course requires technology imports, particularly from developed market economies. The former is contingent on imports from countries outside the CMEA area, primarily developing countries. If reforms get under way, the level, commodity composition and geographical distribution of trade will increasingly result from greater exploitation of the comparative advantages of each country. This would open opportunities for significant boosts of imports of traditional, labour-intensive manufactures from developing countries. Fuller exploitation of these opportunities may require that CMEA developing countries, as some of the newly industrialized countries have already demonstrated in practice, adopt new organizational and financial approaches. But the potential for significantly lifting exports is certainly there. These revenues could in turn provide the platform upon which the planned economies could build export markets in developing countries for medium-level technologies.

37 See *Rudé Právo* (Prague), 8 July 1988, p. 2.
38 See *Izvestia* (Moscow), 8 July 1988, pp. 1 and 4.
39 See *Pravda* (Moscow), 6 July 1988, p. 4.
40 See *Izvestia* (Moscow), 8 July 1988, p. 4.

To normalize their increased integration in international trade, CMEA countries are likely to seek fuller participation in the existing trade order, including the General Agreement on Tariffs and Trade (GATT). Five members (Cuba, Czechoslovakia, Hungary, Poland and Romania) are already full contracting parties, but for various reasons they have remained in a special status. Market-oriented reforms anchored to decentralization, commercial decision-making, explicit government preferences and a direct link-up between domestic and trade prices will certainly justify a revision of their status. Bulgaria, at present an observer, lodged a request for full accession in 1986.

Other CMEA members that are not yet contracting parties, including the Soviet Union, are exploring ways and means of becoming more intimately involved with GATT and its legal and negotiating machinery. Again, meaningful domestic reforms of the market type would facilitate accession to the Agreement, if only in terms of clarifying the issues related to most-favoured-nation status, non-discrimination and reciprocity in the accession negotiations. Because the domestic and CMEA reform process, if adhered to, is bound to be protracted, the Contracting Parties might wish to seek a firm transition mechanism, both to facilitate accession and to support ongoing economic reforms in potential applicants. Such a process of examination, deliberation and experimentation, with a transition phase for countries that cannot immediately be brought fully under the discipline of GATT, would at the very least better prepare the Contracting Parties for dealing with new overtures to GATT.

During the transition phase, non-discrimination and reciprocity could be based on the commitment of the planned economies to giving maximum scope to commercial decision-making by largely autonomous enterprises, to making explicit government preferences that influence the determination of domestic retail prices relative to trade prices, and to setting clear guidelines for how trading companies are expected to assist with maintaining some desirable degree of domestic price stability through the intertemporal management of profits. Once those elements of the situation are understood and agreed, the prime element of reciprocity could be that of ensuring a tight link between domestic and trade prices. This avenue could usefully be explored also because import commitments in physical terms, such as were negotiated earlier for Poland and Romania, would be inconsistent with the spirit of present economic and trade reforms. If improving stability and strengthening multilateralism in global trade become key concerns of the Soviet Union,[41] the Contracting Parties to GATT should benefit.

The link between reform and membership of the planned economies in the multilateral financial institutions is more complex. However, there is a clear need for structural adjustment in virtually all CMEA countries; the International Monetary Fund and the World Bank could build upon their wide experience with developing country adjustment programmes and be of assistance to CMEA countries too. They might even be instrumental in helping these countries to work out a realistic transition to currency convertibility in the long run and a more beneficial regional monetary régime for the transferable rouble in the short to medium, and perhaps even the long, run. The CMEA members that are members of the Bretton Woods institutions (Hungary, Poland, Romania and Viet Nam) have not been adversely affected. They have benefited from Fund drawings, loans from the World Bank and its affiliates, and the ability to participate in development projects financed by the World Bank. The CMEA members that are not members of the Bretton Woods institutions have shown interest in accession. Market-oriented reforms would facilitate such a step, but it would be unrealistic to expect the developed planned economies to be admitted under article XIV of the Fund's Articles of Agreement without clarifying the transition toward currency convertibility, which would be a difficult process under the most propitious of circumstances.

### Framework agreement between CMEA and the European Economic Community

After 15 years of on-off negotiations about the establishment of formal diplomatic relations between the European Economic Community (EEC) and CMEA, both sides initialled a framework agreement on 9 June 1988 in Moscow and signed it on 25 June 1988 in Luxembourg. The joint declaration, drawn up in no fewer than 17 authoritative versions, states essentially that the two sides "will develop co-operation in areas which fall within their respective spheres of competence and where there is common interest".[42] This is a meagre result of the protracted negotiations on normalizing relations between the two parts of Europe.

Apart from its obvious diplomatic and political demonstration angles, one may question whether the framework agreement really matters, especially since it is no more than a simple statement of mutual recognition. It settles nothing regarding trading, financial, transportation, ecological, scientific, technological, informational and other relations between the two politico-economic groups. It is questionable whether a significant impact on East-West trade could be expected from it. What will happen depends on the strength and impact of the probable links between the framework agreement and what might be possible economically and politically, perhaps even strategically. As Mr. Willy de Clercq, the EEC Commissioner for External Relations, noted, the accord represents "a great change in attitude" and will contribute to East-West "détente".[43]

41 See Vladimir N. Cheklin, "SSSR i GATT", *Vneshnyaya torgovlya* (Moscow), No. 7 (1987), pp. 37-39; Mikhail S. Pankin, "SSSR i GATT: perspektivy vzaimodeystvia", *Ekonomicheskaya gazeta* (Moscow), No. 49 (1986), p. 23; and the discussion with key advisers of Mr. Gorbachev reported in Gianni Corbi, "Un impero che bussa alle porte del capitale – Mosca si prepara allo choc del mercato", *La Repubblica* (Rome), 16 April 1988, p. 13.

42 See the text of the agreement in *European Community News*, No. 16 (1988), p. 1.

43 See *European Community News*, No. 16 (1988), p. 2.

The most important immediate consequence is that the framework agreement provides the go-ahead for individual CMEA countries to sign bilateral trade and co-operation agreements with the EEC. The Soviet Union appears to be keen on concluding such an arrangement in the very near future, and pushed for the CMEA-EEC framework agreement as a necessary preliminary step. Even before the signing of the agreement, Bulgaria, Czechoslovakia, the German Democratic Republic and the Soviet Union had informed the Commission of the European Communities that they wished to establish diplomatic relations. Other European CMEA members are expected to follow suit shortly.

The formal treaty powers of EEC are limited to commercial policy as traditionally understood; hence the reference in the framework agreement to the "respective spheres of competence".[44] All other international economic relations, including credits, technology, the environment, information and so on, remain within the competence of the EEC Governments. The same is true for CMEA members, even for commercial policy.[45] Even so, now that the EEC Governments have resolved to move towards a truly unified European market by the end of 1992, greater harmonization of other components of international economic relations is bound to come to the fore in the years ahead. This could in due course provide more scope for CMEA/EEC co-operation.

Several CMEA members (including Czechoslovakia and Hungary) have in the meantime already concluded their bilateral agreement with EEC and others have drafts in an advanced stage of negotiations. These bilateral trade and co-operation agreements revolve around such things as some form of most-favoured-nation treatment for the planned economies; more favourable quota allotments for some products instead of lifting quantitative import restrictions, some of which are in conflict with GATT obligations; and a relaxation of EC quantitative restrictions maintained, in particular, against the planned economies that are already full contracting parties to GATT—Czechoslovakia, Hungary, Poland and Romania. If the CMEA countries can capitalize on such overtures through effective shifts in their export supply to EC markets, they might thus set in train a sequence of productive economic co-operation with EC.

Viewing the potential impact of the CMEA/EEC agreement and the follow-up bilateral agreements in a longer-term perspective, it may be instructive to look beyond the purely commercial aspects of these protocols and take a fresh look at the politics and history of East-West relations. In endorsing the CMEA/EEC agreement, both sides have obvious political aims that transcend their economic interests and even go beyond the purely European aspects of the matter. Western Europe has been firmly entrenched in the Atlantic Alliance and the market economies share many political values, security interests and strategic objectives, but there may now be slightly more room for Western Europe to assert itself.

Although the parallel between 1992 as the magic date for Western European integration efforts and the similar objective of CMEA integration is not completely artificial, it should not be overdrawn. EEC has been pursuing integration since 1958 and has attained, by any standard of reference, a high degree of policy co-ordination, particularly in matters concerning trade, labour mobility and capital markets. In a sense, therefore, 1992 is simply placing a capstone on a long and difficult enterprise. In CMEA, the creation of a common market so far amounts to little more than the expression of a policy intention in a protracted and tedious germination stage.

## Towards a new integration strategy and mechanism: a perspective

The fortieth anniversary of CMEA will undoubtedly be a year of decisions on substantive matters of co-operation. A third economic summit for the 1980s will be convened in mid-1989 at Prague.[46] It will consider a number of issues of regional integration that have not so far received an unambiguous answer either in national economic reforms or at the CMEA level.

The forty-third and forty-fourth Council Sessions and their aftermath have shown that the policy debate on the process of socialist economic integration is very far from over. The next summit and the summer Session of the Council, which may coincide, should be illuminating. Even if a swift decision with broad implications for socialist economic integration can be reached soon, a rapid change in the CMEA concert is not to be expected, in view of the lack of consensus on the far-reaching reform of CMEA and the reluctance of some Eastern European leaders to entertain meaningful economic reform at home. Considerable organizational, legal and technico-economic problems also arise in moving away from the traditional central planning environment. This holds true at the national level and even more so regionally. This may be illustrated by highlighting the technical problems of inter-firm relations.

Inter-firm relations cannot progress far unless the enterprise leadership is given the authority and the means to decide upon inputs and outputs in respect of both price and quantity. When such relations are fostered, the firms should not have to concern themselves with exchange rates or ways of settling accounts. These issues need to be tackled at the macro-economic level. Some countries have already set special exchange rates for these selected inter-firm transactions, although their suitability for the exchanges envisaged has yet to be ascertained, and have created an environment in which it is hoped that autonomous micro-economic deci-

44 See the text of the agreement in *European Community News,* No. 16 (1988), p. 1.

45 The Commission of the European Communities used this for many years as a pretext to refuse to come to terms on an agreement with CMEA.

46 It was first announced for late March 1989, but the divergences among the members on the question of integration evidently remained too wide for a summit to be successful.

sions can be reached without stultifying bureaucratic interference. What is not yet agreed, however, is how to cope with imbalances incurred on these special accounts.

The proposals of the past two years do not entail convertibility in any proper sense of the term. All that is envisaged is that imbalances on special accounts should be offset against transferable rouble holdings at the International Bank for Economic Co-operation in Moscow, which is the CMEA clearing agency for transactions in non-convertible currencies.

The shortcoming of previous attempts to introduce multilateralism in CMEA has been that accruals on transferable rouble accounts are unusable in the short run, unless goods and services are earmarked in *ex ante* bilateral trade and payments agreements. Furthermore, there is as yet no agreement on the exchange rates to be utilized for these transactions. In as much as there is no possibility of converting bilateral claims, the new limited settlements proposal essentially aims at facilitating simple clearing of one category of decentralized transactions. Without incentives to enforce convertibility and ensure its expansion by imposing some form of convertible currency settlement on deficit countries,[47] this otherwise promising step is likely to remain a constructive initiative without follow-up.

However, the prevailing pragmatism in external trade and foreign policy exhibited in recent years by several CMEA countries, particularly the USSR, may produce a revised version of the convertibility proposal. Such a proposal, even if it were applied only to two or three CMEA members bent on moving ahead, could demonstrate the possibility of market criteria enhancing effective economic integration. This possibility was publicly entertained by key leaders at the forty-third Council Session in Moscow in 1987 and has since been gaining support.

47 This does not necessarily require that such convertible currency transactions actually be settled and possibly diverted to trade with market economies. An alternative scheme can be imagined in which, for example, convertible currency claims can be borrowed from a common convertible currency fund to be created, and chronic deficits are to be settled in increasing proportion to the cumulative liability in convertible currency.

# Chapter VII

## INTEREST RATES IN THE 1980s

In the 1980s, developments in international financial markets have been the most far-reaching of the changes in the world economy. Changes on the international financial scene have shaped the pattern and influenced the magnitude of world economic growth. They have been manifested in international financial flows among countries unprecedented in both size and nature, most particularly in the size of the capital flows among the developed market economies and in the reverse net transfer of resources from developing to developed countries. Both of these flows have acquired a longevity and magnitude that would have been considered unsustainable in the 1970s.

These developments have been paralleled by increasing government emphasis on national and international monetary policy. Indeed, in many of the developed market economies, fiscal policies have fallen into a state of relative unimportance as a means of controlling the level of economic activity. International policy co-ordination among the leading industrial countries has been effected primarily through monetary means. In setting these monetary policies, attention has been focused on the two prices that are most important in international financial markets—interest rates and exchange rates.

Both interest rates and exchange rates have shown an unusual degree of volatility in the 1980s. In the early years of the decade, nominal interest rates in domestic and international markets were also high by historical standards, primarily as a result of the anti-inflationary monetary policies adopted by many of the developed market economies. As the 1980s progressed, inflation in developed market economies fell. Nominal interest rates fell as well, but not by as much as inflation rates. The result has been persistently high levels of "real" interest rates throughout the 1980s. Much of this persistence in high real interest rates can be traced to downward shifts in private savings and upward shifts in government deficits that appeared during the 1980s.

High interest rates have been a leading cause of the debt crisis of the developing countries. In the 1970s, rates of inflation were often higher than nominal interest rates, creating negative real interest rates. In the 1980s, with this situation sharply reversed, the real sacrifice involved in repaying debt presents both a burden on those with accumulated past debts and an obstacle to new finance.

Even at high real rates of interest, profitable investment opportunities will continue to present themselves, but they will be fewer than at lower interest rates. In particular, many long-term projects of an infrastructural nature yield low annual rates of return and may be neglected in an era of high real interest rates unless concessional financing can be obtained. This suggests that the lower average rates of growth of the world economy in the 1980s can be attributed at least in part to the high real interest rates that have prevailed. From a developmental perspective, therefore, the reasons for the transition from low real interest rates in the 1970s to high real interest rates in the 1980s warrant examination.

This chapter focuses on interest rates in the developed market economies. However, as net importers of capital, the majority of developing countries are directly affected by these external interest rates. Even though the developing countries have a negligible role in their determination, interest rates in the developed market economies have a direct bearing on the developing countries' ability to draw upon foreign savings to finance their development. High rates of interest in international markets will place a heavier debt-servicing burden on borrowing countries and will reduce the number of viable development projects. As a result, their borrowing will be decreased and their growth impaired.

The chapter reviews three questions regarding the levels and volatility of interest rates in the developed market economies and their interrelationships over the past decade. First, why have "real", that is, inflation-adjusted, interest rates been persistently high in the 1980s? Second, why have interest rates become so volatile, even in real terms? Third, why have interest rates in different countries diverged so much in the 1980s and what does that imply about the functioning and efficiency of international capital markets? This discussion of relative interest rates between countries is inextricably connected to current and prospective movements in exchange rates between these countries. This raises questions about the connections between real interest rates, exchange rates and capital flows among different countries. Misalignments in real exchange rates and the development of current account imbalances appear to be systematically related to swings in the differences between the real interest rates of the individual developed market economies.

### Nominal and real interest rates

With very few exceptions, the interest rates borrowers and lenders use as a basis of contract, which traders quote and which are reported in the financial press, are money, or "nominal", interest rates. They are percentages per annum of the principal amount, without adjustment for changes that may occur in the prices of goods or services during the term of the loan or credit. On the other hand, most borrowing and lending decisions also involve some consideration of prospective price changes during the lending period. When interest rates are adjusted to reflect changes in the prices of goods and services, they are conventionally referred to as "real" interest rates. If actual price changes are employed in the calculation (which can be done only after the interest period is over), they are known as *ex post* real interest rates; if forecasts of future price changes are employed, the results are known as *ex ante* real interest rates. Forecasts will rarely

Box VII.1. Real interest rates and developing countries

Interest rates in the developed countries are of concern to developing countries because the developing countries' international borrowing normally must be done in the currency, and at the interest rates, of the developed countries. In addition, the real rate of interest on developing countries' international borrowing will not be the same as that of the lender, nor the same as the domestic real interest rate within the borrowing country. These discrepancies between the real interest gain from the point of view of the lender and the burden from the point of view of the borrower can be large.

Nominal and real effective rates of interest on outstanding debt of groups of developing countries, 1981-1988

(Annual percentage rates)

| | 1981 | 1982 | 1983 | 1984 | 1985 | 1986 | 1987 | 1988 |
|---|---|---|---|---|---|---|---|---|
| LIBOR[a] | 16.2 | 16.3 | 10.1 | 10.5 | 10.4 | 8.0 | 6.3 | 7.7 |
| Real effective rate of interest[b] | | | | | | | | |
| Energy-exporting developing countries | 10.3 | 19.1 | 28.9 | 10.5 | 14.3 | 80.7 | 0.9 | 9.8[c] |
| Non-energy exporting developing countries | 27.1 | 23.3 | 11.3 | 14.8 | 18.0 | 6.6 | .. | .. |
| Fifteen heavily indebted countries | 21.7 | 18.9 | 19.8 | 12.1 | .. | .. | .. | .. |
| Small low-income developing countries | 19.8 | 30.8 | 6.8 | 6.8 | 23.2 | 12.3 | .. | .. |

*Source:* IMF, *International Financial Statistics: Supplement on Trade Statistics* (Washington, D.C., 1988). Changes in the price index are percentage differences of fourth-quarter average export value indexes.

a London interbank offered rate on six-month dollar deposits.

b Calculated according to the formula shown in the note to table VII.1, using LIBOR as the nominal interest rate and the change in the unit value of exports as the inflation rate.

c First six months only.

be accurate, so *ex ante* and *ex post* interest rates for the same period will usually be different.

The relevant real interest rate—whether *ex ante* or *ex post,* and whatever prices it is adjusted for—depends on the nature of the decision to be taken or the analysis to be performed. Those who are concerned with movements in aggregate economic variables and who consider the "average" decisions of broad groups of economic actors usually employ real interest rates that incorporate changes in the prices of bundles of goods or services, as reflected in price indexes. For example, in analysing the attractiveness for households (in the aggregate) to save, the concept of the real interest rate that is typically employed embodies the expected rate of change in the consumer price index over the same period. The logic is that the typical consumer can earn the nominal interest rate by abstaining from consuming from the basket of goods which makes up the consumer price index. However, the "real" value of the money he receives at the end of the period for deferring consumption will be reduced (or increased) by the average rise (or drop) in the price of the goods in the basket. Thus, the prospective "real" return can be thought of as the nominal interest rate minus the expected (i.e., *ex ante*) rate of change in the consumer price index.

The typical non-financial business credit decision is somewhat different. The nominal interest rate normally represents a borrowing opportunity and whether it will contribute positively to the value of the firm will depend not only on how successfully the firm produces, but also what happens to the price of its output. Although the price index for calculating the real interest rate may be specialized—for instance, for the import or export sectors of an economy, an index of import or export prices may be required—a common aggregate approach is to deduct inflation as measured by the wholesale or producers' price index to estimate the real interest rate.

In these cases, it is the *ex ante,* or forecast, real interest rate that is relevant to the decision. For other problems, the *ex post* rate may be the more useful concept. The *ex post* real interest rate is appropriate to determine how much the real burden of an old debt has actually risen over time. One example of the use of an *ex post* real interest rate is the calculation of the real financing cost to the developing countries during the 1980s of their outstanding external debt (see box).

Domestic nominal interest rates in some developing countries are heavily administered and are often held below market levels that would be consistent with prevailing rates of inflation. International capital flows are also often subject to administrative controls in developing countries. This reduces these countries' degree of integration into international capital markets, although experience shows that such controls do not eliminate market-oriented flows. Rather, the effect of such administration is to raise transactions costs, sometimes resulting in wide disparities between the domestic and international interest rates. Although domestic real interest rates are in principle calculated as in developed market economies (i.e., by subtracting domestic inflation), these real rates are often not true market rates: domestic lenders' opportunity costs are often more closely tied to foreign interest rates and credit is frequently not available at these rates.

Other factors combine with disparities in nominal interest rates to create substantial differences in the real interest rates that are faced by the developed market economies and developing countries. Developing countries have to earn sufficient foreign exchange through exports in order to repay loans denominated in the lenders' currency. To judge the burden that this outflow of real goods and services places on the borrowing country, the relevant price deflator is that of average export prices measured in the currency value of the lending country.

During the 1970s, domestic real interest rates in many developing countries were negative because domestic prices were rising faster than the rate of interest. At the same time, there was a borrower's market in international financial markets as the commercial banks endeavoured to lend the liquid assets they had accumulated from the deposits of the energy-exporting countries. The commercial banks were eager to lend these funds, many of the middle-income developing countries needed the financing for balance-of-payments purposes, and there was a broad consensus in the international community at the time that this was an appropriate means of meeting the large external imbalances of the developing countries. Loans from the commercial banks to the borrowing countries were usually denominated in one of the key currencies (primarily dollars) in order to transfer the risk of changes in the exchange rate from the lenders to the developing countries (thereby removing any incentive the borrowing country might have to reduce the real value of the obligation through inflation).

In the the first half of the 1980s, falling commodity prices and a rising dollar caused the terms of trade for most developing countries to deteriorate. This raised the burden of the outstanding debt in terms of the goods and services that had to be forgone in order to service it—that is, the "effective" or real interest cost of servicing the debt was greater than indicated by the nominal interest rate (see table).

This was illustrated most clearly in the case of the energy-exporting countries in 1986, when the collapse in the price of oil presented some of them with increased debt-servicing problems. On the other hand, the general improvement in many commodity prices since 1987 has decreased the burden of external debt for some developing countries and is reflected in their effective rate of interest being less than the nominal LIBOR.

### Measures of short-term and long-term rates

The choice between *ex ante* and *ex post* interest rates is often made on the basis of practical rather than theoretical considerations. The *ex ante* rate is not observable except to individual transactors. Its calculation requires the analyst to decide what the forecast must be or must have been. The main issues are the degree of foresight and the sophistication to be attributed to the agents who make or made the decisions. These considerations will be influenced by the maturity of the credit instruments that offer the nominal rate. For instance, it is implausible to assume that investors in long-term bonds regularly forecast long-term inflation accurately. In this case, *ex ante* and *ex post* real long-term interest rates are likely to be far apart; the *ex post* rate cannot be calculated for the years late in the sample period (since future inflation has not yet occurred) and analysts must therefore use a survey or other forecast of prices in order to construct the real interest rate. Purchasers of three-month government bills, on the other hand, will generally err in their forecasts of the three-month inflation rate, but such short-term forecast errors may cancel out over one or two years. In such cases, *ex post* and *ex ante* short-term real interest rates may not be far apart.

In the early 1980s, nominal interest rates in the developed market economies assumed their highest levels in modern financial history before falling back to the levels of the early 1970s (see figure VII.1). In many countries, these interest rates have also been more volatile than in the 1970s. At the same time, interest rates for financial instruments issued in different domestic markets and denominated in different currencies became more sensitive to each other as linkages between developed countries' financial markets tightened. Nevertheless, despite this greater integration, interest rates among countries were more, rather than less, dispersed in the 1980s than in the 1970s.

There are also major differences in both short-term and long-term real interest rates across countries and over time (see table VII.1 and figure VII.2). There has been a dramatic reversal between the 1970s, when real interest rates were low and often negative, and the 1980s, when they have moved upward to high positive levels. Since 1985, real rates appear to have fallen somewhat in the United States of America and to a certain extent in Japan, but they have remained high in Europe.

## Reasons for the high real interest rates of the 1980s

There are many possible explanations for the high real interest rates of the 1980s. These include a monetary explanation, centreing on the abrupt shift in the United States and some other countries to strongly disinflationary monetary policies after September 1979; the pressure exerted by the heavy borrowing by the United States to finance its fiscal deficit; an increase in private investment demands, particularly in the United States and motivated at least in part by tax incentives; and a miscellaneous set of explanations as varied as the post-1970s' decrease in the incomes of high-saving, oil-producing countries and heightened risk awareness on the part of lenders. Each explanation has important implications for world growth and stability.

Table VII.1. Alternative measures of short-term and long-term real interest rates for selected developed market economies, 1973-1988

(Percentage)

| | Short-term rate[a] | Long-term rate[b] | Long-term rate[c] |
|---|---|---|---|
| France | | | |
| 1973-1979 | -1.13 | -0.47 | -0.46 |
| 1980-1982 | 2.34 | 2.14 | 1.45 |
| 1983-1985 | 5.01 | 3.07 | 5.33 |
| 1986-1988 | 4.67 | 5.26 | 6.70 |
| Germany, Federal Republic of | | | |
| 1973-1979 | -1.51 | 2.71 | 2.89 |
| 1980-1982 | 3.55 | 4.14 | 4.27 |
| 1983-1985 | 3.42 | 3.84 | 4.61 |
| 1986-1988 | 3.06 | 5.25 | 4.87 |
| Japan | | | |
| 1973-1979 | -1.63 | -2.74 | -1.25 |
| 1980-1982 | 4.46 | 3.24 | 2.67 |
| 1983-1985 | 4.30 | 4.61 | 4.44 |
| 1986-1988 | 3.74 | 3.67 | 3.94 |
| Netherlands | | | |
| 1973-1979 | -5.41 | 0.65 | .. |
| 1980-1982 | 3.96 | 4.82 | 4.26 |
| 1983-1985 | 3.50 | 4.29 | 4.89 |
| 1986-1988 | 5.04 | 5.75 | 6.03 |
| Switzerland | | | |
| 1973-1979 | .. | -0.10 | .. |
| 1980-1982 | 0.40 | 0.57 | 0.87 |
| 1983-1985 | 0.89 | 0.60 | 1.42 |
| 1986-1988 | 1.91 | 2.35 | 2.63 |
| United Kingdom | | | |
| 1973-1979 | -3.79 | -1.06 | 1.69 |
| 1980-1982 | 3.87 | -0.15 | 1.77 |
| 1983-1985 | 4.85 | 4.74 | 4.56 |
| 1986-1988 | 4.93 | 5.27 | 5.60 |
| United States | | | |
| 1973-1979 | -1.72 | 0.40 | 0.40 |
| 1980-1982 | 4.66 | 1.62 | 2.76 |
| 1983-1985 | 4.71 | 7.02 | 6.41 |
| 1986-1988 | 2.41 | 5.26 | 4.95 |

*Source:* IMF, *International Financial Statistics*, various issues, and OECD, *Economic Outlook*, various issues.

*Note:* Real interest rates are calculated from the formula $[(1+i)/(1+p)]-1$, where $i$ is the nominal interest rate and $p$ is the percentage rate of inflation, both expressed as decimals.

a *Ex post* quarterly short-term rate.

b Conventional long-term rate (i.e., with inflation assumed to be the average growth of the consumer price index over the past two years).

c Long-term real interest rate, where the inflation rate is assumed to be that forecast by OECD for the next year.

Figure VII.1. Long-term and short-term interest rates in selected developed market economies

A. *Long-term rates*

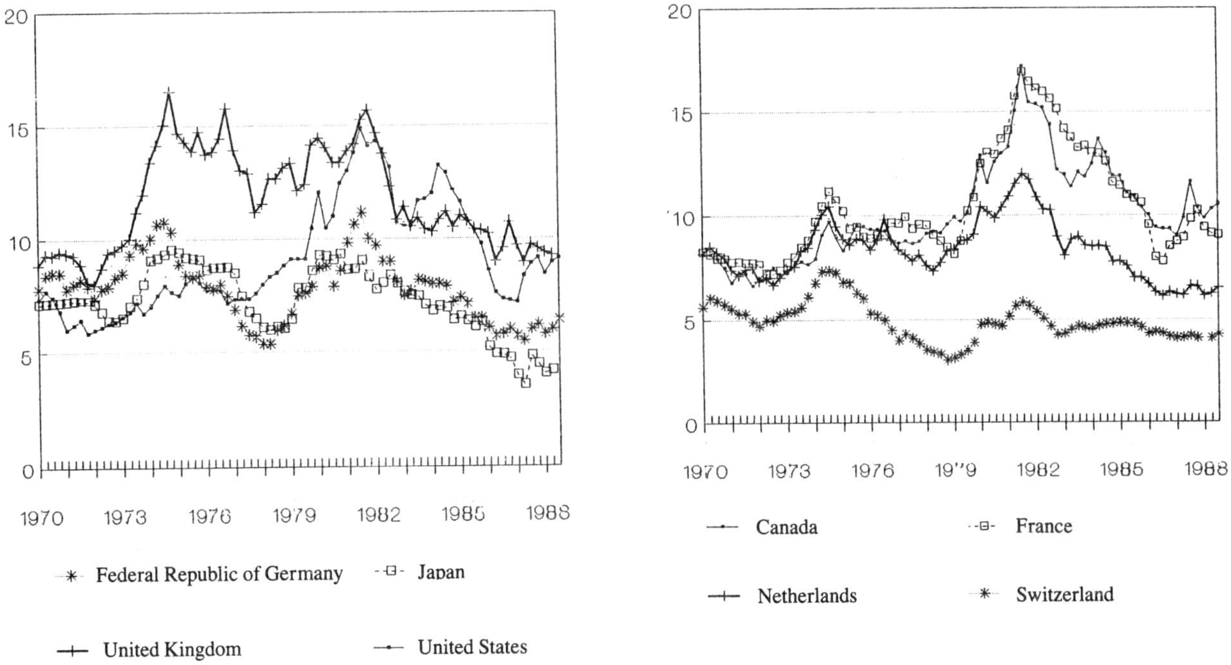


B. *Short-term rates*

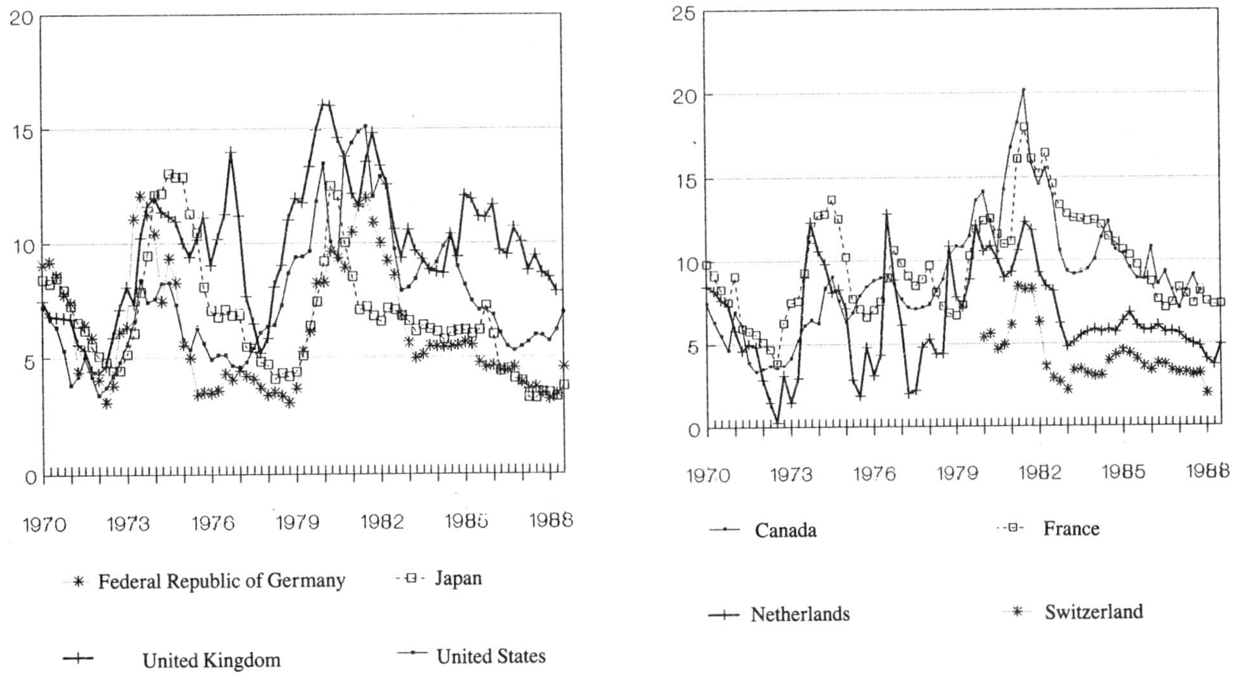


*Source:* IMF, *International Financial Statistics*, various issues.

Figure VII.2. Long-term and short-term real interest rates
in selected developed market economies

A. *Long-term rates*[a]

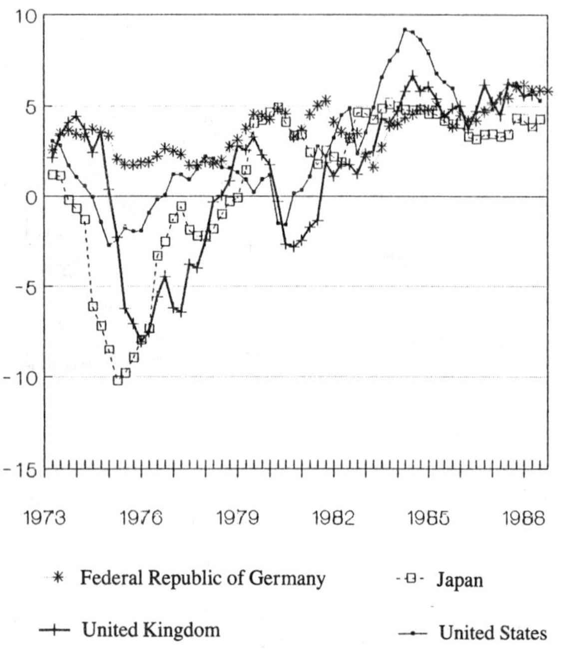


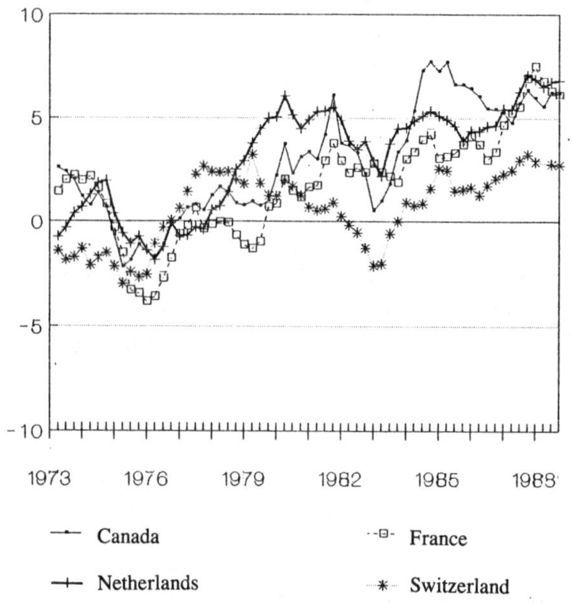


B. *Short-term rates*[b]

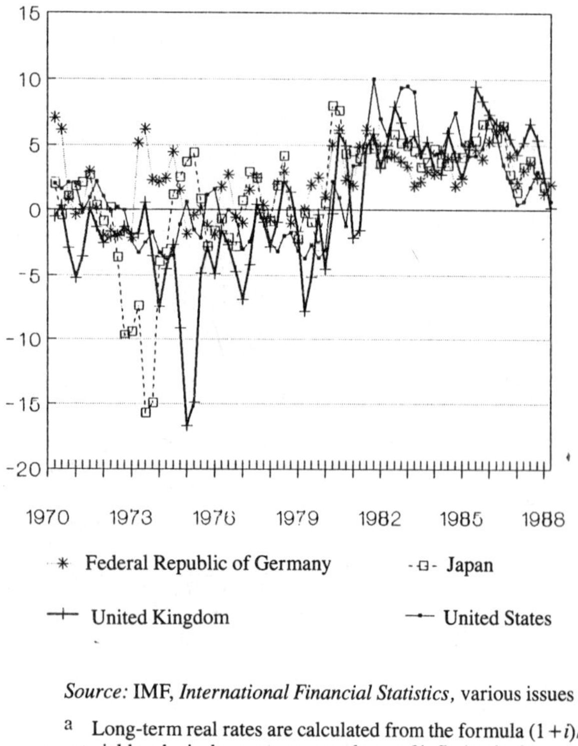


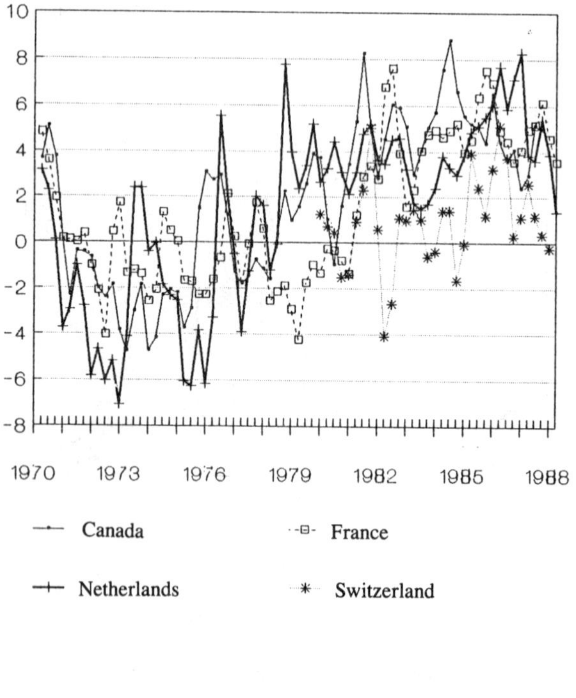


*Source:* IMF, *International Financial Statistics,* various issues

[a] Long-term real rates are calculated from the formula $(1+i)/(1+p)-1$, where $i$ is the nominal long-term government yield and $p$ is the average annual rate of inflation in the consumer price index for two years up to the present quarter.

[b] Short-term real rates are calculated as above, except that inflation is defined as the average annualized growth of the quarterly consumer price index between the previous quarter and the next quarter.

## The monetary explanation

There is strong evidence that changes in monetary growth have an inverse relationship to real interest rates in the short run. The reason given for this is that prices tend to be "sticky", that is, slow to adjust to long-run, market-clearing levels. When the rate of growth of money supply changes rapidly, the real (price-deflated) values of people's money-holdings also change. Both theory and historical experience indicate that prices eventually tend to rise or fall in proportion to money supply, but in the meantime people have either a surplus or deficit in their liquidity, which tends to depress or raise real interest rates.

The restrictive shift in monetary policies may have been the principal explanation for the rise of real interest rates in the early 1980s. However, the experience of the United States makes it seem less plausible for the later years of the decade. By 1985, real interest rates in the United States remained high and showed no tendency to fall. This made the period 1980-1985 in the United States unusual by historical standards. In the past, high real interest rates had led to major and protracted recessions in the United States, which in turn had resulted in drops in real interest rates.[1] A recession occurred in 1982, but it was brief and was followed by the present extended recovery. If monetary restriction had been the explanation for the high real interest rates that have prevailed from 1980 to the present, it would have been expected to have had strongly depressive effects on real growth in the United States. This has not occurred.

The inadequacy of the monetary policy explanation is further supported by an examination of the mix of real interest rates, exchange rates and current account balances of the United States from 1982 to early 1985. During this period, the real trade-weighted value of the United States dollar increased by about 24 per cent, while the current account of the United States went into large deficit. Real interest rates in the United States were not only high at this time, but exceeded those of most other developed countries (see table VII.1). The only plausible way of reconciling these observations is a driving force of strong aggregate demand in the United States. This would jointly explain the high real interest rates (which occurred because of demands for finance), the high exchange rate for the dollar (because of the international differential in interest rates and the resulting capital flows) and the United States current account deficit (because of excess demand).

Table VII.2. Share of fiscal balances in GNP/GDP for the major developed market economies, 1980-1988

(Percentage)

| | Seven major countries[a] | Federal Republic of Germany | Japan | United States |
|---|---|---|---|---|
| 1980 | -3.3 | -1.9 | -6.2 | -2.3 |
| 1981 | -3.5 | -2.5 | -5.9 | -2.4 |
| 1982 | -4.6 | -2.4 | -5.9 | -4.1 |
| 1983 | -5.3 | -1.9 | -5.6 | -5.6 |
| 1984 | -5.0 | -1.6 | -4.7 | -5.1 |
| 1985 | -4.9 | -1.3 | -3.9 | -5.3 |
| 1986 | -4.4 | -1.2 | -3.6 | -4.8 |
| 1987 | -3.5 | -1.4 | -3.3 | -3.3 |
| 1988 | -3.1 | -1.8 | -2.5 | -3.1 |

*Source:* IMF, *World Economic Outlook* (Washington, D.C., April 1989).

[a] Canada, France, the Federal Republic of Germany, Italy, Japan, the United Kingdom and the United States.

Table VII.3. Changes in real domestic demand in the major developed market economies, 1980–1988

(Percentage)

| | Seven major countries[a] | Federal Republic of Germany | Japan | United States |
|---|---|---|---|---|
| 1980 | -0.1 | 1.1 | 0.8 | -1.8 |
| 1981 | 1.0 | -2.6 | 2.2 | 2.2 |
| 1982 | -0.3 | -2.0 | 2.8 | -1.9 |
| 1983 | 3.3 | 2.3 | 1.8 | 5.1 |
| 1984 | 5.7 | 2.0 | 3.8 | 8.7 |
| 1985 | 3.4 | 0.8 | 3.9 | 3.8 |
| 1986 | 3.7 | 3.5 | 4.0 | 3.7 |
| 1987 | 3.7 | 3.1 | 5.1 | 3.0 |
| 1988 | 4.2 | 3.2 | 7.4 | 3.0 |

*Source:* IMF, *World Economic Outlook* (Washington, D.C., April 1989).

[a] Canada, France, the Federal Republic of Germany, Italy, Japan, the United Kingdom and the United States.

## The United States fiscal deficit and world savings

The obvious source of the demand stimulus in the United States was its fiscal deficit, which reached 4.1 per cent of GNP in 1982 (see table VII.2). In absolute magnitude, at $125.7 billion, this was equal to nearly 70 per cent of the combined fiscal deficits of the six other large industrial countries. It represented more than one quarter of United States gross capital formation in 1982, almost 40 per cent of that of Japan, almost all of that of the Federal Republic of Germany, and more than the total gross capital formation of the four other leading industrial countries. Moreover, the United States fiscal deficit grew after 1982, exceeding 5 per cent of GNP in 1983-1985 and reaching a maximum absolute annual level of $209.6 billion in 1986.[2]

1 On this point, see William Poole, "Monetary policy lessons of recent inflation and disinflation", *Journal of Economic Perspectives*, vol. 2, No. 3 (Summer 1988), p.88. High real interest rates were associated with recession and falling prices in 1929-1932, 1920-1921, 1907 and 1893-1894.

2 The United States deficits discussed here are federal deficits only and omit state and local fiscal balances (which tend to be in surplus). Combining the two significantly reduces the deficit of the United States government sector in aggregate; for instance, the aggregate deficit in 1986 was $144.4 billion, compared with a federal deficit of $205.6 billion.

Aggregate demand in the United States was strongly stimulatory after 1982 (see table VII.3). This was also a period of high real interest rates in the United States, which suggests that the source of this stimulus was a net upward shift in aggregate spending. Growth rates outside the United States tended to be lower during this period, while the differences between United States real interest rates and those of other developed market economies were positive and widened after 1982. This suggests that a stimulus from expenditure demand in the United States was the cause of high real interest rates world wide.

What sort of expenditure demand shifts were at work, and is it clear that the United States fiscal deficit was behind them? Government expenditure has been fairly stable as a percentage of GNP in the United States, ranging between 19 per cent and 20 per cent over the period 1974-1982. Most of the variation in the share of the deficit as a proportion of GNP has arisen from reductions in taxes and growth in transfer payments. These changes may have induced private spending to increase, but only to the extent that private savings did not rise—that is, government dissaving will impinge on society's overall savings only if private savings do not rise to compensate. A fall in total domestic savings (private and public) because of increased government dissaving must be reflected in the form of either a drop in domestic expenditure or a deterioration in the current account position. An excess of domestic investment expenditure over domestic savings must be financed with a current account deficit, and vice versa.

Gaps between investment spending and savings in the United States appear prominently after 1982, as do large current account deficits. Three observations arise from an analysis of the individual and relative movements of the ratios of investment and savings to GNP in the Federal Republic of Germany, Japan and the United States for the period 1974-1982 (see figure VII.3). First, in all three countries, movements in the private investment ratios before 1983 were more clearly associated with total domestic savings (i.e., including government savings) than with private savings alone. This suggests that changes in fiscal deficits tended to be reflected in changes in private investment in the opposite direction. Before 1982, when massive current account financing among the developed market economies began, government deficits appear to have impinged on private investment and were not compensated for by private savings. This phenomenon is referred to as "crowding out". Second, the United States investment ratio was rather steady throughout the period 1974-1987, but there was a drop in the private savings ratio. Maintenance of the investment ratio was made possible after 1982 by growing current account deficits financed largely by the surpluses of the Federal Republic of Germany and Japan. Third, investment ratios in the Federal Republic of Germany and Japan moved downwards after 1982, despite these countries' having maintained (and slightly increased) their private savings ratios.

The joint implication of these observations is that the United States fiscal deficits absorbed significant amounts of savings, from both domestic and external sources. Domestic savings in the Federal Republic of Germany and Japan that might otherwise have been used for capital investment in these countries were instead allocated towards building up financial claims on the United States.

Movements in exchange rates both reflected and helped determine how much of the United States fiscal deficit would be financed from external sources. The growth of the trade and fiscal deficits caused interest rates and returns on dollar-denominated financial instruments to increase. This raised both the demand for these instruments and the real exchange rate for the dollar. The rise in the real exchange rate helped provide the net increase in United States imports needed to balance the current account financing flow. Until 1985, the key variables moved in directions consistent with this explanation based on the driving force of the United States fiscal deficit: fiscal deficits (as percentages of GNP) were rising, real interest rates were high, the real exchange value of the dollar was high, and the current account was in substantial deficit.

After early 1985, real exchange rates, real interest rates, the difference in real interest rates across countries and the United States fiscal deficit changed course. The United States fiscal deficit fell as percentage of GNP. The value of the dollar fell, average real interest rates fell and the difference between interest rates in the United States and elsewhere narrowed. These events might be interpreted as a reversal of developments in the period 1982-early 1985: the declining fiscal deficit reduced the real interest rate spread, which in turn pushed down the value of the dollar. Two differences in the later period, however, belie this interpretation. First, as noted earlier, the drop in private savings largely offset the impact of the improving fiscal deficit on total savings in the United States. Second, most of the period from 1985 to mid-1988 was characterized by monetary ease relative to the previous several years, especially in the United States. This helped to reduce the interest rate differential in favour of dollar assets and contributed to bringing down the dollar. At the same time, it also helped to sustain demand in the United States and contributed to the persistent United States current account deficit, even while the real exchange rate of the dollar was falling. The United States current account deficit peaked at 3.7 per cent of GNP in 1987.

Monetary policies in the developed countries reversed in mid-1988, leading to higher real interest rates in general and a return to a positive spread of United States real interest rates over those of other developed countries. These developments were accompanied by a moderate rise in the real value of the dollar relative to most other currencies.

### A private investment boom?

Another explanation for the high real interest rates, given by some policy makers in the United States during the mid-1980s, was that there was an upward shift in United States investment demand. Investor confidence was often cited as one reason for this, but tangible incentives were also provided by the 1981-1982 Economic Recovery Act. According to this explanation, the factors leading to the upward shift in investment could be permanent, so that expectations of the

Figure VII.3. Private and public savings ratios for the Federal Republic of Germany, Japan and the United States, 1974-1987

(Percentage shares of gross national product)

A. *Federal Republic of Germany*

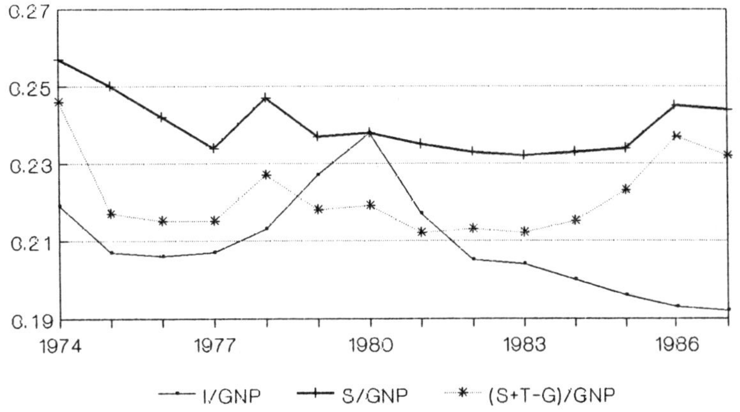


B. *Japan*

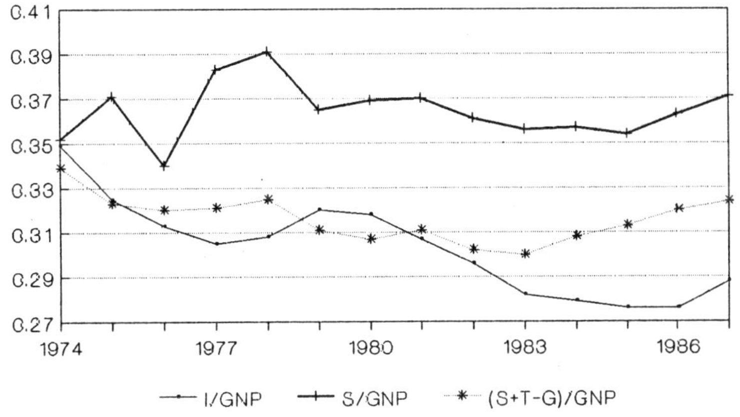


C. *United States*

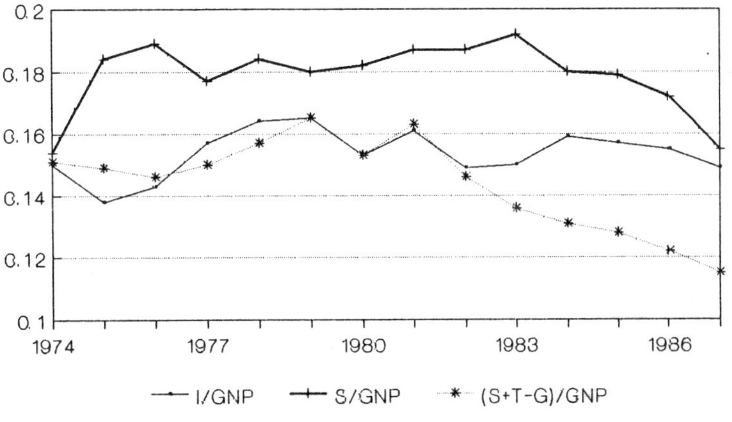


*Source:* Department of International Economic and Social Affairs of the United Nations Secretariat, based on IMF, *International Financial Statistics*, various issues.

long-run real value of the dollar might have increased permanently in the period 1982-1985. The argument can also explain the decline in the real value of the dollar after 1985, as tax reform in the United States in 1986 may have stifled some of the incentive to invest.

This investment-boom explanation for high real rates is not supported by the data. In the United States, the ratio of gross private capital formation to GNP did not increase (see figure VII.3). Any positive shift in United States investment demand seems to have been sufficient at most to compensate for the negative effects of the high real interest rates. Meanwhile, the investment ratios in the Federal Republic of Germany and Japan continued their downward trend as domestic savers in those countries acquired claims on the United States rather than on domestic business.

Many observers have attributed the decline in investment ratios of the Federal Republic of Germany and Japan during the 1980s to a shift in investors' preferences towards the United States. The investment rates in the United States fell less than those in the Federal Republic of Germany and Japan, so that inter-country shifts in investor preferences are probably part of the reason for the relative changes in the investment ratios among the three countries. Shifts in preferences towards capital investment in the United States cannot, however, be the main explanation, since United States investment ratios did not shift upward when the others decreased. Moreover, the very phenomenon of rising real interest rates suggests that the net pressure on credit markets must have been positive, again pointing to the apparent role of the United States fiscal deficit in absorbing savings.

### Other explanations for high real interest rates

Between the 1970s and the 1980s, oil-exporting countries experienced a drop in their export and current account surpluses due to changes in the structure of the international oil market and falling oil prices. Previously, these countries' surpluses had been recycled back to industrialized countries' money markets. The disappearance of those surpluses is sometimes suggested as a reason for higher real interest rates in the 1980s on the grounds that the shift in income from the high-saving, oil-exporting countries to lower-saving countries would reduce the share of global savings in world output. However, it is questionable whether the shift in the energy-exporting countries' revenues mattered much in comparison with the United States fiscal deficit and its drag on world savings. During the 1970s, the maximum annual current account surplus of the energy-exporting countries was $53.6 billion, compared, for example, with the United States fiscal deficit of $205.6 billion in 1986. However, this direct comparison of magnitudes does not provide an accurate indication of the impact on world saving. This is because the reduction in world savings that would be brought about by the shift in oil revenues away from the producing countries would depend on the difference between the fraction of those revenues that the producing countries saved and the fraction saved by other countries. In contrast, the income flow captured by the United States fiscal deficit represents a direct, dollar-for-dollar drain on world savings.[3]

Another explanation for high real interest rates centres on market perceptions of volatility and risk. Substantial risk premiums may have arisen as a result of increasing concerns about the risks of holding financial assets. There are several lines of argument. First, macro-economic instability may reduce incentives to save because uncertainty weakens confidence in financial assets; the downward shift in savings may drive up real interest rates.[4] A second possible effect stems from uncertainty regarding inflation. Errors in forecasting inflation make the return to savers uncertain; if this uncertainty reduced the willingness to save more than the desire to invest, real interest rates would rise. The debt crisis which erupted in 1982 also increased uncertainties regarding the return on financial assets.

Neither of these two arguments is easy to evaluate empirically, but doubt is cast on the validity of the second by the fact that the volatility of inflation increased during the 1970s, whereas real rates of interest were higher in the 1980s. Moreover, short-term real interest rates should be less influenced than long-term rates by uncertainty regarding forecasts of inflation. However, short-term real rates have been persistently high in the 1980s and not much lower than long-term rates.

## The volatility of real interest rates

Volatility in interest rates has negative implications. It raises the risks of both financial and real investment, increasing required rates of return and stifling investment in productive capital. At the international level, volatility in interest rates causes and interacts with volatility in exchange rates and so interferes with the international allocation of investment and with world trade. The extent to which financial markets are responsible for these negative consequences is a controversial issue. The ultimate sources of movements in interest and exchange rates are private decisions and public policies. The markets can be considered responsible for creating instability only in the sense that, in their present highly developed state, they increase the possibilities for unreasonable speculation or misguided policies.

Nominal interest rates became more volatile during the 1970s and, with some exceptions, notably the Federal Republic of Germany and Japan, this volatility increased in the

3 The oil-producing countries' maximum annual surplus was $89 billion in 1981. This is larger than the surplus cited in the text, but it occurred at a time when real interest rates were already rising. The timing therefore seems inconsistent with the argument at hand.

4 The effect of real economic uncertainty on saving is not unambiguous, however. It is also conceivable that households would choose to save more—for example, if the major risk were unemployment rather than the security of financial assets. Further, if real interest rates rise because of real economic uncertainty, one has to assume that any downward shift in investment must be less than the downward shift in savings.

1980s. Several causes of the volatility have been suggested, including supply shocks, shifting macro-economic policies, cumulative debts, and interactions with volatile exchange rates. There has, however, been little investigation of the extent to which the volatility reflected fluctuations in the real rate of interest or fluctuations in the rate of inflation.

It is often assumed that real interest rates are approximately constant; only recently has the variability of real interest rates gained attention.[5] The assumption of constancy in short-term real interest rates seems broadly valid for Canada and the United States in the 1970s because the variance of short-term real interest rates in those countries was smaller than the variance of inflation (see table VII.4). In several countries, however, the data suggest that the real interest rate was not constant or stable in the 1970s. In the 1980s, the variance of short-term real interest rates has risen in some countries (e.g., the United States), but fallen in others (e.g., the Federal Republic of Germany and Japan). In general, it would be difficult to argue that real interest rates have been constant except in the case of a few specific countries and periods. It follows that the volatility of nominal interest rates cannot be explained merely by volatility in inflation rates.

## Differences in real interest rates among countries

Nominal interest rates have also exhibited an increasing tendency to diverge across countries (see table VII.5). The differences between the nominal interest rates in different countries on both long-term and short-term government securities have been greater in the 1980s than between 1973 and 1979. The divergence seems most pronounced for long-term interest rates.

The differences are partially explained by differences in inflation rates: the divergence in real interest rates across countries has tended to be less than the divergence in nominal rates. In addition, the divergence in most real rates has been somewhat less in the 1980s than in the 1970s (see table VII.6), suggesting that the globalization and integration of capital markets in the 1980s has had some effect on harmonizing interest rates across national boundaries. Nevertheless, the cross-country divergences remain large, with the average absolute difference between the short-term real interest rate in the United States and the average in seven other major countries being almost 3 percentage points.

Divergence in real interest rates does not necessarily imply a lack of financial market integration. Most investors are resident within one set of national boundaries and for them the relevant price deflator for the nominal interest rate is the change in their local prices. For example, the real interest rate in the United States is not of direct concern to an investor in the Federal Republic of Germany. For such an investor, the real return comprises the nominal return from investing in the United States in dollar-denominated assets, adjusted for changes in the exchange rate, less the rate of inflation in the Federal Republic of Germany. A difference (or "spread") between the real rate of interest in the United States and that in the Federal Republic of Germany does not itself imply a wasted opportunity since there is no direct means by which the investor in the Federal Republic of Germany can earn the former rate.

It is this inability of investors to be able to take advantage of differences in national real interest rates that makes it possible for countries to conduct independent financial policies. If there were no such tolerance of spreads and no other imperfections in capital markets, there would be only one real interest rate on assets with a given class of risk. Individual countries would have little or no power to influence that rate.

The existence of a difference in real interest rates among countries, even when international capital markets are highly integrated, is consistent with a number of studies that have examined the behaviour of domestic savings and investment. These studies have found that these two variables are too closely correlated to be consistent with a situation in which the reactions of savers and investors quickly eliminate any difference in real interest rates.[6] It appears that domestic factors can have simultaneous effects on a country's levels of savings and investment that are independent of developments in the rest of the world, suggesting that it is inappropriate to think in terms of a single world pool of funds with costs and returns that are the same for all countries.

### Real interest rates, capital flows, and exchange rates

The supposed actions of both savers and investors are not the only factors that might have been expected to eliminate the spread between real interest rates in different countries. In theory, real interest rates in different countries should move to equality because of two conditions, known as uncovered interest parity (UIP) and purchasing power parity (PPP). The former concept posits that investors will shift

5 The evidence to support the assumption that United States real interest rates were approximately constant is contained in Eugene F. Fama, "Short-term interest rates as predictors of inflation", *American Economic Review*, June 1975, pp. 269-282. For an article rejecting constancy but suggesting that the variance of United States real interest rates is small relative to that of inflationary expectations, see Eugene F. Fama and Michael R. Gibbons, "Inflation, real returns and capital investment", *Journal of Monetary Economics*, May 1982, pp. 297-323.

6 The seminal papers are M. Feldstein, "Domestic saving and international capital movements in the long run and the short run", *European Economic Review*, vol. 21, March/April 1983, pp. 129-151, and M. Feldstein and C. Horioka, "Domestic saving and international capital flows", *Economic Journal*, 90, 1980, pp. 314-329. The logic is that, if all savers and investors had access to a world pool of funds at the same real costs and returns, sources and uses of funds would be independent of origin and place of use. If local real interest rates are somewhat independent, as seems to be the case, local factors can have simultaneous effects on both domestic savings and investment that are at least partially independent of the rest of the world's savings and investment.

Table VII.4. Components of the fluctuations in short-term interest rates for selected developed market economies, 1973-1988

| Country and period | Variance of nominal rate[a] | Variance of inflation rate[b] | Variance of real rate | Covariance between real rate and inflation rate |
|---|---|---|---|---|
| Canada | | | | |
| 1973-1988 | 9.87 | 10.03 | 7.39 | -3.77 |
| 1973-1978 | 4.86 | 5.67 | 3.64 | -2.25 |
| 1979-1988 | 9.36 | 3.00 | 9.47 | -1.56 |
| France | | | | |
| 1973-1988 | 8.91 | 11.42 | 8.03 | -5.93 |
| 1973-1978 | 5.47 | 6.15 | 1.96 | -1.33 |
| 1979-1988 | 8.60 | 15.46 | 7.01 | -6.93 |
| Germany, Federal Republic of | | | | |
| 1973-1988 | 7.13 | 3.59 | 4.75 | -0.61 |
| 1973-1978 | 8.37 | 3.01 | 2.74 | 1.31 |
| 1979-1988 | 6.06 | 1.54 | 4.88 | -0.18 |
| Japan | | | | |
| 1973-1988 | 6.12 | 27.29 | 14.77 | -17.98 |
| 1973-1978 | 7.27 | 29.33 | 12.83 | -17.49 |
| 1979-1988 | 4.47 | 5.20 | 1.38 | -1.05 |
| Netherlands | | | | |
| 1973-1988 | 8.15 | 12.17 | 10.36 | -7.19 |
| 1973-1978 | 11.69 | 12.00 | 4.67 | -2.50 |
| 1979-1988 | 6.95 | 6.65 | 5.59 | -2.65 |
| Switzerland | | | | |
| 1980-1988 | 3.15 | 3.39 | 2.29 | -1.27 |
| United Kingdom | | | | |
| 1973-1988 | 7.35 | 29.69 | 26.26 | -24.30 |
| 1973-1978 | 6.56 | 26.59 | 16.23 | -18.13 |
| 1979-1988 | 4.84 | 21.58 | 9.16 | -12.95 |
| United States | | | | |
| 1973-1988 | 7.64 | 10.16 | 8.77 | -5.65 |
| 1973-1978 | 1.97 | 5.80 | 1.81 | -2.82 |
| 1979-1988 | 7.86 | 13.75 | 7.36 | -6.63 |

*Source:* Department of International Economic and Social Affairs of the United Nations Secretariat, based on IMF, *International Financial Statistics*, various issues.

a Based on data of quarterly averages.

b Based on the inflation rate for the current and the past four quarters as measured by the consumer price index.

their purchases between securities denominated in different currencies until the difference in nominal interest rates on comparable securities is equal to the expected percentage depreciation (over the same period as the interest rate) of the currency whose security carries the higher nominal interest rate. This approach assumes that the investor's objective is to maximize his nominal expected return—which implies he is indifferent to foreign exchange risk—in a market free from transactions costs and regulatory interferences. The term "uncovered" refers to the assumption that the expected change in currency values is the investor's forecast rather than the result of prearranged prices transacted in futures contracts or forward markets in foreign exchange.[7]

The concept of PPP is based on the assumption that market forces align exchange rates and the prices of goods in different countries so that the "real exchange rate", that is, the rate at which one country's exports buy imports, will be

7 In futures markets, investors agree to take or render delivery of deposits denominated in one currency in exchange for cash payments in another currency at specific dates. "Forward" currency deposits are prearranged exchanges of deposits with commercial banks in different currencies at prearranged rates of exchange.

Table VII.5. Dispersion of short-term and long-term nominal interest rates for selected developed market economies, 1973-1988[a]

(Percentage)

| | Short-term rates | Long-term rates |
|---|---|---|
| Overall dispersion[b] | | |
| 1973-1979 | 2.06 | 1.39 |
| 1980-1982 | 3.02 | 2.18 |
| 1983-1985 | 2.71 | 3.13 |
| 1986-1988 | 2.17 | 2.80 |
| 1980-1988 | 2.61 | 2.70 |
| Deviations from the United States rate[c] | | |
| 1973-1979 | 2.59 | 1.75 |
| 1980-1982 | 3.45 | 2.22 |
| 1983-1985 | 2.75 | 3.14 |
| 1986-1988 | 2.27 | 3.19 |
| 1980-1988 | 2.86 | 2.83 |

*Source:* Department of International Economic and Social Affairs of the United Nations Secretariat, based on data from IMF, *International Financial Statistics.*

a Eight countries are included: Canada, France, the Federal Republic of Germany, Japan, the Netherlands, Switzerland, the United Kingdom and the United States. Calculations are based on quarterly average interest rates.

b Average absolute difference from the overall average interest rate for all countries for each quarter.

c Average absolute difference between the quarterly average interest rate in the United States and those in the seven other countries.

Table VII.6. Dispersion of short-term and long-term real interest rates for selected developed market economies, 1973-1988[a]

(Percentage)

| | Short-term rates | Long-term rates |
|---|---|---|
| Overall dispersion[b] | | |
| 1973-1979 | 2.63 | 1.75 |
| 1980-1982 | 2.26 | 1.61 |
| 1983-1985 | 1.61 | 1.43 |
| 1986-1988 | 1.60 | .99 |
| 1980-1988 | 2.19 | 1.36 |
| Deviations from the United States rate[c] | | |
| 1973-1979 | 3.25 | 2.13 |
| 1980-1982 | 3.42 | 2.46 |
| 1983-1985 | 2.05 | 3.37 |
| 1986-1988 | 2.43 | 1.13 |
| 1980-1988 | 2.92 | 2.39 |

*Source:* Department of International Economic and Social Affairs of the United Nations Secretariat, based on data from IMF, *International Financial Statistics.* Nominal interest rates are quarterly averages. Short-term real interest rates are *ex post:* the inflation component is taken as the percentage growth in the (quarterly average) consumer price index, annualized (times four). The inflation components of the long-term interest rates are taken to be the average growth in countries' (quarterly average) consumer price indices for two years ending with the current quarter.

a Eight countries are included: Canada, France, the Federal Republic of Germany, Japan, the Netherlands, Switzerland, the United Kingdom and the United States. Calculations are based on quarterly average interest rates.

b Average absolute difference from the overall average interest rate for all countries for each quarter.

c Average absolute difference between the quarterly average interest rate in the United States and those in the seven other countries.

constant.[8] This "purchasing power parity" usually requires the assumption that foreign exchange and goods markets are highly efficient and that this relative price is not affected by changes in the money supply or by other factors that influence nominal demand in different countries. Constancy of real exchange rates implies that nominal exchange rates and relative price levels must grow at offsetting rates. When PPP is combined with UIP, the theoretical result is that real interest rates should be the same in the two countries.[9]

There is, however, abundant evidence that these conditions are not satisfied in practice. The invalidity of PPP is the more obvious: real exchange rates oscillate widely (see those shown for the United States *vis-à-vis* Japan and *vis-à-vis* the Federal Republic of Germany in figure VII.4). The usual explanation is that the prices of goods are sticky in the short run, while nominal exchange rates are much more volatile because they are affected by factors besides the relative prices of goods (such as interest rates and capital flows).

One influential theory rejects the proposition of short-run PPP (on the grounds that prices are sticky), but retains the proposition of PPP for the long run (on the grounds that prices can adjust fully if there is enough time) and accepts UIP.[10] This combination of assumptions not only explains why spreads between real interest rates among countries might reasonably exist, but also makes these spreads into key indicators of the direction of capital flows and major determinants of short-run movements in exchange rates. One implication of this theory is that the value of a country's currency, measured against that of a country with lower real interest rates, should be higher than the long-run equilibrium. The expected correlation between differences in real

8 Stricter versions of PPP require that prices of individual goods be equal after the appropriate exchange rate conversion. The version in the text is based on the average price of a basket of goods measured relative to some base year, i.e., a price index. PPP in this context requires the expression $E(P_1/P_2)$ to be constant, where $E$ is the the price of the currency of country 1 in terms of the currency of country 2 and $P_1$ and $P_2$ are the domestic price indices of countries 1 and 2, respectively.

9 If the real exchange rate remains constant, it implies that $e^* + (p_1^* - p_2^*) = 0$, where $e$, $p_1$ and $p_2$ represent average percentage changes of $E$, $P_1$ and $P_2$ respectively (see note 8 above) and * represents their expected values. UIP requires that $i_2 = i_1 + e^*$. Replacing e* in this equation with its value from the first one gives $i_2 - p_2^* = i_1 - p_1^*$, i.e., the real interest rates must be equal.

10 Rudiger Dornbusch, "Expectations and exchange rate dynamics", *Journal of Political Economy,* 84, 1976, pp. 1161-1176.

Figure VII.4. Real exchange rates, short-term real interest rate spreads and current account ratios in the Federal Republic of Germany, Japan and the United States

A. *Real exchange rates*[a]

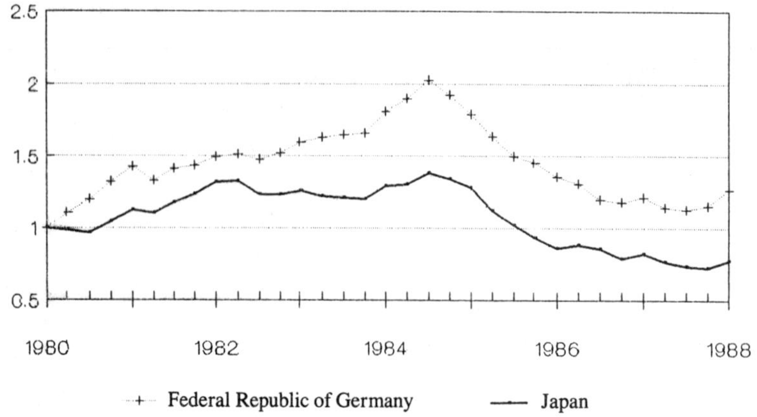


B. *Differences in short-term real interest rates*[b]

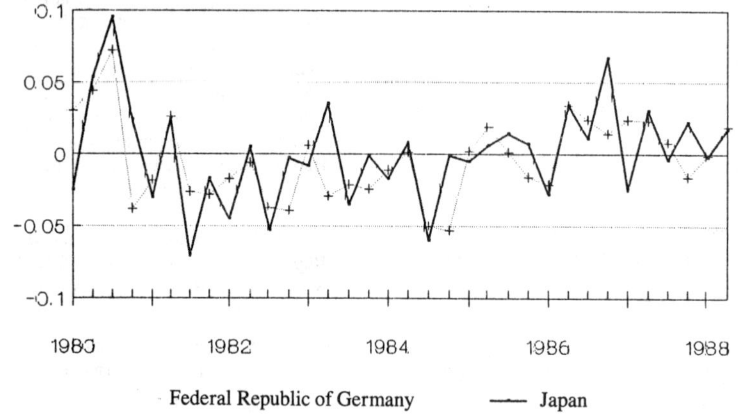


C. *Current account balances as a percentage of GNP*

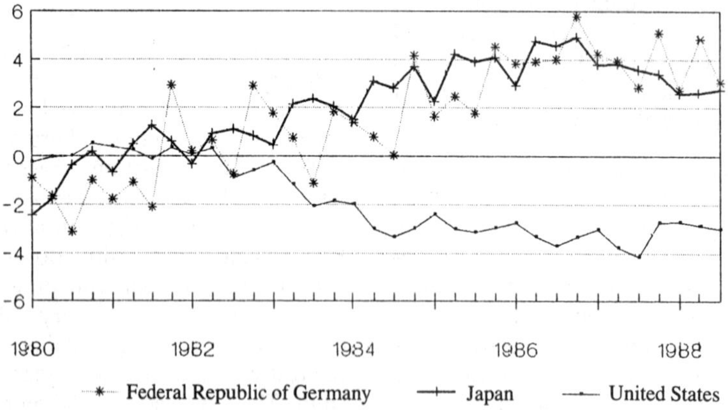


*Source:* Department of International Economic and Social Affairs of the United Nations Secretariat, based on IMF, *International Financial Statistics*, various issues.

a Real exchange rates are expressed as the price of the dollar in foreign currency multiplied by the ratio of the United States consumer price index to that in the Federal Republic of Germany and Japan, respectively. The resulting series is expressed with base 1980 = 1.

b The difference refers to the excess, expressed as a decimal, of short-term real interest rates in the Federal Republic of Germany and Japan over the United States rate. Inflation is defined as the average annualized growth of the quarterly consumer price index between the previous quarter and the next quarter.

Figure VII.5. Differences in short-term nominal rates of return on dollar and non-dollar financial instruments[a]

(Percentage)

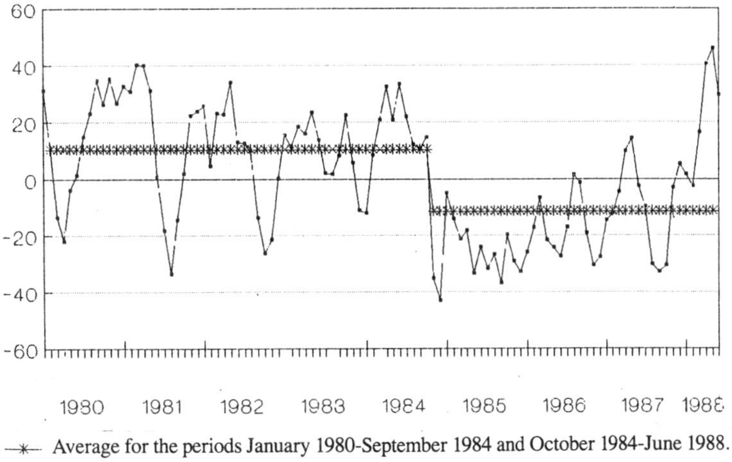


*Source:* Department of International Economic and Social Affairs of the United Nations Secretariat, based on IMF, *International Financial Statistics,* various issues.

[a] The difference is defined as the United States short-term nominal interest rate minus the average of the corresponding rate for seven countries (Canada, France, the Federal Republic of Germany, Japan, the Netherlands, Switzerland and the United Kingdom), with each of the latter rates adjusted for the average quarterly annualized change in the value of their currency *vis-à-vis* the dollar.

interest rates and real exchange rates clearly exists for the Federal Republic of Germany and Japan *vis-à-vis* the United States (see figure VII.5). Moreover, the relationship is not restricted to the United States and other countries: it holds tightly on a bilateral basis between many countries (see table VII.7).

The approach also provides some insight into the apparent overvaluation of the dollar in the mid-1980s. If UIP and gradual adjustment of real exchange rates to PPP are assumed to prevail, the spread in the real interest rate between two countries provides a theoretical forecast of the real depreciation of the currency of the country with the higher interest rate. A comparison of the real interest rates on United States Government bonds with those on comparable bonds issued by other developed countries, together with other information, suggests that the dollar was overvalued in real terms in early 1985 by about 35 per cent relative to currencies of the other leading industrial countries.[11] As of early 1985, the real value of the dollar had risen by approximately that amount relative to the real values of the other currencies since about 1980 (when the United States current account had been roughly in balance).

Nevertheless, the events of the 1980s call into question some aspects of this approach. The fall in the real exchange value of the dollar since early 1985 has not been sufficient to keep the United States current account deficit from growing. It appears that the calculation of a long-run equilibrium real exchange rate requires more detailed analysis and that the connection between the differences in real interest rates in early 1985 and the dollar's supposed "overvaluation" relative to a base year of 1980 is a matter of coincidence.

Empirical data have never given strong support to UIP, and the volatile movements in interest rates and exchange rates in the 1980s cast particular doubt on its validity. UIP predicts that, on average, returns on comparable assets denominated in different currencies should be equal after exchange rate conversion. However, the difference between the returns on non-dollar and dollar-denominated assets, after adjustments for changes in the exchange rate, has been large and persistent in the 1980s (see figure VII.5). In particular, in the period to late 1984 (when the dollar appreciated rapidly), the nominal return on dollar-denominated short-term assets, adjusted for changes in the exchange rate, appears to have exceeded the returns on similar assets in other currencies by about 10 per cent, while the opposite occurred (in the amount of about 11 per cent) as the dollar fell after 1984. These systematic deviations were large in relation to the differences in interest rates.

11 See Rudiger Dornbusch and Jeffrey Frankel, "The flexible exchange rate system: experience and alternatives", National Bureau of Economic Research Working Paper No. 2464, p. 18. The authors estimated elsewhere that this real exchange rate tended to adjust the gap between its current and long-run value by about 14 per cent annually. Since the real interest rate spread of 5 per cent implied an annual 5 per cent depreciaion in the dollar real exchange rate and this should equal about 14 per cent of the gap, it followed that the current real exchange rate was about 35 per cent (5/0.14) higher than its long-run value.

Table VII.7. Correlations between differences in short-term real interest rates[a] across countries and the corresponding real exchange rates[b] for selected developed market economies, 1970-1988

| Country *j* \ Country *i* | Canada | France | Federal Republic of Germany | Japan | Netherlands | Switzerland | United Kingdom | United States |
|---|---|---|---|---|---|---|---|---|
| Canada | | -0.23* | 0.33* | 0.13* | 0.65** | 0.25* | 0.15* | -0.32** |
| France | | | 0.16* | 0.06 | 0.34** | 0.64** | 0.45* | 0.17* |
| Germany, Federal Republic of | | | | 0.41** | 0.66** | 0.78** | 0.51** | 0.75** |
| Japan | | | | | 0.04 | 0.59** | 0.25** | 0.41** |
| Netherlands | | | | | | 0.66** | 0.44** | 0.63** |
| Switzerland | | | | | | | 0.09 | 0.57** |
| United Kingdom | | | | | | | | 0.12* |
| United States | | | | | | | | |

*Source:* Department of International Economic and Social Affairs of the United Nations Secretariat, based on IMF, *International Financial Statistics,* various issues.

*Note:* A positive correlation in this table indicates that a larger real interest rate spread in favour of one country (e.g., a bigger difference between real interest rates in the United States and those in the Federal Republic of Germany) is associated with a higher real exchange rate for the currency of that country (i.e., the dollar). The real exchange rate is defined here as the nominal exchange rate of country *i's* currency in terms of country *j's* currency (e.g., if country *i* is the United States and country *j* is the Federal Republic of Germany, it is the number of dentsche mark required to buy one United States dollar) multiplied by the ratio of the consumer price index in country *i* to the consumer price index in country *j.* The real short-term interest spread is defined here as the rate in country *i* minus the rate in country *j.*

a Measured as the difference in the average of four quarterly *ex post* short-term interest rates ending in the quarter over which the nominal interest rate applies.

b Measured as the exchange rate between the two countries deflated by the ratio of their consumer price indices.

* indicates statistically significant correlation at the 0.3 level.

** indicates statistically significant correlation at the 0.05 level.

In summary, the evidence suggests that both PPP and UIP hold up poorly in practice, though not so poorly as to render real interest rates in different countries completely independent of each other, nor so poorly as to make exchange rates independent of differences between real interest rates. An upward shift in a country's fiscal deficit, as occurred in the United States beginning in 1982, will still raise domestic real interest rates and the real value of the domestic currency. These imperfections in markets simply imply that we should expect no straightforward arithmetic relationship between the difference in real interest rates and the market's expectation of future changes in the real value of the currency. After 1985, the excess of real interest rates in the United States over those elsewhere declined and, as would be predicted, so did the real value of the dollar.

## Conclusions

High levels of interest rates—real interest rates in particular—are usually considered to augur ill for the economy, but this depends on the reasons for their being high. If high real interest rates reflect strong demand for funds for investment, the implication is that borrowers regard future growth and profits as also being sufficiently high to cover their payments to lenders. High rates under these circumstances imply a favourable view of the economic future. If, on the other hand, high real interest rates reflect a low availability of savings in the world at large, the prognosis is less favourable.

The foregoing analysis suggests that the increase in real interest rates in the 1980s is a symptom of macro-economic imbalance associated with the United States fiscal deficit. The key data—investment and savings ratios, spreads in real interest rates between the United States and other countries, exchange rate movements in relation both to these ratios and to spreads in interest rates—point to the United States fiscal deficit as a major drag on world savings. In the absence of an increase in other sources of world savings, further large United States fiscal deficits will continue to "crowd out" world investment and retard growth. In addiiton, failure to increase the flow of world savings and the persistence of high real interest rates will continue to be a major obstacle to the objective of reversing the net transfer of resources from the heavily indebted countries.

Although the United States fiscal deficit has declined as a share of the United States GNP, this boost to total savings in the United States has been substantially offset by a decline in the private savings rate.[12]. At the same time, the difference in short-term real interest rates between the United States and other countries has narrowed, which implies (and has been accompanied by) a drop in the real value of the dollar. The decline in United States real interest rates relative to those abroad suggests that the maintenance of United States demand betwen 1986 and 1988 was driven largely by monetary policy. This, in turn, helps to account for the increase in the United States current account deficit.[13]

In this instance and in general, real interest rates appear to be important determinants of real exchange rates. A higher domestic real interest rate relative to another country's leads to a higher exchange value of domestic goods when traded for the other country's goods. The mechanism appears to work through the capital market, with the higher rate on domestic assets increasing their attractiveness. Because the Governments of the major developed market economies have committed themselves to co-ordinated efforts aimed at stabilizing exchange rates, real interest rates should be useful indicators for this purpose.

However, recent history also indicates that real interest rates should be used as a policy indicator with great care. A particular difference in real interest rates among countries can be consistent with a variety of current account balances and real exchange rates, depending on the mix of monetary and fiscal policies in and between countries. The policy mix chosen by the Governments of the major industrial countries after 1985 succeeded in reducing the value of the dollar (primarily by monetary policy), but it also helped to perpetuate the United States current account deficit. Although spreads in real interest rates are becoming recognized as important indicators for economic policy, reliance on monetary policy to manipulate these spreads and real exchange rates cannot substitute for domestic fiscal policy reform.

12 The savings rate is likely to continue to decline in many developed market economies for demographic reasons. The proportion of older people in these populations is increasing (see Special Issues, sect. I, below) and this age group tends to save less than younger age groups, or even to dissave.

13 As indicated in figure VII.5, the ratio of the current account to GNP showed essentially no trend between 1986 and 1988.

# Chapter VIII

## ECONOMIC ADJUSTMENT AND THE NET TRANSFER OF RESOURCES FROM DEVELOPING COUNTRIES

For large parts of the developing world, the 1980s have been a period of economic retrogression. Many countries—concentrated in Africa and Latin America and the Caribbean, but also some Asian and European developing countries—have lost the momentum of development gained in the 1960s and 1970s and have seen standards of living deteriorate. Other developing countries have charged ahead, both in terms of average income per head and levels of technological sophistication. In the 1990s, per capita income in Asia, long known as the poorest continent on earth, will begin to exceed that of Africa.

The split in the economic performance of the developing countries has prompted many investigations, including some in the *World Economic Survey,*[1] and has affected international discussions of development policy. The countries whose economic performance has lagged are sometimes viewed as having been trapped in an economic adjustment process through which other countries have progressed more quickly or have been able, thus far, to evade due to differences in their economic circumstances. The fact that the adjustment process in the world economy is still far from complete is important, especially in the United Nations where preparations are now under way for a new intergovernmental pact on development, the International Development Strategy for the Fourth United Nations Development Decade, as discussed in chapter I above.

The collective understanding of economic development and the adjustment process is not very far advanced. There is a consensus that the economic performance of developing countries has multiple determinants: some reside within them and some in the external economic environment; some are policy-related and some the results of resource endowments and the state of technology; some respond quickly to domestic policy measures and others require a long time to change. Still others can only be addressed at the policy level by the international community.

One factor that has been a focus of attention in intergovernmental discussions is the net transfer of financial resources from developing to developed countries, also referred to as the "negative transfer of financial resources", in contrast to the traditional positive transfer to developing countries.[2] At the level of the aggregate of the capital-importing developing countries, 1989 will mark the seventh consecutive year of negative transfers.[3] As noted in chapter IV, the negative transfer is not everywhere related to economic distress. In rapidly growing economies such as the Republic of Korea, it is a sign of growing economic maturity and success. But in most cases, the negative transfer is due to adverse changes in credit-related flows that are intimately related to the developing country debt crises of the 1980s.

If the capital-importing developing countries are divided into those that have experienced debt-servicing difficulties and those that have not, the negative transfer is seen to be very much the experience of the former group of countries. Table VIII.1 illustrates this clearly in terms of two groups of developing countries as defined by the International Monetary Fund (IMF)[4] and in terms of the two common definitions of the net financial transfer of resources. Viewing the net transfer as the net capital flow minus the net payment of investment income, the group of countries that have not had recent debt-servicing problems has continuously registered a net financial resource inflow, whereas the aggregate of the debt-problem group of countries last received a net resource inflow in 1982. In terms of the expenditure definition—which is the one most closely related to concepts of national income accounting, such as gross domestic investment and saving—the net transfer of the countries without debt problems turned negative in 1987, as these countries applied their trade surpluses to building up reserves. Indeed, these latter countries have added to their aggregate reserves in each year of the decade, whereas the debt-problem countries have had to draw down their reserves, in aggegate, as often as they were able to add to them.

That there is a close relationship between the change in the net financial transfer and the adjustment problem is clear: not a single developing country that experienced serious debt-servicing difficulties in the early 1980s and was adjusting by mid-decade has been able to recover sufficiently to restore the confidence of its international creditors and regain normal access to international finance. But the solution to the adjustment problem is not merely to return financial

1 See, in particular, "The fast-growing developing countries of the 1980s", in *World Economic Survey 1987* and "Growth and adjustment in small and medium-sized developing countries during the 1980s", in *World Economic Survey 1988* (United Nations publications, Sales Nos. E.87.II.C.1 and E.88.II.C.1), pp. 155-167 and 141-149, respectively.

2 One sign of continuing intergovernmental interest in the subject of the net transfer of resources from developing to developed countries is Economic and Social Council decision 1988/160, in which the preparation of this chapter was called for. That decision was the latest in a series of decisions on the subject adopted by the Council and the General Assembly (see, in particular, Council resolution 1987/93 and General Assembly decision 42/429).

3 In some presentations, the net transfer of resources is understood to include the effect of changes in the terms of trade as well as changes in financial flows. The concept as used here is restricted to the financial flow effect in order that the impact of changes in the terms of trade may be addressed separately. For further details on the definition of the net transfer, see the report of the Secretary-General on the net transfer of resources from developing to developed countries (E/1988/64) and *World Economic Survey 1986* (United Nations publication, Sales No. E.86.II.C.1), pp. 163-164.

4 The Fund classifies a country as having had recent debt-servicing difficulties if it has incurred external payments arrears or entered official or commercial bank debt rescheduling agreements during 1985-1987 (see IMF, *World Economic Outlook 1989* (Washington, D.C., April 1989), Statistical Appendix).

Table VIII.1. Net transfer of financial resources of developing countries with and without debt-servicing difficulties, 1981-1988

(Billions of dollars)

| | 1981 | 1982 | 1983 | 1984 | 1985 | 1986 | 1987 | 1988 |
|---|---|---|---|---|---|---|---|---|
| Countries with debt-servicing difficulties (73 countries) | | | | | | | | |
| Net financial transfer[a] | | | | | | | | |
| Capital account definition | 33.4 | 4.4 | -6.3 | -12.7 | -28.0 | -12.1 | -14.8 | -28.5 |
| Expenditure definition | 56.9 | 46.1 | -6.9 | -28.1 | -29.4 | -4.9 | -19.7 | -21.9 |
| Use of official reserves | 23.5 | 41.7 | -0.6 | -15.4 | -1.4 | 7.2 | -4.9 | 6.6 |
| Countries without debt-servicing difficulties (53 countries) | | | | | | | | |
| Net financial transfer[a] | | | | | | | | |
| Capital account definition | 33.6 | 29.1 | 30.6 | 14.5 | 26.1 | 10.1 | 3.9 | 12.0 |
| Expenditure definition | 29.2 | 25.4 | 26.2 | 13.3 | 21.6 | 9.6 | -10.7 | -7.5 |
| Use of official reserves | -4.4 | -3.7 | -4.4 | -1.2 | -4.5 | -0.5 | -14.6 | -19.5 |

*Source:* Data and country groups from IMF, *World Economic Outlook,* April 1989.

a Capital account definition is the net flow of all forms of capital in and out of the sample countries, minus net capital servicing, including IMF flows, but excluding changes in official reserve assets. Expenditure definition is the negative of the balance of payments of goods, private transfers and all services excluding capital-related payments. The change in official reserve assets is the difference between the two measures. Data in this table are approximations in that IMF does not include payments of direct investment income in its measure of net investment income; net resource transfer data in subsequent tables in this chapter include those payments.

transfers to their previous levels. About that there is no controversy. The key question is how to find the appropriate mix of policy reforms and how much international finance to supply in support of reform.

With this in view, the present chapter looks into the economic adjustment process and the role played by international transfers of financial resources. The approach taken here is to analyse broad aggregates of countries and specific country case histories in an effort to explore why the adjustment problem still exists in so much of the developing world and how it might be overcome.

## The net transfer and adjustment

The phrase "economic adjustment" has come to have a multitude of definitions. The kernel of meaning that the various authors seem to share is that adjustment is a set of responses of an economy to policies that were themselves adopted in response to adverse economic developments. First there is a disturbing economic shock and then an attempt to recover economic balance. The recovery need not aim at restoring the *status quo ante;* indeed, in some cases the shock was especially disruptive because it revealed weaknesses in existing economic structures and policies. In such cases, adjustment becomes structural adjustment, which in policy terms often becomes indistinguishable from long-run development planning.

### The goal of adjustment: sustained development

For purposes of the present analysis, economic adjustment is defined as the changes needed to place an economy on a sustained path of economic growth and development. For growth to be sustained, adjustment must proceed on two broad fronts: structural and macro-economic. The latter includes monetary and fiscal policy-making. On the fiscal side, government budget balances need not be reduced to zero, but deficits must become small enough to allow the economy to absorb smoothly the growth of the government debt that finances the deficits. This does not mean that government expenditures must everywhere be curtailed, especially if cutbacks have already been instituted, but it does mean that government revenues must rise to carry the overwhelming bulk of the cost of expenditures.

On the monetary side of economic policy, one looks for adequate stability of prices and positive but not excessive real interest rates. This also makes exchange rate management easier. To give proper signals for business decisions, changes in domestic prices need to reflect changes in international prices and in relative domestic scarcities. On a sustainable growth path, inflation need not be reduced to zero, but investors must not be so distracted by inflationary worries that they cease to make long-run commitments of funds to projects. In addition, as the financial system is usually intended as a mechanism for effective mobilization and allocation of capital resources, individuals and enterprises should be willing to buy and hold financial assets, for which they naturally expect a real return.[5] Economic agents will remove their wealth if they think its value is endangered, particularly at a time when the technology of international finance has made it relatively easy to do so.

The international financial aspect of sustainability requires that foreign claims can be serviced without undue strain on the foreign exchange earnings of the economy. Countries that achieve this condition will regain normal access to international financing, and creditors and investors would make decisions on resource commitments on the usual basis, which concentrates on the soundness of individual projects and programmes. In contrast, today lending of almost any type is banned to a country that has not overcome its adjustment problems, for fear of macro-economic restrictions on transferring earnings abroad.

For most developing economies, international prices are exogenous variables to which they can adjust but which they cannot control. Indeed, part of the structural aspect of economic adjustment is changing the mix of goods produced for export and imported for domestic use in response to changes in international price trends. This aspect of the structural problem can be viewed in different ways. One is to increase the production of tradable goods as opposed to non-tradables; another is to increase the interlinkages between sectors in an economy so that, for example, an increasing proportion of inputs to a production process are purchased from domestic suppliers. A third aspect is to diversify the production structure and emphasize economic activities that are not overly specialized, so that the economy can shift relatively quickly in response to adverse international circumstances or newly emerging opportunities. In an uncertain and volatile international economy, the value of diversified agriculture and a strong manufacturing base need hardly be stressed.

Another of the structural dimensions of adjustment is that for sustained growth a developing country needs a robust official sector that is able to provide necessary public services and build and maintain essential infrastructure, such as road networks. However large the role accorded the private sector in a country's development strategy, the Government must provide services that the private sector cannot supply.[6] It is also the essential role of the Government to promote and protect the common good; public action against environmental polluters is a classic case in point. In addition, the Government is traditionally the major source of financing of education, a primary underwriter of research and is responsible for public health measures, all of which would be provided in adequate measure in a country undergoing sustained growth.

It is also traditional to look to the Government for an overall perception of the direction in which an economy is and should be going. Whatever the degree of popular participation, the Government is the forum in which decisions are made on directions and paths of development, on what economic sectors to encourage, on what economic behaviour to prohibit. Action to ensure that the environment is defended can be taken only at the governmental level. Whether or not Governments engage in formal development planning, they make the decisions that together form the development policy package. And by monitoring performance they can discern when development takes a direction that is not sustainable. Moreover, in countries experiencing sustained growth, the people seem to devote considerable attention to how their Government is functioning, questioning shortcomings and searching for techniques to improve its effectiveness.

Finally, countries undergoing sustained growth would be on a trend of rising average incomes and rising wage rates. Competitiveness is maintained as workers gain in productivity since investment expands and renews the capital stock. Indeed, a high rate of investment would occur in all key sectors of the economy, financed for the most part by domestic savings that increase more easily when incomes themselves are rising. In this setting, entrepreneurship is encouraged by the growth of markets at home as well as abroad and by the generally buoyant conditions. Farsighted and humane policies for reducing poverty would be more readily adopted and financed when aggregate income is rising significantly.

### Investment resources: a key element in growth-oriented adjustment

The picture presented of an economy undergoing sustained growth is not meant as an unattainable ideal. For most developing countries in the 1980s, however, it might seem to be such. The differences among economic situations can be highlighted by dividing the developing countries that are usually thought of as net users of foreign capital into three analytical subgroupings of countries, namely, those that have not experienced recent debt-servicing and adjustment crises, a group of 15 heavily indebted countries that is often associated with the "Baker Plan" of the former United States Secretary of the Treasury, and a group of low-income African countries.[7]

The countries that have avoided debt-servicing crises have been able to maintain high rates of economic growth for long periods. Their per capita GDP has even grown more rapidly in the 1980s (4.2 per cent a year on average from 1981 to 1988) than it did in the 1970s (3.6 per cent a year on average

5 This is not necessarily an argument against subsidization of credit, although it is probably best used when it can be effectively targeted; but subsidization should be an explicit policy whose costs are clearly seen in the government budget.

6 Governments may contract almost any public service to a private firm, but the expenditure decision would remain a governmental one.

7 The country groupings and the data estimates in this discussion are those of the International Monetary Fund, as published in its *World Economic Outlook.* Countries without debt-servicing problems are the same as those in table VIII.1. The 15 country sample comprises Argentina, Bolivia, Brazil, Chile, Colombia, Côte d'Ivoire, Ecuador, Mexico, Morocco, Nigeria, Peru, the Philippines, Uruguay, Venezuela and Yugoslavia. The sub-Saharan grouping comprises 46 countries, excluding Nigeria and South Africa. The groupings are solely for analytical convenience and do not express an opinion about what types or degrees of financial assistance might be required by any individual country.

Figure VIII.1. Growth and investment in developing countries, 1980-1988

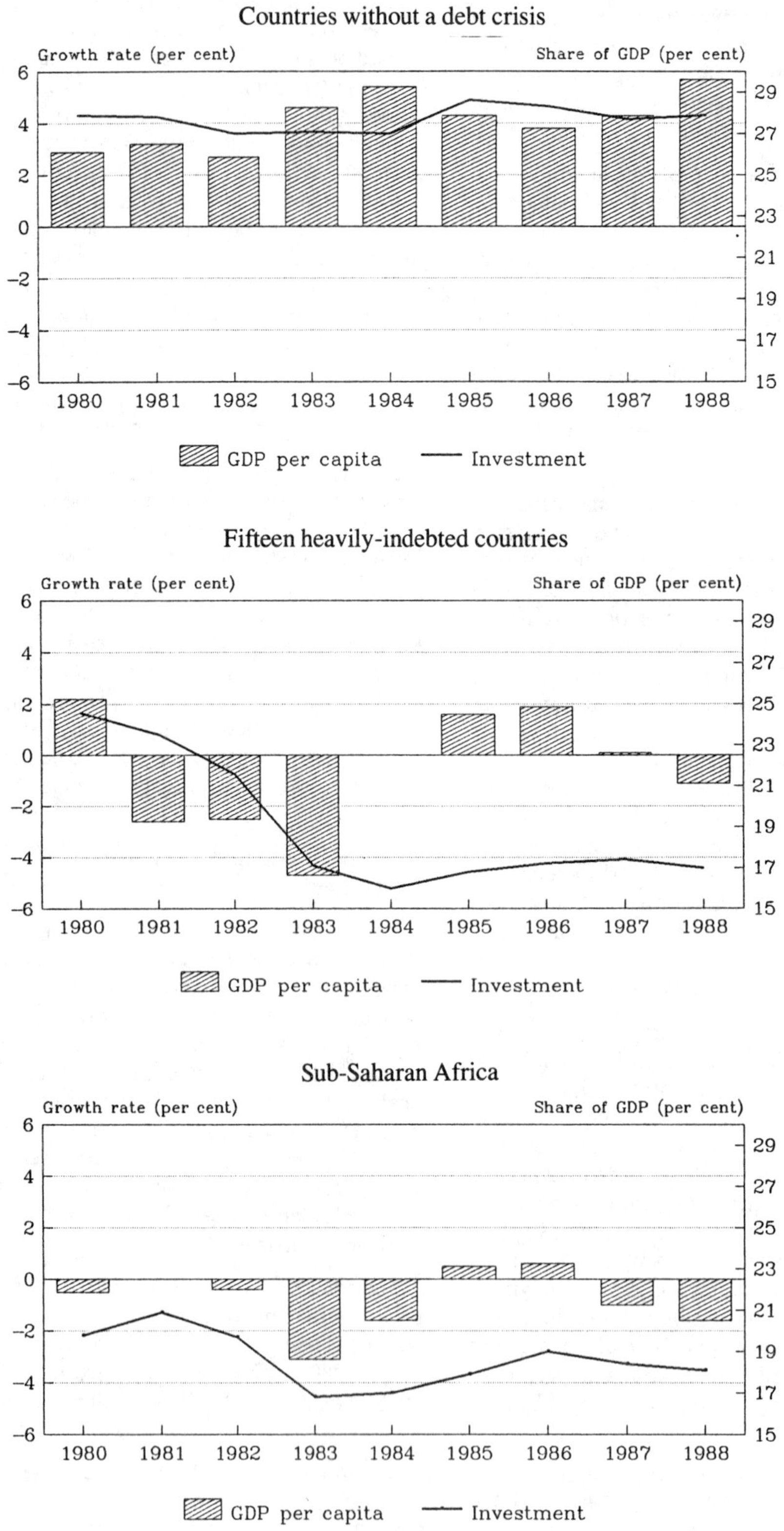


*Source:* Department of International Economic and Social Affairs of the United Nations Secretariat, based on IMF data and country groupings.

from 1971 to 1980). Growth of per capita output of the other groups has been quite different. For the 15-country sample, it dropped from 3.1 per cent on average in the 1970s to -0.9 per cent a year in the 1980s. For the African sample, GDP per capita did not grow at all in the 1970s, and has been declining at an average rate of 0.8 per cent a year in the 1980s.

A crucial difference among the country groups is their investment levels. In contrast to the steady rate of investment of over 27 per cent of GDP by the countries that evaded debt-servicing crises, the investment rates in the other two groups fell drastically. Investment efforts seem impossible to maintain in the face of declining per capita output (see figure VIII.1). In the case of the 15 country sample, the fall was from pre-crisis levels of 24 per cent of GDP or more to about 17 per cent or less. In the case of the African grouping, investment began the decade at the already relatively low level of about 20 per cent of GDP, from which its fall to 17 per cent was especially costly. By 1988 the investment share was hardly above that in 1983, and as per capita GDP itself has fallen, it cannot be said that recovery of investment has begun. Of course, the rate of growth of an economy depends on much more than the rate of investment; but without adequate levels of investment, especially over long periods of time, a country's capacity to grow is severely curtailed.

The relationship of investment to the net transfer of resources is that the financing of investment must come from domestic savings or the net financial transfer.[8] As can be seen in figure VIII.2, the country group with the highest average growth rate and the highest investment share also had the highest rate of savings.[9] With hindsight, it is clear that these countries did not rely excessively on foreign resources for investment. When international financial conditions deteriorated sharply in the early 1980s they were generally less vulnerable.

There is a virtuous circle here, as rapid growth of income per capita fosters a rising savings rate and high investment, which provide support for further rapid growth of output and income. When the net transfer of this group of countries became negative in 1987, they were able to absorb it with a higher savings rate and without sacrificing investment (see figure VIII.1).

The contrast with the other two groupings of countries could not be more dramatic. In the 15-country sample, the net transfer of resources dropped sharply from a pre-crisis average of 2 per cent of GDP in 1979-1981 to a low of -4 per cent in 1984-1985 and a level of at least -2 per cent since. A drop of that magnitude could not have been offset by an increase in savings. In any case, after first declining a small amount, savings have held fairly steady at roughly 20 per cent of GDP since 1981.

A similar story can be told about sub-Saharan Africa, except that the savings rate was much lower to begin with and the dependency on foreign resource transfers was—and is—much higher. Net transfers on average remained positive, if reduced, although for many countries in the region they became significantly negative.

The resource transfer problem has hobbled the countries facing the adjustment imperative in two ways. First, they were deprived of foreign resources and as such their "absorptive capacity"—that is, their expenditure capacity—was cut back. The drop in resources available for investment would itself cause investment levels to fall, but in addition, declining total spending sours the economic outlook, which also deters investment. After some years of reduced investment, the second hobbling factor takes effect: the capacity to produce is curtailed. Not only does capacity not rise to employ the ever-growing work force, but the existing stock of equipment becomes increasingly obsolete.

The implication of this analysis is that without an important improvement in the net transfer of resources, developing countries have not been able—and will not be able—to undertake investments that are necessary for the adjustment process. In the circumstances, domestic savings cannot replace the foreign resources lost. It is not politically conceivable that after incomes and consumption have already fallen so much, average consumption levels could be squeezed further to free the resources for investment, nor should they be in most countries. Indeed, there is a strong case for increasing expenditures to raise the consumption standards of the lowest income and most vulnerable groups in the debt-crisis countries.[10]

### Effective adjustment policy: the confidence problem

There is an international consensus that economic adjustment requires economic policy changes.[11] Indeed, most developing countries in economic crisis have adopted policy

8 The relationship is a precise one in national income accounting terms, as gross domestic investment equals gross domestic savings plus the net financial transfer. An alternative formulation—perhaps a more common one in industrialized countries—is that gross domestic investment equals gross national savings plus net foreign investment. Since gross national savings is gross domestic savings minus net factor payments abroad, the two formulations are identical.

9 The savings rates shown in figure VIII.2 and discussed here should be interpreted as very approximate indicators, subject to considerable margins of error. However, even under the best systems for data collection and analysis, savings estimates are relatively weak, not to mention subject to considerable definitional controversy (see, for example, Robert Eisner, "Divergences of measurement and theory and some implications for economic policy", Presidential Address, American Economic Association, 29 December 1988, in *The American Economic Review*, March 1989, pp. 1-13).

10 A sufficient reason would be simple human solidarity, but it is also a farsighted development policy to improve the productivity of the labour force. As the United Nations Committee for Development Planning concluded, "The pendulum has swung too far towards the neglect of human development. When Governments face the need of adjusting to short-term economic and fiscal constraints, there *are* policy choices to be made" (*Human Resources Development: A Neglected Dimension of Development Strategy, Views and Recommendations of the Committee for Development Planning* (United Nations publication, Sales No. E.88.II.A.11), p. 2).

11 Although the discussion in this chapter is restricted to actions of developing countries, adjustment also has a global dimension and there is a contribution to be made by policy changes in industrialized countries; for example, relating to interest rates in international money centres and to protectionist restrictions on imports from developing countries.

Figure VIII.2. Savings and net transfers of financial resources, 1980-1988

### Countries without a debt crisis

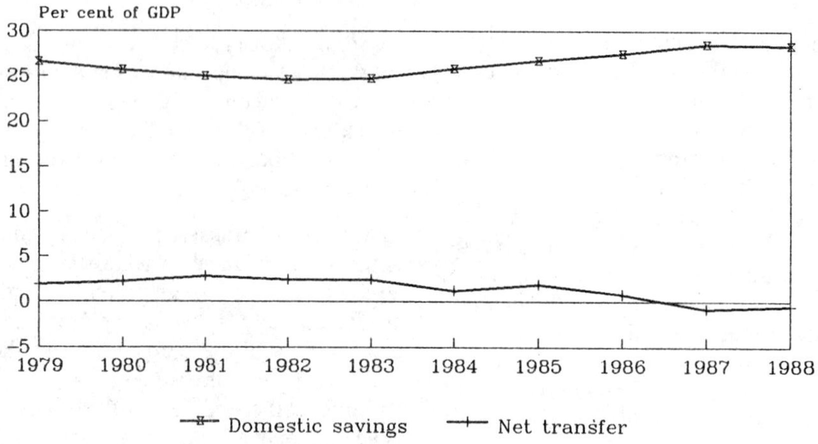


### Fifteen heavily-indebted countries

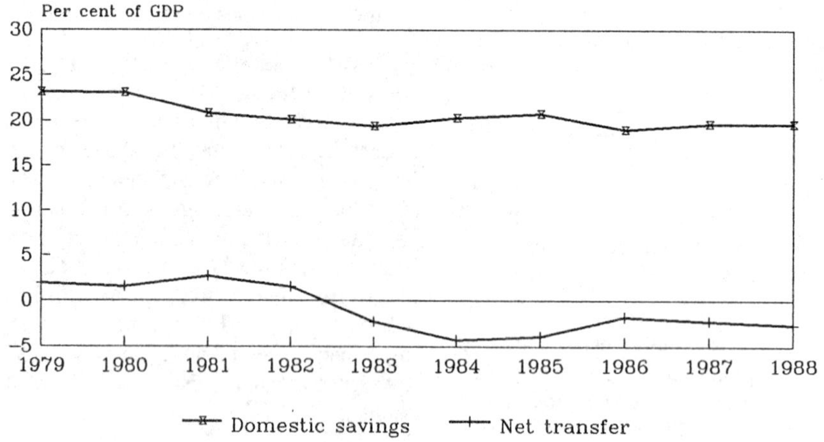


### Sub-Saharan Africa

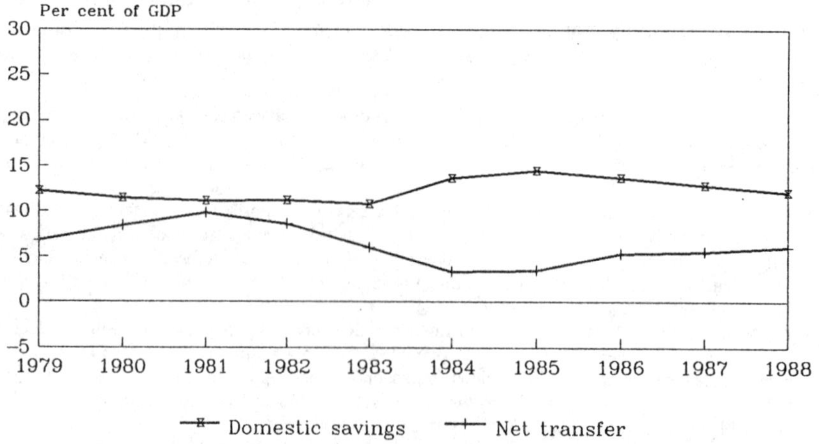


*Source:* Department of International Economic and Social Affairs of the United Nations Secretariat, based on IMF data and country groupings.

reform programmes that have been actively supported by the international community. These programmes may not have encompassed all the aspects of adjustment listed above, especially those formulated in the early years of the decade. However, the emphases of these adjustment programmes have begun to change as the deep and intractable nature of the adjustment problem has been increasingly appreciated. But, the hubris of multilateral policy advice is still only partly acknowledged. The models on which the policy advice is based have been technical economic abstractions, often devoid of the political and social considerations that shape actual policy-making in developing, as well as in developed, countries. Structural limitations on economic flexibility are also often insufficiently appreciated. It is not credible that there were only errors in parameter estimates in all the failed adjustment programmes that were thought to meet each country's adjustment needs (including financing packages). The models are clearly an incomplete guide to policy formulation.

One factor that seems to crystallize several of the missing elements is that sometimes an adopted package of policy changes with international financial support does not win the confidence of important elements of the adjusting country. Adjustment requires that various social and economic groups in a country take losses in income and accept risks to future earnings prospects. If the losses are certain and the possibilities of recouping them highly uncertain, the incentive to impede or derail the adjustment programme may be high. And these groups can be powerful enough to be effective.

The problem of confidence has been addressed elsewhere, although usually indirectly. For example, various analysts have taken note of the phenomenon of capital flight from developing countries, attributing it, *inter alia,* to differences in risk-adjusted expected returns from holding assets in source and recipient countries.[12] Private bank creditors of some developing countries have complained about being pressured to increase their lending exposure to countries in debt crisis when those countries' resident citizens and enterprises—some of which are, of course, affiliates of transnational corporations—are taking their capital out. In this regard, wealth holders from developed and developing countries seem to operate on the same basic principles and assumptions.

A more slowly moving phenomenon that in part reflects similar sentiments as those underlying capital flight is the emigration of people from countries in crisis, both the middle class and entrepreneurial strata that pass through the world's major airports and the poor that sneak across borders.

But there is an additional dimension to emigration of the poor, which is more straightforward: the inability to make a minimally adequate income at home. In many countries, people do not leave the country, but leave the economy, or more precisely the legal economy. In a few countries, large numbers of people have been attracted into a flourishing illicit drug sector, swamping international efforts to control that plague. In some cases, the economic situation became so distorted that a large-scale underground economy emerged, particularly when wages in the formal sector fell far behind actual living costs. The informal economy even became a major participant in the international trade of some countries; for example, smuggling domestic production across borders where goods could be sold for foreign exchange which could be converted into local currency at black market rates.[13]

One major focus of policy makers might thus be how to design adjustment programmes that would rebuild the confidence of economic actors that they could earn an adequate income in the formal economy so they would turn their creativity and energy to productive economic activity in the legal sectors. The adjustment programme would generally include familiar policy reforms such as have been advocated by the international community and a substantial improvement of the net transfer of financial resources in order that essential investments could be undertaken. But if the private sector—workers, farmers and entrepreneurs—did not come to have confidence in an adjustment programme, they were undoubtedly focusing on some things that the policy makers were not taking into account. Discerning what those are and acting on them is the function of the political process in each country.

### Case experiences of adjustment in the 1980s

The discussion presented above is a distillation of the experiences of a great many countries that have sought to bring about economic adjustment. But there are important aspects of the socio-economic process called adjustment that aggregative analysis fails to capture. It is thus necessary to look at actual experiences of adjustment in order to gain insight into the process, particularly to deepen understanding of how it has operated in the economic conditions of the 1980s.

---

12 The extent of the phenomenon and its causes have been disputed, but policy recommendations to stem capital flight have been less controversial; for example, many authors point to the need for macro-economic stabilization and international co-operation in taxation, while some also emphasize the contribution that can be made by foreign exchange controls. For policy and analytical reviews, see John Williamson and Donald R. Lessard, *Capital Flight: the Problem and Policy Responses,* Policy Analyses in International Economics, No. 23 (Washington, D.C.: Institute for International Economics, 1988), and Michael Deppler and Martin Williamson, "Capital flight: concepts, measurement and issues", *Staff Studies for the World Economic Outlook* (Washington D.C., International Monetary Fund, August, 1987), pp. 39-58; on technical aspects of international policy to stem tax evasion, see *Contributions to International Co-operation in Tax Matters* (United Nations publication, Sales No. E.88.XVI.1).

13 Indeed, in many countries at one time or another, official data on the legal economy became poor indicators of actual levels of domestic economic activity.

Five cases are presented, each of which seems to stress a different aspect of the nature of adjustment. In each, adjustment has been a prolonged and difficult process, where policy efforts have been severe but ultimately have had positive results. In none of the cases, however, could the adjustment process be judged complete. A conscious effort was made to choose both large and small countries, countries with different average income levels and from different developing country regions.[14] One of the objectives of the exercise is to reflect on the process of adjustment as it occurs—not in abstract economies but in real ones—as a way to indicate the breadth of issues that needs to be taken into account in the design of economic adjustment programmes.

Figure VIII.3. Gross national income per capita of Mexico, 1967-1988
(Index, 1980=100)

*Source:* Based on data from World Bank, *World Tables,* 1988-1989 edition (1988 estimated by the United Nations Secretariat).

**Mexico: complexities of adjustment to negative transfers**

In the 1970s, Mexico enjoyed almost a steady rise in income per capita; in the 1980s, it has fallen in most years, ending in 1988 almost a fifth below the 1980 level (see figure VIII.3).[15] In the 1980s, the policy imperative dominating the economy has been economic stabilization and finding a sustainable economic growth path. Correction of macro-economic imbalances had also been a concern in some years of the 1970s, but achieving a rapid rate of economic growth was a constant goal, especially as the labour force was growing by almost 4.5 per cent a year in that decade.

Indeed, with the discovery of large oil reserves, the 1977-1978 stabilization effort was given less priority, expansionist policies were launched, and imports rose so much that the trade balance remained in deficit despite the considerable increase in export revenues brought about by the oil sector. The weight of accumulated debt also started to be felt on the balance of payments, as foreign interest payments increased; but income losses from net interest payments abroad were offset by the terms-of-trade gains from rising petroleum prices. The stock of external debt soared, espe-

14 No claim is made that this is a scientific sample or that one could even be meaningfully defined for such a complex economic, social and political process.

15 In this and each of the subsequent cases presented in this chapter, per capita income refers to gross national income per person, which is GDP per capita adjusted for changes in the terms of trade and net factor payments abroad, which are, in essence, net payments of profits and dividends.

Table VIII.2. The Mexican economy in the 1980s

| | 1980 | 1981 | 1982 | 1983 | 1984 | 1985 | 1986 | 1987 | 1988[a] |
|---|---|---|---|---|---|---|---|---|---|
| *Domestic economic activity* | | | | | | | | | |
| Gross domestic product, real (annual percentage change) | 8.4 | 8.8 | -0.6 | -4.2 | 3.6 | 2.6 | -4.0 | 1.4 | -0.4 |
| Investment (per cent of GDP) | 27.2 | 27.4 | 22.9 | 20.8 | 19.9 | 21.9 | 18.5 | 18.5 | 20 |
| Gross domestic savings (per cent of GDP) | 24.9 | 24.9 | 27.9 | 30.3 | 27.7 | 26.8 | 23.2 | 24.6 | 23 |
| Public finances (per cent of GDP) | | | | | | | | | |
| Total revenue, of which | 26.9 | 26.7 | 28.9 | 32.9 | 32.2 | 31.2 | 30.3 | 30.0 | .. |
| Oil revenue | 7.3 | 7.3 | 9.9 | 14.2 | 13.0 | 11.5 | 9.0 | 9.7 | 9.8 |
| Current expenditure[b] | 19.8 | 21.4 | 25.2 | 20.6 | 20.2 | 21.1 | 21.5 | 19.0 | .. |
| Capital expenditure | 9.6 | 12.9 | 10.2 | 7.5 | 6.7 | 6.0 | 6.0 | 5.5 | .. |
| Primary balance | -3.1 | -8.0 | -7.1 | 4.3 | 4.8 | 3.5 | 2.0 | 5.3 | 7.1 |
| Domestic interest paid | 2.4 | 2.9 | 4.9 | 7.7 | 8.0 | 7.8 | 12.1 | 15.2 | .. |
| External interest paid | 1.1 | 2.1 | 3.3 | 4.6 | 3.9 | 3.7 | 4.4 | 4.3 | .. |
| Financial balance | -7.5 | -14.1 | -16.9 | -8.6 | -8.5 | -9.6 | -16.0 | -15.8 | -10.8 |
| Real wage, manufacturing (index, 1980=100) | 100.0 | 103.5 | 104.4 | 80.7 | 75.4 | 76.6 | 72.3 | 72.8 | .. |
| Manufacturing employment (annual percentage change) | 7.4 | 5.6 | -2.4 | -9.6 | -1.1 | 2.3 | -4.0 | -3.4 | .. |
| Consumer price increases (annual percentage change) | 25.7 | 28.0 | 59.7 | 101.6 | 65.5 | 57.7 | 86.2 | 131.9 | 114.2 |
| *International economic activity* | | | | | | | | | |
| Import volume, including non-factor services (annual percentage change) | 31.9 | 17.7 | -37.8 | -33.8 | 17.8 | 13.4 | -14.4 | 3.5 | 38 |
| Export volume, including non-factor services (annual percentage change) | 6.1 | 11.6 | 21.8 | 13.6 | 5.7 | -4.0 | 1.5 | 12.2 | 4 |
| Terms of trade, merchandise (annual percentage change) | 16.3 | 6.5 | -3.1 | -6.4 | 0.7 | 0.5 | -32.2 | 5.7 | -10 |
| Real effective exchange rate (index, 1980-1982=100) | 102.1 | 113.9 | 84.0 | 78.5 | 91.4 | 90.4 | 64.8 | 66.5 | 74 |
| Foreign exchange earnings[c] (billions of dollars) | 22.3 | 27.9 | 27.8 | 28.9 | 32.7 | 29.9 | 24.1 | 30.2 | 30 |
| Net financial transfer[d] (billions of dollars) | 4.9 | 7.4 | -9.5 | -11.5 | -10.8 | -11.9 | -5.5 | -4.9 | -11 |
| Net financial transfer[e] (per cent of GDP) | 2.3 | 2.5 | -5.0 | -9.6 | -7.8 | -4.9 | -4.8 | -6.1 | -3 |
| Gross foreign debt (billions of dollars) | 57.5 | 78.3 | 86.1 | 93.1 | 94.9 | 96.9 | 101.1 | 107.9 | 107.4 |

*Source:* Data and estimates of Banco de México, IMF, the World Bank, Morgan Guaranty Trust Co., the United Nations Economic Commission for Latin America and the Caribbean and the Department of International Economic and Social Affairs of the United Nations Secretariat.

a Preliminary estimates.
b Excluding interest payments.
c Goods, services and private transfer inflows.
d Capital account definition (see table VIII.1).
e Expenditure definition (see table VIII.1).

cially in 1980 and 1981, not only to cover the current account deficits but also to compensate for capital flight which started to pick up in 1980.[16]

In 1981, the oil bonanza ended as the world economy entered a recession. Oil prices started to decline, and it became increasingly difficult for Mexico to attract new financing.

16 During the period 1977-1982, the current account deficit was significantly less than the inflow of external credit, which means that—measurement problems apart—some Mexican capital was leaving the country. However, the order of magnitude changed after 1980; for example, "errors and omissions" in the balance of payments jumped from rather small positive values to –$9 billion in 1981 and –$7 billion in 1982. Meanwhile, Mexico's stock of total external debt increased from $31 billion in 1977 to $86 billion in 1982 (see E. Z. Ponce de Leon, "Mexico's recent balance-of-payments experience and prospects for growth", *World Development,* vol. 14, No. 8 (August 1986), pp. 963-991).

International reserves were depleted and a three-month moratorium on debt-servicing was declared in August 1982. The net transfer of financial resources turned negative and economic adjustment became the elusive policy goal of the 1980s.

**A sequence of stabilization efforts: 1982-1987**

The first of the stabilization programmes prompted by the 1982 crisis aimed at correcting a profound disequilibrium in government finances and an excessive reliance on oil, while also strengthening a sheltered private sector. Stabilization measures adopted in 1982 and 1983 included a very tight fiscal and monetary policy, real exchange rate devaluation, and reduction of aggregate demand. The programme also envisaged a rescheduling of the Mexican external debt so that repayments could be smoothed out over the decade.

Adjustment of public finances proved to be spectacular. The "primary balance," which is the government budget balance excluding the servicing of the government debt and new borrowing, went from a deficit of 7 per cent of GDP in 1982 to a surplus of over 4 per cent in 1983 (see table VIII.2). With public saving replacing "dissaving", gross domestic saving also rose significantly, although it was not available for use in higher domestic investment as it had to be transferred abroad.

The trade balance quickly responded to the adjustment measures as well and exhibited a surplus of $14 billion in 1983, which financed a net financial transfer out of Mexico of almost $10 billion or 5 per cent of GDP. The apparent success of this external adjustment in 1983, however, rested on two fragile foundations that also characterized the weakness of the economic structure of Mexico. First, on the export side, crude oil, the earnings from which are basically determined outside the Mexican economy, accounted for over 70 per cent of merchandise exports. In the face of stagnant oil earnings, even an expansion of manufactured exports of some 50 per cent above levels in the early 1980s helped push up total foreign exchange earnings by only 4 per cent. Second, most of the adjustment in the trade accounts had occurred on the import side, where a drastic reduction in capital goods imports played a major role in generating the trade surplus.[17]

In addition, the adjustment programme had aggravated some of the other disequilibria of the Mexican economy. Inflation rose for the year, just reaching the three-digit level, helped by cuts in food subsidies, increases in indirect taxes and the exchange rate devaluation. Real wages in the manufacturing sector fell by almost one quarter in 1983 and unemployment rose, thus exacerbating social inequality. Compensation of employees fell from 36 per cent of GDP in 1982 to 28 per cent in 1984. Real GDP itself declined by 4 per cent in 1983.

The stabilization effort continued throughout 1984 and 1985, but the Government's main attention now shifted from external imbalances to the control of inflation, the restructuring of the economy and a return to economic growth. A mild recovery did take place in 1984 and 1985 and the inflation rate fell back to roughly the 1982 level. Private investment responded favourably to fiscal incentives, but it was apparently not oriented towards the expansion of productive capacity.[18] Exchange rate devaluation and depressed home market conditions brought about a further expansion of manufactured exports. The trade balance, however, deteriorated in 1985 as imports increased and as foreign demand for exports in 1985, particularly in the United States, receded. The balance-of-payments was once again approaching crisis.

By the end of 1985 a renewed stabilization effort focusing once more on the external accounts had to be undertaken as adequate new lending was not forthcoming, which meant that Mexico had to continue transferring resources out of the country if it was to meet its debt-servicing obligations. The new stabilization programme contained the same elements as the previous one, with the added component of trade liberalization. This time, however, the measures adopted failed to increase the trade surplus because international oil prices plunged by 50 per cent in 1986, and the value of Mexican foreign exchange earnings declined by one fifth. Inflation soared to 86 per cent, real output fell back 4 per cent and public finances deteriorated sharply. In sum, hard-won progress in the fiscal sphere was set back and import compression again had to be applied.

This cycle of shifting the focus of policy suggests that these first adjustment programmes had certain built-in inconsistencies. Indeed, despite the success in moving the fiscal balance into surplus in the period 1983-1985, inflation hardly slowed. It seems that the overall effect of the package of adjustment measures was offsetting the positive effect that balanced public finances might have had in controlling inflation. To further complicate matters, the persistence of inflation was undermining government efforts to stimulate non-oil exports as gains obtained through exchange rate devaluations were eroded by the inflation. Repeated devaluation of the peso as an instrument to promote exports was constrained by the high import content of Mexican manufacturing. And further depreciation of the peso would transmit new inflationary shocks to the economy. Moreover, as inflation accelerated, the nominal cost of servicing the domestic public debt increased, which itself put pressure on the budget and made it difficult not to increase government borrowing.

With external financing unavailable and fiscal deficits rising, the supply of available domestic funds was being increasingly absorbed by the public sector, crowding out the private sector, which had been targeted to replace the Gov-

---

17 See N. Lustig, and J. Ros, "Stabilization and adjustment in Mexico: 1982-1985", paper prepared for the Conference on Stabilization and Adjustment Programmes and Policies, World Institute for Development Economics Research of the United Nations University, Helsinki, 19-21 August 1986.

18 There is some evidence that fiscal incentives obtained through accelerated depreciation allowances were mainly used to replace the stock of automobiles of private firms, (see N. Lustig and J. Ros, "Stabilization and adjustment in Mexico ...").

ernment as the major promoter of investment. As further curbs in public investments were made to compensate for the increase in government financial expenditures,[19] overall investment in the economy plunged. The share of investment in GDP declined from 27 per cent in 1981 to 18.5 per cent in 1986, while GDP declined as well. The net effect is that the volume of gross investment in 1986 was about half what it was before the crisis in 1981.

Not only was the private sector unable to substitute for the declining government activity on this front, private investment itself declined during the period. Complementarity between private and public investment was not sufficiently appreciated. And the existence of idle capacity, depressed domestic markets and volatile external demand also acted as serious deterrents to the expansion of investment.

Macro-economic policy for 1987 was formulated as the experience of the previous four years was being digested. The Government aimed at recovering from the 1986 recession with a moderate economic growth of 2 to 3 per cent, and a continuation of the restructuring of the economy towards greater emphasis on the private sector and export-oriented, non-oil activities. Economic growth, albeit modest, was to generate jobs and help to begin a recovery of labour income. It was now the fifth year of a six-year government term of office and improvements in living conditions began to have a political imperative.

According to the Government,[20] controlling inflation required a continuation of the policy of strengthening public finances, correcting relative prices, and carefully monitoring interest and exchange rates so that costs—and therefore prices—would not be pushed up. The further liberalization of the trade régime was to discourage the private sector from setting domestic prices above their external counterparts.

Further fiscal restraint was also called for so that total government borrowing requirements could be reduced. In addition, government borrowing from domestic sources was expected to be less in 1987 due to an agreement Mexico was negotiating with its external creditors which included $10.7 billion of new money from foreign commercial banks and multilateral institutions. With a lighter presence of the public sector in the financial markets, nominal interest rates were to go down and credit would be extended to the private sector.

The above targets, however, were not met. Inflation even accelerated. Unions pressed for wage increases as labour income was quickly deteriorating, and wage rates began to be revised quarterly. As prices rose, so did inflationary expectations.

Nominal interest rates also rose. Indeed, they had to, as lower real interest rates would decrease the differential between internal and external interest rates and encourage capital flight. Government interest payments then rose and absorbed 65 per cent of total revenues. Together with lower than expected tax revenues and delays in receiving the external funds—anticipated for December but available only the following April—the Government had to continue to rely on domestic sources to finance the public deficit. Relief from public sector crowding out of private sector borrowers was thus not realized.

Meanwhile, the exchange rate was gradually becoming more misaligned as the nominal devaluations of the peso lagged behind inflation. The exchange rate, however, was not under serious attack until the Mexican stock market crumbled.

The effects of the world stock market crash of 19 October 1987 were immediately felt in the Mexican market. The market had absorbed a great deal of liquidity in recent years and Mexican stock prices had soared.[21] Already nervous because of Mexico's inflation rate, stockholders panicked. They tried to convert their capital into dollars, and pushed the exchange rate down.

Mexico was maintaining a dual exchange rate system with private capital transactions except for debt servicing and some imports carried out in a virtually free market managed by Mexico's commercial banks, and the rest—about 80 per cent of external transactions—effected under a controlled rate. In one month, the peso fell 39 per cent against the dollar in the free market. The spread between the free market and the controlled rate, which had been practically nil during the year, jumped to almost 30 per cent. The general perception became that the peso was overvalued and if not corrected it would erode gains hoped for in non-oil exports, stimulate capital flight and put Mexico's foreign reserves under pressure. Yet, caught once again trying to satisfy too many targets with too few instruments, policy makers understood that devaluing the exchange rate would have a negative impact on the general price level and would lead to a higher domestic cost of servicing the public external debt. Devaluation was thus postponed, albeit temporarily.

Nevertheless, private sector confidence had been eroded and in order to counter capital flight, the Government increased the interest rates paid on Treasury Certificates (Cetes) which went up by 15 percentage points from October to November. Higher interest rates, of course, would raise the cost of servicing the domestic public debt. Meanwhile, the increase granted in the minimum wage in October was quickly being eroded by inflation, and the unions were pressing once again for wage adjustments. With inflation going out of control, pressure mounting on the exchange rate and wages and the presidential election approaching, the Government devalued the peso by 22 per cent on 14 De-

19 The orders of magnitude here are quite striking: external plus domestic interest payments by the public sector jumped from 3.5 per cent of GDP in 1980 to 12.3 per cent in 1983 and to 16.5 per cent in 1986 (see table VIII.2).

20 See "Criterios generales de política económica para 1987: consideraciones técnicas complementarias", *El Mercado de Valores* (Nacional Financiera), 5 January 1987, p. 1.

21 The general stock price index rose at rates well above inflation since 1983. In 1986, the index rose by 421 per cent (December to December). In the nine months to September 1987, the index increased by 729 per cent.

cember and on the following day announced the Economic Solidarity Pact.

### An additional instrument for adjustment in 1988

The Economic Solidarity Pact combined familiar elements of macro-economic policy—in this sense it was a continuation of the readjustment effort pursued by the Mexican Government since 1982—with new components of price management.[22] The Pact called for yet another dose of fiscal contraction that would free more resources for debt servicing. The surplus in the primary budget balance was to be expanded by 3 percentage points of GDP. This would be achieved by an increase in government revenues and reduction of public expenditures. The former included some changes in tax policy, but a major part of the additional revenues would come from increases in the prices and fees for goods and services supplied by the public sector. Public expenditures would be reduced by the elimination of certain subsidies, the accelerated restructuring of the public enterprise sector (privatization, merging and closure of state companies) and cuts in planned investment. A much hoped-for decrease in inflation would also help rein in government expenditure.

The innovative part of the Economic Solidarity Pact began when public sector fees and the exchange rate were adjusted in December and then frozen. Future public-sector price increases were to be co-ordinated with those of wages, and the prices of those items to be included in a basic consumption basket. Real agricultural prices were maintained, while the minimum wage was raised by 15 per cent in December, and an extra 20 per cent increase was granted for January. To counter the inflationary effects of peso devaluation, tariffs and taxes on imported goods were reduced. If the private sector raised prices unduly, or if artificial shortages and speculation arose, imports were expected to increase and exert a countervailing force.

The Government was aware that planned price realignments would send inflation up in January and February. However, as future price increases were to be carried out in co-ordination and by negotiation with the various sectors of the economy, abrupt price changes could be avoided. Moreover, the freeze of some prices for a limited period was intended to make people lower their inflationary expectations. Thus, it was expected that monthly inflation rates would fall to 2 per cent by the end of the year, from 15 per cent in December 1987.

Although the Government-business-labour-farmer pact was initially agreed to last only for the first three months of the plan, it was renewed in March and again in August and was maintained throughout the year, with some adjustments introduced in August to address a deterioration of workers' income. Open wage increases could not be granted because it would justify price increases by the private sector, thereby undermining efforts to keep inflation down. Instead, the Government reduced taxes paid by workers. The private enterprise sector in turn agreed to reduce the prices of 100 goods—mainly food and clothing—by 3 per cent. All other provisions of the Pact would remain in operation; that is to say, the freeze on wages, exchange rate, controlled prices and public sector fees and prices.[23]

The Pact succeeded in reducing inflation as planned, but at a cost of deteriorated external accounts as imports swelled (see figure VIII.4). Indeed, per capita income fell for the third consecutive year as the economy stagnated. Industrial activity was hurt by lower domestic demand, competition from imported goods and tight credit. To make matters worse, agricultural output suffered from a severe drought. The construction sector contracted as a result of the cuts in government spending, and the oil sector again had to face declining international prices. The only buoyant activities were the non-oil, export-oriented sectors, particularly the *industria maquiladora* or "in-bond" industries.[24] However, their performance was not enough to provide a major stimulus to the economy. Investment contracted yet again in 1988.

Public finances, however, improved, especially so far as the primary balance was concerned. The Government had nevertheless been obliged to cut expenditures more than anticipated as oil revenues decreased. But even with austerity on the side of programmatic expenditures, the financial balance did not improve to the degree anticipated owing to rising interest payments as international interest rates rose.

On the domestic side, with the decline of inflation, nominal interest rates fell, but not as fast as inflation, and thus real interest rates became increasingly high. Nominal interest rates could not be pushed down, it was felt, owing to the need to maintain the willingness of savers to buy and hold Treasury notes and bonds. In addition, as the Economic Solidarity Pact froze the exchange rate, the peso was appreciating in relation to the dollar and thus high domestic interest rates were needed to prevent capital flight.

The trade balance registered a surplus of $2 billion, which was $6.5 billion lower than in 1987. Exports had been hurt by decreasing oil prices while imports soared due to the frozen exchange rate, lower tariffs and higher local food prices. As interest payments rose and there were no new capital inflows, the net transfer out of Mexico reached $11 billion.[25] The country thus entered 1989 having made some progress once more in internal adjustment but facing the possiblity of yet one more balance-of-payments crisis.

### International finance: a key to the adjustment strategy

It is important to emphasize that the Economic Solidarity Pact could not even have been launched if not for a tempo-

22 See "Pacto de solidaridad económica", *El Mercado de Valores* (Nacional Financiera), ano XLVII, Suplemento al num. 51, 21 December 1987.

23 See "Pacto de solidaridad económica: concertación para septiembre", *El Mercado de Valores* (Nacional Financiera), 1 September 1988.

24 For details on this sector, see *Mexico: In-Bond Industry/Industria Maquiladora* (Mexico, D.F., Administración y servicios internacionales, S.A., 1988).

25 This is the net transfer using the capital account definition. The net outward transfer viewed from the expenditure definition was about $5 billion, as about $6.5 billion of reserves were expended. In other words, $11 billion was transferred abroad, of which $6.5 billion came from official reserves and $5 billion came from the surplus on trade in goods and non-factor services.

Figure VIII.4. Inflation, the trade balance and reserves of Mexico, 1988
(Monthly data: end-month stocks)

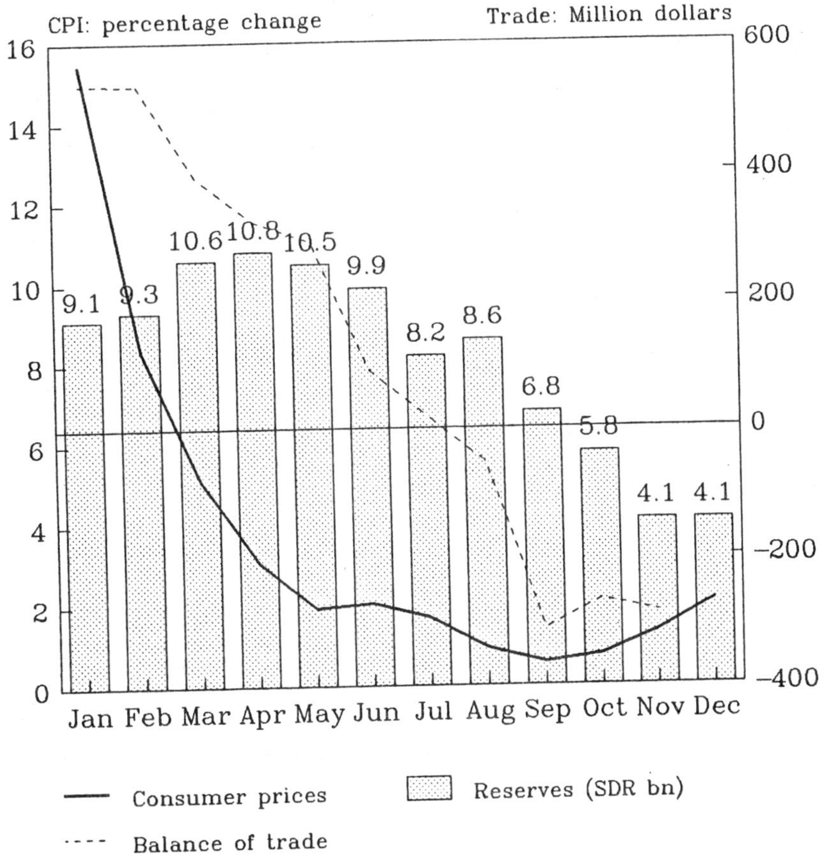


*Source:* Department of International Economic and Social Affairs of the United Nations Secretariat, based on IMF data.

rary financial breathing space created by the external debt renegotiations of 1986-1987. Under these negotiations, principal repayments were rescheduled and Mexico received commitments of $7.7 billion from commercial banks which, combined with a $4 billion recovery of the trade surplus in 1987, led to large additions to official foreign exchange reserves.

With a reserve cushion equal to six months' expenditure on imports of goods and services (including interest), the Government could work out an anti-inflation plan that included a freeze of the exchange rate and would permit a higher level of imports. These two elements were crucial if the freeze of wages and controlled prices were to be maintained. Competition from imported goods was to prevent the private sector from raising prices. Moreover, with the exchange rate frozen, pressure on costs would recede. Labour, in turn, would have less of a case for wage increases based on current or expected inflation. Lower inflation, finally, was fundamental to the Government's plan to decrease its financial borrowing requirements. Burgeoning financial deficits rising to 16 per cent of GDP had been generated by the need to service the domestic debt at increasing nominal interest rates.

Many economists believe that when inflation becomes chronic as it had in Mexico by 1988, only an anti-inflationary strategy that combines nominal monetary targets with fiscal policy goals can succeed.[26] According to these authors, orthodox fiscal discipline is not enough to guarantee the control of inflation; it must be complemented by a policy directed at a key nominal parameter of the economy, such as the money supply or the exchange rate.

The Mexican authorities chose the exchange rate as the nominal anchor for their programme. By using the exchange rate to help control prices, the domestic problem of inflation was eased, but this exacerbated the external problem; that is, the trade balance weakened. As the peso appreciated,

26 See Miguel A. Kiguel and Nissan Liviatan, "Inflationary rigidities and orthodox stabilization policies: lessons from Latin America", *The World Bank Economic Review*, vol. 2, No. 3 (September 1988), pp. 273-298, and references cited therein.

imports increased. But the length of time over which such a policy can be maintained while the inflationary expectations are squeezed out of the system depends on what else is happening to the trade balance. In Mexico in 1988 the pressure on the trade balance from the stabilization plan was joined by the deterioration of the terms of trade and the rising interest-cost of servicing the external debt.

Despite these added factors, the Government had to remain faithful to its nominal anchor in order to build and maintain confidence in the plan, which was essential if it was to have any chance of success. However, wealth holders could see the balance of payments weakening and the peso becoming increasingly overvalued. Some kind of measure was thus needed to reinforce their willingness to keep capital at home. In this sense, the increase of real interest rates noted above was a compensation for the appreciation of the peso—a price the Government had to pay even if this could compromise its efforts to bring the budget's financial deficit down.

In any case, Mexico's rapid drawdown of its international reserves—they fell by almost SDR 5 billion from May to October, or about one half—was already a sign that the Economic Solidarity Pact was coming to an end, unless some financing could be obtained abroad. A bridge loan offered by the authorities of the United States in October—and never used by Mexico—played a major role in keeping the plan credible up to the end of the year.

In short, Mexico's adjustment efforts in the 1980s seem to illustrate well the difficulties a country may face in undertaking a stabilization programme under two sets of adverse circumstances: first, a sharp shift from positive to negative transfers of financial resources, and second, being subject to volatile external accounts. Mexico's adjustment difficulties were very much compounded by oscillations in policy and the dependence of the overall fiscal position on monetary developments, in particular interest rate changes. Moreover, to meet the adverse contingencies that would otherwise undermine its adjustment programme, Mexico has needed access to a substantial line of foreign credit.

In other words, since adverse international shocks tend to occur and since Mexico remains vulnerable to them, there should be a way in which the net transfer of financial resources could improve substantially, if needed, during the confidence-building period of the adjustment programme. If the terms of trade should move in favour of Mexico at this stage, the enhanced net financial transfer would not be needed. If the terms of trade turned against it, compensatingly larger net transfers would be required. The need to provide for the contingencies is itself so crucial, however, because the need to marshal the resources to effect the negative transfer has left so little room for policy to manoeuvre. That is, adjustment is exceedingly difficult under a sharp external financial constraint.

## Bolivia: adjustment without growth

In 1981, Bolivia's inflation rate was 29 per cent, roughly the same as it had been for many years. By 1985, the annual inflation rate had risen above 12,000 per cent. By 1987, inflation had fallen back to 15 per cent (see table VIII.3). The hyperinflation meant that there was an economic adjustment crisis that had to be faced, and it was. There was also a drain of resources being paid abroad, but in 1986—unlike the case of Mexico—that was reversed. But although the economy has been essentially stabilized, it is not yet on a path of sustainable and adequate growth and development. In particular, gross income per head continues unchanged, at about two thirds of the level it had reached at the beginning of the decade (see figure VIII.5).

Regaining a positive net transfer of financial resources is only one of many determining factors in adjustment. Policy directions, in particular, matter a great deal. Indeed, the Government of Bolivia has set policy to turn the economy towards a new development strategy, albeit one that even under favourable assumptions, requires a long period before the goals to be achieved through adjustment fall within reach.

### Roots of an adjustment crisis

The origins of the modern Bolivian economy can be traced to the Revolution of 1952, which swept away feudal landlords and a government mostly backed by a landed élite and mine-owners. As peasants carved up the highland estates and miners took more control of the mineral wealth, a new state took charge and a new development strategy was put into effect. The political and economic structure of the country was permanently altered. A large state apparatus emerged, as did a strong and politically independent military and labour unions. Economic power shifted away from the traditional centres of population in the Bolivian highlands (the Altiplano), which stretch from La Paz in the north, not far from the Peruvian border, to the mining and marginal agricultural grazing regions of Oruro and Potosi to the south. The new wealth arose in the labour-intensive tea and coca plantations on the eastern slopes of the Andes and the rich eastern agricultural lands that were opened up to cotton and soybean cultivation with modern machinery and technology.

By the early 1970s, the Bolivian State had become the dominant economic actor. It was the owner of banks and mines, provider of credit, producer of energy, and the major partner in agriculture and agro-industrial enterprises. It had become the major employer, directly through the public administration as well as through its manufacturing and mining enterprises. The State also intervened heavily in the economy in indirect ways through governmental budgetary processes; for example, through differentiated rates of taxation, pricing policies and subsidization of state enterprises.

The private sector developed as a junior partner, relying more on government resources than on its own creativity. Prices were regulated, loans, subsidies and lands granted, and segments of the market reserved for what became a

Table VIII.3. The Bolivian economy in the 1980s

| | 1980 | 1981 | 1982 | 1983 | 1984 | 1985 | 1986 | 1987 | 1988[a] |
|---|---|---|---|---|---|---|---|---|---|
| *Domestic economic activity* | | | | | | | | | |
| Gross domestic product, real (annual percentage change) | -0.9 | 0.9 | -4.4 | -6.5 | -0.3 | -0.1 | -2.9 | 2.4 | 2.5 |
| Investment (per cent of GDP) | 14.2 | 11.9 | 9.7 | 3.4 | 5.7 | -0.8 | 8.0 | 9.5 | 9 |
| Gross domestic savings (per cent of GDP) | 20.0 | 11.3 | 14.1 | 6.2 | 8.7 | 0.1 | 3.0 | 1.5 | 5 |
| Public finances (per cent of GDP) | | | | | | | | | |
| Government expenditure | 18.3 | 15.0 | 33.3 | 23.7 | 35.9 | 52.6 | 12.2 | 11.5 | 11 |
| Deficit (-) or surplus | -8.3 | -6.3 | -28.5 | -20.7 | -33.5 | -44.9 | -1.8 | -0.4 | 0 |
| Consumer price increases (annual percentage change) | 47 | 29 | 133 | 369 | 700 | 12 400 | 276 | 15 | 16 |
| *International economic activity* | | | | | | | | | |
| Import volume, including non-factor services (annual percentage change) | 37.9 | 37.8 | -34.5 | 2.3 | -10.4 | 44.4 | -21.2 | -8.8 | 2 |
| Export volume, merchandise (annual percentage change) | -4.8 | 8.0 | -8.3 | -10.8 | 3.7 | -9.9 | 5.0 | -7.6 | 11 |
| of which, tin | -15.3 | 8.0 | -10.2 | -27.2 | 27.3 | -20.6 | 4.0 | -40.4 | 13 |
| Terms of trade, merchandise (annual percentage change) | 4.9 | -4.8 | -4.0 | -1.1 | 0.0 | -7.0 | -27.7 | -15.8 | 11 |
| Real effective exchange rate (index, 1985=100) | 35.8 | 45.0 | 48.9 | 44.8 | 58.2 | 100.0 | 29.4 | 28.3 | 27 |
| Foreign exchange earnings[b] (millions of dollars) | 1 059.6 | 1 036.1 | 936.4 | 940.6 | 871.1 | 759.4 | 703.7 | 634.3 | 670 |
| Net financial transfer[c] (millions of dollars) | -299.0 | 135.4 | -161.8 | -108.2 | -79.0 | -88.8 | 374.1 | 234.6 | 155 |
| Net financial transfer[d] (per cent of GDP) | -5.8 | 0.6 | -4.4 | -2.8 | -3.1 | -0.9 | 5.0 | 8.0 | 4 |
| Gross foreign debt (billions of dollars) | 2.7 | 3.2 | 3.3 | 4.1 | 4.3 | 4.7 | 5.5 | 5.5 | 5.7 |

*Source:* Data and estimates of IMF, the World Bank, the United Nations Economic Commission for Latin America and the Caribbean, the Board of the Cartagena Agreement (Modelo Econométrico del Grupo Andino) and the Department of International Economic and Social Affairs of the United Nations Secretariat.

a Preliminary estimates.

b Goods, services and private transfer inflows.

c Capital account definition (see table VIII.1).

d Expenditure definition (see table VIII.1).

group of private-sector interests that were close to and dependent upon the post-revolutionary State.

Workers associated with the State or with privileged branches of the private sector shared in the benefits with steady employment, high wages, and union protection. However, almost half the labour force—unorganized peasants and urban workers of the informal sector—remained outside the privileged circles. They remained impoverished, operating with outmoded technology in agriculture, crafts or trade on their own lands, or moved to the towns or the capital city in search of a livelihood.

Bolivia has thus developed over the past three decades, in essence, as a mixed economy in which the State was the major actor, protector and protagonist. By the early 1980s, the public sector consisted of 570 agencies, 120 belonging to the central Government and 350 to regional and local levels. It included 50 financial and other public enterprises, the state oil and mining companies and national airlines. Private participation in manufacturing was minor, the private entrepeneurs sharing the already protected markets with the government agencies.

While always staying within this framework, a sequence of Governments shifted the thrust of economic policy back and forth from the early 1970s. Some sought to promote economic growth through government subsidies to the private sector. Those régimes resisted higher wages, reduced public activities and taxes, and borrowed heavily from foreign sources. Other administrations attempted to use the state directly to redistribute income and benefits to the poor and to the workers, raised wages in the public enterprises

Figure VIII.5. Gross national income per capita of Bolivia, 1967-1988 (Index, 1980=100)

*Source:* Based on data from World Bank, *World Tables,* 1988-89 edition (1988 estimated by the United Nations Secretariat).

and mines, inflating the economy to finance expansionist activities. They also borrowed from foreign sources.

Foreign financing was attractive as the terms of lending did not seem onerous in the latter 1970s and as export earnings alone did not support the country's import growth. The terms of trade of Bolivia rose almost 4 per cent a year on average in the 1970s. However, export volume peaked in 1972 and essentially stagnated or declined during the remainder of the 1970s and the early 1980s.

Official foreign borrowing in the 1970s mainly took the form of supplier credits, commercial bank loans and official export credits. Argentina lent to Bolivia to accelerate exploitation and export of natural gas. Brazil supported the expansion into new cotton and soybean lands. Multilateral official lenders financed the infrastructure. Commercial banks lent for a wide range of activities, at least until 1981. The external debt, which in the mid-1970s had equalled less than half of GDP, doubled its share by 1982. Interest payments, which had once required only 5 per cent of exports, required 20 per cent.

For as long as it lasted, essentially the 1970s, an overvalued exchange rate encouraged imports, discouraged new exports, and in effect subsidized an international style of living by the wealthy. Dollars were made available at a favourable rate for those who wished to travel or transfer their money abroad. When no longer able to continue supporting the appreciating exchange rate, reserves fell and foreign creditors halted lending.

In 1982, after nearly 18 years of military government, civilian elections were held. GDP per capita had been falling since 1979, but buoyant export prices and terms-of-trade gains had held up gross national income per capita until 1981; 1982 was to be less propitious (see figure VIII.5). It had become evident earlier, however, that the economy was on an unsustainable course and a series of adjustment plans had been designed for economic correction, beginning with the December 1979 programme that was supported by an IMF stand-by arrangement and a World Bank structural adjustment loan. But, as elsewhere in Latin America, the military was unable to carry out the required economic changes in the face of rising popular discontent. Nine persons served as president from 1979 to 1981. During that period, the human rights situation deteriorated and became a focus of international concern.[27] Finally, the military returned the Government to civilian control.

The new Government immediately implemented populist policies. Public spending increased, including significant wage increases as organized labour had supported the new administration. Worker co-ownership of Corporación Minera de Bolivia (COMIBOL), the state mining corporation, was also introduced. The economic adjustment problem was acknowledged, although it was not successfully handled: six different plans under seven different finance ministers and Central Bank presidents were tried within three years.

There were, also, multiple possibilities for abuse. An artificially maintained exchange rate, for example, obliged exporters to turn over their dollars to the State in return for a relatively low equivalence in local currency, permitting the State to then import necessities and to retail the dollars at low rates to selected recipients. Public agencies and private individuals purchased those dollars cheaply at the official rate. They could then be sold in the black market at handsome profits.

Meanwhile, export revenues dropped as the effect of declining export volumes was compounded by falling international prices of tin and oil. The fiscal deficit swelled and without new inflows of foreign credit—indeed, with the net transfer of resources turning negative in 1982—the Government stepped up seignorage financing, also known as the inflation tax.[28] The rate of inflation had already begun to pick up before the new administration took over, but the unrestrained printing of money to finance state operations resulted in growing and finally rampant inflation. Prices rose 29 per cent in 1981, rose at almost a 400 per cent rate in 1983, 700 per cent in 1984 and finally over 12,000 per cent in 1985. Revenues could not be collected, enterprises collapsed, and the State in effect became bankrupt. Indeed, in 1984, the Government announced that servicing of foreign debt would be unilaterally held to 25 per cent of export earnings, to which the foreign commercial banks responded by cutting off all credit.

The real economy went underground, dollarizing its transactions to provide stability, and a commodity that had been grown for domestic use for centuries became newly important to the economy. Highly valued, grown locally, requiring much local labour and few imported materials, coca-growing, harvesting and refining became a main staple of the underground economy.

By 1984, inflation was clearly out of control. Prices were rising 60 per cent per month and per capita income had fallen to one third of the 1979 level. As the government deficit rose to over 30 per cent of GDP, goods were driven into the black market. Price ceilings were raised with a lag, creating a severe shortage of basic staples. Government loans under such inflationary conditions were virtually grants to the private sector. The hyperinflation left the large government sector bereft of criteria for correct management, and the peasants and working people, whose incomes were not indexed to price changes, became increasingly impoverished.

**Stabilization by shock treatment**

In an increasingly chaotic situation, the Government called new elections and one of the original leaders of the 1952 Revolution, Víctor Paz Estenssoro, became President. Within three weeks after taking office in August 1985, Decree 21060 established a New Economic Policy which stopped the price spiral almost immediately.[29] Inflation fell to 15 per cent in 1987 and remained at that level in 1988.

Under the new policy, public spending was undertaken only when matched with revenues. The budget was slashed, with no protection for essential health, education or other basic services. Ministries adhered to the public budget. Workers were discharged from the public sector, including 20,000 of the 27,000 miners in COMIBOL. Of COMIBOL's 23 mines, 19 were either shut down or sold to worker co-operatives.

The new Government at first financed itself largely on the basis of revenues from hydrocarbons, as the basic retail price of gasoline was raised from heavily subsidized levels. The exchange rate was decontrolled and an auction system was established for allocating foreign currency. The immediate effect was a devaluation of 93 per cent. Wages in the entire public sector were reduced. Growth of the money supply slowed and a high real rate of interest was established. This was to encourage the return of flight capital, but it also discouraged private investment.

Domestic markets were deregulated, and imports and exports were freed of quantitative restrictions. Tariffs were reduced to a maximum of 20 per cent and then to 10 per cent. The Ministry of Labour removed itself from labour market intervention, allowing employers to negotiate directly with unions. Prices were thus freed internally, but in addition, all dollar-linked indexes and dollar-specified contracts were suspended.

In October 1985, just as the internally directed stabilization programme was beginning to take hold, tin prices on the London Metal Exchange collapsed, and to the internal shock was added an external shock. In the light of the collapse of tin prices, the anticipated payment of the Christmas 1985 bonus to workers raised fears of renewed inflationary fi-

27 See, for example, two studies (the second conducted after this period had ended) by the Special Envoy of the United Nations Commission on Human Rights on the human rights situation in Bolivia, (documents E/CN.4/1500 of 31 December 1981 and E/CN.4/1983/22 of 13 December 1982, and references cited therein).

28 See, for example, Jeffrey Sachs, "The Bolivian hyperinflation and stabilization", National Bureau of Economic Research, Working Paper No. 2073, Cambridge, Massachusetts, November 1986.

29 For an account of the programme and its implementation, see Juan Antonio Morales, "Inflation and stabilization in Bolivia," in M. Bruno, G. Di Tella, R. Dornbusch and S. Fischer, eds., *Inflation and Stabilization: The Experience of Israel, Argentina, Brazil, Bolivia and Mexico (Cambridge, Massachusetts, MIT Press, 1988), and commentaries thereon by Gail E. Mackinen and Joseph Ramos.*

nancing and speculation that there would be an exchange rate crisis. But inflationary financing was not used and the Central Bank defended the exchange rate with dollar sales.

By February 1986, it became clear that the stabilization was truly sticking. The vicious circle of the past had been replaced with a virtuous circle of a stable exchange rate, an effective ceiling on the government deficit, and enough credibility in foreign official circles to merit new credits, in particular, a new IMF agreement and World Bank structural adjustment assistance.

### Foreign debt and the net financial transfer during adjustment

When the Paz Estenssoro administration was inaugurated, interest payments due each year on the total stock of Bolivia's foreign debt amounted to more than 10 per cent of GDP, while the Government's tax revenue was less than 2 per cent of GDP. Debt relief was a necessity.

The large debt overhang also made the Government's budget reduction plans politically more difficult to implement. To the extent that the public would have concluded that budget cutting was done for the sake of foreign banks and not for the needs of the domestic economy, fiscal austerity was bound to meet intense opposition. Indeed, the trade unions had opposed the adjustment programme and called for a general strike. The Government declared a temporary state of siege and the strike was unsuccessful. The sense of crisis prevailed above all and the need for austerity was widely accepted.

When the programme began, the Government approached the multilateral financial institutions for support. For this, it was necessary to remain current in its debt-servicing obligations on credits outstanding to them. But as it could not afford economically or politically to continue to pay its full interest obligations, debt servicing of commercial bank debt remained unilaterally suspended. Intense pressure was put on the Government to resume normal interest payments, but in the end IMF accepted the arguments and an agreement was reached on a stand-by arrangement in mid-1986, with Bolivia's relations with its commercial bank creditors still unresolved.[30]

A rescheduling of Bolivia's debts owed to bilateral official creditors quickly followed in the Paris Club in July. A Consultative Group of major donor Governments, co-ordinated by the World Bank, had been formed. It met in Paris as well, in December, to discuss funding of investment programmes, including anti-narcotics projects. Thus, additional financial assistance came to be provided by bilateral and multilateral sources and included assistance from other Latin American countries through the Andean Group.

A method was also found for regularizing Bolivia's relations with its commercial bank creditors. As it had become clear that Bolivia would not and could not return to normal debt servicing, a special arrangement was negotiated during 1987 for a major reduction of the debt.[31] In November, IMF set up a special Voluntary Contribution Account for Bolivia into which donor Governments put grant assistance and from which the Bolivian Government could draw in order to buy back its commercial bank debt at a discount. The banks formally agreed to the plan and specified how the discounts would be alloted and the debt extinguished. In 1988, the Government repurchased about 40 per cent of its bank debt at 11 cents on the dollar. Since Bolivia had not been servicing its commercial bank debt and was not expected to begin doing so soon, the debt buy-back operation did not directly improve the net transfer of financial resources to Bolivia. However, by removing some of Bolivia's debt-servicing obligations, it was expected to hasten an improvement in the climate for new lending to Bolivia, albeit not medium-term, sovereign risk (i.e., unsecured) lending by banks.[32] Indeed, the remaining portion of Bolivia's outstanding commercial bank debt remains to be addressed and it is expected that Bolivia will repeatedly call on the Paris Club to reschedule official credits.[33]

Nevertheless, Bolivia has undergone a major improvement in its net transfer of financial resources. In place of the negative transfers experienced through much of the 1980s, the net transfer turned positive in 1986 and has remained positive since, averaging over 5 per cent of GDP up to 1988 (see table VIII.3). As domestic savings have been quite low as a share of GDP compared to Bolivia's own history as well as compared to other developing countries, the positive net transfer has been important in returning gross investment to almost 10 per cent of GDP. Certainly, this is a far less dynamic investment situation than obtained in the 1970s, when investment averaged 27 per cent of GDP, but it is above the average for the 1980s and represents in that sense the stirrings of economic recovery.

### Where to next

Bolivia's stabilization programme can be said to have been orthodox internally since the Government severely cut the state budget, but unorthodox externally since it suspended interest payments to commercial creditors and successfully eliminated about half the commercial bank debt through a

30 At the time, this was highly unusual. The separability of IMF agreements and commercial bank debt renegotiations was only suggested as a general policy option in 1989 as part of the new debt initiative of the United States Secretary of the Treasury (see chap. IV).

31 A noteworthy but minor reduction in the debt was also arranged in 1987, when $0.7 million of bank debt was retired by Conservation International, a non-governmental organization based in the United States. The debt, which had been purchased on the secondary market at a very large discount, was returned to the Government in exchange for its commitment to expand natural conservation areas by almost 1.5 million hectares.

32 For an assessment of the financial aspects of the plan, see chap. IV.

33 Bolivia agreed outside the Paris Club to a debt rescheduling with its largest bilateral official creditor. This was Argentina, which had underwritten natural gas development and export to Argentina through a specially constructed pipeline. As Argentina had itself fallen into arrears on payment for its natural gas imports, the debt rescheduling was part of a comprehensive agreement on natural gas trade between the two countries, reached in September 1987.

pioneering buy-back plan. The depreciation of the exchange rate has kept pace with local and foreign inflation rates, maintaining a spread of not more than 1 per cent between official and parallel markets and a relatively constant real effective exchange rate. Fiscal policy has been cautious and the public sector deficit has been reduced to less than 1 per cent of GDP. In short, austerity has been carried out for the sake of Bolivia's stability, as is frequently said in Bolivia, not for the sake of paying back the foreign creditors.

However, despite the success in stabilizing the economy, the social situation remains desperate. High infant mortality, low life expectancy, poor nutrition, housing and health, and high unemployment are structural characteristics of Bolivia. Bolivia ranks below the average for low-income developing countries in terms of many social indicators, including daily calorie supply per capita, life expectancy at birth, and infant and maternal mortality.[34] Poverty on the Altiplano is the most extreme in Latin America.

When to a situation that begins with widespread poverty, one adds a major reversal of aggregate economic output and income that is unlikely to be recuperated in the near term, the social dimensions of Bolivia's crisis stand out. It is natural that under such conditions, cocaine cultivation would flourish in the less accessible regions of the country. This activity and its derivatives have become a deep economic issue as well as a social issue.[35] It is estimated that the Bolivian economy earned $375 million from coca-related exports in 1987, which may be compared with annual merchandise exports recorded in balance-of-payments data over the past three years, which averaged $518 million. The attraction of the industry is straightforward: estimated returns per hectare from these crops can exceed by 10 to nearly 20 times those from traditional crops. For poor farmers, former miners and others, the crop is apparently well worth the risk of engaging in an illegal activity.

Aside from being a problem in itself, the emergent coca sector is a symptom of the incomplete adjustment of the Bolivian economy. The austerity of 1985-1989 has stabilized macro-economic variables, but it has created something of an institutional vacuum. It has reduced the State's role as employer and appropriator of the nation's wealth without a dynamic private sector emerging to replace it. Nor has it addressed the major structural problems of agriculture or of the conditions of poverty.

The real challenge for structural adjustment is still to deliver on the promises of the 1952 Revolution. Land has again become concentrated and large landholders have become dominant in the eastern provinces. The problem of low productivity on the Altiplano has never been successfully addressed, just as the inefficiency in the mines was attacked by severing workers rather than renovating the capital stock and expanding operations. Open unemployment, estimated at 20 per cent since 1986 and underemployment close to 60 per cent, is especially severe in the highland cities where the public sector was once important. In addition to the middle-level civil servants whose jobs have been cut, one quarter of the rural teachers have abandoned their schools.

The private sector, which has so long been a junior partner in Bolivia, has not yet assumed a leading role despite the effort to create an environment conducive to private initiative. The modest economic growth of the past two years may be encouraging, but the major structural problems of poverty, the duality of peasant and modern sectors, and an alternative to the income and employment generated by coca cultivation and illicit exports all remain on the agenda of the Government.

## Adjustment in the Philippines: the cost of political crisis

Like so many other countries, the Philippines began the 1980s with an economic adjustment problem. As the country's terms of trade fell sharply in 1980 and again in 1981, imports stopped growing and the economy slowed (see table VIII.4). Nevertheless, output had been growing rapidly; even as the economy slowed, output per capita kept rising until 1982. On the other hand, terms-of-trade losses, coupled with higher interest payments to foreign creditors, caused the beginning of a decline in gross domestic income per capita (see figure VIII.6). What is remarkable, however, is what came next, as a stagnating economy in 1983 became a collapsing one in 1984 and 1985. In only two years, gross national income per capita fell back below the level of 1973. At the same time, the Government lost political legitimacy in the eyes of its own people and was overthrown in a popular uprising. This and the recovery that followed underline the fundamental importance of political stability to implementation of a credible economic adjustment policy.

### Development of conditions for crisis

The sudden economic contraction in 1984 and 1985 was a remarkable contrast to the 1970s, when the expansion of real GDP averaged 6 per cent yearly and agriculture grew at an annual rate of almost 5 per cent. In 1978, the country had attained self-sufficiency in rice, its major food crop.[36] The industrial sector expanded rapidly at 9 per cent per year. Non-traditional manufactured exports, led by electronics and garments, rose strongly and increased their share of total exports from small amounts to almost 50 per cent by the early 1980s. The level of public investment had also risen appreciably, expanding infrastructure and social services.

---

34 Based on data and categories of "World development indicators", in World Bank, *World Development Report 1988* (New York, Oxford University Press, 1988).

35 See the 1989 report on the world social situation (E/CN.5/1989/2), p. 158. To be issued as a United Nations publication.

36 Indeed, the Philippines was one of the birthplaces of the Green Revolution, in which high-yield varieties of seeds suitable for developing country climates were developed in the 1960s.

Table VIII.4. The Philippine economy in the 1980s

| | 1980 | 1981 | 1982 | 1983 | 1984 | 1985 | 1986 | 1987 | 1988[a] |
|---|---|---|---|---|---|---|---|---|---|
| *Domestic economic activity* | | | | | | | | | |
| Production (annual percentage change) | | | | | | | | | |
| Gross domestic product | 5.0 | 3.4 | 1.9 | 1.1 | -6.8 | -3.8 | 1.5 | 4.7 | 6.7 |
| Agricultural GDP | 4.9 | 3.8 | 3.2 | -2.0 | 2.0 | 3.4 | 3.3 | -1.1 | 3.5 |
| Industrial GDP | 4.7 | 4.8 | 2.0 | 0.8 | -10.3 | -10.3 | -2.2 | 7.7 | 8.1 |
| Investment (per cent of GDP) | 30.7 | 30.6 | 28.3 | 26.7 | 17.0 | 13.9 | 12.9 | 15.3 | 18.1 |
| Gross domestic savings (per cent of GDP) | 25.0 | 25.1 | 21.6 | 19.9 | 16.7 | 16.9 | 19.1 | 16.2 | 18.3 |
| Public finances (per cent of GDP) | | | | | | | | | |
| Expenditure | 12.3 | 12.7 | 12.0 | 11.7 | 9.8 | 10.5 | 13.3 | 15.4 | 14.8 |
| Budget deficit | -1.3 | -4.0 | -4.2 | -1.9 | -1.8 | -1.8 | -5.0 | -2.4 | -2.0 |
| Consumer price increases (annual percentage change) | 18.3 | 13.2 | 10.1 | 10.0 | 50.4 | 23.2 | 0.8 | 3.8 | 8.8 |
| *International economic activity* | | | | | | | | | |
| Import volume, c.i.f. (annual percentage change) | 3.1 | -1.5 | 2.4 | 0.3 | -17.3 | -13.9 | 5.5 | 15.6 | 24 |
| Export volume, of which (annual percentage change) | 18.8 | 3.6 | -4.8 | -5.2 | 2.3 | 0.0 | 7.7 | -1.2 | 11 |
| Copra and coconut oil | 8.7 | 10.0 | -5.5 | -5.8 | -34.7 | 4.7 | 85.1 | -10.5 | -18 |
| Terms of trade (annual percentage change) | -13.0 | -8.0 | -3.2 | 9.0 | 8.2 | -12.7 | 3.5 | 3.1 | 9.2 |
| Real effective exchange rate (index, 1980-1982=100) | 92.1 | 101.3 | 106.7 | 96.2 | 107.9 | 114.3 | 89.9 | 86.5 | 89.9 |
| Foreign exchange earnings[b] (billions of dollars) | 8.4 | 9.0 | 8.5 | 8.6 | 8.3 | 8.3 | 9.0 | 9.7 | 11 |
| Net financial transfer[c] (billions of dollars) | 2.4 | 1.1 | 0.8 | -0.7 | -0.5 | -1.7 | -1.6 | -1.8 | -1.3 |
| Net financial transfer[d] (per cent of GDP) | 5.7 | 5.4 | 6.8 | 6.8 | 0.1 | -3.0 | -6.2 | -0.9 | -0.2 |
| Gross foreign debt (billions of dollars) | 17.4 | 20.8 | 24.3 | 24.1 | 24.4 | 26.2 | 28.9 | 30.0 | 30.2 |

*Source:* Data and estimates of IMF, the World Bank, the Asian Development Bank, the United Nations Economic and Social Commission for Asia and the Pacific, Morgan Guaranty Trust Co. and the Department of International Economic and Social Affairs of the United Nations Secretariat.

a Preliminary estimates.
b Goods, services and private transfer inflows.
c Capital account definition (see table VIII.1).
d Expenditure definition (see table VIII.1).

The overall investment effort had been quite strong, averaging 30 per cent of GDP in the second half of the 1970s. Most of it was financed out of domestic resources, although international lending to the Philippines had been substantial, raising the net transfer of financial resources to an average 5.5 per cent of GDP during that period. This too changed dramatically after 1983, as investment and the net transfer plummeted, the latter turning negative in 1984 (see figure VIII.7).[37] From 1983 to 1986, the net financial transfer fell from an inflow of 7 per cent of GDP to an outflow of 6 per cent.

If the strong net transfer of financial resources through the early 1980s was beneficial in supporting the high rate of investment, it also was a source of vulnerability to the economy, as the support vanished when the inflow of new private lending was cut back with the onset of the crisis. Thus, instead of a net transfer of resources to the Philippines of about

37 Using the capital-account definition, as in table VIII.4, the net financial transfer became negative in 1983. It remained highly positive from the perspective of expenditures because official reserves were drawn down by about $2 billion to finance the expenditures. The expenditure measure showed an insignificantly positive net transfer in 1984, rather than a negative one as shown by the capital-account measure, owing to differences in measurement methodologies. Both measures, however, lead to the same conclusion of a major shift to a net outward transfer of financial resources by 1985.

Figure VIII.6. Gross national income per capita of the Philippines, 1967-1988

(Index, 1980=100)

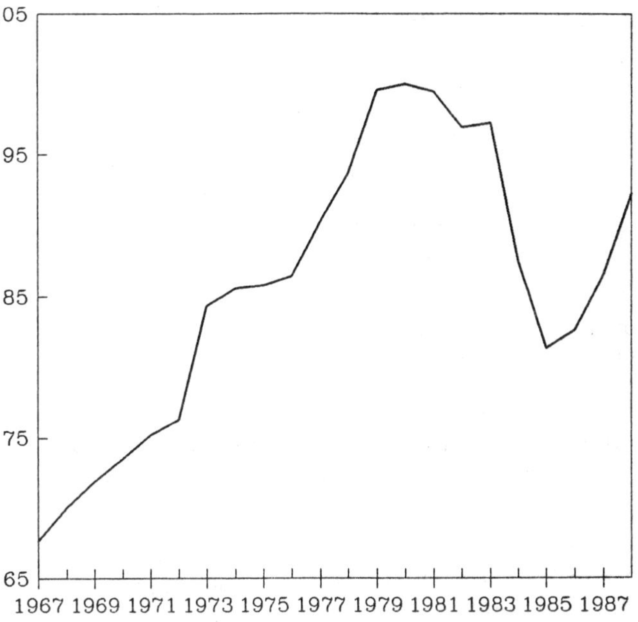


*Source:* Based on data from World Bank, *World Tables,* 1988-1989 edition (1988 estimated by the United Nations Secretariat).

Figure VIII.7. Investment, net resource transfers and savings in the Philippines, 1975-1988

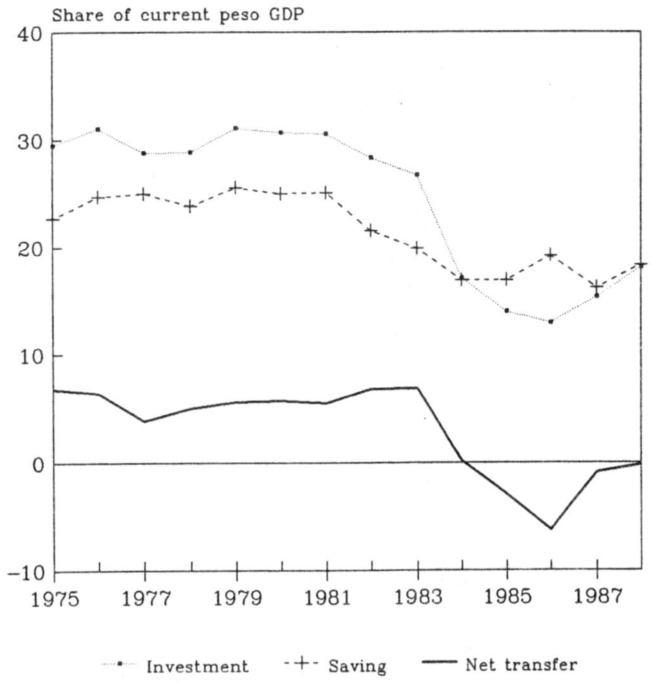


*Source:* Based on data from World Bank, *World Tables,* 1988-1989 edition, and IMF, *International Financial Statistics.*

$500 million a year on average in 1982 and 1983 from the medium-term lending commitments of the financial markets, the Philippines began transferring resources to these creditors in 1984 and has continued to do so since.

The Government had looked to new external financing to support a countercyclical expansion of the public sector in 1981 and 1982, based on over-optimistic assumptions about how quickly and strongly the world economy would recover from recession. About $7 billion were added to total external debt in 1981 and 1982, $5 billion from private banks, of which almost $4 billion had been short-term borrowing.[38] Added to already high foreign borrowing for investment projects, this rapidly built up a heavy debt-servicing burden.[39]

As was seen in the case of Mexico, a sudden and sharp drop in the net transfer of financial resources puts great strain on economic policy-making. In the Philippines, this strain was applied to a fragile political situation—which included operation in the countryside of two separate guerilla armies—as acute social pressures were not alleviated.

The Philippines is an overwhelmingly rural nation, whose emphasis on coconut and sugar exports and a highly protected and capital-intensive industrial sector in the cities has created an extremely unequal income distribution. In 1987, almost 60 per cent of the population still lived in rural areas, where the proportion of people living in absolute poverty had increased from one half to two thirds between 1971 and 1985. The share of the urban population living in absolute poverty had risen from 36 per cent to 50 per cent during the same period. In the countryside, 46 per cent of the population had no access to safe drinking water and even in the cities 17 per cent were in the same situation. The buoyant years of economic growth noted above had thus generated great wealth for the few, and swelled the numbers of those living in poverty. The wealthiest fifth of the families in the Philippines received 53 per cent of all income, while the bottom fifth received 5 per cent.[40]

While benefiting from the Philippines' development strategy, the high- income groups were not necessarily confident of its sustainability. The Government had begun an economic adjustment programme in 1980 with IMF support, aimed at sustaining the rate of economic growth while regaining external equilibrium, in the face of the economy's vulnerability to adverse terms-of-trade and interest-rate changes. However, some policy changes such as exchange rate adjustment lagged, and public sector investments continued to expand by relying on domestic and external credit. Moreover, certain large investment projects that proved unviable nevertheless raised the debt burden of official financial institutions and absorbed ever-larger budgetary resources. Increasingly, the response of the affluent private sector was capital flight.[41]

In short, a crisis was clearly brewing in the early years of the 1980s. It was in part a foreign debt crisis, in part a crisis that stemmed from certain weaknesses in the past pattern of development, and in part the economic manifestation of a political crisis.

### The crisis and the response

By 1983, foreign exchange reserves, which were being used to support an overvalued exchange rate, had dwindled; and with debt-service ratios increasing, external creditors grew hesitant to extend additional finance. When a political crisis, caused by the assassination of a major political figure, erupted in August 1983, foreign commercial banks refused to roll over short-term credits or extend new medium-term or long-term loans and thereby precipitated a debt-servicing crisis. Confidence in the economy—and its leadership—was badly shaken and capital flight accelerated. Depleted reserves were not sufficient to cover the resulting balance-of-payments deficit and the Government was forced to declare a moratorium on debt repayment and seek a negotiated rescheduling of the debt.

The Government, whose 1980 IMF stand-by arrangement had expired at the end of 1981, also returned to IMF. The policy prescriptions agreed with the Fund were of the conventional type: devaluation of the currency; liberalization of the import régime and removal of tariff barriers; budget austerity to reduce the deficit; and the restructuring of the coconut and sugar sectors to improve efficiency in operations.

But if the agreement by the Government to these policy measures was prompt, its implementation was erratic, piecemeal or marred by long delays. Relations with IMF deteriorated and the release of later tranches of the IMF loan was held up as terms of conditionality were not met. Some policies were politically too difficult to enforce. For instance, budgetary restrictions were not applied to public corporations and the Government hesitated to dismantle public

---

38 Most of the rest of the lending was accounted for by the World Bank, whose loans outstanding to the Philippines rose almost $1 billion in those two years (see World Bank, *World Debt Tables*, 1988-89 edition, vol. II (Washington, D.C., December 1988)).

39 Interest payments, as recorded in the balance of payments, doubled from $1 billion in 1980 to $2 billion in 1982.

40 These data are drawn from UNICEF, Manila, "Redirecting adjustment programmes toward growth and the protection of the poor: the Philippine case", in G. Cornia, R. Jolly and F. Stewart, eds., *Adjustment with a Human Face*, vol. II, *Country Case Studies* (Oxford, Clarendon Press, 1988), especially pp. 193-196; UNICEF, *Statistics on Children in UNICEF Assisted Countries* (New York, UNICEF, April 1989); and World Bank, *Social Indicators of Development* (Washington, D.C., September 1988).

41 The extent of capital flight became apparent only after the crisis had begun. For example, one estimate in September 1983 placed the level of capital flight at a relatively small amount of $0.9 billion, which was roughly the difference between the officially reported total external debt of $16.3 billion and the sum of current account deficits from 1970 to 1983 of $15.3 billion. This $0.9 billion figure was also not very far from an estimate based on the sum of errors and omissions of $1 billion for the period 1970 to 1982. However, two months later, in November 1983, the Government announced that the total foreign debt was $24.8 billion. When compared to the total current account deficit mentioned above, estimated capital flight totals $9.5 billion, more than 38 per cent of total external debt (see Manuel F. Montes, Philippines, Country Study No. 2 of *Stabilization and Adjustment Policies and Programmes*, (Helsinki, World Institute for Development Economics Research of the United Nations University, 1987, p. 3).

sector monopolies in sugar and coconut, a condition regarded as vital to the recovery of these depressed sectors.[42]

In 1984, widespread business failures led to massive layoffs. Inflation rose sharply to 50 per cent in consequence of the series of currency devaluations and the expansion in the money supply of the previous year. Investments as a percentage of GDP fell sharply to 17 per cent and real GDP contracted by 7 per cent. The economic dislocation and inconsistent policy measures noted above added further to the already intense political and social pressures. Business confidence remained depressed. A severe financial crisis erupted as many financial institutions failed because of large-scale withdrawal of deposits. A government attempt to rescue the ailing financial institutions rendered the austere budget policy ineffective as the additional expenditure aggravated the already huge budget deficits.

In the end, the need for important efforts of economic and financial adjustment was widely seen as imperative and a new stabilization programme was designed and supported by IMF through a $603 million IMF stand-by facility in December 1984. The economic policy objectives in 1985 entailed a restrictive monetary policy and control of the fiscal deficit.

The measures were effective and led to a drastic compression of domestic demand. Inflation receded to 23 per cent for the year. But the greatly reduced level of economic activity also led to the further contraction of real GDP by 4 per cent. The contraction in aggregate demand was accomplished mainly through a drop in both public and private investment. Total investments thus fell sharply again, to 14 per cent of GDP. The industrial sector experienced a 10 per cent contraction for two consecutive years. However, the current account balance improved dramatically from deficits of about $3 billion in 1982 and 1983, to $1.3 billion in 1984 and near balance in 1985.

Thus, finally, the adjustment effort launched in 1980 became effective in so far as the external payments balance of the Philippines contracted in 1985. Put in different terms, as there was little new financing, the net transfer of financial resources became a substantial net outflow (see table VIII.4). This was accomplished mainly through the compression of domestic demand, which led to a drastic drop in capacity utilization, an increase in unemployment and a decline in per capita income to levels of the mid-1970s.

Two years of severe economic decline after a number of years of stagnation made conditions unbearable for a large segment of the population. The dissatisfaction and disenchantment with the economic conditions were manifested in workers' strikes for higher wages, the clamour for a boycott of the Administration's surprise call for elections and the increased influence of the guerilla movement in the rural areas. In January 1986, the political situation deteriorated further and a peaceful revolt of the urban population deposed the Government and swept a new administration into power.

### A new beginning

The new régime faced the task of rehabilitating institutions that had collapsed and an economy in disarray, while the political climate did not fully stabilize for at least the initial 18 months. Attempts were made to overthrow the new Government and a rash of strikes disrupted the economy. But the new Government survived and began to implement its main economic policy objectives, which included the development of the rural economy through extensive support for labour-intensive, rural-based industries, improvement of infrastructure and the reduction in the direct economic role of the Government through privatization and disposal of certain government assets.

Efforts have also been made to set a new standard of civic behaviour and to recover illicitly obtained assets of the former President and senior government officials.[43] In addition, action was taken in foreign courts to recover payments on certain international business transactions.[44] For the future, the watchful eye of an informed public is to be an important ally of the Government in maintaining the new standards.

Soon after the change in Government, official inflows resumed, led by drawings from an IMF stand-by facility. In addition, development aid was either pledged or received from several industrial country donors.

### A return of optimism

The two-year decline of the economy ended with small positive growth in 1986, but economic recovery itself began in 1987. GDP rose 5 per cent that year and 7 per cent in 1988 led by industrial production in both years. Investment too has been recovering and the net transfer, while still negative, has become far less so. The short-term outlook is for continued strong recovery in 1989 and 1990, with real GDP growing 5 to 6 per cent each year (and thus per capita output rising 3 to 4 per cent a year), and with rising investment and

---

42 By the start of 1984, two discoveries had come to light that further damaged credibility. One was the overstatement of official reserves by as much as $600 million, which might have been done to cover illicit foreign exchange dealings by senior government officials. The other was an inexplicable surge in the money supply of 20 per cent and, more important, a rise of 26 per cent in money in circulation between October and November 1983 alone.

43 After only a year in operation, the Presidential Commission on Good Government has sequestered shares in 286 firms and recovered cash and property valued at $400 million. Some associates of the former President have negotiated agreements to return assets, or in some instances, to surrender control of corporations they once headed. The sequestered assets will be confiscated and sold by the Government if proved to be illegally acquired. They will be returned, if shown to have been legitimately obtained.

In October 1988, a United States federal grand jury in New York indicted the former President and his wife for fraud and racketeering. They were charged with diverting $103 million in government funds to buy personal property and real estate in the United States, fraudulently borrowing $16.5 million from United States banks, and illegally transferring assets that had been frozen by the federal court.

44 In particular, the Government has filed suit in the United States against a United States multinational corporation for fraud and bribery in the procurement of a contract to build a nuclear power plant in the Philippines and for technical faults in its design and construction.

domestic savings ratios. Even inflation, which was 9 per cent in 1988, is expected to moderate this year and next.[45]

There is, furthermore, a palpable sense of optimism in the business community of the Philippines. It is evident in the rising real estate and stock market prices, in the large amount of construction now under way, in the first class hotels in Manila that are heavily booked with visitors seeking business opportunities. The political situation is seen to have stabilized and structural economic adjustment is again on the agenda.

However, it is not yet assured that the Philippines will enter a path of long-run, sustained economic growth and development. The basic structure of the economy will take a long time to change. While the terms of trade have recently improved, the Philippines remains vulnerable to a reversal of these changes, not to mention the debt burden that still overhangs both the budgetary and the balance-of-payments outlook.

Furthermore, the guerilla movement continues to be active today. The poor remain poor and the prospects for their incomes rising through reinvigorating the development strategy of the 1970s are not promising. Indeed, the Government accepts that much needs to be done to directly attack the conditions of the poor, including distribution of land to them through land reform. It lists its national development goals expressly in these terms: alleviation of poverty; generation of more productive employment; promotion of equity and social justice; and sustainable economic growth.[46]

Rural development is one centrepiece of Government policy as legislated by the Philippine Congress in the Comprehensive Agrarian Reform Programme. Its full and timely implementation will be important as the prospects for sustained development in the Philippines would be especially helped if the majority of the population participated in the economy in an integral and sustained way.

## Ghana's adjustment: institutions and structures

The economic adjustment project now under way in Ghana is nothing short of revolutionary. To a degree, the adjustment programme that the Government began in 1983 was made necessary—as in other countries—by a sharp deterioration in the terms of trade in 1980-1982 associated with sharply rising petroleum import prices and rapidly deteriorating commodity export prices. It was prompted as well by the effects of the worst drought in Ghana in the twentieth century. But both those crises also served to underline just how far Ghana's economy had deteriorated in the quarter century since the country's birth and the critical need for radical reform.

The economy had all but collapsed by 1983. Per capita income had fallen by one quarter since 1980 alone, when it was already 15 per cent lower than it had been a decade before (see figure VIII.8).[47] Today, the Government has obtained a measure of recovery and its goal is to set Ghana finally on a path of sustained development, which entails not only standard macro-economic stabilization and structural adjustment, but also major institutional rehabilitation and development; indeed, it aims at changing how people behave in their every day economic activities—that is, to change the culture of the society.

Supporting Ghana's economic recovery has also become a major project of the international community of donor countries and official agencies, in which large-scale financial support, technical assistance and ideas on development and adjustment strategies have been proffered. The net transfer of financial resources, in particular, has become significantly positive in recent years. Ghana is one of the few countries in which the social costs of economic adjustment have received explicit consideration and programmatic response. It is a case in which a great deal of progress has been made in a relatively short period of time and in which the net financial transfer has become an aid to adjustment. But whether the ultimate goal will be achieved is still an open question.

### Antecedents: 25 difficult years

The economy of Ghana was once described as severely constrained by what its exports could earn, by the inability of food production to keep pace with the growing population and by shortages of a wide range of middle-level and top-level skills.[48] That could almost be a description of Ghana in the 1980s, but it was written in the 1960s. Ghana has had an adjustment problem ever since.

The story of Ghana's economic performance begins with cocoa. Ghana has been and will continue to be heavily dependent on cocoa exports for foreign exchange earnings and as a major source of income for a large segment of the rural

---

45 This, for example, is the forecast of the Asian Development Bank-ESCAP joint regional modelling project, as presented at the meeting of Project LINK, United Nations Department of International Economic and Social Affairs, New York, 6-8 March 1989.

46 Philippines, National Economic Development Authority, *Updates on the Medium-Term Philippine Development Plan, 1988-1992* (Manila, July 1988), p. 1.

47 Ghanaian economic data suffer from more than the usual statistical limitations and so quantitative results must be interpreted with caution; in particular, the large informal sector, which arose in the 1970s and is largely unaccounted for in official data, distorted results then and can be expected to do so again as it is re-absorbed into the open economy as part of adjustment. In addition, certain inconsistencies exist in population data, which reduce the reliability of per capita information (see Reginald H. Green, *Ghana,* Country Study No. 1 of *Stabilization and Adjustment Policies and Programmes,* (Helsinki, World Institute for Development Economics Research of the United Nations University, 1987), annex). This notwithstanding, the basic trends in the data are considered valid.

48 See, for example, A. Killick and R. Szereszewski, "The economy of Ghana", in P. Robson and D. A. Lury, eds., *The Economies of Africa* (London, George Allen and Unwin, Ltd., 1969), pp. 123-124.

Figure VIII.8. Gross national income per capita of Ghana, 1967-1988

(Index, 1980=100)

*Source:* Based on data from World Bank, *World Tables,* 1988-89 edition (1988 estimated by the United Nations Secretariat).

population. Under the current adjustment programme, production and export of cocoa are recovering from mid-1980s lows, but the levels being attained are only those of the first half of the 1950s (200,000 to 250,000 tons annually).[49] New plantings in the 1950s and improvements in disease control had raised production and export to over 400,000 tons a year in the 1960s. In the 1950s, cocoa accounted for about 63 per cent of exports, roughly the same as today. Production and export are expected to be of the order of 300,000 tons a year, but in any case, with significant production increases from Ghana and other cocoa producers, cocoa prices are expected to remain soft. The success of adjustment in Ghana will thus be contingent on the success of recovery in other traditional exports and diversification into new products.

Food production is another area in which the problems of the 1960s are still the problems of the 1980s. Traditionally, food crops in Ghana have mostly been produced in a highly land-intensive manner, using "slash-and-burn" techniques to clear and fertilize fields which would produce for a few years with annually declining productivity and then be left fallow to regenerate for three years or more. By the 1960s, with population growth beginning to put pressure on land resources, new agricultural techniques were needed which, with more capital inputs, would make labour more productive. Research and extension work to disseminate technological improvements were also easily identified needs, as was adequate rural credit on appropriate terms. While many programmes were designed in the ensuing years, implementation fell short and by 1982 (before the worst effects of the drought), production of most food commodities was no higher—and in some crops was much less—than in 1970 and yields per hectare were also roughly the same. Meanwhile, the population had grown steadily and average land per person had fallen 30 per cent. The rural transportation sector was also in general disrepair. The ratio of food self-sufficiency measured against basic consumption requirements plummeted from 83 per cent in 1964-1966 to 71 per cent in 1978-1980 and to 60 per cent in 1982.

Following the drought, food production recovered and has surpassed output levels of 1970, but the sector remains a major focus of the structural adjustment effort. Indeed, it must. Not only is food an important tradable good, increased production of which frees foreign exchange for other imports, but it is a major part of the national economy. Smallholder agriculture, including export crops as well as food, still accounts for roughly half of GDP and employment, and food production remains the chief occupation of the large number of rural poor. Moreover, a recommendation of one of Ghana's earliest development advisers is still

49 The *caveat* in footnote 47 about data applies in particular to cocoa production, as smuggled exports are believed to have been substantial.

sound, namely, that a rapidly developing rural economy provides an important market base for industrial development.[50]

In the 1960s, the Government of Ghana had been accused of failing in an intensified effort at development planning in part because of being too ambitious, given the limited administrative capacity of government at that time.[51] It had only emerged from colonial status in 1957. But a similar concern has recently been raised by senior Ghanaians and others, namely, that the current structural adjustment programme is demanding too much of the State in terms of the comprehensiveness of the reform package being implemented and the multitude of studies of various policy areas that must be completed and digested.[52]

Whether or not this view is representative, it is important because it highlights two central issues: first, although a large number of Ghanaians have been trained and educated over the decades, virtually a generation of them were lost to Ghanaian society as they were not absorbed by the public service or private enterprise because of a quarter century of economic and political decay. They emigrated or spent much of their effort in the parallel market rather than the open economy, as did Ghanaians of all walks of life. Indeed, in 1983, at the depths of Ghana's economic crisis, Nigeria's own crisis forced repatriation of roughly 1 million Ghanaians from that country. Second, the civil service and, more generally, people from all income classes, have been driven by a heavily distorted economy into excesses or abuses.

Cleansing the system was a major commitment of the new Government that came to power at the end of 1981. The temper of the time seems well reflected in a speech made by the head of Government in 1986, in which he recalled that five years earlier selfishness and the pursuit of power for exclusive personal reasons had taken hold of the ship of state.[53] The drive to stop corrupt practices was very popular and, as it had some effect, disrupted the economic system then operating and the interests that benefited from it. The initial effort also undoubtedly laid the foundation for public acceptance of the adjustment programme begun in 1983.

### The adjustment effort

Adjustment began with an emergency programme that included moving cocoa from producing areas that had been closed off, demonetizing the largest denomination Ghanaian currency note, which is a distributionally interesting means to reduce liquidity, attacking corrupt practices, and mobilizing communities for activities ranging from cocoa and oil palm rehabilitation to garbage disposal and cleaning up choked sewer drains.[54] In addition, as the economy had been starved for imports, an adjustment programme with several traditional features—but also some innovations—was set in motion. Although discussions with IMF had begun in July 1982, the Economic Recovery Programme began without Fund support in April 1983 with the first devaluation of the national currency, the cedi. By August, however, a stand-by arrangement with the Fund went into effect and Ghana's programme has since been supported by a sequence of loans from IMF and the World Bank and substantial bilateral support.

Key measures of the adjustment programme included, first, a sequence of major devaluations of the cedi, leading in 1986 to the initiation of a foreign exchange auction system. The intent was not only to give appropriate price signals to the economy, but also to encourage the flow of foreign exchange back into legal channels. Second, import controls were relaxed, ensuring that scarce goods could be imported, shortages could be reduced, and inordinate price increases deterred. Third, prices paid farmers for cocoa were increased and 25,000 "ghost" workers were pared from the payroll of the Ghana Cocoa Marketing Board (GCMB); this was followed by the release of 29,000 workers in 1987 (39 per cent of the total staff), among other steps taken to reduce the cost and increase the efficiency of the Board.

Fiscal measures were a third area of policy reform. Taxes were increased on incomes and commodities, and expenditures were restricted. Subsidies were reduced, notably on petroleum, which had supported substantial smuggling of oil products to neighbouring countries; but fertilizer subsidies were also cut. Fees were introduced in the health sector and tariff rates for utilities and transport were raised. As civil service salaries had fallen in real terms during the crisis to levels that forced state employees to have other incomes (legal or otherwise) to survive, salary levels were raised about 60 per cent. On the other hand, the size of the civil service is being contracted at a rate of about 12,000 jobs a year from 1987 to 1989, and perhaps beyond. A major examination of state enterprises is also under way to decide which to retain, divest or form into joint ventures. At the same time, sector rehabilitation and other public investment programmes have been set in motion in tradable goods sectors and basic infrastructure.

Finally, among the conventional vectors of adjustment policy, monetary policy sought to slow the growth of credit

---

50 W. Arthur Lewis, *Report on the Industrialization of the Gold Coast* (Accra, Government Printing Office, 1953).

51 See Elliot J. Berg, "Structural transformation versus gradualism: recent economic development in Ghana and the Ivory Coast", in Philip Foster and Aristede R. Zolberg, eds., *Ghana and the Ivory Coast: Perspectives on Modernization* (Chicago, University of Chicago Press, 1971), pp. 187-230.

52 See John Loxley, *Ghana: Economic Crisis and the Long Road to Recovery* (Ottawa, The North-South Institute, February 1988), p. 36.

53 Flight-Lieutenant J. J. Rawlings, Chairman of the Provisional National Defence Council, 31 December 1986, as reported in *West Africa,* 12 January 1987, pp. 59-61.

54 Several discussions of Ghana's adjustment programme from different perspectives have been published. See, in particular, Tsatsu Tsikata, "Ghana's country experience" (ECA/ICHD/88/51), paper prepared for the International Conference on the Human Dimension of Africa's Economic Recovery and Development, Khartoum, 5-8 March 1988; UNICEF, Accra, "Adjustment policies and programmes to protect children and other vulnerable groups in Ghana", in G. Cornia, R. Jolly and F. Stewart, eds., *Adjustment with a Human Face,* Vol. 2, *Country Case Studies* (Oxford, Clarendon Press, 1988), pp. 93-125; *Ghana: Policies and Programme for Adjustment* (Washington, D.C., World Bank, 1984); Green, *op. cit.*, and Loxley, *op. cit.*

Table VIII.5. The Ghanaian economy in the 1980s

| | 1980 | 1981 | 1982 | 1983 | 1984 | 1985 | 1986 | 1987 | 1988[a] |
|---|---|---|---|---|---|---|---|---|---|
| *Domestic economic activity* | | | | | | | | | |
| Gross domestic product, real (annual percentage change) | 0.5 | -2.9 | -6.5 | -4.4 | 8.7 | 4.5 | 5.0 | 4.4 | 6 |
| Agricultural GDP (annual percentage change) | 2.2 | -2.6 | -5.5 | -7.0 | 9.7 | 0.6 | 3.3 | 0.0 | 6 |
| Industrial GDP (annual percentage change) | 0.3 | -16.0 | -17.0 | -11.9 | 8.9 | 17.7 | 7.7 | 11.3 | .. |
| Investment (per cent of GDP) | 5.6 | 4.6 | 3.4 | 3.8 | 6.9 | 9.6 | 9.6 | 10.7 | 12.5 |
| Gross domestic savings (per cent of GDP) | 4.9 | 4.0 | 3.7 | 0.6 | 4.2 | 6.7 | 5.8 | 4.2 | 5.5 |
| Overall budget deficit (-) (per cent of GDP) | -4.2 | -6.5 | -5.6 | -2.7 | -1.8 | -2.2 | 0.1 | 0.5 | 0.4 |
| Domestic budget deficit[b] (-) (per cent of GDP) | -4.2 | -6.5 | -5.7 | -2.7 | -2.1 | -2.7 | -0.7 | -0.3 | -0.7 |
| Real wage[c] (index, 1985=100) | 115.4 | 68.6 | 61.0 | 47.1 | 69.5 | 100.0 | 162.8 | .. | .. |
| Consumer price increases (annual percentage change) | 50.7 | 116.4 | 22.3 | 122.9 | 39.8 | 10.3 | 24.6 | 39.8 | 30 |
| *International economic activity* | | | | | | | | | |
| Import volume, c.i.f. (annual percentage change) | 9.2 | -5.4 | -32.5 | -11.4 | 8.8 | 16.3 | 10.5 | -4.7 | .. |
| Export volume (annual percentage change) | 32.6 | -0.7 | -2.2 | -47.5 | 1.4 | 24.5 | 48.4 | 6.0 | -4 |
| of which, cocoa beans (annual percentage change) | 11.3 | -9.2 | 23.9 | -32.9 | -6.1 | 14.8 | 13.5 | 5.2 | -10 |
| Terms of trade (annual percentage change) | 24.9 | -17.7 | -11.1 | 22.0 | 7.7 | -5.7 | -4.1 | -2.8 | 11 |
| Real effective exchange rate[d] (index, 1985=100) | 1 214 | 1 452 | 1 471 | 2 118 | 172 | 100 | 60 | 29 | 19 |
| Foreign exchange earnings[e] (millions of dollars) | 1 217 | 836 | 718 | 483 | 633 | 712 | 895 | 1 112 | 1 119 |
| Net financial transfer[f] (millions of dollars) | -136 | 394 | 104 | 171 | 225 | 322 | 47 | 135 | 210 |
| Net financial transfer[g] (per cent of GDP) | 0.7 | 0.6 | -0.4 | 3.2 | 2.7 | 2.9 | 3.8 | 6.5 | 7 |
| Gross foreign debt (millions of dollars) | 1 312 | 1 460 | 1 397 | 1 600 | 1 900 | 2 175 | 2 656 | 3 124 | .. |

*Source:* Data and estimates of the Government of Ghana, IMF, the World Bank, the United Nations Economic Commission for Africa, and the Department of International Economic and Social Affairs of the United Nations Secretariat.

a Preliminary estimates.
b Overall deficit, excluding foreign grants.
c Average earnings in December of each year, deflated by average annual inflation in consumer prices.
d Calculated from average official exchange rate *vis-à-vis* the dollar and comparable cross rates with other currencies, and changes in wholesale prices in Ghana and its major trading partners.
e Goods, services and private transfer inflows.
f Capital account definition (see table VIII.1).
g Expenditure definition (see table VIII.1).

and establish positive real interest rates. While interest rates remain low relative to inflation, policies for fiscal correction have helped to slow the growth of credit as public sector borrowing requirements fell. Overall, the goal of greater monetary stability is part of the strategy to rebuild confidence in the financial sector and increase the use of financial institutions for mobilization of savings and allocation of credit.

By almost all conventional measures, the adjustment programme has thus far been a success. In the first year after the programme began, GDP grew 9 per cent and it has grown by 4 per cent to 6 per cent a year since (see table VIII.5). Of course, the ending of the drought in 1984 helped, as did an increasing return to the formal economy by informal economy participants, but economic activity has continued relatively buoyantly, even in years such as 1987, in which adverse weather reduced agricultural output. Overall growth is projected to continue to the end of the present decade at a similar order of magnitude.

Moreover, disastrous declines in import volumes were reversed and exports jumped. Despite weak commodity prices, foreign exchange earnings have recovered steadily. The real effective exchange rate plummeted, which mainly served to underline how irrelevant to the economy the official exchange rate had become in the early 1980s and the serious intention to make the formal economy function well once more.

Investment surged, reaching double-digit shares of GDP for the first time in the decade, and while the investment share remains far below the levels in rapidly growing developing countries elsewhere, it is a major step forward for Ghana. Urban real wages rose, recovering the 1980 level by 1986, and inflation fell from 123 per cent in 1983 to about a quarter of that rate last year. The budget deficit has also been reduced by major proportions, even measured without including foreign grant assistance.

The adjustment programme, nevertheless, was not addressing some problems. The long economic deterioration that culminated in the early 1980s crisis had reduced average living conditions and raised the number of people in poverty. For example, the country lost more than 50 per cent of its doctors between 1981 and April 1984 and about 8.5 per cent of its nurses in 1982 alone.[55] The infant mortality rate is estimated to have risen from 86 per 1,000 in the late 1970s to 107-120 per 1,000 in the 1980s. Child labour became more crucial to family survival, raised drop-out rates from schools, especially among girls, and increased the incidence of irregular attendance and children too tired to benefit from classes. Child labour slipped into a nefarious practice called "child pawning" in which children are put into domestic service in order to reduce the living costs of poor households.

Moreover, the adjustment programme itself had adverse consequences for income distribution as it bypassed some people and hurt others. Low-income farmers not in the cocoa sector, especially in the north of the country, did not for the most part share in the initial benefits of the resurgence of economic growth. Low-income petty traders—often women whose earnings supplemented low family earnings in urban areas—were squeezed by declining retailing margins. In addition, more than 45,000 displaced public sector workers and innumerable underemployed urban workers were unlikely to be absorbed in the short run into the urban private sector. Reduction of subsidies as part of fiscal reforms meant that low-income beneficiaries would lose already modest income supplements, as in the case of the phasing out of the school feeding programme.

The Government acknowledged the difficulties adjustment was causing and sought to address them with international assistance. The Government's proposal to donors was forthright:

> "some components of the [Economic Recovery Programme] have and will exacerbate the economic problems of certain vulnerable groups in the short run, and this may impede the sustainability of the recovery programme itself.[56]

The result was the Programme of Actions to Mitigate the Social Costs of Adjustment (PAMSCAD), which comprised 20 projects costing $84 million, of which $38 million were foreign exchange costs. Projects are aimed at employment generation, rehabilitation of infrastructure and public services for meeting basic needs, such as clean water, sanitation and public health. Priority is given to community initiative projects, especially as they help build confidence in the adjustment programme. PAMSCAD projects are also explicitly designed not to distort the wider goals of the adjustment programme.

### The role of international support

For all its importance as symbol, PAMSCAD is a small expenditure of official international resources and a peripheral part of the international strategy for Ghana's recovery. But Ghana has become a major recipient of international assistance. The net transfer of financial resources rose from less than 1 per cent of GDP at the start of the decade—and that in part from accumulating arrears—to 3 per cent of GDP in the first three years of the adjustment programme; it exceeded 6 per cent in the past two years (see table VIII.5).

Major inflows began with drawings under an IMF stand-by arrangement, followed by other IMF flows and loans from the World Bank. Ghana's initial borrowings were thus mainly standard non-concessional, relatively short-term credits which were inappropriate as a form of balance-of-payments financing for a country in its situation, but they were virtually all that was available at the time. Subsequently, however, Ghana obtained more concessional funds (e.g., from the Enhanced Structural Adjustment Facility of IMF, and World Bank loans from the International Development Association and the Special Facility for Sub-Saharan Africa), followed by stepped-up commitments from the African Development Bank and bilateral sources. All in all, aid commitments to Ghana, which had fallen to little more than $100 million in 1982, almost tripled in 1983, exceeded $600 million in 1987 and $750 million in 1988. Almost $950 million were committed at the meeting of the Ghana Consulta-

55 Information in this paragraph is drawn from UNICEF, Accra, "Adjustment policies and programmes to protect children and other vulnerable groups in Ghana"...

56 Ghana, *Programme of Actions to Mitigate the Social Costs of Adjustment* (Accra, November 1987), p. 1.

tive Aid Group in Paris on 1 March 1989, more than half of which will be bilateral.

These inflows have been essential to the economic recovery programme. They help ensure, for example, that declines in the terms of trade do not disrupt the foreign exchange auction system for want of foreign exchange to offer. More generally, the resources help finance increases in imports and investments far beyond what is attainable based solely on domestic earnings. Indeed, without these international resources, Ghana's aforementioned rise in investment could not have taken place, as domestic savings—although recovered from the recessionary low of 1983—have not yet set a new, higher trend to replace the reduced average savings rate since the late 1970s.

In the light of these funding levels, however, the modest nature of the PAMSCAD exercise stands out, and even that programme was not simple to arrange and will stretch administrative capabilities to implement. PAMSCAD negotiations can be said to have begun in Accra in July 1986 at a meeting convoked by the Government and attended by high-level Ghanaian officials and representatives of the World Bank and the United Nations Children's Fund (UNICEF).[57] One full year later, and after certain false starts, an inter-agency mission to Ghana was assembled comprising the World Bank (as lead agency), UNICEF, the United Nations Development Programme, the World Food Programme, the International Labour Organisation, the World Health Organization, the International Fund for Agricultural Development and the Overseas Development Administration of the United Kingdom. With a mandate from the Ghana Consultative Aid Group, the mission prepared a programme which was discussed with the Government and among the agencies, and finally led in November to a formal proposal for international financing of the portfolio of projects that became PAMSCAD. A pledging conference was held in February 1988. As at early 1989, however, PAMSCAD seems to be developing as a collection of independent projects, each with its own reporting requirements, rather than as a consolidated programme. The additional resources provided under the programme (in contrast to reclassification of existing commitments), is also turning out to be lower than anticipated.

Thus, six years after the adjustment programme began, even a modest programme to ameliorate its social consequences is only beginning to be implemented. Yet it is important as a small monument to the incompleteness of traditional adjustment strategies and it challenges the international community to design social concerns into the fabric of economic adjustment programmes. PAMSCAD can also be seen as an awakening by the international community to the politics of economic adjustment. An explicit goal of the programme is to help mobilize the poor and displaced of Ghana on the side of adjustment policy and deny the opponents of adjustment a potentially important ally. For indeed, there have been opponents:

> "The redistributive impact on incomes ... will strike at powerful vested interests—rentiers and patrons whose opportunities come under threat as these [adjustment] measures bite. That such interests fight back to regain their ascendancy is only to be expected, and the recovery efforts will only be sustained if their political patronage no longer provides the protection they enjoyed in the past. That is why the politics of stabilization is so often also the politics of destabilization, as a Government determined to effect these transformations will face attempts to overthrow it..."[58]

### Towards the long run

Ghana's Economic Recovery Programme is a long-term effort whose success is contingent on substantial, continued financial support from abroad, and is close to a remaking of Ghanaian society. The ambition of the exercise is both a source of confidence—nothing less would be effective ultimately—and a threat to confidence, as it will require persisting in major policy reforms over a long period of time. A key feature of the strategy seems to be explicit recognition of the need to instil new standards of behaviour in the public and private sector, which can only be effective in the end if the belief becomes widespread that national economic development is on the agenda and that its benefits will be widely shared. Such a culture of development will need to spread to all levels of society and become a permanent fixture.

The ultimate signal that the adjustment programme is working will be when Ghanaian investors give the silent but most important vote of confidence by beginning to undertake long-term investments. If this has begun to happen, it is not yet discernible in the data. The long-run success of Ghana's adjustment is thus not yet assured. Many Ghanaians seem to believe that cocoa cannot carry Ghana into the twenty-first century. What can, is the ability to feed itself and export a diversified mix of agricultural and industrial products, including but not restricted to mining.

## Jamaica: structural adjustment as reconstruction

In Jamaica, people are accustomed to economic reconstruction. The Government whose term of office has recently ended had been ushered in with Hurricane Allen in 1980 and it was ushered out soon after Hurricane Gilbert in 1988. But although hurricanes are periodic, it seems that the need for economic adjustment has become chronic. Current efforts are the latest in a sequence that began in the 1970s. Gross income per capita peaked at the midpoint of that decade and fell over a third by the middle of the 1980s (see figure VIII.9). Per capita output had actually peaked earlier,

57 See Richard Jolly, "Poverty and adjustment in the 1990s", in John P. Lewis and others, *Strengthening the Poor: What Have We Learned?* U.S.-Third World Policy Perspectives, No. 10 (Washington, D.C., Overseas Development Council, 1988), pp. 163-175.

58 Tsikata, *op. cit.*, p. 22.

Figure VIII.9. Gross national income per capita of Jamaica, 1967-1988

(Index, 1980=100)

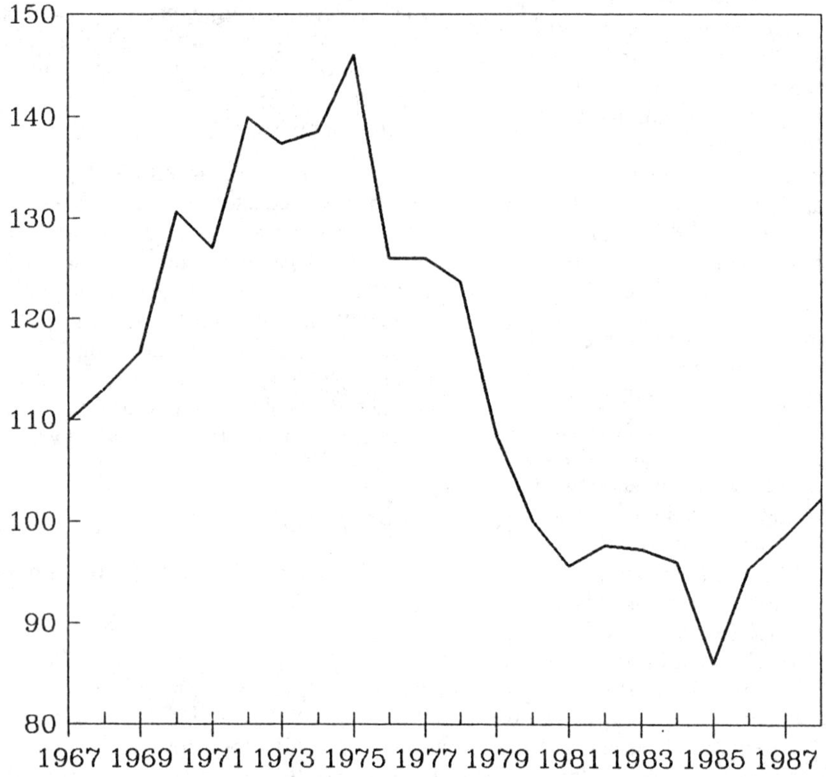


*Source:* Based on data from World Bank, *World Tables,* 1988-89 edition. (1988 estimated by the United Nations Secretariat).

in 1972, but favourable changes in the terms of trade had pushed up gross income per capita for three more years. A turnaround in both production and income per person began in 1986 and despite the hurricane, which virtually eliminated per capita output growth in 1985, both indicators have in essence recovered the already depressed 1980 level.

In one view, the most difficult part of the adjustment process is now over and a period of significant, if not spectacular, economic growth may ensue, barring new terms-of-trade or other economic shocks. Another view sees the structure of the economy as still fragile and subject to many of the same basic weaknesses it had 15 years before, except that Jamaica has now become a much more highly indebted economy. That is the consequence, primarily, of the largely official international credits provided to Jamaica in the 1980s and the positive net transfer of financial resources that it brought about.

**A structural view of the economy**

While economic adjustment difficulties have multiple roots, the underlying economic structure of an economy can make it more or less vulnerable to adjustment problems. In Jamaica, vulnerability has been high for structural reasons that grew out of the implicit development strategy of its colonial past and the modifications of that strategy after independence in 1962. From its origin as a sugar-producing island, Jamaica also had an independent and relatively isolated rural economy of descendants of the Maroon communities of escaped slaves that had prospered out of the direct reach of the colonial authorities.

Today, Jamaica has become a densely populated island with sugar plantations and tourist enclaves on the coast, and impoverished farms and bauxite mining in the interior.[59] The main change after 15 years of adjustment under two government administrations with different economic policy orientations is the addition of a new enclave, namely, manufacturing in export processing zones.

Over the long run, development in Jamaica has meant expansion of the modern sector and decline of the peasant sector, with increasing dependence on earnings from the export enclaves to supply needs through imports, including basic foodstuffs. The rise of bauxite mining was an indirect attack

59 Jamaican bauxite quickly became significant for the world as well as for Jamaica; for example, the first bauxite mine opened in 1952 and by 1970, Jamaica was producing 21 per cent of the world's bauxite supply.

on the rural economy, as the bauxite lay underneath settled communities which, perforce, were displaced.[60] The rise of local manufacturing, which preceded and is not connected to the export-processing zones mentioned above, also accentuated the dual nature of the society, increasing its dependence on imported raw materials which were processed on imported machinery. These goods—processed foods and beverages, textiles and construction materials—have formed the physical basis of the modern sector and competed with the traditional economy in the mountains, which is based on local foods, raw materials and handicrafts.

The development path has also prompted migration to the cities from the countryside, the rapid growth of urban slums, and the spread of poverty and unemployment. The expansion of the modern sector, the growth of government services, the rise of merchant and manufacturing fortunes all contrasted with the difficulties in the countryside and then in the cities. The vast outmigrations from the Jamaican hills in the 1950s and 1960s spilled overseas as hundreds of thousands of Jamaicans emigrated to Great Britain and later to the United States.

Modern economic development meant the expulsion of the peasant farmer and provided no place in his homeland for him to go. The mining sector offered limited opportunities. Modern manufacturing also provided relatively few jobs, as long as its products were limited to a protected domestic or regional market. Indeed, one of the attractions of the new policy thrust towards export processing zones was the possibility of expanding employment. Even tourism employed few local people and required increased imports of foods.

Thus, by the early 1970s Jamaica had developed consistently high unemployment, a highly unequal distribution of income, and great social awareness of the economic cleavages. The partial closing of the escape valve of migration, which had in the past provided an outlet for the social pressures built up by a deteriorating rural economy, has also required that politicians be responsive to the needs of lower income groups.

### A sequence of adjustment policies and the net financial transfer

A first strategy to change Jamaica's economic structure, attempted in the early 1970s, was the inverse of today's orthodoxy of limited government intervention. In the early model, the State would intervene directly in bauxite production and export, and increase taxes on high incomes and property. The higher revenue would then be available to increase public services and investment in public works. Food would be produced locally and land distributed to farmers. The State would become an active partner in the bauxite sector, in manufacturing, banking, the media, and public utilities. Internationally, efforts were made to build up the policy coherence of the International Bauxite Association and to win the support of the international community for stabilizing the commodity producing sectors of Jamaica and other developing countries. Such efforts were envisaged by the United Nations General Assembly in its Declaration and Programme of Action on the Establishment of a New International Economic Order[61] and, in particular, in the Integrated Programme for Commodities adopted by the United Nations Conference on Trade and Development.[62] In the event, world bauxite prices did rise in the 1970s, but fell back sharply in 1981 and 1982.[63]

The economic experience of Jamaica did not, however, follow the script. On the one hand, the unforeseen rise in international oil prices significantly affected Jamaica which was 98 per cent dependent on imported energy. On the other hand, although Jamaica, did impose a bauxite levy, mining production subsequently fell 20 per cent in 1975 and 1976.[64] By the second half of the 1970s, Jamaica was much concerned about budgetary and international payments imbalances and a different set of policies was emphasized. A stand-by agreement was negotiated with IMF in June 1977 and an extended Fund facility in May 1978, although the policy prescriptions of the programmes were ultimately not implemented fully.[65] The Government devalued the Jamaican dollar, froze wages, cut the budget and relaxed price controls. Unemployment rose and capital flight increased despite the attempt to improve the private sector climate. Unprecedented political violence escalated as the 1980 elections approached.

In October 1980, a new Government took power and within 12 months, the new Administration reversed the previous Government's economic programmes. In the domestic economy, it was thought that greater administrative competence would ease the burdens of the poor and that increased availability of foreign exchange would enable the new Government to confer some measure of relief on the population, while enacting an orthodox stabilization programme.

60 See George L. Beckford, ed., *Impact of Bauxite-Alumina on Rural Jamaica, special number of Social and Economic Studies* (University of the West Indies, Jamaica), vol. 36, No. 1 (March 1987).

61 General Assembly resolutions 3201 (S-VI) and 3202 (S-VI) of 1 May 1974.

62 *Proceedings of the United Nations Conference on Trade and Development, Fourth Session*, vol. I, *Report and Annexes* (United Nations publication, Sales No. E.76.II.D.10), part one, sect. A, resolution 93 (IV).

63 More specifically, and citing aluminium prices which are considered more representative than spot market quotations for bauxite itself, prices rose 11 per cent a year on average in the 1970s, and then fell 28 per cent in 1981 and 22 per cent in 1982 (based on data from UNCTAD, *Monthly Commodity Price Bulletin).*

64 Although the multinational aluminium companies were undoubtedly opposed to the bauxite levy, it is possible that they might have shifted production away from Jamaica even without it; for example, the increase in oil prices changed the relative cost of refining bauxite and alumina in different locations (see Omar Davies, "An analysis of the management of the Jamaican economy: 1972-1985", *Social and Economic Studies*, vol. 35, No. 1 (March 1986), pp. 73-109).

65 For an account of Jamaican policy-making and the Government's relationship with IMF in this period, see Norman Girvan, Richard Bernal and Wesley Hughes, "The IMF and the Third World: the case of Jamaica, 1974-80", *Development Dialogue*, 1980:2, pp. 113-155.

Table VIII.6. The Jamaican economy in the 1980s

| | 1980 | 1981 | 1982 | 1983 | 1984 | 1985 | 1986 | 1987 | 1988[a] |
|---|---|---|---|---|---|---|---|---|---|
| | | | | *Domestic economic activity* | | | | | |
| Production (annual percentage change) | | | | | | | | | |
| Gross domestic product | -5.8 | 2.7 | 0.0 | 1.9 | -0.8 | -5.5 | 2.5 | 5.8 | 1.9 |
| Agricultural GDP | -6.3 | 2.2 | 7.9 | 7.3 | 9.3 | -3.4 | -2.0 | 1.1 | -7.5 |
| Mining GDP | 9.9 | 1.3 | -29.0 | 0.6 | 0.7 | -19.5 | 6.6 | 4.8 | -3.0 |
| Manufacturing GDP | -11.6 | 0.9 | 6.9 | 2.1 | -5.1 | 0.9 | 3.2 | 4.7 | -2.5 |
| Construction GDP | -28.3 | 0.4 | 15.9 | 6.7 | -7.1 | -14.3 | 3.3 | 15.2 | 15.0 |
| Investment (per cent of GDP) | 15.7 | 20.4 | 20.9 | 22.3 | 23.4 | 25.3 | 19.3 | 22.6 | .. |
| Gross domestic savings (per cent of GDP) | 13.6 | 10.0 | 9.3 | 10.2 | 16.4 | 14.7 | 20.7 | 22.9 | .. |
| Public finances (per cent of GDP) | | | | | | | | | |
| Expenditure, of which | .. | 31.4 | 31.9 | 34.3 | 30.2 | 28.9 | 28.3 | 28.6 | 27.3 |
| Debt service | 25.5 | 26.3 | 28.4 | 33.2 | 39.7 | 38.8 | 44.1 | 40.4 | .. |
| Education | 20.2 | 20.7 | 20.8 | 18.6 | 16.9 | 16.9 | 16.9 | 16.9 | .. |
| Budget deficit | .. | -14.7 | -13.5 | -15.9 | -6.2 | -6.0 | -2.8 | -0.1 | -3.3 |
| Unemployment (percentage) | 27.3 | 25.9 | 27.6 | 26.4 | 25.5 | 25.0 | 23.7 | 21.0 | .. |
| Employment (index, 1980=100) | 100 | 105 | 105 | 106 | 112 | 112 | 116 | 121 | .. |
| Consumer price increases (annual percentage change) | 28.6 | 4.8 | 7.0 | 16.7 | 31.2 | 23.9 | 10.4 | 6.7 | 8.2 |
| | | | | *International economic activity* | | | | | |
| Import volume, c.i.f. (annual percentage change) | -6.4 | 21.6 | -0.8 | 14.9 | -24.6 | 2.0 | -10.3 | 14.0.. | |
| Export volume (annual percentage change) | 3.5 | 4.4 | -18.9 | -1.6 | 2.0 | -21.5 | -1.1 | 8.3 | 0.0 |
| Tourism earnings, dollars (index, 1980=100) | 100 | 118 | 140 | 164 | 175 | 182 | 227 | 259 | .. |
| Terms of trade (index, 1980=100) | 100.0 | 94.3 | 93.5 | 94.5 | 94.8 | 95.2 | 109.2 | 99.9 | .. |
| Real effective exchange rate (index, 1980=100) | 100.0 | 95.5 | 93.3 | 123.7 | 102.6 | 98.5 | 145.2 | 155.5 | .. |
| Foreign exchange earnings[b] (millions of dollars) | 1 542 | 1 663 | 1 542 | 1 461 | 1 444 | 1 458 | 1 552 | 1 813 | 1 965 |
| of which, bauxite and alumina | 736 | 760 | 484 | 451 | 473 | 293 | 308 | 314 | 342 |
| Net financial transfer[c] (millions of dollars) | -25 | 120 | 238 | 124 | 140 | 79 | -274 | -109 | -46 |
| Net financial transfer[d] (per cent of GDP) | 2.1 | 10.3 | 11.6 | 12.1 | 6.7 | 10.3 | -2.2 | -0.3 | .. |
| Gross foreign debt (millions of dollars) | 1 903 | 2 299 | 2 842 | 3 313 | 3 445 | 3 867 | 3 999 | 4 446 | 4 500 |

*Source:* Data and estimates of the Planning Institute of Jamaica, IMF, the World Bank, the Inter-American Development Bank, the United Nations Economic Commission for Latin America and the Caribbean, and the Department of International Economic and Social Affairs of the United Nations Secretariat.

[a] Preliminary estimates.
[b] Goods, services and private transfer inflows.
[c] Capital account definition (see table VIII.1).
[d] Expenditure definition (see table VIII.1).

Indeed, the Government succeeded in marshalling official international support. The net transfer of resources, which had been very close to zero since 1977, rose to a positive $120 million in 1981 and rose again to $238 million in 1982 (see table VIII.6). New financial commitments began with an IMF agreement in April 1981, which made $700 million available over three years. This opened the door for loans from the World Bank, private commercial banks, and the Caribbean Group for Co-operation in Economic Development. From 1981 to 1985, the net financial transfer to Jamaica was roughly 10 per cent of GDP, a level not seen since the mid-1970s.

The credits were to provide a cushion, and in the meantime market-directed adjustment would occur as policy interferences in market functioning were removed. According to this strategy, the exchange rate had to be set at a realistic level, imports deregulated and taxes lowered, state enterprises divested, and inflation kept in check by high interest rates and a tight money supply. Exports of new goods and services, including promotion of tourism, could be expected to increase if wages were kept low and favourable conditions provided for foreign and local investors.[66]

Circumstances, unfortunately, led to a disappointing outcome. Although inflation fell from 27 per cent in 1980 to 5 per cent in 1981 and little more in 1982, the international recession of 1982 hit Jamaica hard. Rather than double bauxite and alumina exports as projected, the price of bauxite fell on the world market and the aluminium companies cut their exports. Government revenue from bauxite declined from $206 million in 1980 to $137 million in 1982. Sugar exports fell by 50,000 tonnes and banana exports by 11,000 tonnes. At the same time, the lowering of import barriers encouraged a consumer splurge on imports pent-up from the previous decade. Consumer expectations across the entire society were raised. But local manufacturers, unprotected by import restrictions and tariffs, could not compete with the cheaper imports; nor could local farmers compete with the cheap grain imports. The balance of trade turned abruptly negative to a degree unseen in the earlier decade.

The 1983 policy response was, perforce, to tighten stabilization measures. The Government imposed new taxes, cut public spending further, and devalued by creating a two-tier exchange rate and then moving more imports to the more expensive exchange rate category. The World Bank extended two new loans, and the United States Government amplified its strategic reserves with Jamaican bauxite in a show of international solidarity with Jamaica's efforts.

Nevertheless, a further dose of stabilization policy was necessary. In November, the Government devalued by 43 per cent, and a new economic package was designed for 1984. The exchange rate would continue to be devalued in a managed float twice each month. Taxes were raised, food subsidies reduced except for a minumum level on basic commodities, and credit restricted. The Government deficit had risen to nearly 16 per cent of GDP in 1983. By the end of 1984, it was cut to 6 per cent. In March 1984, IMF extended a $143 million credit until the following March, and the Paris Club also rolled forward $135 million of external debt.

By the end of 1984, however, the economy was little improved. Inflation had risen to 31 per cent and unemployment to 24 per cent. The foreign exchange reserves had been spent, and severe austerity was left to show for it. The 6,705 new jobs created by the Investment Promotion Programme barely compensated for the 6,200 government jobs eliminated, not to mention the already high unemployment rate of over 25 per cent. In January 1985 the first sharp public protests began as the prices of cooking fuel and gasoline were raised, burgeoning in June into Jamaica's first general strike since independence. Strikes and pay disputes with the teachers, police and physicians occurred and student protests increased.

Finally, in 1986, the economic decline stopped. The net transfer of financial resources turned negative, but the fall of oil prices gave the Government the foreign exchange to manoeuvre. In a decisive break with past policy, a more growth-oriented policy was adopted in mid-1986. A budget expansion was announced, interest rates were reduced, the exchange rate was held steady, and capital expenditures were increased. In January 1987, Jamaica signed its fourth agreement with IMF for $133 million, now in support of Jamaica's new growth-oriented strategy. In September 1988, a further stand-by arrangement was obtained to continue assistance with growth-oriented adjustment as well as rehabilitation of the social infrastructure and maintenance of tight fiscal management.

### Facing the 1990s

By the end of 1987, Jamaica's economic indicators began to change. Real per capita growth was positive for the first time in 15 years. Inflation had been kept down to 10 per cent in 1986 and fell to 8 per cent in 1987. The change in terms of trade and the new policy had made a major difference.

But central problems had yet to be tackled. First, unemployment remains above 20 per cent. A large population of unemployed males, in particular, continues to be drawn into informal economy activities.[67] Second, Jamaica's foreign debt, which in 1980 amounted to 57 per cent of GNP, had risen to 139 per cent by 1987, and debt service had risen from 26 per cent of the government budget in 1980 to 40 per cent in 1987. Health and education expenditure fell in both absolute and relative terms, as a greater share of the shrinking budget was dedicated to debt service. This notwithstanding, as wages and incomes fell, food subsidies, school lunches, infant nutrition and food stamp programmes had been introduced to provide a safety net for household consumption. Nevertheless, the incidence of mild malnutrition rose from 8 to 39 per cent and the prevalence of stunted growth in infants rose from 6 to 14 per cent from 1978 to 1985.[68] Real expenditure on health fell from 78 to 54 Jamaican dollars per head from 1981 to 1985, a 30 per cent decline.[69] The pass rate of students from primary to secondary school fell from 62 to 34 per cent, suggesting a serious deterioration in the educational system.[70] Migration of Jamaicans to the United States in the 1980s has continued at the rate of 20,000 per year, nearly twice the level in the 1970s,

66 Even before any results were in, the World Bank applauded the new policy of Jamaica in a report on managing adjustment (see World Bank, *World Development Report 1981* (Washington, D.C., August 1981), pp. 72-73).

67 This has been a fertile field for recruitment into the trade in illicit substances as well as "hustling", pointing out once again the social dysfunction of unrealized economic development.

68 UNICEF, *Statistics on Children in UNICEF Assisted Countries* (New York, April 1989).

69 Planning Institute of Jamaica, *Economic and Social Survey, 1987,* table 20.1B.

70 Derick A. C. Boyd, *Economic Management, Income Distribution and Poverty in Jamaica* (New York, Praeger, 1988), p. 121.

resulting in a perceptible drain of entrepreneurship and skilled personnel.

The unevenness of productivity within the Jamaican economy also remains especially high and typical of countries heavily dependent on mining enclaves. Less than 1 per cent of the labour force in mining is responsible for 5 per cent of the national output, while the 31 per cent of the labour force in agriculture produce less than 6 per cent of national output. The productivity attached to the worker associated with mining is six times the national average, compared to one fifth the national level associated with a worker in agriculture (see table VIII.7).

In addition, the structure of exports today is not so different from the earlier era. Bauxite and alumina earn half the nation's foreign exchange, while tourist dollars have nearly tripled since 1980. The export processing zones export primarily garments of limited value added under the Caribbean Basin Initiative and employ mainly young women workers. Judging from the experience in other countries, this form of manufacturing enterprise is "footloose" and may disappear as quickly as it came if wages or taxes begin to rise faster than in a competitor country, leaving behind in Jamaica few skills or other benefits.

In sum, the economy today looks similar in fundamental ways to what it was 15 years ago. It relies on a few export earners, which have few linkages to the rest of the economy, which generate relatively few jobs and which have a high import content—fuels for alumina production, cut textiles for clothing and food for tourism. It is also a relatively specialized economy, relying heavily on imports for direct consumption of rich and poor alike. It has a conspicuously unequal distribution of wealth and persistently high unemployment.

Moreover, Jamaica has been buffeted by the international economy for much of the decade, but the net transfer of financial resources was kept positive, especially through official flows. As a result, Jamaica's debt more than doubled since 1980, and much of it—owed to multilateral institutions—is not subject to rescheduling.

Table VIII.7. Measures of structural disparities in Jamaica, 1980 and 1985

(Percentage)

| | Share of GDP | | Share of labour force | | Relative sector output per worker | |
|---|---|---|---|---|---|---|
| | 1980 | 1985 | 1980 | 1985 | 1980 | 1985 |
| Agriculture | 8.0 | 5.7 | 28.0 | 30.9 | 30 | 20 |
| Mining | 13.8 | 4.9 | 2.0 | 0.8 | 640 | 610 |
| Manufactauring | 15.7 | 19.7 | 16.2 | 13.4 | 100 | 150 |
| Other[a] | 62.5 | 69.7 | 53.8 | 54.9 | 120 | 130 |

*Source:* Department of International Economic and Social Affairs of the United Nations Secretariat and the Inter-American Development Bank.

a Including services and construction.

In the early 1970s, the Government's approach had been to tax the enclave sectors and subsidize the rest to compensate for the lack of real linkages within the economy. That was not sustainable. The approach in the 1980s was to suppress the transfers to the poor and build other enclaves, seeking to create some fresh employment. The present, newly elected Government faces the challenge of augmenting the present direction with programmes that will the address the social and economic distortions.

## Adjustment, structural change and net financial transfers

The review of these five country experiences of adjustment seems to point to certain conclusions about structural adjustment and the role that the net transfer of resources plays in that process. That role is as one factor among several that determine the success of adjustment.

A first conclusion about adjustment was demonstrated well by the experience of Mexico—that is, how difficult it is for a developing economy to adapt to a premature, large and continuous outflow of financial resources that might otherwise have been used for investment and essential consumption at home. The excessive financial constraint arose because the Mexican authorities borrowed heavily from private institutions in the belief that the strong oil prices of 1979-1981 were going to prevail. The Mexican people have paid dearly for that mistake for most of this decade, which perhaps is now being acknowledged by the new willingness of the Governments of countries hosting the commercial bank creditors to look for ways to reduce the debt (see chapter IV). Mexico's difficulty in apportioning the economic losses of negative transfers among its population showed itself in rising inflation and then oscillation of the policy focus between domestic and external imbalances as the international economy itself oscillated.

The case of Bolivia seems to demonstrate that even when internal macro-economic balance is regained, and the net transfer turns positive through increased international assistance and debt relief, significant growth does not necessarily resume. Economic stability may be a prerequisite for development, but it does not necessarily bring on economic growth in itself. The Government of Bolivia is still confronted with the daunting problem of extreme poverty and an informal sector participating in large illicit exports. Under such conditions, Bolivia still faces structural adjustment.

It is clear from the Bolivian case also that if a Government decides to re-orient a largely state-directed economy towards greater reliance on private initiative, the establishment of domestic macro-economic balance and correction of major price distortions are only first steps. For private sector entrepreneurs to undertake to risk private assets requires their confidence that the state sector will be strong enough to carry out its proper function in providing appropriate economic and social services as well as efficient fiscal and monetary management. It takes time to develop such confidence.

The case of the Philippines appears to demonstrate how quickly and severely an economic situation can deteriorate when government officials compromise public responsibility and when policy loses direction. The resulting loss of confidence of foreign creditors and some of the wealthy at home in the Philippines turned a positive net transfer of resources into a substantially negative one, compounding the adjustment difficulties. The Philippine experience also underlines the vulnerability of developing economies that seemed in their gross performance indicators to be quite successful.

Vulnerability seems to be related to economic structures and the institutions for economic management. In the case of Ghana, the formal economy became increasingly unable to provide even the bare necessities of life and people had to turn elsewhere. Economic aspects of government barely functioned. The commitment of the current Government is to rebuild the economy and the polity, reintegrate people into the formal system and recover the promise of development. The international community has come to Ghana's assistance with substantial resource transfers, rising to 7 per cent of Ghana's GDP, underlining a basic appreciation of what negative resource transfers mean for developing countries undertaking adjustment.

But the Ghanaian Government recognizes that economic reconstruction can only be the first stage of adjustment and that continued dependence on a small range of primary products, in this case mainly cocoa, will not generate adequate income growth in the long run and will leave the economy vulnerable to adverse international economic trends. The same may be said for Jamaica, where there has been diversification from plantation-style agriculture into mining, services (tourism), and now manufacturing in export-processing zones. Jamaica has thus developed a diversified set of enclaves, which although a major advance over monocultural production, does not provide the base for sustained development. Indeed, in Jamaica a fifth of the labour force is still unemployed.

All five countries have undergone the austerity of adjustment; but, it can be said that the adjustments have not altered their economic structures in the fundamental way necessary to open the prospect of rapid development in the 1990s and reduce their vulnerability to economic shocks. The objective of adjustment has been to establish macro-economic balance and resurrect what the economy was basically doing before the need for adjustment arose. Governments that have made serious attempts to adjust have been more or less successful in achieving the objective according to the degree to which financial transfers and terms-of-trade changes have been supportive or a hindrance. But a further stage of adjustment remains.

To place developing economies on a path of sustained economic growth and development, in other words, appears to require a more integrated design of development. This is an old message that can be traced to the origins of development economics but one that needs to be refreshed with an explicit recognition of the social and political dimensions of development.

A first principle is that people look to their government to provide certain basic services and to help them provide for their own basic needs. It is a political and social imperative that development policy be designed to try to fully engage the population in economic activities with rising productivities. This approach yields many economic benefits as well. When the local population has rising incomes, it is a potential market for output as well as a supply of labour and its demand will be less volatile than that of the international marketplace. The domestic economy can also become a test market for potential exports, and not only an importer of fads and fashions designed for different environments.

The seductiveness of economic specialization for export has been the promise that domestic consumption levels would be higher because more could be purchased with the export proceeds than otherwise. History has repeatedly proved this argument incomplete, as can be seen also in the five case studies, because an extreme form of specialization often took hold, in which the productive energies of a country became limited to a small range of primary products and imports were relied upon for most other goods. Dealing with the problems of overspecialization is at the core of development economics as it emerged in the post-colonial era, but the limits of overspecialization are still causing several difficulties today. First, foreign exchange earnings are not automatically distributed broadly, so that it is still meaningful in some countries to talk of economic dualism, depressed regions and enclaves. Secondly, the international economy is volatile and the foreign earnings are unassured. In the case of primary commodities with low income and price elasticities, demand shocks have produced major reverberations in the domestic economy. Countries can be easily thrown out of their growth or adjustment path.

From this viewpoint, the essence of adjustment is diversification of production and spreading participation in development widely within the adjusting economy. Both have high investment requirements which underlines the necessity of ensuring that aggregate investment be high. In our volatile world economy, protecting rates of investment in developing countries entails a commitment to provide an international cushion to smooth the impact of international economic shocks and allow deliberate adjustment to them. Over the long run, however, developing countries need to strengthen their capacity for self-reliance so that, for example, domestic savings would supply a growing amount of their investment resources.

For the short-run to medium-run, however, sufficient additional resources for investment cannot be squeezed from the domestic economy and an improved net international transfer of financial resources is imperative. In part this can be met from new flows, but it is no longer controversial that there is a place for debt reduction in improving the net transfers. The international community of creditor countries adopted this position first for the low-income countries, especially in sub-Saharan Africa, at the 1988 Summit Meeting of seven major industrial countries when a commitment was made, *inter alia,* to expand the menu of options available to official creditors undertaking Paris Club debt rescheduling. The menu would now include debt and interest rate reduction. The international response for countries heavily indebted to private banks came in the proposals of several countries, including France, Japan and the United States, all of which came to entertain the concept of interest or debt reduction as part of management of the debt overhang (see chapter IV). As also noted in chapter IV, this leaves one major component of international finance for which neither debt reduction, rescheduling nor refinancing have been introduced, namely, the multilateral lending institutions. As these institutions are the principal creditors of certain developing countries and as arrears to these institutions continue to mount, the problem continues to warrant international attention, as does elaboration and implementation of commitments made with regard to other forms of finance.

But finally, in addition to ensuring the availability of an adequate supply of investment resources, it is essential that those resources be applied most effectively. This involves both export diversification, particularly into products with high income elasticities of demand and efficient import substitution.[71] It also involves an oversight function of economic policy-making that scans the economy for possibilities of increasing inter-industry and intersectoral supply, as well as surveying emerging technologies that may have application to small-scale entrepreneurs as well as large ones.[72] And some activities that may once have been seen as belonging to the domain of large-scale public or private initiatives might also be redesigned to capitalize on the untapped energies of the people.[73]

---

71 It is considered almost blasphemous in some circles to recall the infant-industry argument for protection of a nascent local industry against competition from imports. Although much abused in countries at all stages of development, the argument itself remains sound. The key to effective use is that protection must be applied only for a limited and pre-set period, not be subject to extension, and should be applied selectively to only a few lines of activity, not the whole industry.

72 An example is drip irrigation for smallholder farming, in contrast to its more traditional use in large plantation applications. Significant experimentation in this area has been undertaken by the Rutgers University Research and Development Centre, Bridgetown, New Jersey, United States of America. See also Richard Weisskoff, *Factories and Food Stamps: The Puerto Rico Model of Development* (Baltimore, Maryland, Johns Hopkins University Press, 1985), pp. 152-153.

73 An example has been developed in the urban housing sector, which makes small budgetary claims, has minimal import requirements and is labour-intensive (see United Nations, Department of International Economic and Social Affairs, *Housing and Economic Adjustment* (New York, Taylor and Francis, 1989)).

# SPECIAL ISSUES

# I. SOCIO-ECONOMIC ATTAINMENT OF WOMEN

While the fuller participation of women in the socio-economic process will, as discussed in this section,[1] foster their advancement, development itself will help women, and indeed all members of society, to achieve full enjoyment of social advantage. Development is widely recognized as not being one-dimensional, and therefore not to be summed up by a single statistic, such as GNP per capita. Social and economic development should build a society that is able to provide for the health, shelter and nutrition of its citizens, to extend full educational opportunities to the young and satisfying work opportunities to those of working age, to offer protection to all members of society, especially the young and the aged, grant fair hearing in independent and impartial courts of law and ensure access to cultural facilities.

There is clearly no straight correlation between the prosperity of a country and its socio-economic achievements. However, the process of development, by which a country attains higher standards of living through higher productivity, itself brings about social changes that directly affect women: customs are broken down and new patterns of life develop. In this context, the different cultural traditions of societies can influence the pace and direction of changes in the socio-economic position of women. However it has frequently been noted that the majority of political and religious leaders in a country are men, and their interpretation of what is conformable with religious and cultural traditions could be influenced by gender, or by political considerations.

## The family as a social and economic Unit

It is paradoxical that women's reproductive and caring roles, which are fundamental to society and ensure its future, are so often a main obstacle to their socio-economic advance. The family is traditionally the centre of reproduction and socialization and a basic economic unit of both production and consumption. It is a mechanism for social support based on ties of affection, kinship and mutual need. Yet, as a mechanism for an equitable distribution of benefits, the family will be defective if there is a male bias. The family is a framework for a relationship between men and women who, while living together and therefore having to co-operate, nevertheless have to resolve conflicts of interest in this co-operative setting. Perceptions as to the relative contributions of men and women and the claims generated are of critical importance in determining the outcome of such co-operative conflicts and the division of responsibilities and entitlements within the family. One of the factors forming such perceptions is participation in paid economic activity. In societies where women have outside earnings, as in Africa, gender disparities in the distribution of food and other benefits are less than in those where women have little outside earnings, as in parts of Asia.[2] This is not because women work less: time allocation studies show that women with no outside earnings do astonishingly large amounts of work. Interregional data show that, in general, the higher the rate of participation of women in economic activity, the greater is their life expectancy relative to men; this points to the possibility that female paid productive activity may be positively related to enhanced entitlement for women.[3]

The relationship between gender bias within the family, female survival rates, and female participation in economic activity is complex. Moreover, the issues raised by women's participation in economic activity and the division of responsibilities and benefits within the family have not yet been resolved by economic development anywhere. Studies in Canada, Sweden and the United States of America have shown that married women are far more involved in child care and housework than husbands, even when they both work. In general, the participation of women in economic activity outside the home has not led to a corresponding decrease in their domestic responsibilities or a change in the intra-family division of labour.[4]

In developing countries, the issues are starker: many women combine their domestic responsibilities with domestic agricultural labour and also work in the formal or informal economic sector. For instance, in parts of South Asia, the average working day for a woman is from nine to ten hours, whereas for her husband it is from seven to eight hours.[5] She spends six hours on agricultural labour and on supplying water and fuel for the family, tasks to which the man devotes from three to four hours. From two to three hours of the woman's time is spent on child care, cooking and other household work, to which the man devotes five minutes.

The time women devote to childbearing and the social recognition of this time play a considerable role in determining their economic participation.

---

1 This section is one of a number of contributions of the Department of International Economic and Social Affairs to discussions on the socio-economic attainment of women. The previous *World Economic Survey* gave statistics on, *inter alia*, labour force participation and education (*World Economic Survey, 1988* (United Nations publication, Sales No. E.88.II.C.1)). The *1989 Report on the World Social Situation* contained a chapter on the advancement of women. The Statistical Office issued a *Compendium of Statistics and Indicators on the Situation of Women, 1986* (United Nations publication, Sales No. E/F.88.XVII.6). The Department works in close collaboration with other departments and agencies of the United Nations system in the preparation of its reports and publications.

2 A. Sen, "Gender and cooperative conflicts", WIDER Working Papers, No. 18 (July 1987), p. 30.

3 *Ibid.*, p. 41; and A. Sen, "Africa and India: What do we have to learn from each other?", WIDER Working Paper, No. 19 (August 1987), p. 34.

4 Freda Paltiel, "The family of the future: a model based partnership" in *Interdependence between women and men: report of the Third International Working Seminar, Salzburg, 9-13 July 1987*, p. 34.

5 Population Crisis Committee, "Country rankings on the status of women: poor, powerless and pregnant", Population Briefing Paper No. 20 (Washington, D.C., 1985), p.7.

Table S.I.1. Demographic characteristics of women in developed and developing regions

| | Developed regions | Developing regions | | |
|---|---|---|---|---|
| | | Africa | Asia | Latin America |
| Age at first marriage | 23 | 17 | 17 | 19 |
| Age at first birth | 23 | 19 | 20 | 20 |
| Interval between first and last birth (in years) | 7 | 17 | 16 | 16 |
| Number of live births | 2 | 7 | 7 | 6 |
| Life expectancy at birth of last child | 47 | 29 | 36 | 38 |

*Source:* United Nations Centre for Social Development and Humanitarian Affairs, Division for the Advancement of Women, *Childbearing and Woman's Life Cycle,* Data Highlights, No. 5 (Vienna 1989).

In the developed countries the proportion of a woman's life spent in childbearing has decreased as a result of the decline in the number of births per woman. Currently childbearing accounts for seven years of a woman's life, as shown in table S.I.1. The reduction in the period of childbearing reflects the increase in the age at which the first child is born and also the smaller number of children born, typically two. Moreover, a significant period of time remains after the birth of the last child for women to devote to other tasks. On average, a woman in a developed country can expect to live another 47 years after her last child is born, when she is typically about 30 years old.

The situation is very different in most developing countries. Table S.I.1 shows that on average, women in developing countries marry and have their first child at a young age (19-20 years), have a large family (6-7 children) and spend about 16-17 years in childbearing between the ages of 20-37.

Even when women are able to distribute their tasks among other members of the family, the work is usually assumed by other females. The care of the sick, the disabled or the aged is usually assigned to women.

When such gender stereotyping breaks down, as has happened in the course of development, co-operative conflicts within the family over the division of roles can themselves become more intense. In some societies, the courts have assumed a role in determining family responsibilities, which would have been previously considered a purely internal family matter. The determination of responsibilities by legal precedent rather than by tradition or gender stereotypes might paradoxically strengthen the family by establishing new norms where none had previously been set, and by involving the courts in maintaining the family's integrity.

Many studies have shown a strong positive correlation in non-industrial societies between the sharing of the caring roles within the family and the acceptance of female participation in public authority and decision-making.[6] In societies with significant paternal involvement in family activities, women tend to be active in community decision-making.

The increased participation of women in economic and social activity enhances the need for services and social support structures to help them carry out their reproductive and productive roles. Where the extended family exists, working mothers can leave the care of children and disabled dependents to older-generation relatives. But, this institution is under severe strain even in those regions where it still exists. In other regions, too, maternity is not fully recognized and supported as a social function. Social facilities in general, and child-care arrangements in particular, are generally inadequate, and the available services impose a considerable economic burden on women workers. The centrally planned economy countries have devoted considerable effort to the provision of child-care facilities but they too recognize the need to improve their family and child-support services.

One consequence of economic and demographic change has been an increasing incidence of single-parent households, which are usually headed by females. The ILO estimates that some 35 per cent of the world's households are now headed by women. In some parts of sub-Saharan Africa, 43 per cent of households are headed by women.[7] The Economic Commission for Latin America and the Caribbean estimates that between 20 and 25 per cent of all rural households in that region are headed by women.[8] In Asia, the figures for households headed by women range from 16 to 20 per cent. In developed market economies, the figures are also high: in Belgium, France, Luxembourg, New Zealand and Switzerland, they vary between 20 and 25 per cent. In Austria and in the United States the figure is over 30 per cent, in Norway nearly 40 per cent, and in Sweden over 50 per cent.

6 Scott Coltrane, "Father-child relationships and the status of women: a cross-cultural study", *American Journal of Sociology,* vol. 93 (March 1988), pp. 1060-1095.

7 *The Role of the Family in the Development Process* (The Family, No. 2) (United Nations publication, Sales No. E.86.IV.7), p.10.

8 Economic Commission for Latin America and the Caribbean, Fourth Regional Conference on the Integration of Women into the Economic and Social Development of Latin America and the Caribbean, Guatemala City, 26 to 30 September 1988, *Latin American and Caribbean women: between change and crisis* (LC/L.464 (CRM. 4/2)) p.24.

In the developing countries, women become heads of households due to male migration and rising rates of desertion. In the developed countries, women become heads of households due to divorce and the increased social acceptance of single-parent families. But single-parent families are everywhere likely to be economically disadvantaged, often constituting the poorest segment of the population.

## Trends in female participation in the labour force

The participation of women in different age groups in the labour force is a useful indication of the extent to which social and political changes have affected the socio-economic role of women. The graphs in figure S.I.1 show the participation rates for women and men in nine different groupings of the world. The staples show the rates for women in the years 1970, 1980 and 1985. For the sake of comparison, the activity rates for men are given for the years 1970 and 1985.

For men, activity rates between the ages of 25 and 55 were invariably high and close to 100 per cent (the figures include those who are currently unemployed). At the two ends of the graphs, showing rates for the young and the old, the rates for 1985 were lower than for 1970. This reflects on the one hand increasing attendance at educational institutes, and on the other, earlier retirement from economic activity. The figures for the European developed market economies, for instance, show almost no economic activity among children under 14, a drop from 60 per cent to less than 50 per cent in the rate of participation of those aged 15 to 19, and, among the older workers, a fall from over 60 to 50 per cent in economic activity amongst those aged 60 to 64.

Differences in concepts and definitions are very great and considerable caution should be exercised in making cross-regional comparisons, but, except for China, Eastern Europe and the USSR, activity rates for women never approached 80 per cent for any age group. Among the developing countries activity rates were highest in China and then in sub-Saharan Africa.

Movements over time within regions were of great interest. In sub-Saharan Africa and Asia, excluding China, activity rates fell for all age groups, not only between 1980 and 1985 but also between 1970 and 1980. In that decade activity rates in Latin America and the Caribbean rose sharply, although from a much lower base. But the increase between 1980 and 1985 in that region was marginal.

The decline in activity rates in Africa and Asia, excluding China, not just during the early 1980s, when economic crises affected many countries, but also during the 1970s, would appear to reflect the deep-rooted problems facing women in these regions. Women's activity rates are determined not simply by the growth in employment opportunities generated by the economy as compared to the rate of growth of the female population in the relevant age groups, but also by the division of such opportunities between men and women. In Africa, where women make up more of the recorded economically active population than in Latin America, their share of "new jobs" would have to be greater than in that region for their participation rate to rise.[9] In the matter of female activity rates, the developing countries of Asia should be viewed as a composite of subregions with very different cultural traditions. The overall decline in activity rates in Asia reflects stagnation in eastern South Asia, decline in middle and western South Asia and increases in East Asia (excluding Japan and China).

Activity rates in the developed market economies rose sharply between 1970 and 1980. Yet, as in Latin America, the improvement between 1980 and 1985 was marginal. By 1985, activity rates in North America exceeded 60 per cent for women between 20 and 50 years old. In Europe, activity rates were about ten percentage points lower. The curves in the developed market economies dip between the ages 20 and 24, and about 35 and 39, reflecting the fact that women cease economic activity with the onset of child-rearing, but later resume. This effect was particularly noticeable in Japan. With higher rates of economic activity and with the spacing between the first and last child shrinking, the dip is less pronounced, as in North America between 1970 and 1985.

## Women's employment in major economic sectors

The role of women in labour markets will be studied under the three broad divisions of agriculture, industry and services. In table S.I.2, the percentage of the economically active female population accounted for by these three sectors, is given for 1970 and 1980. Figures in brackets are the corresponding ratios for the total economically active population.

In the developing countries, and indeed in the world as a whole, the majority of women are engaged in agriculture. The only developing regions where this is not the case are Latin America and the Caribbean. In the developed market and centrally planned economies, agriculture is the smallest of the three sectors. Invariably, the services sector is larger than the industrial sector, and in the developed market econ-

9 It was calculated that from 1950 to 1975, women's share of the total increase in employment opportunities was 38 per cent in Africa and 32 per cent in Latin America and the Caribbean. However, women in 1950 made up 42 per cent of the recorded total economically active population of Africa as against 18 per cent in Latin America and the Caribbean, so in Africa the female share of the recorded economically active population fell whereas in Latin America and the Caribbean it rose. See Shirley Nuss *Women in the World of Work: Statistical Analysis and Projections to the Year 2000,* Women, Work and Development Series, No. 18 (Geneva, International Labour Office, forthcoming in 1989).

Figure S.I.1 Female-male activity rates

(Percentages)

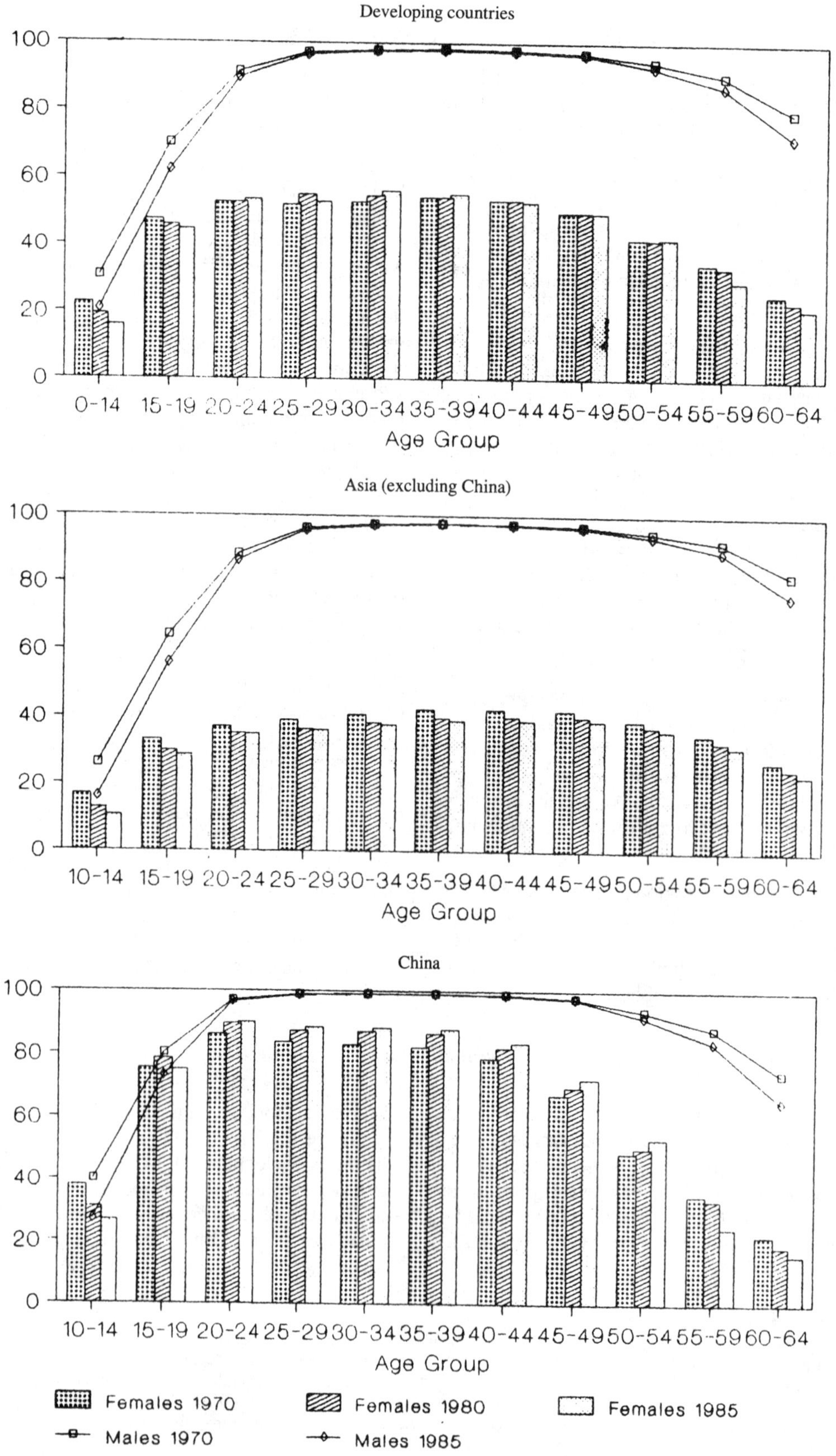

Sub-Saharan Africa

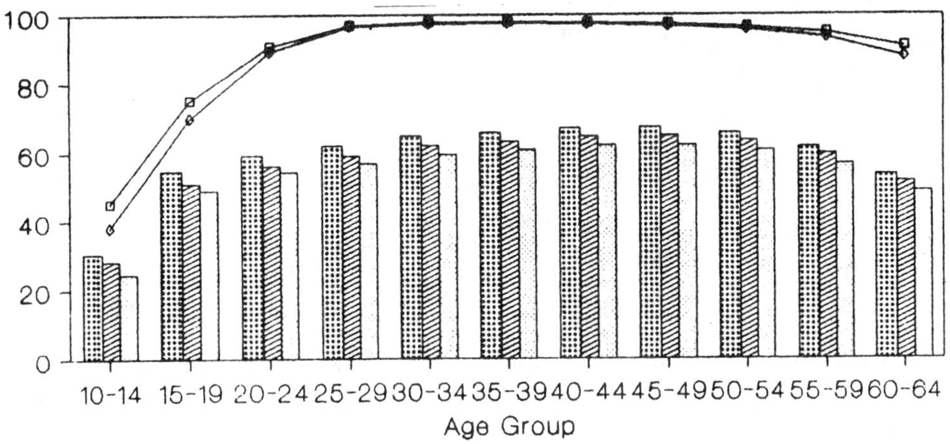


Latin America and Caribbean

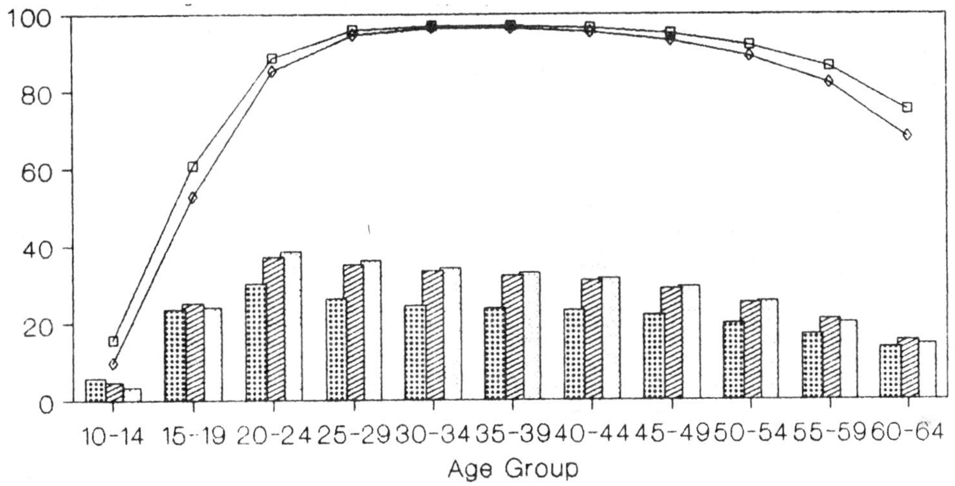


Eastern Europe and USSR

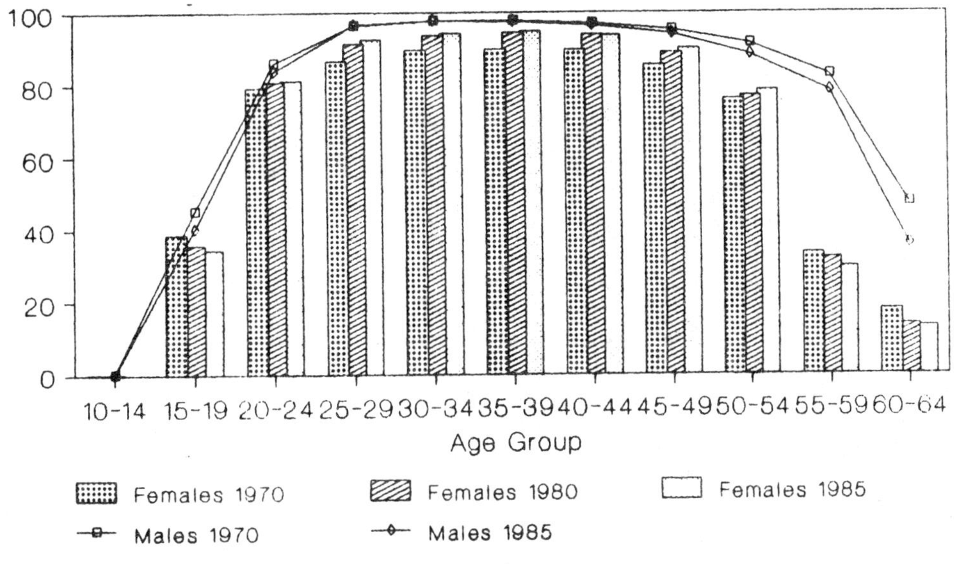

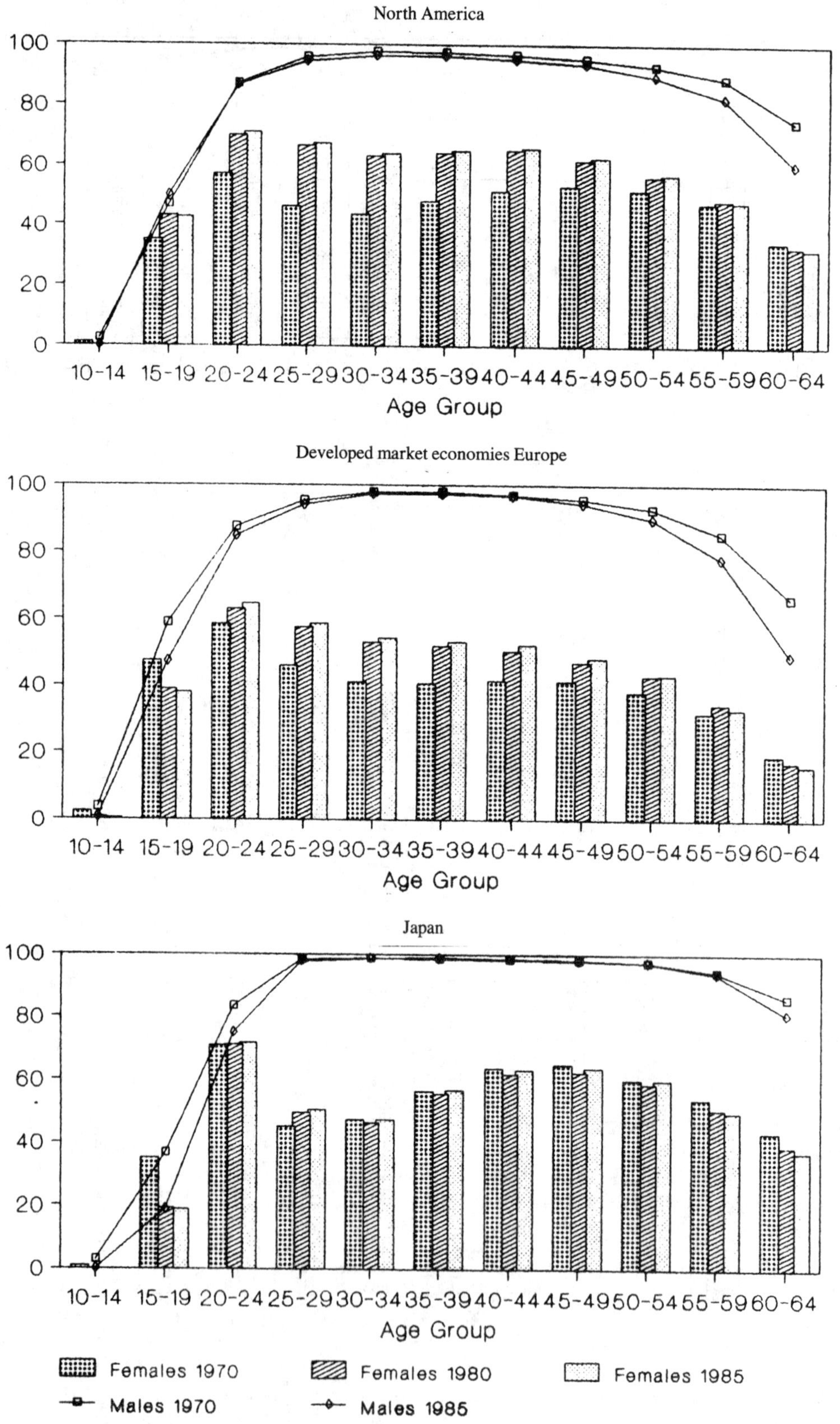


*Source:* International Labour Office, *Economically Active Population, 1950-2025* (Geneva, 1986).

Table S.I.2. Economically active female population in agriculture, industry and services, 1970 and 1980

(Percentages; figures for total male and female employment are given in parentheses)

| Regions | 1970 AGR | 1970 IND | 1970 SER | 1980 AGR | 1980 IND | 1980 SER |
|---|---|---|---|---|---|---|
| **World** | 58.1<br>(55.1) | 15.2<br>(19.7) | 26.7<br>(25.2) | 53.2<br>(50.9) | 16.5<br>(20.9) | 30.2<br>(28.2) |
| **Developing Countries and areas** | 77.0<br>(71.0) | 8.9<br>(12.1) | 14.1<br>(16.9) | 71.3<br>(65.7) | 11.7<br>(14.8) | 17.0<br>(19.5) |
| Sub-Saharan Africa | 87.0<br>(80.8) | 3.1<br>(7.1) | 9.9<br>(12.1) | 83.5<br>(76.2) | 3.9<br>(8.6) | 12.6<br>(15.2) |
| North Africa | 54.0<br>(56.4) | 14.1<br>15.8) | 31.9<br>(27.8) | 44.7<br>(47.5) | 20.5<br>(20.7) | 34.8<br>(31.8) |
| Latin America | 15.7<br>(40.3) | 20.7<br>(23.6) | 63.6<br>(36.1) | 13.3<br>(31.5) | 20.5<br>(26.3) | 66.2<br>(42.2) |
| Caribbean | 33.7<br>(43.3) | 13.6<br>(19.8) | 52.8<br>(36.9) | 25.5<br>(35.4) | 15.2<br>(21.0) | 60.3<br>(43.6) |
| Asia (excluding China) | 74.5<br>(68.4) | 11.1<br>(12.7) | 14.4<br>(18.9) | 68.2<br>(62.9) | 12.4<br>(14.5) | 19.4<br>(22.6) |
| Hong Kong, Malaysia Rep. of Korea, Singapore | 55.2<br>(44.0) | 21.2<br>(22.4) | 23.6<br>(33.6) | 40.3<br>(32.3) | 26.2<br>(28.1) | 33.5<br>(39.6) |
| China | 83.0<br>(78.4) | 7.5<br>(10.1) | 9.5<br>(11.5) | 78.5<br>(74.3) | 12.0<br>(14.0) | 9.5<br>(11.7) |
| **Developed market economies** | 12.8<br>(12.6) | 25.6<br>(37.2) | 61.6<br>(50.2) | 7.7<br>(8.3) | 22.6<br>(34.6) | 69.7<br>(57.1) |
| North America | 2.2<br>(4.6) | 20.6<br>(32.3) | 77.3<br>(63.1) | 1.8<br>(3.6) | 18.9<br>(30.9) | 79.3<br>(65.5) |
| Japan | 26.5<br>(19.7) | 26.2<br>(34.5) | 47.3<br>(45.8) | 14.1<br>(11.2) | 26.3<br>(34.2) | 59.6<br>(54.6) |
| Australia and New Zealand | 4.7<br>(8.7) | 22.7<br>(36.4) | 72.6<br>(54.9) | 5.4<br>(7.6) | 18.4<br>(32.2) | 76.2<br>(60.2) |
| Europe | 14.7<br>(15.4) | 29.1<br>(41.4) | 56.2<br>(43.2) | 11.8<br>(10.8) | 27.4<br>(37.7) | 72.7<br>(51.5) |
| **Centrally planned economies** | | | | | | |
| Eastern Europe | 37.8<br>(32.0) | 29.0<br>(39.4) | 33.2<br>(28.6) | 24.4<br>(22.0) | 34.5<br>(44.1) | 41.1<br>(33.9) |
| USSR | 26.4<br>(25.7) | 31.2<br>(37.6) | 42.4<br>(36.7) | 21.0<br>(20.0) | 32.7<br>(39.0) | 46.3<br>(41.0) |

*Source:* International Labour Office, *Economically active population, 1950-2025* (Geneva, 1986).

omies and Latin America and the Caribbean, it accounts for the overwhelming majority of employed women.

Comparing 1970 with 1980 and the richer with the poorer groups of countries, it can be seen that over time, and with development, the agriculture sector decreases in importance as an employer. Moreover, not only does the services sector increase in importance but also the industrial sector shrinks in importance, as shown in North America and the European developed market economies.

## The agricultural sector

Concepts and methods for defining and measuring female labour participation have received considerable attention within the United Nations system,[10] and Governments are actively involved in data collection and in efforts to reach agreement on concepts and definitions.

Data concepts and methods based on the contemporary experience of developed market economies have been found inadequate when applied to developing countries, where workers are more likely to be self-employed or unpaid family workers rather than wage earners, to work seasonally

10 See, in particular, *Improving Concepts and Methods for Statistics and Indicators on the Situation of Women* (United Nations publication, Sales No. E.84.XVII.3); and the reports of the Thirteenth and Fourteenth International Conferences of Labour Statisticians, held in 1982 and 1987. (*Report of the Fourteenth Conference* (International Labour Organisation document ICLS/14.D.14)).

rather than year-round, to be underemployed rather than formally unemployed, and to engage in multiple economic activities. In developing countries the boundary between production for the household's own consumption and production for sale or exchange is less clearly drawn, especially in rural areas and among women.[11] Major censuses or surveys frequently undercounted a substantial proportion of women's agricultural work. Population census procedures in some cases defined a person's economic activity by his or her stated primary activity. Thus, if women were classified as housewives, no information was recorded on their productive and income-earning occupations, even though these were important. The Agricultural Census in principle covered all agricultural holdings, but in practice often excluded small agricultural holdings in which female labour can be substantial. Moreover, labour force participation data often implicitly used an "economic activity" concept that measured the production of goods and services for the market. Household work was not considered an economic activity unless it was remunerated. As a result, many female agricultural tasks that are generally unpaid and do not bring a marketable output, such as threshing and pounding grain, preserving food, fetching water for livestock and domestic use, collecting wood fuel, dung and wild foods, milking and processing dairy products, were not counted, although these activities represent a vital contribution to increasing family income and welfare.

Women's work sometimes becomes "invisible" because of cultural attitudes about appropriate roles for women. In cultures where a man's social status is higher if his wife is not employed, men, who are often the respondents to censuses or surveys, frequently fail to report a wife's economic activity. It has been found that in developing countries women were more likely to report accurately their own income-earning activities than were male respondents.[12]

For all these reasons, the importance of women as a source of labour in agriculture in all developing regions is much underestimated, and progress must still be made before internationally accepted and comparable figures can be presented. With all those caveats, it may be said that a large proportion (71 per cent in 1980) of the economically active women in developing countries were engaged in agriculture and only 12 and 17 per cent respectively were in industry and services (table S.I.2). The majority of female workers are employed in agriculture in sub-Saharan Africa, North Africa and Asia, and a significant percentage in Latin America and the Caribbean and the centrally planned economies of Eastern Europe and the USSR.

In agriculture, and also in the non-agricultural sectors, women working as own-account or unpaid family workers have more limited access to capital, equipment and transportation to markets, which lowers the returns to their labour. Census data show approximately 40 per cent of the female agricultural labour force in sub-Saharan Africa as self-employed. The figure for Central and South America and the Caribbean is 30 per cent; for Asia, 30 per cent; and for North Africa and the Middle East, 15 per cent.[13]

Women rarely have the title to the agricultural holdings in which they work.[14] This restricts their access to credit. However, where loans have been made to women, their repayment rates have usually been better than men's.[15] Women's co-operatives and savings groups have proved to be an effective means for them to qualify for credit, provided that they obtain the management skills and autonomy required to maintain control of such organizations. Besides credit restrictions, women's access to production inputs is further constrained by institutional and social biases against their attending extension and training courses, operating mechanized farm equipment and handling input supply, marketing and personnel matters.

Agrarian reform laws have not removed the constraints women face. Large inequalities persist, little progress has been made in providing access to land, and landlessness has increased. Since women tend not to be landowners, they are often excluded from agricultural organizations such as co-operatives.

Women's role in food production is growing in most parts of Africa. As farms shrink through inheritance, and men turn to outside work or become part-time farmers, women are increasingly becoming full-time farmers. Yet, as women's agricultural workload has tended to increase, their traditional work of child care, wood-gathering, water-fetching, and staple food pounding has remained the same or even increased as deforestation progresses.

Women's goals and priorities have been stimulated by the impetus and new directions given in the 1985 Nairobi World Conference to Review and Appraise the Achievements of the United Nations Decade for Women. It is recognized that these goals can only be realized if women become fully integrated in economic and social development as a result of efforts at all levels—national, regional, international—and involving non-governmental bodies and both the public and private sectors. At the same time, the attention that developing countries are paying to macro-economic stabilization, structural adjustment, ensuring food supplies to the cities, and saving foreign exchange for productive investment, has led to an increasing recognition of women's economic role in agriculture and particularly of their major role as food producers, processors and traders.

---

11 Ruth Dixon-Mueller and Richard Anker, *Assessing Women's Economic Contribution to Development,* Women, Work and Development Series, No. 6 (Geneva, International Labour Office, 1988), p. 29.

12 Richard Anker, M.E. Khan and R.B. Gupta, *Women's Participation in the Labour Force: a Method Test in India for Improving Its Measurement,* Women, Work and Development Series, No. 16 (Geneva, International Labour Office, 1988), p. 9.

13 Anker, Khan and Gupta, *op. cit.*, p. 59.

14 See *World Economic Survey 1988* (United Nations publication, Sales No. E.88.II.C.1), table A.1.5, p. 154.

15 A. S. Carboni, *Women in Development: AID's Experience 1973-1985,* vol. 1, *Synthesis Paper,* AID Program Evaluation Report, No. 18 (Washington, D.C., United States Agency for International Development, 1987). See also S. Joekes, *Women in the World Economy,* prepared for the International Research and Training Institute for the Advancement of Women (New York, Oxford University Press, 1987), p. 146.

## The service sector

The service sector comprises an extremely wide range of occupations. Some require little training, such as domestic help or street vending, others very high skill levels and higher education as in computer programming. The sector's relative importance tends to increase with economic development and urbanization.

There is a sharp difference between the activity rates recorded for women in predominantly agrarian societies and in middle-income countries where the service sector is larger. Rates as high as 80 to 90 per cent are given for various age groups in different African countries, especially those among the poorest in terms of per capita income, while, in Latin America, the maximum activity rate for any particular age group is usually in the range of 35 to 40 per cent.

Part of the reason for this is that about 80 per cent of the population in the poorer countries is rural whereas about the same percentage is urban in the middle-income developing countries. This rural to urban shift is accompanied by a difference in classification: the number of women classified as "employers and own-account workers" or "unpaid family workers" decreases, while the number of those classified as "employees" increases.[16]

The change from being an unpaid family worker to being an employee usually constitutes an advance for women who thereby obtain a disposable income which allows them to make their own choices in the market place.

Table S.I.3 shows the percentage of total identified female employment accounted for by the service sector, and its division into the four categories, "wholesale/retail trade, restaurants and hotels", "transport, storage and communications", "financing, insurance, real estate and business services" and "community, social and personal services".

On the whole, the higher the per capita income of a country, the larger the share of services in total female employment. Over 80 per cent of women were employed in services in North America, as compared with less than 50 per cent in most of the developing countries listed. The share was higher in some of the higher income developing countries.

In most countries, the "transport, storage and communications" sector accounted for a small percentage of female employment. This was also the case for "financing, insurance, real estate and business services". However, the size of this latter sector is related to the level of economic attainment and is considerably higher in the developed market economies than in the developing countries.

The relative size of the sector "wholesale/retail trade, restaurants and hotels" varied, being less than 20 per cent in India and Pakistan and over 80 per cent in Ghana where the women in this sector are predominantly own account workers, selling their own agricultural produce. It has been calculated that in West Africa, the Caribbean and the southern part of Asia, women sell between 70 and 80 per cent of the domestic farm and marine produce consumed.[17] In the higher income Asian countries and Latin America, the majority of women in this sector are employees.

The sector "community, social and personal services" was, in most countries, the largest of the four, and in some of the low-income Asian countries accounted for over three quarters of employment within the service sector. The overall pattern outlined above reflects the difference between "producer services" and "final consumption services". The former are intermediary inputs to production, or are associated with market access. Examples are management consultancy, legal services, public relations, quality control, accountancy and distribution.[18] Such producer services are included in "financing, insurance, real estate and business services", and on the whole require higher training and educational qualifications than final consumption services. As noted earlier, demand for such services increases with the degree of development. However, the contrast should not be exaggerated, for in the developed market economies, particularly, there has also been a trend towards greater "professionalization" of final consumption services. Restaurants, cleaning and repairs, which can be provided by family concerns, are increasingly provided by chains, applying new management and organizational techniques.

A comparison of different countries in Latin America and the Caribbean indicates how modernization in the service sector affects women, and also how economic crisis has affected employment in the sector.[19] The more modernized the country, the more personal services tended to shrink, although this trend was mitigated by the increase in government social services. In the more modernized countries, salaried domestic work shifted from "resident" to "non-resident" participation, although the former group tended to

16 For instance, in Burundi in 1979, 92.9 per cent of the economically active population was employed in "agriculture, hunting, forestry and fishing"; a total of 1,280,987 women were classified as economically active as compared to 1,137,042 men. Of these, 237,608 were classified as "employers and own-account workers", of whom 233,905 were workers in agriculture, hunting, forestry and fishing. Another 1,027,732 were classified as "unpaid family workers" of whom 1,016,157 worked in agriculture. Only 12,563 women were classified as employees, and of these 10,043 worked in "community, social and personal services".

In Costa Rica, in 1987, agriculture accounted for 27.5 per cent of the economically active population, and 252,195 men and only 16,458 women worked in that sector, with 12,495 of the latter being classified as employees. In the country as a whole, 767,898 men and 269,949 women were classified as economically active, with 215,267 women being classified as employees, of whom about half, 112,973 worked in "community, social and personal services". (Figures from *Yearbook of Labour Statistics 1988* (Geneva, International Labour Office, 1988.)

17 *World Survey on the Role of Women in Development* (United Nations publication, Sales No. E.86.IV.3), p. 162.

18 See "The service sector" in *World Survey on the Role of Women in Development: First Regular Update* (United Nations publication, 1989, forthcoming).

19 See Economic Commission for Latin America and the Caribbean, Fourth Regional Conference on the Integration of Women into the Economic and Social Development of Latin America and the Caribbean, Guatemala City, 26 to 30 September 1988, *Women, work and crisis* (LC/L.458 (CRM. 4/6)).

Table S.I.3. Distribution of female employment in the service sector by major divisions and for selected countries, 1980s

(Percentage)

| | Service sector as percentage of total female employment | Wholesale/ retail trade, restaurants and hotels | Transport, storage and communi-cations | Financing, insurance, real estate and business services | Community, social aid, personal services |
|---|---|---|---|---|---|
| Botswana | 35.6 | 18.8 | 1.0 | 2.7 | 77.7 |
| Ghana | 29.0 | 82.3 | 0.6 | 0.9 | 16.2 |
| Cameroon | 5.1 | 49.6 | 1.3 | 0.7 | 48.4 |
| Costa Rica | 70.3 | 29.6 | 1.9 | 4.1 | 64.3 |
| Peru | 62.0 | 32.7 | 2.1 | 4.4 | 60.8 |
| Colombia | 42.8 | 37.0 | 2.2 | 8.7 | 52.2 |
| Singapore | 64.4 | 36.7 | 7.9 | 17.7 | 37.7 |
| Philippines | 54.2 | 45.6 | 1.2 | 3.5 | 49.8 |
| Rep. of Korea | 46.3 | 61.5 | 2.0 | 7.6 | 29.0 |
| Pakistan | 39.8 | 16.1 | 4.5 | 1.4 | 78.0 |
| India | 9.3 | 19.3 | 3.9 | 2.6 | 74.2 |
| United States | 82.5 | 27.3 | 4.4 | 16.4 | 51.9 |
| Canada | 82.6 | 31.6 | 4.6 | 15.5 | 48.2 |
| Germany, Fed. Rep. of | 67.9 | 31.5 | 4.8 | 11.8 | 51.9 |

*Source:* International Labour Office, *Yearbook of Labour Statistics 1988* (Geneva).

remain the larger. During periods of economic crisis, "non-resident" domestic service tended to increase as it provided a source of income to those who, although qualified for other work, could not find suitable employment.

In the less modernized countries, the proportion of women in domestic service increased, particularly as a result of the employment of young migrant women.

In all countries, as education levels rose, the proportion of women in the professional and technical category increased. Teaching particularly attracted women, and also the number of women engaged as office employees rose with modernization and the expansion of the government bureaucracy. In general, the higher the education level, the higher the activity rate. Among women with more than thirteen years of education, the activity rates of ever-married women were greater than those of single women. The higher income levels resulting from higher education allowed married women to employ other women to carry out domestic work.

The increase in the service sector, and the fact that this sector absorbs the majority of the economically active females in the more developed countries suggests that the social changes involved in modernization will favour the socio-economic advancment of women.

The nature of the service sector changes with economic development from being an employer of "last resort", absorbing in very low skill occupations in the informal sector women moving from rural to urban areas, to being one that can provide employment in the most technologically advanced sectors of the economy. Furthermore, much work in the service industries is compatible with part-time employment, and in the case of advanced countries and computer-based professions, with home-based employment. Tasks requiring high technology equipment, such as text and data processing, are being transferred by banks, airlines and publishing houses from developed to developing countries where pay scales are lower since the information can readily be fed back via satellite equipment.

Women are, however, still under-represented in higher level management positions in the service industry even in the most developed countries.

## Women in the manufacturing industry

The pattern of employment of women in the industrial sector is a reflection of that observed in connection with agriculture and services. Growth in manufacturing output is accompanied by a growth in producer services, and more of the relative decline in the female agricultural labour force goes into services than into manufacturing. In the case of the four fast-growing exporters of manufactures shown separately in table S.I.2 (Hong Kong, Malaysia, Republic of Korea and Singapore) there was a decline of 15 percentage points between 1970 and 1980 in the share of female employment in agriculture: 5 per cent went to manufacturing and 10 per cent to services.

The kinds of manufacturing industry that employ women are much the same in all countries. As table S.I.4 shows, textiles, clothing and fabricated metal products including electronic equipment, account for over half of the paid female employment in manufacturing in almost all countries. However, in the poorer and largely rural developing coun-

Table S.I.4. Distribution of female paid employment in manufacturing by major industry divisions, selected countries and areas, 1980s (latest data available)

| ISIC Division | Botswana | Kenya | Mauritius | Hong Kong | India | Rep. of Korea |
|---|---|---|---|---|---|---|
| (31) | 20.2 | 42.3 | 2.5 | 1.3 | 44.0 | 7.2 |
| (32) | 41.5 | 22.4 | 90.8 | 54.5 | 25.1 | 41.8 |
| (33) | 2.3 | 4.7 | 0.3 | 1.4 | 0.9 | 1.4 |
| (34) | 4.3 | 8.2 | 1.1 | 2.5 | 1.7 | 2.4 |
| (35) | 2.9 | 12.4 | 0.9 | 9.3 | 10.2 | 13.2 |
| (36) | – | 0.6 | 0.1 | 0.2 | 4.1 | 2.3 |
| (37) | – | 0.6 | 0.0 | 0.1 | 2.9 | 0.8 |
| (38) | 16.2 | 5.9 | 1.4 | 29.1 | 9.9 | 25.4 |
| (39) | 12.3 | 0.4 | 2.8 | 2.6 | 1.0 | 5.7 |

| ISIC Division | Singapore | Sri Lanka | Colombia | Cuba | United States | United Kingdom |
|---|---|---|---|---|---|---|
| (31) | 3.5 | 13.4 | 19.6 | 38.9 | 8.5 | 15.0 |
| (32) | 18.7 | 68.8 | 44.3 | 24.6 | 20.9 | 22.7 |
| (33) | 3.2 | 0.4 | 1.4 | 2.4 | 4.5 | 2.6 |
| (34) | 5.5 | 1.1 | 5.8 | 2.8 | 12.9 | 11.1 |
| (35) | 5.5 | 10.3 | 13.6 | 5.7 | 9.6 | 10.9 |
| (36) | 0.7 | 4.7 | 2.9 | 1.2 | 1.8 | 3.4 |
| (37) | 0.3 | 0.0 | 0.8 | 2.0 | 1.6 | 2.0 |
| (38) | 60.0 | 1.5 | 9.8 | 13.2 | 37.3 | 30.0 |
| (39) | 2.6 | 0.8 | 1.8 | 9.2 | 2.7 | 2.4 |

*Note:* ISIC category:
(31) Food, beverages and tobacco
(32) Textile, weaving apparel and leather industries
(33) Wood and wood products
(34) Paper and paper products, printing and publishing
(35) Chemicals and chemical products
(36) Non-metallic mineral products
(37) Base metal industries
(38) Fabricated metal products
(39) Other manufacturing industries

*Source:* International Labour Office, *Yearbook of Labour Statistics, 1988* (Geneva).

tries, such as India and Kenya, food, beverages and tobacco employed a larger percentage of those women employed in manufactures. Also, in almost all the developing countries shown, textiles and clothing was a larger employer than fabricated metal products whereas the reverse was the case in the two developed market economy countries shown, the United States and the United Kingdom.

Singapore, which is a major publishing centre, also had a larger percentage of women employed in paper and paper products, printing and publishing than most of the other developing countries. In developed market economies, such as the United Kingdom and the United States, this sector was similarly large.

As the textile and clothing industry is a very important employer of informal labour, with women preparing garments in their homes, there are serious problems with underreporting. For instance, the garment industry in New Delhi accounts for 60 per cent of the country's annual garment export, and recent official figures reported that it employed 13,563 workers in 353 units of production.[20] However, the Garment Exporters Association gave a figure of 100,000, of whom 25 per cent were women, and even those figures were thought to be too low, as they did not take into account the large number of house-based workers active in the industry.

Within the manufacturing industry, many occupations are performed almost solely by women. Studies have found that

20 R. Rao and S. Husain, "Invisible hands: Women in home-based production in the garment industry in Delhi" in A. M. Sengh and A. K. Viitanen, eds., *Invisible Hands: Women in Home-based Production* (New Delhi, 1987) quoted in *World Survey on the Role of Women in Development: First Regular Update* (forthcoming), chap. 7. The ILO *Yearbook of Labour Statistics 1988* gave a figure for India in 1985 of 16,000 female paid employees working in "manufacture of wearing apparel, except footwear".

in the typical textile factory in Asia, whereas the managers, foremen and technicians are invariably men, the machine operators are invariably women. This division of labour was itself the result of a widespread perception that "women have greater patience and nimbler fingers, can be paid lower wages and are more docile and controllable".[21] Yet, from the case studies reported by ESCAP of the conditions of women workers in a number of textile and garment facilities in Asian countries, this stereotype was seen to be over-simplified. In particular, the docility assumption was found to be incorrect as women workers were found to be more unionized and more willing to organize strikes and take other forms of industrial action in defence of their rights than men. However, the studies indicated that this assertiveness was in turn due to women within the enterprises on the whole being assigned more onerous tasks, being subjected to harsher working environment and having a higher rate of industrial accidents.

The nature of the textiles and clothing and electronics industries are themselves changing in ways that require a much higher skill content on the part of the labour force. With advances in technology, and in particular computer-aided design and computer manufacturing, capital costs have risen considerably in relation to labour costs.[22] In these circumstances, the availability of managerial and technical skills and good research facilities will gain increasingly in importance in decisions by international companies on where to locate their manufacturing facilities and will be major determinants of a country's competitiveness on international markets. The developed market economies have already experienced a rapid shift away from semi- or unskilled labour towards technicians, managers and administrative and clerical staff,[23] and, similarly, in the developing countries the need is to provide greater training for women so that they can assume managerial and highly skilled positions, and continue to update their skills.

## Technology and the future

Technological advances that have had profound impact on women in developed and developing countries have been made in the areas of health and human reproductiom. Modern birth control techniques have been significant in many parts of the developing world and improved health facilities have meant lower infant mortality, fewer pregnancies and higher life expectancy. Such advances relate to rights of parenthood, health, safety and education of women and also raise profound cultural and religious questions.

In agriculture, in many developing countries, men use most of the machines available while for women, the universal tool, apart from baskets and winnowing fans, is the sickle, with which they cut grass, weed and reap grain.[24] Much research has been directed towards improving the efficiency of machines, such as tractors, and inputs, such as seed varieties, fertilizers and herbicides. These are used by men rather than women since the gender-based division of farm management responsibilities gives men the power to decide the use of such machines and inputs.

Technological advances in agriculture, which have raised production and reduced costs, have been accompanied by some social costs in the form of labour displacement. In some instances the consequences affect women with particular harshness, as in the case of women engaged in rice husking in South Asia who were largely from poor households and were displaced by mechanized milling.[25]

In the mouern manufacturing sector, earlier industrial restructuring, largely based on the redeployment of labour-intensive manufactures of low skill content to developing countries is increasingly being replaced by a restructuring that involves (a) a partial relocation "back North" of automated, previously labour-intensive processes; and (b) a new international redeployment of more skill-intensive production processes. The building up of competitive industrial structures and capacities in the developing countries will, therefore, require that the training of technical labour will be done "rapidly enough, and on a large scale enough to foster a second stage of 'off-shore' productive decentralization from the North's industrial base".[26]

Similarly, in the service industries, many routine tasks and even occupations are being eliminated by technology changes, while at the same time new opportunities for women are opening up in the office and commercial sectors, the hotel and tourist industries, data-processing and communications. The international aspects of these changes, as outlined earlier, hold forth the potential for new sources of income for developing countries which have labour forces with the required skills in the new high-technology occupations.

For these reasons, education to provide and update women's skills and abilities is essential to create a flexible labour force, capable of responding to the continuous changes that

21 Economic and Social Commission for Asia and the Pacific, "Young women workers in manufacturing: a case study of rapidly industrializing economies of the ESCAP region" (ST/ESCAP/553, Bangkok, 1987), p. 73.

22 It has been reported that not more than 10 per cent of the ex-factory costs of consumer electronic goods are now labour costs. *World Survey on the Role of Women in Development: First Regular Update* (forthcoming), chap. 7.

23 In the United Kingdom's manufacturing industry, it has been calculated that semi-skilled or unskilled labour will fall from 40 per cent of the total labour force in 1980 to 10 per cent in 1995, and craftsmen from 33 to 15 per cent. Over the same period, managers would increase from 10 to 20 per cent, and technicians, including engineers, from 6 to 40 per cent. (Commission of the European Communities, in connection with the journal *Futures*, "Eurofutures: the challenges of innovation"; *The FAST Report* (London, Butterworth, 1984), p. 100. (Reproduced in *World Survey on the Role of Women in Development: First Regular Update*, chap. 7.)

24 I. Ahmed, "Technology, production linkages and women's employment in South Asia", *International Labour Review*, vol. 126, No. 1 (January-February 1987), (Geneva, International Labour Office), p.23.

25 K. Salahuddin, *Women and technology: Impact of Technology Change in Agriculture on Rural Women of Bangladesh* (1986).

26 M. Castells, "High technology, world development and structural transformation: the trend and the debate", *Alternatives*, vol. 11 (1986), p. 305.

result from economic restructuring propelled by rapid technological change. Education can also ensure that women make a significant contribution to the advancement of scientific knowledge, through research and its application. Statistics reveal, however, that women are grossly under-represented in the sciences, and especially in engineering.[27] Raising women's capabilities to have a more powerful presence in science and technology will do much in terms of advancing equality and assisting the overall development process.

27 International Research and Training Institute for the Advancement of Women, "Women and technology in developing countries: technological change and women's capabilities and bargaining positions" (1985), table 3, p. 27.

# II. EARLY IDENTIFICATION, ANALYSIS AND MONITORING OF WORLD ECONOMIC DEVELOPMENTS

Early identification of macro-economic disturbances is an important element in averting potential crises at both the national and international levels. This annex, prepared at the request of the Economic and Social Council, discusses the mechanisms available within the United Nations system for early identification activities.

## Conceptual issues

### Meaning of "early identification"

The concept of "early identification" would appear to be intuitive and simple. The term connotes the collection of timely and correct information and its proper interpretation, the object of which is to enable Governments or other relevant actors to anticipate events, especially adverse ones, and, therefore, to be in a better position to deal with their consequences, or even to prevent them.

The term "early identification" is a recent variation of the older concept of "early warning". This latter term has multiple meanings. Since the Second World War, it has been related in military parlance to securing information regarding the launching of a nuclear attack in time to make an effective response. It has also been used in connection with the control of damaging drugs, undesirable human behaviour and, in the United Nations World Food Conference of 1974, in relation to food security.[1] It has recently been used in discussions of refugees.[2]

The term "early warning" is also associated with the concept of preventive diplomacy[3] and is used in other fields as well, such as natural disaster prevention. The concept of early warning was frequently used in the late 1960s and early 1970s, particularly in the area of environmental and economic forecasting. Under the auspicies of the Club of Rome, a number of reports were prepared stressing the dangers of depleting the shrinking non-renewable resource base of the globe and people's ability to affect their larger environment in unanticipated and often undesirable ways. These reports were extensively publicized—to the point where, even today, the general public is widely familiar with the expression "limits to growth".[4]

The fact that most of these warnings were rather wide off the mark in their predictions limited their usefulness, however. It also dampened the enthusiasm for this type of early warning. But the accelerating pace of change in all domains and the serious or even disastrous consequences of being caught unprepared and unaware have revived interest in the concept of early warning.[5] Technological advances have also seemingly made early warning more feasible as the expansion in the use of computers has led to an explosion of model-building and forecasting.[6]

The term "early warning" suggests that, when a process has started, the perceived threat will occur with virtually 100 per cent certainty. In the socio-economic sphere, however, events generally happen with less certitude. Therefore, the tendency now is to use the term "early identification" in this context, "early identification" being attached to an event which has a less than certain probability of happening.

Attempts to make the notion of early identification operational have revealed some of its complexities. One of the fundamental problems is the issue of "What is early?". For an early identification system to be useful, the information it provides must be both accurate and timely. Advance information is usually questionable, although it becomes more reliable over time, as new and more data are added. However, waiting longer for more information may mean forgoing the opportunity to take action early enough, which may be a critical factor.

### Leading indicators

The trade-off between accuracy and timeliness is one of the principal concerns in the systems of leading indicators used to predict business cycle swings.[7] These indicators are used as an early identification system for economic recession or recovery and are of interest to job seekers, businessmen, investors, policy makers and other economic actors. In the United States, for example, the Department of Commerce publishes monthly a Composite Index of Leading In-

1 See *Report of the World Food Conference, Rome, 5-16, November 1974* (United Nations publication, Sales No. E.75.II.A.3), chap. II, resolution XVI.

2 Leon Gordenker, "Early warning of disastrous population movement", *International Migration Review*, vol. 20, No. 2, pp. 170-180.

3 In the area of preventive diplomacy, see, for example, the *report of the Secretary-General on the work of the organization* (*Official Records of the General Assembly, Forty-second Session, Supplement No. 1* (A/42/1)).

4 Donella H. Meadows, Dennis L. Meadows, Jorgen Randers and William K. Behrens, III, *Limits to Growth* (New York, Universal Books, 1972).

5 John Renninger, "Early warning: what role for the United Nations?" (UNITAR, September 1988), paper prepared for a United Nations Roundtable entitled "Future role of the United Nations in an interdependent world".

6 For a recent description of forecasting advances over the past 20 years, see Kenneth F. Wallis, "Macroeconomic forecasting: a survey", *The Economic Journal*, vol. 99, No. 394 (March 1989), pp. 28-61.

7 Recently, increasing attention has been given to identifying leading indicators for inflation, particularly to the possible use of changes in commodity prices in this regard. See, for example, James M. Boughton and William H. Branson, "Commodity prices as a leading indicator of inflation", National Bureau of Economic Research, Working Paper No. 2750 (October 1988), and Martine Durand and Sveinbjörn Blondal, "Are commodity prices leading indicators of OECD prices?", OECD, Department of Economics and Statistics, Working Paper No. 49 (February 1988).

dicators, which is a weighted average of 11 different leading indicators. Similarly, the Organisation for Economic Co-operation and Development (OECD) publishes composite leading indicators monthly for 20 countries.[8]

A major concern arising from such composite indicators is the weighting that should be used in constructing an aggregate indicator. Not only do different components measure different aspects of an economy, but the different indicators have varying lead times. On average, for instance, the change in consumer debt, the formation of business enterprises, the stock price index or housing construction indices all have a longer median lead time than the change in business inventories, the average manufacturing work week or profits.

Another question raised by leading indicators is whether they are consistent and accurate predictors of business cycle trends. In general, they tend to retain certain behavioural patterns over time, so that it is highly unusual for an indicator that was once classified as leading to be reclassified as coincident or lagging. Furthermore, the record of such leading indicators has been reasonably good. They have predicted the course of the cycle fairly successfully in the past (though certain variables, such as interest rates, have proved difficult to forecast). However, the historical record of predictive accuracy fails to take into account changing patterns of policy responses, which may have mitigated the predicted fluctuations or, as some suspect, have aggravated them by coming too late and having long delayed effects.

Moreover, leading indicator systems do not incorporate socio-economic trends, in large part because social data are generally available with greater delay than purely economic data. However, various systems of socio-economic and social indicators have been devised in an attempt to measure "social welfare" or the "quality of life". Most such schemes include indicators in the areas of health, education, housing, social security, the use of time and leisure and social stratification. With all social indicator systems, major problems are encountered in selecting indicators that are representative of each area and in weighting them into one overall statistic. The more ambitious the scheme, the more laden it is with value judgements and, hence, the more difficult it is to determine whether the indicator system accurately monitors emerging social and economic issues.

### International surveillance of economic policies

In recent years, increased attention has been given both to economic co-operation and co-ordination among the leading industrialized countries and to the type of conditionality which is associated with lending by international financial institutions to developing countries. In both cases, the result has been closer international surveillance of the economic performance of individual countries; monitoring performance has, in turn, required a reinvestigation of the economic indicators used.

In the case of the Group of Seven industrial countries, agreement was reached at the Economic Summit held at Venice in June 1987 to use "performance indicators to review and assess current economic trends and to determine whether there are significant deviations from an intended course that require consideration of remedial actions".[9] Six indicators (growth of output, trade, budget balances, inflation, interest rates and exchange rates) were initially used to monitor the performance of the seven economies. Subsequently, in order to obtain early warning of an impending acceleration in inflation, a commodity price indicator was added.[10] For the major industrial countries, in addition to using such indicators to oversee individual country performance, there is interest in ascertaining the impact of any changes on the world economy at large.

No comparable indicators for developing countries exist to monitor individual country performance. Although greater flexibility is being introduced, the current performance indicators used by the international financial institutions to monitor the economic performance of borrowing developing countries, particularly those undergoing adjustment programmes, tend to focus on specific aspects of the domestic economy, such as the domestic money supply, the size and financing of the government budget deficit, international reserve holdings and changes in trade and exchange rate restrictions.

### Problems of implementation

In a scheme where policy co-ordination plays a role, as in the Group of Seven, the problem arises of weighing different objectives and reconciling differing perceptions of the efficacy of various solutions. An additional point is that there is a major difference between indicator schemes, leading or otherwise, and an early identification system. Spotting trends is only one aspect of early identification; an equally important—and perhaps even more difficult—task is to predict abrupt changes in trends, or turning points. What is called for is not just prediction of the future in very general terms, but prediction of events or specific developments. These may be either events that one wishes to prevent or at least protect oneself from or events that one wants to benefit from by taking timely action.

Early identification, in the sense of indicators which would show when a critical situation is arising, can be exemplified by the miner's canary, which used to serve as an early warning of gas in mines. In this case, it is not only the danger that is apparent; it is also equally clear who is issuing the warning and who is expected to heed it. In most cases, the situation is less clear. In addition to early warning of disasters, for example, there is the need for the early identifica-

---

8 For a description of the OECD system of indicators, see *OECD Leading Indicators and Business Cycles in Member Countries, 1960-1985* (Paris, 1987).

9 See the Economic Declaration of the Venice Economic Summit, held from 8 to 10 June 1987 (A/42/344, annex), para. 11.

10 See the economic declaration issued on 21 June 1988 at the Toronto Economic Summit (A/43/435-S/19974, annex I), para. 6.

tion of the erosion of a currently acceptable situation. This, though, raises the question of what is "acceptable". What are the minimum levels that Governments or populations or international organizations are willing to accept and what erosion of these minimum levels is tolerable?

Value judgements are involved, and from this perspective it is relevant to ask who issues early warnings or carries out early identification exercises. The question is equally relevant from the angle of liability and costs. There may be a very high cost to issuing warnings which stimulate expensive counter-measures which turn out not to be needed. Even if inherently worth while, the cost of such schemes—the Japanese system for earthquake warnings, for example—can inhibit their general use.[11]

Another aspect of early identification systems is whether they are heeded or not. History is replete with examples of human beings disregarding warnings of unpleasant events on the grounds that they are not likely to occur. Warnings about earthquakes, hurricanes and the outbreak of war are cases in point. Not heeding predictions need not be due to wishful thinking, however. There tend to be economic, social and institutional rigidities in any economy, as well as a degree of resource immobility, which impede a quick and ready response to anticipated difficult problems. Hence, it is often considered easier to deal with an economic, social or environmental disaster after the fact than to take *ex ante* action on the grounds that a disaster might occur.

### Scope and time horizon of early identification mechanisms

Early identification mechanisms vary greatly in scope. On the one hand, they range in subject from the strictly macroeconomic to systems seeking to identify larger socio-economic issues. On the other hand, they also range from the monitoring of developments, which, *ex post,* could serve as the basis for identifying trends, to fully-fledged early identification exercises. Within the United Nations system, an example of the former is the monitoring of commodity prices on a daily basis by the Commodity Division of the World Bank. An instance of the latter is the work done by the United Nations Office at Vienna in forecasting requirements for the legal processing of opium-based substances, along with which goes the power to impose production quotas.

There is a wide range of possible time horizons in early identification and monitoring mechanisms. Population forecasts, for example, come out yearly at most. Gross national product estimates are made quarterly in many instances. Stock or commodity prices are available on a daily basis, as are exchange rates. There is an equally large diversity in the time horizon of early identification mechanisms within the United Nations system. Short-run early identification systems tend either to pertain to more strictly economic developments or to provide early warning of acts of nature. An example of the former is the World Bank's daily monitoring of commodity prices mentioned above. An example of the latter is the work done by the Food and Agricultural Organization of the United Nations (FAO) in continually monitoring the desert locust situation and weather conditions world wide, with the help of the World Meteorological Organization (WMO). Both are major factors affecting global food production.

Early identification in the short run could more properly be called forecasting of what is likely to happen 6 to 18 months in the future. Such shorter-run forecasting tends to be concerned with marginal changes, rather than early identification of drastic long-term shifts in conditions.

An example of early identification work of a long-run nature is the work of the Population Division of the United Nations Secretariat in monitoring population trends, policies and programmes. Similarly, the efforts of the International Labour Organization in encouraging and assisting Governments to collect data on real earnings and unemployment have a long-term horizon. The work of the General Agreement on Tariffs and Trade in monitoring and surveying trade policies is of a medium-term nature. Some of these medium-run and long-run identification systems have the potential to be more socio-economically oriented than do the primarily economic, short-run forecasts.

## Early identification mechanisms and means within the United Nations system

Within the United Nations system, there are a large number of mechanisms and means available for the early identification, monitoring and analysis of world socio-economic developments. The following listing, which presents these mechanisms by type of activity, is not exhaustive, but nevertheless demonstrates that there is a large amount of information available from the system to provide Governments with an indication of likely developments.

### Early identification systems

The prototype of an early identification system is the FAO Global Information and Early Warning System on Food and Agriculture. This system is designed to monitor the supplies of basic food and fertilizer on a continuous basis and to identify imminent food shortages in order to prepare in advance for emergency interventions. As of 1988, over 100 countries participated in the system, as well as intergovernmental organizations, such as the European Economic Community, and some 23 non-governmental organizations. The information provided by the latter is especially valuable for the monitoring of socio-economic indicators and for the identification and evaluation of the severity of localized food supply difficulties. All information flows into a central computerized system which provides a quantitative assessment of demand and supply levels for the world as a whole, regions,

11 In this regard, an assessment of the probability of an event occurring may define preparatory action. This approach is frequently used in meteorology where the probability of a given event is used as a weight and combined with other parameters, such as the cost of preventive measures, in order to assess whether an action should be initiated.

countries and areas within countries. It forecasts crop size, deficits or surpluses and food aid requirements for the following year. The information is disseminated in a variety of ways, including special alerts which are sent by telex directly to Governments and donors whenever a possible emergency is foreseen. The monthly publication *Food Outlook* provides comprehensive assessments of the global and regional supply and demand position and the outlook for basic foods. Another monthly report, *Food Crops and Shortages,* contains an up-to-date, country-by-country evaluation of foodcrop conditions, production prospects and cereal import and food aid requirements for the low-income food deficit countries. A special report entitled *Food Supply Situation and Crop Prospects in sub-Saharan Africa,* issued periodically, provides the latest analyses and forecasts for that area. The FAO system, which may be termed both a monitoring and an emergency alert system, is still evolving. In recent years, efforts have been made to improve the quality of information received and to use modern techniques, such as remote sensing, to complement field observations.

For the past few years, the Centre for Science and Technology for Development of the United Nations Secretariat has been developing an Advance Technology Alert System (ATAS) to identify new technologies with major social and economic implications, such as micro-electronics and biotechnology, based on expertise in the scientific and policy-making communities and industry. The data include the trends in each of these technologies, their social and economic consequences, as well as the policy options available, especially in the area of investment in science and technology in developing countries.ATAS differs from most other early identification systems in that it is an effort to identify the benefits that may be lost from failing to take advantage of favourable developments, rather than an attempt to avoid the costs, or be prepared to assume the costs, of a possible adverse event.

The World Health Organization (WHO) provides early warning about the potential side-effects of development projects on health. In the belief that all early warning schemes are more effective at the regional and local levels, WHO has set up regional training centres; the latest of which is in Addis Ababa, called centres for emergency preparedness and response. Similar systems already exist in the Americas and Asia. Using advance information, these centres can take steps before a disaster strikes to move the necessary food and medical supplies into a threatened area.

WMO has long experience in issuing warnings of severe weather and flood events which can have an enormous economic impact. Depending upon the phenomena concerned, these warnings are issued either nationally or internationally by means of specialized centres. As mentioned above, WMO assists FAO in monitoring weather conditions affecting locust breeding and movement in Afria. Under the Convention on Early Notification of a Nuclear Accident, the International Atomic Energy Agency and WMO collaborate in a warning and advisory system using the WMO Global Telecommunication System.

The Population Division of the United Nations Secretariat carries out early identification activities in the form of population projections for all countries and regions in the world—at present, up to the year 2025. These projections are updated every two years so that the impact of changes will be visible. In addition to forecasting population size, the age-sex distribution of the population is estimated, as are the two basic demographic indicators—fertility and mortality—and variations thereon. These projections are made in close co-operation with the specialized agencies which use the estimates for their own sectoral projections, one example being the data base on human settlement statistics established by the United Nations Centre for Human settlements (Habitat). The Population Division has a number of studies in progress which investigate the demographic characteristics of various mega cities, examine the nature of their economies and provide growth and migration projections.

In the political area, the Office for Research and Collection of Information of the United Nations Secretariat provides "early warning" by furnishing information and advice relevant to conflict prevention.

**Monitoring**

The great variety of long-run and short-run monitoring of activities carried out within the United Nations system has the potential to be used for early identification purposes, although it does not necessarily lead to action to deal with problems at an early stage.

The United Nations Environment Programme (UNEP) is responsible for identifying emerging environmental problems of global significance, as well as the means required to deal with them. To do this, UNEP monitors and assesses various environmental parameters through the Global Environmental Monitoring System (GEMS). GEMS is a large and growing computer-based system designed to make the voluminous amounts of relevant and available information useful to the world community, individual Governments and other decision makers for management purposes. GEMS works closely with other parts of the United Nations system to obtain relevant information. For example, it works with FAO on data on such parameters as deforestation, desertification, soil degradation and soil loss. It works very closely with WMO in monitoring pollutants in the atmosphere and assessing issues such as the depletion of the ozone layer and climatic change.

ILO has set up an Employment Committee for which it produces a biannual report on the state of employment, unemployment and earnings in the world. This monitoring is directed towards Governments and worker and employer organizations. WHO undertakes a monitoring exercise which tracks progress towards attaining the goal of "health for all by the year 2000", while Habitat has started a similiar endeavour in connection with the Global Strategy for Shelter to the Year 2000.

The International Monetary Fund (IMF) has developed operational criteria relating to domestic credit. When there are fiscal or monetary policy slippages, a set of indicators alerts the authorities that a programme is off-target. The World Bank's Risk Management and Financial Policy Department monitors the credit-worthiness of some 50 countries that are borrowing from the Bank. The Bank also undertakes other tracking exercises—for example, in the area of commodity prices. The United Nations Conference on Trade and Development (UNCTAD) and FAO also monitor commodity trends.

The GATT secretariat is involved in the monitoring and surveillance of trade policies, including individual issues such as trade in textiles and clothing. Its most comprehensive current exercise is the biannual report entitled "Developments in the trading system", which takes stock of all trade policy actions on the part of contracting parties. This report investigates trends in global policies—whether protectionist or liberal—and serves as a basis for discussions in the GATT Council of what can, if necessary, be done. The new Trade Policy Review Mechanism involves efforts to enhance the surveillance activity of GATT by regular reviews of contracting parties' trade policies and practices, country by country, and their impact on the functioning of the multilateral trading system.

**Surveys and reports**

The various annual surveys and reports prepared within the United Nations system may also be considered early identification mechanisms. Some of these reports are primarily economic in nature, but others deal with broader socio-economic issues, in keeping with the mandates of the organizations that produce them.

The United Nations *World Economic Survey* is an annual publication which has been prepared at the request of the General Assembly since 1947. It reviews the year's main economic developments, analyses their implications and presents short-term forecasts for the different regions of the world. A major focus is the identification of emerging economic issues of global concern—global in the sense either that they affect a large number of countries or a large proportion of the world population, or that they involve economic interrelationships between countries. It is from this perspective that chapter II of the *Survey* presents an assessment of global prospects for the coming year. In addition, specific issues of topical relevance and their implications for the world economy are discussed, frequently in response to mandates given by the Economic and Social Council and the General Assembly. The 1988 *Survey*, for example, discussed the growth implications of the fall in stock market prices in October 1987, and the present *Survey* examines the severe constraints to growth that a premature net transfer of resources from developing to developed countries implies. This issue was first raised in the 1985 *Survey* and has since become of increasing international concern.

The United Nations *Report on the World Social Situation*, prepared every four years, dates back to 1952. In accordance with guidelines provided in General Assembly and Economic and Social Council resolutions, the report provides a global overview of the world social situation, giving special attention to regional and other perspectives in social and overall development. In the preparation of the report special emphasis is given to the relationship between national, regional and international trends and policies and to turning points in social conditions.

The annual *Trade and Development Report*, introduced in 1981, is prepared by the secretariat of UNCTAD. It provides an integrated review of recent international economic developments, together with forecasts for the world economy, with special emphasis on the trade and development prospects of the developing countries. In addition, each report devotes attention to a selected topic of particular relevance to trade, money, finance and development issues.

The economic and social surveys and reports of the regional commissions provide, generally on an annual basis, information on current conditions in their respective regions, as well as a qualitative assessment of short-term prospects. In some instances, the forward-looking nature of the review takes centre stage; for example, the 1987/88 report of the Economic Commission for Latin America and the Caribbean discussed, among other things, restrictions on sustained development in Latin America and the Caribbean and suggestions for overcoming them.

The *World Development Report* is an annual study prepared by the World Bank since 1978. Part I of the report generally contains a review of recent trends in the world economy and their implications for the future prospects of developing countries. Part II usually deals with a specific policy-oriented theme of current relevance. For instance, the 1987 report examined the role of foreign trade in the industrialization of developing countries, while the 1988 report looked at the role of public finance in development.

The staff of the International Monetary Fund produces the *World Economic Outlook* biannually. The *Outlook* examines the short-term economic prospects of industrialized countries and developing regions. Its projections and analysis are the product of an interdepartmental review which draws on information the staff of the Fund gathers through regular and special consultations with member countries, as well as through econometric modelling.

*International Trade*, prepared by the GATT secretariat, dates back to 1953 and is published annually in two volumes. In the first section of Volume 1, trends in world trade by major product group, major region and individual countries are traced. In the second section, longer-term developments of trade in a specific sector or region are analysed in depth—for example, the latest issue, *International Trade 1987/1988*, provides an analysis of world trade in agriculture. A concluding section addresses specific trade policy issues. Volume II provides more detailed information about developments in world trade.

Most of the specialized agencies publish regular reviews of recent developments and future prospects in their respective areas of expertise, such as *The State of Food and Agriculture*, published annually by FAO. An annual publication of the United Nations Industrial Development Organization, *Industry and Development: Global Report*, provides short-term forecasts of the level of output in a number of branches of industry in regions and in as many countries as possible; an important feature is the attempt to investigate the implications of macro-economic changes at the national and international levels. In addition to reviewing the current situation and providing an assessment of immediate prospects, the *Global Report* examines a special topic each year.

Similarly, the *Global Report on Human Settlements*, prepared by Habitat and issued annually, provides a complete review of human settlements conditions, including an analysis of the forces and trends accounting for both the present development and the continuing creation, maintenance and improvement of human settlements. The 1988 report focused on the forces of urbanization in developing countries and on policies to avert a major crisis and turn the challenge into an opportunity for development.

Also in this category are the following annual reports: *The State of the World's Children*, prepared by the United Nations Children's Organization, *The State of the Environment Report*, prepared by UNEP, which singles out a particular subject or subjects each year, *The State of World Population*, prepared by the United Nations Population Fund, which also focuses particular attention on one or more subjects each year.

Other documents which can be used for early identification purposes are the numerous periodical statistical publications of the United Nations system. Almost all United Nations bodies and agencies compile and periodically publish data in their respective areas of expertise. Although most of this information is not intended for early identification purposes, it provides a quantitative basis for forward-looking analysis. For instance, the ILO publication *Economically Active Population, Estimates and Projections* shows, *inter alia*, labour force trends for 1985-2025.

The Statistical Office of the United Nations Secretariat compiles a wide variety of current statistics from countries on economic output and industrial activity, international trade, prices, population and housing. The latest available data are published in the *Monthly Bulletin of Statistics*. They are also circulated as soon as possible after receipt to users and analysts in the organizations concerned throughout the international system and other units of the United Nations Secretarit for monitoring and assessment purposes.

### Topical reports

Reports published by the organizations of the system on a wide array of subjects may also be used for early identification purposes. These reports are generally far more specific or narrow as far as subject-matter is concerned than are the ones cited in the previous section, and they do not necessarily appear with the same regularity. Not all fall under the rubric of early identification, but some do—for example, the "Overall socio-economic perspective of the world economy to the year 2000". This report, which is prepared by the United Nations with the help of contributions from the specialized agencies, is a periodic assessment of long-term trends in the world's economic and social development. The report issued in 1988 (A/43/554) was intended to serve as a quantitative and qualitative framework for considering a number of long-term issues which the international community should address in the 1990s.

The World Bank has issued a large number of forward-looking studies on specific topics, such as *Prospects for Food Production and Consumption in Developing Countries* (1983) or, jointly with FAO, *Prospects for the World Jute Industry* (1986). Such World Bank publications include books, commodity studies, country studies, discussion papers, policy studies, statistical working papers, symposium papers, World Bank journals and informal documents.

Similarly, the United Nations Educational, Scientific and Cultural Organization publishes numerous studies on specific topics in a wide range of social and socio-economic areas, such as *Reflections on the Future Development of Education* (1985). The United Nations University and its World Institute for Development Economics Research (UNU/WIDER) publish specific study reports on current issues of economic and development concern, such as prospects for development in Africa or the problems of economic openness to the century's end.

### Models

A further group of devices which can be used for early identification purposes are global models. Project LINK is a co-operative, non-governmental, international research activity, whose principal objective has been to integrate independently developed national econometric models into a world modelling system. Initiated in 1968 at the University of Pennsylvania, the project has expanded from 7 country models to 79 models, including 40 models of individual developing countries and regions. As an active participant in Project LINK, the United Nations has made extensive use of the Project's multicountry model for periodic reporting on the short-run outlook for the world economy.

In a similar vein, the World Bank prepares long-run projections annually, based on econometric models. While the nature of the projections varies from year to year, in general a number of alternative scenarios are prepared. The most recent use of this mechanism, published in the *World Development Report 1988*, presented the outlook for the world economy to 1995. Two scenarios were set out: the "base case" which assumed that industrial countries would leave their policies broadly unaltered, and the "high case", which assumed that they would change them to conform to a number of specified criteria, such as reducing payments imbalances.

UNCTAD also has a world model, supported by the System for Interlinked Global Modelling and Analysis (SIGMA), which is used for forecasting. The system comprises 58 macro-economic models for countries and regions, linked by systems of trade flows, financial flows and international trade prices that ensure global consistency. Other United Nations organizations also work with models. For example, IMF uses short-term to medium-term models, while the regional commissions work with medium-range to long-range models.

Models are becoming increasingly relevant to early identification in the political area. A new generation of computer-based global models developed in academia and elsewhere are now better equipped than were earlier models to deal with the question of the interdependence of political, economic and social matters.[12] The Office for Research and Collection of Information of the United Nations Secretariat use computers and draws on such models in developing its early warning system.

### Conclusions

The foregoing analysis demonstrates that there is a plethora of information available within the United Nations system which can be drawn on for early identification purposes. A large part of what the system does in the economic and social sphere can be described as early identification of one sort or another. A key question, however, is how much of this information is comprehensive enough, yet sufficiently synthesized, to be readily usable by policy makers and others. A further factor is that the information is not uniformly distributed, much more being available for developed countries than for developing ones.

In specific sectoral fields, such as agriculture, health or meteorology, early identification tends to work well at the international level. The real issue in many such cases, especially in the social arena, is not detecting the problem, but reacting to it. In the social fields, the need is to ensure an adequate response to problems. For example, regarding health, the need for a greater response to the AIDS epidemic is a case in point. However, in the economic sphere, information is far more fragmented. Hence, though shocks occur which have world-wide repercussions, the international system's capacity for early warning or identification of such potential trouble spots is fairly unfocused.[13] Consequently, in the economic sphere, the first need is to properly identify potential disturbances. Despite all the information that was available, few foresaw—and fewer took action to mitigate—the oil price increase of the mid-1970s, the debt crisis of the early 1980s or the stock market crash of October 1987, even though such economic events can have potentially devastating effects on many economies.[14]

In an increasingly interdependent world, macro-economic disturbances tend to be inexorably transmitted across countries. Early identification of such disturbances—as well as an early assessment of whether they are temporary or permanent—has become ever more important. Yet the problem is not so much the timely grasp of the phenomena as the national and international action to counter them. Partly for this reason, it might be useful to concentrate early identification activities at the sectoral level.

Another conclusion is that early warnings are most fruitful if addressed to the local or regional level because large-scale schemes addressed to Governments may not be heeded. The usefulness of alarms depends on whether anybody is listening. In general, they are useful only if Governments take them seriously. From this perspective, it makes sense to expand early identification activities in response to a perceived demand from Governments.

A final problem is how to ensure that the information garnered is used for early identification purposes rather than for historical retrospectives. A criticism occasionally levied at the United Nations system in the economic and social arena is that, while resources are devoted to the analysis and monitoring of emerging problems, limited success is realized in averting potential difficulties. Repeated and well-documented warnings are often issued and disregarded. More effective pursuit of early identification activities may lead to improvements in this area by enabling greater progress to be made in anticipating and dealing with identified socio-economic concerns. Indeed, international organizations are in a unique position to provide a global perspective to emerging problems and issues, from an angle which might be lacking, or overlooked, at the national level.

---

12 See, for example, Stuart A. Bremer, ed., *GLOBUS Model—Computer Simulation of Worldwide Political and Economic Development* Frankfurt-am-Main, (Campus Verlag, 1987).

13 This may also be indicative of the need for research linking economic forecasts with socio-economic trends. For instance, ILO is attempting to develop a system of employment forecasting based on indicators of both the output cycle and conditions affecting the labour market.

14 In the area of energy, for example, the developed countries have established their own "early warning system" within the International Energy Agency. The Organization of the Petroleum Exporting Countries also has its own early identification scheme. However, the energy-deficient developing countries have no such system, though they would be among the hardest hit in the event of a crisis. This suggests the need for co-operation among Governments in these countries to provide up-to-date information on their energy situation and plans in order to provide an early warning system in this area.

# III. SELECTED DEMOGRAPHIC INDICATORS

It is generally agreed that there is a significant but not necessarily simple or direct relationship between population changes and economic development. The following tables show demographic trends up to 1990. To typify country situations at the regional level, the median rather than weighted regional averages has been used.

For mid-1989, the total population of the world is projected to reach 5.2 billion; 4.0 billion in the countries of the developing regions and 1.2 in the developed. The world's population is currently increasing by an annual increment of some 89 million, 83 million of whom are added to the populations of the developing regions. After a period of deceleration from its historic peak (2 per cent per year) in the late 1960s, the rate of population growth has levelled off at about 1.7 per cent per year and is expected to remain there into the early 1990s.

The available evidence indicates that mortality measured at the national level is continuing to decline in the countries of all regions; the global expectation of life at birth was rising by 2.9 years per decade through the first half of the 1980s. Differences in mortality remain very large, however, with Africa lagging significantly behind other regions.

The world's population has entered a period of demographic aging; only in Africa is the average age continuing to drop, chiefly as a result of very high fertility. Overall, the ratio of persons in the dependent years to those in the more productive years is declining. The burden of dependency is about 40 per cent heavier in the developing than in the developed regions.

The urban population of the world is projected to be 2.26 billion for 1990. Each year, the global urban population increases by about 50 million persons, growing at a rate of 2.5 per cent per year—twice the rate of growth of the world's rural population.

The data used to prepare the population estimates and projections are based on information derived from censuses, vital statistics, population registries and representative sample surveys. The estimates and projections are revised by the Population Division of the United Nations Secretariat every two years on a country-by-country basis, to take into account all new relevant data. In general, the supply of demographic data has improved substantially during recent decades. During the 1980 census decade, 191 countries or areas took at least one population census and over 95 per cent of the world's population were enumerated. Nevertheless, demographic data remain insufficient in both quantity and quality for the countries of some developing regions—most notably Africa.

In preparing the estimates and projections for each country, the statistical data are examined for reliability and internal consistency. The assumptions used to make population projections are based on demographic experience relevant to each specific country. On the whole, the reliability of population estimates and projections has proved to be quite high over recent decades. Population trends have a considerable amount of internal momentum and, with the exception of migration, major famines or armed conflicts, the range over which demographic variables may vary is constrained by known biological parameters.[1]

Table S.III.1. Population and population growth, 1975-1990, medium variant

| Region and country or area[a] | Population 1990 (Thousands) | Annual rate of change 1975-1980 (Percentage) | 1980-1985 | 1985-1990 |
|---|---|---|---|---|
| World | 5 286 714 | 2.23 | 2.30 | 2.35 |
| | (5 292 178) | (1.74) | (1.74) | (1.73) |
| Developing countries | 4 071 001 | 2.53 | 2.59 | 2.64 |
| Africa | 611 901 | 2.93 | 2.95 | 2.95 |
| Algeria | 25 364 | 3.06 | 3.01 | 3.12 |
| Angola | 10 020 | 3.39 | 2.51 | 2.70 |
| Benin | 4 741 | 2.77 | 2.96 | 3.15 |
| Botswana | 1 285 | 3.55 | 3.58 | 3.51 |
| Burkina Faso | 9 007 | 2.30 | 2.49 | 2.67 |
| Burundi | 5 451 | 1.80 | 2.82 | 2.88 |
| Cameroon | 11 245 | 2.57 | 2.71 | 2.60 |

1 More detailed information on population estimates and projections, data sources and methods can be found in World Population Prospects, 1988 (United Nations publication, Sales No. E.88.XIII.7).

Table S.III.1. (Continued)

| Region and country or area[a] | Population 1990 (Thousands) | Annual rate of change 1975-1980 (Percentage) | 1980-1985 | 1985-1990 |
|---|---|---|---|---|
| Cape Verde | 379 | 0.87 | 2.17 | 2.81 |
| Central African Republic | 2 913 | 2.22 | 2.28 | 2.46 |
| Chad | 5 678 | 2.10 | 2.28 | 2.47 |
| Comoros | 519 | 3.40 | 3.05 | 3.11 |
| Congo | 1 994 | 2.46 | 2.59 | 2.73 |
| Côte d'Ivoire | 12 596 | 4.19 | 4.16 | 4.12 |
| Djibouti | 406 | 4.48 | 3.09 | 2.96 |
| Egypt | 54 059 | 2.69 | 2.72 | 2.55 |
| Equatorial Guinea | 440 | 1.99 | 2.15 | 2.34 |
| Ethiopia | 46 743 | 2.43 | 1.74 | 2.01 |
| Gabon | 1 171 | 4.70 | 4.01 | 3.45 |
| Gambia | 858 | 3.15 | 3.01 | 2.83 |
| Ghana | 15 020 | 1.76 | 3.58 | 3.14 |
| Guinea | 6 876 | 2.17 | 2.33 | 2.48 |
| Guinea-Bissau | 987 | 5.04 | 1.91 | 2.08 |
| Kenya | 25 130 | 3.82 | 4.04 | 4.22 |
| Lesotho | 1 774 | 2.41 | 2.78 | 2.85 |
| Liberia | 2 554 | 3.09 | 3.21 | 3.18 |
| Libyan Arab Jamahiriya | 4 544 | 4.37 | 4.37 | 3.65 |
| Madagascar | 11 980 | 2.90 | 3.05 | 3.18 |
| Malawi | 8 428 | 3.00 | 3.18 | 3.31 |
| Mali | 9 362 | 2.19 | 2.81 | 2.94 |
| Mauritania | 2 024 | 2.46 | 2.60 | 2.73 |
| Mauritius | 1 103 | 1.91 | 1.60 | 1.25 |
| Morocco | 25 139 | 2.27 | 2.64 | 2.56 |
| Mozambique | 15 663 | 2.83 | 2.51 | 2.65 |
| Namibia | 1 876 | 2.97 | 3.08 | 3.19 |
| Niger | 7 109 | 2.59 | 2.82 | 3.01 |
| Nigeria | 113 016 | 3.49 | 3.34 | 3.43 |
| Réunion | 595 | 0.95 | 1.45 | 1.72 |
| Rwanda | 7 232 | 3.27 | 3.34 | 3.40 |
| Senegal | 7 369 | 3.46 | 2.55 | 2.69 |
| Sierra Leone | 4 151 | 2.15 | 2.32 | 2.49 |
| Somalia | 7 555 | 5.06 | 3.57 | 3.32 |
| Sudan | 25 195 | 3.08 | 3.11 | 2.88 |
| Swaziland | 789 | 3.12 | 3.30 | 3.43 |
| Togo | 3 455 | 2.52 | 2.95 | 3.09 |
| Tunisia | 8 169 | 2.58 | 2.57 | 2.36 |
| Uganda | 18 442 | 3.19 | 3.32 | 3.49 |
| United Republic of Tanzania | 27 328 | 3.42 | 3.74 | 3.67 |
| Zaire | 35 990 | 3.27 | 3.04 | 3.17 |
| Zambia | 8 456 | 3.40 | 3.99 | 3.76 |
| Zimbabwe | 9 721 | 2.96 | 3.03 | 3.15 |
| South and East Asia | 2 801 466 | 2.13 | 2.23 | 2.24 |
| Afghanistan | 16 557 | 0.87 | -2.02 | 2.63 |
| Bangladesh | 115 593 | 2.83 | 2.73 | 2.67 |
| Bhutan | 1 516 | 1.70 | 1.80 | 2.15 |
| Burma | 41 675 | 2.11 | 2.09 | 2.09 |
| China | 1 135 496 | 1.43 | 1.23 | 1.39 |
| Democratic Kampuchea | 8 246 | -2.07 | 2.59 | 2.48 |
| East Timor | 737 | -2.91 | 2.50 | 2.24 |
| Fiji | 749 | 1.77 | 1.87 | 1.60 |
| Hong Kong | 5 841 | 2.73 | 1.59 | 1.36 |
| India | 853 373 | 2.08 | 2.21 | 2.08 |
| Indonesia | 180 514 | 2.14 | 1.96 | 1.62 |
| Korea | 66 519 | 1.87 | 1.80 | 1.59 |
| Democratic People's Republic of Korea | 22 937 | 2.57 | 2.46 | 2.36 |
| Republic of Korea | 43 582 | 1.55 | 1.48 | 1.19 |
| Lao People's Democratic Republic | 4 071 | 1.16 | 2.29 | 2.49 |
| Malaysia | 17 339 | 2.32 | 2.31 | 2.31 |
| Mongolia | 2 227 | 2.82 | 2.75 | 3.09 |
| Nepal | 19 143 | 2.67 | 2.59 | 2.47 |
| Pakistan | 122 666 | 2.64 | 3.82 | 3.45 |
| Papua New Guinea | 4 011 | 2.70 | 2.58 | 2.66 |

Table S.III.1. (Continued)

| Region and country or area[a] | Population 1990 (Thousands) | Annual rate of change 1975-1980 (Percentage) | Annual rate of change 1980-1985 (Percentage) | Annual rate of change 1985-1990 (Percentage) |
|---|---|---|---|---|
| Philippines | 62 409 | 2.53 | 2.63 | 2.48 |
| Singapore | 2 702 | 1.30 | 1.16 | 1.09 |
| Sri Lanka | 17 209 | 1.71 | 1.67 | 1.32 |
| Thailand | 55 702 | 2.44 | 1.99 | 1.53 |
| Viet Nam | 67 171 | 2.23 | 2.24 | 2.24 |
| West Asia | 130 489 | 3.56 | 3.85 | 3.47 |
| Bahrain | 515 | 4.87 | 4.27 | 3.64 |
| Democratic Yemen | 2 491 | 2.36 | 2.76 | 3.07 |
| Iran (Islamic Republic of) | 56 585 | 3.08 | 4.05 | 3.45 |
| Iraq | 18 920 | 3.75 | 3.58 | 3.48 |
| Israel | 4 581 | 2.31 | 1.75 | 1.58 |
| Jordan | 4 270 | 2.34 | 3.64 | 3.94 |
| Kuwait | 2 090 | 6.24 | 4.36 | 4.02 |
| Lebanon | 2 965 | -0.72 | -0.01 | 2.11 |
| Oman | 1 468 | 5.01 | 4.67 | 3.34 |
| Qatar | 367 | 5.84 | 5.29 | 4.15 |
| Saudi Arabia | 14 131 | 5.13 | 4.26 | 3.96 |
| Syrian Arab Republic | 12 501 | 3.36 | 3.45 | 3.57 |
| United Arab Emirates | 1 588 | 13.97 | 5.69 | 3.26 |
| Yemen | 8 017 | 2.53 | 2.78 | 3.04 |
| Mediterranean | 80 519 | 1.48 | 0.92 | 0.83 |
| Cyprus | 701 | 0.65 | 1.11 | 1.04 |
| Malta | 353 | 2.09 | -1.11 | 0.49 |
| Turkey | 55 616 | 2.09 | 2.50 | 1.99 |
| Yugoslavia | 23 849 | 0.87 | 0.72 | 0.62 |
| Western hemisphere | 446 626 | 2.11 | 2.05 | 1.99 |
| Argentina | 32 322 | 1.61 | 1.43 | 1.27 |
| Barbados | 261 | 0.28 | 0.31 | 0.62 |
| Bolivia | 7 314 | 2.59 | 2.69 | 2.76 |
| Brazil | 150 368 | 2.31 | 2.23 | 2.07 |
| Chile | 13 173 | 1.48 | 1.68 | 1.66 |
| Colombia | 31 819 | 2.14 | 2.14 | 2.05 |
| Costa Rica | 3 015 | 2.98 | 2.91 | 2.64 |
| Cuba | 10 324 | 0.84 | 0.44 | 0.75 |
| Dominican Republic | 7 170 | 2.42 | 2.38 | 2.22 |
| Ecuador | 10 782 | 2.88 | 2.87 | 2.79 |
| El Salvador | 5 252 | 2.05 | 1.04 | 1.93 |
| Guadeloupe | 340 | -0.12 | 0.47 | 0.34 |
| Guatemala | 9 197 | 2.77 | 2.82 | 2.88 |
| Guyana | 1 040 | 2.07 | 1.95 | 1.74 |
| Haiti | 6 504 | 1.76 | 1.80 | 1.88 |
| Honduras | 5 138 | 3.46 | 3.59 | 3.18 |
| Jamaica | 2 521 | 1.24 | 1.45 | 1.52 |
| Martinique | 331 | -0.14 | 0.12 | 0.18 |
| Mexico | 88 598 | 2.57 | 2.40 | 2.20 |
| Nicaragua | 3 871 | 2.81 | 3.32 | 3.36 |
| Panama | 2 418 | 2.26 | 2.17 | 2.07 |
| Paraguay | 4 277 | 3.20 | 3.20 | 2.93 |
| Peru | 22 332 | 2.63 | 2.60 | 2.51 |
| Puerto Rico | 3 709 | 1.33 | 1.51 | 1.44 |
| Suriname | 403 | -0.54 | 1.10 | 1.46 |
| Trinidad and Tobago | 1 283 | 1.64 | 1.58 | 1.59 |
| Uruguay | 3 128 | 0.56 | 0.70 | 0.76 |
| Venezuela | 19 736 | 3.42 | 2.84 | 2.61 |
| Developed market economies | 810 904 | 0.42 | 0.49 | 0.29 |
| Australia | 16 746 | 1.51 | 1.40 | 1.22 |
| Canada | 26 525 | 1.04 | 1.17 | 0.88 |
| Japan | 123 457 | 0.93 | 0.66 | 0.44 |
| New Zealand | 3 379 | 0.17 | 0.84 | 0.79 |
| South Africa | 35 248 | 2.22 | 2.21 | 2.19 |
| United States | 249 235 | 1.06 | 0.99 | 0.81 |

Table S.III.1. (Continued)

| Region and country or area[a] | Population 1990 (Thousands) | Annual rate of change 1975-1980 | 1980-1985 | 1985-1990 |
|---|---|---|---|---|
| | | (Percentage) | | |
| Europe | 356 314 | 0.33 | 0.39 | 0.19 |
| Austria | 7 492 | 0.08 | -0.13 | -0.03 |
| Belgium | 9 938 | 0.11 | 0.10 | 0.07 |
| Denmark | 5 120 | 0.25 | 0.00 | -0.01 |
| Finland | 4 975 | 0.29 | 0.51 | 0.29 |
| France | 56 173 | 0.44 | 0.47 | 0.36 |
| Germany, Federal Republic of | 60 539 | -0.09 | -0.18 | -0.16 |
| Greece | 10 047 | 1.28 | 0.60 | 0.23 |
| Iceland | 253 | 0.91 | 1.13 | 0.97 |
| Ireland | 3 720 | 1.18 | 0.87 | 0.92 |
| Italy | 57 322 | 0.36 | 0.24 | 0.07 |
| Luxembourg | 367 | 0.09 | 0.15 | 0.04 |
| Netherlands | 14 752 | 0.70 | 0.47 | 0.37 |
| Norway | 4 212 | 0.39 | 0.32 | 0.28 |
| Portugal | 10 285 | 1.43 | 0.78 | 0.25 |
| Spain | 39 333 | 1.06 | 0.56 | 0.38 |
| Sweden | 8 339 | 0.29 | 0.10 | -0.03 |
| Switzerland | 6 521 | -0.25 | 0.45 | 0.15 |
| United Kingdom | 56 926 | 0.04 | 0.10 | 0.11 |
| Centrally planned economies | 404 809 | 0.75 | 0.36 | 0.35 |
| Albania | 3 245 | 1.94 | 2.07 | 1.83 |
| Bulgaria | 9 010 | 0.32 | 0.22 | 0.11 |
| Czechoslovakia | 15 667 | 0.68 | 0.25 | 0.21 |
| German Democratic Republic | 16 649 | -0.13 | -0.11 | 0.01 |
| Hungary | 10 552 | 0.32 | -0.12 | -0.18 |
| Poland | 38 423 | 0.89 | 0.90 | 0.65 |
| Romania | 23 272 | 0.88 | 0.47 | 0.48 |
| USSR | 287 991 | 0.82 | 0.84 | 0.78 |

*Source: World Population Prospects, 1988* (United Nations publication, Sales No. E.88.XIII.7).

a Data for small countries or areas, generally those with population of 300,000 or less in 1985, are not given in this table separately. Data for regions are total population and respective median values for countries or areas listed. For the world, data in parentheses represent total population, including small countries or areas not listed here and respective weighted average values. The original source contains data for all countries or areas.

Table S.III.2. Infant mortality rates, 1970-1990, medium variant[a]

| Region and country or area[b] | 1970-1975 | 1975-1980 | 1980-1985 | 1985-1990 |
|---|---|---|---|---|
| World | 94 | 82 | 71 | 59 |
| | (94) | (86) | (79) | (71) |
| Developing countries | 110 | 96 | 84 | 73 |
| Africa | 138 | 126 | 116 | 106 |
| Algeria | 132 | 112 | 88 | 74 |
| Angola | 173 | 160 | 149 | 137 |
| Benin | 151 | 130 | 120 | 110 |
| Botswana | 95 | 82 | 76 | 67 |
| Burkina Faso | 173 | 162 | 149 | 138 |
| Burundi | 135 | 130 | 124 | 112 |
| Cameroon | 119 | 111 | 103 | 94 |
| Cape Verde | 103 | 87 | 75 | 66 |
| Central African Republic | 148 | 145 | 142 | 132 |
| Chad | 166 | 154 | 143 | 132 |
| Comoros | 106 | 97 | 88 | 80 |
| Congo | 90 | 85 | 81 | 73 |
| Côte d'Ivoire | 129 | 116 | 105 | 96 |
| Djibouti | 154 | 143 | 132 | 122 |
| Egypt | 150 | 120 | 100 | 85 |
| Equatorial Guinea | 160 | 149 | 137 | 127 |

Table S.III.2. (Continued)

| Region and country or area[b] | 1970-1975 | 1975-1980 | 1980-1985 | 1985-1990 |
|---|---|---|---|---|
| Ethiopia | 155 | 149 | 159 | 154 |
| Gabon | 132 | 122 | 112 | 103 |
| Gambia | 179 | 166 | 154 | 143 |
| Ghana | 107 | 103 | 98 | 90 |
| Guinea | 181 | 171 | 159 | 147 |
| Guinea-Bissau | 163 | 154 | 143 | 132 |
| Kenya | 98 | 88 | 80 | 72 |
| Lesotho | 130 | 123 | 111 | 100 |
| Liberia | 119 | 107 | 96 | 87 |
| Libyan Arab Jamahiriya | 117 | 107 | 97 | 82 |
| Madagascar | 172 | 150 | 130 | 120 |
| Malawi | 191 | 177 | 163 | 150 |
| Mali | 203 | 191 | 180 | 169 |
| Mauritania | 160 | 149 | 137 | 127 |
| Mauritius | 55 | 38 | 28 | 23 |
| Morocco | 122 | 110 | 97 | 82 |
| Mozambique | 168 | 160 | 153 | 141 |
| Namibia | 134 | 126 | 116 | 106 |
| Niger | 166 | 157 | 146 | 135 |
| Nigeria | 148 | 124 | 114 | 105 |
| Réunion | 41 | 19 | 16 | 14 |
| Rwanda | 140 | 140 | 132 | 122 |
| Senegal | 162 | 154 | 142 | 128 |
| Sierra Leone | 193 | 179 | 166 | 154 |
| Somalia | 155 | 149 | 143 | 132 |
| Sudan | 145 | 131 | 118 | 108 |
| Swaziland | 144 | 140 | 129 | 118 |
| Togo | 121 | 111 | 102 | 94 |
| Tunisia | 120 | 88 | 71 | 59 |
| Uganda | 116 | 114 | 112 | 103 |
| United Republic of Tanzania | 130 | 125 | 115 | 106 |
| Zaire | 127 | 117 | 107 | 98 |
| Zambia | 100 | 94 | 88 | 80 |
| Zimbabwe | 93 | 86 | 80 | 72 |
| South and East Asia | 103 | 88 | 75 | 62 |
| Afghanistan | 194 | 183 | 183 | 172 |
| Bangladesh | 140 | 137 | 128 | 119 |
| Bhutan | 153 | 147 | 139 | 128 |
| Burma | 100 | 90 | 80 | 70 |
| China | 61 | 41 | 39 | 32 |
| Democratic Kampuchea | 181 | 263 | 160 | 130 |
| East Timor | 183 | 254 | 183 | 166 |
| Fiji | 45 | 37 | 31 | 27 |
| Hong Kong | 17 | 13 | 10 | 8 |
| India | 135 | 126 | 110 | 99 |
| Indonesia | 114 | 105 | 95 | 84 |
| Korea | 47 | 35 | 30 | 25 |
| Democratic People's Republic of Korea | 47 | 35 | 30 | 24 |
| Republic of Korea | 47 | 35 | 30 | 25 |
| Lao People's Democratic Republic | 145 | 135 | 122 | 110 |
| Malaysia | 42 | 34 | 28 | 24 |
| Mongolia | 71 | 62 | 53 | 45 |
| Nepal | 153 | 147 | 139 | 128 |
| Pakistan | 140 | 130 | 120 | 109 |
| Papua New Guinea | 105 | 85 | 74 | 59 |
| Philippines | 64 | 54 | 51 | 45 |
| Singapore | 19 | 13 | 10 | 9 |
| Sri Lanka | 56 | 48 | 39 | 33 |
| Thailand | 65 | 56 | 48 | 39 |
| Viet Nam | 120 | 90 | 76 | 64 |
| West Asia | 85 | 68 | 57 | 46 |
| Bahrain | 55 | 38 | 32 | 26 |
| Democratic Yemen | 168 | 150 | 135 | 120 |
| Iran (Islamic Republic of) | 122 | 100 | 78 | 63 |
| Iraq | 96 | 83 | 77 | 69 |
| Israel | 23 | 18 | 14 | 12 |

Table S.III.2. (Continued)

| Region and country or area[b] | 1970-1975 | 1975-1980 | 1980-1985 | 1985-1990 |
|---|---|---|---|---|
| Jordan | 82 | 65 | 54 | 44 |
| Kuwait | 43 | 34 | 23 | 19 |
| Lebanon | 48 | 48 | 48 | 40 |
| Oman | 160 | 135 | 117 | 100 |
| Qatar | 57 | 46 | 38 | 31 |
| Saudi Arabia | 120 | 100 | 85 | 71 |
| Syrian Arab Republic | 88 | 70 | 59 | 48 |
| United Arab Emirates | 57 | 38 | 32 | 26 |
| Yemen | 168 | 144 | 130 | 116 |
| Mediterranean | 37 | 28 | 23 | 19 |
| Cyprus | 29 | 20 | 16 | 12 |
| Malta | 26 | 18 | 13 | 10 |
| Turkey | 138 | 120 | 92 | 76 |
| Yugoslavia | 45 | 35 | 30 | 25 |
| Western hemisphere | 55 | 48 | 38 | 34 |
| Argentina | 49 | 41 | 36 | 32 |
| Barbados | 27 | 14 | 11 | 11 |
| Bolivia | 151 | 138 | 124 | 110 |
| Brazil | 91 | 79 | 71 | 63 |
| Chile | 70 | 46 | 23 | 20 |
| Colombia | 65 | 55 | 50 | 46 |
| Costa Rica | 51 | 30 | 20 | 18 |
| Cuba | 36 | 23 | 17 | 15 |
| Dominican Republic | 94 | 84 | 75 | 65 |
| Ecuador | 95 | 82 | 70 | 63 |
| El Salvador | 97 | 82 | 70 | 59 |
| Guadeloupe | 42 | 25 | 14 | 12 |
| Guatemala | 95 | 82 | 70 | 59 |
| Guyana | 56 | 49 | 36 | 30 |
| Haiti | 155 | 139 | 128 | 117 |
| Honduras | 110 | 95 | 82 | 69 |
| Jamaica | 36 | 25 | 21 | 18 |
| Martinique | 35 | 22 | 14 | 13 |
| Mexico | 69 | 60 | 53 | 47 |
| Nicaragua | 100 | 93 | 76 | 62 |
| Panama | 43 | 32 | 26 | 23 |
| Paraguay | 53 | 49 | 45 | 42 |
| Peru | 110 | 105 | 99 | 88 |
| Puerto Rico | 25 | 20 | 17 | 15 |
| Suriname | 49 | 44 | 36 | 31 |
| Trinidad and Tobago | 30 | 26 | 24 | 20 |
| Uruguay | 47 | 44 | 30 | 27 |
| Venezuela | 49 | 43 | 39 | 36 |
| Developed market economies | 17 | 13 | 10 | 9 |
| Australia | 17 | 12 | 10 | 8 |
| Canada | 16 | 12 | 9 | 7 |
| Japan | 12 | 9 | 7 | 5 |
| New Zealand | 16 | 14 | 12 | 11 |
| South Africa | 110 | 95 | 83 | 72 |
| United States | 18 | 14 | 11 | 10 |
| Europe | 17 | 13 | 9 | 9 |
| Austria | 24 | 16 | 12 | 11 |
| Belgium | 19 | 13 | 11 | 10 |
| Denmark | 12 | 9 | 8 | 7 |
| Finland | 12 | 9 | 6 | 6 |
| France | 16 | 11 | 9 | 8 |
| Germany, Federal Republic of | 22 | 15 | 11 | 9 |
| Greece | 34 | 25 | 15 | 17 |
| Iceland | 12 | 9 | 6 | 5 |
| Ireland | 18 | 15 | 9 | 9 |
| Italy | 22 | 15 | 13 | 11 |
| Luxembourg | 16 | 13 | 9 | 10 |
| Netherlands | 12 | 10 | 8 | 8 |
| Norway | 12 | 9 | 8 | 7 |
| Portugal | 45 | 30 | 20 | 15 |

Table S.III.2. (Continued)

| Region and country or area[b] | 1970-1975 | 1975-1980 | 1980-1985 | 1985-1990 |
|---|---|---|---|---|
| Spain | 21 | 16 | 11 | 10 |
| Sweden | 10 | 8 | 7 | 6 |
| Switzerland | 13 | 10 | 8 | 7 |
| United Kingdom | 17 | 14 | 11 | 9 |
| Centrally planned economies | 27 | 25 | 20 | 15 |
| Albania | 58 | 50 | 45 | 39 |
| Bulgaria | 26 | 22 | 17 | 16 |
| Czechoslovakia | 21 | 19 | 16 | 15 |
| German Democratic Republic | 17 | 13 | 11 | 9 |
| Hungary | 34 | 27 | 20 | 20 |
| Poland | 27 | 23 | 20 | 18 |
| Romania | 40 | 31 | 26 | 22 |
| USSR | 26 | 28 | 26 | 24 |

*Source: World Population Prospects, 1988* (United Nations publication, Sales No. E.88.XIII.7).

a Number of deaths of children less than one year old, per 1,000 live births.

b Data for small countries or areas, generally those with population of 300,000 or less in 1985, are not given in this table separately. Data for regions are median values for countries or areas listed. For the world, data in parentheses are weighted average for all countries or areas.

Table S.III.3. Life expectancy at birth, males and females, 1970-1990, medium variant

*(In years)*

| Region and country or area[a] | 1970-1975 | | 1975-1980 | | 1980-1985 | | 1985-1990 | |
|---|---|---|---|---|---|---|---|---|
| | M | F | M | F | M | F | M | F |
| World | 56.2<br>(55.6) | 59.1<br>(57.8) | 58.8<br>(56.9) | 62.4<br>(59.4) | 60.5<br>(58.2) | 64.0<br>(61.1) | 62.6<br>(60.0) | 66.0<br>(63.0) |
| Developing countries | 51.1 | 53.7 | 53.6 | 57.1 | 56.2 | 59.8 | 58.7 | 61.9 |
| Africa | 43.2 | 46.8 | 45.2 | 48.9 | 49.2 | 50.7 | 49.2 | 52.9 |
| Algeria | 52.5 | 54.5 | 55.0 | 57.1 | 58.5 | 61.6 | 61.0 | 64.1 |
| Angola | 36.5 | 39.6 | 38.5 | 41.6 | 40.4 | 43.6 | 42.9 | 46.1 |
| Benin | 38.5 | 41.6 | 40.4 | 43.6 | 42.4 | 45.6 | 44.9 | 48.1 |
| Botswana | 49.0 | 53.0 | 51.0 | 56.0 | 53.0 | 59.0 | 55.5 | 61.5 |
| Burkina Faso | 39.7 | 42.8 | 41.6 | 44.9 | 43.7 | 46.8 | 45.6 | 48.9 |
| Burundi | 43.0 | 46.2 | 43.4 | 46.6 | 44.9 | 48.1 | 47.4 | 50.7 |
| Cameroon | 43.0 | 47.0 | 45.0 | 49.0 | 47.0 | 51.0 | 49.0 | 53.0 |
| Cape Verde | 51.7 | 54.0 | 54.9 | 58.3 | 57.3 | 60.8 | 59.3 | 62.8 |
| Central African Republic | 39.4 | 42.6 | 40.4 | 43.6 | 41.4 | 44.6 | 43.9 | 47.1 |
| Chad | 37.5 | 40.6 | 39.4 | 42.6 | 41.4 | 44.6 | 43.9 | 47.1 |
| Comoros | 44.9 | 48.1 | 46.4 | 49.7 | 48.3 | 51.7 | 50.3 | 53.8 |
| Congo | 40.9 | 44.1 | 42.9 | 46.1 | 44.9 | 48.1 | 46.9 | 50.2 |
| Côte d'Ivoire | 43.9 | 47.1 | 46.4 | 49.7 | 48.8 | 52.2 | 50.8 | 54.2 |
| Djibouti | 39.4 | 42.6 | 41.4 | 44.6 | 43.4 | 46.6 | 45.4 | 48.7 |
| Egypt | 50.8 | 53.4 | 54.3 | 57.0 | 56.8 | 59.5 | 59.3 | 62.0 |
| Equatorial Guinea | 38.5 | 41.6 | 40.4 | 43.6 | 42.4 | 45.6 | 44.9 | 48.1 |
| Ethiopia | 39.4 | 42.6 | 40.4 | 43.6 | 38.4 | 41.6 | 39.4 | 42.6 |
| Gabon | 43.4 | 46.6 | 45.4 | 48.7 | 47.4 | 50.7 | 49.9 | 53.2 |
| Gambia | 35.5 | 38.6 | 37.5 | 40.6 | 39.4 | 42.6 | 41.4 | 44.6 |
| Ghana | 48.3 | 51.7 | 49.3 | 52.7 | 50.3 | 53.8 | 52.2 | 55.8 |
| Guinea | 35.2 | 38.3 | 36.7 | 39.8 | 38.7 | 41.8 | 40.6 | 43.8 |
| Guinea-Bissau | 38.0 | 41.1 | 39.4 | 42.6 | 41.4 | 44.6 | 43.4 | 46.6 |
| Kenya | 49.0 | 53.0 | 51.5 | 55.5 | 54.0 | 58.0 | 56.5 | 60.5 |
| Lesotho | 44.0 | 53.0 | 46.5 | 55.5 | 49.0 | 58.0 | 51.5 | 60.5 |
| Liberia | 46.0 | 49.0 | 48.5 | 51.5 | 51.0 | 54.0 | 53.0 | 56.0 |
| Libyan Arab Jamahiriya | 51.4 | 54.5 | 54.1 | 57.5 | 56.6 | 60.0 | 59.1 | 62.5 |
| Madagascar | 45.0 | 48.0 | 48.0 | 51.0 | 50.0 | 53.0 | 52.0 | 55.0 |
| Malawi | 40.3 | 41.7 | 42.4 | 43.7 | 44.4 | 45.7 | 46.3 | 47.7 |
| Mali | 37.0 | 40.1 | 38.5 | 41.6 | 40.4 | 43.6 | 42.4 | 45.6 |

Table S.III.3. (Continued)

| Region and country or area[a] | 1970-1975 M | 1970-1975 F | 1975-1980 M | 1975-1980 F | 1980-1985 M | 1980-1985 F | 1985-1990 M | 1985-1990 F |
|---|---|---|---|---|---|---|---|---|
| Mauritania | 38.5 | 41.6 | 40.4 | 43.6 | 42.4 | 45.6 | 44.4 | 47.6 |
| Mauritius | 60.7 | 65.3 | 62.6 | 67.3 | 64.3 | 69.2 | 66.4 | 71.7 |
| Morocco | 51.4 | 54.5 | 54.1 | 57.5 | 56.6 | 60.0 | 59.1 | 62.5 |
| Mozambique | 40.9 | 44.1 | 41.9 | 45.1 | 42.9 | 46.1 | 44.9 | 48.1 |
| Namibia | 47.5 | 50.0 | 50.0 | 52.5 | 52.5 | 55.0 | 55.0 | 57.5 |
| Niger | 37.5 | 40.6 | 39.0 | 42.1 | 40.9 | 44.1 | 42.9 | 46.1 |
| Nigeria | 42.9 | 46.1 | 44.9 | 48.1 | 46.9 | 50.2 | 48.8 | 52.2 |
| Réunion | 60.4 | 68.1 | 63.5 | 72.5 | 65.5 | 74.0 | 67.0 | 75.0 |
| Rwanda | 43.0 | 46.2 | 43.4 | 46.6 | 44.9 | 48.1 | 46.9 | 50.2 |
| Senegal | 38.5 | 41.6 | 39.7 | 42.9 | 41.7 | 44.9 | 44.2 | 47.4 |
| Sierra Leone | 33.5 | 36.5 | 35.5 | 38.6 | 37.5 | 40.6 | 39.4 | 42.6 |
| Somalia | 39.4 | 42.6 | 40.4 | 43.6 | 41.4 | 44.6 | 43.4 | 46.6 |
| Sudan | 41.4 | 43.9 | 43.9 | 46.4 | 46.6 | 49.0 | 48.6 | 51.0 |
| Swaziland | 45.1 | 49.6 | 47.6 | 52.3 | 51.2 | 54.8 | 53.7 | 57.3 |
| Togo | 43.9 | 47.1 | 46.4 | 49.7 | 48.8 | 52.2 | 51.3 | 54.8 |
| Tunisia | 55.1 | 56.1 | 59.6 | 60.6 | 62.6 | 63.6 | 64.6 | 66.1 |
| Uganda | 45.4 | 48.6 | 46.4 | 49.7 | 47.4 | 50.7 | 49.4 | 52.7 |
| United Republic of Tanzania | 44.9 | 48.1 | 47.3 | 50.7 | 49.3 | 52.7 | 51.3 | 54.7 |
| Zaire | 44.4 | 47.6 | 46.4 | 49.7 | 48.3 | 51.7 | 50.8 | 54.2 |
| Zambia | 45.7 | 49.0 | 47.7 | 51.0 | 50.4 | 52.5 | 52.4 | 54.5 |
| Zimbabwe | 49.8 | 53.2 | 52.0 | 55.6 | 54.0 | 57.6 | 56.5 | 60.1 |
| South and East Asia | 51.1 | 53.6 | 53.6 | 57.4 | 56.3 | 60.2 | 58.8 | 62.7 |
| Afghanistan | 38.0 | 38.0 | 40.0 | 40.0 | 40.0 | 41.0 | 41.0 | 42.0 |
| Bangladesh | 45.6 | 44.1 | 47.1 | 46.1 | 49.1 | 48.1 | 51.1 | 50.4 |
| Bhutan | 43.0 | 41.5 | 44.6 | 43.1 | 46.6 | 45.1 | 48.6 | 47.1 |
| Burma | 51.0 | 54.1 | 53.4 | 56.7 | 55.8 | 59.3 | 58.3 | 61.8 |
| China | 62.5 | 63.9 | 65.5 | 66.2 | 66.7 | 68.9 | 68.0 | 70.9 |
| Democratic Kampuchea | 39.0 | 41.7 | 30.0 | 32.5 | 42.0 | 44.9 | 47.0 | 49.9 |
| East Timor | 39.2 | 40.7 | 30.0 | 32.5 | 39.2 | 40.7 | 41.6 | 43.4 |
| Fiji | 63.6 | 66.7 | 65.5 | 69.0 | 67.0 | 71.0 | 68.2 | 72.7 |
| Hong Kong | 68.5 | 75.6 | 70.5 | 76.8 | 72.6 | 78.3 | 73.4 | 79.1 |
| India | 51.2 | 49.3 | 53.3 | 52.4 | 55.6 | 55.2 | 57.8 | 57.9 |
| Indonesia | 46.4 | 48.7 | 48.7 | 51.3 | 52.2 | 54.9 | 54.6 | 57.4 |
| Korea | 59.2 | 64.0 | 62.4 | 68.8 | 64.6 | 71.0 | 66.2 | 72.6 |
| Democratic People's Republic of Korea | 59.2 | 64.0 | 62.4 | 68.8 | 64.6 | 71.0 | 66.2 | 72.7 |
| Republic of Korea | 59.2 | 64.0 | 62.4 | 68.8 | 64.6 | 71.0 | 66.2 | 72.5 |
| Lao People's Democratic Republic | 39.1 | 41.8 | 42.1 | 45.0 | 44.5 | 47.5 | 47.0 | 50.0 |
| Malaysia | 61.4 | 64.7 | 63.5 | 67.1 | 66.0 | 70.0 | 67.5 | 71.6 |
| Mongolia | 59.1 | 62.3 | 59.3 | 62.8 | 60.0 | 64.1 | 61.5 | 65.6 |
| Nepal | 44.0 | 42.5 | 46.5 | 45.0 | 49.0 | 47.5 | 51.5 | 50.3 |
| Pakistan | 50.0 | 48.0 | 52.0 | 51.0 | 54.0 | 54.0 | 56.5 | 56.5 |
| Papua New Guinea | 47.7 | 47.6 | 50.5 | 50.0 | 51.2 | 52.7 | 53.2 | 54.8 |
| Philippines | 56.4 | 59.4 | 58.3 | 61.5 | 60.2 | 63.7 | 61.6 | 65.4 |
| Singapore | 67.4 | 71.8 | 68.6 | 73.1 | 69.2 | 74.6 | 70.2 | 75.7 |
| Sri Lanka | 64.0 | 66.0 | 65.0 | 68.5 | 67.0 | 71.0 | 68.3 | 72.5 |
| Thailand | 57.7 | 61.6 | 59.3 | 63.2 | 60.7 | 64.8 | 63.0 | 67.1 |
| Viet Nam | 47.7 | 53.1 | 53.7 | 58.1 | 56.7 | 61.1 | 59.2 | 63.6 |
| West Asia | 56.2 | 58.5 | 60.0 | 62.7 | 61.7 | 65.0 | 64.6 | 67.4 |
| Bahrain | 61.7 | 65.4 | 65.6 | 69.5 | 67.1 | 71.4 | 68.6 | 72.9 |
| Democratic Yemen | 42.5 | 44.3 | 44.7 | 47.1 | 46.9 | 49.9 | 49.4 | 52.4 |
| Iran (Islamic Republic of) | 56.2 | 55.5 | 58.2 | 59.0 | 59.4 | 63.0 | 65.0 | 65.5 |
| Iraq | 56.1 | 57.9 | 60.5 | 62.3 | 61.5 | 63.3 | 63.0 | 64.8 |
| Israel | 70.1 | 73.3 | 71.4 | 74.9 | 72.8 | 76.2 | 73.6 | 77.2 |
| Jordan | 54.9 | 58.3 | 59.4 | 63.0 | 61.9 | 65.5 | 64.2 | 67.8 |
| Kuwait | 65.3 | 69.3 | 67.5 | 71.7 | 69.6 | 73.7 | 70.7 | 75.0 |
| Lebanon | 63.1 | 67.0 | 63.1 | 67.0 | 63.1 | 67.0 | 65.1 | 69.0 |
| Oman | 45.2 | 47.6 | 48.0 | 50.8 | 51.0 | 53.7 | 54.1 | 56.8 |
| Qatar | 60.7 | 64.4 | 63.5 | 67.6 | 65.4 | 69.8 | 66.9 | 71.8 |
| Saudi Arabia | 52.4 | 55.5 | 56.2 | 59.7 | 59.2 | 62.7 | 61.7 | 65.2 |
| Syrian Arab Republic | 55.4 | 58.7 | 58.3 | 61.9 | 60.8 | 64.4 | 63.2 | 66.9 |
| United Arab Emirates | 60.7 | 64.4 | 64.7 | 68.9 | 67.1 | 71.4 | 68.6 | 72.9 |
| Yemen | 42.5 | 44.3 | 44.7 | 47.1 | 46.9 | 49.9 | 49.5 | 52.4 |

Table S.III.3. (Continued)

| Region and country or area[a] | 1970-1975 M | 1970-1975 F | 1975-1980 M | 1975-1980 F | 1980-1985 M | 1980-1985 F | 1985-1990 M | 1985-1990 F |
|---|---|---|---|---|---|---|---|---|
| Mediterranean | 67.3 | 71.9 | 68.2 | 73.1 | 69.0 | 73.5 | 70.1 | 70.4 |
| Cyprus | 70.0 | 72.9 | 72.0 | 75.5 | 72.5 | 77.5 | 73.3 | 78.2 |
| Malta | 68.5 | 72.8 | 68.8 | 73.3 | 70.0 | 73.4 | 71.0 | 47.6 |
| Turkey | 55.9 | 60.0 | 58.0 | 62.5 | 60.0 | 63.3 | 62.5 | 65.8 |
| Yugoslavia | 66.0 | 70.9 | 67.6 | 72.9 | 67.9 | 73.5 | 69.1 | 75.0 |
| Western hemisphere | 62.3 | 67.1 | 64.0 | 68.8 | 65.7 | 70.7 | 66.9 | 72.3 |
| Argentina | 64.1 | 70.7 | 65.4 | 72.1 | 66.4 | 73.1 | 67.3 | 74.0 |
| Barbados | 66.9 | 72.0 | 68.7 | 73.9 | 70.0 | 75.4 | 71.0 | 77.0 |
| Bolivia | 44.6 | 49.0 | 46.5 | 50.9 | 48.6 | 53.0 | 50.9 | 55.4 |
| Brazil | 57.6 | 62.2 | 59.5 | 64.3 | 60.9 | 66.0 | 62.3 | 67.6 |
| Chile | 60.5 | 66.8 | 63.9 | 70.6 | 67.6 | 74.6 | 68.1 | 75.1 |
| Colombia | 58.2 | 62.7 | 60.0 | 64.5 | 61.4 | 66.0 | 62.6 | 67.2 |
| Costa Rica | 66.1 | 70.2 | 68.6 | 73.1 | 71.3 | 75.9 | 72.4 | 77.0 |
| Cuba | 69.3 | 72.6 | 71.1 | 74.4 | 71.8 | 75.2 | 72.2 | 75.8 |
| Dominican Republic | 58.1 | 61.8 | 60.3 | 64.0 | 62.2 | 66.1 | 63.9 | 68.1 |
| Ecuador | 57.4 | 60.5 | 59.7 | 63.2 | 62.3 | 66.4 | 63.4 | 67.6 |
| El Salvador | 56.6 | 61.1 | 52.4 | 62.6 | 50.7 | 63.9 | 58.0 | 66.5 |
| Guadeloupe | 64.7 | 70.9 | 66.4 | 73.4 | 68.9 | 76.1 | 70.1 | 76.7 |
| Guatemala | 52.6 | 55.5 | 54.5 | 58.4 | 56.8 | 61.3 | 59.7 | 64.4 |
| Guyana | 61.9 | 66.4 | 64.1 | 68.9 | 65.8 | 70.8 | 67.3 | 72.3 |
| Haiti | 47.1 | 50.0 | 49.1 | 52.2 | 51.2 | 54.4 | 53.1 | 56.4 |
| Honduras | 52.2 | 55.8 | 55.8 | 59.6 | 60.0 | 64.0 | 61.9 | 66.1 |
| Jamaica | 66.0 | 69.7 | 67.0 | 71.0 | 70.3 | 75.7 | 71.3 | 76.7 |
| Martinique | 66.7 | 71.0 | 68.9 | 73.3 | 71.0 | 75.5 | 72.0 | 76.5 |
| Mexico | 60.4 | 64.9 | 62.6 | 68.2 | 64.2 | 70.6 | 65.7 | 72.3 |
| Nicaragua | 53.7 | 55.8 | 55.3 | 57.3 | 58.7 | 61.0 | 62.0 | 64.6 |
| Panama | 65.0 | 67.8 | 67.6 | 70.9 | 69.2 | 72.9 | 70.1 | 74.1 |
| Paraguay | 63.7 | 67.6 | 64.1 | 68.1 | 64.4 | 68.6 | 64.8 | 69.1 |
| Peru | 53.9 | 57.3 | 55.2 | 58.8 | 56.8 | 60.5 | 59.5 | 63.4 |
| Puerto Rico | 69.0 | 76.2 | 70.2 | 77.0 | 70.5 | 77.6 | 71.5 | 78.4 |
| Suriname | 62.7 | 67.3 | 63.8 | 68.6 | 65.6 | 70.6 | 67.1 | 72.1 |
| Trinidad and Tobago | 64.4 | 68.7 | 65.1 | 70.0 | 66.2 | 71.3 | 67.7 | 72.8 |
| Uruguay | 65.6 | 72.2 | 66.4 | 73.0 | 67.1 | 73.7 | 67.8 | 74.4 |
| Venezuela | 63.5 | 69.1 | 64.9 | 70.7 | 66.0 | 72.1 | 66.7 | 72.8 |
| Developed market economies | 69.0 | 75.2 | 69.9 | 77.0 | 71.3 | 78.0 | 72.4 | 78.9 |
| Australia | 68.4 | 75.2 | 70.1 | 77.0 | 71.9 | 78.7 | 72.9 | 79.5 |
| Canada | 69.7 | 76.8 | 70.5 | 78.1 | 72.4 | 79.6 | 73.3 | 80.3 |
| Japan | 70.6 | 76.2 | 72.8 | 78.2 | 74.2 | 79.7 | 75.4 | 81.1 |
| New Zealand | 68.7 | 74.8 | 69.3 | 75.7 | 70.7 | 76.9 | 71.8 | 77.9 |
| South Africa | 51.0 | 57.0 | 53.0 | 59.0 | 55.0 | 61.0 | 57.5 | 63.5 |
| United States | 67.5 | 75.3 | 69.4 | 77.2 | 70.9 | 78.3 | 71.9 | 79.0 |
| Europe | 69.1 | 75.2 | 70.1 | 76.8 | 71.2 | 77.7 | 72.4 | 78.6 |
| Austria | 67.0 | 74.3 | 68.5 | 75.6 | 69.6 | 76.8 | 70.6 | 77.8 |
| Belgium | 68.2 | 74.7 | 69.1 | 75.7 | 70.4 | 77.2 | 71.5 | 78.1 |
| Denmark | 70.9 | 76.4 | 71.3 | 77.3 | 71.6 | 77.5 | 72.6 | 78.3 |
| Finland | 66.6 | 75.0 | 68.0 | 76.6 | 70.0 | 77.9 | 71.0 | 78.8 |
| France | 68.6 | 76.3 | 69.0 | 77.8 | 70.7 | 78.9 | 71.7 | 79.8 |
| Germany, Federal Republic of | 67.6 | 73.7 | 69.0 | 75.8 | 70.6 | 77.3 | 71.6 | 78.2 |
| Greece | 70.6 | 74.2 | 71.7 | 75.8 | 72.7 | 76.9 | 73.5 | 77.9 |
| Iceland | 71.4 | 77.4 | 73.4 | 79.3 | 73.9 | 79.8 | 74.8 | 80.4 |
| Ireland | 68.9 | 73.8 | 69.6 | 74.6 | 70.4 | 75.9 | 71.5 | 76.9 |
| Italy | 69.2 | 75.2 | 70.4 | 76.9 | 71.4 | 78.0 | 72.4 | 79.1 |
| Luxembourg | 67.0 | 74.1 | 68.2 | 75.5 | 70.0 | 76.7 | 71.0 | 77.7 |
| Netherlands | 71.1 | 77.0 | 72.1 | 78.6 | 72.8 | 79.5 | 73.5 | 80.2 |
| Norway | 71.4 | 77.6 | 72.2 | 78.6 | 72.7 | 79.5 | 73.5 | 80.2 |
| Portugal | 64.9 | 71.3 | 66.7 | 73.8 | 68.8 | 75.8 | 70.0 | 76.8 |
| Spain | 70.2 | 75.7 | 71.4 | 77.4 | 72.8 | 78.9 | 73.6 | 79.7 |
| Sweden | 72.1 | 77.5 | 72.3 | 78.3 | 73.4 | 79.3 | 74.2 | 80.1 |
| Switzerland | 70.8 | 77.0 | 72.0 | 78.6 | 73.0 | 79.7 | 73.8 | 80.4 |
| United Kingdom | 69.0 | 75.2 | 69.7 | 76.0 | 71.0 | 77.2 | 72.4 | 78.1 |
| Centrally planned economies | 66.9 | 73.5 | 67.0 | 73.7 | 67.0 | 74.0 | 67.5 | 74.6 |
| Albania | 66.0 | 69.5 | 66.8 | 71.2 | 68.0 | 73.0 | 69.2 | 74.2 |

Table S.III.3. (Continued)

| Region and country or area[a] | 1970-1975 M | 1970-1975 F | 1975-1980 M | 1975-1980 F | 1980-1985 M | 1980-1985 F | 1985-1990 M | 1985-1990 F |
|---|---|---|---|---|---|---|---|---|
| Bulgaria | 68.7 | 74.1 | 68.5 | 74.1 | 68.5 | 74.4 | 69.2 | 75.0 |
| Czechoslovakia | 66.6 | 73.5 | 67.0 | 74.1 | 67.0 | 74.4 | 67.5 | 75.0 |
| German Democratic Republic | 68.6 | 73.9 | 68.8 | 74.6 | 69.3 | 75.2 | 70.4 | 76.2 |
| Hungary | 67.0 | 72.9 | 66.8 | 73.3 | 65.8 | 73.5 | 66.5 | 74.0 |
| Poland | 67.0 | 74.1 | 67.0 | 75.0 | 67.0 | 75.0 | 67.5 | 75.5 |
| Romania | 66.8 | 71.3 | 67.3 | 72.0 | 66.9 | 72.5 | 67.5 | 73.0 |
| USSR | 64.0 | 73.5 | 63.0 | 73.0 | 63.0 | 73.0 | 65.0 | 74.2 |

*Source: World Population Prospects, 1988* (United Nations publication, Sales No. E.88.XIII.7).

a Data for small countries or areas, generally those with population of 300,000 or less in 1985, are not given in this table separately. Data for regions are median values for countries or areas listed. For the world, data in parentheses are weighted averages for all countries or areas.

Table S.III.4. Child and old-age dependency ratios, 1975-1990, medium variant

| Region and country or area[c] | Child[a] 1975 | Child 1980 | Child 1985 | Child 1990 | Old age[b] 1975 | Old age 1980 | Old age 1985 | Old age 1990 |
|---|---|---|---|---|---|---|---|---|
| World | 77.5 | 73.7 | 69.4 | 64.7 | 6.7 | 6.7 | 6.7 | 6.7 |
| | (64.2) | (59.9) | (55.4) | (52.6) | (9.9) | (10.1) | (9.9) | (10.1) |
| Developing countries | 81.3 | 77.8 | 77.0 | 76.4 | 6.1 | 6.2 | 6.2 | 6.3 |
| Africa | 83.4 | 84.3 | 86.6 | 87.0 | 5.6 | 5.7 | 5.9 | 5.9 |
| Algeria | 98.8 | 93.8 | 90.1 | 85.2 | 8.7 | 7.9 | 7.2 | 6.6 |
| Angola | 81.2 | 83.6 | 85.1 | 86.2 | 5.5 | 5.6 | 5.7 | 5.8 |
| Benin | 86.9 | 90.1 | 92.8 | 95.7 | 6.8 | 6.0 | 5.7 | 5.5 |
| Botswana | 105.8 | 99.5 | 100.9 | 100.7 | 4.5 | 10.8 | 8.1 | 7.1 |
| Burkina Faso | 82.5 | 82.2 | 82.0 | 82.4 | 5.2 | 5.3 | 5.4 | 5.6 |
| Burundi | 78.3 | 82.3 | 86.3 | 89.3 | 5.9 | 6.2 | 6.4 | 6.6 |
| Cameroon | 75.9 | 78.8 | 82.1 | 82.9 | 6.9 | 7.2 | 7.4 | 7.4 |
| Cape Verde | 97.9 | 96.0 | 78.5 | 76.6 | 11.4 | 12.8 | 9.6 | 7.3 |
| Central African Republic | 73.2 | 76.4 | 79.3 | 81.8 | 7.1 | 7.2 | 7.2 | 7.2 |
| Chad | 76.1 | 76.9 | 78.2 | 79.9 | 6.6 | 6.6 | 6.6 | 6.7 |
| Comoros | 87.7 | 88.8 | 90.2 | 90.4 | 5.5 | 5.5 | 5.6 | 5.6 |
| Congo | 79.3 | 80.8 | 82.3 | 83.5 | 6.1 | 6.2 | 6.3 | 6.4 |
| Côte d'Ivoire | 95.6 | 97.7 | 100.0 | 102.3 | 4.6 | 4.6 | 4.6 | 4.6 |
| Djibouti | 83.7 | 85.9 | 87.8 | 88.4 | 4.0 | 4.1 | 4.3 | 4.6 |
| Egypt | 71.7 | 71.5 | 72.8 | 74.0 | 7.6 | 7.3 | 7.0 | 7.0 |
| Equatorial Guinea | 71.5 | 74.0 | 76.1 | 78.0 | 7.7 | 7.6 | 7.6 | 7.6 |
| Ethiopia | 83.8 | 84.0 | 93.0 | 87.1 | 4.9 | 5.0 | 8.2 | 6.8 |
| Gabon | 52.3 | 53.1 | 57.3 | 52.0 | 9.3 | 9.6 | 9.8 | 9.4 |
| Gambia | 76.4 | 78.2 | 80.8 | 82.7 | 5.2 | 5.2 | 5.3 | 5.5 |
| Ghana | 87.5 | 85.7 | 87.2 | 87.6 | 5.2 | 5.3 | 5.4 | 5.5 |
| Guinea | 78.3 | 79.0 | 79.7 | 81.7 | 5.2 | 5.3 | 5.4 | 5.6 |
| Guinea-Bissau | 67.7 | 72.2 | 74.0 | 75.9 | 7.5 | 7.6 | 7.7 | 7.8 |
| Kenya | 104.1 | 107.7 | 111.9 | 115.3 | 7.8 | 7.3 | 6.7 | 6.2 |
| Lesotho | 76.2 | 77.0 | 79.3 | 81.2 | 6.5 | 6.6 | 6.8 | 6.9 |
| Liberia | 83.0 | 85.0 | 87.0 | 89.5 | 6.0 | 6.1 | 6.2 | 6.3 |
| Libyan Arab Jamahiriya | 89.0 | 91.3 | 90.5 | 88.6 | 4.4 | 4.4 | 4.5 | 4.7 |
| Madagascar | 82.9 | 83.2 | 84.6 | 86.8 | 5.6 | 5.6 | 5.7 | 5.7 |
| Malawi | 93.4 | 90.9 | 89.6 | 89.9 | 4.3 | 4.5 | 5.0 | 5.2 |
| Mali | 87.7 | 89.7 | 90.7 | 92.1 | 5.2 | 5.4 | 5.3 | 5.4 |
| Mauritania | 80.5 | 82.1 | 83.7 | 85.2 | 5.6 | 5.7 | 5.8 | 5.9 |
| Mauritius | 68.9 | 54.3 | 46.5 | 42.1 | 4.8 | 4.9 | 5.3 | 6.2 |
| Morocco | 96.0 | 82.0 | 78.2 | 73.0 | 7.4 | 7.7 | 7.2 | 6.5 |
| Mozambique | 82.7 | 81.3 | 82.2 | 83.5 | 5.9 | 5.9 | 6.0 | 6.1 |
| Namibia | 82.4 | 84.9 | 87.4 | 89.7 | 6.1 | 6.2 | 6.3 | 6.4 |
| Niger | 87.7 | 91.3 | 93.4 | 94.8 | 7.9 | 7.5 | 6.5 | 5.7 |

Table S.III.4. (Continued)

| Region and country or area[c] | Child[a] 1975 | Child[a] 1980 | Child[a] 1985 | Child[a] 1990 | Old age[b] 1975 | Old age[b] 1980 | Old age[b] 1985 | Old age[b] 1990 |
|---|---|---|---|---|---|---|---|---|
| Nigeria | 95.3 | 97.3 | 97.8 | 98.6 | 4.8 | 4.9 | 4.9 | 5.0 |
| Réunion | 77.5 | 66.1 | 53.7 | 49.4 | 7.1 | 7.6 | 7.6 | 8.3 |
| Rwanda | 97.7 | 99.8 | 100.6 | 100.6 | 4.9 | 4.9 | 4.9 | 4.9 |
| Senegal | 82.3 | 83.4 | 84.2 | 84.6 | 5.5 | 5.5 | 5.6 | 5.7 |
| Sierra Leone | 78.2 | 80.6 | 82.8 | 84.7 | 5.8 | 5.9 | 5.9 | 6.0 |
| Somalia | 84.2 | 81.2 | 89.3 | 95.8 | 5.9 | 5.4 | 5.3 | 5.3 |
| Sudan | 84.1 | 85.6 | 86.9 | 87.1 | 5.1 | 5.2 | 5.3 | 5.5 |
| Swaziland | 88.5 | 90.6 | 93.1 | 95.2 | 5.6 | 5.7 | 5.9 | 5.9 |
| Togo | 83.0 | 84.6 | 86.1 | 88.2 | 5.9 | 6.1 | 6.1 | 6.2 |
| Tunisia | 83.1 | 76.2 | 70.0 | 64.9 | 6.7 | 6.9 | 6.8 | 6.9 |
| Uganda | 94.6 | 96.2 | 97.3 | 99.2 | 5.1 | 5.1 | 5.1 | 5.1 |
| United Republic of Tanzania | 96.0 | 98.1 | 98.9 | 101.2 | 4.7 | 4.7 | 4.7 | 4.8 |
| Zaire | 84.8 | 90.1 | 89.9 | 90.0 | 5.4 | 4.9 | 4.9 | 5.0 |
| Zambia | 91.5 | 102.4 | 99.3 | 101.2 | 5.1 | 5.0 | 4.8 | 4.7 |
| Zimbabwe | 101.2 | 96.5 | 90.6 | 85.4 | 5.4 | 5.2 | 5.3 | 5.2 |
| South and East Asia | 76.1 | 71.3 | 66.9 | 62.2 | 6.1 | 6.2 | 6.1 | 6.3 |
| Afghanistan | 81.2 | 78.9 | 75.3 | 75.9 | 4.4 | 4.7 | 4.8 | 5.0 |
| Bangladesh | 90.8 | 91.6 | 89.4 | 82.5 | 7.1 | 6.8 | 6.0 | 5.5 |
| Bhutan | 71.7 | 71.6 | 70.7 | 69.7 | 5.7 | 5.7 | 5.8 | 5.9 |
| Burma | 73.4 | 70.3 | 68.9 | 63.3 | 6.9 | 7.1 | 6.7 | 7.0 |
| China | 70.3 | 59.3 | 45.8 | 38.6 | 7.8 | 7.9 | 8.1 | 8.6 |
| Democratic Kampuchea | 74.7 | 51.0 | 50.2 | 56.0 | 5.1 | 3.9 | 4.1 | 4.7 |
| East Timor | 76.0 | 54.0 | 55.3 | 57.9 | 4.9 | 3.7 | 4.2 | 4.7 |
| Fiji | 69.3 | 63.2 | 62.8 | 61.8 | 4.6 | 5.2 | 5.9 | 6.6 |
| Hong Kong | 47.2 | 37.5 | 33.3 | 31.8 | 8.4 | 9.5 | 10.9 | 12.7 |
| India | 70.6 | 67.2 | 64.8 | 61.8 | 6.8 | 7.1 | 7.3 | 7.6 |
| Indonesia | 76.6 | 73.7 | 66.8 | 57.4 | 5.8 | 6.0 | 6.2 | 6.3 |
| Korea | 67.8 | 59.8 | 52.1 | 46.0 | 6.2 | 6.2 | 6.4 | 6.7 |
| Democratic People's Republic of Korea | 75.9 | 71.8 | 67.0 | 62.6 | 6.4 | 6.3 | 6.2 | 6.4 |
| Republic of Korea | 64.4 | 54.7 | 45.6 | 38.5 | 6.2 | 6.1 | 6.5 | 6.9 |
| Lao People's Democratic Republic | 76.2 | 76.2 | 78.3 | 78.6 | 4.8 | 5.1 | 5.3 | 5.5 |
| Malaysia | 77.7 | 69.0 | 64.6 | 60.3 | 6.9 | 6.4 | 6.5 | 6.4 |
| Mongolia | 82.6 | 80.2 | 75.5 | 76.2 | 6.1 | 5.9 | 5.9 | 6.1 |
| Nepal | 79.7 | 73.9 | 77.2 | 77.1 | 6.1 | 5.4 | 5.5 | 5.7 |
| Pakistan | 88.2 | 84.1 | 84.9 | 88.4 | 5.7 | 5.5 | 5.3 | 5.2 |
| Papua New Guinea | 76.4 | 77.4 | 74.2 | 75.6 | 5.7 | 2.8 | 4.4 | 4.7 |
| Philippines | 78.5 | 77.1 | 74.1 | 70.9 | 5.0 | 6.2 | 6.1 | 6.0 |
| Singapore | 52.1 | 39.7 | 34.8 | 31.9 | 6.5 | 6.9 | 7.4 | 7.8 |
| Sri Lanka | 69.6 | 58.4 | 55.7 | 52.2 | 7.2 | 7.2 | 7.7 | 8.3 |
| Thailand | 86.1 | 70.9 | 60.9 | 51.4 | 5.7 | 6.3 | 6.1 | 6.2 |
| Viet Nam | 83.5 | 80.8 | 74.0 | 69.6 | 7.7 | 9.1 | 8.1 | 7.8 |
| West Asia | 84.5 | 82.9 | 82.0 | 84.1 | 5.5 | 5.3 | 5.4 | 5.2 |
| Bahrain | 78.6 | 54.8 | 51.5 | 49.9 | 4.1 | 3.3 | 3.0 | 3.0 |
| Democratic Yemen | 95.3 | 89.5 | 86.5 | 85.1 | 5.3 | 5.3 | 5.4 | 5.4 |
| Iran (Islamic Republic of) | 88.4 | 85.1 | 80.6 | 83.0 | 6.5 | 6.4 | 6.1 | 6.1 |
| Iraq | 91.5 | 93.3 | 93.1 | 91.5 | 4.9 | 5.1 | 5.3 | 5.4 |
| Israel | 55.3 | 57.1 | 55.5 | 51.4 | 13.1 | 14.8 | 15.0 | 14.8 |
| Jordan | 94.5 | 104.1 | 97.7 | 96.4 | 5.7 | 6.6 | 5.6 | 5.0 |
| Kuwait | 82.1 | 68.9 | 68.2 | 64.8 | 2.9 | 2.4 | 2.2 | 2.5 |
| Lebanon | 76.4 | 73.6 | 65.3 | 59.2 | 9.2 | 9.9 | 8.9 | 8.6 |
| Oman | 84.9 | 82.5 | 83.3 | 88.6 | 5.2 | 4.9 | 4.7 | 4.9 |
| Qatar | 51.7 | 48.6 | 52.5 | 55.6 | 3.1 | 1.7 | 2.5 | 2.8 |
| Saudi Arabia | 84.0 | 83.3 | 85.4 | 87.5 | 5.7 | 5.3 | 5.0 | 5.0 |
| Syrian Arab Republic | 101.5 | 96.4 | 97.9 | 97.5 | 7.7 | 6.5 | 5.6 | 5.3 |
| United Arab Emirates | 40.4 | 40.8 | 45.8 | 46.2 | 2.9 | 1.8 | 2.2 | 2.5 |
| Yemen | 92.1 | 96.2 | 98.5 | 98.9 | 6.4 | 6.6 | 6.6 | 6.6 |
| Mediterranean | 39.7 | 37.4 | 38.0 | 37.3 | 13.9 | 14.1 | 13.8 | 14.4 |
| Cyprus | 40.3 | 37.3 | 39.4 | 39.9 | 15.3 | 15.7 | 16.6 | 16.0 |
| Malta | 37.6 | 34.4 | 36.6 | 34.7 | 14.6 | 14.7 | 14.9 | 15.3 |
| Turkey | 72.4 | 70.0 | 61.2 | 56.0 | 8.2 | 8.4 | 7.1 | 6.9 |
| Yugoslavia | 39.1 | 37.4 | 35.8 | 33.7 | 13.1 | 13.5 | 12.6 | 13.4 |

Table S.III.4. (Continued)

| Region and country or area[c] | Child[a] 1975 | 1980 | 1985 | 1990 | Old age[b] 1975 | 1980 | 1985 | 1990 |
|---|---|---|---|---|---|---|---|---|
| Western hemisphere | 81.0 | 72.2 | 63.9 | 59.6 | 6.9 | 6.9 | 6.8 | 7.1 |
| Argentina | 46.2 | 48.6 | 50.0 | 49.1 | 12.0 | 13.2 | 14.1 | 14.9 |
| Barbados | 53.6 | 49.5 | 43.6 | 39.2 | 16.8 | 17.6 | 17.1 | 15.8 |
| Bolivia | 80.6 | 81.6 | 82.5 | 83.0 | 6.2 | 6.1 | 6.0 | 6.1 |
| Brazil | 71.4 | 64.8 | 61.4 | 58.6 | 5.6 | 6.9 | 7.3 | 7.7 |
| Chile | 63.6 | 54.7 | 50.2 | 48.3 | 9.3 | 9.2 | 9.3 | 9.5 |
| Colombia | 78.5 | 69.1 | 62.9 | 60.5 | 5.9 | 6.1 | 6.4 | 6.7 |
| Costa Rica | 77.5 | 67.4 | 62.1 | 60.7 | 6.2 | 6.3 | 6.6 | 7.1 |
| Cuba | 65.2 | 51.0 | 38.7 | 31.3 | 11.5 | 11.9 | 12.0 | 12.0 |
| Dominican Republic | 87.8 | 77.4 | 69.5 | 64.5 | 5.8 | 5.7 | 5.7 | 5.7 |
| Ecuador | 86.4 | 81.7 | 76.7 | 73.0 | 7.0 | 6.8 | 6.8 | 6.7 |
| El Salvador | 89.5 | 90.3 | 91.0 | 85.7 | 5.6 | 6.0 | 6.7 | 7.1 |
| Guadeloupe | 80.4 | 51.6 | 43.7 | 40.6 | 11.1 | 12.1 | 12.7 | 13.8 |
| Guatemala | 88.9 | 89.5 | 89.7 | 88.4 | 5.4 | 5.6 | 5.7 | 6.2 |
| Guyana | 82.9 | 69.3 | 62.5 | 56.4 | 6.5 | 6.6 | 6.6 | 6.8 |
| Haiti | 77.4 | 75.5 | 71.7 | 68.8 | 6.9 | 6.9 | 6.8 | 6.8 |
| Honduras | 98.1 | 95.9 | 92.0 | 85.5 | 5.4 | 6.0 | 6.4 | 6.3 |
| Jamaica | 92.4 | 75.7 | 64.1 | 57.7 | 11.8 | 10.8 | 10.7 | 10.0 |
| Martinique | 75.3 | 45.2 | 36.7 | 36.1 | 11.7 | 13.3 | 13.8 | 15.1 |
| Mexico | 92.8 | 84.1 | 73.7 | 63.1 | 6.8 | 6.8 | 6.5 | 6.5 |
| Nicaragua | 96.5 | 94.6 | 92.1 | 89.0 | 4.8 | 4.8 | 5.0 | 5.3 |
| Panama | 81.3 | 73.1 | 64.8 | 58.0 | 7.4 | 7.5 | 7.7 | 7.9 |
| Paraguay | 84.9 | 77.3 | 73.8 | 72.0 | 6.7 | 6.3 | 6.3 | 6.4 |
| Peru | 81.3 | 76.5 | 72.3 | 68.5 | 6.6 | 6.6 | 6.4 | 6.4 |
| Puerto Rico | 55.9 | 52.2 | 47.9 | 45.6 | 10.5 | 13.0 | 13.3 | 13.7 |
| Suriname | 98.3 | 71.3 | 63.6 | 56.3 | 8.0 | 8.0 | 7.3 | 7.4 |
| Trinidad and Tobago | 63.9 | 57.4 | 53.4 | 51.2 | 6.9 | 9.2 | 8.8 | 8.6 |
| Uruguay | 44.2 | 43.3 | 43.1 | 41.9 | 15.4 | 16.7 | 17.2 | 18.0 |
| Venezuela | 81.3 | 73.8 | 69.2 | 65.9 | 5.8 | 5.7 | 6.0 | 6.3 |
| Developed market economies | 38.1 | 34.3 | 31.6 | 28.9 | 19.0 | 19.2 | 18.8 | 19.6 |
| Australia | 43.3 | 38.8 | 35.6 | 33.2 | 13.6 | 14.7 | 15.3 | 16.4 |
| Canada | 40.7 | 33.2 | 31.6 | 31.0 | 13.1 | 14.3 | 15.3 | 16.9 |
| Japan | 35.8 | 34.9 | 31.6 | 26.5 | 11.6 | 13.4 | 15.1 | 16.8 |
| New Zealand | 48.9 | 42.2 | 37.4 | 33.7 | 14.2 | 15.7 | 16.1 | 16.5 |
| South Africa | 71.2 | 67.2 | 65.0 | 62.9 | 6.9 | 6.9 | 7.0 | 7.1 |
| United States | 39.1 | 34.0 | 32.7 | 32.6 | 16.3 | 17.1 | 18.0 | 19.1 |
| Europe | 37.6 | 33.2 | 28.7 | 27.7 | 19.7 | 20.7 | 20.0 | 20.8 |
| Austria | 37.7 | 31.8 | 27.6 | 26.3 | 24.2 | 24.0 | 21.0 | 22.3 |
| Belgium | 34.8 | 30.8 | 28.3 | 26.9 | 21.8 | 21.9 | 20.5 | 21.9 |
| Denmark | 35.3 | 32.2 | 28.1 | 25.2 | 20.9 | 22.3 | 22.5 | 22.9 |
| Finland | 32.7 | 30.0 | 28.5 | 28.5 | 15.8 | 17.7 | 18.3 | 19.5 |
| France | 38.2 | 34.9 | 32.2 | 30.6 | 21.5 | 21.9 | 19.7 | 20.8 |
| Germany, Federal Republic of | 33.5 | 27.4 | 22.4 | 21.3 | 22.6 | 23.4 | 21.1 | 22.0 |
| Greece | 37.4 | 35.6 | 32.6 | 29.6 | 19.1 | 20.5 | 20.3 | 20.7 |
| Iceland | 49.5 | 43.9 | 41.7 | 38.7 | 15.1 | 15.7 | 15.8 | 16.2 |
| Ireland | 54.0 | 52.2 | 49.7 | 44.5 | 19.0 | 18.3 | 17.7 | 16.7 |
| Italy | 38.0 | 34.5 | 28.9 | 24.9 | 18.9 | 20.4 | 18.8 | 20.7 |
| Luxembourg | 33.0 | 28.2 | 24.9 | 24.5 | 20.0 | 20.0 | 19.0 | 19.3 |
| Netherlands | 39.7 | 33.7 | 28.4 | 25.8 | 16.9 | 17.4 | 17.6 | 18.6 |
| Norway | 38.1 | 35.1 | 31.9 | 28.9 | 21.9 | 23.4 | 24.2 | 25.3 |
| Portugal | 44.9 | 40.8 | 36.5 | 32.2 | 15.9 | 16.4 | 18.6 | 19.5 |
| Spain | 44.3 | 42.4 | 35.2 | 30.7 | 16.1 | 17.0 | 18.7 | 19.6 |
| Sweden | 32.2 | 30.6 | 27.1 | 25.4 | 23.5 | 25.4 | 27.6 | 28.1 |
| Switzerland | 34.3 | 29.7 | 24.7 | 24.1 | 19.4 | 20.8 | 21.2 | 22.4 |
| United Kingdom | 37.2 | 32.6 | 29.3 | 28.9 | 22.2 | 23.5 | 23.0 | 23.7 |
| Centrally planned economies | 36.3 | 37.6 | 37.7 | 35.5 | 15.6 | 17.2 | 15.8 | 16.6 |
| Albania | 71.8 | 60.8 | 57.3 | 52.5 | 8.1 | 8.9 | 8.7 | 8.6 |
| Bulgaria | 32.8 | 33.5 | 31.5 | 30.0 | 16.3 | 18.0 | 16.8 | 19.4 |
| Czechoslovakia | 36.3 | 38.3 | 37.9 | 35.7 | 18.8 | 19.7 | 17.1 | 17.7 |
| German Democratic Republic | 34.8 | 30.5 | 28.7 | 29.4 | 26.1 | 24.7 | 20.2 | 19.5 |

Table S.III.4. (Continued)

| Region and country or area[c] | Child[a] 1975 | 1980 | 1985 | 1990 | Old age[b] 1975 | 1980 | 1985 | 1990 |
|---|---|---|---|---|---|---|---|---|
| Hungary | 30.3 | 33.9 | 32.5 | 29.8 | 18.8 | 20.8 | 18.7 | 20.1 |
| Poland | 36.2 | 37.0 | 39.3 | 38.8 | 14.4 | 15.4 | 14.5 | 15.4 |
| Romania | 38.7 | 42.3 | 37.4 | 35.2 | 14.7 | 16.3 | 14.4 | 15.5 |
| USSR | 40.4 | 38.1 | 38.7 | 39.2 | 14.8 | 15.8 | 14.7 | 14.8 |

*Source: World Population Prospects, 1988* (United Nations publication, Sales No. E.88.XIII.7).

a $\frac{\text{Population age 0-14}}{\text{Population age 15-64}}$

b $\frac{\text{Population age 65+}}{\text{Population age 15-64}}$

c Data for small countries or areas, generally those with population of 300,000 or less in 1985, are not given in this table separately. Data for regions are median values for countries or areas listed. For the world, data in parentheses are weighted averages for all countries or areas.

## Table S.III.5. Population in urban areas, 1975-1990, medium variant[a]

*(Percentage)*

| Region and country or area[b] | 1975 | 1980 | 1985 | 1990 |
|---|---|---|---|---|
| World | 41.6<br>(38.5) | 43.7<br>(39.8) | 46.4<br>(41.2) | 49.8<br>(42.7) |
| Developing countries | 34.3 | 37.4 | 41.1 | 44.0 |
| Africa | 21.4 | 27.0 | 31.3 | 34.3 |
| Algeria | 40.3 | 41.2 | 42.6 | 44.7 |
| Angola | 17.8 | 21.0 | 24.5 | 28.3 |
| Benin | 21.5 | 28.2 | 35.2 | 42.0 |
| Botswana | 12.0 | 15.3 | 19.2 | 23.6 |
| Burkina Faso | 6.3 | 7.0 | 7.9 | 9.0 |
| Burundi | 3.0 | 4.1 | 5.6 | 7.3 |
| Cameroon | 26.9 | 34.7 | 42.4 | 49.4 |
| Cape Verde | 30.2 | 42.4 | 53.3 | 61.5 |
| Central African Republic | 34.2 | 38.2 | 42.4 | 46.6 |
| Chad | 15.2 | 20.8 | 27.0 | 33.3 |
| Comoros | 21.3 | 23.2 | 25.2 | 27.6 |
| Congo | 35.8 | 37.3 | 39.5 | 42.2 |
| Côte d'Ivoire | 32.2 | 37.1 | 42.0 | 46.6 |
| Djibouti | 68.5 | 73.7 | 77.7 | 80.7 |
| Egypt | 43.5 | 44.7 | 46.5 | 48.8 |
| Equatorial Guinea | 46.6 | 53.7 | 59.7 | 64.5 |
| Ethiopia | 9.5 | 10.5 | 11.6 | 12.9 |
| Gabon | 30.6 | 35.8 | 40.9 | 45.7 |
| Gambia | 16.6 | 18.1 | 20.1 | 22.5 |
| Ghana | 29.8 | 30.7 | 31.5 | 33.0 |
| Guinea | 16.3 | 19.1 | 22.2 | 25.6 |
| Guinea-Bissau | 20.8 | 23.8 | 27.1 | 30.8 |
| Kenya | 12.9 | 16.1 | 19.7 | 23.6 |
| Lesotho | 10.8 | 13.6 | 16.7 | 20.3 |
| Liberia | 30.4 | 34.9 | 39.5 | 44.0 |
| Libyan Arab Jamahiriya | 46.8 | 56.6 | 64.5 | 70.2 |
| Madagascar | 16.3 | 18.9 | 21.8 | 25.0 |
| Malawi | 7.7 | 9.7 | 12.0 | 14.8 |
| Mali | 16.2 | 17.3 | 18.0 | 19.2 |
| Mauritania | 19.6 | 26.9 | 34.6 | 42.1 |
| Mauritius | 43.6 | 42.9 | 42.2 | 42.3 |
| Morocco | 37.8 | 41.3 | 44.8 | 48.5 |
| Mozambique | 8.6 | 13.1 | 19.4 | 26.8 |

Table S.III.5. (Continued)

| Region and country or area[b] | 1975 | 1980 | 1985 | 1990 |
|---|---|---|---|---|
| Namibia | 39.2 | 45.2 | 51.3 | 57.0 |
| Niger | 10.6 | 13.2 | 16.2 | 19.5 |
| Nigeria | 23.4 | 27.1 | 31.0 | 35.2 |
| Réunion | 49.6 | 54.9 | 59.8 | 63.9 |
| Rwanda | 4.0 | 5.0 | 6.2 | 7.7 |
| Senegal | 34.2 | 34.9 | 36.4 | 38.4 |
| Sierra Leone | 21.1 | 24.5 | 28.3 | 32.2 |
| Somalia | 25.6 | 28.9 | 32.5 | 36.4 |
| Sudan | 18.9 | 19.7 | 20.6 | 22.0 |
| Swaziland | 14.0 | 19.8 | 26.3 | 33.1 |
| Togo | 15.8 | 18.8 | 22.1 | 25.7 |
| Tunisia | 47.6 | 52.2 | 53.0 | 54.3 |
| Uganda | 8.3 | 8.7 | 9.4 | 10.4 |
| United Republic of Tanzania | 10.1 | 16.5 | 24.4 | 32.8 |
| Zaire | 32.2 | 34.2 | 36.6 | 39.5 |
| Zambia | 36.3 | 42.8 | 49.5 | 55.6 |
| Zimbabwe | 19.4 | 21.9 | 24.6 | 27.6 |
| South and East Asia | 20.9 | 21.9 | 22.5 | 23.6 |
| Afghanistan | 13.1 | 15.6 | 18.5 | 21.7 |
| Bangladesh | 9.1 | 10.4 | 11.9 | 13.6 |
| Bhutan | 3.5 | 3.9 | 4.5 | 5.3 |
| Burma | 23.9 | 23.9 | 23.9 | 24.6 |
| China | 20.2 | 20.4 | 20.6 | 21.4 |
| Democratic Kampuchea | 10.3 | 10.3 | 10.8 | 11.6 |
| East Timor | 10.4 | 10.9 | 11.8 | 13.1 |
| Fiji | 36.7 | 38.7 | 41.2 | 44.0 |
| Hong Kong | 90.6 | 91.6 | 92.4 | 93.2 |
| India | 21.5 | 23.4 | 25.5 | 28.0 |
| Indonesia | 19.4 | 22.2 | 25.3 | 28.8 |
| Korea | 50.2 | 57.8 | 64.8 | 70.4 |
| Democratic People's Republic of Korea | 55.1 | 59.7 | 63.8 | 67.4 |
| Republic of Korea | 48.0 | 56.9 | 65.3 | 72.0 |
| Lao People's Democratic Republic | 11.4 | 13.4 | 15.9 | 18.6 |
| Malaysia | 30.5 | 34.2 | 38.2 | 42.3 |
| Mongolia | 48.7 | 51.1 | 50.8 | 51.2 |
| Nepal | 4.8 | 6.1 | 7.7 | 9.6 |
| Pakistan | 26.4 | 28.1 | 29.8 | 32.0 |
| Papua New Guinea | 11.9 | 13.0 | 14.3 | 15.8 |
| Philippines | 35.6 | 37.4 | 39.6 | 42.4 |
| Singapore | 100.0 | 100.0 | 100.0 | 100.0 |
| Sri Lanka | 22.0 | 21.6 | 21.1 | 21.4 |
| Thailand | 15.2 | 17.3 | 19.8 | 22.6 |
| Viet Nam | 18.8 | 19.3 | 20.3 | 21.9 |
| West Asia | 60.1 | 66.6 | 71.8 | 77.6 |
| Bahrain | 79.3 | 80.5 | 81.7 | 82.9 |
| Democratic Yemen | 34.3 | 36.9 | 39.9 | 43.3 |
| Iran (Islamic Republic of) | 45.7 | 49.1 | 51.9 | 54.9 |
| Iraq | 61.4 | 66.4 | 70.6 | 74.2 |
| Israel | 86.6 | 88.6 | 90.3 | 91.6 |
| Jordan | 55.4 | 60.1 | 64.4 | 68.1 |
| Kuwait | 83.8 | 90.2 | 93.7 | 95.6 |
| Lebanon | 68.6 | 75.5 | 80.4 | 83.7 |
| Oman | 6.1 | 7.3 | 8.8 | 10.6 |
| Qatar | 83.6 | 86.1 | 88.0 | 89.5 |
| Saudi Arabia | 58.7 | 66.8 | 73.0 | 77.3 |
| Syrian Arab Republic | 45.4 | 47.4 | 49.5 | 51.8 |
| United Arab Emirates | 79.8 | 81.2 | 77.8 | 77.8 |
| Yemen | 11.0 | 15.3 | 20.0 | 25.0 |
| Mediterranean | 42.5 | 45.1 | 47.9 | 51.5 |
| Cyprus | 43.4 | 46.3 | 49.5 | 52.8 |
| Malta | 80.7 | 83.4 | 85.4 | 87.1 |

Table S.III.5. (Continued)

| Region and country or area[b] | 1975 | 1980 | 1985 | 1990 |
|---|---|---|---|---|
| Turkey | 41.6 | 43.8 | 45.9 | 48.4 |
| Yugoslavia | 38.5 | 42.3 | 46.3 | 50.2 |
| Western hemisphere | 44.5 | 47.1 | 51.1 | 54.2 |
| Argentina | 80.6 | 82.7 | 84.6 | 86.2 |
| Barbados | 38.6 | 40.1 | 42.2 | 44.7 |
| Bolivia | 41.5 | 44.3 | 47.8 | 51.4 |
| Brazil | 61.8 | 67.5 | 72.7 | 76.9 |
| Chile | 78.3 | 81.1 | 83.6 | 85.6 |
| Colombia | 60.8 | 64.2 | 67.4 | 70.3 |
| Costa Rica | 42.2 | 46.0 | 49.8 | 53.6 |
| Cuba | 64.2 | 68.1 | 71.8 | 74.9 |
| Dominican Republic | 45.3 | 50.5 | 55.7 | 60.4 |
| Ecuador | 42.4 | 47.3 | 52.3 | 56.9 |
| El Salvador | 40.4 | 41.5 | 42.7 | 44.4 |
| Guadeloupe | 41.8 | 43.5 | 45.7 | 48.5 |
| Guatemala | 37.1 | 38.5 | 40.0 | 42.0 |
| Guyana | 29.6 | 30.5 | 32.2 | 34.6 |
| Haiti | 22.1 | 24.6 | 27.2 | 30.3 |
| Honduras | 32.3 | 35.9 | 39.7 | 43.6 |
| Jamaica | 44.1 | 46.8 | 49.4 | 52.3 |
| Martinique | 60.6 | 66.4 | 71.1 | 74.7 |
| Mexico | 62.8 | 66.4 | 69.6 | 72.6 |
| Nicaragua | 50.3 | 53.4 | 56.6 | 59.8 |
| Panama | 49.1 | 50.5 | 52.4 | 54.8 |
| Paraguay | 39.0 | 41.7 | 44.4 | 47.5 |
| Peru | 61.4 | 64.5 | 67.4 | 70.2 |
| Puerto Rico | 62.8 | 67.0 | 70.7 | 73.9 |
| Suriname | 44.8 | 44.8 | 45.7 | 47.5 |
| Trinidad and Tobago | 48.4 | 56.9 | 63.9 | 69.1 |
| Uruguay | 83.0 | 83.8 | 84.6 | 85.5 |
| Venezuela | 77.8 | 83.3 | 87.6 | 90.5 |
| Developed market economies | 73.7 | 74.7 | 75.9 | 76.7 |
| Australia | 85.9 | 85.8 | 85.5 | 85.5 |
| Canada | 75.6 | 75.7 | 75.9 | 76.4 |
| Japan | 75.7 | 76.2 | 76.7 | 77.0 |
| New Zealand | 82.8 | 83.3 | 83.7 | 84.2 |
| South Africa | 50.5 | 53.2 | 56.0 | 58.9 |
| United States | 73.6 | 73.7 | 73.9 | 74.0 |
| Europe | 71.3 | 73.0 | 74.6 | 76.4 |
| Austria | 53.1 | 54.6 | 56.1 | 57.7 |
| Belgium | 94.6 | 95.4 | 96.3 | 96.9 |
| Denmark | 82.1 | 83.8 | 85.1 | 86.4 |
| Finland | 55.1 | 59.6 | 64.0 | 67.9 |
| France | 73.0 | 73.2 | 73.4 | 74.1 |
| Germany, Federal Republic of | 83.1 | 84.4 | 85.5 | 86.4 |
| Greece | 55.3 | 57.7 | 60.1 | 62.6 |
| Iceland | 86.8 | 88.2 | 89.4 | 90.5 |
| Ireland | 53.6 | 55.3 | 57.0 | 59.1 |
| Italy | 65.6 | 66.5 | 67.4 | 68.6 |
| Luxembourg | 73.7 | 78.4 | 81.8 | 84.3 |
| Netherlands | 88.4 | 88.4 | 88.4 | 88.5 |
| Norway | 68.2 | 70.5 | 72.8 | 74.4 |
| Portugal | 27.8 | 29.5 | 31.2 | 33.3 |
| Spain | 69.6 | 72.8 | 75.8 | 78.4 |
| Sweden | 82.7 | 83.1 | 83.4 | 84.0 |
| Switzerland | 55.7 | 57.0 | 58.2 | 59.6 |
| United Kingdom | 89.8 | 90.8 | 91.7 | 92.5 |
| Centrally planned economies | 56.4 | 60.2 | 63.3 | 65.4 |
| Albania | 32.8 | 33.4 | 34.0 | 35.3 |
| Bulgaria | 57.5 | 62.5 | 66.5 | 70.3 |
| Czechoslovakia | 58.7 | 62.2 | 65.5 | 68.6 |

Table S.III.5. (Continued)

| Region and country or area[b] | 1975 | 1980 | 1985 | 1990 |
|---|---|---|---|---|
| German Democratic Republic | 75.2 | 76.2 | 77.0 | 78.0 |
| Hungary | 50.1 | 53.5 | 57.0 | 60.3 |
| Poland | 55.2 | 58.2 | 61.0 | 63.2 |
| Romania | 46.2 | 48.1 | 49.0 | 50.4 |
| USSR | 60.0 | 63.1 | 65.6 | 67.5 |

*Source: World Population Prospects, 1988* (United Nations publication, Sales No. E.88.XIII.7).

a Population living in areas defined as urban by national authorities (in per cent of total population).
b Data for small countries or areas, generally those with population of 300,000 or less in 1985, are not given in this table separately. Data for regions are median values for countries or areas listed. For the world, data in parentheses are weighted averages for all countries or areas.

Table S.III.6. The world's largest urban agglomerations

| Rank in 1985 | Agglomeration | Country or area | Population (Millions) 1970 | 1985 | 2000 | Percentage of national population 1970 | 1985 | 2000 |
|---|---|---|---|---|---|---|---|---|
| 1 | Tokyo/Yokohama | Japan | 14.87 | 19.04 | 21.32 | 14.3 | 15.8 | 16.5 |
| 2 | Mexico City | Mexico | 8.74 | 16.65 | 24.44 | 16.6 | 21.0 | 22.8 |
| 3 | New York | United States | 16.19 | 15.62 | 16.10 | 7.9 | 6.5 | 6.0 |
| 4 | Sao Paulo | Brazil | 8.06 | 15.54 | 23.60 | 8.4 | 11.5 | 13.1 |
| 5 | Shanghai | China | 11.41 | 12.06 | 14.69 | 1.4 | 1.1 | 1.1 |
| 6 | Buenos Aires | Argentina | 8.31 | 10.76 | 13.05 | 34.7 | 35.5 | 36.0 |
| 7 | London | United Kingdom | 10.55 | 10.49 | 10.79 | 19.0 | 18.5 | 18.8 |
| 8 | Calcutta | India | 6.91 | 10.29 | 15.94 | 1.2 | 1.3 | 1.5 |
| 9 | Rio de Janeiro | Brazil | 7.04 | 10.14 | 13.00 | 7.3 | 7.5 | 7.2 |
| 10 | Seoul | Republic of Korea | 5.31 | 10.07 | 12.97 | 16.7 | 24.5 | 27.0 |
| 11 | Los Angeles | United States | 8.38 | 10.04 | 10.91 | 4.0 | 4.2 | 4.1 |
| 12 | Osaka/Kobe | Japan | 7.60 | 9.56 | 11.18 | 7.3 | 7.9 | 8.7 |
| 13 | Greater Bombay | India | 5.81 | 9.47 | 15.43 | 1.0 | 1.2 | 1.5 |
| 14 | Beijing | China | 8.29 | 9.33 | 11.47 | 1.0 | 0.9 | 0.9 |
| 15 | Moscow | USSR | 7.11 | 8.91 | 10.11 | 2.9 | 3.2 | 3.3 |
| 16 | Paris | France | 8.33 | 8.75 | 8.76 | 16.4 | 15.9 | 15.1 |
| 17 | Tianjin | China | 6.87 | 7.96 | 9.96 | 0.8 | 0.8 | 0.8 |
| 18 | Cairo/Giza | Egypt | 5.33 | 7.92 | 11.77 | 16.1 | 16.6 | 17.6 |
| 19 | Jakarta | Indonesia | 4.32 | 7.79 | 13.23 | 3.6 | 4.7 | 6.4 |
| 20 | Milan | Italy | 5.53 | 7.50 | 8.74 | 10.3 | 13.1 | 15.1 |

*Source:* Department of International Economic and Social Affairs of the United Nations Secretariat, based on *World Population Prospects, 1988* (United Nations publication, Sales No. E.88.XIII.7).

# Annex

## STATISTICAL TABLES

## Table A.1. Developed market economies: annual rates of growth of real gross domestic product, 1983-1990

(Annual percentage change)

| Country or country group | 1983 | 1984 | 1985 | 1986 | 1987 | 1988[a] | 1989[b] | 1990[b] |
|---|---|---|---|---|---|---|---|---|
| All developed market economies[c] | 2.7 | 4.7 | 3.1 | 2.7 | 3.0 | 4.1 | 2.8 | 2.6 |
| Excluding United States | 2.1 | 3.5 | 3.3 | 2.5 | 3.1 | 4.2 | 3.2 | 2.7 |
| Major industrial countries[c] | 3.0 | 4.9 | 3.1 | 2.8 | 3.1 | 4.2 | 2.8 | 2.6 |
| Canada | 3.3 | 6.3 | 4.5 | 3.3 | 3.9 | 4.3 | 2.3 | 3.3 |
| France | 0.7 | 1.4 | 1.7 | 2.1 | 2.3 | 3.6 | 2.6 | 2.6 |
| Germany, Federal Republic of[c] | 1.9 | 3.3 | 1.9 | 2.3 | 1.8 | 3.5 | 2.7 | 2.2 |
| Italy | 1.1 | 3.2 | 2.9 | 2.9 | 3.1 | 3.8 | 3.2 | 3.1 |
| Japan[c] | 3.2 | 5.1 | 4.7 | 2.5 | 4.4 | 5.7 | 4.5 | 3.3 |
| United Kingdom | 3.6 | 2.1 | 3.7 | 3.1 | 4.6 | 4.5 | 3.0 | 2.2 |
| United States[c] | 3.6 | 6.4 | 2.7 | 2.9 | 3.3 | 3.9 | 2.2 | 2.4 |
| Smaller industrial countries | 1.3 | 3.6 | 2.9 | 2.2 | 2.5 | 3.2 | 2.7 | 2.2 |

*Source:* Department of International Economic and Social Affairs of the United Nations Secretariat.

a Preliminary estimates.

b Forecasts, based on Project LINK.

c Measure used is real gross national product.

## Table A.2. Developed market economies: unemployment rates, 1980-1988

(Percentage of total labour force)

| | 1982 | 1983 | 1984 | 1985 | 1986 | 1987 | 1988 |
|---|---|---|---|---|---|---|---|
| Australia[a] | 7.1 | 9.9 | 8.9 | 8.2 | 8.0 | 8.1 | 7.2 |
| Austria | 3.5 | 4.1 | 3.8 | 3.6 | 3.1 | 3.7 | 4.0[b] |
| Belgium[a] | 12.6 | 12.1 | 12.1 | 11.3 | 11.2 | 11.1 | 10.2 |
| Canada[a] | 10.9 | 11.8 | 11.2 | 10.4 | 9.5 | 8.8 | 7.7 |
| Denmark | 11.0 | 11.4 | 8.5 | 7.3 | 6.3 | 6.3 | 6.8[b] |
| Finland[a] | 5.3 | 5.4 | 5.2 | 5.0 | 5.3 | 5.0 | 4.5 |
| France[a] | 8.1 | 8.3 | 9.7 | 10.2 | 10.4 | 10.5 | 10.3 |
| Germany, Federal Republic of[a] | 6.1 | 8.0 | 7.0 | 7.2 | 6.5 | 6.2 | 6.2 |
| Greece | 5.8 | 7.9 | 8.1 | 7.8 | 7.4 | 7.8 | 8.0[b] |
| Iceland | 0.7 | 1.0 | 1.3 | 0.9 | 0.7 | 0.7 | 0.7[b] |
| Ireland | 11.4 | 14.1 | 15.6 | 17.4 | 18.0 | 19.4 | 20.2[b] |
| Italy[a] | 9.0 | 9.8 | 10.2 | 10.5 | 10.9 | 11.6 | 12.2[b] |
| Japan[a] | 2.4 | 2.6 | 2.7 | 2.6 | 2.8 | 2.8 | 2.5 |
| Luxembourg | 1.2 | 1.6 | 1.7 | 1.6 | 1.4 | 1.6 | 1.5[b] |
| Netherlands[a] | 11.4 | 12.0 | 11.8 | 10.6 | 9.9 | 9.6 | 9.5 |
| New Zealand | 3.5 | 5.6 | 5.7 | 4.1 | 5.5 | 7.2 | 8.7[b] |
| Norway[a] | 2.6 | 3.4 | 3.1 | 2.6 | 2.0 | 2.1 | 3.2 |
| Portugal[a] | 7.3 | 7.9 | 8.4 | 8.5 | 8.5 | 7.0 | 5.7[b] |
| Spain | 15.8 | 17.2 | 20.0 | 21.4 | 21.0 | 20.1 | 19.4[b] |
| Sweden | 3.2 | 3.5 | 3.1 | 2.8 | 2.7 | 1.9 | 1.6 |
| Switzerland | 0.4 | 0.9 | 1.1 | 0.9 | 0.8 | 0.8 | 0.9[b] |
| United Kingdom[a] | 11.3 | 12.5 | 11.7 | 11.2 | 11.2 | 10.3 | 8.3 |
| United States[a] | 9.5 | 9.5 | 7.4 | 7.1 | 6.9 | 6.1 | 5.4 |

*Source:* OECD, *Employment Outlook* (Paris, September), table 1.6; and OECD, *Main Economic Indicators* (Paris, March 1989).

a Data for these countries are standardized by the OECD to preserve comparability over time and to conform to the definitions of the International Labour Office (see *Standardized Unemployment Rates: Sources and Methods* (OECD, Paris, 1985)).

b Estimates by the Department of International Economic and Social Affairs of the United Nations Secretariat.

## Table A.3. Developed market economies: rates of change of GDP deflator and consumer prices, 1982-1988

(Annual percentage change)

| Country or country group | 1982 | 1983 | 1984 | 1985 | 1986 | 1987 | 1988[a] |
|---|---|---|---|---|---|---|---|
| GDP deflators | | | | | | | |
| All developed market economies[b] | 7.2 | 5.3 | 4.8 | 4.5 | 3.7 | 3.6 | 3.7 |
| Major industrial countries[b] | 6.7 | 4.8 | 4.2 | 4.0 | 3.0 | 2.9 | 3.2 |
| Canada | 8.7 | 5.0 | 3.1 | 2.9 | 2.5 | 4.3 | 3.8 |
| France | 11.7 | 9.7 | 7.5 | 5.9 | 5.1 | 2.5 | 2.2 |
| Germany, Federal Republic of[c] | 4.4 | 3.3 | 2.0 | 2.2 | 3.1 | 2.1 | 0.9 |
| Italy | 16.2 | 15.0 | 11.3 | 8.9 | 7.5 | 5.6 | 5.5 |
| Japan[c] | 1.9 | 0.8 | 1.2 | 1.5 | 1.9 | -0.3 | 1.3 |
| United Kingdom | 7.6 | 5.2 | 4.3 | 5.9 | 3.7 | 4.4 | 4.8 |
| United States[c] | 6.4 | 3.9 | 3.9 | 3.7 | 2.0 | 3.1 | 3.7 |
| Other industrial countries[b] | 10.0 | 8.1 | 7.5 | 7.0 | 7.4 | 6.2 | 6.0 |
| North America[b] | 6.7 | 4.1 | 4.2 | 3.7 | 2.1 | 3.5 | 3.7 |
| Western Europe[b] | 9.6 | 7.6 | 6.3 | 5.8 | 5.3 | 4.0 | 3.7 |
| Developed Asia[b] | 2.6 | 2.0 | 2.1 | 2.4 | 3.1 | 1.8 | 2.7 |
| Consumer prices | | | | | | | |
| All developed market economies[b] | 7.9 | 5.7 | 5.4 | 4.9 | 3.2 | 3.6 | 3.8 |
| Major industrial countries[b] | 7.3 | 4.8 | 4.8 | 4.2 | 2.2 | 2.9 | 3.3 |
| Canada | 10.8 | 5.8 | 4.3 | 4.0 | 4.2 | 4.3 | 4.1 |
| France | 11.8 | 9.6 | 7.5 | 5.7 | 2.5 | 3.3 | 2.7 |
| Germany, Federal Republic of | 5.2 | 3.4 | 2.4 | 2.2 | -0.2 | 0.3 | 1.1 |
| Italy | 16.5 | 14.7 | 10.8 | 9.2 | 6.0 | 4.6 | 5.0 |
| Japan | 2.7 | 1.8 | 2.3 | 2.0 | 0.6 | 0.1 | 0.7 |
| United Kingdom | 8.6 | 4.6 | 5.1 | 6.0 | 3.4 | 4.2 | 4.9 |
| United States | 6.2 | 3.2 | 4.3 | 3.5 | 2.0 | 3.6 | 4.0 |
| Other industrial countries[b] | 11.0 | 9.4 | 8.3 | 8.0 | 7.3 | 6.3 | 6.0 |
| North America[b] | 6.5 | 3.5 | 4.3 | 3.6 | 2.2 | 3.7 | 4.0 |
| Western Europe[b] | 10.1 | 8.0 | 7.0 | 6.1 | 3.8 | 3.6 | 3.8 |
| Developed Asia[b] | 4.7 | 3.8 | 3.3 | 4.1 | 3.7 | 3.4 | 3.2 |

*Source:* IMF, *International Financial Statistics;* and OECD, *Economic Outlook.*

a GDP deflators for 1988 are estimates by the Department of International Economic and Social Affairs of the United Nations Secretariat, based on Project LINK and official national and international sources.

b Rates of change in individual countries are aggregated by using the value of output in 1982 in dollars as weights.

c GNP deflator.

Table A.4. Centrally planned economies of Eastern Europe: selected macro-economic indicators, 1982-1989

(Annual percentage rate of growth)

| | 1982 | 1983 | 1984 | 1985 | 1986 | 1987 | 1988[a] | 1989[b] |
|---|---|---|---|---|---|---|---|---|
| *Total output* | | | | | | | | |
| Bulgaria | 4.2 | 3.0 | 4.6 | 1.8 | 5.3 | 5.0 | 6.2 | 6.2 |
| Czechoslovakia | 0.2 | 2.3 | 3.5 | 3.0 | 2.6 | 2.2 | 2.5 | 1.4 |
| German Democratic Republic | 2.6 | 4.6 | 5.5 | 5.2 | 4.3 | 3.6 | 3.0 | 4.0 |
| Hungary | 2.6 | 0.3 | 2.5 | -1.4 | 0.9 | 4.1 | 0.5 | 0.0 |
| Poland | -5.5 | 6.0 | 5.6 | 3.4 | 4.9 | 1.9 | 4.7 | 4.2 |
| Romania | 2.7 | 3.7 | 7.7 | 5.9 | 7.3 | 4.8 | 3.2 | 8.5 |
| Eastern Europe | 0.1 | 3.9 | 5.3 | 3.7 | 4.6 | 3.3 | 3.5 | 4.5 |
| *Industrial output* | | | | | | | | |
| Bulgaria | 4.6 | 4.3 | 4.2 | 3.2 | 4.0 | 4.2 | 5.2 | 5.0 |
| Czechoslovakia | 1.1 | 2.8 | 4.0 | 3.5 | 3.2 | 2.5 | 2.0 | 1.9 |
| German Democratic Republic | 3.1 | 4.1 | 4.2 | 4.4 | 3.7 | 3.1 | 3.7 | 3.5 |
| Hungary | 2.5 | 1.2 | 3.2 | 0.7 | 1.9 | 3.5 | 0.0 | -0.5 |
| Poland | -2.1 | 6.4 | 5.2 | 4.5 | 4.7 | 3.4 | 5.4 | 4.2 |
| Romania | 1.1 | 4.7 | 6.7 | 4.9 | 7.7 | 4.5 | 3.6 | 6.5 |
| Eastern Europe | 1.2 | 4.4 | 4.8 | 4.1 | 4.6 | 3.5 | 3.7 | 3.9 |
| *Agriculture* | | | | | | | | |
| Bulgaria | 5.2 | -7.2 | 7.0 | -12.3 | 11.7 | -5.1 | -0.1 | 8.9 |
| Czechoslovakia | 4.4 | 4.2 | 4.4 | -1.6 | 0.6 | 0.9 | 2.2 | 0.3 |
| German Democratic Republic | -4.0 | 4.1 | 7.7 | 3.2 | 0.0 | -0.7 | -4.0[c] | .. |
| Hungary | 7.3 | -2.7 | 2.9 | -5.5 | 2.4 | -2.0 | 4.5 | 0.5 |
| Poland | -2.8 | 3.3 | 5.7 | 0.7 | 5.0 | -2.3 | 0.6 | 2.8 |
| Romania | 7.6 | -1.6 | 13.3 | 0.1 | 12.8 | 2.3 | 2.9 | 5.2 |
| Eastern Europe | 1.6 | 0.9 | 7.0 | -1.1 | 5.3 | -0.9 | 0.9 | .. |
| *Investment* | | | | | | | | |
| Bulgaria | 3.6 | 0.7 | 0.3 | 8.6 | 8.0 | 7.2 | 3.9 | .. |
| Czechoslovakia | -2.3 | 0.6 | -4.2 | 5.4 | 1.4 | 4.4 | 4.5 | -3.5 |
| German Democratic Republic | -5.1 | -0.3 | -4.9 | 3.4 | 5.3 | 8.0 | 5.0 | .. |
| Hungary | -1.6 | -3.4 | -3.7 | -3.0 | 6.5 | 9.8 | -7.7 | 1.5 |
| Poland | -12.1 | 9.4 | 11.4 | 6.0 | 5.1 | 4.2 | 6.0 | 5.2 |
| Romania | -3.1 | 2.4 | 6.0 | 1.6 | 1.2 | 0.9 | -1.3 | 4.2 |
| Eastern Europe | -4.4 | 2.3 | 2.2 | 3.9 | 3.9 | 4.7 | 2.5 | .. |

*Source:* Department of International Economic and Social Affairs of the United Nations Secretariat, based on national and international sources.

a Preliminary estimates.

b Planned.

c Secretariat estimate.

## Table A.5. World trade: annual rates of change in volume and prices, 1976-1989

(Percentage)

| | 1976-1980 | 1981-1988 | 1986 | 1987 | 1988[a] | 1989[b] |
|---|---|---|---|---|---|---|
| *Volume of exports* | | | | | | |
| World | 5.1 | 3.5 | 3.8 | 5.7 | 8.3 | 6.0 |
| Developed market economies | 6.6 | 3.8 | 2.0 | 4.3 | 8.0 | 6.0 |
| Developing countries | 1.9 | 2.3 | 8.8 | 10.8 | 10.1 | 6.5 |
| Capital surplus countries | -1.6 | -5.7 | 18.5 | 4.1 | 10.2 | .. |
| Other net energy-exporters | 2.1 | 1.5 | 6.0 | 4.1 | 6.8 | .. |
| Net energy importers | 7.4 | 8.7 | 6.5 | 15.3 | 10.5 | .. |
| China | .. | 12.7 | 7.6 | 26.8 | 18.8 | 12.2 |
| Centrally planned economies | 5.7 | 3.4 | 4.4 | 1.9 | 4.6 | 4.0 |
| *Volume of imports* | | | | | | |
| World | 5.5 | 4.1 | 3.1 | 6.8 | 8.7 | 6.3 |
| Developed market economies | 5.6 | 4.9 | 6.8 | 8.0 | 8.7 | 6.5 |
| Developing countries | 5.5 | 2.2 | -7.2 | 5.4 | 10.3 | 5.5 |
| Capital surplus countries | 11.4 | -4.2 | -19.0 | -4.8 | -3.1 | .. |
| Other net energy-exporters | 6.1 | -1.4 | -14.2 | 0.1 | 3.8 | .. |
| Net energy importers | 3.8 | 4.6 | 1.0 | 10.2 | 13.0 | .. |
| China | .. | 8.4 | -23.1 | -2.7 | 24.2 | 9.0 |
| Centrally planned economies | 4.8 | 2.2 | -0.6 | -0.4 | 4.2 | 3.7 |
| *Unit value of exports* | | | | | | |
| World | 12.2 | 0.8 | 5.9 | 10.9 | 3.9 | 4.0 |
| Developed market economies | 9.8 | 1.9 | 14.4 | 12.0 | 5.7 | 4.2 |
| Developing countries | 19.0 | -2.7 | -16.7 | 10.1 | 0.6 | 4.2 |
| Capital surplus countries | 23.5 | -6.9 | -37.6 | 14.7 | -15.7 | 9.0 |
| Other net energy-exporters | 20.9 | -4.8 | -29.2 | 14.5 | -8.7 | 7.1 |
| Net energy importers | 11.2 | -0.6 | -1.2 | 6.6 | 8.7 | 2.1 |
| China | .. | -1.6 | -4.7 | 6.3 | 2.3 | 4.4 |
| Centrally planned economies | 8.7 | 0.7 | 5.9 | 7.2 | -1.4 | 1.0 |
| *Unit value of imports* | | | | | | |
| World | 11.7 | 0.3 | 5.9 | 9.6 | 4.5 | 4.3 |
| Developed market economies | 12.1 | 0.1 | 5.9 | 9.6 | 4.5 | 4.3 |
| Developing countries | 12.5 | 0.4 | 6.3 | 10.2 | 4.3 | 4.2 |
| Capital surplus countries | 10.8 | 1.2 | 9.9 | 10.3 | 5.8 | 4.0 |
| Other net energy-exporters | 11.1 | 1.3 | 9.9 | 10.7 | 5.8 | 4.2 |
| Net energy importers | 13.4 | 0.0 | 2.8 | 10.9 | 4.1 | 4.3 |
| China | .. | 0.0 | 18.7 | 7.2 | 2.1 | 5.2 |
| Centrally planned economies | 6.8 | 1.5 | 11.5 | 8.4 | 1.4 | 1.0 |
| *Terms of trade* | | | | | | |
| Developed market economies | -2.1 | 1.8 | 8.0 | 2.1 | 1.1 | -0.1 |
| Developing countries | 5.8 | -3.1 | -21.6 | -0.2 | -3.5 | -0.1 |
| Capital surplus countries | 11.5 | -8.0 | -43.2 | 4.0 | -20.3 | 4.8 |
| Other net energy-exporters | 8.8 | -6.1 | -35.6 | 3.5 | -13.7 | 2.9 |
| Net energy importers | -2.0 | -0.6 | -3.9 | -3.8 | 4.5 | -2.0 |
| China | .. | -1.1 | -19.7 | -0.8 | 0.2 | -0.8 |
| Centrally planned economies | 1.7 | -0.8 | -5.0 | -1.1 | -2.8 | 0.0 |

*Source:* Department of International Economic and Social Affairs of the United Nations secretariat.

a Preliminary estimates.

b Forecast.

## Table A.6. Indices of prices of non-fuel primary commodities exported by developing countries, 1980-1988

(1979-1981 = 100)

| | Food | Tropical beverages | Vegetable oilseeds and oils | Agri-cultural raw materials | Minerals and metals | Combined index: Dollar | Combined index: SDR | Prices of manufactures[a] | Real prices of commodities[b] |
|---|---|---|---|---|---|---|---|---|---|
| 1980 | 123 | 104 | 96 | 109 | 109 | 110 | 106 | 106 | 104 |
| 1981 | 99 | 85 | 92 | 95 | 94 | 93 | 99 | 99 | 94 |
| 1982 | 71 | 81 | 72 | 82 | 85 | 79 | 90 | 97 | 81 |
| 1983 | 74 | 85 | 88 | 88 | 84 | 83 | 98 | 93 | 89 |
| 1984 | 64 | 97 | 119 | 86 | 78 | 84 | 103 | 91 | 92 |
| 1985 | 57 | 89 | 82 | 77 | 76 | 75 | 93 | 92 | 82 |
| 1986 | 62 | 110 | 51 | 77 | 71 | 79 | 85 | 108 | 73 |
| 1987 | 66 | 72 | 60 | 96 | 82 | 76 | 74 | 122 | 62 |
| I | 63 | 75 | 56 | 88 | 72 | 73 | 72 | 119 | 61 |
| II | 64 | 69 | 59 | 95 | 76 | 74 | 71 | 121 | 61 |
| III | 64 | 67 | 59 | 100 | 84 | 75 | 74 | 121 | 62 |
| IV | 71 | 74 | 64 | 102 | 97 | 84 | 78 | 128 | 65 |
| 1988 | 83 | 73 | 78 | 104 | 110 | 90 | 84 | 130 | 69 |
| I | 76 | 76 | 71 | 104 | 103 | 87 | 80 | 131 | 66 |
| II | 82 | 73 | 77 | 110 | 112 | 91 | 84 | 131 | 69 |
| III | 87 | 69 | 86 | 103 | 105 | 88 | 86 | 125 | 71 |
| IV | 84 | 73 | 78 | 103 | 121 | 92 | 86 | 132 | 70 |

*Source:* UNCTAD, *Monthly Commodity Price Bulletin;* and United Nations, *Monthly Bulletin of Statistics*, December 1986 and March 1989.

a Unit values of exports of manufactures from developed market economies. The base of the original index was shifted to 1979-1981.

b Dollar index deflated by prices of manufactures.

Table A.7. Balance of payments on current account:[a] developed market economies, 1980-1988

(Billions of dollars)

| | 1980 | 1981 | 1982 | 1983 | 1984 | 1985 | 1986 | 1987 | 1988[b] |
|---|---|---|---|---|---|---|---|---|---|
| Major industrial countries[c] | | | | | | | | | |
| Merchandise exports | 895.9 | 905.2 | 846.2 | 836.6 | 897.7 | 926.1 | 1 070.5 | 1 235.7 | 1 431.3 |
| Merchandise imports (f.o.b.) | -929.4 | -905.4 | -845.8 | -848.8 | -944.3 | -965.2 | -1 069.6 | -1 247.6 | -1 430.1 |
| Balance of trade | -33.5 | -0.2 | 0.4 | -12.2 | -46.6 | -39.1 | 0.9 | -11.9 | 1.2 |
| Net services and private transfers | 22.2 | 21.0 | 13.9 | 14.4 | 6.6 | 14.2 | 13.1 | 6.2 | -16.2 |
| Current account | -11.3 | 20.8 | 14.3 | 2.2 | -40.0 | -24.9 | 14.0 | -5.6 | -15.0 |
| Other developed market economies | | | | | | | | | |
| Merchandise exports | 340.1 | 317.0 | 302.6 | 309.1 | 323.5 | 333.0 | 394.3 | 474.4 | 529.1 |
| Merchandise imports (f.o.b.) | -376.6 | -348.3 | -327.7 | -319.2 | -323.6 | -332.2 | -398.5 | -485.3 | -549.1 |
| Balance of trade | -36.5 | -31.3 | -25.2 | -10.2 | -0.1 | 0.8 | -4.3 | -11.0 | -20.0 |
| Net services and private transfers | 12.0 | 5.7 | 4.6 | 6.1 | 0.9 | -0.7 | 6.1 | 8.7 | 11.6 |
| Current account | -24.4 | -25.6 | -20.5 | -4.1 | 0.8 | 0.1 | 1.8 | -2.3 | -8.4 |

*Source:* IMF, *International Financial Statistics* and *World Economic Outlook,* national data and Secretariat estimates.

a Balance on goods, services and private transfers.

b Preliminary estimates.

c Canada, France, Federal Republic of Germany, Italy, Japan, United Kingdom and United States.

## Table A.8. Balance of payments of the United States, 1980-1988

(Billions of dollars)[a]

| | 1980 | 1981 | 1982 | 1983 | 1984 | 1985 | 1986 | 1987 | 1988[b] |
|---|---|---|---|---|---|---|---|---|---|
| Merchandise exports | 224.3 | 237.1 | 211.2 | 201.8 | 219.9 | 215.9 | 224.0 | 249.6 | 319.9 |
| Merchandise imports, f.o.b. | -249.7 | -265.1 | -247.6 | -268.9 | -332.4 | -338.1 | -368.5 | -409.9 | -446.4 |
| Balance of trade | -25.5 | -28.0 | -36.4 | -67.1 | -112.5 | -122.1 | -144.5 | -160.3 | -126.5 |
| Net services and private transfers, of which: | 32.8 | 40.0 | 33.9 | 27.2 | 14.1 | 18.3 | 17.6 | 16.4 | 1.3 |
| Net investment income | 30.4 | 34.1 | 28.7 | 24.9 | 18.5 | 25.9 | 23.1 | 20.4 | 2.6 |
| Current account balance[c] | 7.4 | 12.0 | -2.6 | -39.9 | -98.4 | -103.8 | -127.0 | -143.9 | -125.2 |
| Official transfers (net) | -5.5 | -5.1 | -6.1 | -6.4 | -8.7 | -11.3 | -11.8 | -10.1 | -10.1 |
| Current account balance[d] | 1.9 | 6.9 | -8.7 | -46.2 | -107.1 | -115.1 | -138.8 | -154.0 | -135.3 |
| Net private capital flows | -30.2 | -22.6 | -19.9 | 35.4 | 85.6 | 105.1 | 89.4 | 80.2 | 79.7 |
| United States private capital | -72.8 | -100.7 | -110.1 | -43.6 | -13.7 | -25.9 | -96.3 | -86.3 | -92.0 |
| Direct investment | -19.2 | -9.6 | 2.4 | -0.4 | -2.8 | -18.1 | -27.8 | -44.5 | -20.4 |
| Securities | -3.6 | -5.7 | -8.0 | -6.8 | -4.8 | -7.5 | -4.3 | -4.5 | -7.5 |
| Banking flows | -46.8 | -84.2 | -111.1 | -29.9 | -11.1 | -1.3 | -60.0 | -40.5 | -57.5 |
| Non-banking flows | -3.1 | -1.2 | 6.6 | -6.5 | 5.0 | 0.9 | -4.2 | 3.1 | -6.6 |
| Foreign private capital | 42.6 | 78.1 | 90.2 | 79.0 | 99.5 | 131.1 | 185.7 | 166.5 | 171.7 |
| Direct investment | 16.9 | 25.2 | 13.8 | 11.9 | 25.4 | 19.0 | 34.1 | 42.0 | 42.2 |
| Securities, of which: | 8.1 | 9.8 | 13.1 | 16.9 | 35.6 | 71.4 | 74.8 | 34.6 | 46.8 |
| Equity shares | 4.2 | 5.1 | 3.6 | 6.4 | -1.3 | 4.3 | 17.2 | 15.5 | -0.7 |
| Banking flows | 10.7 | 42.1 | 65.6 | 50.3 | 33.8 | 41.0 | 79.8 | 87.8 | 78.9 |
| Non-banking flows | 6.9 | 0.9 | -2.4 | -0.1 | 4.7 | -0.4 | -2.9 | 2.2 | 3.8 |
| Net official flows | 3.3 | -4.2 | -7.5 | -0.4 | -5.5 | -7.9 | 33.8 | 55.3 | 39.1 |
| Foreign official capital | 15.5 | 5.0 | 3.6 | 5.8 | 3.1 | -1.2 | 35.5 | 45.0 | 39.0 |
| United States official reserves | -7.0 | -4.1 | -5.0 | -1.2 | -3.1 | -3.9 | 0.3 | 9.1 | -3.6 |
| Other U.S. Government assets | -5.2 | -5.1 | -6.1 | -5.0 | -5.5 | -2.8 | -2.0 | 1.2 | 3.6 |
| Statistical discrepancy | 25.0 | 19.9 | 36.1 | 11.2 | 26.8 | 17.8 | 15.6 | 18.5 | 16.5 |
| Memorandum item | | | | | | | | | |
| Net transfer of resources[e] | 23.0 | 22.1 | 31.3 | 64.7 | 116.9 | 129.8 | 150.1 | 164.3 | 127.8 |

*Source:* United States Department of Commerce, *Survey of Current Business.*

a Minus sign (-) indicates payment outflow from the United States or increase in United States official reserves.

b Preliminary estimates.

c Balance on goods, services and private transfers.

d Including official transfers.

e Expenditure definition (negative of balance on goods and services, excluding investment income).

## Table A.9. Balance of payments of the Federal Republic of Germany, 1980-1988

(Billions of dollars)[a]

| | 1980 | 1981 | 1982 | 1983 | 1984 | 1985 | 1986 | 1987 | 1988[b] |
|---|---|---|---|---|---|---|---|---|---|
| Merchandise exports | 182.2 | 165.6 | 164.9 | 159.0 | 160.4 | 171.4 | 229.0 | 276.1 | 304.6 |
| Merchandise imports, f.o.b. | -174.3 | -150.2 | -140.9 | -138.5 | -138.8 | -144.3 | -175.1 | -207.9 | -230.8 |
| Balance of trade | 7.9 | 15.3 | 24.0 | 20.6 | 21.6 | 27.2 | 53.9 | 68.1 | 73.8 |
| Net services and private transfers, of which: | -15.0 | -12.9 | -12.9 | -9.9 | -5.5 | -4.7 | -7.4 | -13.1 | -13.9 |
| Net investment income | 2.0 | 0.5 | -1.2 | 1.6 | 3.6 | 3.2 | 4.0 | 3.7 | 4.2 |
| Current account balance[c] | -7.1 | 2.4 | 11.1 | 10.6 | 16.1 | 22.5 | 46.5 | 55.0 | 60.0 |
| Official transfers (net) | -6.7 | -5.9 | -6.0 | -5.3 | -6.2 | -6.0 | -7.4 | -10.1 | -11.6 |
| Current account balance[d] | -13.8 | -3.6 | 5.1 | 5.3 | 9.8 | 16.4 | 39.1 | 45.0 | 48.4 |
| Long-term capital, net | 3.2 | 3.7 | -5.8 | -2.7 | -7.0 | -4.6 | 15.3 | -13.1 | -47.6 |
| German investment abroad | -15.5 | -11.9 | -11.7 | -14.3 | -15.8 | -21.0 | -25.4 | -34.7 | -53.0 |
| Direct investment | -4.0 | -3.9 | -2.5 | -3.2 | -4.4 | -4.8 | -9.3 | -9.2 | -10.4 |
| Securities | -4.2 | -2.7 | -4.7 | -4.1 | -5.5 | -10.7 | -10.0 | -13.8 | -40.3 |
| Long-term credit transactions | -6.1 | -4.3 | -3.6 | -5.8 | -5.0 | -4.4 | -4.7 | -10.3 | -0.8 |
| Other | -1.1 | -1.1 | -0.9 | -1.3 | -0.9 | -1.0 | -1.4 | -1.5 | -1.4 |
| Foreign investment in the Federal Republic of Germany | 18.7 | 15.6 | 5.8 | 11.6 | 8.9 | 16.4 | 40.7 | 21.6 | 5.4 |
| Direct investment | 0.4 | 0.3 | 0.8 | 1.8 | 0.6 | 0.6 | 1.0 | 1.9 | 0.9 |
| Securities | 0.5 | 0.4 | 1.1 | 5.3 | 6.1 | 13.0 | 34.1 | 18.5 | 4.3 |
| Long-term credit transactions | 17.9 | 14.8 | 3.9 | 4.5 | 2.2 | 2.8 | 5.6 | 1.3 | 0.2 |
| Other | -0.1 | 0.0 | 0.0 | -0.1 | 0.0 | 0.0 | -0.1 | 0.0 | -0.1 |
| Short-term capital, net | -3.4 | -1.2 | 4.5 | -4.5 | -6.2 | -14.2 | -52.2 | -11.4 | -20.7 |
| Net bank flows | -4.9 | -4.5 | 3.3 | 0.7 | 0.0 | -9.4 | -27.2 | -3.4 | -11.5 |
| Enterprises, individuals | 1.2 | 2.6 | 1.3 | -3.5 | -5.7 | -4.8 | -24.6 | -6.5 | -9.9 |
| Official | 0.2 | 0.8 | -0.1 | -1.7 | -0.6 | 0.0 | -0.4 | -1.5 | 0.7 |
| Errors and omissions | -1.3 | 0.0 | -2.5 | 0.3 | 2.3 | 2.9 | 0.5 | 2.5 | 0.2 |
| Reserve-related flows | 15.3 | 1.0 | -1.3 | 1.6 | 1.1 | -0.6 | -2.7 | -22.9 | 19.7 |
| Memorandum item | | | | | | | | | |
| Net transfer of resources[e] | 9.1 | -1.9 | -12.3 | -9.0 | -12.4 | -19.2 | -42.5 | -51.3 | -55.8 |

*Source:* Federal Republic of Germany, *Statistical Supplements to the Monthly Report of the Deutsche Bundesbank.*

a Minus sign (-) indicates outflow from the Federal Republic of Germany or increase in reserves; dollar values are converted from deutsche marks at average annual exchange rates.

b Trade data are partly estimated.

c Balance on goods, services and private transfers.

d Including official transfers.

e Expenditure definition (negative of balance on goods and services, excluding investment income).

## Table A.10. Balance of payments of Japan, 1980-1988

(Billions of dollars)[a]

| | 1980 | 1981 | 1982 | 1983 | 1984 | 1985 | 1986 | 1987 | 1988[b] |
|---|---|---|---|---|---|---|---|---|---|
| Merchandise exports | 126.7 | 149.5 | 137.7 | 145.5 | 168.3 | 174.0 | 205.6 | 224.6 | 259.6 |
| Merchandise imports, f.o.b. | -124.6 | -129.6 | -119.6 | -114.0 | -124.0 | -118.0 | -112.8 | -128.2 | -164.8 |
| Balance of trade | 2.1 | 20.0 | 18.1 | 31.5 | 44.3 | 56.0 | 92.8 | 96.4 | 94.8 |
| Net services and private transfers | -11.6 | -13.8 | -9.9 | -9.3 | -7.9 | -5.4 | -5.5 | -6.7 | -12.3 |
| of which: | | | | | | | | | |
| Net investment income | 0.9 | -0.8 | 1.7 | 3.1 | 4.2 | 6.8 | 9.5 | 16.7 | 21.1 |
| Current account balance[c] | -9.5 | 6.2 | 8.1 | 22.2 | 36.4 | 50.5 | 87.3 | 89.7 | 82.5 |
| Official transfers (net) | -1.3 | -1.4 | -1.3 | -1.4 | -1.4 | -1.4 | -1.5 | -2.7 | -3.0 |
| Current account balance[d] | -10.7 | 4.8 | 6.9 | 20.8 | 35.0 | 49.2 | 85.8 | 87.0 | 79.5 |
| Long-term capital, net | 2.3 | -9.7 | -15.0 | -17.7 | -49.6 | -64.5 | -131.5 | -136.5 | -130.3 |
| Japanese investment abroad | -10.8 | -22.8 | -27.4 | -32.5 | -56.8 | -81.8 | -132.1 | -132.8 | -149.3 |
| Direct investment | -2.4 | -4.9 | -4.5 | -3.6 | -6.0 | -6.5 | -14.5 | -19.5 | -34.1 |
| Trade credits | -0.7 | -2.7 | -3.2 | -2.6 | -4.9 | -2.8 | -1.8 | -0.5 | -6.7 |
| Loans | -2.6 | -5.1 | -7.9 | -8.4 | -11.9 | -10.4 | -9.3 | -16.2 | -14.9 |
| Securities | -3.8 | -8.8 | -9.7 | -16.0 | -30.8 | -59.8 | -102.0 | -87.8 | -87.1 |
| Other | -1.4 | -1.3 | -2.0 | -1.8 | -3.2 | -2.3 | -4.5 | -8.8 | -6.4 |
| Foreign investment in Japan | 13.1 | 13.1 | 12.4 | 14.8 | 7.1 | 17.3 | 0.6 | -3.7 | 19.0 |
| Direct investment | 0.3 | 0.2 | 0.4 | 0.4 | 0.0 | 0.6 | 0.2 | 1.2 | -0.5 |
| Securities[e] | 13.1 | 13.2 | 11.9 | 14.1 | 7.2 | 16.7 | 0.5 | -6.1 | 20.3 |
| Other[f] | -0.3 | -0.3 | 0.2 | 0.2 | -0.1 | -0.1 | -0.1 | 1.2 | -0.9 |
| Short-term capital, net | 16.3 | 8.7 | -1.5 | -3.5 | 13.3 | 9.9 | 56.9 | 95.7 | 64.0 |
| Non-bank transactions | 3.1 | 2.3 | -1.6 | 0.0 | -4.3 | -0.9 | -1.6 | 23.9 | 19.5 |
| Foreign exchange banks | 13.1 | 6.4 | 0.0 | -3.6 | 17.6 | 10.8 | 58.5 | 71.8 | 44.5 |
| Errors and omissions | -3.1 | 0.5 | 4.7 | 2.1 | 3.7 | 4.0 | 2.5 | -3.9 | 2.3 |
| Reserve-related flows | -4.7 | -4.2 | 4.9 | -1.6 | -2.4 | 1.5 | -13.7 | -42.3 | -15.5 |
| Memorandum item | | | | | | | | | |
| Net transfer of resources[g] | 10.3 | -6.9 | -6.4 | -19.1 | -32.1 | -43.7 | -77.8 | -73.0 | -61.4 |

*Source:* Bank of Japan, *Balance of Payments Monthly.*

a Minus sign (-) indicates outflow of capital from Japan or addition to reserves.

b Provisional.

c Balance on goods, services and private transfers.

d Including official transfers.

e Excluding Gensaki transactions, which are included in short-term capital.

f Mainly loans.

g Expenditure definition (negative of balance on goods and services, excluding investment income).

## Table A.11. Balance of payments on current account:[a] centrally planned economies, 1980-1988

(Billions of dollars)

| | 1980 | 1981 | 1982 | 1983 | 1984 | 1985 | 1986 | 1987 | 1988[b] |
|---|---|---|---|---|---|---|---|---|---|
| A. Eastern Europe | | | | | | | | | |
| Merchandise exports | 32.5 | 32.6 | 33.0 | 33.1 | 34.6 | 32.9 | 32.9 | 35.8 | 40.7 |
| Merchandise imports (f.o.b.) | -35.3 | -31.8 | -27.8 | -27.4 | -27.5 | -28.9 | -30.9 | -32.6 | -36.5 |
| Balance of trade | -2.8 | 0.8 | 5.2 | 5.7 | 7.1 | 4.0 | 2.0 | 3.2 | 4.2 |
| Net services and private transfers | -3.8 | -5.9 | -4.5 | -3.5 | -3.4 | -2.7 | -2.9 | -2.0 | -3.1 |
| Current account | -6.6 | -5.1 | 0.7 | 2.2 | 3.7 | 1.3 | -0.9 | 1.2 | 1.1 |
| B. Soviet Union | | | | | | | | | |
| Merchandise exports | 38.2 | 39.1 | 43.4 | 44.2 | 43.3 | 36.9 | 34.7 | 37.8 | 43.1 |
| Merchandise imports (f.o.b.) | -34.8 | -39.9 | -39.1 | -38.0 | -36.6 | -36.2 | -33.3 | -29.4 | -38.9 |
| Balance of trade | 3.4 | -0.8 | 4.3 | 6.2 | 6.7 | 0.7 | 1.4 | 8.4 | 4.2 |
| Net services and private transfers | -0.6 | -0.9 | -0.8 | -0.3 | -0.1 | -0.1 | -0.5 | -1.8 | -0.4 |
| Current account | 2.8 | -1.7 | 3.5 | 5.9 | 6.6 | 0.6 | 0.9 | 6.6 | 3.8 |
| C. Estimated net investment Income of CMEAbanks | -0.5 | -0.6 | -0.5 | -0.4 | -0.4 | -0.2 | -0.2 | -0.5 | -0.4 |
| D. Regional current account | -4.3 | -7.4 | 3.7 | 7.7 | 9.9 | 1.7 | -0.2 | 7.3 | 4.5 |

*Source:* United Nations Economic Commission for Europe, *Economic Survey of Europe in 1988-1989* (United Nations publication, Sales No. E.89.II.E.1).

a Balance on goods, services and private transfers in convertible currencies.

b Preliminary estimates.

## Table A.12. Balance of payments on current account:[a] developing countries, 1980-1988

(Billions of dollars)[a]

| | 1980 | 1981 | 1982 | 1983 | 1984 | 1985 | 1986 | 1987 | 1988[b] |
|---|---|---|---|---|---|---|---|---|---|
| Surplus energy exporters (8 economies) | | | | | | | | | |
| Merchandise exports | 215.9 | 197.5 | 155.9 | 121.2 | 110.5 | 94.5 | 60.5 | 76.1 | 72.0 |
| Merchandise imports (f.o.b.) | -75.1 | -91.5 | -95.3 | -86.4 | -74.5 | -60.4 | -52.0 | -50.9 | -53.0 |
| Balance of trade | 140.8 | 106.0 | 60.6 | 34.8 | 36.0 | 34.1 | 8.5 | 25.2 | 19.0 |
| Net services and private transfers | -36.5 | -44.6 | -42.7 | -40.0 | -36.3 | -26.9 | -18.3 | -20.4 | -20.5 |
| Current account | 104.3 | 61.4 | 17.9 | -5.2 | -0.3 | 7.2 | -9.8 | 4.8 | -1.5 |

Table A.12 (continued)

| | 1980 | 1981 | 1982 | 1983 | 1984 | 1985 | 1986 | 1987 | 1988[b] |
|---|---|---|---|---|---|---|---|---|---|
| Deficit energy exporters (19 economies) | | | | | | | | | |
| Merchandise exports | 140.4 | 140.1 | 125.9 | 121.4 | 132.4 | 126.6 | 90.2 | 107.3 | 112.5 |
| Merchandise imports (f.o.b.) | -108.0 | -128.4 | -116.0 | -97.0 | -96.3 | -91.2 | -79.9 | -84.3 | -99.5 |
| Balance of trade | 32.4 | 11.7 | 9.9 | 24.4 | 36.1 | 35.4 | 10.3 | 22.9 | 13.0 |
| Net services and private transfers | -32.8 | -41.1 | -44.8 | -34.9 | -37.1 | -37.2 | -30.7 | -26.6 | -29.5 |
| Current account | -0.4 | -29.4 | -34.9 | -10.6 | -1.0 | -1.8 | -20.3 | -3.6 | -16.5 |
| Energy-importing countries (99 economies) | | | | | | | | | |
| Merchandise exports | 200.9 | 214.7 | 204.1 | 211.5 | 240.5 | 236.8 | 261.5 | 327.1 | 398.5 |
| Merchandise imports (f.o.b.) | -258.8 | -271.5 | -249.8 | -240.7 | -248.2 | -241.9 | -257.2 | -320.2 | -388.0 |
| Balance of trade | -57.9 | -56.8 | -45.7 | -29.2 | -7.7 | -5.1 | 4.4 | 6.9 | 10.5 |
| Net services and private transfers | -11.4 | -15.2 | -18.9 | -16.0 | -21.9 | -17.7 | -14.6 | -14.5 | -15.0 |
| Current account | -69.2 | -72.0 | -64.6 | -45.2 | -29.9 | -22.8 | -10.2 | -7.6 | -4.5 |
| Recent surplus economies (4 economies)[c] | | | | | | | | | |
| Merchandise exports | 74.7 | 84.7 | 83.1 | 90.7 | 107.6 | 108.6 | 129.4 | 174.2 | 218.5 |
| Merchandise imports (f.o.b.) | -83.9 | -93.7 | -90.5 | -93.2 | -101.0 | -99.8 | -110.5 | -148.3 | -198.0 |
| Balance of trade | -9.2 | -9.0 | -7.4 | -2.5 | 6.6 | 8.8 | 18.9 | 26.0 | 20.5 |
| Net services and private transfers | 0.2 | 1.9 | 4.5 | 4.0 | 0.2 | 1.6 | 4.2 | 4.6 | 5.5 |
| Current account | -8.9 | -7.1 | -2.9 | 1.5 | 6.7 | 10.4 | 23.1 | 30.5 | 26.0 |
| Other energy importers (95 economies) | | | | | | | | | |
| Merchandise exports | 126.1 | 130.0 | 121.0 | 120.8 | 132.9 | 128.2 | 132.1 | 152.9 | 180.0 |
| Merchandise imports (f.o.b.) | -174.9 | -177.8 | -159.3 | -147.5 | -147.1 | -142.1 | -146.6 | -172.0 | -190.0 |
| Balance of trade | -48.7 | -47.8 | -38.3 | -26.7 | -14.2 | -13.8 | -14.5 | -19.0 | -10.0 |
| Net services and private transfers | -11.6 | -17.0 | -23.4 | -20.0 | -22.1 | -19.3 | -18.8 | -19.1 | -20.5 |
| Current account | -60.3 | -64.8 | -61.7 | -46.7 | -36.3 | -33.2 | -33.3 | -38.1 | -30.5 |
| China | | | | | | | | | |
| Merchandise exports | 18.5 | 22.0 | 21.1 | 20.7 | 23.9 | 25.1 | 25.8 | 34.7 | 45.0 |
| Merchandise imports (f.o.b.) | -21.2 | -20.3 | -16.9 | -18.7 | -23.9 | -38.2 | -34.9 | -36.4 | -50.5 |
| Balance of trade | -2.8 | 1.7 | 4.2 | 2.0 | 0.0 | -13.1 | -9.1 | -1.7 | -5.5 |
| Net services and private transfers | 0.3 | 0.3 | 1.6 | 2.4 | 2.4 | 1.6 | 2.0 | 2.0 | 2.5 |
| Current account | -2.4 | 2.0 | 5.9 | 4.4 | 2.4 | -11.5 | -7.2 | 0.33 | -3.0 |
| Long-term capital-importing countries (119 economies) | | | | | | | | | |
| Merchandise exports | 359.8 | 376.8 | 351.2 | 353.6 | 396.8 | 388.5 | 377.5 | 469.2 | 556.0 |
| Merchandise imports (f.o.b.) | -388.0 | -420.2 | -382.7 | -356.4 | -368.3 | -371.3 | -371.9 | -440.9 | -538.0 |
| Balance of trade | -28.2 | -43.4 | -31.6 | -2.8 | 28.5 | 17.2 | 5.6 | 28.2 | 18.0 |
| Net services and private transfers | -43.8 | -56.0 | -62.1 | -48.5 | -56.7 | -53.3 | -43.3 | -39.1 | -42.0 |
| Current account | -72.0 | -99.4 | -93.7 | -51.3 | -28.2 | -36.1 | -37.7 | -10.9 | -24.0 |
| All developing countries (127 economies) | | | | | | | | | |
| Merchandise exports | 575.7 | 596.4 | 528.2 | 495.5 | 531.2 | 508.1 | 463.7 | 580.0 | 673.0 |
| Merchandise imports (f.o.b.) | -463.1 | -532.0 | -494.9 | -461.5 | -466.7 | -469.9 | -458.8 | -528.2 | -641.5 |
| Balance of trade | 112.6 | 64.4 | 33.3 | 34.0 | 64.5 | 38.2 | 4.9 | 51.8 | 31.5 |
| Net services and private transfers | -80.3 | -102.3 | -109.0 | -90.5 | -93.0 | -67.0 | -52.4 | -57.8 | -57.0 |
| Current account | 32.3 | -38.0 | -75.8 | -56.5 | -28.5 | -28.9 | -47.5 | -6.1 | -25.5 |

*Source:* Department of International Economic and Social Affairs of the United Nations Secretariat, based on data from IMF, and official national and other sources.

a Balance on goods, services and private transfers.

b Preliminary estimates, rounded to nearest half-billion dollars.

c Hong Kong, Republic of Korea, Singapore and Taiwan Province of China.

## Table A.13. Official reserves and ratios of reserves to current expenditures of the capital-importing developing countries

| | 1980 | 1981 | 1982 | 1983 | 1984 | 1985 | 1986 | 1987 | 1988[a] |
|---|---|---|---|---|---|---|---|---|---|
| | *Billions of dollars* | | | | | | | | |
| Level of reserves[b] | 113.9 | 111.0 | 100.8 | 109.2 | 127.4 | 138.9 | 157.1 | 206.8 | 209.1 |
| of which: | | | | | | | | | |
| Energy exporters | 44.5 | 39.8 | 28.8 | 31.3 | 36.4 | 38.9 | 33.0 | 41.9 | 28.8 |
| Energy importers | 66.3 | 65.7 | 60.1 | 62.4 | 73.2 | 86.9 | 112.2 | 148.0 | 161.2 |
| Recent surplus countries and area[c] | 11.9 | 17.6 | 20.0 | 23.6 | 29.0 | 38.5 | 62.8 | 96.0 | 103.5 |
| Other | 54.4 | 48.1 | 40.2 | 38.8 | 44.2 | 48.4 | 49.3 | 52.0 | 57.7 |
| China | 3.1 | 5.6 | 11.8 | 15.5 | 17.8 | 13.2 | 12.0 | 16.9 | 19.1 |
| Miscellaneous groupings | | | | | | | | | |
| Fifteen heavily-indebted countries[d] | 50.0 | 41.7 | 26.3 | 27.5 | 39.6 | 40.9 | 34.4 | 38.6 | 32.3 |
| Sub-Saharan Africa[e] | 3.4 | 2.8 | 3.0 | 3.1 | 4.1 | 5.1 | 5.9 | 6.3 | 7.4 |
| | *Number of months* | | | | | | | | |
| Coverage of current expenditures[f] | 2.7 | 2.2 | 1.8 | 2.1 | 2.4 | 2.7 | 2.7 | 2.8 | 2.5 |
| of which: | | | | | | | | | |
| Energy exporters | 3.2 | 2.4 | 1.8 | 2.4 | 2.7 | 3.0 | 2.9 | 3.5 | 2.2 |
| Energy importers | 2.4 | 2.1 | 1.9 | 2.0 | 2.3 | 2.6 | 2.6 | 2.4 | 2.5 |
| 15 heavily-indebted countries[d] | 3.1 | 2.3 | 1.6 | 2.1 | 3.0 | 3.3 | 2.8 | 3.0 | 2.4 |
| Sub-Saharan Africa[e] | 1.1 | 1.0 | 0.9 | 1.1 | 1.1 | 1.5 | 1.6 | 1.8 | 1.7 |

*Source:* Department of International Economic and Social Affairs of the United Nations Secretariat, based on data from IMF and national and regional estimates.

a Partly estimated.

b Total reserves, end of period (with gold valued at SDR 35 per ounce).

c Republic of Korea, Singapore and Taiwan Province of China (data for Hong Kong unavailable).

d Argentina, Bolivia, Brazil, Chile, Colombia, Côte d'Ivoire, Ecuador, Mexico, Morocco, Nigeria, Peru, Philippines, Uruguay, Venezuela and Yugoslavia.

e Excluding Nigeria.

f Expenditures on goods and services (including interest payments) for given year relative to total reserves at end of year, sample of 98 countries.

Table A.14. Resource commitments of multilateral development institutions, 1980-1988[a]

(Millions of dollars)

| | 1980 | 1981 | 1982 | 1983 | 1984 | 1985 | 1986 | 1987 | 1988 |
|---|---|---|---|---|---|---|---|---|---|
| Financial institutions | | | | | | | | | |
| African Development Bank | 571 | 636 | 766 | 899 | 897 | 1 154 | 1 640 | 2 140 | 2 176 |
| Asian Development Bank | 1 452 | 1 694 | 1 702 | 1 922 | 2 257 | 1 845 | 2 044 | 2 508 | 3 241 |
| Caribbean Development Bank | 45 | 42 | 45 | 48 | 65 | 50 | 67 | 41 | 74 |
| Inter-American Development Bank | 2 341 | 2 534 | 2 793 | 3 099 | 3 615 | 3 102 | 3 057 | 2 408 | 1 738 |
| International Fund for Agricultural Development | 394 | 377 | 338 | 282 | 211 | 131 | 147 | 233 | 244 |
| World Bank Group | 12 780 | 13 385 | 12 695 | 15 786 | 13 255 | 17 527 | 18 005 | 19 310 | 20 182 |
| International Bank for Reconstruction and Development | 8 148 | 8 905 | 9 398 | 11 721 | 9 448 | 12 952 | 13 593 | 14 066 | 14 411 |
| International Development Association | 3 817 | 3 688 | 2 832 | 3 112 | 3 222 | 3 541 | 3 373 | 3 841 | 4 350 |
| International Finance Corporation | 815 | 792 | 465 | 953 | 585 | 1 034 | 1 039 | 1 403 | 1 421 |
| Subtotal | 17 583 | 18 668 | 18 339 | 22 036 | 20 300 | 23 809 | 24 960 | 26 640 | 27 655 |
| Operational agencies of the United Nations | | | | | | | | | |
| United Nations Development Programme[b] | 639 | 696 | 621 | 527 | 531 | 567 | 656 | 809 | 942 |
| United Nations Population Fund | 146 | 127 | 115 | 117 | 134 | 141 | 116 | 134 | 169 |
| United Nations Children's Fund | 279 | 295 | 405 | 182 | 204 | 452 | 248 | 330 | 454 |
| World Food Programme | 479 | 543 | 613 | 696 | 925 | 642 | 629 | 621 | 779 |
| Subtotal | 1 543 | 1 661 | 1 754 | 1 522 | 1 794 | 1 802 | 1 649 | 1 894 | 2 344 |
| Total commitments | 19 126 | 20 329 | 20 093 | 23 558 | 22 094 | 25 611 | 26 609 | 28 534 | 29 999 |
| Memorandum item | | | | | | | | | |
| Commitments in units of 1980 purchasing power[c] | 19 126 | 21 627 | 21 840 | 26 470 | 25 691 | 29 780 | 25 834 | 24 598 | 24 389 |

*Source:* Annual reports and information supplied by individual institutions.

a Loans, grants, technical assistance and equity participation, as appropriate; all data are on a calendar year basis.

b Including UNDP-administered funds.

c Total commitments deflated by the United Nations index of manufactured export prices in dollars of developed market economies, 1980 = 100 (see United Nations, *Monthly Bulletin of Statistics,* March 1989).

## Table A.15. Resource commitments of Arab national and regional development institutions,[a] 1982-1988

(Millions of dollars)

| | 1982 | 1983 | 1984 | 1985 | 1986 | 1987 | Two thirds 1988 |
|---|---|---|---|---|---|---|---|
| Functional composition | | | | | | | |
| Project finance (loans, equity or grants) | 2 085.8 | 1 410.2 | 1 158.2 | 999.6 | 1 163.1 | 1 011.7 | 625.4 |
| Technical assistance (grants and loans) | 52.9 | 24.2 | 20.9 | 42.1 | 37.1 | 85.2 | 24.1 |
| Import financing grants, loans and leasing) | 436.4 | 506.0 | 768.3 | 603.9 | 658.6 | 529.8 | 363.0 |
| Balance of payments (mainly OPEC Fund loans) | 83.5 | 25.5 | 3.7 | - | 5.8 | 11.4 | 13.2 |
| Other (grants)[b] | 35.0 | 6.4 | 7.4 | 6.1 | 0.9 | 1.0 | 0.2 |
| Total | 2 693.6 | 1 972.3 | 1 958.5 | 1 651.7 | 1 865.5 | 1 639.1 | 1 025.8 |
| Geographical distribution | | | | | | | |
| Africa | 1 458.4 | 841.7 | 864.5 | 616.4 | 1 008.5 | 748.1 | 534.7 |
| West Asia | 425.6 | 424.1 | 544.0 | 485.8 | 378.1 | 419.2 | 285.3 |
| Other Asia and Pacific[c] | 655.0 | 507.3 | 393.4 | 393.6 | 314.1 | 343.2 | 186.9 |
| Other[d] | 154.6 | 199.2 | 156.6 | 156.0 | 164.8 | 128.6 | 19.0 |
| Total | 2 693.6 | 1 972.3 | 1 958.5 | 1 651.7 | 1 865.5 | 1 639.1 | 1 025.8 |

*Source:* Department of International Economic and Social Affairs of the United Nations Secretariat, based on data from the Co-ordination Secretariat of Arab National and Regional Development Institutions (Kuwait).

a Abu Dhabi Fund for Arab Economic Development, Arab Bank for Economic Development in Africa, Arab Fund for Economic and Social Development, Iraqi Fund for External Development (1982), Islamic Development Bank, Kuwait Fund for Arab Economic Development, OPEC Fund for International Development and Saudi Fund for Development. (The funds included here account for roughly a third (1982) of official development assistance (ODA) commitments by developing countries as reported by OECD (i.e. data exclude contributions to most multilateral institutions and bilateral ODA outside the listed institutions and ODA by non-Arab donors.)

b Including contributions to IFAD, subscriptions to the UNCTAD Common Fund on behalf of low-income countries and research projects to be undertaken by various institutions.

c Including China.

d Including international agencies and organizations.

## Table A.16. Net IMF lending to developing countries: by facility, 1980-1988

(Billions of dollars)

| | 1980 | 1981 | 1982 | 1983 | 1984 | 1985 | 1986 | 1987 | 1988 |
|---|---|---|---|---|---|---|---|---|---|
| Regular facilities | 2.3 | 6.2 | 4.2 | 8.4 | 4.4 | 1.1 | 0.1 | -3.8 | -3.8 |
| Credit tranche drawings | 1.5 | 3.9 | 1.9 | 3.5 | 1.2 | 1.1 | 1.0 | -1.8 | -1.0 |
| Extended facility drawings | 0.7 | 2.4 | 2.3 | 4.9 | 3.2 | - | -0.9 | -1.9 | -2.8 |
| Special facilities | 1.2 | - | 1.4 | 2.2 | -0.2 | -0.8 | -2.1 | -1.0 | -0.7 |
| Buffer stock financing | - | - | 0.1 | 0.3 | 0.0 | -0.2 | -0.2 | -0.1 | - |
| Compensatory financing | 0.3 | 0.6 | 1.7 | 2.1 | - | -0.4 | -1.4 | -0.7 | -0.4 |
| Oil facility | -0.7 | -0.7 | -0.4 | -0.1 | - | - | - | - | - |
| Trust Fund | 1.6 | 0.4 | - | - | -0.2 | -0.3 | -0.6 | -0.7 | -0.7 |
| Structural adjustment facility | - | - | - | - | - | - | 0.1 | 0.5 | 0.5 |
| Total | 3.4 | 6.6 | 5.7 | 10.6 | 4.2 | 0.2 | -2.0 | -4.7 | -4.7 |
| Memorandum items | | | | | | | | | |
| Selected characteristics of higher conditionality lending agreements | | | | | | | | | |
| Number initiated during year | 28 | 31 | 19 | 33 | 20 | 26 | 31 | 25 | 28 |
| Average length (months) | 20 | 23 | 14 | 18 | 14 | 16 | 22 | 26 | 25 |
| Total amount committed | 7.5 | 24.4 | 2.6 | 15.7 | 4.0 | 3.4 | 4.0 | 4.4 | 5.4 |

*Source:* Data from IMF, *International Financial Statistics and IMF Survey.*

## Table A.17. Value of oil exports of OPEC member countries,[a] 1970-1988

(Millions of dollars)

| Country | 1970 | 1980 | 1985 | 1986 | 1987 | 1988[b] |
|---|---|---|---|---|---|---|
| Algeria | 681 | 12 647 | 9 170 | 4 810 | 5 920 | 2 700 |
| Ecuador | 1 | 1 563 | 1 927 | 983 | 820 | 1 200 |
| Gabon | 58 | 1 876 | 1 668 | 725 | 955 | 800 |
| Indonesia | 446 | 15 595 | 9 083 | 5 501 | 6 335 | 3 700 |
| Iran (Islamic Republic of) | 2 358 | 13 286 | 13 115 | 7 199 | 10 000 | 6 900 |
| Iraq | 788 | 26 296 | 11 380 | 7 238 | 11 300 | 11 400 |
| Kuwait | 1 596 | 17 678 | 9 817 | 6 378 | 7 520 | 5 600 |
| Libyan Arab Jamahiriya | 2 357 | 21 396 | 10 523 | 6 139 | 5 650 | 4 700 |
| Nigeria | 715 | 25 262 | 12 327 | 6 176 | 7 166 | 6 300 |
| Qatar | 228 | 5 405 | 3 584 | 1 669 | 1 781 | 1 500 |
| Saudi Arabia | 2 418 | 108 174 | 25 936 | 17 794 | 20 481 | 19 900 |
| United Arab Emirates | 485 | 19 558 | 11 799 | 7 509 | 8 721 | 6 500 |
| Venezuela | 2 371 | 18 248 | 10 352 | 6 713 | 9 050 | 6 000 |
| Total | 14 502 | 286 984 | 130 681 | 78 834 | 95 699 | 77 200 |

*Source:* OPEC, *Annual Statistical Bulletin, 1987* for 1970, 1980, 1985, 1986 and 1987; and *Petroleum Intelligence Weekly,* 14 November 1988, supplement for 1988 estimates.

a Including, where applicable, oil product exports. For some countries, exports of condensate may be included.

b Estimate.

## Table A.18. OPEC crude oil production, 1988

(Thousands of barrels per day)

| Country | Jan. | Feb. | March | April | May | June | July | Aug. | Sep. | Oct. | Nov. | Dec. |
|---|---|---|---|---|---|---|---|---|---|---|---|---|
| Algeria | 600 | 600 | 600 | 600 | 650 | 650 | 650 | 650 | 650 | 650 | 650 | 650 |
| Ecuador | 300 | 310 | 310 | 310 | 310 | 310 | 310 | 310 | 310 | 310 | 310 | 310 |
| Gabon | 175 | 175 | 175 | 175 | 175 | 175 | 175 | 175 | 175 | 175 | 175 | 175 |
| Indonesia | 1 220 | 1 210 | 1 220 | 1 320 | 1 320 | 1 320 | 1 320 | 1 320 | 1 220 | 1 220 | 1 220 | 1 320 |
| Iran (Islamic Republic of) | 2 000 | 1 900 | 2 000 | 2 200 | 2 200 | 2 150 | 2 300 | 2 300 | 2 500 | 2 400 | 2 500 | 2 500 |
| Iraq | 2 400 | 2 500 | 2 500 | 2 650 | 2 600 | 2 650 | 2 600 | 2 600 | 2 700 | 2 700 | 2 700 | 2 700 |
| Kuwait[a] | 1 300 | 1 100 | 1 105 | 1 300 | 1 212 | 1 463 | 1 325 | 1 570 | 1 660 | 1 650 | 1 750 | 1 650 |
| Libyan Arab Jamahiriya | 950 | 1 000 | 900 | 950 | 1 000 | 1 000 | 1 000 | 1 000 | 1 050 | 1 100 | 1 100 | 1 100 |
| Nigeria | 1 397 | 1 385 | 1 352 | 1 319 | 1 373 | 1 394 | 1 350 | 1 400 | 1 450 | 1 450 | 1 300 | 1 500 |
| Qatar | 325 | 300 | 300 | 300 | 300 | 300 | 300 | 300 | 300 | 350 | 350 | 350 |
| Saudi Arabia | 4 230 | 4 350 | 4 105 | 4 550 | 4 562 | 4 415 | 4 525 | 5 170 | 5 260 | 5 950 | 6 650 | 6 550 |
| United Arab Emirates | 1 205 | 1 015 | 1 215 | 1 385 | 1 365 | 1 365 | 1 450 | 1 865 | 1 925 | 1 960 | 2 060 | 1 960 |
| Venezuela | 1 730 | 1 735 | 1 750 | 1 750 | 1 750 | 1 750 | 1 805 | 1 805 | 1 880 | 1 880 | 2 030 | 2 030 |
| Total | 17 832 | 17 580 | 17 532 | 18 809 | 18 817 | 18 942 | 19 110 | 20 465 | 21 080 | 21 795 | 22 795 | 22 795 |

*Source:* Department of International Economic and Social Affairs of the United Nations Secretariat, based on *Petroleum Economist,* vol. LVI, No. 2 (February 1989), p. 76.

a Includes share of neutral zone.

## Table A.19. OPEC crude oil production quotas

(Thousands of barrels per day)

| Country | March 1983 | October 1984 | September 1986 | November 1986 | January 1987 | July 1987 | January 1989 |
|---|---|---|---|---|---|---|---|
| Algeria | 725 | 663 | 663 | 669 | 635 | 667 | 695 |
| Ecuador | 200 | 183 | 183 | 221 | 210 | 221 | 230 |
| Gabon | 150 | 137 | 137 | 160 | 152 | 159 | 166 |
| Indonesia | 1 300 | 1 189 | 1 189 | 1 193 | 1 133 | 1 190 | 1 240 |
| Iran (Islamic Republic of) | 2 400 | 2 300 | 2 300 | 2 317 | 2 255 | 2 369 | 2 640 |
| Iraq[a] | 1 200 | 1 200 | 1 200 | 1 466 | 1 466 | 1 540 | 2 640 |
| Kuwait | 1 050 | 900 | 900 | 999 | 948 | 996 | 1 037 |
| Libyan Arab Jamahiriya | 1 100 | 990 | 990 | 999 | 948 | 996 | 1 037 |
| Nigeria | 1 300 | 1 300 | 1 300 | 1 304 | 1 238 | 1 301 | 1 355 |
| Qatar | 300 | 280 | 280 | 300 | 285 | 299 | 312 |
| Saudi Arabia | 5 000 | 4 353 | 4 353 | 4 353 | 4 133 | 4 343 | 4 524 |
| United Arab Emirates | 1 100 | 950 | 950 | 950 | 902 | 948 | 988 |
| Venezuela | 1 675 | 1 555 | 1 555 | 1 574 | 1 495 | 1 571 | 1 636 |
| Total | 17 500 | 16 000 | 16 000 | 16 505 | 15 800 | 16 600 | 18 500 |

*Source:* Department of International Economic and Social Affairs of the United Nations Secretariat, based on various OPEC press releases.

a Theoretical quota for Iraq from September 1986 through July 1987.

## Table A.20. United States petroleum industry indicators, 1980-1988

| Year | 1980 | 1981 | 1982 | 1983 | 1984 | 1985 | 1986 | 1987 | 1988 |
|---|---|---|---|---|---|---|---|---|---|
| Proved oil reserves (billion barrels) | 26.40 | 29.79 | 29.79 | 27.30 | 27.30 | 28.00 | 24.56 | 25.27 | 26.50 |
| Crude oil production (million barrels per day) | 8.60 | 8.57 | 8.65 | 8.69 | 8.88 | 8.97 | 8.68 | 8.35 | 8.17 |
| Reserves/production ratio (years) | 8.41 | 9.52 | 9.43 | 8.61 | 8.42 | 8.55 | 7.75 | 8.29 | 8.89 |
| Natural gas liquids and other supply (million barrels per day) | 1.62 | 1.66 | 1.60 | 1.61 | 1.68 | 1.67 | 1.61 | 1.66 | 1.68 |
| Oil consumption (million barrels per day) | 17.06 | 16.06 | 15.30 | 15.23 | 15.73 | 15.73 | 16.28 | 16.67 | 17.00 |
| Net crude oil and petroleum products imports[a] (million barrels per day) | 6.37 | 5.40 | 4.30 | 4.31 | 4.72 | 4.29 | 5.44 | 5.91 | 6.44 |
| Net imports as percentage of oil consumption | 37.3 | 33.6 | 28.1 | 28.3 | 30.0 | 27.3 | 33.4 | 35.5 | 37.9 |
| Completion of exploration and development wells | 69 486 | 89 234 | 83 889 | 75 738 | 84 983 | 70 806 | 38 870 | 34 927 | 34 579 |

*Source:* Department of International Economic and Social Affairs of the United Nations Secretariat, based on United States Department of Energy, Energy Information Administration, Monthly *Energy Review,* various issues; and *Oil and Gas Journal,* various issues.

a Net import equals imports minus exports.

## Table A.21. World proved oil reserves, end-1979 to end-1988

| | End 1979 | | End 1988 | |
|---|---|---|---|---|
| | Millions of barrels | Percentage of world | Millions of barrels | Percentage of world |
| Developed market economies | 58 796 | 9.2 | 53 373 | 5.4 |
| Centrally planned economies | 70 000 | 10.9 | 60 250 | 6.1 |
| Developing countries | 512 545 | 79.9 | 875 325 | 88.5 |
| OPEC member countries | 435 611 | 67.9 | 758 019 | 76.6 |
| Non-OPEC oil exporting | 69 930 | 10.9 | 101 418 | 10.3 |
| Oil importing | 7 004 | 1.1 | 15 888 | 1.6 |
| Total | 641 341 | 100.0 | 988 948 | 100.00 |

*Source:* Department of International Economic and Social Affairs of the United Nations Secretariat, based on *Oil and Gas Journal,* 27 December 1979 and 26 December 1988; and *Middle East Economic Survey,* 16 January 1989.

## Table A.22. World coal reserves as of end-1988[a]

(Million metric tons)

| Region and country | Reserves | Percentage of world |
|---|---|---|
| Developed market economies | 226 694 | 39.1 |
| United States | 92 000 | 15.8 |
| Australia | 55 800 | 9.6 |
| South Africa | 30 000 | 5.2 |
| Federal Republic of Germany | 25 500 | 4.4 |
| United Kingdom | 14 000 | 2.4 |
| Others | 9 394 | 1.6 |
| Centrally planned economies | 240 018 | 41.4 |
| USSR | 172 248 | 29.7 |
| Poland | 47 400 | 8.2 |
| German Democratic Republic | 13 000 | 2.2 |
| Czechoslovakia | 6 000 | 1.0 |
| Others | 1 370 | 0.3 |
| Developing countries | 113 736 | 19.6 |
| China | 70 720 | 12.2 |
| India | 19 505 | 3.4 |
| Others | 23 511 | 4.0 |
| Total | 580 448 | 100.0 |

*Source:* Department of International Economic and Social Affairs of the United Nations Secretariat, based on International Energy Agency, *Coal Information 1988* (Paris, 1988), p. I.82.

a Accessible coal reserves; includes bituminous coal and anthracite, sub-bituminous coal, brown coal, lignite.

**كيفية الحصول على منشورات الأمم المتحدة**

يمكن الحصول على منشورات الأمم المتحدة من المكتبات ودور التوزيع في جميع أنحاء العالم . استعلم عنها من المكتبة التي تتعامل معها أو اكتب إلى : الأمم المتحدة ، قسم البيع في نيويورك أو في جنيف .

**如何购取联合国出版物**

联合国出版物在全世界各地的书店和经售处均有发售。请向书店询问或写信到纽约或日内瓦的联合国销售组。

**HOW TO OBTAIN UNITED NATIONS PUBLICATIONS**

United Nations publications may be obtained from bookstores and distributors throughout the world. Consult your bookstore or write to: United Nations, Sales Section, New York or Geneva.

**COMMENT SE PROCURER LES PUBLICATIONS DES NATIONS UNIES**

Les publications des Nations Unies sont en vente dans les librairies et les agences dépositaires du monde entier. Informez-vous auprès de votre libraire ou adressez-vous à : Nations Unies, Section des ventes, New York ou Genève.

**КАК ПОЛУЧИТЬ ИЗДАНИЯ ОРГАНИЗАЦИИ ОБЪЕДИНЕННЫХ НАЦИЙ**

Издания Организации Объединенных Наций можно купить в книжных магазинах и агентствах во всех районах мира. Наводите справки об изданиях в вашем книжном магазине или пишите по адресу: Организация Объединенных Наций, Секция по продаже изданий, Нью-Йорк или Женева.

**COMO CONSEGUIR PUBLICACIONES DE LAS NACIONES UNIDAS**

Las publicaciones de las Naciones Unidas están en venta en librerías y casas distribuidoras en todas partes del mundo. Consulte a su librero o diríjase a: Naciones Unidas, Sección de Ventas, Nueva York o Ginebra.


Litho in United Nations, New York
40395—June 1989—6,625

04500
ISBN 92-1-109116-0

United Nations publication
Sales No. E.89.II.C.1
E/1989/45
ST/ESA/211